PSYCHOLOGY LIBRARY EDITIONS: COGNITIVE SCIENCE

Volume 15

PERSPECTIVES ON PERCEPTION AND ACTION

PERSPECTIVES ON PERCEPTION AND ACTION

Edited by
HERBERT HEUER AND ANDRIES F. SANDERS

LONDON AND NEW YORK

First published in 1987 by Lawrence Erlbaum Associates, Inc.

This edition first published in 2017
by Routledge
2 Park Square, Milton Park, Abingdon, Oxon OX14 4RN

and by Routledge
711 Third Avenue, New York, NY 10017

Routledge is an imprint of the Taylor & Francis Group, an informa business

© 1987 by Lawrence Erlbaum Associates, Inc.

All rights reserved. No part of this book may be reprinted or reproduced or utilised in any form or by any electronic, mechanical, or other means, now known or hereafter invented, including photocopying and recording, or in any information storage or retrieval system, without permission in writing from the publishers.

Trademark notice: Product or corporate names may be trademarks or registered trademarks, and are used only for identification and explanation without intent to infringe.

British Library Cataloguing in Publication Data
A catalogue record for this book is available from the British Library

ISBN: 978-1-138-19163-1 (Set)
ISBN: 978-1-315-54401-4 (Set) (ebk)
ISBN: 978-1-138-64564-6 (Volume 15) (hbk)
ISBN: 978-1-138-64570-7 (Volume 15) (pbk)
ISBN: 978-1-315-62799-1 (Volume 15) (ebk)

Publisher's Note
The publisher has gone to great lengths to ensure the quality of this reprint but points out that some imperfections in the original copies may be apparent.

Disclaimer
The publisher has made every effort to trace copyright holders and would welcome correspondence from those they have been unable to trace.

PERSPECTIVES ON PERCEPTION AND ACTION

Edited by
HERBERT HEUER
Universität Bielefeld

ANDRIES F. SANDERS
Institut für Psychologie der RWTH Aachen

LEA LAWRENCE ERLBAUM ASSOCIATES, PUBLISHERS
1987   Hillsdale, New Jersey   London

Copyright © 1987 by Lawrence Erlbaum Associates, Inc.
All rights reserved. No part of this book may be reproduced in
any form, by photostat, microform, retrieval system, or any other
means, without the prior written permission of the publisher.

Lawrence Erlbaum Associates, Inc., Publishers
365 Broadway
Hillsdale, New Jersey 07642

Library of Congress Cataloging in Publication Data

Perspectives on perception and action.

  Includes bibliographies and indexes.
  1. Perceptual-motor processes. 2. Human information
processing. I. Heuer, H. (Herbert), 1948–   .
II. Sanders, A. F. (Andries Frans), 1933–   .
BF295.P45   1987   153.7   86-29317
ISBN 0-89859-694-7

Printed in the United States of America
10 9 8 7 6 5 4 3 2 1

Contents

Preface

I: PERCEPTION AND THE CONTROL OF MOVEMENT

1. Information and Control: A Macroscopic Analysis of Perception-Action Coupling   3
J. A. S. Kelso and B. A. Kay

    1. Introduction   3
    2. Control   4
    3. Information   6
    4. Introduction to Nonlinear Dynamics   8
    5. A Brief Survey of Nonlinear Dynamics Applied to Movement Control   10
    6. Control of Action Dynamics Via Perception (Kinematic Specification)   24
    7. Common Principles Linking Dynamic Events in Perception and Action?   25
    References   27

2. Catching   33
Claes von Hofsten

    Perception—Action Systems   33
    The Catching Task   34
    Conclusion   44
    References   45

3. Ideo-Motor Action   47
Wolfgang Prinz

    1. Introduction   47
    2. Ideo-Motor Phenomena   49
    3. Views on the Ideo-Motor Hyphen   56
    4. An Event Generation Approach   72
    References   73

CONTENTS

**The Acquisition of Skill: Some Modifications to the
Perception-Action Relationship Through Practice**   77
Richard A. Schmidt

   Shifts Among Information Sources with Practice   *78*
   The Learning of Error Detection Capabilities   *81*
   Acquiring Automaticity   *85*
   Concluding Remarks   *100*
   References   *100*

5. **Brain Potentials Related to Preparation and Action**   105
C. H. M. Brunia

   Introduction   *105*
   Potentials Related to Simple Ballistic Movements   *107*
   Localization of Sources   *112*
   Conclusion   *117*
   Potentials Related to Complex Movements   *117*
   Conclusion   *127*
   References   *128*

6. **Sensorimotor Integration: The Role of Pyramidal Tract Neurons**   131
Christoph Fromm

   I. The Somatic Sensorimotor Cortex   *135*
   II. Input-Output-Relationship of Pyramidal Tract Neurons   *146*
   III. Patterns of PTN Activity with Different Types of
       Motor Behavior   *154*
       References   *162*

II: MOTOR PROCESSES IN PERCEPTION

7. **Muscle Sense and Innervation Feelings: A Chapter in the
History of Perception and Action**   171
Eckart Scheerer

   Introduction   *171*
   The Discovery of the Muscle Sense   *172*
   Innervation Feelings: A Sketch of their Rise and Fall   *186*
   The Final Act   *190*
   References   *192*

8. An Ecological Efference Mediation Theory of Natural Event Perception — 195
Wayne L. Shebliske

Visuomotor Coordination: Efference-Based Determinants *196*
Visuomotor Coordination: Light-Based Determinants *200*
Visuomotor Coordination: Interaction of Efference-Based and Light-Based Determinants *203*
An Ecological Efference Mediation Theory *205*
Modern Applications *208*
Conclusions *210*
References *211*

9. Oculomotor Information and Perception of Three-Dimensional Space — 215
D. Alfred Owens

Introduction *215*
Theoretical Background *216*
The Resting State of the Eyes *221*
The Functional Value of Oculomotor Information *231*
Theoretical Implications *241*
References *244*

10. Perceptual Learning by Saccades: A Cognitive Approach — 249
Peter Wolff

Introduction *249*
Saccadic Reafference and Perception *251*
Function of Saccadic Reafference *252*
A Cognitive Approach *254*
Conclusion *267*
References *267*

11. Information-Processing Theory and Strong Inference: A Paradigm for Psychological Inquiry — 273
Dominic W. Massaro

Introduction *273*
Information-Processing Theory *273*
Integrating Information and Information Processing *276*
Research Strategy *279*
Speech Perception by Eye and Ear *282*
Conclusion *296*
References *297*

12. Asymmetries in the Relationship Between Speech Perception and Production   301
Donald G. MacKay

The Structural Issue: Common Components   302
Functional Issue I: A Theory of Output Processes Involving Mental Nodes   307
Structural Issue II: Bottom-Up Connections For Perception   314
Functional Issue II: The Processes Underlying Perception   316
The Principle of Higher Level Activation   316
Perceptual Errors   321
Asymmetries Between Production and Perception   324
Conclusions   328
References   331

13. Information Stores and Mechanisms: Early Stages of Visual Processing   335
D. J. K. Mewhort

The Nature of the Model   335
Buffers and Processors in Tachistoscopic Tasks   337
Examples of Working Systems   338
The Whole-Report Task   338
An Analysis of Two Partial-Report Tasks   344
The Bar-Probe Task   345
The Digit-Probe Task   350
Evidence Concerning the Separation of Stages   352
Concluding Remarks   354
References   355

III: ATTENTION AND THE CONTROL OF ACTION

14. Beyond Capacity: A Functional View of Attention   361
Odmar Neumann

Introduction   361
Why is Capacity Limited? A Survey of Some Answers   362
A Functional View of Attention   373
Conclusion   386
References   387

15. **Selection for Action: Some Behavioral and Neurophysiological Considerations of Attention and Action**   **395**
    Alan Allport
    - I. Introduction: Behavioral Considerations   *395*
    - II. Considerations of Representation and Selection in the Brain   *400*
    - III. Selection for Action and Theories of Attention   *407*
    - References   *415*

16. **Central Selection in Vision**   **421**
    A. H. C. van der Heijden
    - I. Introduction   *421*
    - IIa. Partial Report 1   *423*
    - IIb. Early Selection and LC Processing   *425*
    - IIc. LC or UC Processing   *426*
    - IIIa. Partial Report II   *429*
    - IIIb. Late Selection—UC Processing   *432*
    - IIIc. Late or Early Selection   *434*
    - IV. Early Selection and UC Processing   *438*
    - References   *441*

Author Index   **447**
Subject Index   **461**

Contributors

J. A. S. KELSO, Haskins Laboratories, 270 Crown Street, New Haven, CT 06510

B. A. KAY, Haskins Laboratories, 270 Crown Street, New Haven, CT 06510

C. VON HOFSTEN, Department of Psychology, University of Umea, Umea, Sweden

W. PRINZ, Abteilung für Psychologie, Universität Bielefeld, Postfach 8640, 4800 Bielefeld 1, West Germany

R. A. SCHMIDT, Department of Kinesiology, University of California, Los Angeles, CA 90024

C. H. M. BRUNIA, Department of Psychology, University of Tilburg, P. O. Box 90 153, 5000 LE Tilburg, The Netherlands

C. FROMM, Max-Planck-Institut fur Biophysikalische Chemie, Postfach, 3400 Göttingen, West Germany

E. SCHEERER, Psychologisches Institut, Universität Oldenburg, Birkenweg 3, 2900 Oldenburg, West Germany

W. L. SHEBILSKE, Department of Psychology, Texas A & M University, College Station, TX 77840

D. A. OWENS, Department of Psychology, Franklin and Marshall College, Lancaster, PA 17604

P. WOLFF, Zentrum für interdisziplinäre Forschung (ZiF), Wellenberg 1, 4800 Bielefeld 1, West Germany

D. W. MASSARO, Program in Experimental Psychology, University of California, Santa Cruz, CA 95064

D. G. MACKAY, Department of Psychology, University of California, Los Angeles, CA 90024

D. J. K. MEWHORT, Department of Psychology, Queen's University, Kingston, Ontario K7L 3NG Canada

O. NEUMANN, Abteilung für Psychologie, Universität Bielefeld, Postfach 8640, 4800 Bielefeld 1, West Germany

A. ALLPORT, Department of Experimental Psychology, University of Oxford, South Parks Road, Oxford OS1 3UD, Great Britain

A. H. C. VAN DER HEIJDEN, Department of Psychology, University of Leiden, Hooigracht 15, Leiden, The Netherlands

Preface

There is a long-standing tradition in the different disciplines like Psychology and Physiology to separate sensory and perceptual processes on the one, and efferent and motor processes on the other hand. This tradition is reflected in conventional subdivisions like Perception, Sensory Physiology, and Motor Control. Moreover, the usual emphasis is on the input side of this dichotomy. In particular in Psychology, human motor actions have often been treated as some appendix to the more interesting aspects of mental life.

There is a growing awareness, however, that the human mind may like dichotomies but that nature does not; and in particular not a dichotomy between clearly separated input and output processes. This awareness suggests to spend some effort for a more detailed examination of the relations between afferent and efferent processes, between perception and movement, between cognition and action, or between whatever other levels there may be to characterize input and output. This effort was channeled into the organizational format of a project group on Perception and Action at the Center for Interdisciplinary Research (ZiF) at the University of Bielefeld in the academic year 1984/85.

One of the aims of the project group was to obtain an obviously eclectric and biased account of the present status of perception-action relationships in various fields. The outcome is this book. The chapters are intended to be eclectric in that they do not represent a unified approach nor center around a single topic. Rather they cover different approaches, ranging from single cell analysis via the information-processing approach to the ecological one; focussing on different approaches, of course, implies different levels of analysis. In addition the chapters cover different issues ranging from very simple skills like choice reaction or perception of the distance of a single point in space to complex questions about catching or speech perception. The diversity reflects the state of the art in the field. Although some of the approaches may seem antagonistic, at least to their proponents, there are also several cases of "unity in diversity."

The chapters can be broadly divided into three sections. The first focuses on motor control, a neglected topic in the past and hence deserving the role of the starting point of this volume. In addition motor control provides a good background to discuss the clear sensory and perceptual effects.

However, motor processes are also highly relevant to perception, which is usually less emphasized in the literature. Therefore a special section is devoted to motor processes in perception together with the issue of integrating information from different sources. The book concludes with a section on attention and selection of perceptual information for subsequent action.

We are indebted to the directors and the staff of the Center for Interdisciplinary Research (ZiF), Bielefeld, for providing the resources without which this book would not have been possible. We deeply appreciate the cooperation of the authors.

Bielefeld, Aachen

PERCEPTION AND THE CONTROL OF MOVEMENT

Information and Control: A Macroscopic Analysis of Perception-Action Coupling

J. A. S. Kelso
Center for Complex Systems, Florida Atlantic University, Boca Raton, FL, and
Haskins Laboratories, New Haven, CT

B. A. Kay
University of Connecticut, Storrs, CT, and
Haskins Laboratories, New Haven, CT

1. INTRODUCTION

In this chapter we address problems pertaining to the current or ongoing control of action—problems that, fundamentally, rest with understanding how perception and production are linked in biological activities. There have been a number of quite recent treatments, both behavioral and physiological, of motor control of simple limb movements performed in relatively uncomplicated environments. Rather than review that material again (see, e.g., Keele, 1981; Kelso, 1982a; Schmidt, 1982, for largely behavioral treatments; and, e.g., Houk & Rymer, 1981; Stein, 1982, for a largely neurophysiological-engineering analysis), we try to expand the horizons of "control" a bit in this chapter—a larger sweep of the brush, as it were (see also Reed, 1982). To a certain extent, we consider goal-directed activities like reaching for a cup, driving a car, climbing stairs—activities that involve very large numbers of degrees of freedom on both the motor and perceptual side of things. Thus, on the performance side were one to count, say, the number of neurons, neuronal connections, and muscle fibers involved (even in so-called simple actions like moving a finger), the result would be a large number. Likewise, on the perception side the light rays to the eye, the retinal mosaic, and the neural processing structures involved amass into a problem of huge dimensionality. Yet somehow—in spite of the large dimensionality on both sides of the coin (or perhaps because of it)—control is possible. Somehow, this high dimensionality gets compressed, as it were, into lower dimensional control. How this is realized, of course, is the challenge faced, not only by students of perception and action, but in other realms of science as well.

In this chapter we have this challenge in focus as we (1) present what an understanding of control in the larger context of perception-action systems might entail; (2) show how an approach based in dynamical systems theory can, on the action side, offer useful ways to describe the behavior of multidegree of freedom systems; and (3) using concepts developed in (2) along with recent empirical analyses of visually guided actions, try to reveal something about the nature of the linkage between perceiving and acting. Questions such as: What *kind* of information is used to regulate action? *When* and *where* in a given action is such information used, and *how* is it used? receive our primary attention. We argue, as have various colleagues (Fitch & Turvey, 1978; Fowler & Turvey, 1978; Kugler, Kelso, & Turvey, 1980; Kugler & Turvey, in press; Saltzman & Kelso, 1983a; Solomon, Carello, & Turvey, in press) that by appropriate *macroscopic* descriptions of perceptual and motor parameters, the potentially complex, high-dimensional control problem seen at the level of the microscopic degrees of freedom can be simplified.

Before proceeding we should mention that in making these moves, we stand on the shoulders of giants. On the perception side, Gibson (1961, 1966, 1979) developed the idea of the optical flow field as a relevant macroscopic description of the light to an eye (any eye) that is specific to the layout of surfaces and the activity of a moving point of observation. On the action side, Bernstein—at least in his later work (1967; Whiting, 1984)—pursued a macroscopic analysis of movement in terms of the essential and nonessential parameters governing large ensembles of neuromuscular elements, namely, those parameters that remain stable during the course of an activity and those that do not. In each case, as we shall see, singular macroscopic quantities emerge that play a key role in the control of activity. But first, let us turn briefly to the meaning of control—both in its conventional form, as something that is imposed on a system by external means—and in the way we would like to view it, as arising intrinsically from the dynamics of the perception-action system itself.

2. CONTROL

The concepts of regulation and control have played a central role in efforts to understand how the many neuromuscular degrees of freedom are harnessed to produce coherent behavior. In a cybernetic system, regulators and controllers serve closely related yet quite distinct functions. On the one hand, given a desired state of affairs in such a system, and a source of variability that can perturb the system away from that state, a regulator maintains that state within acceptable tolerance limits. For example, a thermostat regulates an oven's most important state variable, temperature, in the face of heat fluxes perturbing that temperature. On the other hand, control presupposes the existence of regulation capabilities in a system: The controller sets the particular values that the regulator tries to maintain. As a prosaic example, a chef controls a thermostat on an oven, to cook a meal slowly at a low temperature or more quickly at a higher temperature. Control function is most often provided by a logical separation between the controlling device and the controlled system (i.e., the plant dynamics). Hence, it is not appropriate to consider the controller to be a part of the system in the same sense as a regulator: Whereas a regulator must be sensitive to apposite aspects of the system's dynamics in order to function at all, the specification of control algorithms is in principle arbitrary with respect to those dynamics (see Tomovic, 1978, for informed discussion of the plant-controller problem). Thus, the controller is extrinsic to the system and *prescribes* the system's behavior.

In the motor systems' literature, we see this view of control quite clearly expressed, for example, in Stein's (1982) *Behavioral and Brain Sciences* article on "What muscle variable(s) does the nervous system control?" in limb movements. For Stein and others (see Commentaries, ibid) the skeletomuscular apparatus is the system being controlled, and it is assumed that the nervous system is the controlling device. Control proceeds prescriptively, according to executive command programs, for example. We have argued (e.g., Kelso & Saltzman, 1982; Kugler, Kelso, & Turvey, 1980) that such a strategy offers little explanatory power, because it attributes the coherence and adaptability of coordinated movements to the coherent actions of an external controller that themselves are not explained. Thus, control in this classical engineering sense is an example of allonomy, literally, "external law." Its complement is autonomy or "self-law" (Varela, 1983). Successful biological systems are autonomous in that no external controllers are necessary for their survival. Energy flows figure significantly in the survival of any organism (Morowitz, 1968), and as Yates, Marsh, and Iberall (1972) argue, in order to obtain efficient operation, a controller must be coupled to the system being controlled via an appropriate match or scaling between the energy flows of controllers and controlled systems. This criterion of energy flow commensurability applies to any control situation in which systems dissipate significant amounts of energy, a condition satisfied for biological motions. The criterion is clearly *not* met by the cybernetic theory of control and regulation, in which low energy signals (e.g., in microprocessor circuits) prescribe the large energy flows for the controlled systems (e.g., in torque motors for industrial robot arms). However, autonomous control, in which control resides "inside" the system as a natural consequence of its self-organization, does afford the possibility of satisfying this energy commensurability criterion.

Allonomic control theories imply an extrinsic view of control precisely because of the way they compartmentalize systems. For example, the perceptual and motor "apparatii" are treated as fundamentally distinct components of a larger system (an organism), and organisms and their environments are also treated separately. Decompositions of this kind, though the trademark of analytic reductionism, can carry serious consequences for measurement and understanding (see Rosen, 1978). The problem is that such decomposition obscures the nature of the overall system's dynamics: An analysis of the system's parts may not lead to an understanding of the behavior of the system as a whole. Furthermore, the observables chosen to describe the parts may have nothing to do with those that are appropriate for the description of the system in toto. We are not repeating here the well-known adage that the whole is greater than the sum of the parts. Rather, we want to emphasize that in open, complex, multidegree of freedom systems, novel properties emerge at more global levels that cannot be known or predicted from knowledge of component processes. Thus not only do we have *more* of something as complexity increases, but that "more" is different (Anderson, 1972). This is an inevitable consequence of *broken symmetry:* Systems with large numbers of microscopic degrees of freedom may undergo sharp, discontinuous transitions leaving behind usually few, qualitatively different modes of behavior. Such systems are subject to constraints that arise during the transitions and thus cannot assume all those configurations that were possible before symmetry breaking. We return to this theme later because it affords a way of intuiting how the degrees of freedom of perception-action systems can be "compressed" as it were, so that coordination may be defined over a smaller number of variables.

One major consequence of viewing control as autonomous and self-organized is that the definition and role of *information* is drastically changed. In conventional control theory, information is arbitrary with respect to the activities that it serves. More generally, neither environmental events nor the perceiver's own movements are assumed to structure perceptually relevant energy distributions in ways that are intrinsically meaningful to the organism. Rather, information must be interpreted and disambiguated. An autonomous view of control, however, mandates that information be: (1) unique and specific to the facts about which it informs, (2) meaningful to the control requirements of the activity (i.e., it carries its own "semantics" as it were), and (3) scaled to the system's physical dimensions and behavioral repertoire (see Kugler, Kelso, & Turvey, 1982). In a deep sense, information for a self-organizing, autonomous theory of control is "information," the formation of structure in the system as a whole (Varela, 1983).

But how can we understand information as viewed within such a framework? How can these formulations be grounded in experimental analyses? To proceed further, we must make one additional, yet perhaps crucial, distinction—namely between a view of information as *indicational/injunctional* and a view of information as *specificational.*

3. INFORMATION

Information theory is still a powerful tool in many branches of science where it is used to obtain a measure for the amount of information contained in a system. It has had its application in the motor skills field as well, particularly through the stimulus of the late Paul Fitts (e.g., Fitts, 1954). Here is not the place to discuss the details of this theory except to make a few points. First, the formalisms derived from information theory (e.g., I = k·log(Ro), where I is the information metric, Ro is the number of equiprobable events and k is an arbitrary constant) refer to the scarcity of an event; "information" is thus a measure of *ignorance* about a system (Ashby, 1956). Second, and importantly, the events dealt with in information theory are symbolic, not dynamic, events. Even in physics, and certainly in other fields like biology and psychology, "information" takes the form of a set of symbolic elements organized by a grammar. The role that such symbolic structures play can be termed *injunctional/indicational* (see Reed, 1981; also, Kugler, Kelso, & Turvey, 1982; Turvey & Kugler, 1984). On the one hand states may be indicated symbolically and, on the other, states can be commanded. In contemporary theories of motor control, for example, the motor program tells the muscles when to turn on, how much, and when to turn off. Emphasis here is clearly on the injunctional mode of description with little or no attention given to the rate-dependent, dynamical processes that are prescribed to or directed by the injunctional mode. Further, the symbolic or indicational mode of description greatly underestimates (to the point of ignoring) the information required to actually perform an activity. As Turvey and Kugler (1984) note, a stop sign indicates to a driver that the car should be stopped but provides no information about *how* to stop the car, i.e., how, where, and by how much to decelerate, apply the brakes, etc.

But as just suggested and as repeatedly emphasized in the writings of Pattee (e.g., Pattee, 1972, 1973, 1977), complex systems (the focus here) are to be fundamentally understood in terms of two *complementary* modes of description—the discrete, symbolic rate-independent mode and the continuous, dynamical, rate-dependent mode where the flow of time is included. In spite of the dualism implied by complementarity, the significance of Pattee's analysis for students of perception and action (see Kugler, Kelso, & Turvey, 1982) is his emphasis on dynamical processes, that is, information in the symbolic sense plays a minimum role; it acts as a constraint on dynamics but does not explicitly control them. Thus, although both modes of description are crucial to Pattee, the dynamical mode should be exploited to the fullest. Paraphrasing Emerson, hitch your wagon to a star—and see the chores done by the Gods themselves (quoted by Greene, 1982, in the context of arm movement control).

As we have noted previously and elsewhere (e.g., Kelso, Holt, Rubin, & Kugler, 1981) most of the theoretical effort in the field of movement science has stressed the symbolic, indicational mode. The contribution of dynamical processes is given a fairly limited treatment. For example, there have been many proposals for the "contents" of the motor program (see Kelso, 1981 for a critical review of putative candidates). Little attention has been paid to the processes by which these "contents" interface to the large-scale muscular machinery that carries out their instructions. More important, such theorizing lacks a rationale for how it is and by what means the *particular* contents of the program are created. What is missing is an account of the program that is priviledged with respect to the dynamics that it directs, that is, the origins of the program's code must, it seems, be lawfully derived from dynamics (see Kugler, Kelso, & Turvey, 1982; Turvey & Kugler, 1984). In summary, what we are saying amounts to this: (1) Information in the conventional, symbolic sense is not sufficient to control ongoing action; (2) *Ergo,* information in a nonsymbolic sense must play a significant role; (3) Such information is dynamical in the sense that it is unique and specific to the dynamics of activities themselves, that is, information is implicit in the dynamics, not imposed upon it as a sequence of symbol strings from the outside. In the following sections we provide a short tutorial of what is meant by dynamics, list some of the advantages of dynamic description, and provide some specific examples of its use in the movement field.

4. INTRODUCTION TO NONLINEAR DYNAMICS

Nonlinear (qualitative) dynamics is fundamentally concerned with the appropriate description for forms of motion in complex, multidegree of freedom systems. These forms of motion are specified, roughly, by the qualitative shapes observed in phase portraits of a system's behavior. The phase portrait constitutes the totality of all possible phase plane trajectories generated by a particular dynamical system under a particular parameterization. Phase plane trajectories have been used to varying degrees by engineers over the years, though their full significance is just being realized—at least in the West (see Abraham & Shaw, 1982, for a brief historical treatment). On the other hand, many developments in nonlinear dynamics have been pioneered by Russian workers (e.g., Andronov & Chaikin, 1949; Minorksy, 1962).

A phase plane trajectory is generated by plotting the position (x) of an articulator (say the end of a finger, the tip of the tongue, etc.) against its instantaneous velocity ($\dot{x}$). These quantities act as coordinates that describe the ongoing motion of the articulator in two-dimensional space; for a (deterministic, classical mechanical) system composed of one macroscopic degree of freedom, these two variables represent the state of the system at any point in time. As time varies, the point $P(x,\dot{x})$ moves along a certain path or trajectory on the phase plane. For different initial conditions (such as a given starting position) and parameter values (such as a given level of articulator stiffness) the motion will describe different phase paths. For a given system and set of parameter values, the form of the phase portrait (the ensemble of all the trajectories arising from all possible initial conditions) is specified by the relations among underlying dynamic parameters (for examples, see following). Such patterned forms or topologies can be categorized as low-dimensional *attractors* even though the system they describe is high dimensional.

This brings us to an important point: One reason, it seems, why dynamics has been of little interest to motor behavior theorists is that it has been conceived as local and concrete, pure biomechanics as it were. This bias is misplaced: Dynamics, by definition, constitutes the *simplest and most abstract description of the motion of a system* (Maxwell, 1877, p. 1). There is no logical reason why dynamics, though rate dependent and nonsymbolic, cannot be abstract. Quite to the contrary, as any cursory perusal of the field of dynamical systems will reveal (e.g., Guckenheimer & Holmes, 1983; Haken, 1983; Rasband, 1983). Indeed, as many researchers are now discovering, complex systems composed of very different materials can share the same underlying dynamic structure (for many examples in physics, chemistry, and biology, see Haken, 1975; 1977; in movement science, see Kelso & Tuller, 1984a,b).

An example of the dynamical approach in the field of motor systems was Fel'dman's (1966) insight that, in certain types of tasks, the motor apparatus behaves in a qualitatively similar way to a simple physical system, a mass-spring. Though a system of neuromuscular components differs greatly from a system of masses and springs, they can be shown to share the same abstract functional organization, i.e., an equivalent dynamic, that of Hooke's law relating stresses and strains. As Rosen (1970) remarks, there is nothing unscientific or speculative about the dynamic approach, any more than, say, the hard sphere model for describing the behavior of gases, regardless of each gas's individual molecular structure. Indeed, if one's primary focus is function and behavior then it is the search for appropriate dynamical descriptions of system behavior ("laws") that takes precedence over any particular material embodiment. Such a strategy has played a major role in the development of science. Prigogine and Stengers (1984), for example, propose that Fourier's law, a mathematical description of the propagation of heat in materials (proposed in 1811), was the start of "a science of complexity" (p. 104). This simple law, which states that heat flow is proportional to the gradient of temperature, applies to all matter regardless of its state—solid, liquid, or gas. Also, the chemical composition of the substances to which it applies is immaterial; although each substance has its own proportionality coefficient, the same law holds nevertheless. Here again we see that in spite of a great deal of diversity at a molecular level, the macroscopic behavior is described by a single law, with particular variants resulting from changes in only a single parameter. The framework of nonlinear dynamics follows this macroscopic, law-based orientation to microscopic diversity. It offers a way of characterizing regularities in action problems in terms of relatively abstract, functionally specified control schemes.

5. A BRIEF SURVEY OF NONLINEAR DYNAMICS APPLIED TO MOVEMENT CONTROL

5.1. Generative Properties and Low-dimensional Control—Point Attractors

Attractors represent the asymptotic behavior of a whole family of system trajectories. As a simple example, referred to briefly earlier, a damped mass-spring system with only a single degree of freedom can have many trajectories depending on its initial conditions and its parameter values. For example, the linear mass-spring system

$$m\ddot{x} + b\dot{x} + kx = 0 \tag{1}$$

may simply oscillate without being damped out (if the linear damping term, b, equals zero), or be underdamped, overdamped, or critically damped, depending on the mass (m), the damping (b), and stiffness (k) parameter values (for actual examples of discrete movements displaying these types of behavior, see Kelso & Holt, 1980). For b greater than zero (corresponding to a real system having some frictional component), such a system is called a *point attractor,* a generic dynamical category that reflects the fact that all trajectories converge to an asymptotic, static equilibrium state (see Figure 1a). Such systems exhibit the property of equifinality—the tendency to achieve an equilibrium state regardless of initial conditions. Importantly, however, a multidegree of freedom system whose trajectories converge to a single rest position can also be described as a point attractor. One can imagine, for example, the high dimensionality involved in a simple finger movement, were one to include the neurons, muscles, and their interconnections, yet the resultant behavior would be described as a low-dimensional point attractor. Thus, point attractors also provide low-dimensional descriptions of the asymptotic patterns produced by potentially high-dimensional systems.

Saltzman and Kelso (1983b) have recently shown how a point attractor dynamical regime defined at a task level can control the behavior of a multidegree-of-freedom system in such activities as reaching, cup-to-mouth tasks, and postural stability (see also Saltzman & Kelso, in press). This demonstration seems significant given criticisms that the mass-spring model (so-called "end-point control," Bizzi, Chapple, & Hogan, 1982) for single-joint motions is inadequate for motions involving two or more joints (e.g., the arm and shoulder). The latter display (roughly) straight line trajectories of the hand (e.g., Bizzi et al., 1982; Morasso, 1981). However, though point attractor dynamics defined for each joint could generate the final target configuration, they would also result in a *curved* rather than quasi-straight line trajectory of the hand.

Part of the problem here may be the narrow definition of the mass-spring

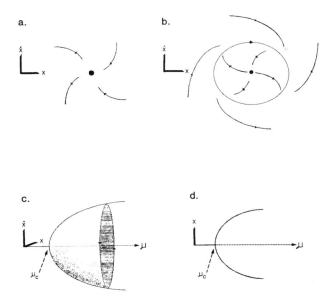

FIG. 1.1 Phase plane portraits for (a) a point attractor and (b) a limit cycle oscillator. Bifurcation diagram of the (c) Hopf and (d) pitchfork bifurcations: As the parameter μ is increased, behavior shifts from a point attractor regime to a periodic regime, in two dimensions for the Hopf and one dimension for the pitchfork bifurcation.

model. Some (a little naively, we note with 20/20 hindsight) have restricted the model to single, discrete movements in which muscles are represented by a pair of springs acting across a hinge in the agonist–antagonist configuration. The final equilibrium point is established by selecting the length-tension characteristics of opposing muscles (e.g., Bizzi, Polit, & Morasso, 1976, Cooke, 1980; Kelso, 1977; Schmidt & McGown, 1980). This view, at best, may work for deafferented muscle but, as pointed out by Fel'dman and Latash (1982), it is inadequate for muscles operating in natural conditions. Clearly, the parallel between a single muscle and a spring should not be taken too literally. The mass-spring model—as intimated above—is better viewed as an account of equifinality, a property shared by mass-springs and a complex, multivariable system's ability to generate targeting behavior (see Kelso, Holt, Kugler, & Turvey, 1980). By adopting this approach and specifying point attractor dynamics in *task* space, Saltzman and Kelso (1983b/in press) show how sets of dynamic parameters, which are constant at the *task* level, can be used to define *changing* patterns of dynamic parameters at the articulator level (e.g., joint stiffness, dampings, rest angles). Thus, via this strategy a low-dimensional control scheme is realized that possesses generative properties. Once the relations among dynamic parameters are set up according to particular task demands, a wide variety of trajectories can be generated. Moreover, this rich set of trajectories emerges from an underlying task dynamic that does not contain detailed, step-by-step trajectory plans (e.g., Hollerbach, 1982) of any kind.

Thus, just as early work on single discrete motions showed that variables like duration and velocity did not need to be conceived as contents in the motor program, but were rather consequences of a simple, point attractor (mass-spring) dynamical system (e.g., Fitch & Turvey, 1978; Fowler, Rubin, Remez, & Turvey, 1980; Kelso, 1977; Kelso & Holt, 1980; Kelso, Holt, & Flatt, 1980; Schmidt & McGown, 1980), so this recent extension of dynamics by Saltzman and Kelso (1983b/ in press) demonstrates how program candidates for two-joint motions (such as trajectory) can arise from an appropriately specified dynamical regime. A very similar analysis holds for tasks involving multidegree of freedom interlimb coordination (Kelso, Putnam, & Goodman, 1983; Kelso, Southard, & Goodman, 1979).

5.2. Generative Properties and Low-dimensional Control—Periodic Attractors

The theme that kinematic diversity can arise from an underlying "simple" dynamic control structure can be readily extended to rhythmical movements. Several years ago, we showed that bimanual, cyclical movements of the hands possess behaviors that are realizable by coupled nonlinear limit cycle oscillators (Kelso, Holt, Rubin, & Kugler, 1981). Of course, a variety of rhythmical behaviors, such as locomotion in both vertebrates (e.g., Miller & Scott, 1977; Patla, Calvert, & Stein, in press; Willis, 1980, for reviews) and invertebrates (e.g., Cohen, Holmes, & Rand, 1982) can and have been modeled in similar ways— far more explicitly in fact than in the Kelso et al. (1981) paper (but see Haken, Kelso, & Bunz, 1985; Schöner, Haken, & Kelso, 1986).

The limit cycle oscillator is called a *periodic attractor* in the dynamics literature because it displays orbital stability. Like a point attractor, all trajectories converge to a single limit set, in this case, a single cyclic orbit on the phase plane $(x,\dot{x})$, the limit cycle (see Fig. 1.1b). "Equifinality" for a limit cycle is caused by a nonlinearity in the damping term (sometimes called the escapement). If the system's initial conditions are outside the limit cycle, the trajectories decay until they reach the limit cycle. Energy is dissipated until a balance between kinetic and potential energy occurs. Likewise, if the initial conditions are inside the limit cycle, trajectories grow or spiral out to the attractor (see Jordan & Smith, 1977; Minorsky, 1962). Mathematically, there are many kinds of equations describing stable periodic motion, most typically in differential form like equation (1). However, they are all topologically the same; that is, they all exhibit orbital stability, because the structure of the equations (in terms of the internal relations among parameters) is identical, though the parameters values themselves may

1. INFORMATION AND CONTROL   13

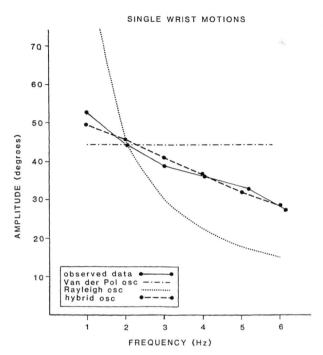

FIG. 1.2 Amplitude-frequency relationship for single hand movements around the wrist joint, and three oscillator models.

change. It is the feature of topological invariance [1] that allows for the classification of dynamical systems into generic categories (Abraham & Shaw, 1982), and that perhaps afford a classification of movement tasks as well (for examples see Kelso & Tuller, 1984a; Saltzman & Kelso, 1983b/in press).

In some cases a single parameter in a dynamic control structure can regulate

---

[1] Dynamical organizations can be used to categorize movement tasks into distinct topological forms. Topology is the branch of mathematics that categorizes, for example, geometrical shapes, on the basis of the loosest possible criterion: continuity of form. A circle, ellipse, square, and any simple closed curve in the plane are topologically indistinguishable, whereas a line and a circle fall into separate topological categories (although they are all one dimensional curves). To transform a circle into a line requires breaking the circle, i.e., a change in the continuity of the circle. Applied to movement, the kinematics of tasks may be treated as shapes, which can be put into topological classes, or topologies. Plotting position versus velocity on the phase plane, one can see that discrete movements to a target exhibit asymptotic behavior to a point topology (hence are characterized as a point attractor), whereas repetitive movements are similar to circles and ellipses and form a periodic attractor topology. Other kinds of movements may require the definition of other topologies, e.g., a chaotic attractor (see Shaw, 1981) for physiological tremor. Different dynamical organizations can thus generate different movement topologies.

14 KELSO AND KAY

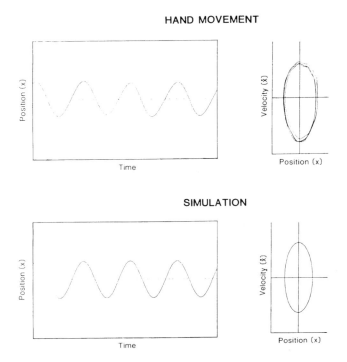

FIG. 1.3 Time series and phase plane plots of a real hand movement (top) and a hybrid oscillator (bottom), both operating at 3 Hz.

the space–time behavior of the system. In recent work at Haskins Laboratories we have inquired how spatiotemporal changes occur in single and bimanual cyclical movements in response to an externally required change in frequency. Basically subjects performed cyclical movements in response to a metronome whose frequency was manipulated (in 1 Hz steps) between 1 and 6 Hz. We wanted to try to understand a very basic question (but for which little information exists in the literature, see Freund, 1983): How do space (in terms of movement amplitude) and time (in terms of movement duration) covary as the task requires the hands to move faster? Subjects grasped a manipulandum with one or both hands—the forearms were stabilized and the task required movement around the wrist joint(s) in the horizontal plane. Transducers situated above the axes of rotation of the joints provided ongoing measures of angular displacement over time. The data on four subjects tested on two separate occasions revealed a reciprocal relationship between cycling frequency and amplitude for both single and bimanual movements (Kay, Kelso, Saltzman, & Schöner, in press). Using a nonlinear, limit cycle oscillator of the form

1. INFORMATION AND CONTROL   15

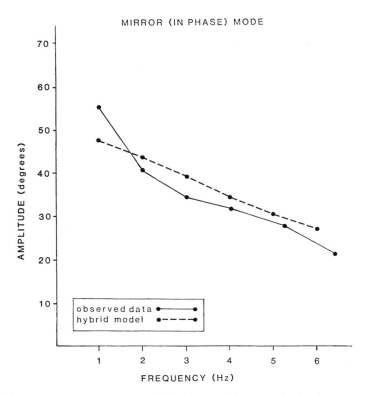

FIG. 1.4 Amplitude-frequency relationship for inphase (two-handed) movements, and the coupled hybrid oscillator model.

$$\ddot{x} + (Vx^2 + R\dot{x}^2 - a)\dot{x} + kx = 0 \qquad (2)$$

o model these data, the covariation between frequency and amplitude is mimicked by changing only a single parameter, k, the linear restoring force (stiffness) of the oscillator (see Fig. 1.2 for single wrist data, and Fig. 1.3 for examples of observed and simulated movements in the time domain and on the phase plane). Note that this dynamic structure is actually a combination of the classic van der Pol and Rayleigh oscillators, which are also shown in Fig. 1.2. These differ in the form of the nonlinear damping term. For the van der Pol oscillator,

$$\ddot{x} + (Vx^2 - a)\dot{x} + kx = 0 \qquad (3)$$

amplitude remains constant across changes in oscillator frequency; that is, the frequency-amplitude function (see Fig. 1.2) has a finite y- (amplitude-) intercept, but the slope is everywhere zero. For the Rayleigh oscillator,

$$\ddot{x} + (R\dot{x}^2 - a)\dot{x} + kx = 0 \qquad (4)$$

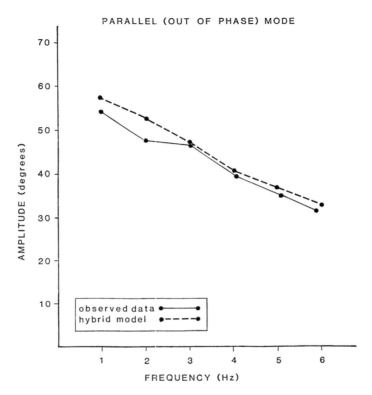

FIG. 1.5 Amplitude-frequency relationship for antiphase (two-handed) movements, and the coupled hybrid oscillator model.

on the other hand, amplitude is inversely proportional to frequency, that is, the slope is everywhere negative but the y-intercept is infinitely large. (Infinite movement amplitude at zero movement frequency seems very unrealistic, both from intuition and our data.) The hybrid dynamics (equation (2)) map onto the real data rather well both in terms of slope and intercept. When two such hybrid oscillators are coupled together (via terms proportional to the other oscillator's position and velocity) (see Haken, Kelso & Bunz, 1985), once more a variation in system stiffness produces space–time behavior mimicking that observed for the two modes, mirror (in phase) shown in Fig. 1.4, and parallel (antiphase) shown in Fig. 1.5.

Although the physiological underpinnings of the nonlinear parameters (or indeed system stiffness, assumed to be linear here) are opaque at the moment, these models allow us to make a simple, but we think important, point. Namely, that what we illustrate here is how a rather simple dynamical control structure, requiring variations in only one system parameter, can describe the spatiotemporal behavior of the limbs singly and together. It should not be lost on the reader that, regardless of its physiological origins, the nonlinearity is crucial to guarantee the particular frequency-amplitude relationship observed.

5.3. Generative Properties—Bifurcations

Fixed point and periodic attractors, as illustrated earlier, generate some of the behavioral characteristics observed in discrete and rhythmical movements, respectively. A nontrivial correspondence between model and reality is the feature of the stable behavior in spite of perturbations and small changes in parameters. Thus the shape of a limit cycle may change a bit or the time needed to complete a cycle may exhibit small variations as a parameter is varied. In such cases, the attractor can be said to change *smoothly* without altering its topological form. However, the topology of an attractor may change abruptly when a key parameter crosses a bifurcation point—a distinct change to a new form may occur. At the bifurcation point (after the Latin, to branch), the system's behavior is ill defined; it may show the old behavior or the new one. For example, Fig. 1.1c shows the bifurcation diagram of the much-studied Hopf bifurcation (for many illustrations see Cvitanovic, 1984). On the phase plane (see Section 4 above), the system exhibits only a point stability at first, but upon changing the key parameter, μ, of the system past a certain value, a limit cycle trajectory ensues, as well as an unstable fixed point. In Fig. 1.1c, the straight line represents an equilibrium or steady state solution, for values of $\mu < \mu_c$. At the critical point μ_c, the system loses its prior stability—a steady state becomes oscillatory, as illustrated by the circle. A similar bifurcation—called the Pitchfork bifurcation—is shown in Fig. 1.1d (see e.g., Haken, 1983). Here again a stable fixed point loses its stability and gives rise to a stable periodic orbit as the parameter is changed.[2]

Similar phenomena abound in nature, including biological motion, from the transitions in phase observed in simple materials (e.g., from solid to liquid to gas) to the transitions in gait patterns observed in horses (walk to trot to gallop, see Hoyt & Taylor, 1981) to transitions in human posture (see Nashner & McCollum, 1985; and, for a bifurcation interpretation, Saltzman & Kelso, 1985). Parametrically scaled bimanual movements have been shown to exhibit bifurcation (Kelso, 1981, 1984). Thus, starting in an antiphase modal pattern (i.e., right flexion [extension] accompanied by left extension [flexion]), subjects in Kelso's studies voluntarily increased the cycling frequency of the two hands in a continuous manner. As frequency increased, the antiphase mode became less stable, as indicated by an increase in phase variance between the hands. At a

---

[2] Mathematically the difference between a Hopf and Pitchfork bifurcations rests in whether a pair of eigenvalues or a single eigenvalue, respectively, crosses the imaginary axis when the parameter passes through a critical value (see Eckmann, 1981), i.e., whether the bifurcation occurs, at a fundamental level, in a space of two dimensions or one.

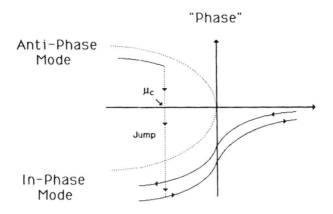

FIG. 1.6 Bifurcation diagram of the bimanual phase transition: As the parameter μ is increased, the antiphase mode becomes unstable (dashed lines), the inphase mode stable. If μ is then decreased, behavior remains in the inphase mode, i.e., the system stays on the same branch of the bifurcation picture.

critical parameter value (which the data suggested to be a dimensionless function of each individual's preferred cycling rate) the system bifurcated, and a different, in-phase modal pattern emerged. Though not given a bifurcation interpretation, similar results have been obtained by Cohen (1971), MacKenzie and Patla (1983), and Baldissera, Cavallari, and Civaschi (1982).

The bifurcation diagram shown in Fig. 1.6 reflects the basic results of the Kelso experiments. If the bimanual system is "prepared" in the antiphase mode (upper left quadrant), loss of stability occurs at the parameter value μ_c, i.e., when cycling frequency reaches a critical point, and a switch to the in-phase modal pattern occurs. The system then remains on the stable branch as μ is further increased (at least within limits). A further feature of the experiments shown in Fig. 1.6, is that when cycling frequency is reduced, the system remains in the symmetric, in-phase mode, i.e., it exhibits the phenomenon of hysteresis. Using nonlinear oscillators similar to the one described in (2), and a *nonlinear coupling*[3] between them, Haken, Kelso, and Bunz (1985) have explicitly modeled bimanual phase transition behaviors and generated novel, but testable predictions regarding their underpinnings (cf. Kelso & Scholz, 1985).

In summary, we have illustrated here how it is possible for simple dynamical

---

[3] Using terms proportional to the product of the position squared and velocity of the other oscillator, similar to a van der Pol damping structure. Current work is underway that tries to account for the previously mentioned frequency-amplitude data in terms of this nonlinear coupling structure. If successful, a single model would then describe both the stable and transition behavior. *Note added in proof.* This step has been successfully accomplished. The full details are reported in Kay, Kelso, Saltzman & Schöner, in press.

structures to generate a diversity of stable kinematic forms within a restricted region of their parameter spaces. In addition, we have shown how it is possible to explain the sometimes abrupt emergence of new kinematic forms when a critical bifurcation point is reached and the system enters a different region of parameter space. This analysis also hints at a kind of universal experimental strategy, viz. "tweak" system-sensitive parameters (externally or internally) to discover "new" spatiotemporal patterns. One is tempted to think that this is precisely what the emergence of skill is all about, and, parenthetically, what gifted teachers and coaches are all about as well. For it is they that often do the "tweaking" and it is they that have differentiated and become attuned to what some of the key parameters are (see Chapters 10–13 in Kelso, 1982b).

5.4. Inferring Dynamic Structure from Kinematic Analysis

A problem for investigators is that the dynamic parameters themselves are seldom, if ever, directly observed but can only be inferred from kinematic events. How can we go from kinematics to dynamics? By looking at key relationships (or *relational invariants;* see Kelso, 1981) among kinematic variables, one can gain valuable insights into the nature of the dynamics. For example, the mass-*nonlinear* spring system,

$$m\ddot{x} + kx + lx^3 = 0 \qquad (4)$$

shows an invariant relationship between frequency and amplitude, depending on the sign of l, the nonlinear restoring force parameter. If l is positive, the spring force is termed *hard* because for larger amplitudes the observed frequency is higher than for smaller amplitudes, and if negative, it is a *soft* spring with larger amplitude movements being slower than smaller amplitude ones (Jordan & Smith, 1977).

Kelso, Putnam, and Goodman (1983) applied the *soft*-spring model to their data on two-handed discrete movements of different amplitudes (see also Corcos, 1984; Marteniuk & MacKenzie, 1980; Marteniuk, MacKenzie, & Baba, 1984). The slight differences in movement time between simultaneously initiated short and long movements of the two limbs, fall out, as it were, from a nonlinear model in which stiffness *decreases* with increasing distance from the equilibrium position. Thus movements of large amplitude will be slightly slower than those of short amplitude, because they have smaller average stiffnesses over the range of motion. Moreover, a prediction of this model—yet to be tested—is that the greater the amplitude differences between the two limbs the greater should be deviations from isochrony.

In the case of cyclical movements, the hybrid oscillator of Equation (2) displays the frequency-amplitude relationship observed in the Kay et al. (in press) data (see Haken et al., 1985). The importance of nonlinearities is apparent here: Autonomous oscillators (i.e., without explicit time-dependent forcing terms) with only linear springs and linear damping terms show no preferred relationship between frequency and amplitude. If, phenomenologically, there is some tight correlation between space and time, for example, then immediately nonlinear dynamics have to be invoked, the particular form of such a relationship giving insight into the particular nature of such dynamics. In this sense, observed kinematic relationships between amplitude and frequency allow us to infer underlying dynamical control structures.

Another way of uncovering the dynamic control structure is to use kinematic relations evident in phase plane trajectories (see previous section) to index dynamic parameters. For example, in a system of constant mass, the slope of the peak velocity-displacement relationship provides an estimate of system stiffness. A recent kinematic study by Kelso, V.-Bateson, Saltzman, and Kay (1985) of reiterant speech, i.e., a subject inserts a simple syllable /ba/ for the real syllables in the utterance, performed at different rates revealed a very systematic scaling relation between an articulatory gesture's peak velocity and its displacement. The finding that the relationship is linear throughout the movement range indicates that the stiffness is constant, supporting the notion that an invariant underlying dynamic is present. Further quantitative analysis of articulatory movement as a function of speaking rate and stress showed that both could be accounted for by a model with only two controllable parameters, system stiffness and equilibrium position. Preliminary modeling was consonant with this perspective. A major implication of the Kelso et al. (1985) studies (as well as much other evidence from unimanual and bimanual motor skills, some of which is discussed earlier) is that time per se is not directly controlled; rather it is a consequence of the system's dynamic structure and parameterization.

Many other systems besides the lip–jaw complex exhibit a linear relationship between peak velocity and amplitude, for example, natural reaching movements (Jeannerod, 1984), drawing and handwriting (Lacquanti, Terzuolo, & Viviani, 1983; Viviani & McCollum, 1983), violin bowing (Nelson 1983), trombone playing (Wadman, Denier van der Gon, Geuze, & Mol, 1979), tongue movements (Ostry & Munhall, 1985), and eye movements (Bahill, Clark, & Stark, 1975). One can imagine that the structures involved all share the fundamental property of elasticity: Any strains imposed upon them are met by linearly proportional forces, a force-displacement law that is precisely stated by the mass-spring dynamic. These examples show that a single dynamic structure can hold quite generally across a wide range of material structures sometimes involving multiple degrees of freedom and in many different kinds of action. Importantly, the data illustrate how kinematic relations can be used to infer (or as we prefer to say, to specify) dynamics.

5.5. Some hard problems for the dynamical approach

The preceding sections seem to promise a bright future for the dynamical approach to movement control. However, there are some outstanding problems standing in the way of success. First, given that we are looking at dynamical systems when we are observing behaving organisms, how can we be sure of the *uniqueness* of the descriptions we apply? Many dynamical structures can give rise to similar kinematic consequences: For example, limit cycle-type behavior is exhibited both by nonlinear autonomous oscillators of the form of equation (2), and by the forced Duffing equation,

$$m\ddot{x} + b\dot{x} + kx + lx^3 = f\cos(\omega t) \tag{5}$$

which contains a time-dependent forcing term on the right hand side, rendering the equation nonautonomous and therefore very different in structure from the hybrid oscillator. Both of these oscillators settle down to an invariant limit cycle trajectory and return to that cycle after perturbation. Distinguishing these two options on the basis of actual behavior is problematical, but hope lies in the fact that other behavioral properties differ. In particular, the forced Duffing oscillator shows a jump in amplitude at a certain frequency, whereas the hybrid oscillator shows no such discontinuity in its frequency-amplitude curve.

Given the possibility of multiple dynamical descriptions, one of the investigators' tasks in the dynamical approach is to become familiar with the behavioral characteristics of various classes of dynamical systems and to obtain data addressing their similarities and differences. This is the approach we have taken in our work. The reader should beware, however, of the difficulties involved. Dynamics typically starts with a set of equations and evaluates their solutions under various conditions such as changes in parameters and initial conditions. Nonlinear dynamical systems, however, generally defy exact solutions and only approximate (via numerical methods) and/or qualitative solutions are possible. In movement science we are faced with an even more difficult problem: Given a solution—a particular spatiotemporal event produced by an organism in an environment—what kinds of equations would produce this particular solution? This is where dynamical analogy (see Section 4 above) seems so crucial, i.e., an insight is needed into the similarity between the real event and something we know—such as a nonlinear oscillator. Then, when the latter is appropriately adapted, at least a qualitative model of the data becomes possible.

Another problem concerns the role of *information* in a dynamical system. In Section 5.1 above we argued that a functional grouping of muscles exhibits behavior qualitatively similar to a (nonlinear) mass-spring system. Such systems are intrinsically self-equilibrating in the sense that the end point of the system or its "target" is achieved regardless of initial conditions. In such a model, the target is not achieved by means of conventional, closed-loop control, though targeting behavior can certainly be described by such a system. But sensory feedback, comparators, and reference levels have no role whatsoever in the dynamical systems considered here.

However, this is not to say that propriospecific *information* is unimportant—only to raise the question of how it is to be conceptualized and used within the present framework. As elaborated by Kelso, Holt, and Flatt (1980), standard views of peripheral mechanoreceptors are that they provide feedback about variables such as position, rate, and acceleration. Such feedback in a closed-loop system is referential to a structural entity, typically a setpoint that the system is trying to attain. Regulation and control are then effected by means of error detection and correction processes. There are good reasons to believe that this view has been greatly overvalued for biological systems. For example, although recognizing that setpoints can play a useful role in certain engineering applications, Cecchini, Melbin, and Noordergraaf (1981) state with reference to biological control that "there is no basis to conclude the existence of separate structural entities . . . that define setpoints" and that setpoints are better considered "an arbitrary convenience" (p. 393; see also Kelso, 1981; Kugler, Kelso, & Turvey, 1982; Yates, 1979).

As discussed earlier, we believe that a conception of information is required that is unique and specific to the state of the system's dynamics (Kelso, Holt, Kugler, & Turvey, 1980; Kugler, Kelso, & Turvey, 1980). It is possible that such information is not given in terms of dimension-specific receptor codes but rather, in geometrical terms, i.e., in the form of the gradients and equilibrium points in the system's potential energy function, which is an alternative representation of its dynamic structure (e.g., Hogan, 1980; Kugler et al., 1980). A task's potential energy function can be visualized as a surface with various hills and valleys, hills corresponding to less stable states, valleys to more stable states. Recently Fel'dman and Latash (1982) have presented a model emphasizing the intrinsic relationship between afferent and efferent signals in postural control which they feel "is in good correspondence with ideas [expressed here and elsewhere] about the dynamic nature of motor control and with the general concept that information in the nervous system reflects different forms of dynamic state and intrinsic metrics of control" (p. 188). This view of information as geometrically and/or topologically specified in the system's dynamic qualities is obviously novel (Thom, 1975) and has yet to be fully explored, but it offers an alternative to simplistic coding schemes in which receptor signals on a single dimension are fed back to a setpoint or a system comprised of multiple setpoints.

Interestingly, it appears that the dynamical approach is now being exploited in robotics research. In a recent conference entitled *"Robotics Research: The Next Five Years and Beyond,"* Coleman (1985) reports that new methods for path planning are now being successfully implemented. Path planning has conventionally required that the robot possess a world model of its environment and a complex series of algorithms to compute the optimal path through (or around!) a series of obstacles. Such methods require a prior representation of the entire work space that often cannot be known completely in advance. Moreover, this kind of path planning is complicated from a computational point of view and does not produce good trajectories.

The new alternative—entirely consonant with the aforementioned discussion—is called the *potential field approach* and eliminates many of the problems of conventional methods. To guide the robot through a cluttered environment requires the specification of two sets of objects, goals, and obstacles, which have potential fields associated with them (akin to a magnet's magnetic field). A goal, like a *task* in Saltzman and Kelso (1983b/in press) is defined by an attractor (whose strength and direction are a function of its parameters), whereas the strength and direction of an obstacle is defined by an *avoidance vector* (or in dynamical language, a *repellor*). The sum of the attractor and avoidance vectors creates an acceleration vector for the robot to follow. Adaptive changes to the environment are also possible. Apparently, this method can be shown not only to reduce the computational complexity typical of path planning approaches but also improves considerably the quality of the resultant trajectories.

In addition, the view that information is available in the geometry of the system's dynamics also has been voiced by Boylls and Greene (1984) in their assessment of Bernstein's (1967) significance for the movement field today. With reference to impedance or end-point control, they hypothesize that such theories "will soon be recast in terms of potential functions (with endpoints identifiable as the extrema of such functions to be "sought," gradient fashion by the *state of the skeletomotor system*)" (p. xxiii, emphasis ours).

Clearly, this view of propriospecific information is not anything like conventional notions of sensory feedback, and we can look forward to its elaboration in the near future. Moreover, a different image of perceptual-motor learning is suggested—one in which the learner actively explores a task's potential energy function in order to *discover* its topology and identify its extrema. Learning (from the learner's perspective) is a problem of becoming sensitive to the information carried in the gradients and equilibrium points of potential surfaces (see e.g., Kugler, 1983).

A final problem considered here is that nonlinear dynamics classifies its attractors, by definition, in terms of *families* of trajectories and their asymptotic behavior. On the one hand this is a very powerful strategy, but on the other it begs the question of how a *particular* trajectory is elected. Once the dynamic parameters are set up for a task and the initial conditions defined, the dynamical approach provides a good account of the space–time behavior of the movement system. But how are the necessary conditions established? In the next section we look to the world of perception for insights into this issue.

6. CONTROL OF ACTION DYNAMICS VIA PERCEPTION (KINEMATIC SPECIFICATION)

In the preceding sections we have shown that dynamics can serve as a rich framework for theories of control, in that it affords low-dimensional control possibilities, and yet can generate a wide variety of behavior. We have also shown how the dynamics of movement control can be studied, via analysis of kinematically stable relationships. We now come to the rather difficult problem raised in the previous section: How do the dynamic structures underlying action arise, and how are they modulated (i.e., how are their parameters set)? It has been argued (e.g., Runeson & Frykholm, 1982; Turvey, 1977; Turvey, Shaw, Reed, & Mace, 1981; Warren & Shaw, 1981) that perception provides the properties necessary to solve this problem for animals. However, perceptual events involve no forceful interactions: the events occurring in the flow of the optic field, for example, are purely kinematic in nature (Gibson, 1966, 1979; Runeson, 1977). Similar to the problem investigators have in determining the dynamics of action, organisms have the problem of perceiving the dynamic structure of events solely from the kinematic array. But, as illustrated in the following examples, critical properties of *kinematic* flow fields define information specific to the *dynamical* interactions of organism and environment (Runeson & Frykholm, 1982; Yates & Kugler, in press).

Consider the problem of driving a car up to an intersection. There are two ways to stop the car: (1) by forceful interaction, e.g., by hitting a nearby tree; or (2) by using the flow of optical texture in the visual field to determine when contact might occur and what to do to avoid contact (Yates & Kugler, in press, provide this example). Lee (1976) has identified the kinematic property of the optic flow field that specifies time-to-contact of an object approaching an observer at a constant relative velocity along the line of sight. The rate of magnification of the object *relative* to the point of observation is this significant optical property. After Lee (1976, 1980) we can designate the *inverse* of this variable as τ (tau), the time-to-contact itself. Tau's importance is that it is a directly available, nonderived property of the optical flow field. Its powerful role in the guidance of biologically significant activities has been demonstrated in numerous studies (see von Hofsten & Lee, 1985; Lee, 1980; Lee & Young, in press; Solomon, Carello, & Turvey, in press; Turvey & Kugler, 1984; for reviews). For example, the gannet is a large seabird that dives for its prey from considerable heights, at variable speeds, and in the face of changing wind conditions. Because the gannet is accelerating under gravity, if its wings were not retracted appropriately, it would annihilate itself upon hitting the water's surface. However, the gannet has been shown to be remarkably sensitive to τ and, in fact, initiates wing retraction when τ reaches a certain critical value.

Relatedly, flies have been shown to begin to decelerate prior to contact with a surface at a critical value of τ (Wagner, 1982). In addition, Wagner shows that no other combination of kinematic variables (which might feasibly be picked up perceptually) is as effective as τ. Returning to our driving example, Lee (1976) has further demonstrated that τ and its rate of change $\dot{\tau}$ provide the necessary information to avoid collisions with an obstacle. Thus the value of $\dot{\tau}$ specifies whether braking is sufficiently hard: below $\dot{\tau} = -.5$, safety is assured. Above it, however, the applied decelerative forces are inadequate to avoid collision. From these examples, we see that τ and its rate of change are key parameters for the regulation of action. Not only do they provide continuous information for *modulating* activity, but they also effect bifurcations to different (and adaptive) modes of behavior.

Time-to-contact is not the only aspect of the optic field that has been found to regulate actor dynamics. Warren (1984) had short and tall subjects visually rate the "climbability" of sets of stairs of varying riser heights. He found that observers of widely different dimensions chose those stairs that optimally matched their body size. The measure of "sameness" in this case was *intrinsic* to the observer, i.e., the same ratio of riser height/leg length indexed climbability in both tall and short people. This ratio is an intrinsic metric akin to the time-to-contact variable τ in the preceding examples. According to Warren (1984), two competing factors may determine the fit between organism (climber) and environment (stairs) in this task. As the ratio of riser height to leg length increases, more energy must be expended to raise the subject's body mass a given vertical distance. On the other hand, as the ratio decreases more steps must be made to accomplish the same amount of work. These competing tendencies may serve to establish an optimum point of minimum metabolic demand for the organism-environment system. Warren found that subjects differed greatly in their oxygen consumption when climbing a series of moving, escalator-like stairmills (analogous to a treadmill) whose tread-to-riser height was varied. However, when the data were scaled to conform with the subjects' body dimensions, the oxygen consumption *minimum* occurred at precisely the same ratio that corresponded to their preferred perceptual judgments. In Warren's work we see a beautiful example of optical specification in body-scaled (intrinsic) terms, providing the observer with information about the fit between his or her dimensions and the stair (see also Warren & Kelso, 1985; Warren & Shaw, 1985, for reviews). In addition and importantly for the present discussion, Warren shows that by enlarging the frame of reference to include animal *and* environment, perceptual category boundaries (*critical* points cf. Sect. 5.3)—separating climbable and nonclimbable stairs—are also predicted by his biomechanical model.

7. COMMON PRINCIPLES LINKING DYNAMIC EVENTS IN PERCEPTION AND ACTION?

Drawing from many of the examples presented in earlier sections we see some impressive parallels between the dynamics of movement control and the perception of dynamic events. Remember, the thrust of this chapter as with much of the work referred to herein has been to identify (relatively abstract) functional organizations common to structurally very different subsystems. The equivalence between the behavior of a complex neuromuscular system and a nonlinear oscillator, as discussed in Section 4, is abstract and functional, rather than concrete and structural. In the context of this chapter such an approach seeks principles that apply not just to movement control or perception alone, but to the perception-action system as a whole. Could it be that perception and action—typically treated as independent domains of inquiry—are really coupled by virtue of sharing common (dynamical) principles? If so, what are they?

We saw earlier that the optic flowfield is literally a global morphology (a velocity vector field) or form that uniquely *informs* (in the sense of Varela, 1983, and Section 2 above) the organism of the many ways it can adjust to its environment. Real or artificially induced global optical changes can be shown to produce lawfully related perceptual experiences. Similarly, we saw how the *forms of motion*, given in phase portraits, allow the scientist to uncover an underlying dynamical control structure. In both cases it is the form of the kinematics that informs—in the sense of a lawful mapping—dynamical states of affairs. We say, after Runeson, that kinematics *specify* dynamics.

We saw, in Section 5, that a criterion for the stability of an attractor is that it exhibits smoothness in the fact of parameter changes and perturbations. But we also saw that when a parameter crosses a critical threshold, bifurcation occurs— there is a switch from one type of behavior to another. Literally, a behavioral phase transition occurs. Both perception and action subsystems share the features of stability on the one hand and criticality on the other. Which behavior is observed depends on which regions of the parameter space the system occupies. From Warren's and others' work we see that stable and critical behavior arise not just in the perception and action subsystems individually but arise from the dynamics of the animal-environment system as a unit.

The individual analyses of production and perception show how enormously detailed *microscopic* descriptions are, in each case, reduced to low-dimensional, *macroscopic* descriptions. And in Lee, Lishman, and Thompson's (1982) analysis of skilled long jumping we see a conflation of macroscopic parameters. Only one macroscopic optical property appears to be pertinent to the jumper's adjustment to the upcoming board, the time-to-contact, τ. And only one macroscopic movement parameter appears to reflect the jumper's motoric adjustments, the impulse generated during the stance phase of the gait cycle. Thus a highly complex control problem reduces to a coupling between just two macroscopic parameters (see also Fitch, Tuller, & Turvey, 1982; Solomon et al., in press). Whether other tasks are amenable to a similar kind of analysis is open to question. Kelso et al. (1985) suggest that the stiffness changes they observe between stressed and unstressed speech gestures may specify listener's perception of stress, an hypothesis that can be tested directly by articulatory synthesis (Rubin,

Baer, & Mermelstein, 1981; Browman, Goldstein, Kelso, Rubin, & Saltzman, 1984). Similarly, the phasing structure of articulatory movements may map directly onto listener's perception of speaking rate (Kelso, 1985; Kelso, Saltzman, & Tuller, 1986a, 1986b).

Are the various parallels mentioned here between perception and production just that, parallels, or is there a deeper dynamical structure linking them together? A quote from Feynman's (1967) classic, *The Character of Physical Law*, may leave the reader with an impression of our position: "This kind of game of roughly guessing at family relationships. . .is illustrative of the kind of preliminary sparring which one does with nature before really discovering some deep and fundamental law" (p. 155). Action and perception have evolved together. Just because we *analyze* them separately is no reason to divorce them from each other, or not to search for the lawful basis of their linkage.

ACKNOWLEDGMENTS

Much of the work referred to herein was supported by NIH Grant NS-13617, Biomedical Research Support Grant RR-05596, and U.S. Office of Naval Research N00014-83-C-0083. We appreciate very helpful comments by Herbert Heuer, Elliot Saltzman, and Michael Turvey on an earlier draft of this chapter.

REFERENCES

Abraham, R. H. & Shaw, C. D. (1982). *Dynamics—The geometry of behavior*. Santa Cruz, CA: Aerial Press.
Anderson, P. W. (1972). More is different. *Science, 177*, 393–396.
Andronov, A., & Chaiken, C. E. (1949). *Theory of oscillations*. Princeton, NJ: Princeton University Press.
Ashby, W. R. (1956). *An introduction to cybernetics*. London: Metheun.
Bahill, A. T., Clark, M. R., & Stark, L. (1975). The main sequence: A tool for studying human eye movements. *Mathematical Biosciences, 24*, 191–204.
Baldissera, F., Cavallari, P., & Civaschi, P. (1982). Preferential coupling between voluntary movements of ipsilateral limbs. *Neuroscience Letters, 34*, 95–100.
Bernstein, N. A. (1967). *The coordination and regulation of movements*. London: Pergamon Press.
Bizzi, E., Chapple, W., & Hogan, N. (1982). Mechanical properties muscles: Implications for motor control. *Trends in Neurosciences, 5*, 395–398.
Bizzi, E., Polit, A., & Morasso, P. (1976). Mechanisms underlying achievement of final head position. *Journal of Neurophysiology, 39*, 435–444.
Boylls, C. C., & Greene, P. H. (1984). Introduction: Bernstein's significance today. In H. T. A. Whiting (Ed.), *Human motor actions: Bernstein reassessed*. Amsterdam: North–Holland, xix–xxix.
Browman, C. P., Goldstein, L., Kelso, J. A. S., Rubin, P., & Saltzman, E. (1984). Articulatory synthesis from underlying dynamics. *Journal of the Acoustical Society of America, 75*, S22–S23. (Abstract)

Cecchini, A. B. P., Melbin, J., & Noordergraaf, A. (1981). Setpoint: Is it a distinct structural entity in biology control? *Journal of Theoretical Biology, 93,* 387-394.

Cohen, A. H., Holmes, P. J., & Rand, R. H. (1982). The nature of the coupling between segmental oscillators of the lamprey spinal generator for locomotion: A mathematical model. *Journal of Mathematical Biology, 13,* 345-369.

Cohen, L. (1971). Synchronous bimanual movements performed by homologous and non-homologous muscles. *Perceptual and Motor Skills, 32,* 639-644.

Coleman, A. (1985, February). Robotics research: The next five years and beyond. *Robotics Age, 7(2),* 14-19.

Cooke, J. D. (1980). The organization of simple, skilled movements. In G. E. Stelmach & J. Requin (Eds.), *Tutorials in motor behavior.* Amsterdam: North-Holland.

Corcos, D. M. (1984). Two-handed movement control. *Research Quarterly For Exercise and Sport, 55,* 117-122.

Cvitanovic, P. (Ed.). (1984). *Universality in chaos.* Bristol, England: Adam Hilger.

Eckmann, J. -P. (1981). Roads to turbulence in dissipative dynamical systems. *Reviews of Modern Physics, 53,* 643-654.

Fel'dman, A. G. (1966). Functional tuning of the nervous system with control of movement or maintenance of a steady posture. III. Mechanographic analysis of execution by man of the simplest motor tasks. *Biophysics, 11,* 766-775.

Fel'dman, A. G., & Latash, M. L. (1982). Interaction of efferent and afferent signals underlying joint position sense: Empirical and theoretical approaches. *Journal of Motor Behavior, 14,* 174-193.

Feynman, R. (1967). *The character of physical law.* Cambridge, MA: MIT Press.

Fitch, H. L., Tuller, B., & Turvey, M. T. (1982). The Bernstein perspective: III. Tuning of coordinative structures with special reference to perception. In J. A. S. Kelso (Ed.), *Human motor behavior: An introduction.* Hillsdale, NJ: Lawrence Erlbaum Associates.

Fitch, H., & Turvey, M. T. (1978). On the control of activity: Some remarks from an ecological point of view. In D. Landers & R. Christina (Ed.), *Psychology of motor behavior and sports.* Urbana, IL: Human Kinetics.

Fitts, P. M. (1954). The information capacity of the human motor system in controlling the amplitude of movement. *Journal of Experimental Psychology, 47,* 381-391.

Fowler, C. A., Rubin, P., Remez, R. E., & Turvey, M. T. (1980). Implications for speech production of a general theory of action. In B. Butterworth (Ed.), *Language production.* New York: Academic Press.

Fowler, C. A., & Turvey, M. T. (1978). Skill acquisition: An event approach with special reference to searching for the optimum of a function of several variables. In G. Stelmach (Ed.), *Information processing in motor control and learning.* New York: Academic Press.

Freund, H. -J. (1983). Motor unit and muscle activity in voluntary motor control. *Physiological Reviews, 63,* 387-436.

Gibson, J. J. (1961). Ecological optics. *Vision Research, 1,* 253-262.

Gibson, J. J. (1966). *The senses considered as perceptual systems.* Boston, MA: Houghton-Mifflin.

Gibson, J. J. (1979). *The ecological approach to visual perception.* Boston: Houghton-Mifflin.

Greene, P. H. (1982). Why is it easy to control your arms? *Journal of Motor Behavior, 14,* 260-286.

Guckenheimer, J., & Holmes, P. (1983). *Nonlinear oscillations, dynamical systems, and bifurcations of vector fields.* New York: Springer-Verlag.

Haken, H. (1975). Cooperative phenomena in systems far from thermal equilibrium and in nonphysical systems. *Review of Modern Physics, 47,* 67-121.

Haken, H. (1977). *Synergetics: An introduction.* Heidelberg: Springer-Verlag.

Haken, H. (1983). *Advanced synergetics.* Heidelberg: Springer-Verlag.

Haken, H., Kelso, J. A. S., & Bunz, H. (1985). A theoretical model of phase transitions in human hand movements. *Biological Cybernetics, 51,* 347–356.
von Hofsten, C., & Lee, D. N. (1985). Dialogue on perception and action. In Warren, W. H., & Shaw, R. E. (Eds.), *Persistence and change: proceedings of the first international conference on event perception.* Hillsdale, NJ: Lawrence Erlbaum Associates.
Hogan, N. (1980). Mechanical impedance control in assistive devices and manipulators. In *Proceedings of the Joint Automatic Control Conferences (Vol. 1).* San Francisco, TA-108.
Hollerbach, J. M. (1982). Computers, brains, and the control of movement. *Trends in Neurosciences, 5,* 189–192.
Houk, J. C., & Rymer, W. (1981). Neural control of muscle length and tension. In V. B. Brooks (Ed.), *Handbook of physiology: Sec. 1. Motor control: Vol. 11,* Part 1 (pp. 257–323). Bethesda, MD: American Physiology Society.
Hoyt, D. F., & Taylor, C. R. (1981). Gait and the energetics of locomotion in horses. *Nature, 292,* 239–240.
Jeannerod, M. (1984). The timing of natural prehension movements. *Journal of Motor Behavior, 16,* 235–254.
Jordan, D. W., & Smith, P. (1977). *Nonlinear ordinary differential equations.* Oxford: Clarendon Press.
Kay, B., Kelso, J. A. S., Saltzman, E. L., & Schöner, G., (in press). The space–time behavior of single and two-handed rhythmical movements: A limit cycle model. *Journal of Experimental Psychology: Human Perception and Performance.*
Keele, S. W. (1981). Behavioral analysis of movement. In V. B. Brooks (Ed.), *Handbook of physiology: Sec. 1. The nervous system: Vol. II. Motor control, Part 2.* Baltimore, MD: American Physiological Society.
Kelso, J. A. S. (1977). Motor control mechanisms underlying human movement reproduction. *Journal of Experimental Psychology: Human Perception and Performance, 3,* 529–543.
Kelso, J. A. S. (1981). Contrasting perspectives on order and regulation in movement. In J. Long & A. Baddeley (Eds.), *Attention and performance* (IX). Hillsdale, NJ: Lawrence Erlbaum Associates.
Kelso, J. A. S. (1982a). Overview of skilled performance: Coming to grips with the jargon. In J. A. S. Kelso (Ed.), *Human motor behavior: An introduction.* Hillsdale, NJ: Lawrence Erlbaum Associates.
Kelso, J. A. S. (Ed.). (1982b). *Human motor behavior: An introduction.* Hillsdale, NJ: Lawrence Erlbaum Associates.
Kelso, J. A. S. (1984). Phase transitions and critical behavior in human bimanual coordination. *American Journal of Physiology: Regulatory, Integrative and Comparative, 246,* R1000–R1004.
Kelso, J. A. S. (1985, February 14). *A note on coarticulation and related issues.* Unpublished manuscript for an in-house conference on "Units of speech production and perception: Origins and functions of their coarticulation." Haskins Laboratories.
Kelso, J. A. S., & Holt, K. G. (1980). Exploring a vibratory systems analysis of human movement production. *Journal of Neurophysiology, 43,* 1183–1196.
Kelso, J. A. S., Holt, K. G., & Flatt, A. E. (1980). The role of proprioception in the perception and control of human movement: Toward a theoretical reassessment. *Perception & Psychophysics, 28,* 45–52.
Kelso, J. A. S., Holt, K. G., Kugler, P. N., & Turvey, M. T. (1980). On the concept of coordinative structures as dissipative structures: II. Empirical lines of convergence. In G. E. Stelmach & J. Requin (Eds.), *Tutorials in motor behavior* (pp. 49–70). New York: North-Holland.
Kelso, J. A. S., Holt, K. G., Rubin, P., & Kugler, P. N. (1981). Patterns of human interlimb coordination emerge from the properties of nonlinear limit cycle oscillatory processes: Theory and data. *Journal of Motor Behavior, 13,* 226–261.

Kelso, J. A. S., Putnam, C. A., & Goodman, D. (1983). On the space-time structure of human interlimb coordination. *Quarterly Journal of Experimental Psychology, 35A,* 347-376.

Kelso, J. A. S., & Saltzman, E. L. (1982). Motor control: Which themes do we orchestrate? *The Behavioral and Brain Sciences, 5,* 554-557.

Kelso, J. A. S., & Scholz, J. P. (1985). Cooperative phenomena in biological motion. In H. Haken (Ed.), *Complex systems: Operational approaches in neurobiology, physics and computers.* (pp. 124-149). Berlin: Springer.

Kelso, J. A. S., Saltzman, E. L., & Tuller, B. (1986a). The dynamical perspective on speech production. *Journal of Phonetics, 13.*

Kelso, J. A. S., Saltzman, E. L., & Tuller, B. (1986b). Intentional contents, communicative context and task dynamics: a reply to the commentators. *Journal of Phonetics, 13.*

Kelso, J. A. S., Southard, D. L., & Goodman, D. (1979). On the nature of human interlimb coordination. *Science, 203,* 1029-1031.

Kelso, J. A. S., & Tuller, B. (1984a). Converging sources of evidence for common dynamical principles in speech and limb coordination. *American Journal of Physiology: Regulatory, Integrative, and Comparative, 246,* R928-935.

Kelso, J. A. S., & Tuller, B. (1984b). A dynamical basis for action systems. In M. S. Gazzaniga (Ed.), *Handbook of cognitive neuroscience* (pp. 321-356). NewYork: Plenum.

Kelso, J. A. S., V.-Bateson, E., Saltzman, E. L., & Kay, B. (1985). A qualitative dynamic analysis of reiterant speech production: Phase portraits, kinematics, and dynamic modeling. *Journal of the Acoustical Society of America, 77,* 266-280.

Kugler, P. N. (1983). *A morphological view of information for the self-assembly of rhythmic movement: A study in the similitude of natural law.* Unpublished doctoral dissertation, University of Connecticut.

Kugler, P. N., Kelso, J. A. S., & Turvey, M. T. (1980). On the concept of coordinative structures as dissipative structures: I. Theoretical lines of convergence. In G. E. Stelmach & J. Requin (Eds.), *Tutorials in motor behavior* (pp. 3-47). New York: North-Holland.

Kugler, P. N., Kelso, J. A. S., & Turvey, M. T. (1982). On the control and coordination of naturally developing systems. In J. A. S. Kelso & J. E. Clark (Eds.), *The development of movement control and coordination* (pp. 5-78). Chichester: Wiley.

Kugler, P. N., & Turvey, M. T. (in press). *Information, natural law, and the self-assembly of rhythmic movement: Theoretical and experimental investigations.* New Jersey: Lawrence Erlbaum Associates.

Lacquanti, F., Terzuolo, C., & Viviani, P. (1983). The law relating the kinematic and figural aspects of drawing movements. *Acta Psychologica, 54,* 115-130.

Lee, D. N. (1976). A theory of visual control of braking based on information about time-to-collision. *Perception, 5,* 437-459.

Lee, D. N. (1980). Visuo-motor coordination in space-time. In G. E. Stelmach & J. Requin (Eds.), *Tutorials in motor behavior.* New York: North-Holland.

Lee, D. N., Lishman, J. R., & Thomson, J. A. (1982). Regulation of gait in long jumping. *Journal of Experimental Psychology: Human Perception and Performance, 8,* 448-459.

Lee, D. N., & Young, D. S. (in press). Gearing action to the environment. *Experimental Brain Research Supplement.*

MacKenzie, C. L., & Patla, A. E. (1983). Breakdown in rapid bimanual finger tapping as a function of orientation and phasing. *Society for Neuroscience.* (Abstract).

Marteniuk, R. G., & MacKenzie, C. L. (1980). A preliminary theory of two-handed movement control. In G. E. Stelmach & J. Requin (Eds.), *Tutorials in motor behavior.* Amsterdam: North-Holland.

Marteniuk, R. G., MacKenzie, C. L., & Baba, D. M. (1984). Bimanual movement control: Information processing and interaction effects. *Quarterly Journal of Experimental Psychology, 36A,* 335-365.

Maxwell, J. C. (1877). *Matter and motion*. New York: Dover Press (1952 reprint).
Miller, S., & Scott, P. D. (1977). The spinal locomotor generator. *Experimental Brain Research, 30*, 387–403.
Minorsky, N. (1962). *Nonlinear oscillations*. Princeton, NJ: Van Nostrand.
Morasso, P. (1981). Spatial control of arm movements. *Experimental Brain Research, 42*, 223–227.
Morowitz, H. (1968). *Energy flow in biology*. New York: Academic Press.
Nashner, L. M., & McCollum, G. (in press). The organization of human postural movements: A formal basis and experimental synthesis. *The Behavioral and Brain Sciences*.
Nelson, W. L. (1983). Physical principles for economies of skilled movements. *Biological Cybernetics, 46*, 135–147.
Ostry, D. J., & Munhall, K. (1985). Control of rate and duration in speech. *Journal of the Acoustical Society of America, 77*, 640–648.
Patla, A. E., Calvert, T. W., & Stein, R. B. (in press). A model of a pattern generator for locomotion in mammals. *American Journal of Physiology*.
Pattee, H. H. (1972). Laws and constraints, symbols and language. In C. H. Waddington (Ed.), *Towards a theoretical biology*. Chicago: Aldine.
Pattee, H. H. (1973). Physical problems for the origin of natural controls. In A. Locker (Ed.), *Biogenesis, evolution, homeostasis* (pp. 41–49). Heidelberg: Springer–Verlag.
Pattee, H. H. (1977). Dynamic and linguistic modes of complex systems. *International Journal of General Systems, 3*, 259–266.
Prigogine, I., & Stengers, I. (1984). *Order out of chaos: Man's new dialogue with Nature*. New York: Bantam.
Rasband, P. (1983). *Dynamics*. New York: Wiley.
Reed, E. S. (1981). *Indirect action*. Unpublished manuscript, University of Minnesota, Center for Research in Human Learning.
Reed, E. S. (1982). An outline of a theory of action systems. *Journal of Motor Behavior, 14*, 98–134.
Rosen, R. (1970). *Dynamical system theory in biology: (Vol. 1). Stability theory and its applications*. New York: Wiley.
Rosen, R. (1978). *Fundamentals of measurement and representation of natural systems*. New York: North–Holland.
Rubin, P., Baer, T., & Mermelstein, P. (1981). An articulatory synthesizer for perceptual research. *Journal of the Acoustical Society of America, 70*, 321–328.
Runeson, S. (1977). *On visual perception of dynamic events*. Unpublished doctoral dissertation, University of Uppsala.
Runeson, S., & Frykholm, G. (1982). Kinematic specification of dynamics as an informational basis for person and action perception: Expectations, gender recognition, and deceptive intention. *Uppsala Psychological Reports*, Dept. of Psychology, University of Uppsala, Sweden.
Saltzman, E. L., & Kelso, J. A. S. (1983a). Toward a dynamical account of motor memory and control. In R. Magill (Ed.), *Memory and control of action* (pp. 17–38). Amsterdam: North–Holland.
Saltzman, E., & Kelso, J. A. S. (1983b/in press). Skilled actions: A task dynamic approach. *Haskins Laboratories Status Report on Speech Research, SR-76*, 3–50. *Psychological Review*, in press.
Saltzman, E., & Kelso, J. A. S. (1985). Stabilities, instabilities, and modes. *The Behavioral and Brain Sciences*.
Schmidt, R. A. (1982). *Motor control and learning: A behavioral emphasis*. Champaign, IL: Human Kinetics.
Schmidt, R. A., & McGown, C. (1980). Terminal accuracy of unexpectedly loaded rapid movements: Evidence for a mass-spring mechanism in programming. *Journal of Motor Behavior, 12*, 149–161.

Schöner, G., Haken, H., & Kelso, J. A. S. (1986). A stochastic theory of phase transitions in human hand movement.*Biological Cybernetics, 53,* 247–257.
Shaw, R. (1981). Modeling chaotic systems. In H. Haken (Ed.), *Order and chaos in nature* (pp. 218–231). New York: Springer–Verlag.
Solomon, J., Carello, C., & Turvey, M. T. (in press). Flow fields: Optical support for skilled activities. To appear in: W. F. Straub & J. Williams (Eds.), *Cognitive sports psychology.* Lansing, NY: Sport Science Associates.
Stein, R. B. (1982). What muscle variables does the central nervous system control? *The Behavioral and Brain Sciences, 5,* 535–577.
Thom, R. (1975). In D. H. Fowler (Trans.), *Structural stability and morphogenesis.* Reading, MA: Benjamin.
Tomovic, R. (1978). Some central conditions for self-organization—what the control theorist can learn from biology. *American Journal of Physiology: Regulatory, Integrative, and Comparative, 235,* R205–R209.
Turvey, M. T. (1977). Preliminaries to a theory of action with reference to vision. In R. Shaw & J. Bransford (Eds.), *Perceiving, acting and knowing: Toward an ecological psychology.* Hillsdale, NJ: Lawrence Erlbaum Associates.
Turvey, M. T., & Kugler, P. N. (1984). Information and the ecological approach to perception and action. In H. T. A. Whiting (Ed.), *Human motor actions: Bernstein reassessed.* Amsterdam: North–Holland.
Turvey, M. T., Shaw, R. E., Reed, E. S., & Mace, W. M. (1981). Ecological laws of perceiving and acting: In reply to Fodor and Pylyshyn (1981). *Cognition, 9,* 237–304.
Varela, F. J. (1983). *Principles of biological autonomy.* New York: North–Holland.
Viviani, P., & McCollum, G. (1983). The relation between linear extent and velocity in drawing movements. *Neuroscience, 10,* 211–218.
Wadman, W. J., Denier van der Gon, J. J., Geuze, R. H., & Mol, C. R. (1979). Control of fast goal-directed arm movements. *Journal of Human Movement Studies, 5,* 3–17.
Wagner, H. (1982). Flow-field variables trigger landing in flies. *Nature, 297,* 147–148.
Warren, W. H. (1984). Perceiving affordances: Visual guidance of stair climbing. *Journal of Experimental Psychology: Human Perception and Performance, 10,* 683–703.
Warren, W. H., & Kelso, J. A. S. (1985). Report of the work group on perception and action. In W. H. Warren, & R. E. Shaw, (Eds.), *Persistence and change: Proceedings of the First International Conference on Event Perception.* Hillsdale, NJ: Lawrence Erlbaum Associates.
Warren, W. H., & Shaw, R. E. (1981). Psychophysics and ecometrics. *The Behavioral and Brain Sciences, 4,* 209–210.
Warren, W. H., & Shaw, R. E. (Eds.) (1985). *Persistence and change: Proceedings of the First International Conference on Event Perception.* Hillsdale, NJ: Lawrence Erlbaum Associates.
Whiting, H. T. A. (1984). *Human motor actions: Bernstein reassessed.* Amsterdam: North–Holland.
Willis, J. B. (1980). On the interaction between spinal locomotor generators in quadrupeds. *Brain Research Reviews, 2,* 171–204.
Yates, F. E. (1979). Physical biology: A basis for modeling living systems. *Journal of Cybernetics and Informations Science, 2,* 57–70.
Yates, F. E., Marsh, D. J., & Iberall, A. S. (1972). Integration of the whold organism: a foundation for a theoretical biology. In J. A. Behnke, (Ed.), *Challenging biological problems: Directions toward their solution* (pp. 110–132). New York: Oxford University Press.
Yates, F. E., & Kugler, P. N. (in press). Signs, singularities, and significance: A physical model for semiotics. *Semiotica.*

2 Catching

Claes von Hofsten
University of Umeå, Sweden

PERCEPTION—ACTION SYSTEMS

Traditionally, perception has been conceived of as a kind of a general purpose device, the task of which is to tell the mind something about the world outside, something that could be used by the subject in different ways in adopting him or herself to the environment. To a certain extent this is of course true. However, even when it comes to such a fundamental aspect as space, perception comes easier to some tasks than to others. Subjects can be trained to throw balls, horse shoes, or darts with great precision to places in the surrounding that require precise information about distance. When asked to estimate distances metrically the precision is much less impressive even after training (Gibson & Bergman, 1954; Gibson, Bergman & Purdy, 1955). Another example of how task-related perception can be has been given by Skravenski and Hansen (1978). They found that the inability to localize a target flashed during a saccade is not valid for all situations. If the subject, instead of being asked to verbally report the location of the target, is given the task to strike the target with a hammer this will be done with very little error.

The difference between the verbal report and the perceptually guided action in the two examples given above is not only a question of spatial precision. It is also the time required to perform the task. Perceiving the distance and direction to the target when throwing a ball or striking the hammer does not seem to take any time. This is important. Perception did not only evolve to give us knowledge about the world but to do so under severe time constraints, i.e., in the context of our actions (Hofsten, 1985).

It is reasonable to assume that perception and action evolved together. The problems perception had to solve were often very specific and time precision was as important as for instance spatial precision. The solutions favored were not necessary applicable to other apparently similar tasks. In lower animals this is rather obvious. According to Arbib (1980) the frog may be said to possess a number of specific visual systems: one for prey catching, one for threat avoidance, one for barrier negotiation, etc. In higher vertebrates perception is undoubtly less specific than that. However, the point is that human perception still may be specialized enough to make it appropriate to speak of a number of perception-action systems instead of regarding perception as a unitary process separate from action. If so, then the problems to be solved will not primarily be how perception makes contact with action, but how the different perception-action systems work and how they together compose what sometimes may appear to be two separate processes: perception and action. It is of course true that one can attach almost any simple movement to any simple stimulus in a learning or reaction task. However, to believe that the study of, for instance, arbitrary finger movements as response to displayed letters or numbers will reveal anything essential about the coordination between perception and action is doubtful. It may actually be as erroneous as the belief that verbal memory could be studied through the use of nonsense syllable lists.

Instead, perception should be studied in the context of the actions for which it evolved. Inquiries should be made to identify the separate perception-action systems, define their areas of operation, and determine their strengths and limitations. Further, questions should be asked about on what kind of information each specific perception-action system is based and how that information is used to guide action. Finally, questions should be asked about the natural history of perception-action systems, their evolution and the development of them in children. In the present chapter, catching is examined from this perspective.

THE CATCHING TASK

To be able to catch a ball, the subject not only needs to perceive the position of the ball at an instant but also where the ball is traveling and how fast. A thrown ball does not travel with constant speed. To catch it you need to take into account the acceleration and deceleration of the ball. Further, the thrower may induce all kinds of distortions of the ball trajectory by getting the ball to spin.

All these facts have to be known within a fraction of a second. Even a just lightly thrown ball will travel with something like 8–10 meters a second. Let alone baseball: The speed of a cleverly thrown baseball will be around 35–40 m/sec, i.e., the ball will arrive at the catcher within half a second.

The only way to catch a thrown ball is to somehow predict a forthcoming position of the ball within the action space of the subject and to get there, open the hand, and close it around the ball as it gets there. If the hand closes too late the ball will bounce off and if the hand closes too early it will hit the knuckles of the hand. Obviously, timing has to be extremely precise.

From this description, catching a ball seems to be an almost impossible task and yet we all know that we can do it. Many of us spend a lot of time exercising ballcatching and with the greatest joy. The timing accuracy in ball catching is quite impressive. Alderson, Sully, and Sully (1974) analyzed catches filmed with high-speed photography and found that the temporal precision in catching a lightly thrown ball was around 14 msec. The hand started to close some 30 msec before the ball made contact with the hand. The closing hand was open enough to admit the arriving ball into it and just after hitting the palm the hand was closed around it. With faster balls like in baseball the timing has to be much more precise of course. Tyldesley and Whiting (1975) found that the timing accuracy in table tennis was around 4 msec.

The Natural History of Catching Skills

Obviously, catching is a very special and a very basic skill. Perceiving an object moving in the air is not just perceiving its motion but also perceiving how to act on it. The functional significance is also obvious. It is of great advantage to a predator to be able to predict future positions of a prey and intercept its flight. This kind of intelligence is definitely present in many higher mammals. Dogs, for instance, are good ball catchers. They like to jump up in the air and catch a ball in its flight.

When catching skills start to appear in evolution is difficult to say. There is one set of observations by Ingle, Cheal, and Dizio (1979) suggesting that its presence is correlated with the evolution of the neocortex. They studied the ability of animals to predict the course of a fast moving visual target by orienting ahead of these targets and pursuing a collision course. He found that this kind of skill was present in the mongolian gerbil but not in frogs and toads. The latter species would strike well behind an object moving at 30 deg. per second, having been guided by the target location of the prey just prior to initiation of the strike. Ingle (1977), also found that moderate damage to visual cortex abolishes the ability of gerbils to turn ahead of moving targets, without affecting speed or accuracy of turns toward stationary targets, again pointing to the crucial importance of the neocortex for predictive behavior.

The generality of this conclusion is questioned by Lanchester and Mark (1975). They studied the movements of a teleost fish (the leather jacket, Acanthaluteres spilomelanurus) approaching and taking food. It was true that the fish did not systematically predict an intersection with the food by following a direct path towards it, in spite of the obvious advantage that would have given them. However, the fish was clearly able to move in a more economical path being directed ahead of the target rather than at the instantaneous position of it. This was especially true when the fish approached the food from below. Thus,

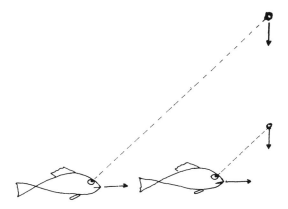

FIG. 2.1 If body tracking is set at an appropriate angle to eye tracking, the fish would not need to change its course during the approach of the target.

however constrained, the teleost fish do seem to possess some kind of anticipatory tracking system. Lanchester and Mark suggested that the fish has an eye-tracking and a body-tracking system and some ability to set the body-tracking system at an angle to the eye-tracking system. If that angle is set appropriately the fish would not need to change its course during approach as shown in Fig. 2.1. The fish doesn't seem to be able to set the angle appropriately but clearly has tendencies toward such a behavior.

The Development of Catching Skills

Developmental psychologists who have been thinking about the ontogenesis of ball catching have mostly been struck by the complexity of the task. Kay (1970), for instance, suggested that catching ability would appear at the earliest around 5 years of age.

However, in a series of studies I have found that young infants already possess a remarkable capacity to catch objects (Hofsten, 1980, 1983; Hofsten & Lindhagen, 1979). Hofsten and Lindhagen (1979) studied this problem longitudinally in a group of 11 infants. They were 12 to 24 weeks old at the first session, were seen at 3-week intervals until 30 weeks old, and were finally seen at 36 weeks of age. The subjects were presented with an object moving at infant's nose height in a horizontal circular path of 115 cm in diameter. The object passed the infant at a nearest distance of either 11 or 16 cm. It moved at 3.4, 15, or 30 cm/sec and stopped moving when it was grasped. For each condition the object was placed randomly to one side and was then moved back and fourth from one side to the other until the infant grasped it. This procedure was repeated until three reaches were secured or the object had passed in front of the subject at least six times.

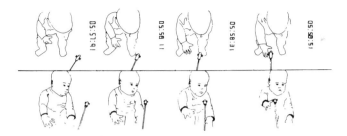

FIG. 2.2 The performance of a well-aimed reach by L. I. at 21 weeks of age. The frame to the far left is the start of the reach. The interval between the frames is 0.2 sec. The velocity of the object is 30 cm/sec. Note how the infant tracks the object with the eyes and head during the reach. From Hofsten (1980).

We found that from the very age when infants start to master reaching for stationary objects, they will also reach successfully for fast moving ones. Eighteen-week-old infants caught the object as it moved at 30 cm/sec. To be able to catch such an object, at least some predictive ability is necessary. As the length of the infant's arm at that age is less than 20 cm, the infant needs to start reaching for the target before it is actually within reach.

To be able to evaluate the predictive skill reflected in these reaches, a quantitative analysis of the three-dimensional trajectories were performed (Hofsten, 1980). The movements were divided into units each consisting of one acceleration and one deceleration phase. The aiming of each unit relative to the meeting point was then calculated. The analysis showed that most reaches were aimed for the meeting point right from the beginning, i.e., a perfect predictive strategy was employed. This was true for all agegroups (Hofsten, 1980). The predictive reaching was typically performed with the hand contralateral to the direction from which the object arrived. (See Fig. 2.2.)

Over the period observed, it was mainly the mobility aspects of reaching that improved. This development was most clearly reflected in the decreasing variability of the initial aiming of reaches with more than one unit. Number of units per reach decreased with age, too, and the trajectory became straighter. I also found a paradoxical dependency between motor performance and target velocity, which is shown in Fig. 2.3. Trajectories straighten out and approach time decreases with target velocity. It is as if the subject performs better when he or she needs to. Wade (1980) found a similar relationship in older children. Their task was to strike a target moving from right to left by rolling an aluminium "doughnut" down a trackway. Especially the younger subjects (7–9 years old) showed much better performance with faster than with slower targets both in terms of absolute and variable error.

In the reviewed longitudinal study of infants catching behavior aiming was studied but not timing. That leaves many questions related to the principles used by the infant in catching fast objects open. To answer some of these questions, a

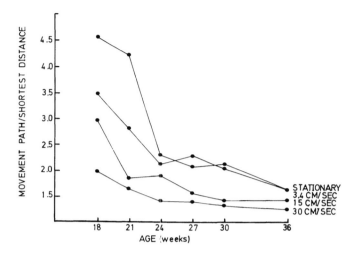

FIG. 2.3 Relative length of movement path as a function of age for each velocity condition (means). From Hofsten (1979).

second study was performed that took both aiming and timing into account (Hofsten, 1983).

Fifteen, healthy, full-term infants took part in the experiment. At the time of the study the subjects were between 34 and 36 weeks of age. A similar setup was used as before. The target moved in a horizontal circular path of approximately 153 cm in diameter. Velocity and starting position was systematically varied. Velocity was either 30, 45, or 60 cm/sec. A subgroup was also tested with 90 and 120 cm/sec targets. The starting position was either 30, 60, or 90 deg. off the sagittal plane corresponding to 40, 80, and 120 cm from the nearest position to the object.

Aiming was calculated as before. The "best" angle ahead was expressed as the angle between the position of the object at the start of the movement unit (A), the position of the hand at the same time (B), and the position of the object at the end of the reach (C) (see Fig. 2.4). The obtained angle ahead was expressed as the angle between A, B, and the position of the hand at the end of the movement unit (D). To estimate timing, the time at which the reach ended was compared with the time at which the hand was closest to the target. The end of the reach was thereby defined as the time after the end of the approach when the hand came to a standstill or when its deceleration had stopped.

The initial aiming of reaches in the different velocity conditions of the experiment is shown in Table 2.1. Table 2.1 shows that although the required angle ahead increases with increasing velocity of the target, so does the obtained angle ahead. The reaches are at all instances directed close to the meeting point with

TABLE 2.1
The Initial Aiming and the Timing of Reaches for Moving Objects in Hofsten (1983)

Object Velocity (cm/sec)	Initial Aiming (degrees) α	Initial Aiming (degrees) β	Timing (msec) Systematic error	Timing (msec) Variable error
30	33.2	38.1	9.4	54
45	39.4	48.3	4.4	57
60	52.0	55.6	-17.0	59

the target. Table 2.1 also shows the systematic and variable timing errors. It can be seen that at no velocity was the systematic timing error greater than 17 msec. The variable timing error was found to be between 54 and 59 msec.

It is interesting to compare these figures with the timing errors found by Dorfman (1977) in another timing and anticipation task with much older children. The task was to direct a cursor dot on an oscilloscope screen to intercept a moving target dot. This was done with the aid of a manual slide control. The absolute timing error of the 6–7 year-old's was 121 msec and the variable error 129 msec. The sensomotor processes involved in this task are obviously much less precise than those involved in infants' catching of moving targets. The aim of Dorfman's study was to learn about development of skilled behavior. If the perception-action systems involved are as task specific as I have suggested earlier and as the discrepancy between Dorfman's and my results indicate, then there is little hope in learning anything about, for instance, catching from studying interceptive skill on an oscilloscope screen.

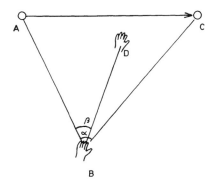

FIG. 2.4 How aiming was calculated. A is the position of the object at the beginning of the reach, B the hand at the same time, C the position of the object at the end of the reach, and D is the position of the hand at the end of the initial step of the reach. α is "best direction ahead and β is obtained direction ahead.

40   von HOFSTEN

The Sensomotor Mechanism for Catching

The result of Hofsten (1983) rules out the possibility that the catching observed in infants is a kind of pseudoskill governed by some simplified strategy. One such strategy would be that the subject always reaches out and intercepts the trajectory of the target when the target passes some landmark. If the subject would catch all the targets by such a strategy the hand would have had to wait at least a quarter of a second for the slower ones. This was not the case. (See Table 2.1).

Another simplified strategy would be for the subject to remember the time it took for the target to arrive and use that to time the reach. Reaches for the object the first time it passes in front of the subject in a given condition should be bad but the subsequent ones good. The result showed that reaches performed at the first passage, were just as precisely timed and coordinated as those performed later.

All kinds of simplified strategies have to assume that the target is caught in a more or less fixed position. This was not what the subjects did (Hofsten, 1983). The objects were caught in a variety of positions within reach. The only plausible explanation for the catching we observed is that the infant somehow extrapolates the trajectory of the target and gets there in time. This can be done in at least two different ways.

First, it is conceivable that the child somehow calculates future positions of the target and at the same time knows how long it would take to get there. A position in front of the target could then be chosen for which the movement time of the hand matches the motion time of the target. If the subject during the approach finds that the calculation is wrong, a new meeting point could be calculated.

It is also conceivable that the child has to his or her disposal a sensomotor system for anticipatory tracking. The one suggested by Lanchester and Mark (1975), however, is insufficient. It would work very well for any species which has its catching instrument, e.g., the mouth, in a fixed relation to the eye. This is not true for the human being. The distance between the eye and the hand is variable indeed. The system I would suggest is slightly more complicated. It is one that tracks and approaches the target at the same time as shown in Fig. 2.5. This does not imply that the subject performs two movements at once, but rather that the performed movement has two determinants. Such a system can most easily be thought about in terms of two coupled servomechanisms or two coupled open-loop mechanisms. There is continuous input to both mechanisms: For one it is the distance to the target and for the other it is its distal motion. If the tracking of the target in 3-D space is correct then the reach will always be directed toward the meeting point. The only constraint of the approach system is that the approach has to be completed while the target is within reach. If this kind of solution to the problem of anticipation is applied, the subject only needs correct perception of the motion of the target in 3-D space. He does not need to use this

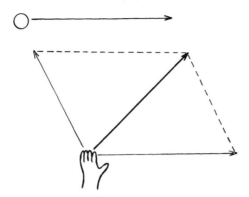

FIG. 2.5 A predictive reach can be described as a simultaneous tracking of the target and approaching of it. If the tracking component corresponds to the distal velocity of the target, the hand will move toward the meeting point with the target.

knowledge to calculate future target positions, nor does he need to know the time it takes to reach out.

The Visual Information Used in Catching

The two models of the catching mechanism outlined previously both presuppose veridical perception of the distal motion of the target. How necessary is this? Is it not sufficient to perceive the time it takes the object to arrive at the subject?

Retinal Expansion. Lee (1976) has shown that the inverse of the rate of dilation of the image specifies time-to-contact with, for instance, an object that moves toward the subject but it does not specify the absolute velocity or distance to the target. However, if time is the crucial variable it seems unnecessary for the subject to work out time-to-contact from perceived distance and velocity of object. Lee has shown that retinal expansion is a potent determiner of timing behavior and determines such diverse timing phenomena as the adjustment of gait in long jumping (Lee et al., 1982), the control of a punch to a falling ball (Lee et al., 1983) and the folding of the wings by gannets plummeting into the sea (Lee & Reddish, 1981). Todd (1981) has also shown that the pattern of expansion together with the retinal displacement of a thrown ball, for instance a baseball, will inform the observer how to move to get to the site of the touch-down so the ball can be caught. If the ball always was caught just in front of the eyes, the subject would only need to center the expansion pattern to succeed with the task. This is perhaps how Lee's ball punchers solved the problem (Lee et al., 1983). However, in most cases, catching is more flexible than that. The object will be caught in a variety of positions within reaching distance. The solution of the problem under such unconstrained conditions needs something more than retinal expansion. Retinal expansion may inform the catcher of time-to-contact and in which direction the hand should be moved but not how far from the eye the object is going to arrive. It could be a large object moving fast and passing far to the side or a small object moving slow and passing close by. To determine the scale of the event, the catcher needs veridical information about the motion of the object, at least at some point during its approach. Thus, retinal expansion could contribute in an important way to the timing performance in catching an approaching object but only in the limiting case of a direct approach toward the eye is it a sufficient determiner of catching.

Is retinal expansion a necessary determiner of timing performance in catching then? No, there are situations where the target does not approach the subject but circles around or passes in front of him or her. No retinal expansion is produced but catching is still possible. Timing will at least in those cases be based on some other kind of visual information than retinal expansion.

Absolute Distance Information. According to the previous discussion, the subject needs information to scale the event relative to his or her own body. Body-scaled space information is normally specified by a number of parameters contained in the retinal flow from a textured environment. However, when catching a ball coming from above in an open field, there is very little textured environment in view. Yet such a ball does not seem to give the catcher extra trouble. Thus, the catcher must have access to body-scaled information about space by other means. Is a textured environment necessary at all? In order to answer that question, an experiment was performed together with Herbert Pick at University of Minnesota in which vision of the environment was prevented by having subjects catch luminant balls in the dark. A throwing machine was used to throw the balls that passed within reaching distance from the subjects. Performance was surprisingly good although understandably poorer than in normal illuminated conditions. If the subject was allowed to use both hands the ball was caught in 46% of the trials and touched but lost in 43% of the trials in the dark compared to 93% caught and 7% touched but lost in the light. In a series of studies, Whiting (1969) found essentially the same thing. Subjects were quite able to catch luminant balls in the dark. As the expansion pattern of the ball itself doesn't give absolute distance information, what source of information does the subject rely on?

In principle, the vergence angle to the target could supply the subject with such information. That vergence can determine perceived distance was shown by Hofsten (1976). In another experiment, Hofsten (1977) found that vergence would determine the point in space toward which infants would direct their reaches. The reaching was carried out while the infant was wearing vergence altering prism spectacles. In adults, Shebilske, Karmiohl, and Proffitt (1983) found that inducing an esophoric shift in eye vergence would alter perceived distance to targets in the surrounding also understructured viewing conditions. In these experiments perceived distance was measured by pointing with the unseen hand.

The change in vergence angle when viewing an approaching target might in itself be an important contributing factor for perceiving the distal motion of the target. I studied perceived motion of a dot, the vergence angle of which changed in a continuous way. Perception of translation in depth was unambiguous (Hofsten, unpublished data).

To determine whether vergence is important for catching, another experiment was performed with Herbert Pick in which subjects caught balls with unrestricted vision or with one eye occluded. We found that subjects did considerably worse with one eye occluded. This was true for subjects catching luminant balls in the dark as well as for subjects catching balls under normal light conditions. Thus, binocular vision seem to play an important role in catching. Under lighted conditions there are, of course, other ways of obtaining absolute distance information, but also under these conditions do subjects seem to prefer to use the binocular system.

Viewing Time

Another question concerns the time needed to extract information about the flight of the ball to catch. This has been extensively studied by Whiting and his associates (Sharp & Whiting, 1974; Whiting, 1969; Whiting, Gill, & Stephenson, 1970; Whiting & Sharp, 1974). They used a ball with an internal light that would light up for a certain time period during its flight. The ball was dropped onto a miniature trampoline that caused it to enter on a parabolic flight path. During the experiments the room was blacked out. Whiting, Gill, and Stephenson (1970) studied catching for the ball when lit up for various periods from the bounce during a 0.4 sec flight. They found that performance increased almost linearly up to the full light condition. In other words, the subject could utilize visual information about the motion of the ball at least up to 0.1 sec from the catch. Alderson et. al., found that when sight of the ball was prevented approximately 275 msec before it arrived, deterioration in performance occurred because balls were located correctly but not grasped adequately.

In another set of studies where the ball was lit up for a certain period at various parts of its trajectory, Whiting and Sharp (Sharp and Whiting, 1974, Whiting & Sharp, 1974) found that as long as the subjects could see the ball for at least 40 msec and at a period in its flight about a third of a second before it reached him or her, then performance would be rather good. If you could see the ball for about 250 msec up to that point that improved your performance because it allowed time for your eyes to latch on to it. That subjects need to view the flight of the ball about a third of a second before it arrives is supported by Nessler (1973) in an experiment with somewhat higher ball velocities. The room was lit up during the last part of the ball's flight. As this period increased from 0.3 to 0.4

sec, the catching success went up from 32 to 65%. When the room was lit up just for the last 200 msec of the ball's flight, only 7% of the balls were caught.

Visual Proprioception

Viewing the catching hand during the act does not seem to improve performance. In an experiment performed together with Herbert Pick, we found no difference between subjects catching a luminant ball with and without carrying a luminant glove on the catching hand. In contrast with this result, Smyth and Marriott (1982) found that when sight of the catching hand was prevented during a whole experiment with the aid of an occluding screen, catching performance deteriorated. The errors made were in positioning of the catching hand, which frequently did not contact the ball. The results suggested that the correspondence between vision and proprioception is slowly lost when the hand cannot be seen. This is in accordance with Lee (1978), who pointed out that the nonvisual proprioceptive systems are probably subject to a considerable drift and has to be kept tuned by vision.

CONCLUSION

Catching is a highly optimized skill. It is more than just goal-directed reaching because it also involves a specific strategy for handling events in the environment. Extraction of information for monitoring catching is effecient and its control over action immediate. Catching skill has deep biological roots and develops quite early.

The study of perception and action should take the biology of the system into account. The information-processing approach that has dominated the field doesn't. In spite of its name, it was never interested in information, just how it was processed. It was never really interested in action either, just what led up to it. When I read accounts of action skills from that perspective, I get a queer feeling that the brain is a one-chip lab computer with a number of AD input channels and a number of DA output channels (see e.g., Sanders, 1980 or Sternberg, 1969). Nothing could be more wrong. The brain is quite a sophisticated device. Its solutions to action problems have been elaborated, tested, and modified during hundreds of millions of years of evolution. The solution to one action problem may not be applicable to another one. Increased efficiency on one task does not imply increased efficiency on all tasks. The brain can afford to incorporate different solutions to different problems in order to improve efficiency on each of them.

However, the brain can also, to a certain extent, perform silly artificial tasks like remembering nonsense syllable lists, raising a particular finger in response to a displayed letter, or pressing buttons in response to a some signals. It may even be the case that under such circumstances the boxology of traditional information-processing theory gives a convenient description of the event. The weakness of the approach becomes quite clear first when the researcher tries to generalize to the normal functioning of the subject. When this is tried, subjects' capacity is often grossly misjudged. This is certainly true with, for instance, coincidence-anticipation tasks and catching. Dorfman (1977), as discussed earlier, grossly underestimated the timing capacity of his subjects as they intercepted a moving dot on an oscilloscope screen.

The shortcomings of the information-processing approach has become apparent to more and more researchers traditionally within the information-processing domain. In memory research today task-specific memory is a keyword (Nilsson & Archer, 1985). Even defenders of information processing like Massaro (see chapter in this volume) have become interested in the task of perception. That is a healthy sign.

I finally like to point out that I am not denying the importance of studying mental processing. On the contrary, such studies are essential, but only when taken in reference to the task to be carried out and the information utilized in carrying out that task. My criticism concerns the artificial and oversimplified way in which problems of information processing has been studied in the past and from which we have learned little.

REFERENCES

Alderson, G. J. K., Sully, D. J., & Sully, H. G. (1974). An operational analysis of a one-handed catching task using high speed photography. *Journal of Motor Behavior, 6,* 217–226.

Arbib, M. A. (1980). Perceptual structures and distributed motor control. V. B. Brooks (Ed.). *Handbook of Physiology (Vol. III).*

Dorfman, P. W. (1977). Timing and anticipation: A developmental perspective. *Journal of Motor Behavior, 9,* 67–79.

Gibson, E. J., & Bergman, R. (1954). The effect of training on absolute estimation of distance over the ground. *Journal of Experimental Psychology, 48,* 473–482.

Gibson, E. J., Bergman, R., & Purdy, J. (1955). The effect of prior training with a scale of distance on absolute and relative judgements of distance over ground. *Journal of Experimental Psychology, 50,* 97–110.

Hofsten, C. von. (1976). The role of convergence in space perception. *Vision Research, 16,* 193–198.

Hofsten, C. von. (1977). Binocular convergence as a determinant of reaching behavior in infancy. *Perception, 6,* 139–144.

Hofsten, C. von. (1979). Development of visually guided reaching: The approach phase. *Journal of Human Movement Studies, 5,* 160–78.

Hofsten, C. von. (1980). Predictive reaching for moving objects by human infants. *Journal of Experimental Child Psychology, 30,* 369–382.

Hofsten, C. von. (1983). Catching skills in infancy. *Journal of Experimental Psychology: Human Perception and Performance, 9,* 75–85.

Hofsten, C. von. (1985). Perception and action. In M. Frese and J. Sabini (Eds.), *Goal directed behavior: The concept of action in psychology,* Hillsdale, NJ: Lawrence Erlbaum Associates.

Hofsten, C. von, & Lindhagen, K. (1979). Observations on the development of reaching for moving objects. *Journal of Experimental Child Psychology, 28,* 158–173.
Ingle, D. (1977). Loss of anticipatory orientation following lesions of visual cortex in the gerbil. *Neuroscience Abstracts, 3,* 68.
Ingle, D., Cheal, M., & Dizio, P. (1979). Cine analysis of visual orientation and pursuit by the mongolian gerbil. *Journal of Comparative and Physiological Psychology, 93,* 919–928.
Kay, H. (1970). Analyzing motor skill performance. In K. Connolly (Ed.), *Mechanisms of motor skill development.* London: Academic Press.
Lanchester, B. S., & Mark, R. F. (1975). Pursuit and prediction in the tracking of moving food by a teleost fish (Acanthaluteres spilomelanurus). *Journal of Experimental Biology, 63,* 627–245.
Lee, D. N. (1976). A theory of visual control of braking based on information about time-to-collision. *Perception, 5,* 437–459.
Lee, D. N. (1978). On the functions of vision. In H. Pick & E. Saltzman (Eds.), *Modes of perceiving and processing information.* Hillsdale, NJ: Lawrence Erlbaum Associates.
Lee, D. N., Lishman, J. R., & Thomson, J. A. (1982). Visual regulation of gait in longjumping. *Journal of Experimental Psychology: Human Perception and Performance, 8,* 448–459.
Lee, D. N., & Reddish, P. E. (1981). Plummeting gannets: a paradgm of ecological optics. *Nature, 293,* 293–294.
Lee, D. N., Young, D. S., Reddish, P. E., Lough, S., & Clayton, T. M. H. (1983). Visual timing in hitting an accelerating ball. *Quarterly Journal of Experimental Psychology, 35A,* 333–346.
Nessler, J. (1973). Length of time necessary to view a ball while catching it. *Journal of Motor Behavior, 5,* 179–185.
Nilsson, L. G., & Archer, T. (Eds.). (1985). *Perspectives on learning and memory.* Hillsdale, NJ: Lawrence Erlbaum Associates.
Sanders, A. F. (1980). Stage analysis of reaction processes. In G. E. Stelmach & J. Requin (Eds.), *Tutorials in motor behavior.* Amsterdam: North–Holland.
Sharp, R. H., & Whiting, H. T. A. (1974). Exposure and occluded duration effects in a ball-catching task. *Journal of Motor Behavior, 6,* 139–147.
Shebilske, W. L., Karmiohl, C. M., & Proffitt, D. R. (1983). Induced esophoric shifts and illusory distance in reduced and structured viewing conditions. *Journal of Experimental Psychology: Human Perception and Performance, 9,* 270–277.
Skravenski, A. A., & Hansen, R. M. (1978). Role of eye position information in visual localization. In J. Senders, D. Fisher, & R. Monty (Eds.), *Eye movements and the higher psychological functions* (pp. 15–34). Hillsdale, NJ: Lawrence Erlbaum Associates.
Smyth, M. M., & Marriott, A. M. (1982). Vision and proprioception in simple catching. *Journal of Motor Behavior, 14,* 143–152.
Sternberg, S. (1969). The discovery of processing stages: Extensions of Donder's method. *Acta Psychologica, 30,* 276–315.
Todd, J. (1981). Visual information about moving objects. *Journal of Experimental Psychology: Human Perception and Performance, 7,* 795–810.
Tyldesley, D. A., & Whiting, H. T. A. (1975). Operational timing. *Journal of Human Movement Studies, 1,* 172–177.
Wade, M. G. (1980). Coincidence anticipation of young, normal and handicapped children. *Journal of Motor Behavior, 12,* 103–112.
Whiting, H. T. A. (1969). *Aquiring ball skill.* Philadelphia: Lee & Febiger.
Whiting, H. T. A., Gill, E. B., & Stephenson, J. M. (1970). Critical time interval for taking in flight information in a ball catching task. *Ergonomics, 13,* 265–272.
Whiting, H. T. A., & Sharp, R. H. (1974). Visual occlusion factors in a discrete ball-catching task. *Journal of Motor Behavior, 6,* 11–16.

3 Ideo-Motor Action

Wolfgang Prinz
Universität Bielefeld

1. INTRODUCTION

The term *ideo-motor action* has been used to refer to movements that are performed in accordance with movements that are perceived—i.e., to situations where action is (seems to be) immediately guided by perception. In this chapter there is much reference to classic literature on this matter. Yet, it is not meant as a chapter on the history of the perception/action issue, but rather as a systematic examination of ideo-motor phenomena as well as of their proposed theoretical explanations. Recent literature is scarce due to the fact that the field of ideo-motor action that flourished in the beginning of the century, has been abandoned long since.

It is ironic that William B. Carpenter who in his Principles of Mental Psychology coined the term *ideo-motor action,* at the same time played an important part in discrediting the concept as well as the phenomena subsumed under it. According to Carpenter an action is under ideo-motor control, if it arises without mediation of a separate volitional impulse. Instead, it is solely triggered and guided by a "chain of ideas."

Carpenter offers a wide and a narrow interpretation of this general definition. In the wider sense "ideo-motor" applies to all action that is more or less automatic—ranging from locomotor control of the limbs (guided by the "idea of moving") to the voicing of an utterance (prompted by the "ideas to be expressed"). According to these examples the *immediacy* of the relationship between ideas and movements seems to be the critical defining property of ideo-motor action (cf. Carpenter, 1874, p. 280). In this broad sense, the concept virtually coincides with that of automatic action and therefore becomes dispensible.

However, the concept has not fallen into disrepute because its definition was too wide. Quite on the contrary, it was mainly discredited in its more well-known narrow version. This was not explicitly defined, but rather implicitly introduced through the examples Carpenter used in order to clarify the concept. These examples have had the effect of limiting its scope and narrowing down its meaning.

The limitation of scope resulted from its use as an explicatory concept for a variety of curious phenomena. According to Carpenter, phenomena such as table turning, mind reading or Saint Vitus's Dance lose much of their disquieting and consternating character, if interpreted as examples of ideo-motor action, i.e., of movements that are guided by overstrong, predominant ideas and therefore executed without or even against the voluntary control of the person concerned.

At the same time these examples served to narrow down the meaning of ideo-motor action. In the analysis of these phenomena did Carpenter not only refer to the immediacy of the relationship between ideas and actions, but also to some *correspondence* with respect to their content. In the well-known demonstration of the magic pendulum, a pendulum is suspended on a person's stretched forefinger with the instruction to keep finger and pendulum absolutely immobile. The usual observation is that after some time the pendulum begins to swing. According to Carpenter (1874) the idea of the moving pendulum causes unintentional or even counterintentional movements "in accordance with the idea" (p. 286).

In this narrow sense the predicate *ideo-motor* applies to all movements that are guided by their corresponding ideas. Thus, in order to be ideo-motor, an action must be under the *immediate* control of ideas that *refer to the action itself*.

Carpenter's examples placed the ideo-motor phenomena within the vicinity of the paranormal phenomena of the mind and thereby attached to them a certain odium which, to this day, has impeded their being taken as seriously as they perhaps should be. A case in point is Thorndike's attack on the ideo-motor principle in which he came to the conclusion that the principle is nothing but a modern version of magic thinking. Thorndike (1913) stated: "our belief that an idea tends to produce the act which it is like, or represents, or 'is an idea of', or 'has as its object', is kith and kin with our forebears' belief that dressing to look like a bear will give you his strength" (p. 105). This attack was clearly inspired by the idea to promote contiguity and reinforcement as the principles that govern the forming of associative connections and to oust from this position the principle of similarity as inherent in the idea of ideo-motor action.

As can be derived from Thorndike's heavy attack this idea was very popular at that time. Its popularity was due to William James's Principles of Psychology, which had promoted the idea of ideo-motor action with great emphasis. James strongly objected to ideo-motor action being relegated to the curiosities of mind (1890, II, p. 522). Instead, he used Carpenter's term to denote a specific understanding of action control and movement guidance that had before been discussed by Rudolph Hermann Lotze in his Medicinische Psychologie (1852).

It seems that Thorndike's attack was one of the last battles around the idea of ideo-motor action. The new theoretical approaches that then became dominant were no longer interested in these phenomena. They would either ban notions like "idea" and "similarity" altogether (like Behaviorism) or would not be concerned with motor processes at all (like Gestalt Psychology). Ideo-motor phenomena were shelved as curious borderline effects and gradually fell into oblivion.

In this chapter I want to argue that for a better understanding of the links between perception and action it is worthwhile to study ideo-motor action in some detail—not so much as a general model for the perception/action interface, but rather as a special class of phenomena of motor control. For this purpose I now turn from history to systematics. Section 2 reviews the phenomena covered under the notion of ideo-motor action. Section 3 provides an account of the main theories that have been developed to bridge the gap between ideo and motor. Finally a new version of an old theoretical approach is outlined in Section 4.

2. IDEO-MOTOR PHENOMENA

Let us start with a quotation from Lotze (1852) that gives some examples of ideo-motor phenomena. In James's translation we read: "The spectator accompanies the throwing of a billiard-ball, or the thrust of a swordsman, with slight movements of his arm; the untaught narrator tells his story with many gesticulations; the reader, while absorbed in the perusal of a battle scene, feels a slight tension run through his muscular system, keeping time as it were with the actions he is reading of" (p. 293; cf. James, 1890, II, p. 525). According to Lotze these are examples of "imitative movements (Nachahmungsbewegungen) . . . (which) arise from movement ideas (Bewegungsvorstellungen) without any voluntary determination." (Lotze, l.c.). It seems that Lotze's notion of "Nachahmungsbewegung" roughly corresponds to Carpenter's notion of *ideo-motor action* in its narrower sense. It refers to all cases in which perceived or imagined movements have (or have attained) the capability of immediately effecting the execution of corresponding body movements.

As Lotze's examples show ideo-motor phenomena comprise very different forms of motor control that can be classified in various ways (cf. Richter, 1954,

1957). In this Section a classification along two lines is proposed. The first is a distinction according to the temporal relation between the perceived event and the prompted movement. A person's body movement can either accompany a perceived or imagined event (synkinetic movement) or follow the event with a certain delay (echokinetic movement). The second distinction concerns the nature of the guiding event. Synkinesis and Echokinesis can be prompted by visual events such as perceived or imagined motion, but also by events in nonvisual modalities (tactual patterns, sound patterns, voices, etc.).

The following account of some varieties of *synkinesis* (2.1) and of *echokinesis* (2.2) emphasizes perceptual rather than ideational guidance. In the last part of this section (2.3) the reasons for this and some further *limitations of the scope* of our considerations are discussed.

2.1 Synkinesis

The term synkinesis, as we understand it, refers to the case where some of the body's own movements are synchronized with a perceived or imagined event. Such synchronized movements usually arise unintentionally, frequently even counterintentionally (as in Carpenter's analysis of the swinging pendulum). Depending on the nature of the perceived/imagined event three examples of movement synchronization can be considered typical.

Example 1. In a slapstick movie I am watching a scene in which an actor quite happily walks along the edge of a plunging precipice, completely unaware of the dangerous situation. When the hero inadvertently steps over the edge or when he just misses falling off and manages to catch hold of a tuft of grass, which is slowly but surely getting uprooted, I am, though only a spectator, quite unable to sit still and watch quietly. I find it difficult to resist the movements in my legs and arms and suppress the strain in my muscles and the involuntary displacements of my body weight that occur to me—i.e., slight movements which can be considered rudimental indications of suppressed full movements. My movements give an indication of those I would perform if I were in the hero's place.

Example 2. I am pushing a bowling ball and follow its course. As long as I cannot extrapolate its final course with absolute certainty—that is to say while it is still open whether it will reach its intended position or not—I can hardly prevent myself from moving my hand or twisting my body as if to push the ball in the intended direction or give it the momentum it needs to reach its goal position. This example illustrates that synkinetic movements are not dependent on the perception of organismic self-motion but also extend to physical object motion. Nor are they limited to the motion of objects caused by myself: When the bowling ball is thrown by one of the other players I might synkinetically accompany its course as well.

Example 3. I listen to a rhythm and dance to it or carry out other rhythmic movements (e.g., with my feet, head, or hands). In this case, too, observers may find it very hard to suppress synkinetic accompaniment of the perceived event. As Fraisse (1981) has pointed out the suggestive power of such auditory-motor synchronizations is quite strong and seems to rely on privileged sensory-motor connections. In addition to the previous examples, this one shows that the spontaneous occurrence of event-synchronized movements is not only prompted by perceived or imagined movements but can also be induced by sound patterns, i.e., by auditory events that are either caused by movements or might at least be interpreted in terms of correlative concomitants of movements.

What is it exactly in these examples that specifies the particular correspondence between perception and action that leads us to consider them to represent a peculiar form of motor control?

The examples clearly differ in the degree of correspondence. Some correspondence in the *temporal* structure between the perceived event and the performed movements seems to be inherent in all of them. When movements are guided by auditory events synchrony of perceptual and motor events is the only mode of correspondence that can be achieved at all. As the guiding event has no spatial characteristics at all there can be no spatial correspondence between the guiding and the guided event. In principle, all parts of the body can do the same job of aptly synchronizing auditory rhythm. Synchronization requires an internal representation of the temporal structure of the perceived or imagined event. If this condition is met, synchronized movements reflect the temporal structure of the perceived events, even if no further correspondence or similarity exists.

When movements are guided by visually perceived events the correspondence between action and perception also pertains to aspects of their *spatial* structure. When the bowling ball drifts more to the left than it should the observer will twist his hand or his trunk in the reverse direction. When the model catches hold of a tuft of grass the pattern of movements induced in the observer will involve those parts of his body that correspond to those involved in the observed movement. However, even though in this type of example the spatial correspondence between guiding and guided movements may pertain to both the topology of the body (with respect to the body parts involved), and the geometry of the environmental space (with respect to direction of movement), it is usually not a correspondence in the sense of a copy of the spatial structure of the observed event. It does not repeat the perceived pattern but rather reflects complementary aspects. In this respect, synkinesis is clearly different from echokinesis.

2.2 Echokinesis

The term *echokinesis* was used by David Katz (1960, p. 373) in order to denote a person's imitative copy of another person's movements. Though the term is out of use, we prefer it to the more common concept of imitation because its scope is clearly limited to the copy of simple movements and does not comprise the much more complex forms and mechanisms of modeling and observational learning as discussed within the framework of Social Learning Theory (Bandura, 1977; Bandura & Walters, 1963). The imitative acts considered in this framework usually refer to molar kinds of behavior—i.e., actions, goals, motives, attitudes, or even traits—rather than to movements per se. Obviously, a distinction is needed between imitation of movements and of actions. In the former case the intention is to copy perceived movements as spatiotemporal *events;* in the latter case it is to attain the same goal *states* as the model—quite irrespective of the movements needed for this (Stränger, 1977, ch. 1; Scheerer, 1984a). The term of *echokinesis* is meant to denote the first of these two meanings and thereby to avoid confusion with all "higher" kinds of imitative behavior.

In adults echokinetic movements will normally presuppose an intention to imitate. The imitator's intention refers to the production of a spatiotemporal movement pattern that corresponds (is identical) to a previously perceived event. On the other hand, a lot of unintentional imitation of movements seems to occur in early infancy and is considered rather important for the early stages of sensory-motor and intellectual development (Baldwin, 1895; Guillaume, 1926; Mounoud & Vinter, 1981; Piaget, 1946).

Unlike the synchronic movements of the synkinetic type, imitative movements of the echokinetic type occur asynchronically in relation to the movement of the model. Again, we have to distinguish several examples of imitative movements, depending on the nature of the model event.

Example 1. I imitate the gesticulative and mimic behavior of a person. This is the most typical form of imitative movement—mainly because in this (and the following) case the imitated and imitative movements are carried out with identical means: the apparatus of human voluntary motor control. If I tried to imitate a movement pattern of my dog, for example, this specific condition would no longer be met (cf. example 3).

Example 2. I imitate another person's voice. In this case I perform a sequence of articulatory movements that are not guided by the perception of a corresponding spatiotemporal pattern of movements, but by a merely temporal pattern of acoustic events, instead. That the acoustic pattern has in turn been produced by a pattern of articulatory movements is not contained in what I perceive. I only hear the (temporal) sound pattern but do not see the (spatiotemporal) pattern of movements causing it (if lipreading is precluded). Accordingly, the imitative intention is directed not to the movement pattern itself, but rather to its acoustic concomitants. However, because the acoustic concomitants are strongly correlated with the movement pattern that produces them the imitation of the sound pattern can be adequately realized only by way of performing a specific pattern of articulatory movements. As I have no knowledge of the model's movement pattern, I have no way of knowing whether or not my movements are an echokinetic copy of his. The only thing I can perceive are his voice and its echo produced by myself.

Examples 3 and 4. I imitate the movements (3) or the voice (4) of an animal. In these examples the conditions for echokinetic imitation are less favorable because my apparatus for locomotion and articulation is different from that of the animal in question. Although my imitation is thus limited to selected characteristics of the model I may succeed, if I am good at it, in convincing the audience with my imitations. The structural limitations that affect imitation under these circumstances do not necessarily interfere with the perceived similarity between the model and its copy.

Examples 5 and 6. With my arms and hands I imitate the motion of an object (e.g., a fly's flight) that I have just followed with my eyes (5). An echokinetic motion description like this can be made even more convincing by additionally imitating some of the accompanying noises (6). In this way, motion and/or noise accompanying it can be imitated without the need to postulate a deep structural correspondence between the mechanism that generates the motion of the model and the imitator's motor apparatus that generates its copy.

Different though these examples may seem, when considered in terms of their phenomenal representation they are closely related: I see a movement or hear a noise and know immediately what to do in order to produce as similar a pattern of movement or noise as possible. Unlike synkinesis, echokinesis always requires spatial in addition to temporal correspondence between the model event and its copy, and the spatial correspondence usually pertains to both the topology of the body (use of corresponding parts of the body) and the geometry of environmental space (generation of corresponding movement trajectories).

In imitating a movement I am completely unaware of the highly complicated functional problem of how my motor system knows what to do in order to generate a movement pattern that has a spatiotemporal structure that closely corresponds to the model event. How does this knowledge arise? The analysis of my mental contents gives no reply to this query because I immediately and spontaneously know what I have to do to produce the appropriate effects. Phenomenally speaking, imitation of movements is child's play.

2.3 Some Delimitations of Scope

The phenomena covered under the notions of synkinesis and echokinesis by no means cover the whole range of effects and observations that have sometimes been subsumed under headings like "ideo-motor action" or "imitation." For the subsequent theoretical considerations it should be kept in mind that our account of synkinesis and echokinesis does *not* pertain to the following classes of phenomena.

Actions. It is a truism that the natural units of our activities are actions, not movements. This means that our activities are guided by representations of intended goal states rather than of intended movements. Usually the movements required in order to attain an intended goal seem to happen by themselves. Actions can be considered to be distally focused sections of our activity, whereas movements are proximally focused in the sense of Brunswik (1952).

Imitation of actions is usually quite different from imitation of movements. On the one hand, when I buy the same car as my neighbor, I am said to copy his behavior. But the copying refers to the action of buying a car and not to the body movement required to perform it. Though we cannot purchase a car without any body movements at all, we fortunately need not perform the same movements as someone else in order to buy the same car as he did. On the other hand, a movement can be exactly copied without intending the same goal. For instance, if I drink a concentrated solution of strychnine in the same nonchalant manner as Humphrey Bogart used to drink his whisky, the movement may be a convincing imitation of his, though the action is not. The same holds for parody: The amusement we enjoy from a parody is partially based on the discrepancy between the intentions inherent in the model's actions and those underlying the parodist's copy. In a sense, the act of imitating a movement can be considered to be an action the intention of which does not go beyond the generation of a particular spatiotemporal movement pattern.

"Ideational Guidance." Furthermore, our considerations only refer to perceptual guidance of movements and do not include what Carpenter and James called "ideational guidance," i.e., the guidance of movements by corresponding images, conceptions, or thoughts. There are three reasons for this restriction. First, it is suggested by the scope of this book. Second, for obvious reasons most of the experimental literature refers to perceptual rather than ideational guidance. Third, when extented to include ideational guidance, the notion of ideo-motor action becomes overexpanded and therefore quite diffuse in its meaning.

This last point is neatly illustrated by Lotze's and James's account of voluntary action as a special expansion of ideo-motor action. Having concentrated on the study of specific ideo-motor movement, neither Lotze nor James could resist the temptation to work on the idea that any voluntary movement can be conceived as the result of an imitative ideo-motor process. For this it is sufficient to assume that the execution of a voluntary movement presupposes (in temporal and in functional terms) some image of its execution and that the actual movement is both initiated and controlled by the movement image.

According to Lotze, on the basis of a voluntary impulse directed to a specific goal, the mind forms a conception of what is intended. This intention comprises, among other things, an image of the movements the body has to perform in order to give effect to the intention. Once the movement image has been formed in the mind the body mechanism—according to Lotze an independent being separate from the mind—has no choice but immediately carry out the appropriate movement, without any further voluntary impulse. The movement image is therefore a necessary and at the same time sufficient precondition for the execution of the movement by the body mechanism (Lotze, 1852, p. 301 ff.). This view is supported by James in a somewhat different terminology. According to James, body movement is a natural, direct effect of specific feelings and representations, and it occurs entirely by itself, unless it is impeded by other, simultaneously effective ideas and their corresponding impulses: "Drop this idea (i.e., the competing idea), think of the movement purely and simply, with all brakes off; and presto! it takes place with no effort at all" (James, 1890, II, p. 527).

Though the magic spell of James's words may be tempting we resist their lure and confine ourselves to the case of perceptual guidance of movements. However, in doing so, we should keep in mind that we thereby exclude a variety of phenomena that classical authors and authorities in the field have regarded as prototypical of ideo-motor action (cf. Allers & Scheminzky, 1926; Greenwald, 1970; Jacobson, 1932; Richter, 1954, 1957; Weber, 1906).

Stationary Patterns. It has often been claimed that movements are not only induced by perceived events (i.e., patterns that include the dimension of time), but also by stationary patterns (e.g., Lipps, 1903, in his theory of empathy, or Werner & Wapner, 1949, 1952 in their sensory-tonic field theory of perception). Though the validity of many of the relevant observations cannot be doubted, we do not consider them here because in these cases the observed movements and/or changes in tonus distribution clearly differ in the mode of their perceptual guidance from the examples considered so far. They are state driven rather than event driven and therefore rely on a different basis of control.

Expressive Movements. Occasionally, expressive movements have also been subsumed under ideo-motor action (Richter, 1957). Though it may be argued that expressive movements synkinetically accompany the time course of the person's emotional condition we disregard them because they track "inner," i.e., nonperceptual events. This is not necessarily true for various kinds of empathic movements a second person performs in accordance with expressive movements observed in the first. Such empathic movements (which are sometimes viewed as a necessary link in order to form in the second person an impression that mirrors the emotional condition of the first) may or may not belong to the echokinetic phenomena, depending on whether they are event driven and not only state driven.

Orienting Movements. Furthermore it has been suggested also to include orienting movements in the class of ideo-motor phenomena (Richter, 1954, 1957). When I move my eyes, my head, or my body in accordance with the motion of an object (e.g., a fly's path) in order to obtain or maintain a suitable position of the eyes relative to the object my movements are clearly driven by the perceptual event. However, functionally speaking, they should not be considered unintentional concomitants of the perceived event. Rather, they are attentional responses to the pattern of stimulation and serve the function of maintaining perceptual contact with the event. For this reason we do not include them—though such exclusion may rest on somewhat arbitrary grounds.

3. VIEWS ON THE IDEO-MOTOR HYPHEN

What are the problems we face when attempting to explain phenomena like synkinesis or echokinesis? The central problem is how to bridge the gap between perception and action. How is visual motion translated into body movements that produce corresponding effects? How does the motor system know how to generate a movement pattern matching that of a model event or a model person observed?

For a long time our thinking has been guided by the idea that in order to understand the behavioral organization of animals a sharp distinction is needed between afferent and efferent processes, i.e., perceptual and motor events. This distinction has proved extremely productive in guiding physiological research and psychological reasoning and has therefore been widely accepted. However, the sharpness of the distinction has had the effect of rendering perceptual and motor processes very different and disparate events and has thus generated the question how the gap between them can be bridged.

Some of the basic problems of psychology arise from the fact that one deals with interrelated sets of phenomena which—though perfectly correlated—are obviously completely disparate, or incommensurable by nature. Like sensory-motor relations, intermodal relations, as reflected by synesthetic phenomena are posing just as many questions. The same holds for the relation between stimulus structure and meaning (as observed, for example, in sound symbolism or physiognomic qualities). Eventually, the relation between physical and mental events must be mentioned as the most prominent instance on such a list of sets of incommensurable phenomena.

In the face of such incommensurability two types of reactions can be observed. The first is to give up further inquiry and to postulate certain basic capabilities of mind that underlie the observed correspondences. This is the *petitio principii* position. The second type of reaction is to develop more or less detailed models and metaphors for the underlying mechanisms. In developing such models, one of two general theoretical orientations can be adopted (see Prinz, 1985). The first is to fully recognize the incommensurability of the phenomena involved and to postulate the existence of structural connections. The second is to deny incommensurability and to acknowledge some kind of at least partial commensurability. With this approach, connections are not needed because, in principle, the gap could be bridged by a match between the commensurable aspects of the related phenomena.

In the discussion to follow our emphasis is on the issue of *how* ideo-motor mediation is accomplished rather than *when* and *why* it occurs. Our primary concern is with the mechanism that is hidden in the hyphen, rather than with the conditions under which this mechanism is used. Before we consider in detail some varieties of the *petitio principii* position (in section 3.2) and of the connectionist and the matching view of the ideo-motor hyphen (in sections 3.3 and 3.4) we first turn to two basically different conceptualizations of the actual problem that is to be solved.

3.1 One Hyphen or Two?

3.1.1 Single-Hyphen View. The simplest conceptualization the issue of ideo-motor action can be given is depicted in Fig. 3.1a. So far we have discussed the issue according to this simple scheme. It assumes two different instances, a perceptual event and a motor event and just one hyphen between them. As far as I can see none of the more prominent students of ideo-motor action has actually believed in this simple scheme—probably not because it is too simple, but rather because some of its theoretical implications may be considered to go too far. This is because the hyphen has to link the percept and the movement immediately and thereby to bridge a gap that would be felt too wide to be bridged in one step.

On the other hand the simple conceptualization of the single-hyphen view has been abundantly used in some other theoretical traditions. This does not only apply to the behavioristic approach (which did not believe in ideo-motor action at all) but also to some variants of motor theories of perception. One of the defining features of these theories is the assumption that perception always implies motor processes that cannot be dismissed—either in the sense of obligatory motor coding accompanying the perceptual analysis (as prevalent in the older tradition

58   PRINZ

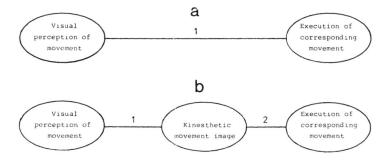

FIG. 3.1 Single versus double-hyphen view of the ideo-motor relationship. In the single-hyphen view, the hyphen stands for a link between perceived and performed movements. In the double-hyphen view the first hyphen (1) stands for the link between perceived movement and kinesthetic movement image, the second (2) for the link between this image and a corresponding body movement.

of motor theorizing; cf. Scheerer, 1984b) or in the sense of common structures and processes used in perception and action control (as prevalent in more recent versions, particularly in the motor theory of speech perception; cf. Halwes & Wire, 1974; Liberman, Cooper, Shankweiler & Studdert-Kennedy, 1967; Weimer, 1977). As becomes apparent later the older conception of obligatory motor coding bears some affinity to the connection view whereas the modern idea of common structures is more closely related to the matching view of the mechanism hidden in the hyphen.

3.1.2 Double-Hyphen View.   At first glance the double-hyphen view depicted in Fig. 3.1b seems to imply an unnecessary complication, simply because it assumes three instances instead of two. According to this scheme the execution of a movement is not directly guided by the perceived event but rather by a kinesthetic image of the movement. Thus the first hyphen stands for the relation between the visual percept and a (somehow) corresponding kinesthetic image that in turn is used to guide a (somehow) corresponding movement pattern.

What are the advantages of this view? Most of the students of ideo-motor action and related phenomena have adopted the position of the double-hyphen view as if it were completely evident. It seems that each of the two mechanisms is easier to conceive than the mechanism of the single-hyphen approach. The first hyphen basically links two sense modalities, viz. vision and kinesthesis. Though incommensurable sets of phenomena, they are both perceptual events (or images derived from percepts, respectively), and they are therefore conceptually less far away from each other than in the first approach.

The second hyphen links kinesthesis and movements. Though conceptually incommensurable, too, these two sets of phenomena are empirically much closer related than vision and movements. This is due to the high correlation between the efferent commands that govern the execution of movements and the afferent kinesthetic information by which the execution is fed back. As these mappings can be repeated and relearned with any body movement it is not unreasonable to assume that kinesthetic and motor codes, though conceptually different, can be empirically equivalent in many respects. If it is further assumed that this correlation does not only allow anticipation of the sensory consequences of ongoing movements but also guidance of movements on the basis of their anticipated kinesthetic image, the second of the two hyphens looks also much less cumbersome than the one in the single-hyphen conceptualization.

Thus, the main advantage seems to be that two smaller and easier bridges are used instead of a single wide one, where the kinesthetic image serves the function of the additional bridge pier. This bridge pier has frequently been used in theorizing about both space perception and motor control. According to Lotze and James the control of voluntary movement is always guided by kinesthetic images. Lotze (1852) states that we can perform a voluntary movement in no other way "than by reproducing within us, if only in outlines, the complex of sensations which earlier used to accompany the ongoing movement and was aroused by it" (p. 302). Correspondingly, according to James (1890) "the bare idea of a movement's sensible effects" is a necessary (and in the case of ideo-motor action even sufficient) "mental cue" to elicit the movement itself (II, p. 522).

In what follows we regard the kinesthetic movement image as a central representation that mediates between the perception and the execution of movements. As this image arises as a by-product of the execution of voluntary movements, i.e., from learning their proprioceptive consequences, it has a particularly prominent place among the possible candidates that might serve the function of this representational mediation. One could not think of any other mediating structure that is more directly and more strongly related to the execution of movements.

If it is taken for granted that the kinesthetic image of a movement (or a class of movements) can immediately govern its execution, the problem of understanding ideo-motor action is basically shifted from the second to the first hyphen, i.e., from the perceptual-motor to the cross-modal bridge. In the two-hyphen approach the critical problem is no longer how the motor system can know what to do in order to follow or to echo the movement of the model event, but rather how the kinesthetic imagery system can know how the execution of a movement like that of the model would feel. From this it is clear that the two-hyphen view does not really bring us closer to an understanding of the ideo-motor mechanism. Rather, it shifts the critical problem to a different locus in that it replaces the ideo-motor gap by a cross-modal gap.

The two-hyphen view is clearly prevalent in the recent literature on phenomena related to ideo-motor action. A couple of years ago Greenwald (1970) presented what he called an ideo-motor theory of performance control. According to this theory, performance in skilled action is directed by anticipatory representations of its feedback. A similar notion has emerged from recent observations on imitation of movements in the neonate and in the infant (see Mounoud & Vinter, 1981 for a summary). As the evidence suggests that visually observed model movements like mouth opening or tongue protrusion can be imitated in the baby's first month of life, it is usually concluded that there must be a large amount of in-built intersensory mapping between vision and kinesthetic proprioception (Abravanel, 1981; Bower, 1977, 1978). A similar idea seems to be inherent in the view that the neonate possesses a body scheme that, within certain limits, enables matching visually perceived model behavior to corresponding proprioceptive representations (Mounoud & Vinter, 1981; Trevarthen, Hubley, & Sheeran, (1975).

3.2 Petitio Principii

Many of the older theories of psychology are considered quite unsatisfactory today because at a certain level of explanation they cut off the analytical inquiry of the phenomena and invoke, instead, the wisdom of nature that is organized so as to produce the phenomena observed. This is illustrated by Lotze's and James's theoretical accounts of ideo-motor action both of which come quite close to a *petitio principii* rather than a satisfactory explanation.

For Lotze (1852) the specific question of how images of movements can produce movements is part of the general question of how the mind influences the body. According to his dualistic framework, the ideas of the mind would not be in any position to influence the physical mechanism of the body, "if the general laws of nature did not connect with these internal movements of the mind (i.e., the movements as imagined) the external ones of the body that is linked with the former" (p. 301). The rule of the mind over the body in general and the rule of the movement image over the movement in particular are characteristics of the basic psychophysical makeup of human nature. The movement image controls the movement because the psychophysical mechanism is constructed so as to enable the image to initiate and guide the corresponding movement. The ideo-motor principle is thus raised to the rank of a basic psychophysical truth at which analytical regress ends.

The explanation of ideo-motor action offered by James (1890) basically paraphrases its descriptive content in an abstract, slightly generalized way: "We may then lay it down for certain that every representation of a movement awakens in some degree the actual movement which is its object; and awakens it in a maximum degree whenever it is not kept from doing so by an antagonistic representation present simultaneously to the mind" (II, p. 526). The ability of the movement representation to provoke the represented movement derives from the fact that all mental phenomena are impulsive by nature so that movement is the direct natural result of all kinds of "feelings."

In ascribing to nature a tendency to produce the observed phenomena and, subsequently, presenting this tendency as an explanation of the phenomena, James gives what might be considered a classical example of pseudo-explanation of the *petitio principii* type. Thus, there is some truth in the caustic remark by Miller, Galanter, & Pribram (1960) that the only bridge James gave us between ideo and motor was the hyphen between them.

Lotze and James were both not particularly explicit about the mechanisms underlying the assumed "natural" relationship between perception and action. Some of their relevant statements seem to refer to the first and some others to the second hyphen in the double-hyphen scheme. Still less explicit about such details have been many students of human and animal imitation who postulated an instinctive basis of imitation (e.g., Morgan, 1891; Romanes, 1891). In all these accounts the phenomena are explained by postulating underlying dispositions to produce them.

3.3 Mapping Views

According to the theories classified in this category the hyphen stands for a set of connections that serve to map specific events on the one side of the gap to specific events on the other side. Due to these connections correspondence between the two sets of events is warranted, notwithstanding their incommensurability. Depending on whether the single- or the double-hyphen view is adopted, the assumed connections either link perceptual with motor processes, or they connect vision with kinesthesis.

Mapping views are quite common in psychological theorizing. With respect to ideo-motor action they have been stated in two versions: nativistic and empiristic.

3.3.1 Mapping "By Nature". The simple assumption of an instinct to imitate or a basic mental faculty of imitation is unsatisfactory because these notions provide words rather than mechanisms. One way to explain their meaning in more functional terms would be to assume the existence of firm inborn connections between specific perceptual patterns and specific patterns of movements. Such assumptions are inherent in the later development of the theory of instinctive behavior (e.g., Tinbergen, 1951). For such a theory of imitation to work, one would have to postulate connections between perceived and performed movement at various levels of integration, i.e., at the level of the finger, hand, forearm, arm . . . etc., which eventually implies assuming the existence of an inborn connective correspondence between two hierarchically organized body schemes: that of the (visually perceived) model and that of the (predominantly kinesthetically perceived) imitator. If such a system of connections existed the two schemes would, via these paths, be mapped to each other in all their components.

The previously mentioned ideas, put forward by Bower (1977) and Trevarthen et al. (1975), are closely related to this view. By assuming a large amount of preestablished mapping, either between perception and action (i.e., stimuli and responses) or across modalities, such theories virtually suggest to talk about nerve fibers rather than hyphens. Though this is certainly justified, it does not really improve our understanding of the underlying mechanisms.

3.3.2 Mapping "By Nurture". The alternative view within the mapping framework is to assume that the gap is bridged by connections that are due to learning—either of perceptual-motor connections or of visual-kinesthetic crossmodal correspondences. Both of these versions start from the assumption that the phenomena of synkinesis and echokinesis have to be explained by the same principles that govern animal learning in general, viz. contiguity and reinforcement, and that no special principle of similarity is needed in addition. The proponents of this line of thinking must therefore be considered Thorndike's immediate successors.

Within the framework of classical S-R theory and the *single-hyphen view* corresponding to it, there have been various attempts to understand imitation as a result of conditioning. The classical approaches in this field have been primarily concerned with more complex forms of imitation and social learning that are beyond our scope (Bandura & Walters, 1963; Miller & Dollard, 1941; Mowrer, 1960). More recently conditioning has also been proposed to explain imitation of simple movements (see Flanders, 1968; Gewirtz & Stingle, 1968; Parton, 1976, and Staats, 1970, for reviews).

In its most straightforward version, as provided by Gewirtz and Stingle, the learning approach assumes that the infant learns imitative responses in the same way as all other behavior, i.e., without any support due to the similarity between stimulus and response. The first imitative response occurs purely by chance and is immediately reinforced by environmental agents. Reinforcement serves both to shape and maintain the response usually on an intermittent schedule. With this approach one need not assume that the infant emits his response in an attempt to copy the parent but rather that the parent reinforces the infant on occasions when the infant happens to behave like himself (or some other model person). Later the collection of specific imitative responses acquired in this way acts as a class of diverse, but functionally equivalent behaviors, and each extrinsic reinforcement of one of the responses from this class then serves to maintain the response class as a whole, thereby laying the ground for generalized imitation.

Tackling the problem in this way is fascinating because, at first glance, it seems to take away a considerable portion of its usual theoretical burden. Learning to imitate is not different from learning to press a bar under particular conditions of stimulation and of reinforcement. However, at a second look, we must not forget that the problem of gap bridging has not disappeared with this approach, but in a sense been transferred from the learner to the reinforcing agent. In order to reinforce the infant appropriately the parent must be able to recognize the similarity between his own behavior and the infant's response. The critical role of the parent's behavior is also emphasized by the results of a systematical study by Pawlby (1977) showing that in very early infancy the parent imitates the infant much more frequently than the infant copies the parent. The same holds for many of Piaget's observations on early occurrence of imitation (Piaget, 1946, ch. 1). These considerations may be taken to suggest that imitation in infancy is at least partially due to the parent's rather than the infant's imitative capabilities.

This brings us back to the learning of crossmodal connections as would be needed within the framework of the *double-hyphen view*. How could we learn to anticipate the kinesthetic image that would be available, if we imitated a visual model's movements? This issue is quite different from the issue of learning crossmodal correspondences as it is usually stated (cf. Marks, 1978). The problem is not how we learn the correlation between visual and kinesthetic information about our own movements (which are simultaneously available when we perform a movement) but rather how visual information about the model's movement and kinesthetic information about our own movement can be coordinated.

This question could be answered in one of two ways. The first answer would assume that this coordination arises as a by-product of the just mentioned operant conditioning procedure, which after some time may take the role of a mediator between the stimulus and the response. This answer is unsatisfactory because it only explains the maintenance of established imitative responses, but not their very origin. The second answer would assume that an individual who has learned crossmodal correspondences between vision and kinesthesis with respect to his own movements can subsequently learn to transfer them to visual model movements by way of stimulus generalization. Basically, this answer has the effect of reducing the problem of learning to imitate a visually perceived movement to the problem of learning crossmodal correspondences between vision and kinesthesis. The operations needed for learning these mappings have recently been analyzed by Bushnell (1981). Unlike the proponents of connections-by-nature she argues that a variety of learning mechanisms of various degrees of complexity are involved in effecting the development of crossmodal mapping, ranging from operant conditioning to inferential and deductive reasoning.

In contrast to the nature version that considers the hyphen connections to be part of the inherited hardware equipment of the system the nurture version of the mapping view assumes that they are implemented under certain conditions. The power of this approach is derived from the fact that it accounts not only for our ability to imitate, but also, at least in principle, for the conditions under which we make use of it. On the other hand, with respect to our understanding of the ability, i.e., of *how* imitation is accomplished, it is no more and no less satisfactory than its counterpart. The only difference seems to be that it gives us arrows in a network of connections, rather than nerve fibers to bridge the ideo-motor gap. As it seems, none of these connectionist metaphors really goes beyond the meaning conveyed by the hyphen they stand for.

3.4 Matching Views

This does not apply when the hyphen is considered to stand for a match. As was discussed earlier, matching presupposes that the events to be matched have some properties in common. Fig. 3.2 depicts the general framework underlying the matching view (for the single-hyphen conceptualization). The critical feature of this scheme is, that, in addition to the representations of the movement perceived and the movement performed, which are incommensurable by their nature, a neutral level of representation is introduced at which shared properties of the perceptual and the motor events are represented. If the assumption of such shared properties were sound, the perceptual and the motor event could be immediately compared at this common level of representation, and the motor event could be generated and guided by copying the perceptual event as far as their common properties permit.

In contrast to the mapping approach in which the language of perceptual events is translated into that of motor events by mapping and connecting the vocabularies of the two languages with the mapping approach, the two languages are translated into the same neutral language, thereby necessitating two translation procedures instead of one. This seems to be an unnecessary complication, unless it is assumed that the mapping required for these translations is easy to accomplish and occurs quite automatically.

Depending on the nature of the assumed common properties two basic forms of matching can be distinguished: matching for categorical equivalence and for structural similarity. Again, both of these forms could in principle be used for both the perceptual-motor and the visual-kinesthetic hyphen.

3.4.1 Matching for Equivalence. The concept of matching for equivalence is readily exemplified by Piaget's account of imitation (Piaget, 1946). According to Piaget the first foundations for imitation are laid by the model imitating the infant. When this occurs the model's imitation begins to be incorporated into the infant's circular action plans. By this the perceived behavior of the model becomes equivalent to the perceived consequences of the infant's own activities and can take their place (assimilation of the model to the plan). Whereas at this stage perceptual similarity between the model's movement and the infant's own movement is required in order to trigger a loop of circular activity, functional equivalence is sufficient in the stages to follow. The infant will then learn to understand the functional equivalence between perceptually different events (e.g., the visual image of a model opening his mouth and the kinesthetic image

3. IDEO-MOTOR ACTION   65

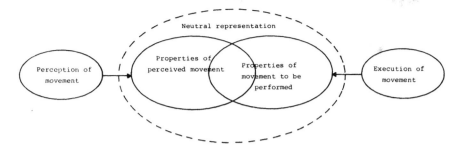

FIG. 3.2 Basic scheme underlying the matching view (see text). In this figure the scheme is outlined for a match between perceptual and motor events, according to the single-hyphen view. An analogous scheme for a match across modalities, as needed for the double-hyphen view, would have to assume a neutral representation of properties of the visually perceived movement and the kinesthetic image corresponding to it.

of himself doing the same). This implies what Piaget calls the accommodation of the plan to the model. In the early stages of development this functional equivalence is preconceptual by nature, because it means equivalence with respect to (sensory-motor) plans (schemes), rather than (cognitive) concepts. However, later these plans become internalized as concepts, and preconceptual equivalence changes to conceptual equivalence.

Ordinary language can give us an idea of how the conceptual language of mind could operate to mediate ideo-motor matching. In ordinary language perceived events and movements can both be described in the same language, using spatial, temporal, and nonspatiotemporal concepts as well. We see movements that are short, large, fast, hasty, or slackish—and we can perform such movements as well. When we see a slackish movement in another person's arm we can immediately copy it. When we see a person kneeling down and bending his body to the floor, thereby stretching his right arm ahead and his left arm to his left side, we can also repeat this movement sequence ourselves—though perhaps not in the sense that we feel we are imitating the movements he made but rather making the same movements as he did. Our movements can be categorically equivalent to those of the model, without necessarily copying them in their detailed structure.

In these examples the neutral language for the common representation of perceived and performed movements is derived from the conceptual framework ordinary language provides for the description of events. This framework is a powerful tool for the description of both the spatiotemporal sectioning of complex events into smaller units and the properties of the units involved. It has often been argued that the verbal descriptions of ordinary language should be considered to mirror the conceptual and propositional nature of the underlying representational structures (Pylyshyn, 1973, 1981). With respect to spatial relations this idea has been worked out in some detail by Palmer (1975) and by Olson and Bialystok (1983). Grammars for the conceptual or propositional representation of events seem to be less developed so far (Cutting & Proffitt, 1981; Johansson, 1978; Johansson, von Hofsten, & Jansson, 1980). Still other kinds of formal languages for the representation of spatiotemporal relationship have been developed in the framework of coding theory (Leeuwenberg, 1969; Leeuwenberg & Buffart, 1983; Restle, 1979).

Such common coding schemes for perceived and performed movements or events should be considered part of the person's conceptual knowledge of the world that has been built up in previous concept learning (which does not mean to exclude the possibility that some of its early roots are built in). Concept learning serves to enable the system to classify each particular event as an instance of one of several categories, depending on whether the event shows the relevant structural properties that define the category. The system of categories is maintained as a network of connections—so that each particular event can immediately be mapped on (i.e., be recognized as an instance of) its category. By such conceptual coding, which is based on mapping, the event is translated into the neutral language of semantic representation in which it can be matched for categorical equivalence with other events. Matching by equivalence therefore always presupposes mapping connections that have been established in previous learning (Prinz, 1984a).

3.4.2 Matching for Similarity. This is not necessarily true for theories that assume that perceived and generated movements can be matched without the mediation of equivalence classes. These theories do not rely on common conceptual codes that are attached to disparate events but rather on common properties that are inherent in these events themselves. To assume such inherent common properties implies that they can be matched for similarity. If this version of the matching view is adopted the two arrows in Fig.3.2 are interpreted in a slightly different way. They are no longer regarded as connections for mapping events to common event categories, but rather as operations for extracting common features from the concerned events.

In contrast to the conceptual matching approach this approach emphasizes analogous and continuous over digital and discrete forms of representation—*per*ception over *con*ception (Turvey, 1977). It is therefore less bound to assumptions about previous learning, and is usually stated with a more nativist than empiricist flavor.

Double-Hyphen View. The similarity-based version of the matching principle has usually been stated in connection with the double-hyphen framework according to which the critical match occurs between the perceptual representation of the model event and the movement image, i.e., the anticipated perceptual consequences of the movement to be performed. Matching for similarity requires that certain features that are extracted from the visual percept can be directly transferred to the image that controls the imitative movements. How could the percept match the image and vice versa?

When percept and image belong to the *same modality* the answer is not too difficult. Typically this occurs in vocal imitation or in the imitation of movements that can be seen, such as movements of the arms or fingers. In these cases the imitating event can be perceived in the same modality as the imitated event; hence there is no need to postulate a match across modalities. One can rather assume that the image, which guides the vocal imitation, coincides with the trace of the perceived auditory event or, respectively, that the movements of the arm and the fingers are guided by the visual trace of the percept. However, whereas the first hyphen poses no specific problem in this case, the second hyphen does. This is because the perfect correlation between perceptual and motor events holds only for the proprioceptive modalities of kinesthesis and does not (at least not always) apply to percepts and images in exteroceptive modalities like vision and audition. The easy solution of the first-hyphen problem shifts the burden to the second-hyphen problem of how a movement image in an exteroceptive modality can gain control over the execution of the corresponding movement.

One solution to this problem is to assume that the coordination between these movement images and their corresponding motor commands is entirely due to learning. Another solution is to assume that in these cases, too, the motor event is always guided by a proprioceptive kinesthetic image that is constructed (via mapping or matching) on the basis of the corresponding visual or auditory movement image. The first solution and the mapping version of the second refer to the mapping view discussed previously. The matching version of the second solution would turn the within-modality match into a match across modalities as is soon discussed.

Independent of which of these two views is adopted, it is obvious that in within-modality imitation the imitator gets immediate feedback about the similarity between the model event and the imitating event, and he can use this feedback in order to modify his imitations and thereby to improve the goodness of their fit. As this does not apply to matches across modalities same-modality matches have usually been considered simpler and to occur earlier in ontogeny than matches involving different modalities. Furthermore, it is often believed that this kind of imitation originates in what Baldwin called "circular activity," i.e., activity by which the infant iteratively repeats (imitates) his self-produced movements or sounds. Circular activity develops into imitation when a model takes over the role of repeating the infant's movements (Baldwin, 1895; Guillaume, 1926; cf. Parton, 1976; Piaget, 1946).

When the percept and the assumed image belong to *different modalities* the matching view is more seriously challenged. Typically this occurs in the imitation of movements one cannot see or hear oneself such as movements of parts of the face as seem to occur even in the neonate (Meltzoff & Moore, 1977, 1983). The challenge is due to the fact that, in order to explain these phenomena by the principle of matching, a *tertium comparationis* is needed between the visual percept and the assumed kinesthetic image.

A case in point is the account Meltzoff and Moore (1977) give of their observations on movement imitation in the neonate. Their conclusion is "that this imitation is based on the neonate's capacity to represent visually and proprioceptively perceived information in a form common to both modalities. The infant could thus compare the sensory information from his own unseen motor behavior to a 'supramodal' representation of the perceived gesture and construct the match required" (p. 78).

The assumed supramodal representation serves a similar function as the conceptual representation of events. The difference is that, whereas conceptual matches are matches for categorical equivalence, intermodal matches are matches for perceptual similarity with respect to spatial and temporal event structure. This view assumes that the (visually) perceived event and the (kinesthetic) image derived from it are commensurable by their structure from the beginning and need not be connected or translated into a neutral language at all. Rather, the image that immediately guides the movement is a structural copy of the percept.

In the case of synkinesis the correspondence between the two events is restricted to their time structure. The synkinetic pattern quite exactly follows the temporal pattern of the perceived event, but not, or only in outline, its spatial pattern (if there is any). For instance, when one moves in accordance with a rhythmic sound pattern we perceive but a temporal pattern of intervals and accents with which we may synchronize a variety of different movements. This applies to all kinds of events that, by their structure, permit some anticipation of their continuation in the immediate future. The phenomena of synkinesis must be understood as resulting from an on-line copy of the perceived/anticipated time structure of the event onto one's own movements.

In the case of echokinesis—as well as in some synkinetic phenomena—the copy also refers to spatial aspects of the model event. As was noted earlier, spatial correspondence can pertain to two reference systems: the topological structure of the body (as in watching a slapstick hero) and/or the geometrical structure of environmental space (as in imitating a moving object's path). It is easy to see how the idea of a match for similarity could be applied to the reference system of environmental space. For this one has to assume that some shared coding dimensions exist for visual motion and kinesthetic movement images (for instance, kinematic dimensions like distance, direction, velocity, etc.). Yet it is more difficult to see how this could be accomplished with respect to the topological structure of the body. This is because topological correspondence does not refer to the structure of the movement pattern as such but rather to the body parts that are involved in its execution. The correspondence is static rather than kinetic, and therefore the principle of intermodal matching of events cannot readily account for it.

Single-Hyphen View. The similarity-based version of the matching approach can also be applied to the single-hyphen framework by postulating a direct match between the perceptual event and the pattern of motor commands required for the execution of corresponding movements. Such a direct bridge over the ideo-motor gap has the advantage of avoiding the notorious kinesthetic image which has so often played the role of a *deus ex machina* in theories of space perception and action control.

Kurt Koffka has been the first to sketch an outline of a matching-for-similarity theory that operates with a single hyphen (Koffka, 1925, ch. V, § 9). Having discussed voluntary and involuntary imitation and critically examined and dismissed as unsatisfactory some of the traditional explanations, Koffka (1925) states:

> If we could assume a direct structural connection between the perception and the movement, all facts could well be understood. The perceptual configuration would produce the configuration of the movement 'because of their inherent similarity.' The movement would then be realized as a phenomenal copy of the perception since the connection between the two distinct configurations (the perception and the movement)—which we have to understand as the production of one by way of the other—must also involve a more or less definite structural connection. (p. 234/235) Such a structural law would then constitute the factual content of the . . . thesis that any idea of a movement has an in-built tendency to produce the movement itself. (p. 236)

Koffka's speculations on the immediate correspondence between the configurations of the perceived and motor event can be considered to result from a transfer of the principle of isomorphism from the psychophysical to the ideo-motor gap (cf. Prinz, 1985). Köhler (1924, 1929) had originally conceived this principle as an attack on the view that the mental and the physical are completely disparate and incommensurable by their nature. According to Köhler certain aspects of spatial and temporal structure are shared by the mental contents and the physical processes in the brain underlying them. For instance, when an object is perceived, spatially and temporally, *between* two other objects we have to assume that in the underlying pattern of physiological processes the object's correlate is also generated, spatially and temporally, *between* the correlates of the other objects.

Our concern is not with the merits of psychophysical isomorphism (see Pomerantz & Kubovy, 1981; Prinz, 1984b; Stadtler, 1981), but rather with its use for bridging the ideo-motor gap. With respect to the *temporal correspondence* between perceived and generated events, ideo-motor isomorphism suggests itself. The temporal patterning of events is an ability not only of our perceptual system for pattern analysis (shared by all modalities, as noted previously), but also of our motor system for pattern generation. In the study of pattern generation the issue of timing or temporal patterning has attracted even more research interest than in the study of pattern analysis. In motor control the problem of proper timing is too obvious to overlook (Schmidt, 1980; Summers, 1975; Wing, 1978).

The ease of synchronizing movement with perceived or anticipated event structure—particularly that of nonspatial events like auditory patterns—has often been considered an indication of an immediate relationship between the temporal patterns of the percept and the movement (Bartlett & Bartlett, 1959; Dunlap, 1910). Event-synchronized movements have even been observed in the neonate (Condon & Sander, 1974). Fraisse (1980, 1981) has stressed the immediate character of motor synchronization with rhythm and also the high degree of its temporal precision (as compared to its precision with respect to the intensity pattern) as first observed by Brown (1911). The immediate and spontaneous occurrence of motor synchronizations with perceptual events seems to suggest that the time pattern of the movement is a direct copy of the time pattern of the visual or auditory event, rather than an indirect result of a crossmodally mediated match, as the double-hyphen view would suggest. As far as time structure is concerned such a mediating link is simply not needed for the explanation of the observed synchrony.

The explanation of *spatial correspondence* by a single-hyphen similarity match is less self-suggesting because it is dependent on the assumption of the identity of the dimensions for the representation of space in perception and motor control. With respect to time such identity has gone unquestioned so far. However, with respect to space the issue is less clear.

Our percepts of environmental events are usually organized in terms of environmental coordinates, and so are our intentions to move. Notwithstanding such commensurability at the phenomenal level, the argument can be raised that at a functional level the mechanisms underlying the spatial patterning of movements might turn out quite disparate from those resulting in the spatial ordering of percepts. A pertinent objection is the position taken by Fitch and Turvey (1978) who argue that it is inappropriate to analyze the mechanisms for the control of movements in kinematic terms (i.e., terms as needed for the spatiotemporal description of the resulting movements). Rather, the problems of motor control should be tackled in dynamic terms (as needed for the description of the physical forces underlying the resulting movements). This is because the parameters that are immediately regulated by the system refer to its dynamic behavior and not to its kinematic behavior that is only its mediated, ultimate result.

Though this may be true at a certain level of molecular analysis of how the system works, it is, of course, also true that at a more molar level the spatial patterning of movements is guided by the spatial layout of the perceived environment. These two truths can be united by assuming (at least) two levels of control: a molar level of kinematic control (at which perceptual and motor space coincide so that perceived events and intended movements share the same spatial reference system), and a molecular level of dynamic control (which, though in itself lacking any spatial qualifications, serves to realize the spatially defined movement intentions).

The existence of such a system for the distal control of movements is indispensable, independent of the proximal machinery by which the distal control is mediated. Distal control of movements refers to control with respect to the same reference system and the same dimension in which the underlying intentions are defined, whereas proximal control refers to the mechanics and dynamics of the apparatus used to realize them. If this is correct, we can adopt the view that spatial aspects of percepts, too, can immediately be copied into corresponding movements. Perceived-event structure, i.e., seen distance, direction, velocity, etc. is directly used for the patterning of the event to be performed. The pattern match bridges the ideo-motor gap directly, and there is no need for support by a kinesthetic bridge pier.

A mechanism like this can explain spatial correspondence between perceived and performed movements with respect to environmental space, but not necessarily with respect to body topology. Though this is not indispensable because other principles can account for such correspondence, we conclude this chapter by speculating how a direct similarity-based match between inflow and outflow could also account for the spontaneous use of corresponding body parts. When I observe a model performing a complex movement with his right arm and then try to copy it, I could find myself thrown upon the use of the corresponding arm simply because this limb is the only instrument suited for the generation of a similar event my motor apparatus has at its disposal. If this line of reasoning is sound, the unequivocality of the use of corresponding body parts would be determined by the complexity of the model event. The more complex it is, the fewer degrees of freedom does the motor system have to generate a similar event.

This view could also lead us to a better understanding of the puzzle of how the neonate can imitate tongue protrusion or mouth opening without previous opportunity to learn. It is certainly not unreasonable to assume that the mouth–tongue system, at birth, is one of the very few (perhaps the only) subsystems of the motor system that can be reliably controlled, possibly even in a more than reflex-like fashion. Thus, when the baby perceives an event with a certain spatiotemporal structure (say, a model opening his mouth), he repeats the structure of this event with the only reliable event generator at his command. According to this interpretation, the baby should not be able to imitate a model's head or the arm movements by moving the corresponding parts of his body—simply because he has no reliable command over the instruments needed for their reproduction. Conversely, it could (and, perhaps, should) occur that he "imitates" certain spatiotemporal features of such events by performing structurally corresponding movements with his mouth–tongue system, thereby using the only event generator under reliable control.

4. AN EVENT GENERATION APPROACH

Having started the chapter with a look back into the history of ideo-motor phenomena we now end with a brief look into their possible future. Our concluding remarks concern the question of how the view of an immediate similarity-based match between perceived- and generated-event configuration could be further elaborated. The following outline is not intended to sketch the theory itself, but rather some of the steps to be taken in order to develop it.

With this approach the mechanism underlying movement control is considered to be a device for the generation of spatiotemporal events. A particular (and possibly rather primitive) mode of operation of this device is to pattern the to-be-generated motor events after certain characteristics of perceptual events. This can either occur as *on-line completion* of ongoing events or as *off-line reproduction* of events that have finished (Synkinesis versus Echokinesis). A basic assumption of the approach is that the perceptual event is coded in terms of certain spatiotemporal parameters that can immediately be used for the generation of the pattern of the corresponding motor event. The difference between event completion and event reproduction suggests that the temporal and spatial characteristics can be used independently. In event completion the time structure of an ongoing event is used for the control of the movements (as in rhythmic dancing), whereas the spatial pattern, if used at all, is only partially relevant (as in empathic accompaniment of seen movements). In event reproduction the temporal and the spatial pattern are always used both at the same time.

If this general view is accepted the next step is to assess *which* of the various possible parameters are actually used for the generation of the motor event. Though these parameters must be empirically determined, it is not unreasonable to assume, on a priori grounds, two general principles underlying their choice. The first is that event generation tends to rely more on pattern in time than pattern in space, and the second is that, with respect to both temporal and spatial pattern, the parameters of the to-be-generated motor event tend to be based on some abstract, high-order representations of the perceived event.

The first of these two principles is derived from the relatively simple structure inherent (at least superficially) in the reference system of time as compared to that of space. As was noted earlier there are two spatial reference systems for body movements, viz. environmental space and body space. The same applies to event perception: Events can be coded either with respect to environmental space or to one of the objects or agents in the event. Furthermore, both of these spatial reference systems have a complex dimensionality. On the other hand, with respect to time, there is but one single system with one single dimension, so that pattern in time should be easier to extract, store, and use than pattern in space.

The second principle implies that the relevant parameters should be extracted from representations of first or second order derivatives of spatial and temporal patterns, rather than from representations of these patterns themselves. For instance, the spatial pattern of an event configuration can be described in terms of path functions established for an arbitrary number of points in the event. In such a function the form of the path produced by the point's movement is specified by assigning coordinate values for spatial position to each point on the movement trajectory. The first and the second order derivatives of this position function would then assign slope and curvature rather than position to each point on the trajectory. In the same way temporal pattern can be defined in terms of movement functions for individual points. The basic movement function specifies distance over time, whereas its first and second derivative assign speed and acceleration to each point on the time scale. If ideo-motor event generation in fact relies on the use of parameters of these higher order representations of spatial and temporal pattern, this should become apparent in closer fits between imitated and imitating movement in the high- as compared to the low-order functions.

The two principles should be taken as general orientations rather than absolute rules. This is because the choice of the parameters used for event generation will also depend on the particular task demands. Task demands may sometimes call for low-order rather than high-order copy, for spatial rather than temporal fidelity—or even for the use of parameters of combined spatiotemporal event representation.

REFERENCES

Abravanel, E. (1981). Integrating the information from eyes and hands: A developmental account. In R. D. Walk & H. L. Pick (Eds.), *Intersensory perception and sensory integration*. New York, London: Plenum.
Allers, R., & Scheminzky, F. (1926). Aktionsströme der Muskeln bei motorischen Vorstellungen und verwandten Vorgängen.*Pflügers Archiv für Physiologie, 212*, 169–183.
Baldwin, J. M. (1895). *Mental development in the child and the race: Methods and processes*. New York, London: MacMillan.
Bandura, A. (1977). *Social learning theory*. Englewood Cliffs, NJ: Prentice-Hall.
Bandura, A., & Walters, R. H. (1963). *Social Learning and Personality Development*. New York: Holt, Rinehart, & Winston.
Bartlett, N. R., & Bartlett, S. C. (1959). Synchronization of motor response with an anticipated sensory event. *Psychological Review, 66*, 203–218.
Bower, T. G. R. (1977). *A Primer of infant development*. San Francisco: Freeman.
Bower, T. G. R. (1978). Perceptual development: Object and space. In E. C. Carterette & M. P. Friedman (Eds.), *Handbook of perception: Vol. VIII*. New York: Academic Press.
Brown, W. (1911). Temporal and accentual rhythm. *Psychological Review, 18*, 336–346.
Brunswik, E. (1952). The conceptual framework of psychology. In O. Neurath, R. Carnap, & Ch. Morris (Eds.), *International Encyclopedia of Unified Science, Vol. 1, No. 10*. Chicago: University of Chicago Press.

Bushnell, E. W. (1981). The ontogeny of intermodal relations: Vision and touch in infancy. In R. D. Walk & H. L. Pick (Eds.), *Intersensory perception and sensory integration*. New York: Plenum.
Carpenter, W. B. (1874). *Principles of mental physiology, with their applications to the training and discipline of the mind and the study of its morbid conditions*. New York: Appleton.
Condon, W. S., & Sander, L. W. (1974). Neonate movement is synchronized with adult speech: Interactional participation and language acquisition. *Sciences, 183*, 99–101.
Cutting, J. E., & Proffitt, D. R. (1981). Gait perception as an example of how we may perceive events. In R. D. Walk & H. L. Pick (Eds.), *Intersensory perception and sensory integration*. New York: Plenum.
Dunlap, K. (1910). Reactions to rhythmic stimuli with attempt to synchronize. *Psychological Review, 17*, 399–416.
Fitch, H. L., & Turvey, M. T. (1978). On the control of activity: Some remarks from an ecological point of view. In R. W. Christina (Ed), *Psychology of motor behavior and sport - 1977*. Champain, Ill.: Human Kinetics Publishers.
Flanders, J. P. (1968). A review of research on imitative behavior. *Psychological Bulletin, 69*, 316–337.
Fraisse, P. (1980). Les synchronisations sensori-motrices aux rythmes. In J. Requin (Ed.), *Anticipation et comportement*. Paris: Centre Nationale de la Recherche scientifique.
Fraisse, P. (1981). Multisensory aspects of rhythm. In R. D. Walk & H. L. Pick (Eds.), *Intersensory perception and sensory integration*. New York: Plenum.
Gewirtz, J. L., & Stingle, K. G. (1968). Learning of generalized imitation as the basis for identification. *Psychological Review, 75*, 374–397.
Greenwald, A. G. (1970). Sensory feedback mechanisms in performance control: With special reference to the ideomotor mechanism. *Psychological Review, 77*, 73–99.
Guillaume, P. (1926). *L'imitation chez L'enfant*. Paris: Félix Alcan.
Halwes, T., & Wire, B. (1974). A possible solution to the pattern recognition problem in the speech modality. In W. B. Weimer & D. S. Palermo (Eds.), *Cognition and the symbolic processes*. Hillsdale, NJ: Lawrence Erlbaum Associates.
Jacobson, L. E. (1932). The electrophysiology of mental activities. *Americal Journal of Psychology, 44*, 677–694.
James, W. (1890). *The Principles of Psychology* (Vols. 1 & 2). New York: Holt.
Johansson, G. (1978). Visual event perception. In R. Held, H. W. Leibowitz, & H. -L. Teuber (Eds.), *Handbook of sensory physiology* (Vol. 8). Berlin: Springer.
Johansson, G., von Hofsten, C., & Jansson. G. (1980). Event perception. *Annual Review of Psychology, 31*, 27–63.
Katz, D. (1960). Sozialpsychologie. In D. Katz & R. Katz (Eds.), *Handbuch der Psychologie* (2nd ed.). Basel/Stuttgart: Schwabe.
Koffka, K. (1925). *Die Grundlagen der psychischen Entwicklung*. Osterwiek: Zickfeldt.
Köhler, W. (1924). *Die physischen Gestalten in Ruhe und im stationären Zustand*. Erlangen: Verlag der Philosophischen Akademie.
Köhler, W. (1929). *Gestalt Psychology*. New York: Liveright.
Leeuwenberg, E. L. J. (1969). Quantitative specification of information in sequential pattern. *Psychological Review, 76*, 216–220.
Leeuwenberg, E. L. J., & Buffart, H. (1983). An outline of coding theory. Summary of some related experiments. In H. G. Geissler (Ed.), *Modern issues in perception*. Berlin: Deutscher Verlag der Wissenschaften.
Liberman, A. M., Cooper, F. S., Shankweiler, D. P., & Studdert-Kennedy, M. (1967). Perception on the speech code. *Psychological Review, 74*, 431–461.
Lipps, Th. (1903). Einfühlung, innere Nachahmung und Organempfindung. *Archiv für die gesamte Psychologie, 1*, 465–519.

Lotze, R. H. (1852). *Medicinische Psychologie oder Physiologie der Seele.* Leipzig: Weidmann'sche Buchhandlung.
Marks, L. E. (1978). *The unity of the senses. Interrelations among the modalities.* New York: Academic Press.
Meltzoff, A. N., & Moore, K. (1977). Imitation of facial and manual gestures by human neonates. *Science, 198,* 75–78.
Meltzoff, A. N., & Moore, K. (1983). The origins of imitation in infancy: Paradigm, phenomena, and theories. *Advances in Infancy Research, Vol. II,* 266–288.
Miller, G. A., Galanter, E., & Pribram, K. -H. (1960). *Plans and the structure of behavior.* New York: Holt, Rinehart, & Winston.
Miller, N. E., & Dollard, J. (1941). *Social learning and imitation.* New Haven, CT: Yale University Press.
Morgan, C. L. (1891). *Animal life and intelligence.* London: Arnold.
Mounoud, P., & Vinter, A. (1981). Representation and sensorimotor development. In G. Butterworth (Ed.), *Infancy and epistemology: An evaluation of Piaget's theory.* Brighton: The Harvester Press.
Mowrer, O. H. (1960). *Learning theory and the symbolic processes.* New York: Wiley.
Olson, D. R., & Bialystok, E. (1983). *Spatial Cognition. The structure and development of mental representations of spatial relations.* Hillsdale, NJ: Lawrence Erlbaum Associates.
Palmer, St. E. (1975). Visual perception and world knowledge: Notes on a model of sensory-cognitive interaction. In D. A. Norman & D. E. Rumelhart (Eds.), *Explorations in cognition.* San Francisco: Freeman.
Parton, D. A. (1976). Learning to imitate in infancy. *Child Development, 47,* 14–31.
Pawlby, S. J. (1977). Imitative interaction. In H. R. Shaffer (Ed.). *Studies in mother–infant interaction.* London: Academic Press.
Piaget, J. (1946). *La Formation du Symbole chez L'enfant.* Paris: Delachaux & Niestlé.
Pomerantz, J. R., & Kubovy, M. (1981). Perceptual organization: An overview. In M. Kubovy & J. R. Pomerantz (Eds.), *Perceptual organization.* Hillsdale, NJ: Lawrence Erlbaum Associates.
Prinz, W. (1984). Modes of linkage between perception and action. In W. Prinz & A. F. Sanders (Eds.), *Cognition and motor processes.* Berlin: Springer.
Prinz, W. (1985). Ideomotorik und Isomorphie. In O. Neumann (Ed.), *Perspektiven der Kognitionspsychologie.* Berlin: Springer.
Pylyshyn, Z. W. (1973). What the mind's eye tells the mind's brain: A critique of mental imagery. *Psychological Bulletin, 80,* 1–24.
Pylyshyn, Z. W. (1981). The imagery debate: Analogue media versus tacit knowledge. *Psychological Review, 88,* 14–45.
Restle, F. (1979). Coding theory of the perception of motion configurations. *Psychological Review, 86,* 1–24.
Richter, H. (1954). Über ideomotorische Phänomene. *Zeitschrift für Psychologie, 157,* 201–257.
Richter, H. (1957). Zum Problem der ideomotorischen Phänomene. *Zeitschrift für Psychologie, 161,* 161–254.
Romanes, G. J. (1891). *Mental evolution in animals.* New York: Appleton.
Scheerer, E. (1984a). Nachahmung. In J. Ritter & K. Gründer (Eds.), *Historisches Wörterbuch der Philosophie* (Vol. 6). Basel/Stuttgart: Schwabe.
Scheerer, E. (1984b). Motor theories of cognitive structure: A historical review. In W. Prinz & A. F. Sanders (Eds), *Cognition and motor processes.* Berlin: Springer.
Schmidt, R. A. (1980). On the theoretical status of time in motor-program representations. In G. E. Stelmach & J. Requin (Eds.), *Tutorials in motor behavior.* Amsterdam: North–Holland.
Staats, A. W. (1970). *Learning, language, and cognition.* London: Holt, Rinehart & Winston.
Stadtler, M. (1981). Feldttheorie heute—von Wolfgang Köhler zu Karl Pribram. *Gestalt Theory, 3,* 185–199.

Stränger, J. (1977). *Beobachtungslernen*. Bochum: Ruhr-Universität, Dissertation.
Summers, J. J. (1975). The role of timing in motor program representation. *Journal of Motor Behavior, 7,* 229–241.
Thorndike, E. L. (1913). Ideo-motor action. *Psychological Review, 20,* 91–106.
Tinbergen, N. (1951). *The Study of Instinct*. Oxford: Pergamon Press.
Trevarthen, C., Hubley, P., & Sheeran, L. (1975). Les activitées innées du nourisson. *La Recherche, 56,* 447–458.
Turvey, M. T. (1977). Perspectives in vision: Conception or perception? In D. D. Duane & M. B. Rawson (Eds.), *Reading, perception, and language*. Baltimore, MD: York Press.
Weber, E. (1906). Das Verhältnis der Bewegungsvorstellung zur Bewegung. *Monatsschrift für Psychiatrie und Neurologie, 20.*
Weimer, W. B. (1977). A conceptual framework for cognitive psychology: Motor theories of the mind. In R. Shaw & J. Bransford (Eds.), *Perceiving, Acting, and Knowing. Toward an Ecological Psychology*. Hillsdale, NJ: Lawrence Erlbaum Associates.
Werner, H., & Wapner, S. (1949). Sensory-tonic field theory of perception. *Journal of Personality, 18,* 88–107.
Werner, H., & Wapner, S. (1952). Toward a general theory of perception. *Psychological Review, 59,* 324–338.
Wing, A. N. (1978). Response timing in hand-writing. In G. E. Stelmach (Ed.), *Information processing in motor control and learning*. New York: Academic Press.

4 The Acquisition of Skill: Some Modifications to the Perception-Action Relationship Through Practice

Richard A. Schmidt
*University of
California, Los Angeles*

The acquisition of skilled movement behaviors via practice or experience has been a topic of considerable interest for many decades, both from a theoretical perspective having to do with the processes underlying motor learning, and from a practical orientation with reference to the efficient structure of practice sessions. Yet, like most of the other topic areas in this volume, the relationship between perception and action has not been of central interest for those studying learning. Most investigators of motor learning have studied practice on a given movement task or problem, with the focus being on changes in movement behavior as a function of variations in the host of variables that impinge on the practice session (e.g., scheduling of practice, instructions, etc.). Seldom has concern been raised about the nature of these changes in terms of different styles of control or mechanisms underlying motor behavior, and the specific questions about the effects of practice on the relationship between perception and action have scarcely been touched.

Yet, a search of the literature dealing with motor learning reveals that a number of experimenters have, either intentionally or not, provided information that can be thought of as contributing to an understanding of the perception-action relationship within the realm of motor learning. This chapter focuses on a number of research areas that seem to bear on how the relationship between perception and action is altered, strengthened, or perhaps even eliminated, by practice. Three of these areas seem to have considerable contributions to this general question. In the first, I discuss the evidence that practice alters the kinds of sensory information selected in support of skilled behavior. Second, sensory information can also act in the evaluation of movement behavior, and here I discuss evidence that practice contributes to an increased capability to detect one's own errors and hence to correct them on subsequent attempts. Finally, a discussion of automaticity is provided, where the learner seems to acquire the capability to function without the performance interfering with other information processing activities.

SHIFTS AMONG INFORMATION SOURCES WITH PRACTICE

It is well known in general terms that various kinds of sensory information contribute to the production of skilled movement behaviors, and that the particular information modality used is highly dependent on the behavior under question. But for a given movement behavior, does the performer shift from one constellation of sensory modalities to another with increased practice and capability at the skill? In many ways, the answers to this question will also probably be highly task specific, because whether one shifts from visual information to proprioceptive information will depend on the kinds of information available in that particular task.

Shifts to Kinesthetic and Proprioceptive Control

One of William James' (1890) many contributions to thinking about movement behavior was that practice in some way changes the control processes in movements so that the behavior becomes less dependent on external sources of information, which he regarded as attention demanding. In exchange, the behavior came to be controlled more strongly by proprioceptive information, which he argues was more "reflex like" and attention free. Although a number of authors have taken a similar stance, even recently (e.g., Adams, 1971), it appears that evidence suggesting an increased role for proprioception as a function of practice is limited to particular kinds of tasks that seem highly feedback dependent. (However, there are newer data suggesting the acquisition of reflex-like proprioceptive loops with practice, which I treat in a subsequent section.) These investigations have used tasks such as linear positioning and force estimation, where there is ample time and opportunity, and potential benefits, for "on–line" sensory information to be used. Adams' work with positioning tasks shows that the "quality" of the response-produced feedback experienced in acquisition has strong effects on performance, and allows the interpretation that proprioception, and particularly vision, were being used to an increasing extent with practice (e.g., Adams & Goetz, 1973; Adams, Goetz, & Marshall, 1972).

Similar findings can be found in other tasks that are not so obviously dependent on proprioceptive feedback. Fleishman and Rich (1963; Fleishman & Hempel, 1955) studied the acquisition of complex movement behaviors such as the two-hand coordination task, in which the subjects had to learn to coordinate two small handwheels (one for each hand) to control the X and Y dimensions of a pointer to follow a randomly moving target. They found that correlations between two-hand coordination performance and a spatial-relations measure decreased with practice, as if control were shifting away from processes involved with orientation in space. But more relevant to the present discussion, a measure called "kinesthetic sensitivity," based on the accuracy in judging differences in small lifted weights, correlated to an increasing extent with two-hand coordination as practice on the latter was increased. Many have taken this latter finding to mean that kinesthetic feedback has taken on an increasingly important role in the two-hand task with practice. Perhaps it did, but it is also possible that an increasing correlation between the kinesthetic-sensitivity task and two-hand coordination skill with practice might simply mean that some third "nonkinesthetic" ability was the common factor here. Also, although the weight-judgment task does appear to have a component that measures the sensitivity to kinesthetic stimuli, there is no independent verification of this; of course, labeling a task *kinesthetic sensitivity* simply because it *seems* to be sensitive to kinesthetic information processing does not necessarily make it so. But in spite of these criticisms, it is still possible that a part of the improvement with practice in two-hand coordination skill is associated with the increased involvement of kinesthetic information. Also a few years ago, I reviewed evidence from the literature on anticipation and timing in tasks where the subject must respond, say, exactly 1 sec after a warning signal; conditions with movement in the interval, as opposed to no movement, generally produce more accurate and consistent timing behavior, suggesting that proprioception may be involved in learning this kind of behavior as well (Schmidt, 1971).

Various studies from the late 1950s were concerned with Bahrick's (1957) notion that the proprioceptive components of the control in tracking tasks could be manipulated by changing the resistances on the control stick (e.g., changing mass affects acceleration cues), allowing a way to study the nature of the sensory information used by the subject in tracking, and the extent to which the use of these cues changed with practice. But this work was disappointing because of the generally small effects of these variables on tracking. The problem is that tracking proficiency is probably determined predominantly by visual information; kinesthetic cues, if they are used at all here, probably have a very small contribution. And, had differences been shown, it would have been difficult to know whether the effect was due to the altered feedback cues, or whether it was due to some mechanical effect of the resistance to the limb. Looking back, it appears that this method had too many difficulties to be a very useful one for our purposes here (Adams, 1968).

Overall, then, the hypothesis that practice results in the shift in control mechanisms so that skills are dependent on kinesthetic information processing does not seem very well supported by the evidence. This contradicts the often heard idea that skill acquisition is critically dependent on an increaed "feel" for the movement, emphasizing the need for kinesthetic information. "Feel" could indeed be important, but perhaps for motor evaluation and not for motor *control,* as discussed in the next major section. Yet, there are undoubtedly some tasks, mainly those involving very careful control and slow movements, where learning may be associated with the increased use of kinesthesis.

Shifts to Higher Order Display Information

One intriguing idea about the changes in sensory information processing with practice was termed the *propression-regression hypothesis* by Fitts, Bahrick, Noble, and Briggs (1961). This view, directed mainly toward tracking tasks in which the performer could be modeled as a closed-loop control system, argued that as the learner progresses, he/she behaves as a more "complicated" servomechanism. In early practice, the learner would respond mainly to positional errors in the display, the simplest form of display information. But with continued practice, the learner would begin to respond to higher order derivatives of the positional error signal, such as velocity, acceleration, or even "jerk" (the derivative of acceleration). This progression to higher order information could be followed by a "regression" in performance during layoffs or with added stress, with the subject becoming systematically more like a simple servomechanism again. Fuchs (1962) showed that the weights assigned to the acceleration term in the transfer function (the equation relating display input to subject output) became systematically larger with practice, whereas the weight for positional information became smaller, providing evidence for the progression hypothesis. Such findings are consistent with the hypothesis that the information used shifted to systematically higher order aspects of the display with practice. And, when stress was added in the form of a simultaneous secondary task, the weight for the positional information increased, implying a regression to a simpler level of control with stress as the regression hypothesis predicts.

One problem with this interpretation is that the link between the nature of the display information used and the weights in the transfer functions (the dependent variables) was both very indirect and required assumptions about the nature of human servo control (so that a closed-loop tracking model could be used). Also, although it is certainly possible to divide the inputs logically into position, velocity, and acceleration components of the track, there is no assurance that the human performer divides up his/her sensory world in the same terms. Most importantly, it would seem that *any* increase in tracking proficiency—i.e., producing responses that are systematically closer to the track (reducing RMS errors)—should necessarily be associated with increased weights for accelerational display information. But it is difficult to ignore Fuchs' finding that the weights for positional information actually *decreased* with practice, as this argument implies that all the weights should increase. This kind of supporting evidence was strengthened recently by an experiment by Jagacinski and Hah (in press), which eliminated several experimental design problems present in the earlier work. Again, their data are easily interpreted in terms of the progression–regression hypothesis. More work is needed in relation to this interesting viewpoint, but the evidence tends to favor it at present.

THE LEARNING OF ERROR DETECTION CAPABILITIES

One common viewpoint, especially during the 1960s and 1970s, was the notion that motor control could be modeled as closed-loop control systems of the type used by engineers. The comparison between some reference of correctness and incoming sensory information (i.e., feedback) defines an error, with this error being the direct controlling agent for future action. Thus these viewpoints propose a strong link between sensory information and action. In addition, because the error is a comparison of *response*-produced feedback against a reference, this error is itself determined jointly by the actions of the performer and the resulting sensory information received. This again emphasizes the strong interaction between perception and action here.

Studies of motor learning under this perspective nearly always employed tracking tasks of various kinds. Although it was seldom clearly stated, the implication was that, in learning to track, sensory information was being evaluated more effectively by virtue of a "stronger" reference of correctness, or perhaps by one which uses a different set of sensory modalities as input (see the previous section). Of course, the nature of the corrective actions could be improved at the same time, so this would not be the only interpretation of improved tracking, and these two sets of processes seem nearly impossibly intertwined here. But Adams' (1971; Adams & Bray, 1970) suggestion that, in *discrete* responses, sensory information available during or immediately after a movement could be evaluated to detect an error, and that the capabilities to detect errors from this sensory information could be learned, added much new life to this area of work. The benefits in such error-detection capabilities could then presumably be seen in a number of ways: (1) as improved performance *during* an action if the movement were sufficiently slow that error information could be used before the movement was completed; or (2) as increased performance on the subsequent trial if the movement were very rapid. As a result, since the early 1970s considerable empirical and theoretical efforts have occurred in relation to the role of error detection in processes associated with learning discrete motor skills. I turn to some of these issues next.

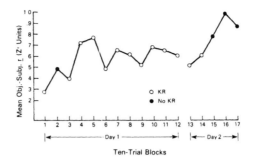

FIG. 4.1 Mean Z'-transformed objective–subjective correlations as a function of practice in a ballistic timing task (from Schmidt & White, 1972).

Error-Detection Capability and Practice

Motivated by Adams' theorizing about closed-loop processes in verbal (Adams & Bray, 1970) and motor (Adams, 1971) learning, Schmidt and White (1972) investigated whether or not error-detection capability could be acquired as Adams claimed. Subjects performed a ballistic timing task, in which a hand-held slide was moved along a trackway with a goal movement time (MT) of 150 ms. We asked subjects to guess their own errors (subjective error) immediately after each trial, and then we provided their actual error (objective error) immediately thereafter. We estimated capabilities for error detection via the within-subject correlation, computed for each block of 10 trials, between the objective and subjective errors. If the subject were becoming more sensitive to his/her own errors, the correlation should rise toward 1.0, with complete insensitivity resulting in a correlation of zero. The mean Z' - transformed correlations increased from about .25 in early practice to about .90 in the last few blocks, suggesting an increased error-detection capability with practice. Newell (1974) has shown similar effects, but using the difference between objective and subjective error as the index of error-detection capability.

The Role of Response-Produced Feedback

Although competing views can be advanced, a leading hypothesis to explain these findings is that the reference of correctness was "strengthened" via practice, and that this allowed the more effective evaluation of the incoming sensory information as practice continued. If so, then experimental variations in the kinds of sensory information available, or variations in the quality of a given kind of information, should interact with practice to determine proficiency in error evaluation. Experiments by Adams' group, already mentioned, have shown that increased quality of visual, auditory, or proprioceptive feedback leads to more

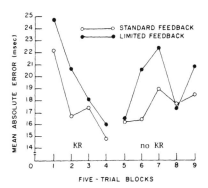

FIG. 4.2 Mean absolute error in ballistic timing during acquisition with KR (left) and when KR is withdrawn in transfer (right) under two conditions of intrinsic feedback (from Schmidt & Wrisberg, 1973).

effective positioning movements, where error evaluation presumably occurs during the response (Adams et al., 1972; Adams, Gopher, & Lintern, 1977). And, when experimenter-imposed errors occur via blocking the movement, subjects are able to recognize the errors more often, correct them more accurately, and be more confident that the blocked movement was incorrect, as a function of both feedback quality and practice.

But in fast movements, time is presumably not available for within-response error detection/correction; does feedback have a role therefore in the accuracy of a *subsequent* response? Schmidt and Wrisberg (1973, Experiment 2) used a ballistic timing task (150-ms MT), with either the visual and auditory channels both intact or blocked. During practice with knowledge of results (KR), this manipulation had no effect on performance, as can be seen in Fig. 4.2. But in a transfer test with KR withdrawn, subjects without vision or audition drifted away from the target across trials, whereas those subjects with the feedback channels operating maintained performance reasonably well, presumably because the latter group could use the acquired error-detection capability in relation to the more salient feedback to detect errors made on a given trial and correct them on a subsequent trial.

Zelaznik and Spring (1976) and Zelaznik, Shapiro, and Newell (1978), in an ingenious method, had one group of subjects listen to the auditory sensory consequences of another subject actively practicing the ballistic slide task. This "listening" group did not see the apparatus or the active subject during these trials. Then, the "listening" subjects were transferred to the active performance of the task. These subjects performed more effectively than active subjects who had not previously listened, and they continued to improve their performances without KR in active practice. The authors argued that listening created a sensory-based error-detection mechanism that was then used in active practice as a basis for error detection and correction. This is similar to certain features of the Suzuki method for teaching young violinists; the child receives extensive experience listening to violin music and then presumably uses the error-detection capabilities developed as a way of correcting his/her own errors in actual practice (Suzuki, 1969).

Movement Time Determines Error-Detection Capabilities

An important interaction exists between the capability of the subjects to learn to detect their own errors and the MT of the response to be produced. When the movement is rapid, presumably controlled largely open-loop, the response-produced feedback cannot be used during the movement to correct errors and is used afterwards by being compared to a learned reference of correctness. However, when the movement is slow, the response-produced sensory feedback can act *during* the movement in relation to the reference of correctness, so that performance is largely determined by the subject's capability to judge his or her own errors; if the subject moves to a position that is judged to be correct during the movement, then after the response the subject will have no *additional* information on which to base a further analysis of error in relation to the target. This supposed relationship between error-detection capabilities and response type was supported by Schmidt and Russell (1972, cited in Schmidt, 1975). Using a paradigm exactly like that of Schmidt and White (1972), but with a slow linear-positioning task, subjects showed no increase in the objective–subjective correlations with 100 trials of practice, with the correlations remaining at about .20—far lower than the .90 found in the ballistic timing task (Fig. 4.1).

These results point out one of many ways that rapid and slow movements are fundamentally different. The perception-action relationship is mainly operating within the response in the slower movements. In rapid movements, though, the error-detection capabilities are not used for movement control, but for detecting one's errors *after* the movement. Then, this knowledge of response correctness can be applied to the next trial, hopefully so that the next movement is programmed more effectively than the previous one.

Theoretical Implications, Practical Applications

The development of error-detection capability with practice, particularly for discrete skills where the sensory information leads to either more effective motor control (slow movements) or more effective next-response motor programming (fast movements) has not received the attention that it deserves and is rather poorly understood as a result. How this capability comes to be acquired, what are the principles of its acquisition, and whether all the sensory information modalities contribute equally, are certainly questions needed for theory development.

But perhaps the acquisition of the capability to detect one's own errors is even more important as a "by product" of the learning process in practical settings. The learner with this capability would be able to evaluate his/her own errors when the teacher is not present and thus make use of extra-class practice time where the feedback from the teacher is not available. Although error-detection capabilities seem to result as a natural consequence of practice for which the major goal is response production, perhaps instruction could be organized so that the acquisition of error detection were more strongly emphasized. Many good teachers seem to instruct in a way that would seem to be effective for the development of error detection. Statements such as "Feel your hand brush your leg at the end of the arm stroke" (in swimming) seem to focus learners' attention on the sensory qualities of the correct action.

ACQUIRING AUTOMATICITY

No discussion of the changes in the relationship between perception and action would be complete without a treatment of the concept of automaticity. Certainly one of the most important changes that occur with gains in proficiency is the apparent reduction of the need for conscious awareness and mental effort in the control of movement responses. Early in practice, we seem to have to control everything consciously; shifting gears in a car when we were beginners involved slow, jerky, hesitant movements. Contrast the shifting behavior of World Driving Champion Niki Lauda, who makes the complex coordination accelerator, brake, and clutch[1] in a fraction of a second, and apparently with little interference with steering or decision making. Peter Vidmar, silver medalist in gymnastics at the 1984 Olympic Games, when asked what he thinks about during his performances, replied,

> As I approach the apparatus . . . the only thing I am thinking about is . . . the first trick. And, as I start the first trick, then my body takes over and hopefully everything becomes automatic and all I have to do is worry about those little adjustments.

This captures the flavor of the notion of the automaticity as it seems to be involved in the control of highly skillful movements, and it is a clear case of a changing relationship between perception and action with practice. But, as we discuss in the next section, the notion of automaticity is not a simple one; and there is considerable disagreement about its defining characteristics, the assumptions involved its study, and in the interpretations of the data. I turn to some of these ideas next.

---

[1]Most race-car drivers simultaneously control the brake *and* accelerator with the right foot in downshifting before a corner; the left foot operates the clutch.

Some Conceptual Issues

At a casual level, automaticity is usually thought of as skilled responding that is free from attention. This seems simple enough, especially when William James (1890) has told us that "Everyone knows what attention is" (pp. 403-404). The problem, as pointed out by Jonides, Naveh-Benjamin, & Palmer (1984) recently, is that everyone may *know* what attention is, but everyone has a different opinion about it. It is not surprising, then, that automaticity, involving the *absence* of attention, would also generate a great deal of definitional disagreement.

It is far beyond the scope of this chapter to review the various arguments about the nature of automaticity (and attention), especially in view of the excellent recent reviews (e.g., Neumann, this volume) and newer alternative viewpoints about it (e.g., Jonides, et al., 1984; Schneider, 1984). But there are a few important conceptual problems that seem to prevent a simple analysis of automaticity and practice. These are dealt with in the next few sections.

Features of Automaticity

Most writers would agree that a number of defining features serve to classify a given performance as "automatic." In his review, Neumann (1984) summarized these features as follows: He argued that automaticity (1) is a *mode of operation*, in that it functions without capacity (attention), neither suffering nor causing interference; (2) it is a *mode of control*, in that it is under the control of stimuli rather than intentions (expectancies, plans, etc); and (3) it is a *mode of representation*, in that it does not necessarily give rise to awareness. In addition to these primary criteria, various secondary criteria can be identified, such as the notion that the processes are relatively "wired in" (or made so by practice?), they are relatively simple and stereotyped, and they are relatively rapid. But certainly the most important of these criteria, and the one that has caused the most difficulties, is the first—the criterion that automatic processes are capacity free.

The Dual-Task Interference Criterion. In the past few decades, the most widely used measure of whether or not a task required capacity (attention) was based on whether or not it suffered or caused interference when paired with some other secondary task. If the two tasks could be performed—perhaps after some practice—as well together as they could separately, then it was argued that at least one did not require attention (Bahrick, Noble, & Fitts, 1954; Bahrick & Shelly, 1958). This kind of definition seemed to make sense under early views of attention, in which tasks interfered because they supposedly tapped some fixed, undifferentiated capacity to process information. So, if two tasks did not interfere, then at least one of them did not require this resource and hence was attention free, or automatic. But McLeod (1977, 1978) and others discovered that the nature of the interference depended on what seemed to be relatively superficial features of the secondary task, such as whether the response to a probe stimulus was with the voice or with the hand. The notion of *pools* of capacity, or relatively specific resources that serve special kinds of behaviors (e.g., spatial localization, memory search), was an attempt to account for data such as McLeod's, but these ideas weakened the dual-task criterion for automaticity: If two tasks do not interfere, are they to be judged as examples of automatic performances, or do they not interfere because they happen to tap different pools of resources?

Neumann (1984), and to some extent Heuer (1984), have been critical of this dual-task test of automaticity, largely because it provides a criterion which is too stringent, and that is unlikely ever to be met. The main problem seems to be that, in order for a task to be classed as automatic, it must suffer no interference from *any* simultaneous secondary task. Neumann (1984) summarized work in this area, saying that, "To my knowledge, no type of process or stage of processing has been reliably identified as interference-free across task combinations" (p. 260); that is, usually when some main task has been shown to be interference free with respect to a second simultaneous task, one can find some other secondary task(s) that interferes with it.

If no process or stage can be shown to meet this criterion, it seems even more unlikely that some *total task,* presumably a collection of processes or stages, will satisfy this criterion (Jonides et al., 1984). It seems too much to ask to have a whole task be automatic, as one of its subprocesses will almost certainly interfere with some other secondary task if one searches long enough to find one. Jonides, et al., argue that we should search for automatic processes within overall performances, and characterize tasks as being made up of various automatic and nonautomatic components.

A related point involves the consistency, or stability, of automaticity across trials. Strictly, tasks will be labeled as automatic only if they suffer *no* interference from some secondary task, usually measured across a series of performance trials. If, on just a few of these trials the two tasks happen to interfere, whether because of a shift in response strategy used by the subjects, or because of various forms of behavioral variability, there will be some small interference on average, sufficient to cause that situation to fail the test of noninterference. Thus, even though the tasks might not interfere at all on the majority of the trials (displaying strong automaticity), the few trials on which they do interfere could result in a failure to classify the behavior as automatic.

Interference in Response Execution. These concerns appear to be particularly serious for studying interference in complex motor tasks, particularly where the movement involves considerably more than a single button press (e.g., piano playing, typing). Using this criterion for automaticity, we must of course show that *any* secondary task we choose will not interfere with our "main" task in order for the latter to be classed as automatic. Yet, there is good reason to believe

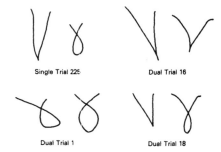

FIG. 4.3 Interference from the production of two simultaneous movements; even after 225 practice trials with each hand separately, subjects were nearly unable to produce the two different figures simultaneously (from Bender, 1980).

that one can always specify a task that will interfere with such a "main" task. This situations would apparently imply that *no* complex movement task could ever be classed as automatic.

As an example, consider an experiment done in our laboratory a few years ago by Bender (1980; see Schmidt, 1982), in which a capital V was drawn with the right hand, and lower case gamma was drawn with the left?[2] In initial trials, these were done by each hand separately, with strong constraints about rapid MT (150 ms) and figure accuracy being imposed on each of 225 practice trials for each hand/figure. Naturally, subjects became quite proficient at making these figures singly, as shown in the upper left of Fig. 4.3. After this practice, subjects were asked to make the same figures, using the same hands, but to do them simultaneously. Examples of various attempts to do this dual task are also shown in Fig. 4.3, and it is fair to say that the interference between hands was massive. There were many kinds of failures, where two Vs or two gammas were drawn, or where the figures were badly distorted, and only rarely were the figures drawn properly according to instruction. Recently, Bender (now Konzem, 1987) has repeated these experiments, finding that the patterns of interference were not appreciably reduced even after 1000 trials of dual-task practice.

A number of interesting interpretations come from these findings. I have argued that these data support a strict single-channel response-execution model, in which only one movement program can be initiated and executed at a time (Schmidt, 1982). (Speech could be an exception.) Because the gamma program and the V program have different temporal structures, and hence are in this view *different* programs (Schmidt, 1982), they cannot be executed together. The dual-task trials are attempts to execute a "new" program that controls both a gamma and a V; and, because this program has had no prior practice, it cannot generate the proper output.

---

[2]Half the subjects had the opposite figure-hand assignment.

Whether or not this viewpoint is accepted, these data suggest that in movement tasks in which a complex, temporally structured, motor output is required, I may always be able to specify another simultaneous secondary task that will interfere with it, just by insuring that the temporal structures of the two movements are different. If so, then by the logic of the dual-task interference criterion discussed earlier, no motor behavior—at least having a temporally structured movement output—can ever be classed as automatic. Of course, such behaviors may be—or may become with practice—interference free with respect to some *other* secondary task that taps, say, response-selection processes (e.g., shadowing, memory search). But according to our strict interference criterion, we must not label that behavior as automatic, as it interferes with another motor response in the other limb. Perhaps we need to specify automaticity *with respect to* some particular process or task; but as it is, the dual-task criterion seems too stringent to be useful (see also Heuer, 1984; Neumann, 1984; Schmidt, in press).

Views of Automaticity in Skilled Movement Control

The general phenomenon of a movement behavior becoming "attention free" can be considered in a variety of ways. Certainly the most common of these is the idea that skills appear to decrease their interference from other concurrent secondary tasks because the many information-processing activities involved in the sensory-to-motor transformations have themselves become "hard-wired," rapid, fast, and (unfortunately) relatively inflexible. In becoming so, they reduce their reliance on the many secondary tasks that we have come to regard as "attention demanding," which are usually those associated with processes in response selection (Heuer, 1984). Thus, when this pattern of decreasing interference with such tasks is found, it has been taken as evidence of decreasing reliance on such capacity-demanding activities, and hence for automaticity.

Heuer (1984) has seen it differently (see also Neumann, 1984, and this volume). He points out that the decreasing pattern of interference seen with some secondary task that is, say, dependent on processes in response selection could simply mean that the development of advanced levels of skill involves tapping some *other* resource to an increasing extent. He presents a convincing case that automaticity in movement skills could be thought of as a *structural displacement*—i.e., a shift of the required resources from those involved in response selection to those involved in response programming, for instance. Because the most commonly used secondary tasks usually tap processing in stages such as response selection, this would account for the commonly seen pattern of decreasing interference in such dual-task situations. But, if researchers had chosen to use as secondary tasks activities that involved processes in response programming, for example, perhaps one would have seen patterns of *increasing* interference with them. Such effects have apparently never been sought (Heuer, 1984), but Bornemann (1942) did show more interference between mental arithmetic and a polishing task as proficiency on the latter increased with practice, which perhaps provides some support for Heuer's (1984) viewpoint. In addition, the patterns of interference seen will probably be a function of the particular tasks one chooses to pair with the main task of interest (Heuer, 1984; Neumann, 1984). This could mean that information processing in the many sensory-to-motor transformations is not becoming automatic at all (in the sense mentioned earlier), but that control is being shifted to other resources that are not so obviously demanding of capacities involved with (conscious) information-processing activities. A variant of this idea is Wickens' (1984) view that the learner acquires a capacity to time share, which is a kind of "resource" to which the dual tasks are shifted with practice.

But a third view is possible, which represents a decidedly different perspective on automaticity, and which has not been considered seriously by those currently studying information processing (see e.g., Neumann's, 1984, review). In this view, the motor system shifts its mode of control from a closed-loop, "data-driven" style of behavior, to a style of control that is primarily open loop; that is, rather than making sensory information processing automatic, the system might reduce the *need* for sensory information by constructing *motor programs* that can handle the details of the movement. Under such a view, practice is seen as the formation of motor programs that are (1) more "comprehensive" in the sense of controlling and coordinating more degrees of freedom, and (2) capable of controlling behavior for a longer duration.

These various viewpoints are probably not mutually exclusive. The development of automaticity could be thought of as a product of a number of separate changes, or it could be seen as changes that are specific to particular kinds of tasks or movement behaviors. In the next section, some of the evidence for these hypotheses about automaticity is discussed.

Making Task-Relevant Information Processing Automatic

Particularly with tasks for which the environment is changing, skilled performances seem to depend on the capability of the performer to detect *patterns* of sensory information and to generate actions quickly that are shaped to the environmental demands. Anecdotal accounts from skilled performers often suggest that patterns of sensory information can be detected quickly and surely, and that these seem to "trigger" appropriate actions without very much mental effort. Good experimental evidence documenting these phenomena is scarce, but some recent work with highly skilled performers in dual-task situations argues for such a viewpoint. Allport, Antonis, and Reynolds (1972), for example, have shown that highly proficient pianists can simultaneously sight-read music and perform an auditory shadowing task without interference (also Shaffer, 1975). These and other studies support the general view that information–processing activities such as sight-reading, which in original learning must have been highly demanding with respect to tasks like auditory shadowing, have become "automatic" with the years of practice devoted to them. Or course, automaticity is with respect to shadowing here and provides no guarantee that other tasks paired with sight reading would not cause interference, as discussed earlier.

Learning to Process Patterns "Automatically." Recent experiments have provided more direct evidence for these changes by charting the course of interference across practice. Schneider and Shiffrin (1977; Shiffrin & Schneider, 1977) broke tradition with the majority of workers in visual information processing when they studied the changes in memory search capabilities across sometimes tens of thousands of practice trials. One of these paradigms involved letter matrices, where the subjects had to respond if a certain target numeral was placed somewhere in the matrix in a location where a letter was expected. Early in practice, subjects used what the authors termed *controlled processing,* in which the search of the matrix for the numeral was serial (apparently letter-by-letter), slow, and produced interference with simultaneous secondary activities such as a running digit-span task (Schneider & Fisk, 1983). However, after much practice, the subject shifted to a qualitatively different style of behavior that the authors called "automatic processing." Here, the information processing of all the letters in the matrix appeared to occur in parallel, and it was very fast and automatic in the sense of producing no interference with the digit-span task. The increases in speed of processing are indeed impressive. In other studies using category search tasks, where the subjects had to determine if a given word (e.g., "Maple") was a member of from one to four categories (e.g., Trees, Foods, etc.) as quickly as possible, the slope of the relationship between number of categories and RT was reduced from 200 ms/category to about 2 ms/category with extended practice. If one regards the slope here as a measure of the time required to make a search of a single category (but see Cheng, 1985), then the speed of information processing was increased 100-fold by practice (Schneider & Fisk, 1983)! These findings together suggest that practice provided a special mechanism that enabled the performance to be highly efficient, fast, and automatic (at least, with respect to simultaneous digit-span and similar tasks).

This kind of work has been very exciting to those concerned with processes involved in skilled movement behaviors. If these processes can be demonstrated in letter matrices and other abstract stimulus materials, it is possible that these results may generalize to the patterns of sensory information that are presented to performers during complex, skilled movement behaviors. For example, patterns of activities involved in the movements of players in a fast game, or involved in the complex displays in an aircraft cockpit, could with extensive practice become automatic in the same sense. Schneider and Fisk (1983) have organized some thoughts on how these learned automatic processes could be relevant to the study of skills, and have described some principles of their acquisition; see also responses to their views in Schmidt (1983) and Cheng (1985).

Principles for Acquiring Automaticity. Perhaps the most important principle in the acquisition of this kind of automatic responding is the idea that the practice must involve what Schneider and Fisk (1983) call *consistent mapping,* so that when a given pattern is presented, the rule defining the response that is called for must be fixed across practice trials. For example, if the subject is directed to respond if a "2" appears in the letter matrix, but not to respond if a "3" appears, then the association of a "2" with a response must always hold. On the other hand, if the subject is told on one block of trials to respond only if a "2" appears, and then on a subsequent block to respond only if a "3" appears (no response to a "2"), such a practice regime will not lead to automatic productions, at least in that particular paradigm.

Practice, S–R Compatibility, and Refractoriness. Another way in which practice has been viewed in relation to information processing has come from older literature on S–R compatibility and refractoriness. For example, Mowbray and Rhoads (1959) showed that extensive practice (42,000 trials) of a choice-RT task resulted in a marked shift in the effect of number of alternatives on RT. Usually, when considerably less practice is given (Hick, 1952), choice RT increases with the $Log_2(N)$, where N is the number of stimulus alternatives (Hick's Law). But Mowbray and Rhoades showed that this relationship became flat after extensive practice, with a four-choice RT being reduced to the level of a two-choice RT. Extensive practice seemed to speed the processing here, to the point that RT became independent of the number of alternatives. In terms of the Schneider and Fisk (1983) notions, it is possible that Mowbray and Rhoads had an early example of learned automatic processing, enabling the subject to deal with added uncertainty in these situations with no increase in RT.

An important "qualification," or complication, of Hick's law is concerned with the *nature* of the relationship between stimulus and response. If the stimulus has a very "natural" relationship to the response it evokes (e.g., an arrow to the right indicates a rightward movement), the S–R compatibility is said to be high, with less natural pairings being classed as having low (or lower) S–R compatibility. Fitts (1964) and others have documented the case that the slope of the Hick relationship depends strongly on S–R compatibility, with lower compatibility leading to steeper slopes. But Leonard (1959) has provided what may be one extreme of this S–R compatibility effect. The subjects' fingers were placed on keys that vibrated to present the stimuli, and then the vibrated finger was pressed as a response, providing what would seem to be a very compatible relationship between stimuli and responses. The RTs for a 2-, 4-, and 8-choice RT task were essentially equivalent (but longer than simple RT), as shown in Fig. 4.4. Once there was more than a single choice, additional choices were handled with no additional time, suggesting a great deal of automatic processing. However, Leonard's finding might not be very general, as ten Hoopen, Aker-

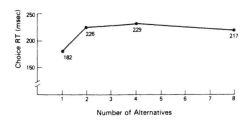

FIG. 4.4 Choice RT as a function of the number of stimulus–response alternatives in a highly compatible task (from Leonard, 1959).

boom, and Raaymakers (1982) found that the slopes were zero in this paradigm only for strong stimuli, with weaker stimuli showing the usual nonzero slope characteristic of situations with variable choices.

It has been tempting to view these data on (1) extended practice and reduced slope of Hick's law, and (2) highly compatible mappings and the zero slope for Hick's law, as showing that one of the effects of practice is to make connections between stimuli and responses "more compatible." Strictly, the notion of S–R compatibility is restricted to a description of the physical pairing between stimulus and response, so it is clear that the *task* (in which this relationship is, by definition, fixed) does not become more compatible with practice. But, of course, I mean here that practice seems to make the learner respond *as if* the task were becoming more compatible, here by making the internal links between the stimulus events and the movement that it is to evoke more "direct" in some way. This fits with our everyday experience where all of the actions required to drive a car or play a musical instrument, which originally seemed very awkward, have become natural (or S–R compatible) as a result of practice. This could also be the basis of so-called *population stereotypes*, in which a particular stimulus–response arrangement is usually seen as "easier" (turning a steering wheel counterclockwise means veering to the left) because of our extensive practice with this particular relationship in many environmental settings.

These changes are similar to some analogous effects seen in the literature on the psychological refractory period that was studied so extensively a few decades ago, in which the RT to the second of two closely spaced stimuli is slowed markedly. The explanation was usually in terms of some rigidly structured attentional limitation (a single channel) for dealing with two responses whose processing overlapped in time. But Gottsdanker and Stelmach (1971), in an experiment with 69 days of practice for a single subject, showed that the PRP effect could be gradually reduced. The effect was never quite eliminated, though, suggesting that there might be some inherent limitation. But that it was reduced markedly suggests that at least the majority of the effect was "plastic," much like the S–R compatibility effects seem to be.

Learning to Time Share

Recent evidence has indicated changes in information processing with practice in two tasks that are time shared (i.e., performed together). Given a time-shared combination of two tasks, it is not surprising that the dual-task performance becomes more effective with practice. As Wickens (1984) points out, this could simply be due to the capability of the subjects to perform each of the component tasks more effectively or more automatically, and may not have anything to do with the processes involved in time sharing. But Damos and Wickens (1980) had subjects practice a digit running-memory task and a digit-classification task, with one group practicing them together in a dual-task situation, and the other group practicing them separately. Then both groups transferred to an unrelated dual-axis tracking task. Subjects with previous dual-task experience performed more effectively on the tracking task, suggesting that a genuine capability (skill) for handling dual-task situations *in general* was developed in dual-task practice. However, the amount of transfer was not very large, indicating that the time-sharing skills were fairly specific to the particular dual-task combinations. Nevertheless, this work does suggest that practice can have marked effects not only on the nature of information processing in a practiced dual task, but also on a genuine time-sharing skill that can be applied to novel time-sharing situations. All this is reviewed by Wickens (1984).

Triggered Reactions: "Automatic" Corrections?

To this point, the discussion has been about how sensory information can be processed "automatically" on the way to response initiation. But another way that automaticity can perhaps be seen is in the patterns of *corrections* that the system produces when perturbed. This topic has held much interest in movement control, and in the past few decades the nature of responses to movement perturbations have been studied extensively. Using a paradigm in which the subject tries to hold a limb in a fixed position, numerous authors have studied the electromyographic (EMG) responses to suddenly presented perturbations that stretch the muscles involved in holding that posture. Three distinct classes of response have been identified (e.g., Marsden, Merton, & Morton, 1972). About 30–50 ms after perturbation, the so-called M1 response is seen as a brief EMG burst in the stretched muscle; this is the well-known monosynaptic stretch reflex. After 50–80 ms, the M2 response occurs, with a somewhat stronger EMG burst; this response is called the "long-loop" reflex, or the trans-cortical stretch reflex, and it is polysynaptic, probably with involvement of the cortex. Finally, at about 120–160 ms the voluntary RT response is seen. The fact that the M2 response can be eliminated by instructions to "let go" although the M1 response is unaffected, and that number of stimulus alternatives affects the RT response but not the M2, argues for separate classifications for these responses.

Crago, Houk, and Hasan (1976) have argued for a fourth category, which "fits" between M2 and the RT response, called the triggered reaction. They have identified responses that are affected by the number of stimulus alternatives as RT is but which are variable in latency and quite fast (from 80–120 ms), and thus presumably too rapid to be RT responses. And, the fact that they are affected by the number of stimulus alternatives, and that they are slower than the 50–80 ms usually seen in the M2 response, argues that they are distinct from this classification as well. The suggestion has been that these triggered reactions are essentially preprogrammed responses initiated by certain stimulus patterns, that they may be learned, and that they are fast and not attention demanding in the sense of interfering with (cognitive) information processing. This has been an interesting suggestion, as it could provide a powerful set of corrective processes for motor control. Unfortunately, the evidence for the distinctiveness of this category can be criticized (see Abbs, Gracco, & Cole, 1984; Schmidt, 1982), no evidence of their acquisition with practice is available, and no experiments have been done examining their qualifications as an automatic process. As important as these triggered reactions could be, they deserve considerably more study.

Phase-Dependent Reflex Responses

Another set of corrective processes with interesting properties was identified by Forssberg, Grillner, and Rossignol (1975) in studies of locomotion in cats. If the animal had just placed its hind foot on the surface to begin the stance phase, a stimulus on the top of the hindpaw caused a slight extension of the joints in the same leg. But, if the *same* stimulus was presented at the moment the cat was lifting the foot to begin the swing phase, the response was a marked *flexion* of the joints in the leg. Thus, the same stimulus led to two different responses, depending on the phase of the step cycle when the stimulus was applied. Other experiments show that the same phenomena occur in spinal animals, so that these corrective actions are not "voluntary" and hence do not involve attention in the sense of interfering with cognitive activities. And, they are fast, and produce coordination across a number of joints. On the surface, they seem similar to triggered reactions, but in this case they are active as a function of the ongoing step cycle.

These reflex reversals do not, at first glance, seem to have much to do with motor learning, as most would agree that these capabilities are largely genetically defined, or "hard wired," in the cat. But they resemble some intriguing findings more recently in speech—a motor control capability that most would argue is highly susceptible to practice. For example, Abbs and Gracco (1983; Abbs et al., 1984) had subjects make utterances such as "afa" or "aba" and then perturbed the trajectory of the lower lip unexpectedly during various portions of the actions. When the lower lip was perturbed during the "aba," a short-latency (25–70 ms) response in the muscles controlling the *upper* lip was observed, sufficient to achieve the closure between the lips necessary to execute the "b" in the action. On the other hand, when the same stimulus was applied to the "afa" action, no such compensation was observed, presumably because lip closure was not a part of "afa". The reactions also depend on when in the action the perturbation is applied, as in the cat locomotion work. But, these results do not strictly indicate reversals in the sense provided by the cat locomotion, because the upper lip showed a positive response during the "aba" action, contrasted with *no* response during the "afa". However, Kelso, Tuller, Vatikiotis-Bateson, and Fowler (1984) later demonstrated that perturbations to the jaw during a "baez" evoked rapid compensations in the tongue muscles but no effect in the lip musculature, whereas the same perturbation during the evocation of a "baeb" produced the reverse pattern—a compensation in the lips, but none in the tongue. These compensations were very rapid, coordinated patterns of adjustment that seemed to have the effect of ensuring that the original pattern of action was carried out faithfully.

These responses have a number of characteristics that qualify them as showing changes in the perception-action relationship with practice. First they occur in speech; and, although we do not have direct evidence from these studies about the acquisition of speech capabilities, most would agree that speech control is learned, and it is reasonable to think that these responses were learned along with the capabilities to speak. Second, the fact that these reactions are task specific, seemingly directed to the achievement of that particular speech sound in the face of perturbations, argues that these reflexes are not "hard-wired" and genetically defined; rather, they seem to be a "soft", but integral, part of the control processes involved in the production of the speech sound. Third, these responses are very fast. Abbs et al. (1984) showed compensations with latencies from 25–70 ms, and Kelso et al. (1984) showed latencies in the lower regions of this range. Fourth, these responses are not *autogenic*—defined as occurring in the same structure as the stimulus (e.g., the monosynaptic stretch reflex)—but rather are coordinated patterns of adjustment in structures often quite remote from the source of stimulation; see also Nashner and Cordo (1981) for examples with postural adjustments. And fifth, these responses seem largely automatic in the sense that they do not interfere with cognitive information-processing activities; subjects seem to be making them with little intention, and in fact with little awareness that they are being produced. Abbs et al.'s subjects claimed that the perturbations were hardly noticeable, and that they often ignored the perturbations (yet faithfully responded to them). And, when asked how many perturbations occurred across a series of trials, subjects estimated that there were only about one-fifth of the perturbations that actually occurred (for 25 perturbations, subjects estimated about 5). Thus, in many ways, these responses resemble the so-called automatic processes discussed by Schneider and Shiffrin (1977), in that they are rapid, apparently involuntary, learned, and result in coordinated outputs in structures often remote from the stimulation. See also Schmidt, in press.

Shifts to Open-Loop Control

One hypothesis for automaticity, which has not in my view been taken very seriously by those interested in the area, holds that the performer shifts to open-loop or motor-program control that does not require (as much) sensory information for behavioral control. Hence, if little sensory information is required for action, then that action can be performed without interfering with other tasks that do require processing of sensory information (e.g., shadowing, sight reading of music, etc.). The argument is that the system acquires, via practice, motor programs that control increasingly long sequences of actions, and that the "running" of these motor programs does not interfere with most other (cognitive) information-processing tasks. Now, program *formation* and *initiation* (in a response-programming stage) causes marked interference with at least some other secondary tasks (e.g., in the PRP paradigm; see Schmidt, 1982). But, because motor programs can be argued to carry our behavior for relatively long durations (Schmidt & McCabe, 1976; Shapiro, 1978), motor-program formation and initiation can occur much less frequently than in early practice, so that the net result is greatly reduced interference with many other secondary tasks. Such a model usually implies skilled switching among resources necessary to perform response programming and those associated with the secondary task (e.g., shadowing), with highly efficient switching producing breaks in behavior which are hardly noticeable.

One important line of work supporting this viewpoint has focused on the nature of the open-loop movement representations to which the subjects presumably shift their control. The recent identification of various movement invariants has both (1) provided hints as to the structure of movement programs, and (2) strengthened this open-loop viewpoint considerably (see, e.g., Schmidt, 1982, in press, Chapter 8 and 9, for a review).

Relative-Timing Invariances. From this perspective, a critical event was an accidental finding by Armstrong (1970), who was interested in various methods of practice for learning a complex movement sequence shown in Fig. 4.5. The subject practiced a pattern of arm movement defined in space and time which had an overall movement duration of 4 sec as shown by the solid line. Occassionally the subject made the entire movement too quickly, as for example in the dotted trace, almost as if the entire movement was sped up as a unit, or "compressed" in time. This finding led Armstrong and his advisor Pew (1974) to suggest that some underlying, temporally structured pattern was learned, and that this structure could be "run off" either quickly or slowly by applying some relatively superficial transformation to the representation to increase or decrease its speed, yet retaining its fundamental structure. This idea also implied that something called *relative timing* was maintained across change in overall MT, in which a ratio of some segment duration (e.g., from first peak to second) divided by MT

98 SCHMIDT

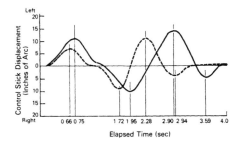

FIG. 4.5 Position-time curve of an arm movement task, showing the correct movement (solid trace) and a trial on which the subject moved too quickly (dotted trace); the dotted trace appears to be temporally "compressed" (from Armstrong, 1970).

should be constant for any MT; and, such a constancy should hold for *any* segment one chooses. Shapiro (1977, 1978) tested this idea more thoroughly in a similar task where subjects were instructed to speed up the movement after they had received considerable practice at the original movement. In Fig. 4.6 are the relative times (i.e., the durations of the segments divided by MT) for the various segments in her task. The Test Trials are the original performances, whereas the Compressed Trials are those for which the subjects were instructed to speed up the movement, and the Speeded-Up trials are those for which the subjects were told to speed up the movement and to ignore the timing learned in acquisition. The relative timing, as measured by the proportions, remained nearly constant, suggesting that the relative timing was a fundamental aspect of these responses.

This work, and other experiments that have followed it (see Schmidt, 1985) have provided considerable support to the idea that when subjects learn movement patterns such as this, one fundamental product of learning is the establishment of a movement program that has a rigidly defined timing structure. This movement, then, can be carried out in a subsequent performance test with somewhat changed superficial features (e.g., altered MT, size, etc.), but the underlying structure tends to remain. Similar findings have been produced in other tasks such as typing (Terzuolo & Viviani, 1979; but see Gentner, 1982, for a rebuttal), locomotion (Shapiro, Zernicke, Gregor, & Diestal, 1981), and various other responses. Most importantly, these findings gave for the first time evidence about the nature of a motor program's structure, allowing the possibility of objective identification of a given movement program (Schmidt, 1985), and allowing the modification to it that occur with practice to be examined experimentally.

Choice of Mode of Control. Inherent in this idea of movement programming and automaticity is the notion that the performer has some *choice* over the mode

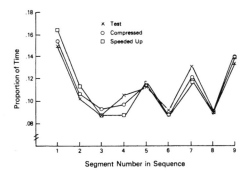

FIG. 4.6 Proportions of time (i.e., segment duration divided by MT) for each of nine segments in a wrist-twist task; Test = normal speed; Compressed = move faster with original timing; Speeded-up = move faster but ignore original timing (from Shapiro, 1977, 1978).

of control that is to be used. Some years ago, I speculated about the various environmental and task conditions that could play a role in such decisions (Schmidt, 1980). One, of course, is practice or experience; unpracticed tasks would have very poorly developed motor programs, thus leading the subject to select closed-loop control to a greater extent. Also, if the environment is very stable, if the "cost" of making errors is low relative to the "benefit" derived from being fast and/or smooth, or if the individual is too fatigued, bored, or lazy to devote the resources necessary to make (conscious) feedback-based corrections, an open-loop mode should be favored. These issues have not been studied very much, but I think they have merit as a means to understanding the determinants of motor behavior capabilities in various settings. And, if it is correct that the choice of open-loop control is associated with reduced demand for resources used for (conscious) processing of sensory information in secondary tasks, then these factors could have a role in the prediction of those conditions that yield automatic responding.

Costs of Automaticity

As with most things in this world, it seems, whenever one receives a "benefit" associated with some method of functioning (here, "automatic" processing), "costs" must invariably be paid. Schneider and Fisk (1983) reported that subjects who learned to make automatic productions for detecting a numeral in a letter matrix also occasionally made such detections when reading outside of the laboratory. It was as if the numeral on the page "jumped out" at them, attracting attention and providing annoying disruptions to the ideas that the words were conveying at the time. In a similar way, perhaps, because automatic processes are supposedly rather rigid (but fast), such a mode of control could lead to more errors if the triggering stimulus is made to occur at a time when its response is inappropriate. Examples are numerous, such as pressing the "clutch pedal" when driving a friend's car with an automatic transmission; also, in rapid ball games, Player 1 attempts to give stimulus information that will lead Player 2 to make an automatic response in one direction, and then Player 1 produces a response that takes advantages of Player 2's committing herself to that course of action. These situations are frequent, sometimes comical, but often deadly serious, as in examples with vehicle control (e.g., Perel, 1976; for reviews, see Mannell & Duthie, 1975; Norman, 1981). Perhaps we focus too heavily on the benefits received from automatic processing in skills without considering sufficiently their costs.

CONCLUDING REMARKS

Although a direct, frontal attack on the relationships between perception, action, and learning has not been of much concern in movement behavior, this chapter points out how a number of areas of research, when viewed from this perspective, do have something to say about how this link might be modified by practice. Although there are a number of potentially important principles than can be suggested from this literature, the experiments are seldom done with this perspective in mind and frequently the interpretations that one would be tempted to make are rivaled by a number of other, perhaps less interesting, possible explanations. These ideas are quite tentative, suggesting how these various experiments might tell us something about practice and the perception-action relationship. If this chapter is to be of much use, I expect that it will be as a stimulus to others to refine and clarify the apparent relationships discussed here, rather than as a set of certain principles. But however these principles are eventually stated, it seems clear that practice will figure heavily in our understanding of the relationship between perception and action in movement behaviors.

ACKNOWLEDGMENTS

The preparation of this manuscript was supported in part by Grant No. BNS 80-23125 from the National Science Foundation, Memory and Cognitive Processes Program. Thanks to Herbert Heuer, Donald MacKay, and Wolfgang Prinz for their comments on an earlier draft.

REFERENCES

Abbs, J. H., & Gracco, V. L. (1983). Sensorimotor actions in the control of multi-movement speech gestures. *Trends in Neuroscience, 6,* 391–395.

Abbs, J. H., Gracco, V. L., & Cole, K. J. (1984). Control of multi-movement coordination: Sensorimotor mechanisms in speech motor programming. *Journal of Motor Behavior, 16,* 195–231.
Adams, J. A. (1968). Response feedback and learning. *Psychological Bulletin, 70,* 486–504.
Adams, J. A. (1971). A closed-loop theory of motor learning. *Journal of Motor Behavior, 3,* 111–149.
Adams, J. A., & Bray, N. W. (1970). A closed-loop theory of paired associate verbal learning. *Psychological Review, 77,* 385–405.
Adams, J. A., & Goetz, E. T. (1973). Feedback and practice as variables in error detection and correction. *Journal of Motor Behavior, 5,* 217–224.
Adams, J. A., Goetz, E. T., & Marshall, P. H. (1972). Response feedback and motor learning. *Journal of Experimental Psychology, 92,* 391–397.
Adams, J. A., Gopher, D., & Lintern, G. (1977). Effects of visual and proprioceptive feedback on motor learning. *Journal of Motor Behavior, 9,* 11–22.
Allport, D. A., Antonis, B., & Reynolds, P. (1972). On the division of attention: A disproof of the single channel hypothesis. *Quarterly Journal of Experimental Psychology, 24,* 225–235.
Armstrong, T. R. (1970). *Training for the production of memorized movement patterns.* University of Michigan, Human Performance Center, Technical Report No. 26.
Bahrick, H. P. (1957). An analysis of stimulus variables influencing the proprioceptive control of movements. *Psychological Review, 64,* 324–328.
Bahrick, H. P., Noble, M. E., & Fitts, P. M. (1954). Extra-task performance as a measure of learning a primary task. *Journal of Experimental Psychology, 48,* 298–302.
Bahrick, H. P., & Shelly, C. (1958). Time sharing as an index of automatization. *Journal of Experimental Psychology, 56,* 288–293.
Bender, P. A. (1980). *Limitations in execution of two-handed movements.* Paper presented at NASPSPA annual meeting, Boulder, CO.
Bornemann, E. (1942). Untersuchungen über den Grad der geistigen Beanspruchung. II. Teil. Praktische Ergebnisse. *Arbeitsphysiologie, 12,* 173–191.
Cheng, D. W. (1985). Restructuring versus automaticity: Alternative accounts of skill acquisition. *Psychological Review, 92,* 414–423.
Crago, P. E., Houk, J. C., & Hasan, Z. (1976). Regulatory actions of the human stretch reflex. *Journal of Neurophysiology, 39,* 925–935.
Damos, D., & Wickens, C. D. (1980). The acquisition and transfer of time-sharing skills. *Acta Psychologica, 6,* 569–577.
Fitts, P. M. (1964). Perceptual-motor skill learning: In A. W. Melton (Ed.), *Categories of human learning.* New York: Academic Press.
Fitts, P. M., Bahrick, H. P., Noble, M. E., & Briggs, G. E. (1961). *Skilled performance.* New York: Wiley.
Fleishman, E. A., & Hempel, W. E. (1955). The relation between abilities and improvement with practice in a visual discrimination reaction task. *Journal of Experimental Psychology, 49,* 301–312.
Fleishman, E. A., & Rich, S. (1963). Role of kinesthetic and spacial-visual abilities in perceptual motor learning. *Journal of Experimental Psychology, 66,* 6–11.
Forssberg, H., Grillner, S., & Rossignol, S. (1975). Phase dependent reflex reversal during walking in chronic spinal cats. *Brain Research, 85,* 103–107.
Fuchs, A. H., (1962). The progression-regression hypothesis in perceptual-motor skill learning. *Journal of Experimental Psychology, 63,* 177–182.
Gentner, D. R. (1982). Evidence against a central control model of timing in typing. *Journal of Experimental Psychology: Human Perception and Performance, 8,* 783–810.
Gottsdanker, R., & Stelmach, G. E. (1971). The persistence of psychological refractoriness. *Journal of Motor Behavior, 3,* 301–312.

Heuer, H. (1984). Motor learning as a process of structural constriction and displacement. In: W. Prinz & A. F. Sanders (Eds.), *Cognition and motor processes*. Berlin-Heidelberg: Springer-Verlag.

Hick, W. E. (1952). On the rate of gain of information. *Quarterly Journal of Experiment Psychology, 4,* 11-26.

Jagacinski, R. J., & Hah, S. (in press). Progression-regression effects in tracking repeated patterns. *Journal of Experimental Psychology: Human Perception and Performance*.

Jonides, J., Naveh-Benjamin, M., & Palmer, J. (1984). *On the cooccurrence of capacity limitations and voluntary control.* Paper at the conference, Action, Attention, and Automaticity at Zentrum für interdisziplinäre Forschung, Universität Bielefeld, Germany, 1984.

James, W. (1890). *The principles of psychology* (Vol. 1), New York: Holt.

Kelso, J. A. S., Tuller, B., Vatikiotis-Bateson, E., & Fowler, C. A. (1984). Functionally specific articulatory cooperation following jaw perturbations during speech: Evidence for coordinative structures. *Journal of Experimental Psychology: Human Perception and Performance, 10,* 812-832.

Konzem, P. B. (1987). *Extended practice and patterns of bimanual interference.* Unpublished doctoral dissertation, University of Southern California.

Leonard, J. A. (1959). Tactual choice reactions. *Quarterly Journal of Experimental Psychology, 11,* 76-83.

Mannell, R. C., & Duthie, J. H. (1975). Habit lag: When "automatization" is dysfunctional. *The Journal of Psychology, 89,* 73-80.

Marsden, C. D., Merton, P. A., & Morton, H. B. (1972). Servo action in human voluntary movement. *Nature, 238,* 140-143.

McLeod, P. (1977). A dual-task response modality effect: Support for multi-processor models of attention. *Quartery Journal of Experimental Psychology, 29,* 651-668.

McLeod, P. (1978). Does probe RT measure central processing demand? *Quarterly Journal of Experimental Psychology, 30,* 83-89.

Marteniuk, R. G., & Romanow, S. (1983). Amplitude, time, and frequency characteristics of sequential movement performance as a function of learning. In R. A. Magill (Ed.), *Memory and control of action.* Amsterdam: North-Holland.

Mowbray, G. H., & Rhoads, M. V. (1959). On the reduction of choice reaction times with practice. *Quarterly Journal of Experimental Psychology, 11,* 16-23.

Nashner, L. M., & Cordo, P. J. (1981). Relation of automatic postural responses and reaction-time voluntary movements of human leg muscles. *Experimental Brain Research, 43,* 395-405.

Neumann, O. (1984). Automatic Processing: A review of recent findings and a plea for an old theory. In W. Prinz & A. F. Sanders (Eds.), *Cognition and motor processes.* Berlin-Heidelberg: Springer-Verlag.

Newell, K. M. (1974). Knowledge of results and motor learning. *Journal of Motor Behavior, 6,* 235-244.

Norman, D. A. (1981). Categorization of action slips. *Psychological Review, 88,* 1-15.

Perel, M. (1976). *Analyzing the role of driver/vehicle incompatibilities in accident causation using police reports.* Technical Report, DOT HS-801,858, Department of Transportation.

Pew, R. W. (1966). Acquisition of hierarchical control over the temporal organization of a skill. *Journal of Experimental Psychology, 71,* 764-771.

Pew, R. W. (1974). Human perceptual-motor performance. In B. H. Kantowitz (Ed.), *Human information processing: Tutorials in performance and cognition.* New York: Lawrence Erlbaum Associates.

Schmidt, R. A. (1971). Proprioception and the timing of motor responses. *Psychological Bulletin, 76,* 383-393.

Schmidt, R. A. (1975). A schema theory of discrete motor skill learning. *Psychological Review, 82,* 225-260.

4. ACQUISITION OF SKILL   103

Schmidt, R. A. (1980). Past and future issues in motor programming. *Research Quarterly for Exercise and Sport, 51,* 122–140.
Schmidt, R. A. (1982). *Motor control and learning: A behavioral emphasis.* Champaign, IL: Human Kinetics Press.
Schmidt, R. A. (1983). On the underlying structure of well-learned motor responses: A discussion of Namikas, and Schneider and Fisk. In R. A. Magill (Ed.), *Memory and control of action.* Amsterdam: North–Holland.
Schmidt, R. A. (1985). Identifying units of motor behavior. *The Behavioral and Brain Sciences, 8,* 163–164.
Schmidt, R. A. (in press). *Motor Control and Learning: A behavioral emphasis* (2nd ed.). Champaign, IL: Human Kinetics Press.
Schmidt, R. A., & McCabe, J. F. (1976). Motor program utilization over extended practice. *Journal of Human Movement Studies, 2,* 239–247.
Schmidt, R. A., & Russell, D. G. (1972). *Error detection in positioning responses.* Unpublished data, University of Michigan.
Schmidt, R. A., & White, J. L. (1972). Evidence for an error detection mechanism in motor skills: A test of Adams' closed-loop theory. *Journal of Motor Behavior, 4,* 143–153.
Schmidt, R. A., & Wrisberg, C. A. (1973). Further tests of Adams' closed-loop theory: Response-produced feedback and the error-detection mechanism. *Journal of Motor Behavior, 5,* 155–164.
Schneider, W. (1984). *A communication theory of attention and skill development: Neural architecture and a mathematical representation of automaticity.* Paper presented at the conference Action, Attention, and Automaticity, Zentrum für interdisziplinäre Forschung, Universität Bielefeld, Germany.
Schneider, W., & Fisk, A. D. (1983). Attention theory and mechanisms for skilled performance. In R. A. Magill (Ed.), *Memory and control of action.* Amsterdam: North–Holland.
Schneider, W., & Shiffrin, R. (1977). Controlled and automatic human information processing: I. Detection, search, and attention. *Psychological Review, 84,* 1–66.
Shaffer, H. (1975). Multiple attention in continuous verbal tasks. In S. Dornic (Ed.), *Attention and performance V.* New York: Academic Press.
Shapiro, D. C. (1977). A preliminary attempt to determine the duration of a motor program. In D. M. Landers & R. W. Christina (Eds.), *Psychology of motor behavior and sport* (Vol. 1). Champaign, IL: Human Kinetics.
Shapiro, D. C. (1978). *The learning of generalized motor programs.* Unpublished doctoral dissertation, University of Southern California.
Shapiro, D. C., Zernicke, R. F., Gregor, R. J., & Diestal, J. D. (1981). Evidence for generalized motor programs using gait-pattern analysis. *Journal of Motor Behavior, 13,* 33–47.
Shiffrin, R. M., & Schneider, W. (1977). Controlled and automatic human information processing: II. Perceptual learning, automatic attending, and a general theory. *Psychological Review, 84,* 127–190.
Suzuki, S. (1969). *Nurtured by love: A new approach to education.* New York: Exposition Press.
ten Hoopen, G., Akerboom, S., & Raaymakers, E. (1982). Vibrotactile choice reaction time, tactile receptor systems and ideomotor compatibility. *Acta Psychologica, 50,* 143–157.
Terzuolo, C. A., & Viviani, P. (1979). The central representation of learned motor patterns. In R. E. Talbot & D. R. Humphrey (Eds.), *Posture and movement.* New York: Raven.
Wickens, C. D. (1984). *Engineering psychology and human performance.* Columbus, OH: Merrill.
Zelaznik, H. N., Shapiro, D. C., & Newell, K. M. (1978). On the structure of motor recognition memory. *Journal of Motor Behavior, 10,* 313–323.
Zelaznik, H. N., & Spring, J. (1976). Feedback in response recognition and production. *Journal of Motor Behavior, 8,* 309–312.

5 Brain Potentials Related to Preparation and Action

C. H. M. Brunia
*Tilburg University,
The Netherlands*

INTRODUCTION

Since the pioneer work of Hans Berger (1929) it has become a usual procedure both in the clinic and in the laboratory to record changes in electrical activity of the brain by means of surface electrodes fixed to the scalp. Electrodes are generally placed at standard positions that are reflected in Fig. 5.1. These positions are indexed by letter-figure combinations, indicating the left or right brain area above which the electrodes are fixed. The write-out of changes in potential recorded between pairs of electrodes is known as the electroencephalogram (EEG). In the present chapter a review is given of potential changes that are coupled with the occurrence of circumscribed events. From the set of event-related potentials (ERPs) we discuss only ERP's related to the planning and execution of a movement.

ERP amplitudes are very small in relation to the amplitudes of the spontaneous brain activity. Therefore averaging procedures are used in order to visualize them. In general they are composites of several negative and positive waves that succeed each other in a systematic way. Waves are called components if changes in amplitude or latency are systematically related to an experimental variable or a set of such variables (Donchin, Ritter, & McCallum, 1978). In principle ERPs can be studied on an exclusively functional basis, i.e., without taking into account the fact that they reflect electrophysiological brain activity. Many psychologists seem to follow such a strategy, partly perhaps, because so much is still unknown about the physiological basis of ERPs. In the present text, however, we try to stay as close as possible to the physiological reality also. This approach implies that we discuss components not only in terms of their func-

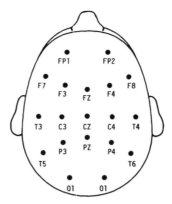

FIG. 5.1 Electrode positions, used in the recording of an electroencephalogram (EEG). F = frontal, C = central, P = parietal, O = occipital, T = temporal. Even subscripts: rigtt side of the scalp. Odd subscripts: left side of the scalp.

tional significance but also in terms of their electrophysiological sources. This latter point needs some further explanation.

It is known that the cortex is built up of cell columns in which cells are aligned in a regular geometric way. Dendrites of large cells in layer IV descend from upper layers almost perpendicularly from the surface. They are targets of afferent axons from other cortical areas, specific and aspecific thalamic nuclei. Graded postsynaptic potentials at the axodendritic synapes form the physiological basis of ERPs. In principle, scalp negativity is based on dendrite depolarization or soma hyperpolarization and scalp positivity on dendrite hyperpolarization or soma depolarization. Because dendrites are nearer to the surface than somata, their graded postsynaptic potentials have a greater impact for the emergence of surface ERPs (Caspers, Speckmann, & Lehmenkühler, 1980). Cells in layer V can act like dipoles: If negative activity is present at the surface, positive activity can be found when the recording electrode is placed in the deeper cortical layers or just below the cortex. Such a polarity inversion points to an electrophysiological source situated between surface and depth. Polarity inversion is an important argument for the localization of an electrophysiological source, as we see later on.

Most research on movement-related potentials concerns simple ballistic movements. Only in the last few years complex movements are studied for which a certain skill is required. We first describe potentials related to simple movements. A distinction is made between potentials recorded prior to movement onset and those following movement onset. Different authors have used different terminologies in order to indicate various components. We class the different components in a schema, which might be of some help if one wants to study the literature in some more detail. Next we describe the possible physiological sources of the potentials, as far as animal research provides information about that. In the second part of the chapter potentials related to complex movements are discussed. Information about their electrophysiological sources is almost completely absent. We discuss potentials related to attentional processes in so far as they are relevant for the guidance of movements. We suggest that different brain areas can be activated depending on the kind of process that controls the movement.

POTENTIALS RELATED TO SIMPLE BALLISTIC MOVEMENTS

Potentials Recorded Prior to Movement Onset

These potentials are usually obtained when subjects make well-defined self-paced movements (e.g., pressing a button) at intervals of 5 seconds or more. These intervals are chosen to prevent the premovement potentials from being influenced by postmovement potentials. Subjects are instructed to refrain from any other movement from at least 2 seconds preceding until 2 seconds after the movement. In this period they fixate a point in the frontal plane without blinking, because eye movements and eye blinks can cause considerable artifacts in the EEG.

Kornhuber and Deecke (1965) were first in describing a number of movement-related potentials. They distinguished a negative Bereitschafts potential (BP), a premotion positivity (PMP), and a negative motor potential (MP). In contrast to using names that suggest a functional meaning, Gilden, Vaughan, and Costa (1966) preferred a strictly sequential indication for the same components: N_1, P_1, and N_2. The letters indicate component polarity (Fig. 5.2). The available evidence suggests the existence of at least 4 premovement potentials since N_1 is composed of a symmetric and an asymmetric slow wave.

The readiness potential (RP) as the BP is called also, starts between 1500 and 1200 milliseconds prior to a unilateral movement. It has a symmetrical distribution over the central and parietal areas. The process reflected by this negativity cannot be a prerequisite for movement execution itself, for manual reaction time, defined as the delay between an imperative stimulus and a response is about 200 msec. Within that time the imperative stimulus is encoded, a movement prepared and executed. One of the factors that might be related to the RP is the timing of the movement, because RPs are mostly recorded under certain timing constraints, as we have seen earlier. The traditional RP recording situation allows the subject to preplan the movement, perhaps by counting silently. Libet, Wright, and Gleason (1982, 1983) suggested that the crucial process might be an intention or preparation to act in the near future (seconds). This process I underlying the type I RP is distinguished from process II, underlying the next component (see Table 5.1).

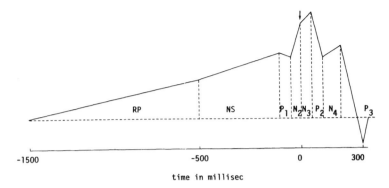

FIG. 5.2 Schematic representation of the 8 movement-related potentials, discussed in the text and represented in Table 5.1. Time axis from 1500 milliseconds preceding EMG onset till 300 milliseconds after that. This representation is a composite of components recorded at various electrode positions. They cannot be derived from one single electrode position.

From about 500 msec preceding EMG onset, amplitudes are larger over the hemisphere contralateral to the movement side, at least with finger or hand movements (Deecke & Kornhuber, 1977; Kornhuber & Deecke, 1965). This part of the slow wave is considered a second component, although not unanimously. Shibasaki, Barret, Halliday, and Halliday (1980a) named it the negative shift (NS). Libet et al. (1982, 1983) supposed that a more specific urge or intention to act is underlying the NS. They called the second component type II RP (see Table 5.1). The second component may or may not be preceded by the first one, depending on the kind of task to be performed.

The next component is the P_1: a bilateral widespread positive wave with a maximal amplitude at P_z (see Fig. 5.1) and larger amplitudes over the ipsilateral parietal and central area as compared to the contralateral regions. Gilden et al. (1966) suggested that this component was related to activation of corticospinal pathways. They called the interval between the onset of P_1 and EMG onset in the agonist the corticomuscular delay. This delay is larger, the larger the length of the neural pathway from the cortex to agonist (Vaughan, 1974) as is shown in Fig. 5.3. Deecke and Kornhuber (1977) suggested that P_1 reflects the command to move. Deecke, Grözinger, and Kornhuber (1976) hypothesized that the command to move is transmitted from the association cortex to the cerebellum and from there via the thalamus to the motor cortex. Another explanation for the emergence of P_1 was proposed by Shibasaki and Kato (1975). These authors suggested that P_1 was related to the inhibition of so-called mirror-movements. They pointed to the fact that if children and hemiplegic patients are asked to make a unilateral hand movement, they frequently are unable to prevent a similar movement on the other side. Comparing slow potentials preceding unilateral and

TABLE 5.1
BALLISTIC MOVEMENT-RELATED BRAIN POTENTIALS

	BP	PMP	MP	N		RAP		
								Bates (1951)
	N₁	P₁	N₂		P₂			Kornhuber & Deecke (1965)
	N₁	P₁		N₂	P₂ₐ		P₂ᵦ	Gilden, Vaughan & Costa (1966)
	N₁	P₁	N₂		P₂		P₃	Gerbrandt, Goff & Smith (1973)
N₁ₐ	N₁ᵦ	P₁	N₂	N₃	P₂ₐ	N₄	P₂ᵦ	Arezzo & Vaughan (1975)
	N₁			MCP				Gerbrandt (1977)
	N₁			P₁' N₂	P₂		P₂'	Papakostopoulos (1978)
	N₁	P₁	N₂ₐ	N₂ᵦ	P₂ₐ		P₂ᵦ P₃	Hazemann, Metral & Lille (1978)
BP	NS	P₋₅₀	N₋₁₀	N₊₅₀	P₊₉₀	N₊₁₆₀	P₃₀₀	Arezzo & Vaughan (1980)
RP I	RP II							Shibasaki, Barret, Halliday & Halliday (1980)
								Libet, Wright & Gleason (1982)

← Movement onset

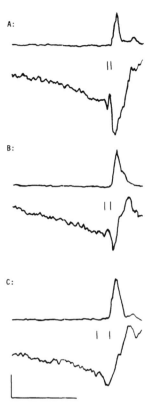

FIG. 5.3 Movement-related potentials and rectified averaged electromyogram (EMG) of the agonist. A: right lower facial contraction, B: clenching right fist, C: dorsiflexion right foot. Upper trace: EMG. Paired lines indicate interval between P1 onset and EMG. Corticomuscular delay increases from A to C. Negativity downward. Time 1 second Voltage: A: 25 μV, B, and C: 50 μV (from Vaughan, 1974).

bilateral opposition movements of the thumb in normal right-handed adults, they found a P_1 sometimes preceding a unilateral movement and never prior to a bilateral movement. Therefore Shibasaki and Kato (1975) interpreted these results as being in favor of the inhibition of mirror-movements. However, recent studies of bilateral movements in right-handed (Kristeva, Keller, Deecke & Kornhuber, 1979) and left-handed subjects (Kristeva & Deecke, 1980) demonstrated the existence of a P_1, thus questioning the interpretation of Shibasaki and Kato.

The last premovement component is the N_2. Kornhuber and Deecke (1965)

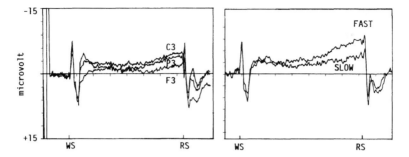

FIG. 5.4 CNV recordings during a foreperiod of 4 seconds. Left: after the evoked potential following the warning signal, an early negativity emerges with maximal amplitudes over the frontal area. In contrast to that, the late wave is maximal over the central area. Right: CNVs preceding fast and slow responses of the same subjects recorded within one session. Only late wave amplitudes are larger preceding fast responses, suggesting a role in motor preparation.

suggested that it presumably reflects the corticospinal outflow initiating the movement. Gilden et al. (1966) were of the same opinion. It has been questioned whether the N_2 was a premovement potential indeed. Gerbrandt, Goff, and Smith (1973) recorded an N_2 that was present after EMG onset, making its role in the initiation of the movement unlikely. In a later study Gerbrandt (1977) agreed upon the existence of a negative wave preceding movement onset (N_2). It was suggested to label the negative wave after EMG onset N_3 (see Table 5.1).

CNV: A Special Premovement Potential?

The EEG in a warned simple reaction time experiment is characterized by the so called contingent negative variation (CNV). If a warning signal (WS) after 4 seconds is followed by an imperative stimulus (RS) two slow waves are found. The first is larger over the frontal areas and shows a peak at about 750 milliseconds after the WS. Its amplitude reflects the alerting properties of the WS. The next slow wave is present during the second part of the foreperiod and is more pronounced over the central and parietal areas (Fig. 5.4). Maximal amplitudes of this CNV late wave are reached at the presentation of RS, contralateral to the responding hand. Rohrbaugh and Gaillard (1983) have argued that the CNV late wave is a RP. Its relation to motor functioning is among others suggested by the fact that larger amplitudes are found preceding short reaction times (see Fig. 5.4). However, the conclusion that cognitive factors are not reflected in the CNV is not warranted. This is even so for the RP. Insofar as the motor aspects of both slow waves are concerned, there is no reason to treat CNV late waves as different from RPs.

Potentials Recorded After Movement Onset

At present there seems to be agreement about the existence of four components, but again the terminology used by various authors is quite different (Table 5.1). Once EMG activity is present in the agonist, a negative–positive–negative–positive wave complex is found in the EEG (Gerbrandt, 1977; Shibasaki et al., 1980b).

The first postmovement onset component is a negative wave, discovered in 1951 by Bates (Table 5.1). This wave has been called originally N_2 by Gerbrandt et al. (1973) and later on N_3, to prevent a mixing up with a premovement potential of the same annotation (Gerbrandt, 1977). N_3 has its largest amplitude over the premotor area. Shibasaki et al. (1980b) found it over the frontal areas, with larger amplitudes over the contralateral side. Gerbrandt et al. (1973) suggested that this wave reflects sensory feedback. Papakostopoulos (1980), using a comparable averaging technique as Gerbrandt et al. (1973), was of the same opinion, but called N_3 the motor cortex potential (MCP).

The next component P_2 is bilaterally symmetrical over the motor cortex and shows larger amplitudes over the contralateral postcentral cortex (Gerbrandt et al. 1973). In the original publication of Kornhuber and Deecke (1965) the authors pointed to the similarity of the positive wave following active and passive movements. Therefore they hypothesized that reafferent activity from the moving muscles might be the explanation for their emergence. This opinion has been challenged by Arezzo and Vaughan (1975) as we see later on when discussing the sources of the different components.

The third component N_4 is present over the parietal, postcentral and precentral regions. Its maximal amplitudes are present over the contralateral parietal cortex, suggesting a sensory function (Shibasaki et al., 1980b).

The fourth component P_3 is a bilateral wave with maximal amplitudes at the vertex or the contralateral precentral electrode. Both Kornhuber and Deecke (1965) and Vaughan, Costa, and Ritter (1968) reported its contralateral predominance. Moreover, they pointed to the similarity of this component and a late component of the somatosensory evoked potential, suggesting its role in a sensory feedback mechanism. Shibasaki et al. (1980b) found the same component with similar latency and amplitude after active and passive finger movements, which suggests a role of sensory feedback too.

LOCALIZATION OF SOURCES

Monkeys show movement-related potentials comparable to those found in man. Recordings from different layers of the monkey cortex provide evidence for the localization of the source of these potentials. If, preceding a movement, nega-

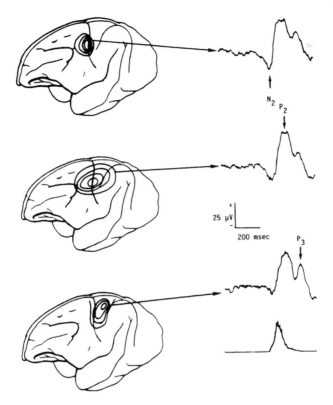

FIG. 5.5 Isopotential lines of N_2, P_2, and P_3 components of contralateral movement related potentials in a monkey. Note the difference in localization of the sources (from Arezzo & Vaughan, 1975).

tivity prevails at the surface, a positive wave can sometimes be found in the deeper layers. Such a transcortical potential inversion is used as an indication of the position of the source that generates the slow wave. If the level at which the inversion takes place is marked, it is possible on the basis of postmortem analysis to indicate which cell group presumably was involved in the generation of the slow wave (Arezzo & Vaughan, 1975; Sasaki, Gemba, & Hashimoto, 1981). Arezzo and Vaughan (1975) also used a large number of epidural electrodes to allow for the mapping of isopotential lines of various components (Fig. 5.5).

In describing the electrophysiological analysis of movement-related potentials we follow the same division as in the foregoing section. First the sources of premovement potentials are discussed, followed by a description of the sources underlying the potentials recorded after agonist EMG onset.

Sources of Potentials Recorded Prior to Movement Onset

The distinction made in the human RP between a symmetric and an asymmetric component has at the moment no clear counterpart in animal research. Arezzo and Vaughan (1975) had difficulties in recording N_1, due to the limited frequency response of their recording system. Yet they suggested that N_1 originates from the precentral cortex, contralateral to the movement side. Hashimoto, Gemba, and Sasaki (1979, 1980) recorded slow premovement potentials from different cortical areas. They found a potential inversion in the premotor, motor and somatosensory cortex. At least some of the figures of this research group show potentials starting at about 1 second prior to the movement. This suggests that as far as the time scale is concerned, we are confronted with both the first and the second component. However, RPs from ipsilateral and contralateral hemispheres are never depicted in such a way that the observer can get an impression of a possible symmetric and asymmetric part of the curve. Also difference curves have not been published. Gemba, Sasaki, and Hashimoto (1980) described, however, contralateral larger RP amplitudes over the motor cortex, and a symmetric RP over the premotor cortex. So it seems likely that only in the motor cortex both components are present.

Symmetric premovement activity suggests a rather generalized excitation of both cortical areas above which potentials are recorded. The asymmetric component, then, reflects perhaps preparatory excitation of dendrites of cells that are going to fire to execute the movement. If that reasoning is correct, it would follow that NS reflects the increasing excitation that leads to the emergence of N_2. It should be noted, however, that this interpretation is a possibility, not a proven fact.

Another point needs some further consideration and that is the presence of RPs over different cortical areas. The fact that the RP is symmetric above the premotor areas and asymmetric above the motor cortex is a first indication that RPs over different cortical areas might represent a different involvement of these areas in the preparation for the movement. From the fact that RP sources are found in the premotor, motor, and somatosensory cortex, it does not follow that the different generators are put into action by one single control mechanism. For example, right cerebellar hemispherectomy decreases the amplitude of the RP in the left motor and somatosensory cortex. The RP in the somatosensory cortex recovers within a few weeks, in contrast to the RP in the motor cortex (Sasaki, Gemba, Hashimoto, & Mizuno, 1979). These data suggest that RPs in motor and somatosensory cortex are controlled in a different way. This is a second argument in favor of possibly different involvement of these cortical areas in motor preparation. A third argument stems from experiments in which movements had to be carried out under different load conditions. Gemba et al. (1980) found larger RP amplitudes when more muscle force was needed to perform the move-

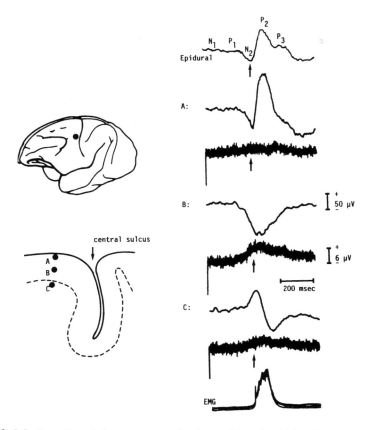

FIG. 5.6 Recording of slow movement-related potentials and multiple unit activity at three different depths (A, B, and C) within the precentral gyrus of a monkey. The leading edge of the averaged multiple unit activity indicates the total voltage. Potential inversion between B and C. Averaged rectified EMGs from each series of trials are depicted below (from Arezzo et al., 1977).

ment. Although load effects were found over all three cortical areas, the strongest increase was found over the somatosensory cortex. Moreover, time of onset was different. RPs start first over the premotor cortex, then over the motor cortex, and finally over the somatosensory cortex. In summary, the available evidence suggests that RPs over different cortical areas reflect different processes indeed, but the nature of these process is still unclear.

Up to now we have seen that an increase in muscle force results in an increase of RP amplitudes, but that this increase might be different for different cortical areas. Reaction time, defined as the delay between an imperative stimulus and the pressing of a button, results also in larger CNV late wave amplitudes (Brunia & Vingerhoets, 1980; Rohrbaugh, Syndulko, & Lindsley, 1976). Because this slow potential can be considered a RP, recorded in a reaction time experiment, there is a parallel with muscle force. The effects of fast reaction times are also rather widespread over both hemispheres. We know that the increase in amplitude reflects an increase in excitation of the dendrites in the upper cortical layers. What we do not know is where that increased activity originates.

As far as the third component P_1 is concerned, no animal data are available related to its possible source.

During the last 2 decades a number of experiments in monkeys are performed, in which neuronal activity in the cortex could be related to certain aspects of motor behavior (for reviews, see: Evarts, 1981; Fuster, 1981; Wiesendanger, 1981). To bridge the gap between recordings of neuronal activity in the monkey cortex and of slow potentials in man, Arezzo, Vaughan, and Koss (1977) and Arezzo and Vaughan (1980) developed a technique with which multiple unit activity and slow potentials can be recorded by the same intracortical electrodes. An example of such recordings is found in Fig. 5.6. If a transcortical potential inversion is found simultaneously with an increase in multiple unit activity in one and the same cortical layer this indicates in all likelihood that the excitation of the dendrites of these cells is the source of the slow potential. Using this technique Arezzo and Vaughan (1980) were able to show that N_2 is indeed caused by a discharge of cells in layer V of the precentral gyrus. This confirms the original idea of Kornhuber and Deecke (1965) that this component is related to the corticospinal outflow, which starts the movement. The NS in man has its counterpart in an asymmetric monkey RP, which is exclusively found over the contralateral motor cortex (Gemba et al., 1980). NS and N_2 might reflect, respectively, the preparatory and final excitation of the agonist pyramidal tract neurons, as we have seen earlier.

Sources of Potentials Recorded After Movement Onset

The first component to be discussed is N_3, which was called N_{2b} by Arezzo and Vaughan (1980). These authors found sources of N_{2b} and P_{2a} in the banks of the central sulcus. They concluded that N_{2b} and P_{2a} could be considered the consequence of a resultant dipole around the sulcus, situated in an about horizontal direction. Thus the two waves are interpreted as one component of the ERP. EMG onset precedes this component by 15–20 milliseconds. Therefore the authors suggested that short latency reafferent activity in precentral and postcentral gyri might be reflected in this component. It is known indeed, that the banks of the central sulcus receive inputs from stretch and joint receptors. Moreover, somatosensory-evoked potentials can be recorded over these areas with half the latency of this component.

About the next component N_4, which is larger over the contralateral parietal area, no animal data are available.

The source of the next component P_{2b} is localized in the motor cortex (areas 4 and 6) and in the somatosensory cortex (areas 2 and 5). Arezzo and Vaughan (1980) recorded multiple unit activity in the upper cortical layers to a wider extent in voluntary movements than when accompanying the somatosensory evoked potential. This suggests a function different from sensory feedback. Moreover, in an earlier paper, Vaughan, Gross, and Bossom (1970) reported that the at that time called P_2 component was resistant to upper limb deafferentiation in monkeys trained to perform wrist movements. This also suggests that P_2 is not just reflecting reafferent information, although such information from other muscles still could have arrived at the cortex. Later Arezzo and Vaughan (1980) suggested that this component, in between called P_{2b} reflects a central feedback from corollary activity anywhere in the central motor structures.

The last component P_3 has a bilateral representation over the somatosensory cortex (area 5). Arezzo et al. (1977) found multiple unit activity in the upper layers of this cortical area, accompanying this surface positive potential. It is presumable that this component reflects reafferent activity, in line with the original proposition of Kornhuber and Deecke (1965). Somatosensory stimulation evokes cell activity in this same area at comparable latency (Sakata, Takaoka, Kawarasaki, and Shibutani, 1973).

CONCLUSION

The introduction indicated that most research of movement-related potentials concerns simple ballistic movements. We have seen that these movements are preceded and accompanied by a number of negative and positive ERP components. We have also seen that the anatomical localization of some of the sources has been clarified and sometimes their functional significance as well. It has become clear that much has to be learned still, about the anatomical, the physiological, and the psychological aspects of these potentials. We have found indications that timing of self-paced movements is reflected in premovement potentials and also that in postmovement potentials reafferent activity and central feedback mechanisms play a role. Especially these aspects seem relevant for complex movements. In complex movements guidance becomes an important factor. After a review of slow potential recordings during various tasks, we come up with a suggestion about how movement can be guided from different cortical areas and how this might be reflected in ERPs.

POTENTIALS RELATED TO COMPLEX MOVEMENTS

Potentials Recorded During Button Press Tasks

A Dual Button-Press Task. The first study on slow potentials related to skilled movements was done by Papakostopoulos (1978). Slow potentials were recorded during a task, in which subjects started a single sweep of an oscilloscope spot by means of their left thumb. A second button press with their right thumb had to be made in order to stop the sweep in the middle portion of the screen within 40–60 milliseconds after sweep onset. Incorrect trials were divided in "too early" (20–39 milliseconds), "too late" (60–79), and "other" (out of these intervals). Early and late errors decreased significantly in the later part of the experiment, but increase in correct trials was not significant. In other words, the behavioral results were ambiguous, which prevents reliable conclusions about a relation between slow potential changes and performance. Slow potentials preceding this task were compared to those preceding a simple button press with one hand or with both hands simultaneously. EEG was recorded at EP_z, C_z, (see Fig. 5.1) and over the pre and postcentral areas on both sides. Epochs of 200 milliseconds prior to and following EMG onset on the left side were used as RP and N_3 values, respectively. Thus, the RP measure in this experiment is a mixture of NS and N_2 (Table 5.1). Both RP and N_3 were larger preceding the skilled task than preceding unilateral or bilateral button presses. Moreover a positive wave was present about 400 milliseconds after EMG onset, which was called the skilled performance positivity (SPP). Because the behavioral results were ambiguous, however, it is difficult to speak about a developing skill. Therefore, it is questionable, whether the positive component is really related to skill. Taylor (1978) argued that a component can only be related to skill if it changes with increasing practice. Because such findings were not offered by Papakostopoulos (1978) his interpretation seems susceptible to criticism. In the next section we see how Taylor (1978) attacked the problem of skill-related potentials.

A Multiple Button-Press Task. Taylor's subjects held on their laps a box in which 2 rows of 3 buttons were mounted. The right index finger rested upon button 1. The experiment consisted of 3 successive conditions. In Condition I a simple button press had to be made and in Condition II a series of 6 button presses in a specified order. Condition III was identical to Condition I. EEG was recorded from F_z, C_z, and the postcentral areas on both sides. EEG was investigated from 2 seconds prior to movement onset until 2 seconds thereafter. RP was calculated over the last second prior to the movement. Taylor's RP is a mixture of RP, NS, and N_2 (Table 5.1). Next, a peak was measured from 50 milliseconds prior to 50 milliseconds after the first button press, thus coinciding with the N_2 and N_3 component. Finally slow potentials were measured over the whole 2-seconds period following the first button press.

The results showed a decrease of total response time over trials, for the serial button press condition. Also time taken for the second response diminished as compared to that for the first in the series. Thus, a learning effect was present and the ERP results could be related to these effects. Moreover, there was no difference in RP between conditions I and III, indicating that here no learning was present. The RP did not show significant differences, but the peak value was significantly larger during the skilled task than during conditions I and III, in line with Papakostopoulos' findings (Papakostopoulos, 1978). Moreover a systematic increase in RP amplitude over trials was found, while response time decreased.

During acquisition of the task the RP increased equally for the four derivations studied. Once the response was learned the RP over the frontal area decreased, in contrast to the one at C_z and the left postcentral area. Taylor interpreted her results in line with Keele and Summers (1976): When a response tends to become automatized, less attention and feedback is necessary to maintain a particular performance level. Taylor's data suggest that the frontal area plays a role in monitoring output and feedback.

So far we can summarize the results as follows. A skilled task is preceded by a larger RP than an unskilled movement. A developing skill is accompanied by increasing RP amplitudes. An acquired skill remains preceded by a centrally localized negativity.

A final point should be referred from this study, that is: the presence of a continued negativity during the series of button presses, lasting for more than 2 seconds. With simple ballistic movements we have seen that almost immediately after movement onset the negative BP, N_2 and N_3 are followed by a positive wave complex. In contrast to that, a skilled performance seems to be accompanied by a sustained surface negativity and not by a positive wave, as Papakostopoulos (1978) claimed.

Taylor suggested that the attentional demands for the skilled movements might be reflected in this sustained negativity. We see next that other investigators came to a comparable conclusion, when studying goal directed movements.

Potentials Recorded During Goal-Directed Movements

Another example of a complex movement is the smooth goal-directed hand movement studied by Grünewald-Zuberbier and Grünewald (1978). In that study subjects moved a rod from a fixed starting point to a contact plate by making a wrist flexion. They were instructed to look at a fixation area in front of them during the movements. After having made contact, subjects returned the rod to the starting position. EEG was recorded bilaterally from precentral and parietal areas. It was analyzed in several epochs: (A) 3 seconds prior to movement onset, (B) from movement onset to contact plate, (C) during stop on plate, (D) during backward movement. In a later comparable study Grünewald and Grünewald-Zuberbier (1983) gave subjects feedback about their performance by means of a visual stimulus 1.5 seconds after the end of the backward movement. This provided an epoch E, in which subjects waited for the feedback. A final 1.5 seconds epoch F terminated the trial. For the moment we only discuss the results obtained during epochs A–D (Fig. 5.7). EEG changes during epochs E and F are described at the end of this chapter, when prefeedback potentials are discussed.

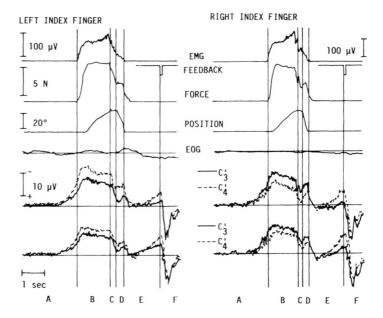

FIG. 5.7 Ramp positioning movements of the left and right index finger. Recording of rectified EMG, force, position, vertical EOG, and slow potential shifts in left and right precentral (C_3', C_4') and postcentral (C_3'', C_4'') EEG. A: premovement interval, B: positioning movement interval, C: stop on target interval, D: return to starting position interval, E: feedback interval, F: post feedback interval. : feedback. Preceding and during the movement (A–D) amplitudes are larger contralateral to the movement side. Preceding feedback amplitudes are larger over the right hemisphere, irrespective of movement side (from Grünewald & Grünewald-Zuberbier, 1983).

Following the bilateral RP a sustained negativity was found during the wrist flexion over all four electrode positions, with larger amplitudes over the precentral areas. Also a consistent hemisphere difference was present over the latter regions with larger amplitudes contralateral to the movement side. The sustained negativity, recorded in this experiment during the execution of a goal-directed movement resembles very much the negative activity during the sequence of button presses, Taylor studied. The Grünewalds suggested that the goal directedness of the movement is crucial for the emergence of the accompanying surface negative activity. In other words these authors underline the attentional demands during the execution of the movement, as Taylor did.

Grünewald and Grünewald-Zuberbier (1983) provided further evidence for this viewpoint in a review, in which three types of motor activity were described: positioning movements, isometric ramp contractions, and hold contractions. We now briefly describe their results.

Positioning Movements. Self-paced flexion movements of the index finger were carried out at different speed, either as a ballistic or as a ramp movement. Preceding EMG onset of both response modes, a bilateral symmetrical RP was followed by an asymmetric NS. After EMG onset of the ballistic movement a short negative wave was found, lasting until the EMG peak was reached. A similar result was found with the ramp movement: The negativity increased until the EMG maximum was reached. After the maximal displacement had been reached, a positive deflection followed the negative waves in both response modes. The authors pointed to comparable results of Vaughan et al. (1970) who studied slow epidural potentials in monkey prior to and during a wrist extension. These authors also found a sustained negative wave over the precentral motor cortex during prolonged contraction, with larger amplitudes contralateral to the movement side. The negative wave was also followed by a positive one at the end of the contraction.

Isometric Ramp Contractions. Because in former experiments joint movements were carried out, Grünewald-Zuberbier, Grünewald, Schuhmacher, and Wehler (1980) investigated whether such movements were a prerequisite for the potentials recorded. Therefore the following isometric ramp contraction was studied. Holding a rod between thumb and index finger, subjects had to press the rod against a force transducer and to relax immediately thereafter. The minimal rod displacement at the beginning and the end of the contraction marked the contraction interval. Again a negative slow wave was found over precentral, postcentral, and parietal regions, both preceding and during the muscle contraction. Over the former two electrode positions amplitudes were larger contralateral to the movement side. The authors concluded that both a change in limb position and an isometric change of force is accompanied by negative EEG activity.

Hold Contractions. In the next experiment it was investigated whether voluntary contraction per se was a sufficient condition for a negative wave to show up. Subjects had to produce a certain force level and to maintain it for some seconds. In the holding period tonic muscle activity was present, not aimed at an external goal. The same electrode positions were used as in the former experiment. Following the RP and NS, amplitudes in the hold condition decreased to even become positive. The contralateral preponderance diminished to become insignificant at about 600 milliseconds. The hold contraction lasted nearly 2 seconds. Thus, a purposeless muscle contraction is not accompanied by surface negative activity in the EEG. A similar conclusion was drawn by Otto, Benignus, Ryan, and Leifer (1977) and Otto and Benignus (1978), who found positive, not negative activity during sustained muscle contraction without an external goal.

Potentials Recorded During Tracking Tasks

In a recent experiment of Deecke, Heise, Kornhuber, Lang, and Lang (1984) slow potentials were recorded preceding voluntary and accompanying stimulus-guided movements. While fixating a point in front of them, subjects held a ballpoint in their right hand equip with a trigger device. The trigger was activated by a self-paced movement, bringing the ballpoint in contact with a piece of paper. Following the trigger activation, a visual or a tactile stimulation was produced. In the visual condition a light spot on a TV screen placed in the left visual field started to move for 1 second, forming a straight line in any direction. Then the light spot changed direction and a second line was produced, again for 1 second, after which the spot disappeared. The V-like figures were generated in randomly changing directions. The subject had to track the lines on his piece of paper (Fig. 5.8). In the tactile condition, a spring-suspended stylus was brought into contact with the volar side of the left hand, invisible to the subject. Two lines in different direction were produced on the palm of the hand, comparable to the visual condition. Again the subject was to follow the lines on his piece of paper. Stimuli in both conditions moved at a speed of 4 cm per second. Some of the subjects were also confronted with the stimuli in a no-tracking visual or tactile control condition. Electrode positions are indicated in Fig. 5.8. EEG was analyzed for 6 seconds, 2 seconds being pretrigger. In the following we deliberately restrict ourselves to the major ERP findings, omitting details that ask for a too elaborate discussion.

In the tracking condition RP was recorded over all electrode positions except at F_3. It should be noted that for the first time a RP has been found over the occipital area. RP onset over the visual cortex was earlier in the visual than in the tactile condition. No other RP differences were found between the visual and tactile tracking condition. Maximum RP amplitudes were found at C_z and FC_z. The overall picture was characterized by three sharp positive waves, which were found during the 6-second recording epoch (Fig. 5.9). The first one, following the self-paced movement, reached a peak at 450 milliseconds after the contact was made between ballpoint and paper. The second positive wave had a similar peak latency after the change in stimulus direction. A third positive deflection was found after the termination of the second tracking movement. The distribution over the midline from F_z to P_z was different from the one found over the convexity of the skull. Over the first group of electrodes the positive wave immediately followed a P_1 component. Over the second group a 200 millisecond negativity followed the trigger, before the positive wave emerged. That negative

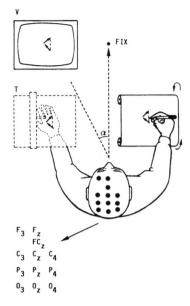

FIG. 5.8 Experimental set-up for the recording of slow potentials during visual and tactile tracking movements. Stimuli are presented on the left side. Movements are carried out on the right side (from Deecke et al., 1984).

component was largest over the hemisphere contralateral to the stimulation side and more pronounced over the respective sensory areas, i.e., P_4 and O_2 in the visual condition and C_4 in the tactile condition.

Following the first positive peak a second negative wave emerged, which was larger in the visual than in the tactile condition. Amplitudes reached maximal values over the hemisphere contralateral to the stimulation side. They were larger over the contralateral occipital electrodes in the visual task and over the parietal electrodes in the tactile task. A second positive deflection followed the negative wave and was succeeded by another negative wave, preceding the resetting of the stimulus. Now no difference in potential distribution was found between tactile and visual conditions.

Both the negative and positive potentials found in these experiments need to be discussed in some more detail. We first call attention upon the negative waves, to discuss the positive waves after that. From the foregoing results it might be concluded that preceding tracking more brain areas are activated than in the no-tracking condition in which only a simple movement was required (placing the ballpoint on the piece of paper). Preceding tracking a negative slow wave is present over the sensory projection areas, where the stimulus to be tracked will be projected upon. In the visual condition this is the right parietal and occipital

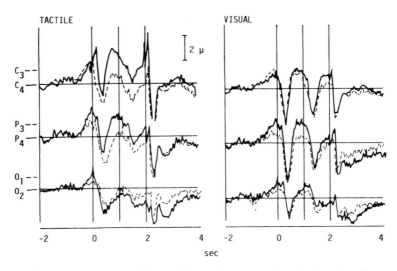

FIG. 5.9 Cerebral potentials preceding and accompanying visual and tactile guiding movements over a 6-seconds period. Monopolar recordings versus linked ears. Baseline 0–500 milliseconds. Onset of movement at 2 seconds. Change in direction of stimulation at 3 seconds. Reset of stimulus at 4 seconds. $P_4 > P_3$ in both conditions, $O_2 > O_1$ in the visual condition, $C_4 > C_3$ in the tactile condition. (from Deecke et al., 1984).

area, in the tactile condition the right central and parietal area. Preceding a simple movement NS is larger over the central area contralateral to the movement side. In the tactile tracking condition the opposite is found, although the movement has to be carried out with the right hand. This can be explained in a more or less similar way as the results of Taylor (1978) and of the Grünewalds (1978, 1983). Remember that these authors suggested an attentional process to be reflected in the sustained negativity found over the contralateral motor cortex during the complex movement. The increased negativity found over the respective projection areas preceding the tracking movements, might also point to an attentional process. Here attention is directed to the sensory stimuli having immediate consequences for the movement to follow. Remember that an increased negativity was found three times. First, prior to the movement used to put the ballpoint on paper. This movement triggered visual or tactile stimuli, that had to be attended to allow for a movement in the correct direction. Second, prior to the change in direction of the visual or tactile stimuli. Here attention had to be directed to the change in stimulation, in order to allow for a second movement in another direction. Third, prior to the reset of the stimulation, indicating the end of the tracking movement.

So far we have seen two different ways in which attention might play a role in the execution of a movement. First to perform the multiple button-press task

(Taylor, 1978) or the goal-directed movements (Grünewald-Zuberbier and Grünewald, 1978) attention seems to be directed to the cortical sensory-motor structures, involved in the execution of the movement. In this case proprioceptive projection areas might be facilitated by attention underlying processes. Second, guiding of movements by exteroceptive stimuli activates cortical areas upon which these stimuli are projected. Here attention directed to these areas, might be accompanied by excitation of superficial dendritic synapses.

Next we see, how, at a more abstract level, still other brain areas might be activated as part of other attentional processes. We start, however, to comment upon the positive waves, recorded during the tracking.

With simple movements the negative RP, NS, N_2, and N_3 are followed by a predominantly positive wave complex. We have seen that most of the underlying neural activity is related to central and peripheral feedback mechanisms (Arezzo & Vaughan, 1975, 1980; Vaughan et al., 1970). The positive wave, described by Papakostopoulos in his dual button-press task could very well be related to the right-finger button press. With longer lasting complex movements the positive waves are postponed until the movement comes to an end. In other words, it is likely that the positive wave complex reflects the end of the movement and not its initiation. In the tracking experiments, however, the positive waves are present earlier than the end of the movement. They are found after the start of tracking the first line, after the start of tracking the second line, and after the lifting of the ballpoint. Whereas the latter positive wave could be related to the end of the movement as the positive waves described earlier, this can not be the case with the first two positive waves. Deecke et al. (1984) called these positive waves relaxation potentials, suggesting that positive waves reflect the end of an activation. Although this suggestion is interesting, it seems not compatible with the increase in cell discharges found in the superficial cortical layers in the somatosensory cortex during postmovement positivity (Arezzo & Vaughan, 1980). For the moment there is no direct evidence for the correctness of the relaxation interpretation.

Potentials Preceding Feedback about Foregoing Movements

The last potentials we want to discuss are recorded preceding feedback giving the subject information about the correctness of his performance. The relevant research was started by the Grünewalds (1983). In Fig. 5.7 it was shown that preceding and during the goal-directed movement negative activity was present over the central areas, amplitudes being larger over the cortex contralateral to the movement side. Once the movement was finished (Fig. 5.7D), subjects had to wait during a 1.5 second interval, until information was given about their results. This information, indicating either a hit, an undershoot, or an overshoot, could be used by the subjects to ameliorate their performance. As can be seen in Fig.

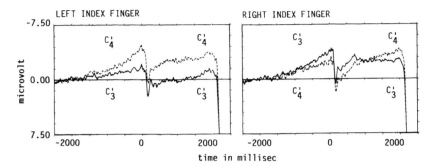

FIG. 5.10 Slow potentials preceding a finger flexion on either side. Subjects had to press a button every 20 seconds. Two seconds following each button press a visual feedback signal indicated whether that button press was too early, in time or too late. Note the contralateral larger amplitudes preceding a unilateral movement and the right hemisphere preponderance preceding the feedback signal, irrespective of movement side (from Brunia & Damen, unpublished).

5.7 prefeedback potentials are negative and larger over the right hemisphere, independent of the hand used to make the movement. The Grünewalds, who have replicated these findings several times, suggest that the meaning of the stimulus for spatial aspects of the action is crucial. This interpretation is based on neuropsychological evidence that the right hemisphere is especially involved in space perception.

Recent experiments done in our laboratory (Brunia & Damen, unpublished) cast some doubt upon this interpretation. In contrast to the Grünewalds, we studied simple ballistic movements, namely a button press with either the right- or the left index finger. The movements had to be made every 20 seconds, allowing a 2 seconds inaccuracy in their timing. Two seconds after each button press a feedback signal provided information about the length of the interval, which was either correct or too short or too long. As can be seen in Fig. 5.10 a right-hemisphere predominance of the prefeedback potentials was found again. Although these results ask for a detailed study of the distribution of the prefeedback potentials, two preliminary hypotheses can be suggested. First, it is possible that both timing and spatial aspects of movements are organized in the right hemisphere. Second, the kind of feedback provided by the Grünewalds and by ourselves, can be categorized as Knowledge of Results. The latter suggestion, then, would imply that for the guidance of movements from a more abstract level, the right hemisphere would play a major role. We realize that much research is needed to clarify this issue. It can be suggested, though, that we have found a third manner for attention to play a role in the preparation for action.

In the experiments discussed in this section feedback has been presented in the form of abstract signs (a light spot, an illuminated line, etc.). One could think of another way of presenting subjects information about their performance, e.g., by using spoken or written words. In that case it could be expected that the left hemisphere would become more important, although it is known that the right hemisphere has some language capabilities. We hypothesize that again negative activity will show up preceding verbal feedback, although we express no opinion about the brain area where it is to be expected. We consider this as yet another way in which attention to information about a preceding performance can play a role in a future action.

CONCLUSION

In contrast to ballistic movements, complex movements are continuously controled by different kinds of feedback. Proprioceptive, kinaesthetic, and exteroceptive information contribute to an immediate control of ongoing movements. Furthermore information about spatial and temporal aspects of the movement can be given after movement execution to influence future movements. We suggest that attention to these different kinds of information is reflected in negative waves recorded over the relevant cortical areas. On the basis of the description of the different kinds of feedback we conclude to the following.

First, we interpret the negative activity over the central somatomotor cortex as an indication of an attentional process directed at the proprioceptive and kinaesthetic feedback during the movement.

Second, we consider the negative activity over the sensory projection areas (visual end tactile) as a reflection of an attentional process directed to the information, that is of immediate relevance for the future movement.

Third, we consider the negative activity over the right hemisphere, preceding spatial or temporal information about passed performance, and relevant for the movement to follow, as a reflection of an attentional process directed to structures, which might be related to Knowledge of Results, or, at least, to the organization of temporo-spatial characteristics of movements.

Fourth, we expect a negativity over a yet unknown cortical area, related to verbal feedback, presented in an auditory or visual way. This could be a special case of Knowledge of Results.

These four possibilities of influencing ongoing or future movements could fit in a distributed motor control system.

Summary

In this chapter movement-related potentials are discussed. A distinction is made between simple ballistic movements and complex movements. Potentials related to simple ballistic movements are distinguished in those preceding and those following movement onset. Because there exists no uniform nomenclature, an attempt is made to categorize the different components, described by different authors in various ways. Research of complex movements did start recently. Guidance of complex movements can be brought about in different ways. The second part of this chapter describes the various kinds of information used to guide movements. It is suggested that attentional processes, directed to these various kinds of information, are reflected in different slow negative waves, each having its specific potential distribution.

ACKNOWLEDGMENTS

The final draft of this study has been written during a stay at the Zentrum für interdisziplinäre Forschung of the University at Bielefeld, F.R.G. The author wishes to thank his co-workers from Tilburg University, Gerhard and Erika Grünewald and Herbert Heuer for their valuable criticism upon an earlier version of the text.

REFERENCES

Arrezzo, J., & Vaughan Jr., H. G. (1975). Cortical potentials associated with voluntary movements in the monkey. *Brain Research, 88,* 99–104.

Arezzo, J., & Vaughan Jr., H. G. (1980). Intracortical sources and surface topography of the motor potential and somatosensory evoked potential in the monkey. In H. H. Kornhuber & L. Deecke (Eds.), *Motivation, motor and sensory processes of the brain. Progress in brain research* (Vol. 54, pp. 77–83). Amsterdam: Elsevier, North–Holland Biomedical Press.

Arezzo, J., Vaughan Jr., H. G., & Koss, B. (1977). Relationship of neuronal activity to gross movement-related potentials in monkey pre and postcentral cortex. *Brain Research, 132,* 362–369.

Bates, J. A. V. (1951). Electrical activity of the cortex accompanying movements. *Journal of Physiology* (London), *113,* 240—257.

Berger, H. (1929). Über das Elektrenkephalogramm des Menschen. *Archiv für Psychiatrie und Nervenkrankheiten, 87,* 527–570.

Brunia, C. H. M., & Vingerhoets, A. J. J. M. (1980). CNV and EMG preceding a plantar flexion of the foot. *Biological Psychology, 11,* 181–191.

Caspers, H., Speckmann, E. J., & Lehmenkühler, A. (1980). Electrogenesis of cortical DC potentials. In H. H. Kornhuber & L. Deecke (Eds.), *Motivation, motor and sensory processes of the brain. Progress in brain research* (Vol. 54, pp. 3–17). Amsterdam: Elsevier, North–Holland Biomedical Press.

Deecke, L., Grözinger, B., & Kornhuber, H. H. (1976). Voluntary finger movement in man: Cerebral potentials and theory. *Biological Cybernetics, 23,* 99–119.

Deecke, L., Heise, B., Kornhuber, H. H., Lang, M., & Lang, W. (1984). Brain potentials associated with voluntary manual tracking: Bereitschaftspotential, conditioned premotion positivity, directed attention potential and relaxation potential. In R. Karrer, J. Cohen, & P. Tueting (Eds.), *Brain and information: Event related potentials* (Vol. 425, pp. 450–464). Annals of the New York Academy of Sciences.

Deecke, L., & Kornhuber, H. H. (1977). Cerebral potentials and the initiation of voluntary movement. In J. E. Desmedt (Ed.), *Attention, voluntary contraction, and event-related cerebral potentials* (pp. 132–150). Basel: Karger.

Donchin, E., Ritter, W., & McCallum, W. C. (1978). Cognitive psychophysiology: The endogenous components of the ERP. In E. Callaway, P. Tueting, & S. H. Koslow (Eds.), *Event-related brain potentials in man,* (pp. 349-411). New York: Academic Press.

Evarts, E. V. (1981). Role of motor cortex in voluntary movements in primates. In J. M. Brookhart & V. B. Mountcastle (Eds.), *Handbook of physiology: Sec. I. The nervous system. Vol. II. 2,* (pp. 1083-1120). Bethesda, MD. American Physiological Society.

Fuster, J. M. (1981). Prefrontal cortex in motor control. In J. M. Brookhart & V. B. Mountcastle (Eds.), *Handbook of physiology: Sec. 1. The nervous system: Vol. II. 2,* (pp. 1149-1178). Bethesda, MD: American Physiological Society.

Gemba, H., Sasaki, K., & Hashimoto, S. (1980). Distribution of premovement slow cortical potentials associated with self-paced hand movements in monkeys. *Neuroscience Letters, 20,* 159-163.

Gerbrandt, L. K. (1977). Analysis of movement potential components. In J. E. Desmedt (Ed.), *Attention, voluntary contraction, and event-related cerebral potentials* (pp. 174-188). Basel: Karger.

Gerbrandt, L. K., Goff, W. R., & Smith, D. B. (1973). Distribution of the human average movement potential. *Electroencephalography and Clinical Neurophysiology, 34,* 461-474.

Gilden, L., Vaughan, Jr., H. G., & Costa, L. D. (1966). Summated human EEG potentials with voluntary movement. *Electroencephalography and Clinical Neurophysiology, 20,* 433-438.

Grünewald, G., & Grünewald-Zuberbier, E. (1983). Cerebral potentials during voluntary ramp movements in aiming tasks. In A. W. K. Gaillard & W. Ritter (Eds.), *Tutorials in ERP research Endogenous components* (pp. 311-327). Amsterdam: North-Holland.

Grünewald-Zuberbier, E., & Grünewald, G. (1978). Goal directed movement potentials of human cerebral cortex. *Experimental Brain Research, 33,* 135-138.

Grünewald-Zuberbier, E., Grünewald, G., Schuhmacher, H., & Wehler, A. (1980). Scalp recorded slow potential shifts during isometric ramp and hold contractions in human subjects. *Pflügers Archiv für die gesammte Physiologie, 389,* 55-60.

Hashimoto, S., Gemba, H., & Sasaki, K. (1979). Analysis of slow cortical potentials preceding self-paced hand movements in the monkey. *Experimental Neurology, 65,* 218-229.

Hashimoto, S., Gemba, H., & Sasaki, K. (1980). Premovement slow cortical potentials and required muscle force in self-paced hand movements in the monkey. *Brain Research, 197,* 415-423.

Hazemann, P., Metral, S., & Lille, F. (1978). Influence of force, speed and duration of isometric contraction upon slow cortical potentials in man. In D. A. Otto (Ed.), *Multidisciplinary perspectives in event-related brain potential research* (pp. 107-111). Washington, DC: U.S. environmental protection agency.

Keele, S. W., & Summers, J. J. (1976). The structure of motor programs. In G. E. Stelmach (Ed.), *Motor control: Issues and trends* (pp. 109-142). New York: Academic Press.

Kornhuber, H. H., & Deecke, L. (1965). Hirnpotentialänderungen bei Willkürbewegungen und passiven Bewegungen des Menschen: Bereitschaftspotential und reafferente Potentiale. *Pflügers Archiv für die gesammte Physiologie, 248,* 1-17.

Kristeva, R., & Deecke, L. (1980). Cerebral potentials preceding right and left unilateral and bilateral finger movements in sinistrals. In H. H. Kornhuber & L. Deecke (Eds.), *Motivation, motor and sensory processes of the brain. Progress in Brain Research* (Vol. 54, pp. 748-754). Amsterdam: Elsevier, North-Holland Biomedical Press.

Kristeva, R., Keller, E., Deecke, L., & Kornhuber, H. H. (1979). Cerebral potentials preceding unilateral and simultaneous bilateral finger movements. *Electroencephalography and Clinical Neurophysiology, 47,* 229-238.

Libet, B., Wright, Jr., E. W., & Gleason, C. A. (1982). Readiness potentials preceding unrestricted 'spontaneous' vs. preplanned voluntary acts. *Electroencephalography and Clinical Neurophysiology, 54,* 322-335.

Libet, B., Wright, Jr., E. W., & Gleason, C. A. (1983). Preparation- or intention-to-act, in relation to pre-event potentials recorded at the vertex. *Electroencephalography and Clinical Neurophysiology, 56,* 367–372.

Otto, D. A., & Benignus, V. A. (1978). Slow positive shifts during sustained motor activity in humans. In D. A. Otto (Ed.), *Multidisciplinary perspectives in event-related brain potential research* (pp. 131–133). Washington, DC: U.S. environmental protection agency.

Otto, D. A., Benignus, V. A., Ryan, L. J., & Leifer, L. J. (1977). Slow potential components of stimulus, response and preparatory processes in man. In J. E. Desmedt (Ed.), *Attention, voluntary contraction and event-related cerebral potentials* (pp. 211–230). Basel: Karger.

Papakostopoulos, D. (1978). Electrical activity of the brain associated with skilled performance. In D. A. Otto (Ed.), *Multidisciplinary perspectives in event-related brain potential research* (pp. 134–137). Washington DC: U.S. Environmental Protection Agency.

Papakostopoulos, D. (1980). A no stimulus, no response, event-related potential of the human cortex. *Electroencephalography and Clinical Neurophysiology, 48,* 622–638.

Rohrbaugh, J. W., & Gaillard, A. W. K. (1983). Sensory and motor aspects of the contingent negative variation. In A. W. K. Gaillard & W. Ritter (Eds.), *Tutorials in ERP research: Endogenous components* (pp. 269–310). Amsterdam: North–Holland.

Rohrbaugh, J. W., Syndulko, K., & Lindsley, D. B. (1976). Brain wave components of the contingent negative variation in humans, *Science, 191,* 1055–1057.

Sakata, H., Takaoka, Y., Kawarasaki, A., & Shibutani, H. (1973). Somatosensory properties of neurons in the superior parietal cortex (area 5) of the rhesus monkey. *Brain Research, 64,* 85–102.

Sasaki, K., Gemba, H., & Hashimoto, S. (1981). Premovement slow cortical potential on self-paced hand movements and thalamo-cortical and cortico cortical responses in the monkey. *Experimental Neurology, 72,* 41–50.

Sasaki, K., Gemba, H., Hashimoto, S., & Mizuno, N. (1979). Influences of cerebellar hemispherectomy on slow potentials in the motor cortex preceding self-paced hand movements in the monkey. *Neuroscience Letters, 15,* 23–28.

Shibasaki, H., Barret, G., Halliday, E., & Halliday, A. M. (1980a). Components of the movement-related cortical potential and their scalp topography. *Electroencephalography and Clinical Neurophysiology, 49,* 213–226.

Shibasaki, H., Barret, G., Halliday, E., & Halliday, A. M. (1980b). Cortical potentials following voluntary and passive finger movements. *Electroencephalography and Clinical Neurophysiology, 50,* 201–213.

Shibasaki, H., & Kato, M. (1975). Movement-associated cortical potentials with unilateral and bilateral simultaneous hand movement. *Journal of Neurology, 208,* 191–199.

Taylor, M. J. (1978). Bereitschaftspotential during the acquisition of a skilled motor task. *Electroencephalography and Clinical Neurophysiology, 45,* 568–576.

Vaughan Jr., H. G. (1974). The analysis of scalp-recorded brain potentials. In R. F. Thompson & M. M. Patterson (Eds.), *Bioelectrical recording techniques. Part B. Electroencephalography and human brain potentials,* New York: Academic Press.

Vaughan Jr., H. G., Costa, L. D., & Ritter, W. (1968). Topography of the human motor potential. *Electroencephalography and Clinical Neurophysiology, 25,* 1–10.

Vaughan Jr., H. G., Gross, E. G., & Bossom, J. (1970). Cortical motor potentials in monkeys before and after upper limb deafferentiation. *Experimental Neurology, 26,* 253–262.

Wiesendanger, M. (1981). Organization of secondary motor areas of cerebral cortex. In J. M. Brookhart & V. B. Mountcastle (Eds.), *Handbook of physiology. Sec. I. The nervous system: Vol. II, 2,* (pp. 1121–1147). Bethesda, MD: American Physiological Society.

6 Sensorimotor Integration: The Role of Pyramidal Tract Neurons

Christoph Fromm
Max-Planck-Institut für biophysikalische Chemie

> *The organs which concur in muscular contraction are the brain, the nerves, and the muscles. We have no means of distinguishing in the brain those parts which are employed exclusively in sensibility, and in intelligence, from those that are employed alone in muscular contraction. The separation of the nerves into nerves of feeling and nerves of motion is of no use: this distinction is quite arbitrary.*
> —Magendie, 1824

The technique of recording from single neurons in conscious animals, pioneered by Jasper, Ricci, & Doane, (1958), Hubel (1959), and Evarts (1964), has decisively narrowed the gap between brain and behavior. Simultaneously, the opportunity of monitoring the conscious brain at work has established a major link between neuroscientists and experimental psychologists interested in problems of motor control. As an outcome of the first decade of neuronal recording in behaving animals, the work session of the Neurosciences Research Program (NRP) on "Central Control of Movement" (Evarts et al., 1971) marks a cornerstone by its departure from previous simplistic and narrow views that existed in the neurobiological domain toward a more multidisciplinary approach. By defining and formalizing the problems of motor behavior this NRP meeting and a symposium 3 years later (Teuber, 1974) ushered to the field of neurophysiology in much of the current concepts and issues of motor control. Likewise, a convergent shift of the psychological approach toward an understanding of the processes and even neuromechanisms underlying movement could be observed (Pew, 1974; Schmidt, 1975; Stelmach, 1976). Undoubtedly, this method and other recently refined techniques to record neuronal activities in man (e. g., Brunia, this vol.) have contributed in setting common concepts and goals that can be approached by the different disciplines including the area of robotics and prosthetic devices.

In stressing the impact of recording neuronal activity in the behaving animal the limitations of this method must not be forgotten. One disadvantage is the use of highly trained animals in order to achieve consistent behavioral events and reproducible motor performance. Consequently, there have been only very few contributions by single unit recordings (e. g., Gilbert & Thach, 1977; Maton, Burnod, & Calvet, 1983) to the important issue of learning of motor skills. The influence of overtraining on correlations found between neuronal discharge frequency and parameters of movement is also largely unknown and must be taken into account by any parametric analysis (see Maton et al., 1983). Furthermore, the inherent restraint in using a stereotype learned task creates one of several sampling errors when recording from a certain brain structure. Although giving a glimpse on the properties of neuronal populations related to a certain behavioral response, the features of so many neurons being unrelated to the particular task remain undetected. Moreover, the correlations between cortical neuron discharge and movement performance are found to be variable and flexible (Evarts & Tanji, 1974; Fetz & Finocchio, 1975; Fromm & Evarts, 1977; Fromm, Wise, & Evarts, 1984; Muir & Lemon, 1983), depending on a variety of behavioral conditions that have to be clearly specified.

We face the problem that even consistent temporal and parametric correlations as found in pretrained tasks cannot necessarily be taken to imply a functional relation between a neuron and a motor response. To dissociate such correlations would be an alternative way and a crucial test for a functional relationship. This has been done by operant conditioning of neuronal activity using reinforcement procedures. For example, monkeys had learned to control differentially the levels of single motor cortex unit activity and of the electromyogram (EMG) of a number of contralateral arm muscles (Fetz & Finocchio, 1975). Operantly reinforced neuronal burst discharges were found to be associated with coactivation of specific arm muscles (or vice versa). The authors found several neurons that exhibited a strong temporal, intense, and consistent covariation with the same muscle even under different behavioral response conditions. However, the dissociation of this relationship by rewarding the monkey for increased neuronal activity and simultaneous suppression of EMG in the coactivated muscle was invariably successful. Of course it remained unknown to what extent the operant conditioning technique itself might have influenced operant control of neuronal discharge and some explanation for this dissociation is given in section III. But the conclusion of Fetz and Finocchio (1975) must be underlined: Even strong temporal or consistent neuron-motor response correlations are neither necessary nor sufficient to establish a direct functional, not to mention a causal relationship.

Likewise, if the input and output connections of recorded neurons have not been verified, no really meaningful conclusion can be drawn as to the functional significance of these neurons. Many single unit studies try to categorize, however, neurons recorded in a restricted brain area into "functional classes" on the basis of their similar or different associations with a particular aspect of behavior. Here, the identification of anatomical connectivity for the same neurons is a prerequisite for any functional interpretation. As to the input site, there have been and will be enormous, possibly insurmountable difficulties due to theoretical and technical limitations, if one considers the vast convergence and complex interactions of inhibitory and excitatory influences from so many different sources impinging upon a neuron. In contrast, the output targets can be much better identified in some cases. In particular, it appeared promising to attack the coding of efferent motor commands, because the "decoding" mechanisms and transformation of efferent signals into muscular force by the motor unit are quite well known.

This is the case for the pyramidal tract neuron (PTN) and one reason why this descending cortical subsystem has attracted so much attention ever since the beginning of cortical neuron recording in the awake monkey and why PTNs are the focus of the present article. Evolutionary, the immense expansion of the pyramidal tract and motor cortex in subhuman primates and in man parallels the development of manual skill, the increasing repertoire of fractionated finger movements to allow their independent and discrete action in almost endless combinations, as has been reviewed by Phillips and Porter (1977). To understand the "truly" human motor skills of the hand and fingers has been the great challenge to those investigating the PTNs in the monkey. The bundling of the efferent axons to form the medullary pyramid gives the classical definition of the pyramidal tract and offers an easy experimental tool to identify PTNs in the monkey by their antidromic activation via chronically implanted stimulating electrodes. Origin, structure and terminal action within the spinal cord of the pyramidal tract have been fairly well delineated. Axons of PTNs may supply collateral branches to various sites of the neuraxis as they descend, but, according to Humphrey and Corrie (1978), to a lesser extent than previously thought. Some PTNs terminate in the brain stem, mainly distributed to the dorsal column nuclei, some nuclei of cranial nerves and to the reticular formation; thus their axons do not continue into the spinal cord. However, about 80% of the PTN population in the monkey have been shown to send their efferents to the spinal cord (Humphrey & Corrie, 1978) termed *corticospinal cells*. It is this close coupling of the PTNs with the spinal sensorimotor apparatus that should permit more meaningful interpretation of their functional relationship. Moreover, a direct cortico-motoneuronal component of the pyramidal tract occurs in the primate evolution in parallel with the precise control of distal movements (cf. Phillips & Porter, 1977). These direct connections of PTNs with the motoneurons in the ventral horn could recently be demonstrated by using the spikes of single PTNs as trigger to average the EMG of limb muscles (Fetz, Cheney, & German, 1976). This cross-correlation technique has proved to be particularly valuable in solving the forementioned problem of causal linkage at least for the subpopulation of cortico-motoneuronal (CM) cells of the pyramidal tract, which indeed appears to be the most significant component in man (Schoen, 1964). This powerful technique and its remarkable results are described in detail (Section II.4, and Fig. 6.4).

At this point, the view must be emphasized that the pyramidal tract constitutes a "multicomponent system" (Wiesendanger, 1981). PTNs are located in different subdivisions of the "sensorimotor" cortex of monkey, which is akin to the perirolandic cortex of the human brain. These different cortical fields of the primary somatosensory, primary motor, and secondary motor cortex serve common functions in sensorimotor integration, but each of these areas receives differential afferent input and might have a specialized function. In the first section I describe in more detail the roles played by these cortical subdivisions in sensorimotor coordination and in the guidance, initiation and preparation of voluntary movement, because the neuronal mechanisms and connectivity of the sensorimotor cortical complex are regarded essential for the understanding of the central issue "perception and action." Moreover, most textbook or review articles lack a comprehensive and actual coverage of this topic. PTNs located in these different fields of the sensorimotor cortex also project to different targets, for example to the dorsal horn of the spinal cord where they can modulate the transmission of ascending somatosensory information (section II.4.). It becomes already clear that any separation into "sensory" and "motor" roles of PTNs is very artificial. The intriguing question has been posed in some of the own experiments (Fromm & Evarts, 1982) whether there is no common denominator for PTNs of different cortical areas except the bundling together of their axons as they descend. Thus the properties of postcentral PTNs in the "sensory" cortex during movement performance are compared to those of their counterparts in the "motor" cortex (section III).

PTNs are incorporated into various internal feedback loops (e. g., Allen & Tsukahara, 1974; Eccles, 1973). PTNs are known to be the targets of learned motor programs and they also receive a fast "response" feedback from somatosensory afferents (section II). The different significance of cutaneous versus proprioceptive inputs to PTNs is discussed in section II.3. This prepares for section III in which some findings on PTN discharge patterns with precise fine movements, during maintenance of postural stability and during accurate control of finely graded muscle forces have been summarized—motor skills for which continuous *proprioceptive* information appears to be critical. The notions of feedforward and feedback controls can indeed be readily exemplified on the PTNs. During performance of fine and precise motor skills the PTN is viewed to operate in a closed-loop control system. For preprogrammed movements (large "ballistic" movements and fast, "triggered" reactions) the PTN is involved in open-loop control, probably confering some additional speed on such movements. Finally, the functional significance of the "transcortical reflex loop," a currently much debated issue, is related to recent findings in human subjects and to the responses of PTNs to kinesthetic inputs that were evoked under different conditions of motor behavior.

I. THE SOMATIC SENSORIMOTOR CORTEX

I.1. The Origin of the Pyramidal Tract

The somatic sensorimotor cortex, as defined here, and also the fields of origin of the pyramidal tract comprise Brodmann's cytoarchitectonic areas 6, 4, 3a, 3b, 1, 2, and 5 in the monkey, which are comparable to Brodmann's (1909) similar map of the human brain. The following subdivisions of the sensorimotor cortical complex can be distinguished (Fig. 6.1) and are in part considered further later: the primary somatosensory cortex (SI) of postcentral gyrus comprising the areas 3, 1, and 2; the caudally adjacent area 5 of the parietal cortex; the second somatic sensory cortex (SII) hidden in the anterior bank of sylvian fissure; the primary motor cortex (MI) of the precentral gyrus being identical with area 4, and immediately rostrally adjacent to MI, the area 6. This cytoarchitectonic area consists of at least two different fields, i.e., the secondary or supplementary motor area (MII) located for the most part on the mesial surface of the hemisphere and the premotor cortex (PM) of the lateral area 6.

Modern anatomical tracer-techniques have demonstrated the location and distribution of corticospinal cells within these cortical fields. Across these different fields of origin corticospinal cells were found to lie exclusively in cortical layer V and to form clusters of three to eight neurons of about 500 µm in extent separated by variable gaps; corticospinal cells are somatotopically organized and show the greatest variation of size and also the largest cell bodies in area 4 whereas more uniform- and small-sized pyramidal cells were labeled in the other cortical fields (Catsman-Berrevoets & Kuypers, 1976; Jones & Wise, 1977; Murray & Coulter, 1981; Toyoshima & Sakai, 1982). Of the pyramidal tract fibers, area 4 gives rise to 31%, area 6 to 29%, and the postcentral-parietal cortex to 40% (Russel & DeMyer, 1961). The relative distribution of corticospinal neurons within these cortical fields is difficult to assess quantitatively. Thus the given proportions vary considerably between two reports on the monkey (Murray & Coulter, 1981; Toyoshima & Sakai, 1982), possibly because of problems in defining the caudal boundary of area 4 with area 3a and its rostral border with area 6. Certainly the primary motor cortex of area 4 contains the largest percentage of corticospinal cells (31–51%) of any single field, thus leaving 27–60% for the postcentral-parietal fields (SI, SII, and all parts of area 5) and 9–22% for area 6 (with the majority lying in the MII region).

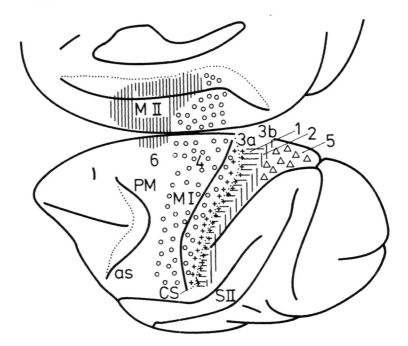

FIG. 6.1 Surface view of the left hemisphere of the rhesus monkey with its mesial aspect shown, inverted, at top. From rostral to caudal: the premotor cortex (PM) and supplementary motor area (MII) of area 6; the primary motor cortex (MI) of area 4; the postcentral fields 3a, 3b, 1, and 2 composing the primary somatosensory cortex; and parietal area 5. Fine dotted lines indicate the bottom of arcuate sulcus (as) and of the central sulcus (cs). Notice that area 3a is buried in the floor, and area 3b in the caudal bank of central sulcus (crosses) whereas area 4 extends deeply into the precentral wall (open circles).

Interestingly, other major corticofugal systems to various subcortical structures also arise largely from the so-defined sensorimotor cortex. Each of the efferent systems is characterized by a specific size of its cell bodies, being uniform across the different sensorimotor fields, and, like the PTNs, the other corticofugal populations are all somatotopically organized and similarly segregate into cluster-like groups of cell colonies, which apparently constitute the *modular arrangement of cortical output neurons* (Jones & Wise, 1977). In providing the common origin for the most important corticofugal systems the subdivisions of the sensorimotor cortex are also extensively interconnected with each other (Jones & Powell, 1970), thus suggesting their unity and common role in motor control. However, one must be aware of the functional specialization of these subdivisions. This view derives from the different thalamic inputs to, and from the multiple representations of the body in, these fields. Thus, there is a need to review some recent findings on these areas in order to understand the specialized roles played by each of those cortical subdivisions in the context of sensorimotor integration.

I.2. The Somatosensory Areas and Parietal Area 5

The following features provide the basis of our current understanding of the postcentral areas: multiple sensorimotor representations of the body in each of the four subfields of SI, instead of the single "body-map" previously shown by Woolsey (1958); in parallel, separate representations of somesthetic submodalities within these SI-subfields; a hierarchical processing of information directed rostro-caudally in SI; and a close cooperation of certain postcentral-parietal fields with the precentral motor cortex (MI).

The thalamic input that relays the somesthetic information of the dorsal column-lemniscal pathway is confined to the four subfields of SI and to SII; the "cutaneous" core of this thalamic nucleus projects most heavily to area 3b whereas a shell region relaying "deep" receptor modalities projects to areas 3a and 2 (Jones, 1983). On the cortical level, somatosensory modalities are thus segregated, with representation of slowly and rapidly adapting mechanoreceptors of the skin in area 3b and 1, with predominantly group I muscle afferents in area 3a, while area 2 receives primarily joint and also muscle afferent input. This modality-segregation is paralleled by separate and complete representations of the body surface in area 3b and area 1, and again by an orderly representation of deep body tissues in area 2; a fourth parallel representation of the body's muscle afferents has been speculated for area 3a (Kaas, Nelson, Sur, & Merzenich, 1981).

In addition, a hierarchical processing of information within SI in the rostro-caudal direction has been evidenced by both cortical connectivity pattern (Jones, Coulter, & Hendry, 1978; Vogt & Pandya, 1978) and single unit recordings in awake monkeys. The area 3 projects mainly backward to area 1 and from there to area 2 and area 5. Cells in area 3b have small, simple receptive skin fields, whereas towards the posterior areas the size, complexity, and submodality convergence of the receptive fields increase; single units in area 2 for example exhibit an enormous specialization as a result of this cortical processing, in responding specifically to the roughness, texture, shape, and geometry of objects (Hyvärinen, 1982; Sakata & Iwamura, 1978). Accordingly, selective lesions of these areas have shown that area 3b as the cutaneous cortical input station is critical for all forms of tactile discrimination whereas area 1 more specifically contributes to surface-texture discrimination and area 2 to the aspects of stereognosis (Carlson, 1981; Randolph & Semmes, 1974), findings that are supported by clinical observations (Roland, 1976). Furthermore, monkeys with ablations of SII are impaired on both texture and shape discrimination learning (Murray & Mishkin, 1984).

The somatosensory cortical areas are normally considered in relation to somesthetic perception. But it is self-evident that the somesthetic sense is naturally used only in connection with "active" touch, the active grasping and exploratory manipulation of objects with the hand and fingers (Gordon, 1978). For one, the somesthetic perception is enhanced in acuity and efficiency by the active movement. On the other side, the exploratory movement itself has to be continuously adjusted on the basis of tactile and proprioceptive inflow. This would call for a close interrelationship between the primary or secondary motor areas (MI, MII) and those regions of SI and adjacent parietal cortex that possess proprioceptive, highly processed tactile information and stereognostic capabilities.

In fact, MI has been shown to be reciprocally via cortical fibers connected with area 2 and rostral part of area 5 and with SII, MI sends also axons to areas 3a and 1 but lacks any connection with area 3b; in addition, MII is linked with caudal SI and area 5 (Jones et al., 1978; Jones & Powell, 1970; Vogt & Pandya, 1978). Recordings from awake monkeys have shown that the responses to the same somesthetic stimulus of neurons in areas 3a, 1, and 2 (but not in area 3b) are different, depending on the "motor set" of the animal (Nelson, 1985), or that sensory responses in area 5 neurons are even contingent upon the subsequent execution of movement (Chapman, Spidalieri, & Lamarre, 1984). Responses of feature-detection neurons in area 2 (to specific forms, material, and edges of objects) are enhanced under the condition of active movement (Iwamura, Tanaka, Sakamoto, & Hikosaka, 1985); and an increasing number of neurons in area 5 become only involved in active manipulation of fingers and reaching forward to objects in the immediate extrapersonal space (Mountcastle et al., 1975). Such neuronal changes that are dependent on the motor context or performance of movement might reflect the mechanisms of "corollary discharge" (Evarts et al., 1971; Sperry, 1950), possibly exerted by MI or MII via those cortico-cortical connections with SI and area 5 and/or by way of corticofugal modulation of the afferent somatosensory pathways (involving, for example, the PTNs). Whatever the exact mechanisms, the concept of "efference copy" (von Holst & Mittelstaedt, 1950) is of importance in this connection. Consider a subject actively scanning with its fingers a textured surface. By using such a task in the monkey, Darian-Smith, Goodwin, Sugitani, & Heywood (1985) have shown that the activity of peripheral mechanoreceptors as well as of SI neurons depends both on the spatial characteristics of the surface and on the pattern of finger movement across the surface. Thus, SI neuronal populations would provide ambiguous information about the spatial features of the surface, being confounded with information concerning the pattern of finger movement. The authors then gave some circumstantial evidence that the independent encoding of the scanning finger movement by MI neurons would contribute to the unique specification of the patterned surface in SI.

Thus, we conclude that especially for exploratory manipulations, reaching, and grasping of objects precentral "motor" areas work in concert with certain postcentral-parietal areas and might have complementary functions. Besides its generally accepted role in somesthetic perception, SI might even compensate temporary dysfunction of MI, which has been induced by local cortical cooling (Sasaki & Gemba, 1985), thus supporting Woolsey's (1958) original idea that the distinctions between MI and SI are relative.

I.3. The Primary Motor Cortex (MI)

Indeed, the aforementioned connection *from SI to MI* appears to constitute the major route by which the fast somatosensory input from the peripheral receptors reaches motor cortex within 10–20 msec. This is the outcome of a number of recent experiments that have been stimulated by a hotly debated question as to the afferent pathways to MI (Jones, 1983; cf. section II.1). This fast somatosensory input is believed to form the afferent link of the transcortical loop in which the PTN is incorporated to constitute the descending limb as is further elucidated in section II.3. The fine organization within MI of this input in relation to the output neurons is considered in section II.2. Although this somatosensory input represents the important peripheral "response" feedback to MI, it is certainly not the only input impinging upon MI.

Other pathways convey the "central motor programs" to MI. Motor programs, as defined here, are assemblies of innate or learned motor commands in a sequence ordered and structured in advance of movement execution, specifying more or less the entire requirements of the evolving movement. The importance of centrally programmed MI activity can be shown by the method of deafferentation. Following dorsal root section initiation and performance of sound-triggered fast ballistic movements that were highly trained and rather uncontrolled as to their target requirements were grossly unaltered (Lamarre, Bioulac, & Jacks, 1978). Pattern and timing of neural activity in MI in advance of the movement was not modified in contrast to the ceasing of discharge associated with voluntary movement in most SI neurons following deafferentation (Bioulac & Lamarre, 1979). Additional ablation of the cerebellum in these monkeys led to a parallel delay of 150 msec of both the onset times of MI discharge and reaction times, which already points to the role of the cerebellum in the initiation of fast ballistic movements; in the same deafferented and cerebellectomized monkeys Lamarre et al. (1978) could further demonstrate that the execution of these ballistic movements depended on the integrity of MI.

Central programs that require MI for execution are transmitted by two major pathways. One is the *thalamic input* to MI relaying signals almost exclusively (with some modest contribution from spinothalamic afferents) *from the cerebellar output nuclei*; the projections of this cerebellar relay nucleus, the "motor" thalamus, are restricted to MI and to some part of lateral area 6, the premotor cortex (Asanuma, Thach, & Jones, 1983; Jones, 1983; Schell & Strick, 1984). The cerebellar dentate-thalamo-cortical pathway is considered important for open-loop control of MI in the initiation of fast learned movements, encoding in particular the timing aspects of skilled movements, and in setting MI to allow for fast "automatic" reactions; the cerebro-cerebellar loop involving the interpositus nucleus is considered in relation to internal feedback to MI (e. g., Brooks & Thach, 1981). The other important input to MI is a *cortical* one from the secondary motor areas, namely *from MII*. MII is an essential link between the frontal lobe and the *basal ganglia*. The major output of the basal ganglia in turn is directed (via a separate thalamic relay) to MII, thus reaching the primary motor cortex only after further processing in MII (DeLong, Georgopoulos, & Crutcher, 1983; Schell & Strick, 1984). The well-known global function of the frontal lobe is the planning of serial future behavior based upon past and present experience (Ingvar, 1975). On the basis of all available experimental and especially clinical evidence, Marsden (1982) pointed out that "the basal ganglia are responsible for the automatic execution of learned motor plans." To achieve a certain motor plan the basal ganglia would normally run sequences of the plan's constituent motor programs (Marsden, 1982).

In summary, MI appears to receive information about the sequences of learned skilled motor acts, elaborated by the basal ganglia together with MII, and motor commands—conveyed by the cerebellar output—that specify particularly timing parameters of the forthcoming movement (start, stop, velocity) (Brooks & Thach, 1981; Evarts, 1981). What is now the special task for MI? It is "a primary device for fast adjustment of programmed motor patterns to afferent signals" (Conrad, 1978). We had specified this broad view by assuming that the PTN in the motor cortex may be a *summing point* for such central programs and afferent response feedback (Evarts & Fromm, 1978). According to this concept, PTN output should signal discrepancies between the actual movement (as revealed by feedback) and the intended movement (corresponding to the central program). This mode of operation is obviously less important for preprogrammed fast movements and when the errors are large (cf. the results on deafferentation referred to previously), but might become significant for other sorts of motor behavior (sections II.3. and III.).

I.4. The Supplementary Motor (MII) and Premotor (PM) Cortex

Investigation of the secondary motor fields, the medial MII and the lateral PM around the arcuate sulcus (Fig. 6.1) has become the major interest of motor neurobiologists during the last years, and research on the "secondary motor areas" is still a rapidly expanding field. Although having intimate reciprocal connections with each other, MI, MII, and PM are nowadays considered distinct entities on the basis of their thalamic connectivity (Asanuma et al., 1983; Schell & Strick, 1984; cf. section I.3.), morphological, neurophysiological properties and on clinical grounds (for recent reviews see Freund, 1984; Roland, 1984;

Wise, 1985; Wise & Strick, 1984; Wiesendanger, 1986, in press). MII and PM also display separate somatotopical representations (Muakassa & Strick, 1979). In the current discussion, the supplementary and premotor areas are readily labeled with "higher" motor processing. However, neither their access to motor executive structures nor the direct sensory input to these areas can be dismissed (see Wiesendanger, 1986, in press). In fact, PM and MII share a number of properties with MI; especially movement-related behavior of PTNs in MI and MII, when directly compared in the same monkey, appears to be quite similar (Tanji & Kurata, 1982). At the single neuron level, a number of features are only quantitatively different in the three fields. Low- and high-level motor controls are always interlaced and cannot be regarded as mutually exclusive. Indeed, one would even postulate for any area involved in motor preparation or planning that it is able to preset and condition the effector apparatus (e. g., for postural changes in advance of movement) and to suppress stimulus-evoked "automatic" reactions if undesired in the context of the motor plan (cf. I.4.3.).

"*Motor planning or preparation*" are often loosely used and ill-defined terms, involving various functional aspects and processes: a decision process to move or not to move after evaluation of external cues or "internally" arising "ideas"; selection of the appropriate strategy to serve the intended goal; addressing of subroutines or programs for sequenced or concurrent movements to be executed, including coordination of distal and proximal limbs and bimanual task-coordination (characteristicly affected by unilateral ablation of MII, Brinkman, 1984); the adaptive setting of motor executive structures for expected environmental events. The available data on the MII and PM of many investigations are all compatible with anyone or several of these aspects. Furthermore, neuronal mechanisms of selective attention cannot easily be distinguished from "motor-set", especially when discussed in relation to PM (Wise & Mauritz, 1985), because lesion of PM has been reported to cause an inattention for both somatosensory and visual modalities (Rizzolatti, Matelli, & Pavesi, 1983).

At the present it seems difficult to summarize the functions of the PM and MII, unless in global terms. Both appear to be involved in the planning and preparation of future action. Let us instead pose the crucial question: What actually is the evidence for some function that is not shared by any other brain area? There are two recent studies, one in man (I.4.1.) and the other on single neurons in the monkey's MII (I.4.2.), that gave exciting new insight into possibly unique roles played by the supplementary motor area. Besides the almost revolutionary impact of these discoveries, the following presentation of these findings should give the reader an impression of the promising avenues that have been opened by new techniques to monitor human brain activities and by using complex paradigms in trained monkeys.

I.4.1. Findings on the Human MII. The local cortical activity changes of the working human brain can be measured by monitoring changes in the amount

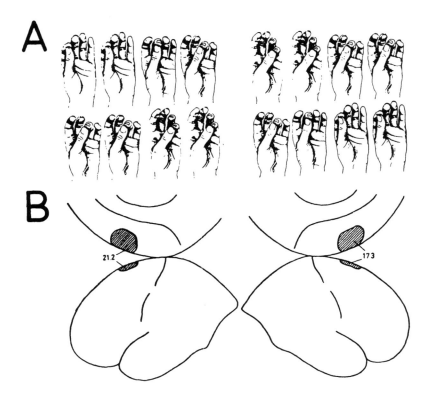

FIG. 6.2 *A:* One run shown of fast isolated finger movements in a sequence to be performed within 10 sec and then repeated (after the first eight on the left, continue with upper row on the right). rCBF measurements were taken while subjects actually performed the motor sequence task or during "internal" rehearsing the task with the same speed. *B:* Mean increase of rCBF in percentage during internal planning the sequence task, values corrected for diffuse increase in blood flow. Solely in a region that corresponds to the human MII there is a significant increase ($p < 0.01$) of blood flow; the left hemisphere is to the left, average of three subjects; right hemisphere average of five subjects. (From Roland et al., 1980). Reprinted by permission.

and regional distribution of radioactively labeled blood. A 254-channel detector system has been used to monitor the regional cerebral blood flow, rCBF[1] (Roland, 1984; Roland, Larsen, Lassen, & Skinhøj, 1980). Recently, a positron emission tomography has been combined with the isotope-inhalation of an inert gas. The combined technique then allowed measurement or rCBF also in subcortical structures, displayed in transverse sections of the brain (Roland et al., 1982).

---

[1]The rCBF is linearly related to the regional cortical oxygen consumption of the human working brain and is thought to reflect the neuronal and glial activity changes. Its spatial resolution is quite good (about 6 mm), but this metabolic technique takes up to 40 sec to measure.

If a complex, self-paced sequence of finger movements is *executed* by subjects (Fig. 6.2 A), there are strong bilateral increases of rCBF in MII, modest in PM cortex and SII, and only contralateral in the hand region of MI and SI (Roland et al., 1980). Moderate to substantial increases of rCBF were seen in addition in subcortical regions comprising the basal ganglia, mostly again bilaterally (Roland et al., 1982). This points to the close cooperation of MII with the basal ganglia, in particular for control of skilled sequenced movements (see Marsden, 1982; section I.3.). During execution of other complex sequenced or concurrent movements or during speech, MII is always bilaterally activated (see references in Roland, 1984). However, if the same motor-sequence task is *only being planned* by the subjects, i.e., mentally conceived, without overt EMG activity, the only area that is activated is the MII cortex (Fig. 6.2 B). Patients with a damage to MII are well known for their paucity of self-generated limb movements and of spontaneous speech (see review by Wiesendanger, 1986). Taken together, the human MII might be implicated in the planning and generation of self-initiated motor acts, specifically, in addressing of subroutines for skilled sequenced movements (Roland, 1984).

1.4.2. Neuronal MII-Processes in Preparation or Suppression of Movement. Following instructions that indicate to the monkey the direction of the next limb movement there are sustained changes of neuronal activity until the onset of movement that is triggered by a subsequent stimulus. Such "motor-set" activity related to the particular direction of ensuing movement was observed in MI (Tanji & Evarts, 1976), MII (Tanji, Taniguchi, & Saga, 1980), in PM (Godschalk & Lemon, 1983; Wise & Mauritz, 1985) and in the prefrontal cortex (Kubota & Funahashi, 1982). Set-related activity in PM might only reflect the motor preparation per se, for the respective direction of impending movement (Wise & Mauritz, 1985). An entirely different and novel property has very recently been discovered for instruction-related responses of neuronal elements in MII (Tanji & Kurata, 1985). The neuronal patterns to be described might reflect an engagement of MII in the preparatory process of "let-go" or prevention of the evolving movement.

In these experiments, the movement to be executed, a key press of the monkey's hand, was always the same. Two instructions (auditory mode and tactile mode) informed the monkey how to deal with two subsequent signals. In the auditory mode (Ins. Aud.) the instruction warned the animal to start the movement in response to a tone ("A" in Fig. 6.3) but to remain motionless if there were an intervening vibrotactile signal ("T" in Fig. 6.3) applied to the hand. A different instruction (tactile mode, Ins. Tac) would tell the monkey to perform promptly the key press in response to the vibrotactile cue but to withhold movement for the auditory signal, thus trigger and nontrigger signals were reversed. In some trials only the movement-trigger signal was delivered, in other trials it would be preceded by the nontriggering signal, which was given at varying times of 2.1–3.9 sec after the instruction. The four different combina-

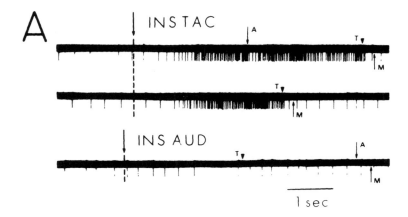

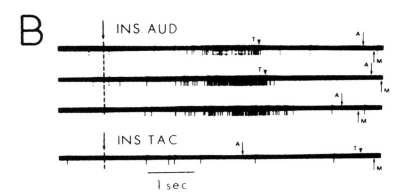

FIG. 6.3 Discharges of two MII neurons illustrated in single trials. The neuron in *A* shows a type I, the neuron in *B* a type II response to two modes of instructions given in this paradigm. For further details see text. Time of instruction (INS. TAC or INS. AUD) indicated by large arrow and dashed line to the left of traces; arrows labeled "A" denote onset of 1000-Hz tone, arrowheads labeled "T" mark occurrence of the vibrotactile signal (40-Hz vibration of the hand), both signals lasting about 200 msec. Upward arrow labeled "M" marks onset of key-press movement of the hand. (From Tanji & Kurata, 1985). Reprinted by permission.

tions (three of them are depicted in Fig. 6.3) of instructions, nontriggering, or triggering signals were given in randomized order. Great care was taken, already during training, to ascertain the absence of any EMG changes in the muscles during the delay period.

Two types of instruction-related responses were seen in MII neurons: a gradual increase of activity after the instruction, continuing until appearance of the triggering signal, regardless of whether an intervening nontrigger signal occurred

(Fig. 6.3 A, type I). Type II neurons (Fig. 6.3 B) showed a postinstruction discharge that gradually increased and then ceased with the appearance of the nontriggering signal (upper two records in B), or the discharge would subside near the time when the nontriggering signal would have been presented (third record), in short, whenever the monkey became assured that the next signal must be the movement trigger. Notice further that (1) the postinstruction responses for both types of neurons were differential, being selective for one kind of instruction (seen in two thirds of these MII cells); and (2) that both neuronal types do not covary activity with movement execution, a common observation for instruction-related neurons in MII but unlike those in MI (Tanji et al., 1980). Direct comparison in the same animal revealed that only 22% of task-related precentral MI neurons displayed postinstruction changes, mostly nondifferential (with both modes) and weak. Nondifferential "anticipatory" activity following both instructions is to be expected for MI neurons, because the same movement is being prepared for. Type II responses were never seen in MI neurons (Tanji & Kurata, 1985).

In interpreting the results of Fig. 6.3, any attentional processes can hardly be inferred nor would discriminatory processing of the different trigger stimuli offer a likely explanation. The cautious conclusion drawn by Tanji and Kurata (1985) seems to be very valid: The MII is "specifically involved in the preparatory process leading to correct initiation or suppression of movement in response to particular modalities of forthcoming sensory signals." In support of this conclusion, short-time dysfunction of MII-cortex by local reversible cooling led to erroneous key presses made by the animal in the same paradigm (Tanji, Kurata, & Okano, 1985).

1.4.3. MII Sets the Responsiveness of Precentral Neurons to Kinesthetic Input. A "gating" influence exerted by MII on the precentral motor cortex had been originally suggested by Wiesendanger (see his reviews, 1986 and in press). He applied electrical stimulation (surface or intracortical microstimulation) to the MII cortex. Following such stimulation, short-latency reflex responses of precentral MI neurons, evoked by muscle stretch in the anesthetized animal or by passive limb displacement in the awake monkey, were then diminished. A possible substrate for this modulatory action has been directly demonstrated by Tanji and Kurata (1985): MII neurons that display the properties illustrated in Fig. 6.3 can send their axons to the precentral MI cortex. Kurata and Tanji (1985) furthermore suggested that through this projection the responsiveness of precentral MI neurons to the kinesthetic (vibrotactile) stimulus might be altered, depending on whether the stimulus is used as movement trigger or not. When the vibrotactile stimulus applied to the hand (cf. the paradigm described in I.4.2.) served as movement trigger, there was a short-latency response in MI neurons being time locked to the vibrotactile signal, followed by a second movement-associated discharge (refer to Fig. 6.9, sketching these precentral responses). But when the monkey was required to refrain from moving, the short-latency response to the same vibrotactile stimulus was often attenuated and the later activity was absent (Kurata & Tanji, 1985).

In conclusion, there is evidence for a modulatory action of the MII cortex on the responsiveness of MI neurons to somatosensory inputs according to the instruction, intent or set. Such a presetting mechanism might also underlie the phenomenon illustrated for a PTN in MI (Fig. 6.7). This influence of MII on other brain areas seems to be central for the adaptive changes of early transcortical reflex responses, observed to vary with the instruction (Evarts & Tanji, 1974) or motor behavior (e. g., Fromm & Evarts, 1978). In addition, fast stimulus-evoked reactions (termed "M3" in Fig. 6.9) and the corresponding late "set-dependent" responses in precentral PTNs (e. g., Evarts & Tanji, 1976) might be either suppressed or let through by this mechanism.

II. INPUT–OUTPUT-RELATIONSHIP OF PYRAMIDAL TRACT NEURONS

II.1. Somatosensory Input to PTNs

Reflex discharges in the pyramidal tract following afferent stimulation have been originally observed by Adrian and Moruzzi in 1939. Following the simultaneous demonstrations in 1973 by Evarts of rapid responses in primate PTNs to peripheral disturbances and of long-loop responses in the human EMG by Marsden's group (see his review, Marsden, Rothwell, & Day, 1983), there has been revived interest in this issue that has stimulated a vast amount of studies. By now it is clear that all kinesthetic joint and proprioceptive muscle afferents as well as cutaneous receptors have fast (10–20 msec) access to motor cortex and its PTNs (see reviews by Asanuma, 1981; Evarts, 1981; Phillips & Porter, 1977; Porter, 1981; Wiesendanger & Miles, 1982).

The ascending pathway of the dorsal column-lemniscal system undoubtedly carries these messages, because section of the dorsal column abolished reflex responses of MI neurons (Brinkman, Bush, & Porter, 1978) and peripherally evoked short-latency potentials over MI (Asanuma, Larsen, & Yumiya, 1980). However, there exists as yet a discrepancy between anatomical and neurophysiological findings as to whether this afferent information might be mediated directly via the motor thalamus to area 4 of MI, or indirectly via SI, or by both routes at unknown proportions (Asanuma & Arissian, 1984; Asanuma et al., 1983; Jones, 1983; Wiesendanger & Miles, 1982). After all, ablation of SI (even sparing areas 3a and 5) can reduce the evoked MI potential by as much as 75% (Asanuma et al., 1980), being consistent with observations on long-loop responses in patients (cf. Marsden et al., 1983). Area 2 as the solely left source for transmitting peripheral input to MI (besides area 5 and SII, see section I.2.)

had never been much in favor for a number of reasons. Area 3a appears to be the "missing link" also in the present debate alluded to earlier. This field that receives the short-latency input from muscle group I afferents within 5 msec had been documented in the cat to project to area 4, but until recently anatomical evidence for such a connection in the primate was missing (cf. Jones, 1983; Jones, Coulter, & Hendry, 1978; Wiesendanger & Miles, 1982). Very small injections of a tracer substance into the forelimb area of MI has been found to label projection cells in area 3a (Porter & Ghosh, 1985). Thus, we can conclude that SI including area 3a is an important relay of short-latency proprioceptive and cutaneous input to MI and to its PTNs.

II.2. Input-Output-Organization within MI

The most important feature that has been discovered in this regard is the *strict input-output-coupling*, the close somatotopical relation between the receptive field of a PTN and its motor action or "motor field" (Asanuma, 1981; Evarts, 1981; Porter, 1981). For example, a PTN controlling wrist movements is likely to receive its input from that joint, or from muscles acting around the wrist, or from a cutaneous field of that zone. PTNs located in a *cluster* (cf. section I.1.) usually have similar inputs and motor targets and also "behave" similarly with voluntary movement (e.g., Asanuma, 1981; Cheney, Kasser, & Fetz, 1985; Evarts & Fromm, 1977, 1978; Lemon, 1981 a,b; Murphy et al., 1978). There is a multiple representation of a particular input zone of the limb within MI cortex that is paralleled by multiple discontinuous clusters of PTNs destined for a particular motor field, with these clusters being distributed over quite a large area of MI and overlapping with cortical colonies for other muscles (Murphy, Kwan, Mackay, & Wong, 1978; Phillips & Porter, 1977).

The *somatotopical arrangement* of the primate forelimb is so that PTNs controlling movements around a certain joint form horseshoe-shaped bands within MI. The outermost band is for the shoulder, the next ring for the elbow surrounding the one for the wrist, and neurons controlling hand and finger muscles are situated within a central core nearest the central sulcus (Lemon, 1981 b; Murphy et al., 1978; Sessle & Wiesendanger, 1982). It became also clear from these and other studies, that for neurons controlling more proximal zones of the limb, deep proprioceptive input is most important while for neurons of the hand-finger core cutaneous input is more significant (Lemon, 1981 a). Interestingly, there appears to be a segregation of cutaneous and kinesthetic inputs at least for the hand representation of the squirrel monkey into two spatially separate regions: a caudal zone receiving cutaneous input (MIc) and a rostral concentration of deep joint and muscle afferent input (MIr). Both zones have the same motor output; thus, there is double representation of the wrist and digits within MI with differential sorting of modalities (Strick & Preston, 1983).

This finding reminds of the multiple representations and modality-segregation in the postcentral cortex (section I.2.).

However, in the macaca forelimb area of MI, such a clear-cut separation of both modalities has not been seen (Lemon, 1981 b; Murphy et al., 1978). Moreover, substantial degree of convergent modality- input onto single PTNs has been evidenced by a number of studies (cf. Lemon, 1981 a; Wiesendanger, 1973; Wiesendanger & Miles, 1982). The proportion of "mixed" PTNs, i. e., those being influenced by deep and cutaneous receptors, could only be underestimated in the experiments referred to earlier due to technical limitations (undetectable subthreshold effects and inhibitory responses that often remained unnoticed). Most importantly, in all these experiments that tried to differentiate the type of afferent input, the peripheral stimuli were not tested during movement performance. It is, however, with different motor strategies and types, and during actively maintained posture where such peripheral response feedback is of relevance and where convergent cutaneous or deep receptor input to PTNs might be used in a different way. We have pointed out that an examination of peripheral response pattern, at least at the cortical level, must be carried out with an understanding of the *muscle activity,* because such activity affects the pattern, magnitude, and even sign of PTN responses to somatosensory stimuli (Fromm, Wise, & Evarts, 1984). Consequently, we must also see the dynamics of the described input–output-organization.

II.3. Significance of Cutaneous Versus Proprioceptive Reflex Responses in PTNs

Differential involvement of two foci in the finger-hand region, in controlling either movements that use kinesthetic (MIr) or tactile feedback (MIc) for their execution and guidance, remains an attractive concept (Strick & Preston, 1983). In seeking analogies between segmental and transcortical loops, Evarts (1981; and in Evarts & Fromm, 1981) stressed the entirely different significance of such proprioceptive and exteroceptive reflexes. He gave credit to Sherrington's earlier definitions in pointing out that exteroceptive reflexes are in response to disturbances and stimuli arising from the environment. They would involve recruitment of the large phasic motoneurons and should be characterized by a rather *flexible* relationship between the strength of the cutaneous stimulus and the sign and strength of the response. Obviously, if an object gets into contact with the fingers it might either trigger an intensified movement toward the object or a withdrawal response. Long-loop EMG responses in man following stimulation of skin receptors seem to be consistent with these considerations (Jenner & Stephens, 1982). Observations on cutaneous PTN reflex responses have been scanty, especially under the condition of active movement in the conscious monkey. PTNs having an input from the glabrous skin of the fingers might either discharge with voluntary flexion of the digits, thus advancing the input zone towards an object, or with finger extension, i. e., withdrawal from the object (cf. Lemon, 1981 a; Murphy et al., 1978). Conversely, PTNs with the similar excitatory receptive field (as revealed in the relaxed monkey by experimenter's testing) may show either excitation or inhibition during active movement leading to touch of the receptive field (Lemon, 1981 a). These observations would suggest a flexible input–output-relation of PTNs in MI for exteroceptively guided finger movements.

Recalling Sherrington's notion that *proprio*-ceptive reflexes operate in relation to events arising from within the organism but only secondarily to the actions of the environment, Evarts (1981) went on to point out that the effects of proprioceptive feedback are "mild," directed towards the tonic small spinal motoneurons and small tonic PTNs. We have postulated (Evarts & Fromm, 1981) the special role of segmental and transcortical proprioceptive reflexes in instantaneous corrections of *small internally generated irregularities* to enable accurate postural stability and the smooth, small transitions from one postural state to another. Internal disturbances arising within the neuromuscular system (like hysteresis and fatigue effects of the muscles) create errors that affect mostly precise small movements. There is overwhelming evidence that the proprioceptive loops can effectively deal with small errors in closed-loop operation and with compensation for variations in muscle properties but become *ineffective* for *compensation* of *large, external load* disturbances and in control of large movements (Bizzi, Polit, & Morasso, 1976; Desmedt & Godaux, 1978; Evarts & Fromm, 1981; Goodwin, Hoffman, & Luschei, 1978; Houk & Rymer, 1981; Marsden et al., 1983; Sanes & Evarts, 1983; 1984). This point is being stressed here, because in the experimental situation torque pulses and external load disturbances were commonly applied to reveal the nature of the transcortical reflex. But a teleological significance of external "load compensation" cannot necessarily be inferred from this fact.

Muscle and partly also joint receptors have nonlinear response characteristics with greatest sensitivity for small amplitude signals (Goodwin et al., 1978; Houk & Rymer, 1981; Matthews, 1972). Thus, proprioceptors appear to be unsuitable for control of large forces and large movements. Recordings of spindle afferent discharge in the human nerves gave dramatic insight into the high sensitivity of these proprioceptors: Spindle afferents responded to smallest deviations during the course of a slow voluntary finger movement in such a way as to maintain smooth shortening of the isotonic contraction (Vallbo, 1973). During slow isotonic contractions the fusimotor drive to the muscle spindles is to some extent linked to the skeletomotor drive to the receptor-bearing muscle. Moreover, the fusimotor drive has been suggested to form a temporal template of the intended movement and also to be adjusted to the load opposing the movement. As a consequence, spindle discharge rate remains about the same at different joint positions during load-bearing position holding in man, even increasing at the *shorter* muscle length with increasing size of the load (Hulliger, Nordh, &

Vallbo, 1982; Prochazka & Hulliger, 1983). Thus, the concomitant fusimotor bias keeps the spindle afferent firing at a constant level, at least in the face of small *slow* voluntary changes of muscle length. However, for faster movements exceeding about 80 degrees/sec of angular joint displacement, the muscle spindle afferent behaves like an unbiased "passive" length transducer (Prochazka & Hulliger, 1983). Thus again, this proprioceptive feedback would seem to be more effective in controlling slow accurate movements and postural maintenance.

This concept of "servo-assistance" of movement (Matthews, 1972; Phillips, 1969) has provided the framework for the proposed positional servomechanism of the transcortical loop. A servomechanism involves a closed-loop system in which the controlling signal is derived from comparison of a reference signal with a feedback signal that specifies the actual output. Subtracting this feedback signal from the input signal leaves an error signal (negative feedback), which indicates the extent to which the actual performance falls short of the desired. There should be a proportional relation between input and output over some range, depending on the gain of the servo-loop. Phillips (1969) specifically proposed a continuous feedback from coactivated spindle afferents to those PTNs whose output is directed to the motoneurons (Fig. 6.9). But the same is possible for the muscle tension receptors, or for both (length and force receptors) to control the parameter of muscular stiffness (e.g., Houk & Rymer, 1981). Here the question arises whether the proprioceptive servo-loop via PTNs would indeed fulfil the two prerequisites: (1) negative feedback and (2) proportional relation between input and output signals.

As to point (1), and in analogy with the known segmental reflexes via spinal motoneurons, one would assume that proprioceptive input signalling a mismatch between intended and actual movement will inhibit PTNs when producing excessive (too fast, too large) displacements and excite PTNs when producing insufficient displacements. In the experimental situation, this hypothesis has been tested by applying loads or torque pulses that assist or oppose voluntary movements. In general agreement with the proposed negative feedback it has been established that external forces slowing or halting that movement with which a PTN would increase its activity would tend to reflexly excite that neuron or vice versa (see Fig. 6.7 and Fig. 6.8, left part). This is the typical response property of MI PTNs if they are closely related to the particular movement being disturbed (for example, Conrad, 1978; Evarts & Fromm, 1978). For cortico- motoneuronal (CM) cells in MI (see following section II.4.) the input–output-relationship is unequivocal: they are always reflexly excited either by events opposing the shortening of their identified target muscle or by passive joint movements that stretch their target muscles (Fig. 6.9; Cheney et al., 1985).

As to point (2), there is a proportional relationship between, for example, spindle afferent input and the strength of PTN reflex response, thus fulfilling the second important requirement of the proprioceptive servo-loop. In the anesthetized baboon, PTNs exhibited graded responses to graded ramp stretches of hindlimb muscles, which these PTNs were shown to be linked with (Sakai & Preston, 1978). And we have seen (Fromm et al., 1984) in the conscious monkey that the dynamic responses of PTNs increased with the velocity of ramp displacements of the forearm. Similar quantitative relations between size of muscle stretch and the long-loop response in the EMG (called M2 in Fig. 6.9) exist in man (Marsden et al., 1983).

II.4. Destination of PTN Output

Like their origin (section I.1.), PTNs lying in those different cortical fields have possibly rather specialized and different projection patterns. Whereas PTNs of precentral MI undoubtedly have the most direct access to the skeleto and fusimotoneuronal pools of the ventral horn and to the intermediate zone of spinal cord, PTNs located in MII and in area 3a seem to terminate within the intermediate zone where they can modulate various interneurons of segmental pathways; but whether their terminations really spare the ventral horn has not yet been decided. PTNs in postcentral areas 3b, 1, 2, and 5 possess terminal branches apparently to specific sites within the dorsal horn (Catsman-Berrevoets & Kuypers, 1976; Cheema, Rustioni, & Whitsel, 1984; Coulter & Jones, 1977; cf. review by Wiesendanger, 1981). PTNs also give off collaterals or project to other relay stations of ascending pathways, namely to the dorsal column nuclei, which are mostly impinged upon by PTNs in postcentral area 3a and precentral MI. Much electrophysiological work has been done on this corticofugal modulation of transmission in somatosensory afferent pathways, but unfortunately, studies done in the behavioral situation are mostly lacking (cf. Wiesendanger, 1981). We can conclude with a formulation by Adkins, Morse, & Towe (1966): "The pyramidal tract . . . constitutes one route by which the cerebral cortex can modify its own afferent input" (p. 1022).

The terminal ramifications, projections, and spinal actions of PTNs in MI have been fairly well delineated by various methods including electrophysiological approaches, intracellular staining, microstimulation, and deoxyglucose metabolic labeling (Asanuma, 1981; Kosar & Asanuma, 1984; Phillips & Porter, 1977; Shinoda, Zarzeki, & Asanuma, 1979). In summary, PTNs destined for control of proximal, especially coaxial muscles have been shown to branch extensively within the spinal cord, with a single PTN activating numerous motor nuclei from the cervical down to the lumbar cord. In contrast, the more a PTN is involved in controlling progressively more distal muscles the greater the probability that it projects only to a single motoneuron pool. Neighboring PTNs in a cluster are likely to have the same target site.

Further insight into the organizational aspects of MI PTNs has been provided by a cross-correlation technique which uses the spikes of PTNs as trigger for averaging the EMG recorded from a number of extensor and flexor muscles of the wrist (Fetz et al., 1976). By this method, those PTNs with a monosynaptic

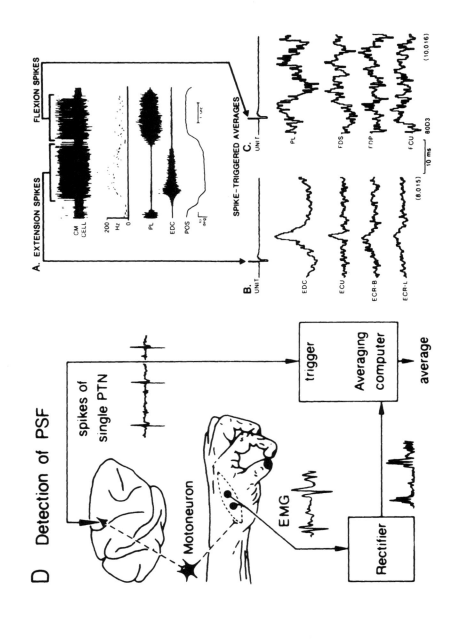

connection or a disynaptic inhibitory coupling with spinal motoneurons can be identified, called CM cells (Fig. 6.4). After postspike averaging of 5000–10,000 sweeps an EMG facilitation appears at a mean onset latency of 6.7 msec, which varies from cell to cell with the conduction and synaptic transmission times, and with a mean amplitude of 9% above EMG baseline; postspike suppression can sometimes be detected in antagonist muscles, typically weaker (4.1% below EMG baseline) and at a longer mean onset latency of 8.9 msec, which suggests an intercalated inhibitory interneuron (Cheney et al., 1985).

Three basic patterns of linkage and synaptic influence on agonist and antagonist wrist muscles were observed (agonist muscles are those with which the CM cell coactivates): (1) pure postspike facilitation in one or several agonist muscles, (2) pure postspike suppression of one or several antagonist muscles, no influence on agonists, (3) reciprocal CM cells that facilitate agonists and inhibit antagonist muscles (this type is shown in Fig. 6.4 A–C). No exception has been noted, in particular no CM cells have been encountered that facilitate both agonists and antagonists. Cheney et al. (1985) furthermore investigated the issue of distribution of CM output to several motoneuron pools. At least 50% of CM cells had a divergent influence on more than one synergistic muscles of the wrist (Fig. 6.4 B), and this proportion could only be underestimated because of the limited number of recorded muscles. However, PTNs projecting to the small hand muscles appear to have more restricted "muscle fields": CM cells involved in the fractionated use of fine finger movements, the precision grip (Fig. 6.4 D), seem to influence single muscles only (Muir & Lemon, 1983). Also consistent with the data mentioned before, neighboring CM cells have similar patterns of terminations within the motoneuron pools (Cheney et al., 1985).

FIG. 6.4 *A–C:* This CM cell normally coactivated with wrist extension (position trace, POS, downward in *A*) and with extensor EMG and was *silent* with flexion. However, to demonstrate effects on the flexor muscles during the antagonist phase of movement, it was necessary to induce "artificial" spike activity by iontophoretical application of glutamate near the cell body. Brackets in *A* indicate gating of spikes such that only those that occurred during wrist extension were accepted as triggers for spike-triggered averages of extensor muscles (shown in *B*), whereas only spikes that occurred during wrist flexion were accepted as triggers for the averages of flexor muscles (shown in *C*). Postspike facilitation of this cell was seen in four extensor muscles, strong in Ext. dig. comm., EDC, weaker in Ext. carp. ulnaris, ECU, in Ext. carp. rad. brevis, ECR-B, and in Ext. carp. rad. longus, ECR-L (*B*). Postspike suppression was seen in one of four flexor muscles, in palmaris longus, PL (*C*). *D* shows the experimental setup for detection of postspike effects in small hand muscles of the monkey during the precision grip. *A–C* (from Cheney, Kasser, & Holsapple, 1982), *D.* From Muir & Lemon (1983). Reprinted by permission.

III. PATTERNS OF PTN ACTIVITY WITH DIFFERENT TYPES OF MOTOR BEHAVIOR

This section is thought to amplify and elucidate some of the issues raised in the previous paragraphs. I describe some observations on PTNs made during an exciting and so stimulating period of collaboration with Edward V. Evarts at the National Institute of Mental Health. In these experiments, special attention had been devoted to the small-sized PTNs in pre and postcentral areas. In contrast to the fact that these small-fiber neurons constitute more than 90% of the pyramidal tract (Lassek, 1954) not much had been known about the functional properties and movement-related features of small PTNs. The reason had been that the two techniques widely used in neurophysiology (electrical stimulation and transdural recording with microelectrodes) preferentially sample the large PTNs, which are only present in MI (see Section I.1). Our recordings of PTNs focused on those cortical fields that are known to receive predominantly noncutaneous input: the rostral MI, "MIr" (see section II.2.), and the postcentral areas 3a, 2, and 5 (see section I.2.). The essential paradigm we used had been a visual pursuit-tracking task in which the monkey rotated a handle, connected to a torque motor, by supination-pronation movements of the forearm.

III.1. Large Ballistic Versus Small Precise Movements

Craik's ratio rule states that for large rapid movements *above* a certain extent the magnitude of error is a fixed proportion of the movement. How can the error become smaller as the volitional change of position becomes smaller and smaller? Our ability to manipulate under a dissecting microscope with an accuracy of small fractions of a millimeter is amazing. What are the cortical controls called into play? These were the questions that led to our experiments in which a monkey had to maintain accurate positional stability within a small hold zone and to position the handle into small target zones (1.5° wide) by 1–2° supination or pronation movements. Notice from the superimposed position traces (Fig. 6.5, lower right) how precisely controlled these small movements were: over or undershooting of the small target zone rarely occurred. These movements were contrasted with large (20°) supination-pronation movements for which speed rather than accurate termination was required; in fact, these ballistic movements were stopped by a physical barrier at the end point. Thus, regarding amplitude, speed, and accuracy both types of conditioned movement can be seen at the extremes of voluntary movement categories.

The striking result was that the fraction of cortical PTNs engaged in control of these fine movements was far larger than the fraction of spinal motoneurons firing with that movement (Fromm & Evarts, 1977, 1981). It was difficult to pick up—in some prime movers—the minute fluctuations of EMG accompanying such small movements, which contrasts with the intense bursts of muscular

6. SENSORIMOTOR INTEGRATION   155

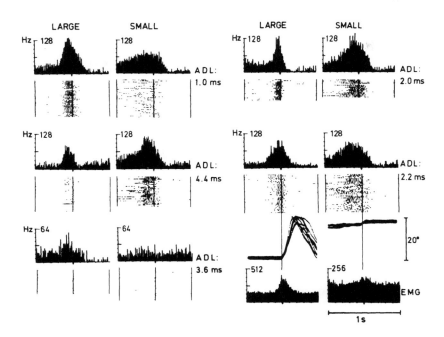

FIG. 6.5 Discharge patterns of five MI PTNs with *large* ballistic and *small* precise movements, respectively, shown in form of rasters (each dot representing a spike) and of time histograms (average discharge frequency in imp./sec). The three PTNs on the left side increased firing with pronations, whereas for the two PTNs on the right, activity increased with large and small supinations. The antidromic latency to pyramidal stimulation (ADL) is given for each PTN (in msec). The center line in all plots marks the onset of large or small movement. In addition, superimposed position records of both types of movement (upward deflection = supination) and the corresponding surface EMG of biceps are depicted (note the different scales of the EMG histograms). The time (1 sec) applies to all plots. (From Fromm & Evarts, 1981). Reprinted by permission.

activity found in many muscles for the large rapid movement (cf. biceps-EMG in Fig. 6.5). As a general observation made under many conditions, maximum firing rates of PTNs rarely exceed 100–150 impulses per second, and such rates were often reached during performance of fine movements. In Fig. 6.5 notice also the prolonged PTN activity starting much earlier before onset of small movement than is the case for the short burst of firing prior to ballistic movement. If one would take the integral of activity modulation it is safe to conclude that much more activity emanates from many PTNs in MI and postcentral areas during control of precise fine movement as compared to large ballistic movement. But even if we (Fromm & Evarts, 1977) measured the peak discharge frequency attained, about 60% of PTNs would exhibit the same maximum discharge rate for both types of movement (like the two PTNs at the right side of

Fig. 6.5). Higher peak firing rates with the small movements were observed in 15% (like the PTN with an antidromic latency, ADL, of 4.4 msec in Fig. 6.5); the PTN with an ADL of 1.0 msec (top left in Fig. 6.5) illustrates the pattern seen in the remaining 25% of PTNs. The antidromic latency (ADL) to pyramidal stimulation gives a clue to the conduction velocity and thus cell size: the smaller a PTN the longer its ADL. There was a statistically significant tendency for the large PTNs to increase further their discharge frequency with the large fast movements, while smaller PTNs exhibited their full dynamic discharge frequency already in association with the fine movements (Fromm & Evarts, 1981).

Is it then possible to determine a "threshold" for each individual PTN with movements becoming ever smaller? The postcentral PTN in Fig. 6.6 exhibited a moderate "static" tonic firing rate of 20 Hz during postural stability, which is interrupted by micromovements. The amplified velocity records of handle movement were used to detect occurrence of such micromovements. There is some decrease of activity with small pronations (upward deflection of velocity trace) and an intense firing with small supinations on which the spike activity has been aligned. Trial-by-trial analysis of the individual movement records corresponding, from top to bottom, to the rows in the spike raster reveals some variations of the dynamic firing rate that is, however, not in a consistent way associated with variations in the amplitude and velocity of the micromovements. There is no apparent "threshold" for minimal postural changes: Especially small PTNs were found to use their *full dynamic frequency* range regardless of how small the micromovement becomes. In addition, we have examined the relation of the *static,* tonic discharge rate of PTNs to steady-state external loads (produced by the torque motor) during positional maintenance (Evarts, Fromm, Kröller, & Jennings, 1983). Many PTNs were found to be most sensitive to small steady forces around zero external load, in exhibiting graded frequency changes over a limited range of low torques, with saturation of tonic discharge rate for larger torques.

We should recall that the pronounced activity changes associated with fine adjustments of muscular force as seen especially in small PTNs might also be devoted to the control of somatosensory relay neurons, spinal interneurons, and of fusimotoneurons (cf. section II.4.), in addition to control of the early-recruited portion of tonic motoneurons. It was therefore not predictable, indeed surprising, that our results obtained on PTNs could be confirmed for CM cells, because one would a priori assume that CM neuronal activity is more rigidly linked with that of their target motoneurons. Nonetheless, a similar remarkable dissociation of CM cell and target muscle activity was noticed when large ballistic movements were compared to slow, accurately performed ramp-and-hold-movements of the wrist (Cheney & Fetz, 1980). Furthermore, much greater CM cell activity was found in relation to the precision grip (Fig. 6.4D), which involves discrete, finely graded movements of the thumb and index finger, than during performance of a "power grip" (Cheney et al., 1985; Muir & Lemon, 1983). The power grip required of the monkey to strongly squeeze a rubber bar which was

6. SENSORIMOTOR INTEGRATION   157

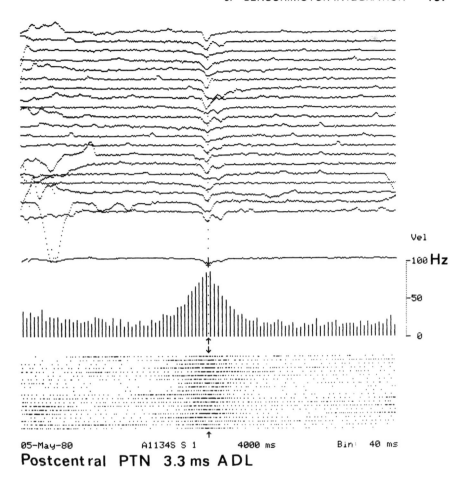

FIG. 6.6 Intense and early firing of a postcentral PTN with small (1°) supinations (downward deflections of velocity traces). This PTN was located in caudal area 2 at the border to area 5. From top to bottom, individual records of velocity of small movement corresponding to the rows in the spike-raster are shown, together with the averaged velocity signal (peak: 5°/sec) and time-histogram (averaged discharge frequency in Hz, bin: 40 msec) of the activity displayed in the raster below. Time of total display: 4 sec. The small arrows indicate detectable change of velocity on which unit discharge has been aligned. (From Evarts & Fromm, 1981). Reprinted by permission.

associated with intense cocontraction of many muscles including the target muscles of these CM cells. The described dissociation of PTN and muscular activity, depending on the motor program or movement strategy, might explain the findings of Fetz and Finocchio (1975) revealed by the technique of operant conditioning (see introduction). We conclude that PTNs have *preferential roles* in

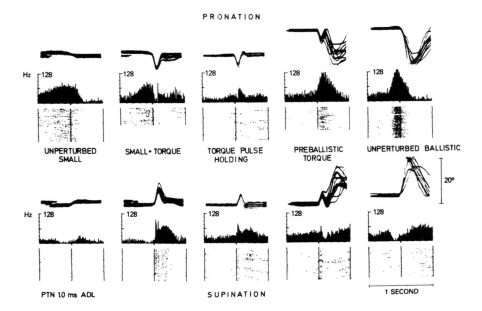

FIG. 6.7 Reflex responsiveness of an MI PTN during postural stability ("holding"), precise small movement and immediately before ballistic movement ("preballistic"). The same 50-msec torque pulse had been applied during the three conditions resulting in a 5° displacement. Three sorts of displays are shown: superimposed position traces representing the handle position (top), histogram of averaged PTN activity (middle), and raster of unit discharges (below). Upper row of displays: active and passive pronation movements; lower row of displays: active movements and torque pulses in supination-direction. Onset of unperturbed movements or of torque pulses marked by center line in the rasters. Time applies to all records (1 sec). In accordance with the sign of feedback postulated for the proprioceptive PTN reflexes, this PTN was reflexly excited by the supinating torque pulse that stretches the pronators (lower row) while it increased activity with voluntary pronation movement; or vice versa, it was inhibited by torque displacements assisting the active movement with which this PTN fired (upper row). Notice further the heightened reflex effects (inhibitory as well as excitatory) when the perturbation is applied during small movements (marked "small + torque") as compared to the other conditions. Latency of reflex response was 20 msec. (From Evarts & Fromm, 1978). Reprinted by permission.

precisely controlled small movements allowing the delicate fractionated use of fine finger movements and in postural adjustments, a hypothesis that is consistent with the results of lesion studies (cf. Wiesendanger, 1981).

Accurate maintenance of position and fine movements might involve similar controls, both depend critically on proprioceptive feedback for their execution, as has been recently found in patients with large fiber sensory neuropathy (Marsden, Rothwell, & Day, 1984; Sanes & Evarts, 1984). Conversely, the striking sensitivity of PTNs to micromovements and to finely graded muscle forces under static conditions might in part reflect the consequences of proprioceptive feedback in closed-loop operation. Operant conditioning of precentral PTN discharge rate by the conscious monkey has demonstrated the critical role played by proprioceptive input in the accurate operant control of PTN discharge (Wyler & Burchiel, 1978; Wyler, Burchiel, & Robbins, 1979). On the other hand, large fast movements might be carried out in the open-loop mode (for reviews see Arbib, 1981; Evarts, 1981). At least the initial phase of large ballistic movements is relatively unaffected by peripheral inputs, whereas load disturbance of slow precise ramp movements elicits a clear M2 response (Fig. 6.9) in the human EMG (Desmedt & Godaux, 1978).

Consistent with these findings and considerations we found that the reflex responsiveness of MI PTNs to the same small perturbations (a 5° pronating or supinating displacement by a torque pulse) was enhanced in the course of small precisely controlled movements, being somewhat less pronounced during positional maintenance, and severely attenuated just prior to large ballistic movements (Fig. 6.7). This and other results (Evarts & Fromm, 1977, 1978; Fromm & Evarts, 1978, 1981) suggest that proprioceptive reflexes continuously modulate PTN discharge rate during the closed-loop mode of control used in accurate positioning and precise fine movement, while such modulation is attenuated before and during (not shown in Fig. 6.7) large fast movements. These findings thus imply an adaptive gain control in the proposed servo loop depending on the motor program or type of movement. Too high gain would lead to oscillations in the servo loop. Performance of ever-smaller movements is thus finally limited by the occurrence of tremor. Such gain control could be exerted by the supplementary motor cortex and/or via corticofugal modulation of the ascending somatosensory pathways, as outlined in the previous sections.

III.2. Comparison of Postcentral PTNs with PTNs in MI

Comparison of PTNs in the different cytoarchitectonic areas of SI with their counterparts in rostral MI led to the following conclusion in Fromm (1983). "Similarities between PTNs in motor cortex and SI appear to transcend the differences that might have been expected on the basis of their location in areas as functionally different as the primary motor and somatosensory cortex" (p. 342). PTNs in areas 4, 3a, and in the most caudal part of SI and in area 5 (refer to Fig. 6.1) were found to change activity well in advance of large or small (see Fig. 6.6) voluntary movements (Fromm & Evarts, 1982). Therefore, this movement-related discharge in postcentral PTNs might carry information about the forthcoming movement, thus adjusting their target neurons to the intended motor act. Such postcentral PTNs also exhibited responses to a brief and randomly occurring halt of volitional movement that was brought about by "clamping" the

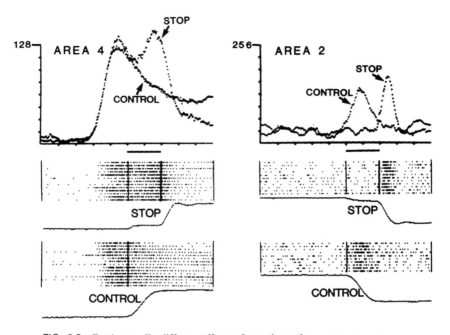

FIG. 6.8 Fundamentally different effects of stopping voluntary movement on two PTNs recorded from area 4 (left column) and from area 2 (right column). Activity with the unimpeded control movements and stopped movements displayed in rasters, centered on the onset of movement or stop, respectively. Beneath each raster, the averaged handle position; at the top of each column, two superimposed averaged discharge frequency (imp./sec) curves that were computed from the respective rasters below, labeled *control* and *stop*. Horizontal bar indicates the 200 msec period of arrest of handle, removal of stop being also marked by second vertical line in the upper rasters. The PTN in area 4 shows the typical transcortical servo response, consistent with the hypothesis for the proprioceptive loop (cf. section II.3.). In contrast, the activity of the PTN in area 2 occurred late, i. e., at the onset of voluntary movement (control); in addition, during the stop period this burst of activity does not occur until removal of stop allowed the movement to proceed.

handle connected to the torque motor just as the movement was starting (Fig. 6.8). Similar servo responses as illustrated for an area 4 PTN (left part of Fig. 6.8) occurred in some postcentral PTNs, indicating that such PTNs may also signal misalignment between actual and intended movement. In contrast, the major difference to PTNs in MI was shown by PTNs in the rostral areas of SI. They discharged late, at or after onset of movement (see control movement, right part of Fig. 6.8). As strongly suggested by the peculiar stop effect displayed for the area 2 PTN in Fig. 6.8, its movement-related activity might be a pure reflection of somatosensory events caused by the movement, implying that the stop prevented the responsible receptors (e.g., joint receptors) from being activated. This postcentral PTN may thus give a signal of movement-detection to subcortical structures.

Short-latency responses of PTNs to passive ramp-and-hold displacements of the forearm were also studied in the awake monkey (Fromm et al., 1984). Across all cortical subdivisions of MI and SI, larger PTNs tended to show dynamic ramp responses, whereas dynamic-static and purely static sustained responses prevailed in smaller PTNs. Smaller PTNs also varied more frequently their steady tonic firing rates as a function of static muscle forces and as a function of actively maintained steady joint position (Evarts et al., 1983; Fromm, 1983; Fromm & Evarts, 1982; Jennings, Lamour, Solis, & Fromm, 1983). In summary, smaller precentral and postcentral PTNs receive continuous somatosensory feedback during posture as well as during the dynamic phase of movement. The pattern of many postcentral PTNs with active and passive movements can best be understood by assuming that they receive a central, "corollary" input in addition to a

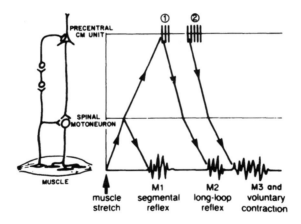

FIG. 6.9 The diagram on the left shows the neural connections of the segmental and transcortical proprioceptive reflex loops that would generate the sequence of events (shown at the right) initiated by muscle stretch in a subject *prepared* to make a voluntary contraction of that muscle. Arrows indicate conduction of neural signals over the segmental, monosynaptic pathway (leading to M1) and over the cortico-motoneuronal (CM) cell that contributes causally to the subsequent M2 and M3 responses of EMG. The 1. CM-cell response (occurring at 20–25 msec) and M2 response (occurring at 28–35 msec, i. e., after a mean efferent conduction time to muscle of 7 msec), both depend on the parameters of limb displacement (e. g., direction). This first phase follows the rules of a closed-loop control system in a negative feedback mode. The 2. CM-cell response (occurring at 40–60 msec) and subsequent M3 contraction (occurring as early as 60 msec), both depend entirely on motor-set adopted by the subject due to intent or prior instruction. This second phase is to be viewed in connection with open-loop control. (From Fetz, 1981). Reprinted by permission.

peripheral input (Evarts & Fromm, 1981). Certainly, the significance of somatosensory feedback to postcentral PTNs must be different from the servo-loop function of PTNs known to address the spinal motoneurons, as shown for CM cells (Fig. 6.9). But because the subcortical projections of postcentral PTNs have not been identified in these experiments, it seems premature to discuss the relative importance of "sensory" as compared to "motor" roles of PTNs in SI.

ACKNOWLEDGMENT

This chapter is in memory of Dr. Edward V. Evarts who died on July 2nd, 1985. The work of the author was supported by the Deutsche Forschungsgemeinschaft (Fr 469/5-2, Fr 469/6-1).

REFERENCES

Adkins, R. J., Morse, R. W., & Towe, A. L. (1966). Control of somatosensory input by cerebral cortex. *Science, 153,* 1020–1022.
Adrian, E. D., & Moruzzi, G. (1939). Impulses in the pyramidal tract. *Journal of Physiology (Lond.), 97,* 153–199.
Allen, G. I., & Tsukahara, W. (1974). Cerebrocerebellar communication systems. *Physiological Reviews, 54,* 957–1006.
Arbib, M. A. (1981). Perceptual structures and distributed motor control: In V. B. Brooks (Ed.), *Handbook of Psychology, Motor Control, (Vol. II, pp. 1449–1480).* Bethesda, MD: American Physiological Society.
Asanuma, H. (1981). The pyramidal tract: In V. B. Brooks (Ed.), *Handbook of Physiology, Motor Control* (Vol. II, pp. 703–733). Bethesda, MD: American Physiological Society.
Asanuma, H., & Arissian, K. (1984). Experiments on functional role of peripheral input to motor cortex during voluntary movements in the monkey. *Journal of Neurophysiology, 52,* 212–227.
Asanuma, H., Larsen, K., & Yumiya, H. (1980). Peripheral input pathways to themonkey motor cortex. *Experimental Brain Research, 38,* 349–355.
Asanuma, C., Thach, W. T., & Jones, E. G. (1983). Distribution of cerebellar terminations and their relation to other afferent terminations in the ventral lateral thalamic region of the monkey. *Brain Research Reviews, 5,* 237–265.
Bioulac, B., & Lamarre, Y. (1979). Activity of postcentral cortical neurons of the monkey during conditioned movements of a deafferented limb. *Brain Research, 172,* 427–437.
Bizzi, E., Polit, A., & Morasso, P. (1976). Mechanisms underlying achievement of final head position. *Journal of Neurophysiology, 39,* 435–444.
Brinkman, C. (1984). Supplementary motor area of the monkey's cerebral cortex: short- and long-term deficits after unilateral ablation and the effects of subsequent callosal section. *The Journal of Neuroscience, 4,* 918–929.
Brinkman, J., Bush, B. M., & Porter, R. (1978). Deficient influences of peripheral stimuli on precentral neurons in monkeys with dorsal column lesions. *Journal of Physiology (Lond.), 276,* 27–48.
Brodmann, K. (1909). *Vergleichende Lokalisationslehre der Großhirnrinde.* Leipzig: J. A. Barth.
Brooks, V. B., & Thach, W. T. (1981). Cerebellar control of posture and movement: In V. B. Brooks (Ed.), *Handbook of Physiology, Motor Control* (Vol. II, (pp. 877–946). Bethesda, MD: American Physiological Society.

Carlson, M. (1981). Characteristics of sensory deficits following lesions of Brodmann's areas 1 and 2 in the postcentral gyrus of Macaca mulatta. *Brain Research, 204,* 424–430.
Catsman-Berrevoets, C. E., & Kuypers, H. G. J. M. (1976). Cells of origin of cortical projections to dorsal column nuclei, spinal cord, and bulbar medial reticular formation in the rhesus monkey. *Neuroscience Letters, 3,* 245–252.
Chapman, C. E., Spidalieri, G., & Lamarre, Y. (1984). Discharge properties of area 5 neurons during arm movements triggered by sensory stimuli in the monkey. *Brain Research, 309,* 63–77.
Cheema, S. S., Rustioni, A., & Whitsel, B. L. (1984). Light and electron microscopic evidence for a direct corticospinal projection to superficial laminae of the dorsal horn in cats and monkeys. *Journal of Comparative Neurology, 225,* 276–290.
Cheney, P. D., & Fetz, E. E. (1980). Functional classes of primate corticomotoneuronal cells and their relation to active force. *Journal of Neurophysiology, 44,* 773–791.
Cheney, P. D., Kasser, R. J., & Fetz, E. E. (1985). Motor and sensory properties of primate corticomotoneuronal cells: In A. W. Goodwin & J. Darian-Smith (Eds.), *Hand function and the neocortex, Experimental Brain Research Suppl.* (Vol. 10, pp. 211–231).
Cheney, P. D., Kasser, R., & Holsapple, J. (1982). Reciprocal effect of single corticomotoneuronal cells on wrist extensor and flexor muscle activity in the primate. *Brain Research, 247,* 164–168.
Conrad, B. (1978). The motor cortex as a primary device for fast adjustment of programmed motor patterns to afferent signals: In J. E. Desmedt (Ed.), *Cerebral motor control in man: Long loop mechanisms, progress in clinical neurophysiology* (Vol. 4, pp. 123–140). Basel: Karger.
Coulter, J. D., & Jones, E. G. (1977). Differential distribution of corticospinal projections from individual cytoarchitectonic fields in the monkey. *Brain Research, 129,* 335–340.
Darian-Smith, I., Goodwin, A., Sugitani, M., & Heywood, J. (1985). Scanning a textured surface with the fingers: Events in sensorimotor cortex: In A. W. Goodwin & I. Darian-Smith (Eds.), *Hand function and the neocortex, Experimental Brain Research Suppl.* (Vol. 10, pp. 17–43).
DeLong, M. R., Georgopoulos, A. P., Crutcher, M. D. (1983). Corticobasal ganglia relations and coding of motor performance. *Experimental Brain Research Suppl., 7,* 30–40.
Desmedt, J. E., & Godaux, E. (1978). Ballistic skilled movements: Load compensation and patterning of the motor commands: In J. E. Desmedt (Ed.), *Cerebral motor control in man: Long loop mechanisms, Progress in clinical neurophysiology* (Vol. 4, pp. 21–55). Basel: Karger.
Eccles, J. C. (1973). *The understanding of the brain.* New York: McGraw-Hill.
Evarts, E. V. (1964). Temporal patterns of discharge of pyramidal tract neurons during sleep and waking in the monkey. *Journal of Neurophysiology, 27,* 152–171.
Evarts, E. V. (1973). Motor cortex reflexes associated with learned movement. *Science, 179,* 501–503.
Evarts, E. V. (1981). Role of motor cortex in voluntary movements in primates: In V. B. Brooks (Ed.), *Handbook of physiology, motor control* (Vol. II, pp. 1083–1120). Bethesda, MD: American Physiological Society.
Evarts, E. V., Bizzi, E., Burke, R. E., DeLong, M., & Thach, W. T. (1971). Central control of movements. *Neurosciences Research Program, Bulletin, 9,* 1–170.
Evarts, E. V., & Fromm, C. (1977). Sensory responses in motor cortex neurons during precise motor control. *Neuroscience Letters, 5,* 267–272.
Evarts, E. V., & Fromm, C. (1978). The pyramidal tract neuron as a summing point in a closed-loop control system in the monkey: In J. E. Desmedt (Ed.), *Cerebral motor control in man: Long loop mechanisms, progress in clinical neurophysiology* (Vol. 4, pp. 56–69). Basel: Karger.
Evarts, E. V., & Fromm, C. (1981). Transcortical reflexes and servo control of movement. *Canadian Journal of Physiology and Pharmacology, 59,* 757–775.
Evarts, E. V., Fromm, C., Kröller, J., & Jennings, V. A. (1983). Motor cortex control of finely graded forces. *Journal of Neurophysiology, 49,* 1199–1215.
Evarts, E. V., & Tanji, J. (1974). Gating of motor cortex reflexes by prior instruction. *Brain Research, 71,* 479–494.

Evarts, E. V., & Tanji, J. (1976). Reflex and intended responses in motor cortex pyramidal tract neurons of monkey. *Journal of Neurophysiology, 39,* 1069–1080.

Fetz, E. E. (1981). Neuronal activity associated with conditioned limb movements: In A. L. Towe & E. S. Luschei (Eds.), *Handbook of behavioral neurobiology* (Vol. 5, pp. 493–526). New York: Plenum.

Fetz, E. E., Cheney, P. D., & German, D. C. (1976). Corticomotoneuronal connections of precentral cells detected by postspike averages of EMG activity in behaving monkeys. *Brain Research, 114,* 505–510.

Fetz, E. E., & Finocchio, D. V. (1975). Correlations between activity of motor cortex cells and arm muscles during operantly conditioned response patterns. *Experimental Brain Research, 23,* 217–240.

Freund, H.-J. (1984). Premotor areas in man. *Trends in Neurosciences, 7,* 481–483.

Fromm, C. (1983). Contrasting properties of pyramidal tract neurons located in the precentral or postcentral areas and of corticorubral neurons in the behaving monkey: In J. E. Desmedt (Ed.), *Motor control mechanisms in health and disease, advances in neurology* (Vol. 39, pp. 329–345). New York: Raven.

Fromm, C., & Evarts, E. V. (1977). Relation of motor cortex neurons to precisely controlled and ballistic movements. *Neuroscience Letters, 5,* 259–265.

Fromm, C., & Evarts, E. V. (1978). Motor cortex responses to kinesthetic inputs during postural stability, precise fine movement and ballistic movement in the conscious monkey: In G. Gordon (Ed.), *Active touch* (pp. 105–117). Oxford: Pergamon Press.

Fromm, C., & Evarts, E. V. (1981). Relation of size and activity of motor cortex pyramidal tract neurons during skilled movements in the monkey. *The Journal of Neuroscience, 1,* 453–460.

Fromm, C., & Evarts, E. V. (1982). Pyramidal tract neurons in somatosensory cortex: Central and peripheral inputs during voluntary movements. *Brain Research, 238,* 186–191.

Fromm, C., Wise, S. P., & Evarts, E. V. (1984). Sensory response properties of pyramidal tract neurons in the precentral motor cortex and postcentral gyrus of the rhesus monkey. *Experimental Brain Research, 54,* 177–185.

Gilbert, P. F. C., & Thach, W. T. (1977). Purkinje cell activity during motor learning. *Brain Research, 128,* 309–328.

Godschalk, M., & Lemon, R. N. (1983). Involvement of monkey premotor cortex in the preparation of arm movements. *Experimental Brain Research Suppl., 7,* 114–119.

Goodwin, G. M., Hoffman, D., & Luschei, E. S. (1978). The strength of the reflex response to sinusoidal stretch of monkey jaw closing muscles during voluntary contraction. *Journal of Physiology (Lond.), 279,* 81–111.

Gordon, G. (Ed.). (1978). *Active Touch: The mechanism of recognition of objects by manipulation.* Oxford: Pergamon Press.

Houk, J. C., & Rymer, W. Z. (1981). Neural control of muscle length and tension: In V. B. Brooks (Ed.), *Handbook of physiology: Motor control* (Vol. II, pp. 257–323). Bethesda, MD: American Physiological Society.

Hubel, D. H. (1959). Single unit activity in striate cortex of unrestrained cats. *Journal of Physiology (Lond.), 147,* 226–238.

Hulliger, M., Nordh, E., & Vallbo, A. P. (1982). The absence of position response in spindle afferent units from human finger muscles during accurate position holding. *Journal of Physiology (Lond.), 322,* 167–179.

Humphrey, D. R., & Corrie, W. S. (1978). Properties of pyramidal tract neurons within a functionally defined subregion of primate motor cortex. *Journal of Neurophysiology, 41,* 216–243.

Hyvärinen, J. (1982). *The parietal cortex of monkey and man: Studies of brain function* (Vol. 8). Berlin–Heidelberg–New York: Springer–Verlag.

Ingvar, D. H. (1975). Patterns of brain activity revealed by measurements of regional cerebral blood flow: In D. H. Ingvar & N. A. Lassen (Eds.), *Brain work* (pp. 397–413). Copenhagen: Munksgaard.

Iwamura, Y., Tanaka, M., Sakamoto, M., & Hikosaka, O. (1985). Functional surface integration, submodality convergence, and tactile feature detection in area 2 of the monkey somatosensory cortex: In A. W. Goodwin & J. Darian-Smith (Eds.), *Hand function and the neocortex, Experimental Brain Research Suppl.* (Vol. 10, pp. 44–58).

Jasper, H., Ricci, G. F., & Doane, B. (1958). Patterns of cortical neurone discharge during conditioned responses in monkeys: In G. Wolstenholme & C. O. Connor (Eds.), *Neurological basis of behavior.* Boston: Little Brown.

Jenner, J. R., & Stephens, J. A. (1982). Cutaneous reflex responses and their central nervous pathways studied in man. *Journal of Physiology (Lond.), 333,* 405–519.

Jennings, V. A., Lamour, Y., Solis, H., & Fromm, C. (1983). Somatosensory cortex activity related to position and force. *Journal of Neurophysiology, 49,* 1216–1229.

Jones, E. G. (1983). The nature of the afferent pathways conveying short-latency inputs to primate motor cortex: In J. E. Desmedt (Ed.), *Motor control mechanisms in health and disease, advances in Neurology* Vol. 39, pp. 263–285). New York: Raven.

Jones, E. G., Coulter, J. D., & Hendry, S. H. C. (1978). Intracortical connectivity of architectonic fields in the somatic sensory, motor and parietal cortex of monkeys. *Journal of Comparative Neurology, 181,* 291–348.

Jones, E. G., & Powell, T. P. S. (1970). An anatomical study of converging sensory pathways within the cerebral cortex of the monkey. *Brain, 93,* 793–820.

Jones, E. G., & Wise, S. P. (1977). Size, laminar and columnar distribution of efferent cells in the sensory-motor cortex of monkey. *Journal of Comparative Neurology, 175,* 391–438.

Kaas, J. H., Nelson, R. J., Sur, M., & Merzenich, M. M. (1981). Organization of somatosensory cortex in primates: In F. O. Schmitt, F. G. Worden, G. Adelman, & S. G. Dennis (Eds.), *The organization of the cerebral cortex* (pp. 237–261). Cambridge, MA: M.I.T. Press.

Kosar, E., & Asanuma, H. (1984). Focal and diffuse metabolic changes in the spinal cord of the monkey elicted by microstimulation of differing motor cortical foci. *Brain Research, 310,* 43–54.

Kubota, K., & Funahashi, S. (1982). Direction-specific activities of dorsolateral prefrontal and motor cortex pyramidal tract neurons during visual tracking. *Journal of Neurophysiology, 47,* 362–376.

Kurata, K., & Tanji, J. (1985). Contrasting neuronal activity in supplementary and precentral motor cortex of monkeys. II. Responses to movement triggering vs. nontriggering sensory signals. *Journal of Neurophysiology, 53,* 142–152.

Lamarre, Y., Bioulac, B., & Jacks, B. (1978). Activity of precentral neurons in conscious monkeys: Effects of deafferentation and cerebellar ablation. *Journal of Physiology, (Paris), 74,* 253–264.

Lassek, A. M. (1954). *The pyramidal tract. Its status in medicine.* Springfield, Ill.: Charles C. Thomas.

Lemon, R. N. (1981a). Functional properties of monkey motor cortex neurones receiving afferent input from the hand and fingers. *Journal of Physiology (Lond.), 311,* 497–519.

Lemon, R. N. (1981b). Variety of functional organization within the monkey motor cortex. *Journal of Physiology (Lond.), 311,* 521–540.

Magendie, F. (1824). *An elementary compendium of physiology.* E. Milligan (Trans.). Philadelphia: J. Webster.

Marsden, C. D. (1982). The mysterious motor function of the basal ganglia. The Robert Wartenberg Lecture. *Neurology, 32,* 514–539.

Marsden, C. D., Rothwell, J. C., & Day, B. L. (1983). Long-latency automatic responses to muscle stretch in man: Origin and function: In J. E. Desmedt (Ed.), *Motor control mechanisms in health and disease, Advances in Neurology* (Vol. 39, pp. 509–539). New York: Raven.

Marsden, C. D., Rothwell, J. C., & Day, B. L. (1984). The use of peripheral feedback in the control of movement. *Trends in Neurosciences, 7,* 253–257.

Maton, B., Burnod, Y., & Calvet, J. (1983). Area 4 cell activity during learning of a new amplitude of movement. *Experimental Brain Research Suppl., 7*, 241–245.
Matthews, P. B. C. (1972). *Mammalian muscle receptors and their central actions.* London: Arnold.
Mountcastle, V. B., Lynch, J. C., Georgopoulos, A., Sakata, H., & Acuna, C. (1975). Posterior parietal association cortex of the monkey: Command functions for operations within extrapersonal space. *Journal of Neurophysiology, 38*, 871–908.
Muakkassa, K. F., & Strick, P. L. (1979). Frontal lobe inputs to primate motor cortex: Evidence for four somatotopically organized "premotor" areas. *Brain Research, 177*, 176–182.
Muir, R. B., & Lemon, R. N. (1983). Corticospinal neurons with a special role in precision grip. *Brain Research, 261*, 312–316.
Murphy, J. T., Kwan, H. C., Mackay, W. A., & Wong, Y. C. (1978). Spatial organization of precentral cortex in awake primates. III. Input-output coupling. *Journal of Neurophysiology, 41*, 1132–1139.
Murray, E. A., & Coulter, J. D. (1981). Organization of corticospinal neurons in the monkey. *Journal of Comparative Neurology, 195*, 339–365.
Murray, E. A., & Mishkin, M. (1984). Relative contributions of S II and area 5 to tactile discrimination in monkeys. *Behavioural Brain Research, 11*, 67–83.
Nelson, R. J. (1985). Sensorimotor cortex responses to vibrotactile stimuli during initiation and execution of hand movement: In A. W. Goodwin & J. Darian–Smith (Eds.), *Hand function and the neocortex, Experimental Brain Research Suppl.* (Vol. 10, pp. 59–76).
Pew, R. W. (1974). Human perceptual-motor performance: In B. H. Kantowitz (Ed.), *Human information processing: Tutorials in performance and cognition.* Hillsdale, NJ: Lawrence Erlbaum Associates.
Phillips, C. G. (1969). The Ferrier Lecture, 1968. Motor apparatus of the baboon's hand. *Proceedings of The Royal Society of London Series B, 173*, 141–174.
Phillips, C. G., & Porter, R. (1977). *Corticospinal neurones.* London: Academic Press.
Porter, R. (1981). Internal organization of the motor cortex for input-output arrangements: In V. B. Brooks (Ed.), *Handbook of physiology, motor control* (Vol. II, pp. 1063–1082). Bethesda, MD: American Physiological Society.
Porter, R., & Ghosh, S. (1985). Relationships between premotor, supplementary motor and precentral motor cortex in primates. *Experimental Brain Research, 58*, A6.
Prochazka, A., & Hulliger, M. (1983). Muscle afferent function and its significance for motor control mechanisms during voluntary movements in cat, monkey and man: In J. E. Desmedt (Ed.), *Motor control mechanisms in health and disease, Advances in Neurology* (Vol. 39, pp. 93–132). New York: Raven.
Randolph, M., & Semmes, J. (1974). Behavioral consequence of selective subtotal ablations in the postcentral gyrus of Macaca mulatta. *Brain Research, 70*, 55–70.
Rizzolatti, G., Matelli, M., & Pavesi, G. (1983). Deficits in attention and movement following the removal of postarcuate (area 6) and prearcuate (area 8) cortex in Macaque monkeys. *Brain, 106*, 655–573.
Roland, P. E. (1976). Astereognosis. *Archives of Neurology, 33*, 543–550.
Roland, P. E. (1984). Metabolic measurements of the working frontal cortex in man. *Trends in Neurosciences, 7*, 430–435.
Roland, P. E., Larsen, B., Lassen, N. A., & Skinhøj, E. (1980). Supplementary motor area and other cortical areas in organization of voluntary movements in man. *Journal of Neurophysiology, 43*, 118–136.
Roland, P. E., Meyer, E., Shibasaki, T., Yamamoto, L., & Thompson, C. J. (1982). Regional cerebral blood flow changes in cortex and basal ganglia during voluntary movements in normal human volunteers. *Journal of Neurophysiology, 48*, 467–480.
Russel, J. R., & De Myer, W. (1961). The quantitative cortical origin of pyramidal axons of macaca rhesus. *Neurology (Minneapolis), 11*, 96–108.

Sakai, T., & Preston, J. B. (1978). Evidence for a transcortical reflex: Primate corticospinal tract neuron responses to ramp stretch of muscle. *Brain Research, 159,* 463–467.
Sakata, H., & Iwamura, Y. (1978). Cortical processing of tactile information in the first somatosensory and parietal association areas in the monkey: In G. Gordon (Ed.), *Active touch* (pp. 55–72). Oxford: Pergamon Press.
Sanes, J. N., & Evarts, E. V. (1983). Effects of perturbation on accuracy of arm movements. *The Journal of Neuroscience, 3,* 977–986.
Sanes, J. N., & Evarts, E. V. (1984). Motor psychophysics. *Human Neurobiology, 2,* 217–225.
Sasaki, K., & Gemba, H. (1985). Compensatory motor function of the somatosensory cortex in the monkey following cooling of the motor cortex and cerebellectomy: In A. W. Goodwin & J. Darian-Smith (Eds.), *Hand function and the neocortex, Experimental Brain Research Suppl.* (Vol. 10, pp. 275–287).
Schell, G. R., & Strick, P. L. (1984). The origin of thalamic inputs to the arcuate premotor and supplementary motor areas. *The Journal of Neuroscience, 4,* 539–560.
Schmidt, R. A. (1975). A schema theory of discrete motor skill learning. *Psychological Review, 82,* 225–260.
Schoen, J. H. R. (1964). Comparative aspects of the descending fibre systems in the spinal cord. *Progress in Brain Research, 11,* 203–222.
Sessle, B. J., & Wiesendanger, M. (1982). Structural and functional definition of the motor cortex in the monkey (Macaca fascicularis). *Journal of Physiology (Lond.), 323,* 245–265.
Shinoda, Y., Zarzecki, P., & Asanuma, H. (1979). Spinal branching of pyramidal tract neurons in the monkey. *Experimental Brain Research, 34,* 59–72.
Sperry, R. W. (1950). Neural basis of the spontaneous optokinetic response produced by visual inversion. *Journal of Comparative and Physiological Psychology, 43,* 482–489.
Stelmach, G. E. (1976). *Motor control: Issues and Trends.* New York: Academic Press.
Strick, P. L., & Preston, J. B. (1983). Input-output organization of the primate motor cortex: In J. E. Desmedt (Ed.), *Motor control mechanisms in health and disease, advances in neurology* (Vol. 39, pp. 321–327). New York: Raven.
Tanji, J., & Evarts, E. V. (1976). Anticipatory activity of motor cortex neurons in relation to direction of an intended movement. *Journal of Neurophysiology, 39,* 1062–1068.
Tanji, J., & Kurata, K. (1982). Comparison of movement-related activity in two cortical motor areas of primates. *Journal of Neurophysiology, 48,* 633–653.
Tanji, J., & Kurata, K. (1985). Contrasting neuronal activity in supplementary and precentral motor cortex of monkeys. I. Responses to instructions determining motor responses to forthcoming signals of different modalities. *Journal of Neurophysiology, 53,* 129–141.
Tanji, J., Kurata, K., & Okano, K. (1985). The effect of cooling of the supplementary motor cortex and adjacent cortical areas. *Experimental Brain Research, 60,* 423–426.
Tanji, J., Taniguchi, K., & Saga, T. (1980). The supplementary motor area: Neuronal response to motor instructions. *Journal of Neurophysiology, 43,* 60–68.
Teuber, H. L. (1974). Key problems in the programming of movements. *Brain Research, 71,* 533–568.
Toyoshima, K., & Sakai, H. (1982). Exact cortical extent of origin of the corticospinal tract (CST) and the quantitative contribution to the CST in different areas. A study with horseradish peroxidase in the monkey. *Journal für Hirnforschung, 23,* 257–269.
Vallbo, A. B. (1973). Muscle spindle afferent discharge from resting and contracting muscles in normal human subjects: In J. E. Desmedt (Ed.), *New developments in electromyography and clinical neurophysiology* (Vol. 3, pp. 251–262). Basel: Karger.
Vogt, B. A., & Pandya, D. N. (1978). Cortico-cortical connections of somatic sensory cortex (areas 3, 1, and 2) in the rhesus monkey. *Journal of Comparative Neurology, 177,* 179–192.
von Holst, E., & Mittelstaedt, H. (1950). Das Reafferenzprinzip (Wechselwirkungen zwischen Zentralnervensystem und Peripherie). *Naturwissenschaften, 37,* 464–476.

Wiesendanger, M. (1973). Input from muscle and cutaneous nerves of the hand and forearm to neurones of the precentral gyrus of baboons and monkeys. *Journal of Physiology (Lond.), 228,* 203–219.

Wiesendanger, M. (1981). The pyramidal tract: Its structure and function: In A. L. Towe & E. S. Luschei (Eds.), *Handbook of behavioral Neurobiology* (Vol. 5, pp. 401–491). New York: Plenum.

Wiesendanger, M. (1986). Recent developments in studies of the supplementary motor area of primates. *Reviews of Physiology, Biochemistry and Pharmacology, 103,* 1–59.

Wiesendanger, M. (in press). The initiation of voluntary movements and the supplementary motor area. *Experimental Brain Research Suppl.*

Wiesendanger, M., & Miles, T. S. (1982). Ascending pathway of low-threshold muscle afferents to the cerebral cortex and its possible role in motor control. *Physiological Reviews, 62,* 1234–1270.

Wise, S. P. (1985). The primate premotor cortex: Past, present, and preparatory. *Annual Review of Neuroscience, 8,* 1–19.

Wise, S. P., & Mauritz, K.-H. (1985). Set-related neuronal activity in the premotor cortex of rhesus monkey: Effects of changes in motor set. *Proceedings of The Royal Society of London Series B, 223,* 331–354.

Wise, S. P., & Strick, P. L. (1984). Anatomical and physiological organization of the non-primary motor cortex. *Trends in Neurosciences, 7,* 442–446.

Woolsey, C. N. (1958). Organization of somatic sensory and motor areas of the cerebral cortex: In H. F. Harlow & C. N. Woolsey (Eds.), *Biological and biochemical bases of behavior* (pp. 63–81). Madison, WI: University of Wisconsin Press.

Wyler, A. R., & Burchiel, K. J. (1978). Operant control of pyramidal tract neurons: The role of spinal dorsal columns. *Brain Research, 157,* 257–265.

Wyler, A. R., Burchiel, K. J., & Robbins, C. A. (1979). Operant control of precentral neurons in monkeys: Evidence against open loop control. *Brain Research, 171,* 29–39.

II MOTOR PROCESSES IN PERCEPTION

7 Muscle Sense and Innervation Feelings: A Chapter in the History of Perception and Action

Eckart Scheerer
Universität Oldenburg
and
Universität Bielefeld

INTRODUCTION

The contribution of efferent and proprioceptive (kinesthetic) factors to perception remains a vital research issue in present-day psychology (e.g., Shebilske, 1984). Owing to the independent rediscovery of Helmholtz's efferent theory of space constancy by Sperry (1950) and v. Holst and Mittelstaedt (1950), most investigators are aware of the fact that in the middle of the last century great emphasis had been given to the role of efferent factors in perception, and that this emphasis somehow became superseded by their complete denial at the end of the last century. However, the historical details of the rise and fall of efferent theorizing in the 19th century are little known. The section "kinesthesis" in Boring's (1942) classical work *Sensation and Perception in the History of Experimental Psychology* is still the most comprehensive treatment of the topic, to which may be added, for readers of German, the article "Kinästhesie" in the *Historisches Wörterbuch der Philosophie* (Lasslop, 1976). In the present contribution, an attempt is made to eleborate the information given by these two authors and to supplement an earlier study presenting a more inclusive outline of the history of motor theorizing in psychology (Scheerer, 1984).

When formulating their "reafference principle," v. Holst and Mittelstaedt employed a terminology that has gained wide acceptance today but was not used in the last century. "Efference" (or "outflow") refers to the impulses generated by the motor centers in the brain and relayed to the skeletal muscles; "afference" (or "inflow") refers to the messages reaching the brain from the sense-organs, and among them a distinction is made between "exafferent" and "reafferent" components, i.e., between those components of afference that are due to external stimulation and to the organism's own activity. When reafference arises from receptors in the movement apparatus (muscles, tendons, joints), it is called *kinesthesis* or *proprioception.* The latter terms were introduced, respectively, by Bastian (1880) and by Sherrington (1906); they were meant to replace the older term *muscle sense,* which had come to be applied to the afferent (or "centripetal," in 19th-century usage) impulses generated in the muscles. "Centripetal" finds its counterpart in "centrifugal," which refers to efference proper. Centrifugal impulses were thought to be accessible to consciousness, and then they were called "innervation sensations," sometimes also "feeling of effort." This clear demarcation between centrifugal and centripetal impulses became obligatory only after the discovery of the entrance of sensory nerves through the posterior roots and of motor nerves via the anterior roots of the spinal marrow: a law that was established, independently of each other, by Bell in 1811 and by Magendie in 1822. Thus, it should not surprise that prior to this discovery the term *muscle sense* was used without paying attention to whether it referred to the afferent or to the efferent side.

The main focus of the present chapter is on the history of the muscle sense concept. Reasons are given why the existence of a "muscle sense" was accepted very late in history, and the slow emergence of the muscle sense concept in the 18th century is documented. Traditional assignments of priority with respect to the "discovery" of the muscle sense are critically evaluated. To provide a link with the other contributions in this volume, the rise and fall of the doctrine of innervation sensations in 19th-century psychology is outlined. A final section briefly discusses why the muscle sense concept became obsolete along with the doctrine of innervation sensations.

THE DISCOVERY OF THE MUSCLE SENSE

Five Senses Only: The Classical Background

Boring (1942) credits Sir Charles Bell (1826) with having given "the classical and most successful argument for the independent status of the muscle sense" (pp. 524 ff). Another authority quoted by him is the "Scottish philosopher, Thomas Brown" (1820), "who insisted that 'our muscular frame' forms a 'distinct organ of sense', without which the perception of spatial extension could not be developed." In mentioning Bell and Brown, Boring echoes an opinion about the discovery of the muscle sense that can be found in 19th-century historical sketches, where physiologists usually give priority to Bell and psychologists to Brown. However, as Hamilton (1846) has shown, the muscle sense concept had been used prior to Bell and Brown. The concept emerged around 1800 and before that period the sensations arising from the movements of the limbs were invariable referred to the sense of touch, despite some earlier attempts, occurring in the 16th century, to show that this was not appropriate. The question then poses itself why the muscle sense was discovered so late in history.

The decisive *negative* influence has been correctly diagnosed by Boring (1942, p. 525). It was *Aristotle,* who insisted that we have five senses only: vision, audition, taste, smell and touch. Boring mentions that Aristotle "might have implied the existence of muscular sensitivity." Aristotle's term for muscles is *flesh* and sometimes *sinew.* Indeed he says (1912, 651 b 4) that "flesh and its analogue are sensory." But his main intention here is to maintain a general tenet of his theory of perception, that all senses require an intermediary or "medium" between external object and sense organ; he thus provides the sense of touch, which has no external medium as all other senses do, with a medium inside the organism. In a very general way, Aristotle connects touch with movement, because all nonstationary living things must possess sensation, and touch is the sense that must be present in all animals because without it they would "not be able to avoid some things and seize others" (1936, 434 b 15). On the other hand, according to Aristotle locomotion certainly is not subserved by the "muscular sensibility" we have alluded to; he "did not recognize the importance of flesh, as muscle, for locomotion. The movement of the limbs he ascribes to the 'sinew.', which might include the harder and stronger muscles, but not the soft 'fleshy' parts" (Preus, 1975, p. 134).

But how about *Galenos,* who summarized most of the physiological knowledge available in the second century A.D.? He had definitely established the muscles as the "organs of voluntary movement" (1964, I 1), he showed their contraction, including their resting tonus, to be controlled by nerves originating in the brain, he distinguished between sensory and motor nerves. Nevertheless, even he did not doubt the classical doctrine of five senses and did not hesitate to subsume muscular sensitivity under touch. For one thing, he "was convinced that each peripheral nerve served both motor and sensory functions" (Siegel, 1970, p. 177). More importantly, he stressed the unity of the receptive and the active function of touch, deriving it from the unity of both the object and the sense organ:

> It was not necessary that there should be one instrument of prehension and another instrument for touch, or that the instrument which holds and lifts external objects should be separate from the one which then distinguishes in them warmth, coldness, hardness, softness, and the other different qualities perceptible to the touch. On the contrary, it was better that as we grasp an object, we should at the same time determine its nature . . . If, then, it was proper for the hand to be an instrument of touch because it was also a prehensile instrument, it was logical that the same parts that make it prehensile should also make it an instrument of touch. (May 1968, Vol. I, p. 125).

Those parts are the hairless skin of the fingers *and* the tendons and muscles densely packed under it.

For many centuries, Aristotle and Galen were the leading authorities in their respective fields. But the tenacity of the five senses doctrine and its corollary, the subsumption of muscular sensitivity under touch, cannot be put to blind belief in authority alone. The doctrine simply rested on solid phenomenological and functional grounds, and it is by no means anachronistic that it should have been revitalized, albeit with a different grouping of the senses, by J. J. Gibson (1966), who comes to the conclusion that there are five basic orientation systems. The type of functional argument for the necessity of five senses and the superfluity of an additional sense that must have appealed to many comes out in the following quotation from a late Renaissance scientist:

> Things that occur are in part near and in part remote. Those that are near either impinge on us from the outside, and for them touch has been installed. Or we take them in, and in order for this not to happen against our will, it is sufficient to explore them by smell; once taken in, they are seized by taste. In order that we may avoid things that cannot be touched, vision and audition have been installed: vision for those directly in front of us, audition for those in an oblique direction . . . It is therefore manifest that we need five senses . . . ; if nature had provided a sixth sense, it would have been of no use. Thus, there will be only five senses. (Cardanus, 1554/1663, p. 570)

Certainly, the senses are taken here, from a purely biological or functional standpoint, as "basic orientation systems."

What are the objects of touch? Hieronymus Cardanus supplemented the traditional list (hot, cold, dry, wet) by pleasure and pain, sexual sensations, and heavy and light. This provoked the protest of his archenemy, *Julius Caesar Scaliger*. No, heaviness cannot be apprehended by touch. Touch is passive; in order to appreciate heaviness, we must resort to the motor faculty. In paralysis, warmth but not heaviness is perceived. If we simply touch a heavy object, we do not perceive its heaviness. A weight suspended by a thread feels heavy, but the hand feels the thread and not the weight. In sum, "the motor power senses without touch" (Scaliger, 1557; quoted after Hamilton, 1846, p. 867).

A contemporary of Scaliger had likewise suggested that the judgment of heavy and light depends on movement, but this did not lead to the general recognition that the muscles are sense organs. Not even Scaliger himself drew such a conclusion. Instead, he introduced the sexual appetite as a sixth special sense. In this he was followed by some other Renaissance scientists. Sensibility of the muscles was acknowledged only as a consequence of those changes in Western thinking that are known as the "scientific revolution," and even in the 18th century it was usually subsumed under the label *touch*.

The muscle sense concept emerged in three intellectual contexts: (1) epistemological uncertainties surrounding the concept of force; (2) the problem of space perception as formulated by British Empiricism; and (3) the emancipation of physiology from the mechanical sciences.

Three Backgrounds for the Muscle Sense

The Concept of Force. In *Galileo Galilei's* "Dialogues Concerning Two New Sciences" (1638/1954, p. 166), we read the following passage: "When one holds a stone in his hand does he do anything but give it a force impelling it upwards equal to the power to gravity drawing it downwards . . . And what does it matter whether this support which prevents the stone from falling is furnished by one's hand or by a table or by a rope from which it hangs?" At a time when the muscle sense (in an afferent or an efferent interpretation) was at the height of its popularity in psychology, this passage of Galilei's was taken to mean that he had developed the notion of acceleratory force out of an analogy with muscular effort. This interpretation can still be found in the last edition of Wilhelm Wundt's *"Logik,"* where we read that Galilei "could not have made a more fortunate choice than to take human and animal muscle force as the prototype of force itself"; a choice that was fortunate because the separation of mass and force is particulary obvious in the case where "human or animal muscle force sets into motion an external load" (Wundt, 1920, pp. 316 f.).

Once force had been accorded the central place in mechanics by Newton, philosophers set themselves the task to explain how we arrive at the concept of force. According to *John Locke* (1690/1823, p. 238) the motions of external bodies can give us only an idea of "passive power"; the idea of "active power," which implies that of the beginning of movement, "we have only from reflection on what passes in ourselves, where we find by experience, that barely by willing it, barely by a thought of the mind, we can move the parts of our bodies which were before at rest." Locke's suggestion to derive the concept of force from the experience of volition soon underwent criticism of a basically skeptical nature, which was intended to show that as a physical concept "force" could only be used in a metaphorical fashion and did not reveal to us the "true" nature of things. *George Berkeley* took this line: "Solicitation and effort or conation belong properly to animate beings alone. When they are attributed to other things, they must be taken in a metaphorical sense; but a philosopher should abstain from metaphor." The only legitimate meaning of "force" applies to "tangible ideas": "While we support heavy bodies we feel in ourselves effort, fatigue, and discomfort. We perceive also in heavy bodies falling an accelerated motion towards the center of the earth; and that is all the senses tell us." Consequently, gravity is an "occult quality" that has no explanatory value (Berkeley 1721/1951, pp. 31 f.). The visual experience of a change in motion serves as a sign for a potential haptic experience of force.

A somewhat different route leading to a similar end was taken by *David Hume* (1740/1886, p. 457). He quotes Locke's doctrine "that we feel an energy, or power, in our own mind; and that having in this manner acquir'd the idea of power, we transfer that quality to matter, where we are not able immediately to discover it." But by transferring the idea of power to matter it is impossible to establish a necessary connexion between force, as a cause, and its effects. The analogy with the will does not work, because "it has no more discoverable connexion with its effects, than any material cause has with its effects." The effect of an act of volition on the motion of the body is forever inexplicable, and all that we perceive is "their constant conjunction; nor can we ever reason beyond it."

The experiences alluded to by Locke and Hume on the one side and by Berkeley on the other side were not the same; the former appealed to the unimpeded functioning of volitional impulses, the latter to "effort, fatigue and discomfort." Thus, Locke and Hume stressed the efferent and Berkeley the reafferent side of the experience. But even the latter never mentions the possibility that the feelings discussed by him might arise in the muscles. It was all touch, like in his theory of vision. Why and when did the muscle sense enter the picture?

The basic reason was an *epistemological* one. Hume's analysis of the idea of force was part of his *skeptical program,* and his skepticism provided the impetus for Kant's *Critique of Pure Reason,* where the concept of force is treated as dependent on the a priori principle of substance. Kant's philosophy met with virulent opposition from many German philosophers who were heavily influenced by the British Empiricists but were little attracted by the Humean skepticism. Thus, their task was to somehow improve on the British empiricist program by confronting it with the Kantian transcendental analysis and above all providing it with a realist (i.e., nonidealist, not necessarily materialist) epistemology.

One of these philosophers was *Johann Jakob Engel,* known to historians of psychology as the author of a treatise on mimics. On December 13, 1802, he read at the Royal Academy in Berlin a paper on the origin of the concept of force. The original paper is in French; it is quoted here on the basis of the German version included in Engel's Collected Works (1802/1844). In it the term *muscle sense (sens musculaire;* the German version has *Muskelnsinn,* a now obsolete form) is introduced as an alternative to the neologism *Gestrebe* (striving), which the author had suggested in a somewhat earlier treatise. The author himself is obviously aware that he is employing not only a new idea but also a new term, and as long as no other evidence will be forthcoming we may adopt *December 13, 1802* as the birthday, Berlin as the birthplace and J. J. Engel as the father of the muscle sense.

Engel wants to show that both Locke and Hume have stopped halfway in their attempts at a psychological derivation of the concept of force. Locke was wrong in assigning the idea of force to reflection rather than to sensation. The criticism leveled at Hume bears quoting: "He ought to use his muscles, but instead he uses his eyes; he ought to grasp and struggle, and instead he is content to watch" (1802/1844, p. 104). Thus, his basic fault was to adopt a purely contemplative attitude. But like Locke, Hume also neglected a careful analysis of the external senses, a neglect he shares with contemporaneous philosophy in general. The so-called sense of touch (*Gefühlssinn*) is by no means homogenous—in fact, Engel had earlier distinguished between coarse and fine touch, thus anticipating Head's distinction between protopathic and epicritic sensibility—, and a more refined analysis reveals that the muscles are organs by which we acquire ideas about external objects. If Locke and Hume had known about that role of the muscles, "they would, while going through the number of external senses, have fixed their attention on this muscle sense . . . and would have found in it the original source of our concept of force" (p. 102).

Engel then briefly sketches a theory of the muscle sense. His basic idea is that the effect we operate in bodies to which we apply muscular force (by bending or breaking them) and the resistance they offer to our effort enter into a "complication," i.e., a special type of association. In order to get aware of this "complication," we need to expend some effort, but the *effort* will only be perceived when it meets some *resistance* on the part of an external object. In modern parlance, it may thus be said that Engel combines the efferent ("effort") and the reafferent ("perceived muscle force") viewpoint on the muscle sense, although it must be conceded that he professes complete ignorance as to how we can tell apart the two terms entering into the "complication."

Engel's analysis was used by the French philosopher *Maine de Biran*, who also wished to refute Hume's elimination of substantial causality. Asking with Engel whether "independently of the effort, or of any exercise of the muscular sense (*sens musculaire*)" it would be possible "to produce some idea of an external force" (Maine de Biran, 1807/1963, p. 147), he comes, like Engel, to a negative answer. Maine de Biran's psychological and metaphysical thinking was centered on the concept of effort, and although he erected an idealist system on this foundation, he also had a keen interest in physiological psychology and was one of the first psychologists to use clinical data from paralysis cases for the purposes of psychological theory. Maine de Biran established the term *muscular sense* in France, and he was responsible for the tendency of many later French writers to include the central motor impulse in the meaning of the term.

There is no need to further pursue the associated notions of effort and the muscle sense in the context of the epistemology of the force concept. In the 19th century, the idea was firmly established, and the philosophical lexicographer Rudolf Eisler was able to quote more than 50 authorities who all maintained the same basic idea derived from Engel through Maine de Biran (Eisler, 1927, p. 866). The idea was soon transferred from epistemology to psychology and physiology, and E. H. Weber (1846/1905) coined the term *Kraftsinn* for the perception of weight insofar as it was mediated by muscular effort rather than by cutaneous sensibility. The point made first by Scaliger was finally driven home.

Eye Movements and Space Perception. The second context for the recognition of the muscle sense is known much better. It started all with *George*

Berkeley's assertion (1709/1910, p. 13) that "it is . . . agreed by all . . . that distance of itself, and immediately cannot be seen." As Berkeley himself conceded, the assertion was far from new. Moreover, the *convergence* of the eyes had already been discovered, by Descartes, as a means to arrive at perceiving the *distance* of objects. What was new was Berkeley's insistence that this cannot be done in virtue of some "natural" and presumably innate "geometry." Instead, the "ideas suggesting distance" are (1) "the sensation arising from turning the eye" (=convergence), (2) "confusion" (=a blurred retinal image), and (3) "straining the eyes" (=accommodation) resulting in the removal of "confusion." More precisely, relative distance is suggested by these "ideas," whereas absolute distance is "measured by the motion of (the) body, which is perceivable by touch" (op.cit., p. 33).

One modern commentator (Pastore, 1971, p. 81) refers to "turning of the eyes" and "straining" as "muscular sensations"; a clear anachronism, because to Berkeley they were "tangible" (i.e., tactile) "ideas," where "idea" means an "immediate object of sense." It is difficult to understand how Berkeley brought his conviction that convergence and accomodation produce tactile sensations into line with his statement that the tangible qualities are "hard or soft, hot or cold, rough or smooth" (op.cit., p. 60). He might have thought of tactile sensations arising from the tissues surrounding the eye; but it is more likely that he was simply following one of the oldest traditions in sensory psychology.

So far, we have been concerned with Berkeley's analysis of depth perception. Turning to *two-dimensional perception*, we notice that he did not believe that it was mediated by eye movements. It was *E. B. de Condillac* (1754/1982) who denied extension and form to visual sensations per se and thus felt impelled to amend Berkeley's theory by an account of the formation of the two-dimensional visual field. Using the fiction of an "animated statue," he postulates a two-stage process of perceptual learning. The first stage has to do with the *acquisition of eye movements*. By a process akin to what we today call "orienting reflex," the attention of his statue will be attracted to one color, and the statue looks at this color until it is fatigued by it. It then switches to another color, and so on. Thus, eye movements serve to analyse the visual field into a layout of color patches, but in themselves they do not give rise to awareness of an external object and its form. The latter is acquired only at a second stage, on the basis of *tactile exploration*. The statue watches its own hand while it is exploring a surface. It sees how a moving color covers and uncovers another color, and it arrives to the judgment that the moving color belongs to its hand and the nonmoving color to the surface.

One might be tempted to think that Condillac had an efferent notion of spatial perception, because he says that without active movement, vision would remain forever nonspatial. On the other side, he obviously denies that the spatial characteristics of eye movements, as such, are accessible to consciousness; all that we are aware of are the changes they produce in the visual sensations. Also, the "education" the eyes receive from "touch" is of a visual nature: changes in perceived brightness, occlusion and reappearance of colors, and so forth. Even if Condillac had known about a "muscular sense," he probably would not have felt obliged to let it enter into the construction of the spatial world. All his statue needs to know is that itself has initiated the movements of its limbs; their extent and direction will then be appreciated on the basis of "reafferent" information.

Many 18th-century authors adopted Berkeley's and Condillac's analyses of space perception, even if they did not go along with the more general philosophical outlook behind them, such as Berkeley's denial that matter exists. But the empiricist approach to space perception was severely challenged in the last decades of the 18th century, in Great Britain by the Scottish Common-Sense Philosophy and in Germany by Kant and his followers. Like in the case of the force concept, *arguments against the nativism* implied by these schools eventually led to the discovery of the muscle sense.

According to Kant, space is the a priori form of intuition of the external senses, and it therefore cannot be derived from experience alone. Kant himself was scarcely interested in presenting psychological evidence in support of this basic principle of his epistemology, but the polemic between his followers and his adversaries was in part conducted at a psychological level. One of his most outspoken adversaries, *Dietrich Tiedemann,* maintained that the notion of space is founded on sensations arising from intended or real movements, among others "a feeling of the movements of the eyes in all directions" (1794, p. 69). Imagined space depends on the same type of sensations. If we try to imagine something extended, "we first feel some effort in the eyes, and then a tendency to movement in various direction; it is as if one was to move the eyes here and there, back and forth . . . If someone looks at something extended of considerable breadth and width, he in fact executes eye movements of that sort" (1798, p. 96). Visual images are accompanied by eye movements because all images arise from movements: "Every sensation is connected with certain movements of the organs . . . We repeat internally these movements, copy what we do while perceiving, and thus we form a mental image" (Tiedemann, 1804, p. 53). Mental images are copies (*Nachbildungen*), but what is copied is not previous sensations but previous movements necessary for sensations. This must be the *earliest "motor theory" of mental imagery.*

How do we get aware of the movements of the sense organs and of other limbs? Tiedemann is obviously indebted to Condillac, but other than Condillac he must be classified among the efferent theoreticians. In an earlier psychological work, he had referred to a "feeling of tension in the skin and the tendons" (1777, p. 222), but in his later works he tends to invoke a *feeling of effort,* which he localizes in "the nerves." In fact, he proclaims that "all nerves have an inner feeling . . . , a feeling of their state" (1804, p. 404). By employing the term *inner feeling,* he dissociates these "feelings of the nerves" from touch, which he calls "external feeling."

Within the Scottish tradition, the breakthrough to the "muscle sense" concept was made in *Thomas Brown's Lectures on the Philosophy of the Human Mind* (Brown, 1820/1846). Brown argues from the premiss that neither touch nor vision are originally spatial. In the case of vision, this had already been stated by Condillac, but it seems that the idea of a *strictly punctiform tactual sensation* was introduced by Brown. Against our presumably immediate perception of extension and figure by touch alone, Brown adduces several arguments. For instance, be it granted that a figure of some magnitude stimulates 100 "physical points of the organs of touch" (op. cit., Vol. I, p. 518), its extension could still not be perceived, because we do not know how densely packed these points are on our sensitive surface. Again, if the organ of touch were able to apprehend figure without the assistance of another sense organ, then this should be true of all figures alike. But experience is contrary to that. The "discovery" of figure is far from being exact even for the most simple figures; it becomes very difficult and next to impossible for complicated or unfamiliar forms (p. 530). In sum, "the knowledge of figure . . . is not the state of the mind originally and immediately subsequent to affections of our organ of touch, any more than the perception of distance is the state of the mind originally and immediately subsequent to affections of our organ of sight" (p. 532).

Given his presumption that both visual and tactile sensations are punctiform, Brown practically had to invent the muscle sense. What he needed was a medium that displayed "continuous divisibility" and could glue together the punctiform sensations. At a general epistemological level, this medium was the "feeling of time," and at a more concrete psychological level, the "gradual" (i.e., graded) movements of the hand, which result in a "series of muscular feelings" (p. 542). These muscular feelings "flow together" with the "tactual feelings," or in the case of vision, with sensations of light and color.

Despite their purely theoretical background, the *muscular feelings* certainly had no hypothetical character for Brown. On their *phenomenology,* he is much more explicit than any of his predecessors. By calling them "feelings," he does not want to imply that they are nonsensory; like every other sensation, they require "a distinct organ of sense," which is the "muscular frame." Brown concedes that muscular sensations are usually "obscure"; nevertheless, "there is probably no contraction, even of a single muscle, which is not attended with some faint degree of sensation that distinguishes it from the contractions of other muscles, or from other degrees of contraction of the same muscle" (p. 511). But would such sensations of muscle contraction not imply some kind of "natural anatomy," a detailed knowledge of the number and locations of our own muscles? By no means, because the motions of our limbs are visible, and these visible motions serve to individualize the otherwise too "complex" muscular feelings. Moreover, the "obscurity" of the muscular feelings obtains only under "common circumstances" and vanishes, for example, in fatigue; because "what is the feeling of fatigue . . . but a muscular feeling?" (p. 512).

Brown's analysis of space perception provided the model for much 19th-century "motor" theorizing by British psychologists like John Stuart Mill, Herbert Spencer, and Alexander Bain. Although Brown himself obviously held an afferent interpretation of the muscle sense, the later British theoreticians tended to switch to an efferent interpretation.

The Effects of Irritability on Sensibility. In the second half of the 18th century the general ideas underlying physiological research underwent a profound change. The conviction that living matter was subject to purely mechanical laws and could profitably be studied by the methods of mathematical physics gave way to a more modest attitude that acknowledged that the reducibility of organic phenomena to mechanical laws had not been adequately demonstrated. At the end of the 18th century, various forms of *vitalism* had emerged that maintained that the phenomena of life were governed by a nonmechanical or supramechanical "vital power" (*Lebenskraft*).

The vitalist tradition was another background for the acknowledgment of the muscle sense. However, such acknowledgment occurred only as the result of a complicated process of defining and redefining the "vital powers" of irritability and sensibility, a process that was initiated by the work of the Swiss physiologist *Albrecht von Haller.* Haller (1753) examined the responses of animals to mechanical and chemical stimulation of various tissues. He found that stimulation of the muscles resulted in contraction, whereas stimulation of peripheral nerves and of tissues provided with nerve endings resulted in symptoms of pain. He concluded that there were two functionally and anatomically distinct vital powers: irritability, defined by the ability to contract, and residing in the muscles; and sensibility, defined by symptoms of pain, and residing in the nervous system.

Most late 18th-century physiologists accepted the distinction between irritability (or contractility, if defined in Haller's terms) and sensibility. However, Haller's doctrine about the anatomocal loci of irritability and sensibility was often criticized. At the beginning of the 19th century, F. M. X. Bichat (1821) asserted the presence of sensibility in the muscles. Nevertheless, it is doubtful whether Bichat should be listed, as was done by Henri (1899, pp. 409-410), among those who pioneered the muscle sense concept prior to Thomas Brown and Charles Bell. Bichat maintained that the muscles displayed a sensibility that was not mediated by the nervous system: clearly, a dead alley rather than a promising avenue. Within the vitalist tradition, the pioneer of the muscle sense concept was *Franz von Paula Gruithuisen,* the author of an *Anthropology; or: On the Nature of Man's Life and Thought; for Beginning Philosophers and Doctors.* This book (Gruithuisen, 1810) contains a completely elaborated doctrine of the muscle sense, under the heading "What Irritability Does Contribute to Sensibility."

Considering terminology first, we notice that Gruithuisen claims priority for the term *muscle sense*. The *Muskelsinn* is one subdivision of "common sensibility" (*Gemeinsinn*, "coenaesthesis," not to be confused with the "common sense" of the Scottish philosophers); alternatively, it may be called "mechanical sense." The "mechanical sense is a true muscle sense or, as it were, a sense of touch residing in the muscle system." It comprises six subdivisions: (a) active: sense of movements and posture (b) passive: sense of orientation and passive movement; (c) mixed: vertigo and sense of resistance (Gruithuisen, 1810, p. 130).

This is certainly a somewhat mixed list, but it turns out to be nearly identical to the one Nagel (1905) gave in replacement of the traditional "muscle sense." At the time, nothing was known about the function of the inner ear in producing vertigo, a discovery made only by Flourens in 1824. The rest of Gruithuisen's list is quite reasonable. The existence of the *active movement sense* is revealed by the locomotor abilities of blind people and by our behavior in judging lifted weights. The *active posture sense* (*Positurensinn*) is the "feeling of the . . . spatial relations among the parts of our skeleton by means of the muscles"; it is particularly well developed in dancers or piano players. The *orientation sense* (*Lagesinn*) concerns the orientation of our body relative to light and gravitation; it regulates the distribution of the contractions of our musculature previously to an intended change in position. That we have a *passive movement sense* is evident in walking, riding, and so forth; it consists in an active use of the *Lagesinn*. The *resistance sense* is introduced by a somewhat curious example— the bat's ability to avoid obstacles—but in man it comprises performances involving tactual exploration. Finally, *vertigo* consists in a disturbance of the unitary action of the muscles in maintaining bodily position; the eye muscles are set in antagonistic motion, the muscles subserving erect posture get unrestful . . . . Obviously, Gruithuisen is describing here the symptoms of vertigo, without adducing evidence that they are caused by a dysfunction of the muscle sense. But his general message is clear: The muscle sense is needed for the patterning of movements, their adjustment to the initial position of limbs, and the maintenance of body equilibrium with respect to gravitation, achievements that for the most part are entirely unintentional (p. 232).

Gruithuisen does away with the idea that there could be a muscle sensibility that was not subserved by the nervous system; every irritable organ depends on the nervous system as far as internal stimuli are concerned (p. 129). The muscle has all attributes of a sense organ, the stimulation of the muscle sense is a purely mechanical effect, and "the entire function of the muscle sense consists in registering the degree of contraction of the muscle fibers in the human and animal body" (p. 363). Consequently, the nerves supplying the muscles must have both motor and sensory components, but Gruithuisen gives no indication concerning their entrance into the spinal marrow.

As a physiological mechanism, the muscle sense became viable only after Sir Charles Bell (1811) had discovered that sensory and motor fibres are kept separate in the peripheral nerves and the spinal marrow—a discovery immortalized by the epitheton "Bell–Magendie's law." The law states that motor nerves enter the spinal marrow by the anterior roots and sensory nerves leave it by the posterior roots; the basic fact underlying it was independently rediscovered, in 1822, by Francois Magendie.

A brief comment is needed on Bell's intellectual background. He knew little of the psychology of his time, and apparently he became aware of Thomas Brown's references to the muscle sense only after his own discoveries had been made (Carmichael, 1926, p. 204). Bell was an anatomist, and his researches were motivated by a deeply religious reverence for the "design evinced" in the human body. As a physiologist, Bell belongs to the tradition of vitalism. In the opening paragraph of his privately printed *Idea of a New Anatomy of the Brain* (1811/1948), Bell disclaims to be "in search of the seat of the soul" and pronounces that he wishes "only to investigate the structure of the brain, as we examine the structure of the eye and ear" (op.cit., p. 113). His aim is to assign separate vital properties like sensation, conduction, and motion, to the parts of the brain, which hitherto had been assigned a unitary function despite its obvious structural heterogeneity. And he uses the methods developed by the vitalist school—vivisection and clinical observation—to establish correlations between structure and vital (i.e., non-mechanical) function in the nervous system.

Bell sets out to show "that the cerebrum and cerebellum are different in function as in form; that the parts of the cerebrum have different functions; and that the nerves which we trace in our body are not single nerves possessing various powers, but bundles of different nerves . . . ; that the nerves of sense, the nerves of motion, and the vital nerves are distinct through their whole course, though they seem sometimes united in one bundle" (p. 114). But he was not able to fulfill this program in its entirety, and his partial failure was responsible for the discovery that afterwards received the epitheton "Bell-Magendie's law." He conjectured that the cerebrum is "the seat of those qualities of the mind which distinguish man" and the cerebellum "corresponds with the frame of the body." Seeing no way to experiment directly on the brain, he instead "injured" the anterior and posterior "portions" of the spinal marrow, which he thought to be connected with the cerebrum and the cerebellum, respectively. An injury to the anterior portion "convulsed the animal more certainly" than a posterior injury, but it proved difficult to produce isolated injuries. Then, working from the premiss that "the properties of the nerves are derived from their connections with the parts of the brain" and "considering that the spinal nerves have a double root," he "cut across the posterior fasciculus of nerves without "convulsing the muscles of the back"; however, "on touching the anterior fasciculus with the point of the knife, the muscles of the back were immediately convulsed" (pp. 119 f.)

Thus, it was established that "the roots of the spinal nerves have different powers," but the possibility remained that the double innervation of muscles was restricted to those that were subserved by spinal nerves. Fifteen years later, Bell took up a study of the "nerves of the encephalon" and arrived at the conclusion that "every muscle has two nerves, of different powers, supplied to it" (1826, p. 164). After having inferred, from anatomical dissection, that a given muscle was supplied by both motor and sensory nerves and that, on the other hand, a given nerve subserved both sensory and motor functions, he asked the following question: "Why are nerves, whose office it is to convey sensation, profusely given to muscles in addition to those motor nerves which are given to excite their motions? and why do both classes of muscular nerves form plexus?" (p. 166). To arrive at an answer, it must first be enquired, "if it be necessary to the governance of the muscular frame, that there be a consciousness of the state or degree of action of the muscles?" (p. 167). Positive evidence on this question is provided by feelings of overexertion and weariness . . . , by our power of weighing in the hand . . . , by the ability of the blind to balance their body.

All these examples had been adduced by previous authors. Bell's new contribution consisted in his demonstration "that a motor nerve is not a conductor to the brain, and that it cannot perform the office of a sensory nerve." "Irritation" of the two nerves of a muscle shows that only one of them will produce a contraction. Cutting across the nerve "which had the power of exciting the muscle" and stimulating the other nerve, the animal will give evidence of pain but will not move the muscle in question (pp. 167 f.). Some clinical cases are relevant. For instance, one woman had "lost the sensibility of the eye and the eve-lid. . . She could not tell whether her eye-lid was open or shut . . . but being asked to shut the eye which already was closed, she acted with the orbicular muscle and puckered the eye-lids" (p. 169).

In sum: "*Between the brain and the muscle there is a circle of nerves; one nerve conveys the influence from the brain to the muscle, another gives the sense of the condition of the muscle to the brain.* If the circle be broken by the division of the motor nerve, motion ceases; if it be broken by the division of the other nerve, there is no longer a sense of the condition of the muscle, and therefore no regulation of its activity" (p. 170).

On the basis of these quotations, it is obvious that the "*sense of the condition of the muscle,*" for Bell, rested on "proprioceptive" information. Leonard Carmichael, who reviewed Bell's work at a time when the concept of innervation sensations was no longer accepted, credits Bell with having provided the "apparently unequivocal facts" that necessitated rejection of the concept. According to Carmichael (1926, p. 206), "it is remarkable that this false view was given credence long after Bell had presented proofs which were sufficient to refute it." Even more remarkable, however, is the fact that Carmichael, though he knew the relevant publication by Bell, was unable to see that Bell himself accepted the doctrine of innervation sensations, if not in words then in substance. As we shall see Bell had a clear notion of what v. Holst and Mittelstaedt called the "efference copy," and he offered one of the classical proofs for its existence.

Concluding Remarks on the Muscle Sense

Who discovered the muscle sense? Perhaps we had better asked: Who invented the muscle sense? It has become clear that the concept of the muscle sense arose in response to some dead alleys of 18th-century science and philosophy. The concept of force, the basis of classical physics, had come under the attack of skepticism; some immediate experience ensuring the reality of cause and effect was needed, and the feeling of muscular effort provided it for Engel and Maine de Biran. In the psychology of perception, sensations had become strictly punctiform, and spatial perception was turned into an intriguing puzzle. In order to keep up an empiricist account of space perception, exploratory activity, in the form of eye and hand movements, had to be invoked. How do we become aware of our own movements? Perhaps vision alone, coupled with an awareness of volitional impulses, was sufficient; but it seemed more safe to assign a specific sense to take care of this achievement. Tiedemann hit on the idea, and Brown baptized it. Mechanical accounts of organic functions had revealed their weakness. It was important to study living matter in its own right, and initially this resulted in a strict division between sensibility and muscle contractions. The division proved unworkable, in the long run. Gruithuisen assembled the reasons why information about the state of muscle contraction was necessary for the organism; despite their obvious heterogeneity, a unitary organic function seemed to be involved, and Gruithuisen did not hesitate to coin a term for it. The concept was there, but was the idea behind it workable? Bell showed that it was; sensory and motor functions could be kept separate in the nervous system yet made to interact in a manner that ensured "the consciousness of the state of our muscles."

Although the obligation to distinguish between afferent and efferent "factors" arose only as a consequence of Bell–Magendie's law, we have occasionally classified earlier conceptions in terms of "afference," "efference," "reafference," and so on. This is legitimate as a means to summarize the opinions held by a given author and to render them intelligible to a modern reader. We have distinguished between three contexts for the emergence of the muscle sense concept, and if a retrospective classification is applied to them, it turns out that emphasis on the various potential components of the muscle sense was not uniformly distributed across the three contexts. "Effort" theories, which by and large are equivalent to modern "efferent" theories, emerged in the "concept of force" context. The study of visual space perception naturally drew attention to potential optical components of the perception of one's own movement, and at least one theory (Condillac's) revealed a clear recognition of the importance of reafferent visual information. Finally, the irritability/sensibility issue resulted in a concern for those aspects of the muscle sense that today would be termed "proprioceptive."

Once the muscle sense concept had become firmly established, such differences of emphasis tended to disappear. Scientists are not exempt from the magics of words, and the presence of a unitary term strongly suggested an underlying unity of the phenomena covered by the term. Although it now seemed important to distinguish between efferent and afferent interpretations of the "consciousness of the state of contraction," the underlying assumption was that once the question was settled, it was settled for all functions of the muscle sense alike.

INNERVATION FEELINGS: A SKETCH OF THEIR RISE AND FALL

Until the middle of the 19th century, there was no definite and universally accepted terminology for distinguishing afferent and efferent interpretations of "the consciousness of the state of contraction." Ideally, the term *muscle sense* should have been restricted to the afferent interpretation. But some French writers remained loyal to the tradition, initiated by Maine de Biran, of covering the effort of the will by the term *sens musculaire*. Alexander Bain (1855), one of the most vociferous defendants of an "outflow" interpretation, continued to subsume the "sense of effort" under "muscular feelings." Apart from these exceptions, in the second part of the century the term *muscle sense* had become restricted to the afferent component, a terminological development made possible by the availability of the term *innervation sensations* for the efferent component.

The term *innervation sensation* was probably coined by Wilhelm Wundt (1863), but the reasoning underlying the term (though not the term itself) can already be found in Johannes Müller's (1838) influential *Handbuch der Physiologie des Menschen*. The following sketch will be organized around issues, rather than around the ramifications of terminology.

The doctrine of innervation sensations did not arise from, nor did it necessarily result in, a denial of muscular sensibility. Rather, it maintained that afference alone, either from the muscles or from other sense organs, was not sufficient to explain various perceptual phenomena that had become associated with the "muscle sense." As a consequence, an efferent contribution to perception had to be postulated. Despite wide variations of individual viewpoints, the theoreticians of innervation sensations shared two common assumptions: The motor (or "outgoing") impulse originating in the brain (1) is available to consciousness, and (2) it somehow combines with afferent impulses to produce a given perceptual phenomenon. In retrospect, it is easy to see that assumptions (1) and (2) are independent of each other, but at a time when psychology was the science of consciousness it seemed almost unavoidable to assume that a cortical impulse subserving perception must in principle be accessible to introspective awareness.

The following perceptual phenomena seemed to require innervation sensations for their explanation.

1. The Stability of the Visual World Despite a Moving Retinal Image Produced By Active Eye Movements. It had been known for a long time (see Grüsser, 1985) that after-images shift their location with eye movements, but this observation was not brought into contact with the problem why we perceive a stable visual world despite eye movements resulting in shifting retinal images. Independently of each other, Bell (1823) and Purkinje (1825) observed that passive eye movements did not result in perceived movement of after-images. Bell (1823, p. 178) deduced that "it is by the consciousness of the degree of effort put upon the voluntary muscles, that we know the relative position of an object to ourselves." Johannes Müller (1838, p. 363), quoting Purkinje's but not Bell's observations, discussed three cases under which a "judgment about the movement of a visual object" is made. If the image on the retina moves when our eye or our body is at rest, the object will be judged to be moving with respect to our body. When we follow a moving object, but the retinal image does not move, then we use "either the sensations from the moving eye muscles or the impulses sent to the eye muscles from the sensorium" to judge that the object moves. When both the retinal image and the eye muscles move in correspondence to each other, then we judge that the objects is at rest and we change our position with respect to it. Thus, Müller accorded the centrifugal impulse a role in egocentric visual localization, but not to the extent that he excluded the contribution of afferent impulses from the eye muscles. He did not mention the observation made by Purkinje (1825) that passive displacement of the eye results in an illusory movement of the visual field in the opposite direction.

2. Differences Between Active and Passive Appreciation of Weights. Quoting E. H. Weber's (1834) pioneer work on differential sensitivity for lifted weights, Müller (1838, p. 500) asked whether it was "entirely certain that the idea of the expended force of muscular contraction depends on sensation only. We have a very precise knowledge . . . of that magnitude of the nervous impulse issued by the brain which is necessary to produce a certain movement." If we have a faulty expectation about the weight of an object, we cannot grasp it correctly, and this seemed to speak for the involvement of a central impulse in the perception of "force." E. H. Weber (1846/1905) put Müller's suggestion to direct test by comparing differential sensitivity for actively lifted weights and for weights put on a hand lying on a table. Active lifting resulted in better discrimination, a result that gave rise to the notion of a sense of force derived from muscular effort. Although Weber (op.cit., p. 148) mentioned the possibility that the "sense of effort might be localized not in the muscle nerves but in those parts of the brain which are subject to the action of the will," he conducted a special experiment to show that a passively provoked extension of the muscles could be used in judging weight. Thus, neither Müller nor Weber ever denied the involvement of muscular sensibility in the sense of force, and the central impulse was only an additional factor needed to explain differences between active and passive movements.

By later authors, two further types of evidence for the existence of innervation sensation were added:

3. Clinical Data from Anesthesia, Paralysis, and Amputation. This rather ill-defined group encompassed the following observations: (1) Certain ataxic patients, whose muscular sensibility to pressure is reduced or abolished, are nevertheless able to discriminate weights and to appreciate, in a somewhat gross manner, the position of their limbs. The same patients make very aberrant active movements with their eyes closed, but they notice their errors only upon opening their eyes. Thus, they possess innervation sensations, but the control from muscle sensations is lacking; (2) Patients suffering from partial paralysis, where there is a discrepancy between the motor impulse and the actual muscle contractions, complain that the affected limb feels "heavy" and they misperceive the actual extent of their movements. The experience cannot be explained by muscular afference alone and seems to require a comparison with the central motor impulse; (3) A patient can have a limb amputated and still feel that he moves it when he intends to move it. There can of course be no muscular sensibility in a limb that does no longer exist; consequently, the feeling of movement is based on the central innervation.

4. Paresis of Eye Muscles. v. Graefe (1854) was the first to draw attention to the mislocalizations experienced by patients suffering from paresis of the external muscular rectus in one eye. When a patient of this type intends to move the affected eye in a direction in which he cannot move it any longer, he experiences an illusory displacement of the visual field in the direction of the attempted movement. Mach (1886) simulated ocular paresis by mechanically preventing the movement of the eye; when he attempted to move his eye, he observed the illusory displacement known from paretic patients.

The arguments reviewed so far relied on empirical evidence, but there was also a general philosophical "climate" fostering acceptance of innervation sensations. In France, Maine de Biran's effort of the will theory remained influential. In Germany, philosophers like Trendelenburg (1840) and George (1846) argued that there had to be an immediate consciousness of our movements that was not mediated by muscular sensibility; both Trendelenburg and George relied on Johannes Müller as a physiological authority, and they were teaching at Berlin when Helmholtz was studying there. In Scotland, Hamilton (1846) proposed to distinguish between the central motor impulse (called "locomotor faculty") and the muscle sense proper; and Bain (1855) felt that the most important conceptual division in psychology, that between the active and the passive side of our mental

7. MUSCLE SENSE AND INNERVATION FEELINGS 189

life, would be lost if muscular feelings were reduced to "ingoing" impulses alone.

Thus, if there was ever a *Zeitgeist* in Boring's sense, then between 1850 and 1880 it dictated belief in the existence of innervation sensations. No wonder, then, that Boring's (1942, p. 528) list of believers reads like a Who is Who of the life sciences during that period. Of the authorities mentioned by him, three are especially important in terms of their influence: Helmholtz (1867), Wundt (1863), and Mach (1886). All of them were convinced that active and passive movements differ from each other with respect to their perceptual effect, and that these differences can and must be explained by the match or mismatch between the efferent impulse and its reafferent effects.

Around 1880, however, a younger generation of scientists began to attack the concept of innervation sensations. The fight was started, among psychologists, by G. E. Müller (1878) and William James (1880), and it was won, by the same authors, around 10 years later (James, 1890; Müller & Schumann, 1889). Because James's definitive statement on innervation sensations is easily accessible (James, 1890, Vol. II, pp. 503–518) but G. E. Müller's is not, emphasis will be given on the latter's arguments.

The innervation sensations dispute occasionally involved doubts about the replicability of observations, but in the main the observations were taken for granted and the task was to offer alternative explanations for them. More specifically, the opponents of the innervation sensations orthodoxy attempted to show that active and passive movements produce different perceptual results not because of an involvement of efferent impulses in the former, but because they do not involve the same afferent situation. Let us use two examples to see how this reinterpretation worked.

Concerning the evidence from weight lifting, Müller (1878) maintained that the paralytics' feelings of heaviness in the limb and the normals' misjudgments about weight were in fact *expectation effects*. Expectation was different from innervation sensations because it involved the memory image of previously encountered weights or muscle sensations and thus did not accompany an efferent impulse but rather the traces of earlier afferent impulses. Müller and Schumann (1889) carefully investigated the effects of expectation and concluded that both veridical and illusionary impressions of weight were based on the velocity of lifting the weights and thus on a sensation of peripheral origin. Bernhardt (1872) had compared discrimination for weights lifted by muscles contracted via local faradization to actively lifted weights and had found better discrimination for active lifting; but Müller (1878) rejected this evidence for innervation sensations by assuming that the faradizing stimulus had exerted various disturbing influences. Thus, the active/passive difference did in fact not exist, and innervation sensations were not involved in judging lifted weights.

Mislocalizations occurring in paresis of the eye muscles, Müller believed, can likewise be put to afferent causes. In gaining a proper perspective on them, we must first note that they typically involve one eye only, and second, that *the muscles of both eyes are innervated in a uniform manner*. Thus, the potential contribution of the nonparetic eye to visual localization must be considered, even though it usually is closed or covered in the relevant experiments. It may then be assumed that the nonparetic eye executes a normal movement to fixate a peripheral target and that the localization of the target is based on the nonparetic eye, in virtue of a presumed principle that when two synergistic muscles are unequally contracted, the afference resulting from the stronger contraction is used. The resulting mismatch between retinal image motion and muscular afference will lead to illusory displacements of the visual field.

Although we have restricted our discussion to two classes of evidence for innervation sensations, it should be clear that Müller had formulated some general principles for "explaining away" innervation sensations, principles that could be extended to other types of evidence as well and that were adopted by most major psychologists of the time. Of course, the existence of central efferent impulses was not denied by Müller and his followers, but it was denied that they were accessible to consciousness and that they were involved in perception and in preparing and planning voluntary action. Inasmuch as central components of perception and voluntary actions existed, they belonged to the afferent side of the mental apparatus: expectation, anticipation, motor set—they were all considered to be "memory images" or to depend on the activation of memory images. The second principle was that presumed conflicts between efference and reafference could be reduced to conflicts between different classes of afference; its application required consideration of the afference resulting from the synergistic innervation of symmetrical muscles, not only of the eyes, but also of the limbs.

THE FINAL ACT

As one contemporaneous reviewer noted, "the presence or absence of an innervation sense has been discussed very frequently. Curiously enough, the partisans of both camps have appealed to the very same facts in order to defend their theories. Occasionally these discussions have been very nit-picking. This alone shows that . . . the admission or refutation of a central innervation sense is a purely hypothetical and subjective matter which only indicates the personal preferences of an author" (Henri, 1899, p. 485).

Even around 1900, there were some authors whose personal preferences still were in favor of innervation sensations. Neither Wundt nor Mach ever abandoned them. Both changed their terminology, however: Wundt talked of "internal tactile sensations," and Mach preferred a theoretical language involving the "will." But these were relicts from an earlier period, and Boring (1942, p. 528) could say that after 1890 "the case was not open and shut."

Given that personal preferences entered the picture, why were they slanted, among the younger psychologists, against the innervation sense? At the end of the 19th century, psychology underwent a definite move towards a *peripheralistic determinism,* where central processes were suspect unless they could be shown to have peripheral antecedents. The innervation sensations were a violation of this principle, they were tied to the notion of spontaneous activity, they seemed to smack of metaphysics and voluntarism. Consequently, as a respectable scientific psychologist, one simply could not *believe* in them: "I disbelieve in (their) existence" (James 1890, Vol. II. p. 493).

There was an additional problem, though. At the end of the 19th century, a common opinion (e.g., Henri, 1899; James, 1890) prevailed that innervation sensations were not "needed," that they had no explanatory value, and that they violated the *principle of parsimony.* This objection contained an element of truth. Although Wundt, Helmholtz and Mach never denied the indispensability of what today would be called reafferent impulses, they failed to exactly specify the functional relationship between the "efference copy" and "reafference." There was, to be sure, the notion that they had to be compared with each other, but not even Helmholtz gave an unambiguous statement to the effect that the efference copy was needed to exactly compensate the reafferent component of the retinal image motion and thus to maintain perceived stability of the exafferent component. Although it should have been said that the innervation sensations are *subtracted* from the afferent sensations, they often were represented as being *added* to the afferent impulses. Such addition, though perhaps meant metaphorically, was indeed superfluous, and Ockham's razor had to be swung.

The demise of the innervation sensations left a theoretical vacuum that was not to be filled by the old-fashioned muscle sense. Whatever the shortcomings of the peripheralistic orientation, it had the salutary effect to direct the attention of investigators to the potential sources of peripheral information about the movement and position of the limbs and of the body. At the height of the innervation sensation doctrine, the "muscle sense" and the movements of the retinal image were the only "ingoing" counterparts of the "outgoing" central impulse. For the sense of force, the skin had earlier been a likely candidate, but it was definitely out of the picture around 1850. Joint or tendon afference was rarely if ever mentioned. Bastian (1880) coined the term *kinesthesis* in order to get rid of innervation sensations. Kinesthesis was thought to be of peripheral origin and leaving central memory images, but Bastian was careful not to assign any single peripheral locus to it; kinesthesis was defined in functional, but not in anatomical terms (Lasslop, 1976). Its anatomical specification was a matter of further empirical work. By means of an extended series of experiments involving a variety of anesthesization and faradization techniques, Goldscheider (1889) established joint receptors as the predominant if not exclusive source of sensations relating to the movement and relative position of the limbs. Sensations of weight and resistance (the "sense of force" of the earlier days) were now separated from sensations of movement; Goldscheider assigned the former to the tendons and the latter tentatively to pressure exerted on the joints.

Goldscheider's conclusions amounted not only to the desintegration, but also to the annihilation of the "muscle sense"; in fact, Goldscheider left virtually no role of muscular sensibility except perhaps muscle pain or fatigue. Although this was a full turn back to 100 years ago, it was inconsistent with physiological evidence in favor of muscle sensibility, which had been provided by Sachs (1874). In the 1890s, the researches of Sherrington and his associates made definitely clear that afference from the muscles is needed for the execution of precise movements of the limbs and established the sensory function of the muscle spindles. However, Sherrington eventually came to reject the "muscle sense" terminology because of its mentalistic connotations; by coining the term *proprioception* (Sherrington, 1906) he focused on the role of muscle sensibility in the reflex regulation, rather than in the conscious representation of movement.

Thus, at the beginning of the 20th century *kinesthesis* and *proprioception* had superceded the "muscle sense." *Kinesthesis* was predominantly used by psychologists, and although it initially was conceived as a functional concept, it rapidly was assimilated to the "psychology of sensory contents" espoused by Titchener and others. *Proprioception* was the physiologist's term; like *kinesthesis*, it encompassed much more than muscular sensibility, but it had no connotations of conscious representation. Both terms had in common that they rested on the fundamental premise of reflex physiology that all activity had to be instigated from the periphery. No room was left for innervation sensations. Their rebirth in the form of "efference copy" or "corollary discharge" had to await the reestablishment of spontaneous activity as a respectable scientific concept, and the first advances toward a cybernetic analysis of behavior and perception.

REFERENCES

Aristotle (1912). De partibus animalium. In J. A. Smith & W. D. Ross (Eds.), *The Works of Aristotle,* (Vol.5). Oxford, Clarendon.
Aristotle (1936). De anima (On the soul). In *Aristotle in 23 Volumes: Vol. 8.* The Loeb Classical Library. London: Heinemann.
Bain, A. (1855). *The senses and the intellect.* London: Parker.
Bastian, Ch. (1880). *The brain as an organ of the mind.* London: Kegan Paul.
Bell, Ch. (1823). On the motions of the eye, in illustration of the uses of the muscles and nerves of the orbit. *Philosophical Transactions of the Royal Society, 113*(2), 166–186.
Bell, Ch. (1826). On the nervous circle which connects the voluntary muscles with the brain. *Philosophical Transactions of the Royal Society, 116*(1), 163–173.
Bell, Ch. (1948). Idea of a new anatomy of the brain (1811). Reprinted in W. Dennis (Ed.), *Readings in the history of psychology.* New York: Appleton–Century–Crofts.
Berkeley, G. (1910). *A new theory of vision* (1709). A. D. Lindsay (Ed.), London: Dent.
Berkeley, G. (1951). De motu (1721). In A. A. Luce & T. E. Jessop (Eds.), *The works of George Berkeley, Bishop of Cloyne* (Vol. 4). London: Nelson.

Bernhardt, M. (1872). Zur Lehre vom Muskelsinn. *Archiv für Psychiatrie, 3,* 618–635.
Bichat, F. M. X. (1831). *Anatomie générale appliquée a la physiologie et la médecine.* 2nd ed., Paris: Brosson & Chaude.
Boring, E. G. (1942). *Sensation and perception in the history of experimental psychology.* New York: Appleton–Century–Crofts.
Brown, Th. (1846). *Lectures on the philosophy of the human mind* (1820). 16th ed., Edinburgh: Tait.
Cardanus, H. (1663). De subtilitate (1554). In *HieronymiCardani opera omnia,* (Vol. 3). Lugduni (Lyon): Huguetan & Ravaud.
Carmichael, L. (1926). Sir Charles Bell: A contribution to the history of physiological psychology. *Psychological Review, 33,* 188–217.
Condillac, E. B. de (1982). Traité des sensations (1754). In F. Philip & H. Lane (Trans.), *Philosophical writings of Etienne Bonnot, Abbe de Condillac.* Hillsdale, NJ: Lawrence Erlbaum Associates.
Eisler, R. (1927). *Wörterbuch der philosophischen Begriffe,* Bd. 1, 4th ed., Berlin: Mittler.
Engel, J. J. (1844). Über den Ursprung des Begriffs der Kraft (1802). In *J. J. Engel's Schriften,* Bd. 10. Berlin: Mylius.
Galenos (1964). De motu musculorum. In C. G. Kühn (Ed.), *Claudii Galeni opera omnia,* (Vol. 4). Reprint Hildesheim: Olms.
Galilei, G. (1954). *Dialogues concerning two new sciences* (1638). (H. Crew & A. de Salvio, Trans.), New York: Dover.
George, L. (1846). *Die fünf Sinne.* Berlin: Reimer.
Gibson, J. J. (1966). *The senses considered as perceptual systems.* Boston, New York: Houghton Mifflin.
Goldscheider, A. (1889). Über den Muskelsinn und die Theorie der Ataxie. *Zeitschrift für klinische Medizin 15,* 82–161.
v. Graefe, A. (1854). Beiträge zur Physiologie und Pathologie der schiefen Augenmuskeln. *Archiv für Ophthalmologie 1*(1), 1–81.
Gruithuisen, F. V. P. (1810). *Anthropologie, oder von der Natur des menschlichen Lebens und Denkens; für angehende Philosophen und Ärzte.* 2nd ed., München: Lentner.
Grüsser, O.-J. (1985, February 18–22). *Possible role of efference copy signals for space and movement perception.* Paper presented at the Conference on Sensorimotor Interactions in Space Perception and Action, Universität Bielefeld, Zentrum für Interdisziplinäre Forschung.
Haller, A. de (1753). De partibus corporis humani sensilibus et irritabilibus. *Commentarii Societatis Regiae Scientiarum Gottingensis 2,* 114–158.
Hamilton, W. (1846). Supplementary dissertations. In W. Hamilton (Ed.), *The works of Thomas Reid, now fully collected, with selections from his unpublished letters.* Edinburgh: Maclachlan & Stewart, London: Longman.
Helmholtz, H. (1867). *Handbuch der physiologischen Optik.* Leipzig: Voss.
Henri, V. (1899). Revue générale sur le sens musculaire. *Année Psychologique, 5,* 399–513.
von Holst, E., & Mittelstaedt, H. (1950). Das Reafferenzprinzip (Wechselwirkungen zwischen Zentralnervensystem und Peripherie). *Die Naturwissenschaften, 37,* 464–476.
Hume, D. (1886). A Treatise of human nature (1740). In T. H. Green & T. Grose (Eds.), *David Hume, The philosophical works* (Vol. 1). London: Longmans.
James, W. (1880). *The feeling of effort.* Boston: Society of Natural History.
James, W. (1890). *The principles of psychology.* New York: Holt.
Lasslop, P. (1976). Kinästhesie. In J. Ritter & K. Gründer (Eds.), *Historisches Wörterbuch der Philosophie,* Bd. 4. Basel, Stuttgart: Schwabe.
Locke, J. (1823). Essay on human understanding (1690). In *The Works of John Locke* (Vol. 1). London: Tegg.
Mach, E. (1886). *Beiträge zur Analyse der Empfindungen.* Jena: G. Fischer.

Magendie, F. (1822). Expériences sur les fonctions des racines des nerfs que naissent de la moelle épinière. *Journal de physiologie expérimentale et de pathologie, 2,* 366–371.
Maine de Biran, F. P. (1963). *De l'aperception immédiate* (Memoire de Berlin 1807), J. Echeverria (Ed.). Paris: Vrin.
May, M. T. (1968). *Galen On the usefulness of the parts of the body,* translated from the Greek with an introduction and commentary. Ithaca, NY: Cornell University Press.
Müller, G. E. (1878). *Zur Grundlegung der Psychophysik.* Berlin: Hofmann.
Müller, G. E., & Schumann, F. (1889). Über die psychologischen Grundlagen der Vergleichung gehobener Gewichte. *Pflügers Archiv für die gesamte Physiologie, 45,* 37–112.
Müller, J. (1838). *Handbuch der Physiologie des Menschen,* 2. Band. Coblenz: Hölscher.
Nagel, W. (1905). Die Lage-, Bewegungs- und Widerstandsempfindungen. In W. Nagel (Ed.), *Handbuch der Physiologie des Menschen,* Bd. 3. Braunschweig: Vieweg.
Pastore, N. (1971). *Selective history of theories of visual perception: 1650–1950.* New York, London, Toronto: Oxford University Press.
Preus, A. (1975). *Science and philosophy in Aristotle's biological works.* Hildesheim, New York: Olms.
Purkinje, J. E. (1825). *Beobachtungen und Versuche zur Physiologie der Sinne,* 2. Band: Neuere Beiträge zur Kenntniss des Sehens in subjectiver Hinsicht. Berlin: Reimer.
Sachs, C. (1874). Physiologische und anatomische Untersuchungen über die sensiblen Nerven der Muskeln. *Reichert und Dubois' Archiv für Anatomie, Physiologie und wissenschaftliche Medicin 41,* 175–209.
Scaliger, J. C. (1846). *De subtilitate, contra Cardanum* (1557); quoted after Hamilton.
Scheerer, E. (1984). Motor theories of cognitive structure: A historical review. In W. Prinz & A. F. Sanders (Eds.), *Cognition and motor processes.* Berlin, Heidelberg, New York, Tokyo: Springer.
Shebilske, W. R. (1984). Context effects and efferent factors in perception and cognition. In W. Prinz & A. F. Sanders (Eds.), *Cognition and motor processes;* Berlin, Heidelberg, New York, Tokyo: Springer.
Sherrington, C. S. (1906). *The integrative action of the nervous system.* Princeton, NJ: Yale University Press.
Siegel, R. E. (1970). *Galen on sense perception.* Basel, New York: Karger.
Sperry, R. W. (1950). Neural basis of the spontaneous optokinetic response produced by inverted vision. *Journal of Comparative and Physiological Psychology, 43,* 482–489.
Tiedemann, D. (1777). *Untersuchungen über den Menschen,* Anderer Theil. Leipzig: Weidmann & Reich.
Tiedemann, D. (1794). *Theätet, oder über das menschliche Wissen.* Frankfurt/M.: Varrentrapp & Wenner.
Tiedemann, D. (1798). *Idealistische Briefe.* Marburg: Neue Academische Buchhandlung.
Tiedemann, D. (1804). *Handbuch der Psychologie.* Leipzig: Barth.
Trendelenburg, A. (1840). *Logische Untersuchungen.* Leipzig: Hirzel.
Weber, E. H. (1834). *De pulsu, resorptione, tactu et auditu.* Annotationes anatomicae et physiologicae. Lipsiae (Leipzig): Koehler.
Weber, E. H. (1905). *Tastsinn und gemeingefühl* (1846), E. Hering (Ed.), Leipzig: Engelmann.
Wundt, W. (1863). *Vorlesungen über die Menschen- und Thierseele.* Leipzig: Voss.
Wundt, W. (1920). *Logik,* Bd. 2: Logik der exakten Wissenschaften. Stuttgart: Enke.

8 An Ecological Efference Mediation Theory of Natural Event Perception

Wayne L. Shebilske
Texas A & M University

A fundamental ability for any mobile animal is visuomotor coordination, the dual ability to (1) convert continually transforming sensory information into a stable representation of natural events and (2) use sensory information to control actions. Since antiquity, people have had ample opportunities to observe the importance of visuomotor coordination. One example that has always been available is the fact that animals living in the wild depend upon visuomotor coordination to find food and to avoid becoming food for a predator. More recent examples include special events such as the Olympic games in which astonishing levels of visuomotor coordination are required to "win the gold" and everyday events such as perceptual errors causing tragedies on modern highways and skyways. Not surprisingly, then, the question of how space perception is dependent upon and altered by self-produced movements has a long history of investigation, a growing body of current research, and application-oriented efforts to use newly generated data (cf. Desmedt, 1983).

A central issue in current visuomotor research is the idea that efferent and afferent innervations interact to determine perception. This chapter concentrates on that issue and its practical implications arguing for an Efference Mediation Theory of visuomotor coordination in natural event perception. Specifically, the chapter argues that visuomotor coordination is determined in the following ways: (1) by efference-based information in some special situations, (2) by invariant transformations of light-based information in other special situations, and (3) by an interaction of light-based and efference-based information in normal everyday conditions.

Secondarily, this chapter argues for the plausibility of an Efference Mediation Theory from an evolutionary point of view and for the importance of Efference

Mediation theory from a practical point of view. Traditionally, experiments on efference-based information and those on invariance in light-based information stemmed from separate traditions. The former were done in large part by Efference Copy theorists and the latter by Direct Perception theorists who argued that Efference Mediation theories are implausible from an evolutionary point of view (Shebilske, 1984; Turvey & Solomon, 1984). Both traditions will have to be modified according to recent research that is reviewed here on the interaction between these two kinds of information. Specifically, this chapter tries to show; (1) that Efference Mediation theory must be elaborated well beyond the limits of Efferent Copy models, (2) that an elaborated Efference Mediation theory is at least as amenable to evolutionary interpretation as is Direct Perception theory and, (3) that advances in knowledge about efference-based and light-based interactive processes is essential to modern applications.

VISUOMOTOR COORDINATION: EFFERENCE-BASED DETERMINANTS

Visuomotor coordination includes many components including the ability to construct a stable representation of an object's direction and distance with respect to the self despite fluctuations of the proximal stimulus caused by movements of the eyes, head, or torso. Comprehensive reviews of many experiments that support efferent factors as determinants of those components are available (Ebenholtz, 1981; Epstein, 1973; Matin, 1972; Shebilske, 1977). Several examples are reviewed here not only because they implicate efferent factors, but also because they illustrate paradigms that have been used to study the interaction between efference-based and light-based information.

In one study, Morgan (1978) presented small luminous targets in an otherwise dark room. The targets, which were presented on a semicircular track within arms reach, were displaced to the right or left of straight ahead by 12, 22, 32, or 42 degrees. The head was fixed in a straight ahead position while subjects fixated the targets binocularly and attempted to point at them with their unseen hand. The mean pointer settings averaged over left and right displacements were 11.81, 20.99, 30.28, and 39.53 degrees.

Under these darkroom conditions, direction is not uniquely specified by retinal information, which is "information in the visual system resulting from stimulation of the retina by light" (Matin, 1982, p. 4). As illustrated in Figure 8.1, retinal information must be combined with extraretinal eye position information (EEPI), which is "any information regarding the position of his eye in the orbit that an observer has available which does not derive from stimulation of the retina by light" (Matin, 1982, p. 4). Morgan's pointing data therefore indicates that direction can be faithfully encoded by means of retinal position information and EEPI. Pointing at targets under similar conditions is even more accurate when a subject is free to move his or her head (Biguer, Prablanc, &

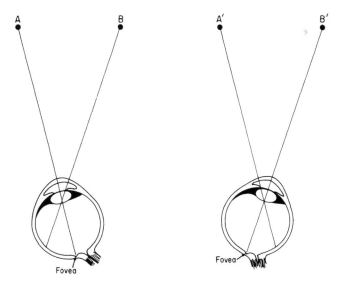

FIG. 8.1 Simplifying assumptions of an algorithm for perceiving visual direction. The assumptions are: (a) Visual location of target [VL(T)]: A and A' are defined as targets located at a spatial location of 0°, B and B' as targets located 30° to the right of A and A'; (b) Retinal location (RL): the fovea is defined as a retinal location of zero. Deviations from the fovea are measured in degrees of visual angle. Target deviations to the right and left produce plus and minus changes in retinal location respectively; (c) Extraretinal eye position information (EEPI): the direction of gaze toward A and A' is defined as zero. For other targets, EEPI is defined in terms of the visual angle between the targets and A or A' (right = plus; left = minus). The algorithm is VL(T) = RL + EEPI. The algorithm specifies the locations of the targets in the figure as follows: VL(A) = 0° + 0° = 0°, VL(B) = 30° + 0° = 30°, VL(A') = −30° + 30° = 0°, VL(B') = 0° + 30° = 30° (reprinted from Shebilske, 1984).

Jeannerod, 1984). These results support the functional significance of efferent factors in the perception of direction under reduced conditions; that is, EEPI is determined by efferent factors either directly by means of a corollary discharge that branches off from an efferent signal before stimulating the muscles, or by means of afferent motor signals that are contingent upon efferent innervations (Matin, 1972, 1982; Shebilske, 1976, 1977).

Other studies of efferent factors have not only controlled retinal information, but they have also manipulated efference-based information by altering the transfer function between efferent commands and oculomotor responses. This transfer function has been altered by means of paralysis (Matin, 1982; Matin, Picoult, Stevens, Edwards, Young, & MacArthur, 1982), external forces on the eyes (Skavenski, Haddad, & Steinman, 1972; Stark & Bridgeman, 1983), and postural aftereffects (Paap & Ebenholtz, 1976; Shebilske, 1979, 1981, 1984). The results from all these paradigms support the functional significance of efferent factors by showing that manipulations of efferent-based information has systematic effects on perception of direction.

Matin and his co-workers injected curare into extraocular muscles to induce partial paralysis. Consequently, they changed the transfer function between efferent innervations and eye position by decreasing muscle responsiveness to efferent innervations. For example, an innervation that held the eye at 40 degrees according to the original transfer function might hold the eye at 30 degrees after curare injections. In other words, the algorithm given in Fig. 8.1 for computing the location of B' would register an EEPI of 40 degrees instead of 30 degrees. As a result, observers should see a 10 degree rightward illusory displacement of B'. Matin supported this prediction by measuring direction illusions under darkroom conditions with three kinds of measurements: (1) visual localization (visually perceived median plane settings and visually perceived eye-level horizontal settings), (2) sensory/motor localization (pointing to a visual target), (3) intersensory localization (auditory/visual match of localization).

In a similar set of experiments, Stark and Bridgeman (1983) changed the oculomotor transfer function by increasing the external load on the eye. Subjects held one eye in a straight ahead position despite a slight external force that subjects caused by pushing their eye with their finger. The other eye was covered, and it manifested where the viewing eye would be without the counteracting force. Fig. 8.1 can be used to predict the visual effects of this manipulation. Position A would be projected on the fovea of the uncovered eye and EEPI would be registered as the position held by the covered eye that might be deviated 5 degrees in opposite direction as the force. Thus, according to the algorithm for predicting the apparent location of A, subjects would see a 5 degree illusory displacement of A in the opposite direction as the force. Stark and Bridgeman confirmed this prediction in darkroom conditions using all three kinds of measurements that had been used by Matin.

A third way to alter the oculomotor transfer function is to induce a postural aftereffect. One induction procedure is to hold the eyes in an eccentric position for an extended duration. For example, Paap and Ebenholtz (1976) had observers hold their eyes to the left or right of straight ahead by amounts of 12, 22, 32, 42 degrees for durations of 30, 60, or 120 seconds. Before and after each induction interval, observers were instructed to put their eyes in their normal straight ahead position. Paap and Ebenholtz then identified which point on a perimeter was in the line of sight when the eyes were held in the subjective straight ahead position. Posttest minus pretest measurements indicated shifts of eye position in the direction of the inducing eye turn. The mean shifts were 1.28, 2.86, 2.53, and 3.33 degrees, respectively, for the four magnitudes of inducing eye turns and 1.88, 2.55, and 3.99 degrees for the three induction durations averaged over all magnitudes of eye turns. Even the weakest inducing condition of 12 degrees for 30 seconds produced slightly more than a 1 degree shift. These discrepancies between the intended eye position and the actual eye position are consistent with the conclusion that the inducing eye turns changed the transfer functions between efferent innervations and eye position by increasing muscle responsiveness to efferent innervations in those muscles that had been strongly activated. A possible mechanism for this effect is posttetanic potentiation, a tendency for muscle tension to remain in a higher than normal resting state after continued contraction (Hughes, 1958).

Notice that the curare aftereffects induced by Matin *decreased* muscle responsiveness, whereas the postural aftereffects induced by Paap and Ebenholtz seemed to *increase* muscle responsiveness; that is, an innervation that held the eye at 25 degrees according to the original transfer function, might mold the eye at 30 degrees after induction of a postural aftereffect. Thus, the algorithm given in Fig. 8.1 for computing the location of B' would register an EEPI of 25 degrees instead of 30 degrees. Observers should therefore see a 5 degree illusory displacement of B' in the opposite direction as the inducing eye turn.

Shebilske (1977) confirmed this prediction. Subjects pointed at targets under darkroom conditions before and after holding their fixation 1 minute on a target that was displaced 60 degrees to the right or left of the median plane. Posttest minus pretest measurements of pointing indicated a shift of 8.33 degrees in the opposite direction as the inducing eye turn.

In summary, the functional significance of efferent factors in perception of direction is supported by two kinds of evidence: (1) Efference-based information (EEPI) sustains accurate perception of direction when light-based information is minimal, and (2) perception of direction in reduced information conditions changes as predicted when efference-based information is manipulated by altering the transfer function between efferent commands and eye position.

In similar studies of distance perception, Ebenholtz (1981) displayed a small luminous target in an otherwise dark environment at six distances from an observer: 28.4, 30.0, 34.4, 38.5, 44.4, and 50.0 cm. Eight observers pointed twice at the target in each of these positions while viewing binocularly. The main result was an excellent linear fit ($r = 998$) to the function relating target distances and pointing distances. Because retinal information alone could not account for this result, the data suggest that vergence and/or accommodation provides a linear signal that faithfully encodes distance.

In a related experiment, Ebenholtz (1981) displayed the same target under darkroom conditions at a distance of 34 cm. Eleven subjects pointed at this target before and after they binocularly fixated a target at a distance of 20 cm for 15 minutes. The same subjects also took phoria test before and after the close fixation. On the bases of previous results, Ebenholtz predicted that the close fixation would induce heterophoria, a latent tendency of the eyes to deviate from parallel positions. The tendency is latent because it is not manifested when both eyes fixate the same object. When a unique stimulus is presented to each eye, however, the ocular axes converge in front of or beyond a given target. The tendencies to converge in front of, beyond, or at the target are called *esophoria, exophoria,* and *orthophoria,* respectively. In Ebenholtz's experiment, the close fixation for 15 minutes induced a 4.82 diopter shift in the esophoric direction. After close fixation, in other words, the eyes viewing separate stimuli converged 4.82 diopters nearer than they had when the eyes viewed the same separate stimuli before close fixation. Ebenholtz attributed this esophoric shift to a change in the steady-state tonus of the vergence and/or accommodation system, which in effect, altered the transfer function between efferent commands and oculomotor responses. Specifically, the new transfer function would cause the efference signal required to converge on any given target to be one that had been associated with less convergence or a greater distance before the change in tonus. Accordingly, under the assumption that the signal provided by vergence and/or accommodation had been calibrated according to the original transfer function, Ebenholtz predicted that subjects would see targets farther after induced esophoric shifts. This prediction was confirmed by a 10.84 cm increase in pointing distance.

In summary, Ebenholtz's experiment showed two things:

1. Efference-based information (EEPI) sustains distance perception when other sources of distance information are reduced, and
2. Distance perception in reduced information conditions changes as predicted when efference-based information is manipulated by altering the transfer function between efferent commands and vergence.

Many of the earlier mentioned studies that implicate efferent factors as determinants of visuomotor coordination also support these conclusions.

VISUOMOTOR COORDINATION: LIGHT-BASED DETERMINANTS

The optic array at an observer's eye changes continuously giving rise to an optical flow pattern when an observer moves through a structured visual environment. Despite this continual transformation, however, there are invariant relationships between parts of the optic array. Gibson (1959) called these invariant relationships higher order variables, and he and others have made a case for the functional significance of higher order light-based information. We do not attempt to review all this work because many comprehensive discussions are available (e.g., Cutting, 1983; Gibson, 1966, 1979; Johansson, Von Hofsten, & Jansson, 1980; MacLeod & Pick, 1974; Michaels & Carello, 1981; Ullman, 1980). Instead we review several examples of studies showing what specific higher order variables can and cannot do.

Observers create potential sources of higher order light-based information when they move toward a textured surface. For example, an object's image expands as an observer approaches the object and the inverse of the rate of expansion that Lee (1976), called τ (tau), corresponds to the time to contact. In principle, therefore, an observer could directly access this important information without computing distance; that is, the observer could know time to contact by processing τ without necessarily knowing the object's distance. A number of correlational studies suggest that observers are in fact sensitive to and attentive to τ. In one study, Lee and Reddish (1981) derived evidence from a film analysis of plunging dives of gannets, which are large seabirds that dive from heights of up to 30 meters into the water to catch fish. The dives begin with the wings outstretched for steering and end with the wings tucked back to avoid injury. Based on the assumption that the timing of the wing tucking response is determined by the optical parameter τ, Lee and Reddish derived a predicted function relating time before contact when gannets start tucking their wings with the duration of the dive. The film analysis supported this prediction.

In another study, Lee, Young, Reddish, Lough, and Clayton (1983) observed visuomotor coordination in subjects jumping to punch a falling ball. They found that differences between functions correlating knee and elbow angles with time for three ball-drop heights could be explained on the basis that subjects were gearing their action to τ. Similar correlational studies supported the use of τ in controlling gait of a long jumper (Lee, Leishman, & Thomson, 1982) and braking of an automobile (Lee, 1976). Correlational studies do not establish cause, of course, so we cannot be sure that τ, as opposed to some correlate of it, is actually being processed to determine actions. Nevertheless, this research strongly suggests a central role of higher order light-based information in determining visuomotor coordination.

Not all potential sources of higher order light-based information are used however. For example, Gibson (1950) speculated along with others before him (Fick, 1905; Mach, 1885) that perception of body parts, including the nose, is an important source of visual information for seeing direction. This speculation is based on a geometrical analysis of an invariant relationship that exists in the optic array. Bower (1974) described this invariance under transformation as follows: "All objects that are straight ahead are symmetrically projected onto the retinas with respect to the projection of the nose and regardless of eye position. All objects that are not straight ahead are asymmetrically projected with respect to the nose. The relative symmetry of the projection of an object could thus serve as the stimulus to specify straight ahead" (p. 54). Accordingly, Bower (1974) advanced the following prediction without providing a test:

> location of objects relative to the observer is possible only if the observer can see himself and the object to be located. We are saying that the retinal position of the nose and orbit specify the observers position to himself. If this information is available, position perception will be accurate. If it is not available, position perception will be inaccurate. (p. 51)

Shebilske and Nice (1976) tested this prediction and found that direction judgments were not improved by nose visibility; that is, absolute error in straight ahead judgments were not reduced by nose visibility when subjects attempted to set a luminous target straight ahead with the nose visible or not visible in an otherwise dark room. Control conditions indicated that this null result was not owing to an insensitive response measure. In these conditions, subjects made judgments with an external surrogate reference on the nose, 3/8 of the way between the target and the observer, or directly in front of the target that was 183cm from the observer. This surrogate reference was ineffective in reducing error when it was on the nose, but it steadily increased in effectiveness as it advanced toward the target. We called this the Pinocchio effect because it suggested that the nose might have become an effective indicator of straight ahead if only it had grown much longer. Natural length human noses, however, seem to be ineffective indicators of visual direction. Future tests will have to determine whether or not direction judgments are influenced by visibility of other body parts. For example, visibility of the hand might have played a role in reducing errors in a dart-throwing experiment (Shebilske, 1984) that is reviewed later in this chapter.

Gibson (1966) also speculated that the center of optical flow might be an important determinant of perceived direction. Regan and Beverley (1982) showed, however, that this speculation is probably wrong. At the same time, Regan and Beverley showed the possible importance of another higher order variable, the point of maximum rate of change.

Observers viewed a cathode-ray tube that displayed simulated transformations of the optic array caused by self movement. The simulated movement was equivalent to the forward view from an automobile traveling at 55 kilometers/hour toward a row of fence posts 76 meters away. Each expanding pattern was presented for 2 seconds while subjects fixated a bar on the screen. Subjects then stated whether the center of the flow pattern was to the left or right of the bar. The results indicated that subjects were not able to use the center of the expanding flow pattern to judge the direction of self motion or that they were able to do so with very poor accuracy of about 5 to 10 degrees. In other conditions, subjects judged whether the maximum rate of change of magnification was to the left or to the right of the black bar. The results indicated that subjects could use relative rate of magnification to judge the simulated direction of self motion to a very high accuracy of 0.03 degrees.

It remains to be seen whether the most important part of this study will be showing what the perceptual system can do or what it cannot do. The finding that the maximum rate of change of magnification can be used will be especially important if experiments under ecologically valid conditions indicate that this source of higher order light-based information is in fact used during natural event perception. The finding that the perceptual system cannot use the center of the optical flow field accurately has already had an impact in steering visual scientists away from the previously held view that the center of optical flow is an important source of information about self direction (e.g., Cutting, 1983).

The negative results concerning the visual significance of the nose and the center of expansion in an optical flow pattern illustrates the importance of empirical tests. The existence of a higher order invariance does not insure that the perceptual system is in fact sensitive to that invariance. Cutting (1983) has also raised the issue of sensitivity with respect to other higher order variables such as texture gradients, which have been proposed as determinants of distance perception. He calls for experiments to determine the limits of perceptual sensitivity to texture gradients in natural environments. This sensitivity will have to be established not only for static conditions, but also for dynamic ones that might reduce sensitivity.

The next section reviews additional support for the functional significance of higher order light-based information. In addition, the research reviewed in the next section suggest that this light-based information interacts with efference-based information such that visuomotor coordination during natural event perception is determined by a synthesis or combination of these two kinds of information.

VISUOMOTOR COORDINATION: INTERACTION OF EFFERENCE-BASED AND LIGHT-BASED DETERMINANTS

Two factors interact when the effect of one factor depends on the level of the second factor. Thus, if efference-based and light-based information interact to determine perception, then one would predict that the visual consequences of changes in efference-based factors would depend on the state of light-based factors and that an observer's response to a given light pattern would depend on the state of efferenced-based factors. Shebilske (1977, 1984) supported these predictions for the perception of direction.

Recall that Shebilske (1977) observed a 8.3 degree shift in pointing at a target in darkroom conditions after a postural aftereffect was induced by having subjects hold their eyes to the left or right for one minute. Another condition was run in a design that was counterbalanced so that the only difference between conditions was whether the pointing tests were done in darkroom conditions or in a fully illuminated, structured visual environment. The pointing shift in the illuminated, structured condition was only 4.3 degrees which was significantly larger than no shift and significantly smaller than the shift in the dark.

More recently, Shebilske (1984) measured the interaction of efference-based and light-based information under more natural conditions in which subjects threw darts instead of pointing with their unseen hand. Specifically, after practicing several dart tosses, subjects threw three darts after each of six intervals, which were either probe or baseline induction intervals. Subjects sat on a stool that was 58 cm high and 146 cm from the target, which was a 1 cm circular

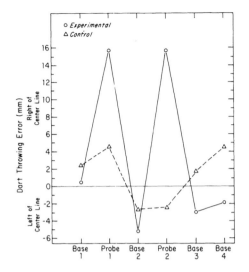

FIG. 8.2 Dart throwing error for experimental and control groups on baseline and probe trials (reprinted from Shebilske and Fisher, 1984).

center on polar coordinate paper. Probe inductions were identical to the leftward induction used in the pointing experiment. Baseline induction was accomplished by having subjects look straight ahead for 1 minute. The trials for an experimental group of subjects were baseline, probe, baseline, probe, baseline, baseline; trials for a control group of subjects were all baseline.

Fig. 8.2 shows the results for each trial for both groups. The dart-throwing error for each trial was the average perpendicular distance of three dart tosses from the target's vertical midline. This error was less than 5 mm on all trials for the control group. For the experimental group, the error was also less than 5 mm on baseline trials, but it was slightly greater than 15 mm on probe trials, which was a statistically significant shift with respect to that of the control group. Although this 15 mm shift is only about 1 degree of visual angle, it was very reliable. In fact, 17 out of 18 experimental subjects shifted to the right on probe trials relative to baseline trials.

The obtained shift on probe trials is consistent with the hypothesis that maintaining a leftward eye position alters efference-based information about direction by changing the transfer function between efferent commands and oculomotor responses. Furthermore, there is no reason to think that the induction procedure altered the proximal light information. Accordingly, responses to equivalent ambient light information depended on the state of efference-based information.

The pointing and dart-throwing experiments also support the conclusion that the visual consequences of changes in efference-based information depends on the state of light-based information. We can assume that the same induction procedure induced the same change in efference-based information in the pointing and dart-throwing experiments. Yet the magnitude of the illusion induced by that change depended on the state of light-based information. The illusory shift in visual direction was 8.3 degrees while pointing with an unseen hand in darkroom conditions, 4.3 degrees while pointing with an unseen hand in a fully illuminated, structured condition, and about 1 degree when throwing darts in an illuminated environment with the throwing hand visible.

In summary, the pointing and dart-throwing experiments show that the perceived direction of objects in a given light pattern depends on the state of efference-based information; and the visual consequences of changes in efference-based information depends on the state of light-based information. This pattern of results is exactly what would be expected if light-based and efference-based information interact to determine visual perception of direction.

Similar experiments support the same conclusions for distance perception. In one experiment, Shebilske, Karmiohl, and Proffitt (1983) measured the effects of induced esophoric shifts on distance perception. The main difference from the Ebenholtz (1981) experiments that were reviewed earlier is that measurements were taken not only in darkroom conditions, but also in a fully illuminated structured environment. The results under darkroom conditions replicated those of Ebenholtz (1981) in that an induced esophoric shift caused a posttest minus pretest shift in distance perception. Specifically, a 4.65-diopter esophoric shift caused a 6.34-cm increase in perceived distance on posttests relative to pretests. The new result was observed in a full illuminated structured environment where the same esophoric shift caused only a 2.31-cm increase in distance perception on posttest relative to pretests. This shift was significantly less than that obtained in the dark indicating that the visual consequences of changes in efference-based information is dependent on the state of light-based information. The 2.11 cm shift was also significantly greater than zero indicating that the perception of distance in equivalent light-based information on pre and posttest depended on the state of efference-based information. Thus, experiments on perception of both direction and distance provide evidence that efference-based and light-based information interact to determine visuomotor coordination.

AN ECOLOGICAL EFFERENCE MEDIATION THEORY

The idea that efference-based information interacts with higher order light-based information to determine perception might be called an "Ecological Efference Mediation Theory." This name emphasizes the fact that evidence supporting the theory calls for a synthesis between two diverging theoretical approaches; (1) the Helmholtzian physiological optics approach with its corresponding theory of mediated or indirect perception, and (2) the Gibsonian ecological optics approach with its corresponding theory of unmediated or direct perception.

Helmholtzian Indirect perception theories are based on the assumption that proximal stimuli have an ambiguous relationship to perception. Thus, mediating operations must supplement a proximal stimulus with information from other sources. As mentioned earlier, an example in visual localization would be the use of efference-based oculomotor position information to supplement visual information. In contrast, Gibsonian Direct perception theories are based on the assumption that the relationship between active animals and real events in the world is such that invariant structures of ambient light specify the perception of events unequivocally. Accordingly, a one-to-one correspondence exists between environmental events, ambient light structures that specify events (proximal information), and perception of the events.

These two theoretical approaches have been contrasted recently (Epstein, 1977; Shebilske, 1979, 1984; Shebilske, Proffitt & Fisher, 1984; Turvey, 1977, 1979; Turvey & Solomon, 1984) with respect to the following issues:

1. The efference mediation postulate that efferent and afferent innervations interact to determine perception is a mainstay of Indirect theories, while it is adamantly rejected by Direct perception theorists.
2. Indirect perception has been proposed to be limited to information-poor, static conditions, in which observers must judge absolute properties of objects, while Direct perception has been identified with information-rich, dynamic conditions in which observers can perceive relative properties of an array.
3. Gibsonian theorists have argued that an evolutionary interpretation is more feasible for a Direct perception theory.

The present article has already argued that the efference mediation postulate is supported in both domains of information-rich and information-poor environments. The present section tries to show that an evolutionary interpretation is at least as feasible for the Ecological Efference Mediation theory as it is for the Direct Perception Theory.

An ecologist seeking an evolutionary interpretation of perceptual information-processing mechanisms would emphasize the relationship between mechanisms and Darwinian fitness. Animals with more efficient perceptual systems should, other things being equal, leave more offspring on the average than animals with lower efficiencies. This differential reproduction should lead to the evolution of highly efficient perceptual systems to the extent that differences between mechanisms are heritable. This view in its most extreme form leads to the prediction that when an animal is tested appropriately, in the environment in which the species evolved or an environment similar to it, perceptual information processing should approach optimal efficiency.

This line of reasoning can lead to more specific predictions when additional assumptions are made. For example, Turvey predicted that ecologically valid tests of humans would indicate that visual perception is directly determined by higher order visual information without any efference mediation (Turvey 1979;

Turvey & Solomon, 1984). He based this prediction upon the empirically unestablished proposition that the specification of surface layout by the lawfully generated optic array is ordinarily sufficient to support successful animal activity. Turvey maintained that it would be inefficient for the perceptual system to contaminate completely reliable visual information with efference-based information that is riddled with anomalous information. Accordingly, it would be illogical to claim that efference-mediation plays a role in natural event perception and Turvey and Solomon (1984) state "it makes more sense to claim that evolution and/or learning would significantly prune or eliminate any voluntarily controlled activity that seriously and repeatedly undercut the accuracy and objectivity of visual perception" (pp. 452–453).

The evidence reviewed earlier in support of the Ecological Efference Mediation theory stands in direct opposition to Turvey's predictions (cf. Shebilske et. al., 1984). Therefore, if we accept this evidence and if we accept that behavior is adaptive and rational, then we must question Turvey's assumption that higher order light-based information is ordinarily sufficient. Indeed this assumption is questionable not only because it is without support, but also because it is unlikely that ecological experiments would indicate even the potential availability of sufficient light-based information in all conditions to which humans are exposed. Perception must guide behavior day and night in highly structured environments such as a forest and in relatively unstructured environments such as a snow covered field or a smooth lake. Studies of optical flow fields available to pilots have already identified certain night landing conditions in which higher order visual information seems to be ambiguous (Kraft & Elworth, 1969). Shebilske et al., (1984) proposed that conditions containing ambiguous light-based information also exist in the endless conditions that influenced the evolution of the human visual system.

Starting with the observation that efference-based and higher order light-based information interacts to determine perception and assuming that behavior is adaptive and rational we can reverse Turvey's logic to infer that the integration or synthesis of efference-based and light-based information is more reliable than either source alone. One source or the other might be more reliable in any given isolated condition, but the synthesis is more reliable over all. Other sensory subsystems such as the retinal rods and cones provide examples of systems that are adaptive overall, but less than ideal in any one isolated condition. A rod-free or a cone-free eye would be better in some situations, but the existing structure described by the duplicity theory is best related to all the conditions in a human's environment. Similarly, studies supporting the Ecological Efference Mediation theory suggest that synthesis of light-based and efference-based information affords an adaptive advantage relative to all the conditions to which humans are exposed.

The available evidence is therefore not only contrary to Turvey's assumption about the information that shaped the development of the visual system, but also suggestive of an alternative proposition that according to Shebilske et al. (1984) "fallibility in both visual and efference-based information function synergistically to shape both the phylogeny and ontogeny of the visual system" (p. 471). This alternative has important implications for basic research because it implies that the criticism of limited generalizability that has often been applied to paradigms that are restricted to information-poor domains (Kelso, 1979, Reed, 1982; Shebilske, 1977, 1984; Turvey, 1977, 1979) applies also to paradigms that are restricted to information-rich domains. As a result of a tradition of restricting research to special domains of either very rich or very poor visual information, we know very little about the wide range of natural conditions between these two extremes or about the processes that combine higher order light-based information and efference-based information. To advance our understanding of these processes, which, according to Ecological Efference Mediation theory, are as ingrained and fundamental as the processes for integrating information from the two eyes, visual scientists will have to broaden their perspectives to include the full range of conditions in the environmental niche of humans. This broadening process will have to include the emergence of paradigms that manipulate and measure under naturalistic conditions both higher order light-based information and efference-based information in order to discover how these sources of information are integrated (see Massaro, this volume).

MODERN APPLICATIONS

Information gained in the elaboration and articulation of the Ecological Efference Mediation Theory has potential applications for clinicians who are concerned with the prediction and optimization of visual performance, computer scientists who are developing artificial visual systems, and human factors engineers who design cockpits and other aspects of our new human environment (Shebilske & Fisher, 1984).

Clinical Applications. Two MMAs that might be especially relevant to clinicians are postural aftereffects influencing the intermediate "bias levels" of the motor systems controlling accommodation and vergence. Owens and Leibowitz (1983) called these "bias levels" dark focus and dark vergence because the levels of bias can be inferred from measurements of accommodation and convergence in the dark or in other empty fields. Owens and Leibowitz also noted that near work induces changes in the levels of both dark focus and dark vergence (see also Ebenholtz, 1981; Owens, 1984; Shebilske, 1981, 1984). Better understanding of these MMAs may lead to insights about (1) induced myopia (Ebenholtz, 1983), (2) orthoptic training (Hung, Cuiffreda, & Semmlow, 1984), and (3) clinical tests of accommodation and vergence anomalies (cf. Schor & Ciuffreda, 1983). Measurements of dark vergence, for example, are similar to clinical heterophoria tests that are in fact affected by MMAs (Ebenholtz, 1981; Shebilske, Karmiohl, & Proffitt, 1983).

Similarly, MMAs may become relevant to clinicians who adopt newly developed tests of dark focus to improve their ability to predict and optimize performance under low visibility conditions. Recent results suggest that such improvements are possible for important conditions such as driving at night (Owens & Leibowitz, 1976) or flying in an empty sky (Post, Owens, Owens, & Leibowitz, 1979). Raymond, Lindblad, and Leibowitz (1982) have also suggested that measurements of dark focus might also be used to improve other clinical tests that use near threshold stimuli. For example, measurements of contrast sensitivity are improved by placing the test field at the optical distance of each individual's dark focus. As such applications increase, so will the demand for better understanding of the interactive effects of MMAs and visual information.

Computer Science Applications. This area of research might also become a concern of computer scientists who have been stymied for almost two decades in their quest to match human vision. Computer-based visual systems depend on the development of computational models of how one form of information is mapped onto different forms during visual processing. Some of the models that have been developed enable robots to "see" simple objects under highly constrained conditions, but no current computer-based visual system could possibly work in the broad range of conditions to which humans are exposed (Ballard & Brown, 1982; Marr, 1982). The quest today therefore is for generality, and a key to that struggle may be a better understanding of how biological visual systems map sensory information onto an internal representation of their environment. Which of all the potential lower and higher order parameters of sensory information are in fact used as building blocks in the construction of an internal representation? The development of successful computer-based visual systems may have to await an answer to this question. And the answer, according to the Ecological Efference Mediation Theory, will require additional research on the interaction between light-based and efference-based information because the building blocks for our perceptions entail a synthesis of these two sources.

Human Factors Applications: As mentioned earlier, Kraft and Elworth (1969) identified night-landing conditions in which higher order visual information seems to be ambiguous. Specifically, they found that optical flow information that ordinarily guides pilots is nullified when pilots are over an ocean or other dark expanse on a descent path approaching an airport at night. This might explain why many planes have crashed under these conditions. It does not necessarily explain, however, why those crashes were always short of the runway. Illusions of visual direction related to MMAs may be the answer. Pilots often tilt their heads forward for extended periods to watch their instruments before looking out the windshield. Similar conditions are known to induce large MMA illusions that could cause pilots to undershoot the runway (Shebilske, 1978; Shebilske & Fogelgren, 1977; Shebilske & Karmiohl, 1978). Research is now being planned, therefore, to investigate interactions between efference-based and light-based information during landing in various conditions.

Research is also being planned to investigate implications of the Ecological Efference Mediation Theory for other human-machine interactions. For example, one such interaction that has not been entirely satisfactory is work involving video display terminals (VDTs). Today, in America alone, more than 7 million people make their living seated in front of VDTs, and many of these people are experiencing eyestrain, muscle fatigue, headaches, and dizziness. These problems are related to how VDT equipment is designed and positioned in the workplace according to a recent report by the National Research Council's Committee on Vision. Many problems have already been identified. Fixed-position keyboards and screens force workers to sit in the same uncomfortable position for long periods; inadequate lighting causes glare on the screen, chairs do not give proper support; and desks are either too high or too low for VDT terminals. One component of the problem of fixed-position screens is that individuals are restricted in selecting a viewing distance that is comfortable for them. Owens (1984) suggested that this inflexibility could be a problem because the best way to ensure optimal visibility and comfort is to match the user's dark focus to the distance of the VDT. One line of evidence leading to this conclusion, is research indicating that prolonged reading at other distances induces MMAs in the accommodative system (Owens & Wolf, 1983). Unpublished data from my laboratory indicates that reading also induces MMAs in the vergence system. Research is being planned therefore to determine the perceptual and motor consequences of these MMAs and how these might be related to discomfort experienced by VDT operators.

CONCLUSIONS

According to the Ecological Efference Mediation Theory visuomotor coordination is determined by an interaction between light-based and efference-based information when both sources of information are available, which they are to varying degrees during normal every day situations. This theory is at least as amenable to evolutionary interpretation as is Direction Perception Theory and perhaps more amenable when one considers the full range of conditions in the environmental niche of humans. Future research to elaborate the Ecological Efference Mediation Theory promises not only to clarify the basic nature of the synthesizing processes that underlie the interaction of light-based and efference-based information, but also to answer important practical questions in the areas of clinical visual assessment, computer science, and human factors engineering.

REFERENCES

Ballard, D. H., & Brown, C. M. (1982). *Computer vision*, Englewood Cliffs, NJ: Prentice–Hall.
Biguer, B., Prablanc, C., & Jeannerod, M. (1984). The contribution of coordinated eye and head movements in hand pointing accuracy. *Experimental Brain Research, 55,* 462–469.
Bower, T. G. R. (1974). *Development in infancy.* (San Francisco: Freeman.
Cutting, J. E. (1983). Four assumptions about invariance in perception. *Journal of Experimental Psychology: Human Perception and Performance, 9,* 310–317.
Desmedt, J. E. (1983). *Motor control mechanisms in health and disease.* New York: Raven Press.
Ebenholtz, S. M. (1981). Hysteresis effects in the vergence control system: Perceptual implications. In D. F. Fisher, R. A. Monty, & J. W. Senders (Eds.), *Eye movements: Cognition and visual perception.* Hillsdale, NJ: Lawrence Erlbaum Associates.
Ebenholtz, S. M. ((1983). Accommodative hysteresis: A precursor for induced myopia? *Invest Ophthalmol Vis Sci, 24,* 513–515.
Epstein, W. (1973). The process of 'taking-into-account' in visual perception. *Perception, 2,* 267–285.
Epstein, W. (1977). Observations concerning the contemporary analysis of the perceptual constancies. In W. Epstein (Ed.), *Stability and constancy in visual perception: Mechanisms and processes.* New York: Wiley.
Fick, E. (1905). Die Verlegungder Netzhautbidler mach aussen. *Zeitschrift fur Psychologie, 102.* XXXIX,
Gibson, J. J. (1959). Perception as a function of stimulation. In S. Koch, Ed., *Psychology: A study of science* (Vol. I). New York: McGraw–Hill.
Gibson, J. J. (1950). *The perception of the visual world.* Boston: Houghton Mifflin.
Gibson, J. J. (1966). *The senses considered as perceptual systems.* Boston: Houghton Mifflin.
Gibson, J. J. (1979). *The ecological approach to visual perception.* Boston: Houghton Mifflin.
Hughes, J. R. (1958). Post-tetanic potentiation. *Psychological Review, 38,* 91–113.
Hung, G. K., Cuiffreda, K. J., & Semmlow, J. C. (1984). Accommodation and vergence in normal and abnormal subjects. In J. L. Semmlow & W. Welkowitz (Eds.), *Frontiers of engineering and computing in health care-1984.* New York: IEEE Publishing.
Johansson, G., von Hofsten, C., & Jansson, G. (1980). Event perception. *Annual Review of Psychology, 31,* 27–63.
Kelso, J. A. S. (1979). Motor-sensory feedback formulations: Are we asking the right questions? *Behavioral and Brain Sciences, 2,* 72–73.
Kraft, C. L., & Elworth, C. L. (1969). *Flight deck workload and night visual approach performance. In Measurement of aircrew performance: The flight deck workload and its relation to pilot performance.* (NTIS 70-19779/AD 699934-DTIC).
Lee, D. N. (1976). A theory of visual control of braking based on information about time-to-collision. *Perception, 5,* 437–459.
Lee, D. N., Leishman, J. R., & Thomson, J. A. (1982). Visual regulation of gait in long jumping. *Journal of Experimental Psychology: Human Perception and Performance, 8,* 448–459.
Lee, D. N., & Reddish, P. E. (1981). Plummeting gannets: A paradigm of ecological optics. *Nature, 293,* 293–294.
Lee, D. N., Young, D. S., Reddish, P. E., Lough, S., & Clayton, T. M. H. (1983). Visual timing in hitting an accelerating ball. *Quarterly Journal of Experimental Psychology, 35,* 516–533.
Mach, E. (1959). *The analysis of sensations.* New York: Dover. (Original edition, 1885).
MacLeod, R. B., & Pick, H. L. (1974). *Perception: Essays in honor of James J. Gibson.* Ithaca: Cornell University Press.
Marr, D. (1982). *Vision.* New York: Freeman.
Matin, L. (1972). Eye movements and perceived visual direction. In D. Jameson & L. M. Hurvich (Eds.), *Handbook of sensory physiology* (Vol. 7). New York: Springer–Verlag.

Matin, L. (1982). Visual localization and eye movement. In W. A. Wagemaar, A. H. Wertheim, & H. W. Leibowitz (Eds.), *Symposium on the study of motion perception.* New York: Plenum.

Matin, L., Picoult, E., Stevens, J. K., Edwards, M. W., Young, D., & MacArthur, R. (1982). Oculoparalytic illusion: Visual-field dependent spatial mislocalization by humans paralyzed with curare. *Science, 216,* 198–201.

Michaels, C. F., & Carello, C. (1981). *Direct perception.* Englewood Cliffs, New Jersey: Prentice–Hall.

Morgan, C. L. (1978). Constancy of egocentric visual direction. *Perception and Psychophysics, 23,* 61–68.

Owens, D. A. (1984). The resting state of the eyes. *American Scientist, 72,* 378–387.

Owens, D. A., & Leibowitz, H. W. (1976). Night myopia: Cause and possible basis for amelioration. *American Journal of Optometry and Physiological Optics, 53,* 709–717.

Owens, D. A., & Leibowitz, H. W. (1983). Perceptual and motor consequences of tonic vergence. In C. M. Schor & K. J. Cuiffreda (Eds.), *Basic and clincial aspects of binocular vergence eye movements.* Boston: Butterworth.

Owens, D. A., & Wolf, K. S. (1983). Accommodation, binocular vergence, and visual fatigue. *Investigative Ophthalmology and Visual Science (Suppl.), 24,* 23.

Paap, K. R., & Ebenholtz, S. M. (1976). Perceptual consequences of potentiation in the extraocular muscles: An alternative explanation for adaptation to wedge prisms. *Journal of Experimental Psychology: Human Perception and Performance, 2,* 457–468.

Post, R. B. L., Owens, R. L., Owens, D. A., & Leibowitz, H. W. (1979). Correction of empty field myopia on the basis of the dark focus of accommodation. *Journal of the Optical Society of America, 69,* 89–92.

Raymond, J. E., Lindblad, I. M., & Leibowitz, H. W. (1982). Contrast sensitivity function of the accommodative system. *Investigative Ophthalmology and Visual Science (Suppl), 22,* 126.

Reed, E. S. (1982). An outline of a theory of action systems. *Journal of Motor Behavior, 14,* 98–134.

Regan, D., & Beverley, K. I. (1982). How do we avoid confounding the direction we are looking and the direction we are moving. *Science, 215,* 194–196.

Schor, C. M., & Ciuffreda, K. J. (Eds.). (1983). *Vergence eye movements: Basic and clinical aspects.* Boston: Butterworth.

Shebilske, W. L. (1976). Extraretinal information in corrective saccades and inflow vs. outflow theories of visual direction constancy. *Vision Research, 16,* 621–628.

Shebilske, W. L. (1977). Visuomotor coordination in visual direction and position constancies. In W. Epstein (Ed.), *Stability and constancy in visual perception: Mechanisms and processes.* New York: Wiley.

Shebilske, W. L. (1978). Sensory feedback during eye movements reconsidered. *Behavioral and Brain Sciences, 1,* 160–161.

Shebilske, W. L. (1979). Oculomotor hysteresis: Implications for testing sensorimotor and ecological optics theories. *Behavioral and Brain Sciences, 2,* 80.

Shebilske, W. L. (1981). Visual direction illusions in everyday situations: Implications for sensorimotor and ecological theories. In D. F. Fisher, R. A. Monty, & J. W. Senders (Eds.), *Eye movements: Cognition and visual perception.* Hillsdale, NJ: Lawrence Erlbaum Associates.

Shebilske, W. L. (1984). Context effects and efferent factors in perception and cognition. In W. Prinz & A. F. Sanders (Eds.), *Cognition and motor processes.* Berlin Heidelberg: Springer–Verlag.

Shebilske, W. L., & Fisher, S. K. (1984). Ubiquity of efferent factors in space perception. In J. L. Semmlow & W. Welkowitz (Eds.), *Frontiers of engineering and computing in health care-1984.* New York: IEEE Publishing.

Shebilske, W. L., & Fogelgren, L. A. (1977). Eye-position aftereffects of backward head tilts. *Perception and Psychophysics,* 1977, *21,* 77–82.

Shebilske, W. L., & Karmiohl, C. M. (1978). Illusory visual direction during and after backward head tilts. *Perception and Psychophysics, 24,* 543–545.

Shebilske, W. L., Karmiohl, C. M., & Proffitt, D. R. (1983). Induced esophoric shifts in eye convergence and illusory distance in reduced and structured viewing conditions. *Journal of Experimental Psychology: Human Perception and Performance, 9,* 270–277.

Shebilske, W. L., & Nice, R. S. (1976). Optical insignificance of the nose and the Pinnochio effect in free scan visual straight ahead judgements. *Perception and Psychophysics, 20,* 17–20.

Shebilske, W. L., Proffitt, D. R., & Fisher, S. K. (1984). Efferent factors in natural event perception can be rationalized and verified: A reply to Turvey and Solomon. *Journal of Experimental Psychology: Human Perception and Performance, 10,* 455–460.

Skavenski, A. A., Haddad, G., & Steinman, R. M. (1972). The extreretinal signal for the visual perception of direction. *Perception and Psychophysics, 11,* 287–290.

Stark, L., & Bridgemen, B. (1983). Role of corollary discharge in space constancy. *Perception and Psychophysics, 34,* 371–380.

Turvey, M. T. (1977). Contrasting orientation to the theory of visual information processing. *Psychological Review, 84,* 67–88.

Turvey, M. T. (1979). The thesis of efference-mediation of vision cannot be rationalized. *Behavioral and Brain Sciences, 2,* 81–83.

Turvey, M. T., & Solomon, J. (1983). Visually perceiving distance: A comment on Shebilske, Karmiohl, & Proffitt (1983). *Journal of Experimental Psychology: Human Perception and Performance, 10,* 449–454.

Ullman, S. (1980). Against direct perception. *Behavioral and Brain Sciences, 3,* 373–415.

9 Oculomotor Information and Perception of Three-Dimensional Space

D. Alfred Owens
*Franklin & Marshall College
and
Universität Bielefeld*

INTRODUCTION

The ability to localize objects in three-dimensional space is fundamental to many of our interactions with the environment. This ability often depends on visual perception of the size, distance, direction, motion, orientation, and shape of distant objects. Under ordinary circumstances, these visual functions are remarkably efficient. Indeed, naive observers often take them for granted, accepting the "commonsense" view that an object's shape, size, and position are simply given by the properties of the object itself. As demonstrated by innumerable spatial illusions, however, space perception is not always so accurate. Rather, its accuracy depends heavily on contextual information provided by the object's surroundings and on the observer's current condition, actions, and past experiences.

This chapter presents some recent evidence concerning the contribution of oculomotor processes to perception of three-dimensional space. These processes are conceptualized as complementing and interacting with information given through the retinal image. Much of the following discussion derives from the rediscovery of a fundamental aspect of oculomotor behavior: namely, that the eyes rest at an intermediate distance rather than at optical infinity. This insight has prompted a new approach to explaining many of the spatial illusions encountered under "reduced cue" conditions, and it suggests a reformulation of the manner in which efferent and afferent processes contribute interactively to space perception. To provide some background for these new arguments, it seems appropriate to begin with a summary of earlier conceptions of the perception of three-dimensional space.

THEORETICAL BACKGROUND

Sources of Distance Information

Since long before the emergence of experimental psychology, space perception has been thought to depend on two types of information: (1) static and dynamic structural characteristics of the retinal image, and (2) an awareness or unconscious "registration" of where the eyes are moving, pointing, and focusing. The first category, which Shebilske (1985) refers to as "light-based" information, can be characterized as *extrinsic* because it is comprised of relationships among components of the stimulus field or "optic array." The second category, which Shebilske (1985) calls "efference-based" information, can be described as *intrinsic* to the observer because it is represented in the neuromuscular events that accompany oculomotor activity. The distinction between extrinsic and intrinsic information should not be relied on too heavily, however, because from a functional standpoint, the two are inextricably related.[1] The availability of extrinsic, light-based information generally requires appropriate visuomotor adjustments, and conversely, effective variation of intrinsic, efference-based information almost always requires adequate light-based stimulation.

Although the distinction is of limited value, it is useful here because it reflects two theoretical emphases whose historical roots have often been parallel and occasionally adversarial (Boring, 1942). Some of the earliest accounts of spatial illusions relied on variations of light-based information, whereas early theories of veridical space perception were inclined to emphasize the contribution of oculomotor processes. In the 13th Century, for example, Roger Bacon observed that filled distances appear longer than empty distances. He applied this observation to the Moon Illusion, arguing that although the moon subtends a constant visual angle throughout its orbit, it appears larger at the horizon because the intervening visual texture makes it appear farther away. Thus, Bacon was among the first to explain celestial illusions on the basis of light-based information and to propose that apparent size depends on perceived distance, a view later known as the "size-distance invariance hypothesis" (Ross and Ross, 1976).[2] About 400

---

[1] Explaining the nature of this interrelation is one of the fundamental problems of space perception and motor control. Despite its centrality, and perhaps because of its complexity, this issue is often neglected in favor of analyzing simpler questions about smaller pieces of the system. Unfortunately, this strategy often fails to provide meaningful insights about the nature of perception or action. For three different and innovative attempts to deal with the larger problem, the reader is referred to Dewey (1896), von Holst (1954), and Gibson (1979).

[2] Ross and Ross (1976) also note that Bacon essentially presented a simplified version of Alhazen's (Ibn al-Haytham, 10th Century) earlier explanation of the celestial illusion. Alhazen used familiarity rather than light-based information as the key variable, however. He argued that when information is reduced, we attribute familiar properties to objects and surfaces. Hence, the sun and moon appear as flat disks on a flat ceiling. It follows that they should appear much closer (and

9. OCULOMOTOR INFORMATION ABOUT SPACE   217

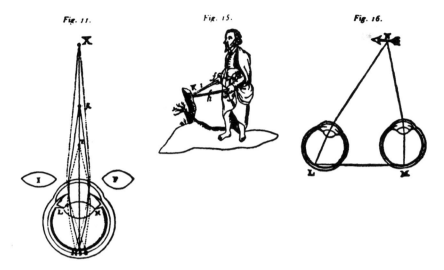

FIG. 9.1 Sketches from Descartes' (1664) *Traite de L'Homme* illustrating the mechanisms to which he attributed distance perception. Forms "I" and "F" in his Fig. 11 indicate the lens shapes that would be necessary to focus points "X" and "T," respectively. The convergence angle and distance when fixating a binocular target (Fig. 16) were thought to be perceived just as the blind man (Fig. 15), knowing the distance between his hands, perceives the angle and distance of the intersecting sticks.

years later, Descartes (1637, 1664) proposed that normal distance perception depends on our innate ability to perceive the convergence angle and the focal distance (accommodation) of the eyes (Fig. 9.1). The British empiricist, Berkeley (1709), subsequently rejected the notion that innate mental geometry is involved. But he agreed that oculomotor adjustments provide important information, and he proposed that space perception is learned through the association of eye muscle sensations and distances experienced through tactual interactions with the environment.

These ideas have echoed through the first century of scientific psychology, generating a large experimental literature that has generally validated the importance of both types of information. There has been considerable controversy, however, over the *relative* importance of optical or "light-based" information as opposed to oculomotor or "efference-based" information. One viewpoint, associated with the phenomenological perspective and, most recently, with Gibson's

---

smaller) when on the heavenly ceiling above our heads than when on the portion of that ceiling near the distant horizon. It is interesting that explanation of the Moon Illusion has been attributed erroneously to Ptolemy by most modern authors, including this one. I thank Herbert Heuer for directing me to the article by Ross and Ross, which helps to set the record straight and to remind us of the dangers of relying on secondary (or higher order) sources for historical perspective.

(1979) "ecological optics," emphasizes the effectiveness of principles of representative painting (e.g., perspective and shadow) and of invariant spatial relations among objects in the visual array that are revealed by movements of the observer (e.g., motion parallax and optical flow). This approach has maintained that oculomotor information is ineffective or misleading and therefore unlikely to survive evolutionary pressures to minimize its role in perception (Turvey, 1979). Another popular viewpoint, which followed more closely the traditions of experimental physiology and physiological optics, has argued that oculomotor activity is of primary importance for space perception (Helmholtz, 1867). According to this approach, oculomotor command signals or proprioceptive feedback provide critical information for the perception of the egocentric distance, direction, and motion of objects in the environment, and thus it is fundamental to all visually guided behavior (Held, 1965; Von Holst, 1954).

As reflected by the theme of the present volume, there is now growing interest in conceptualizing perceptual and motor processes as complementary aspects of a unified system. This viewpoint invites theoretical formulations that incorporate both retinal and extra-retinal information sources. In the preceding chapter, Shebilske (1985) argues for a reconciliation among current theories of visual space perception. He points out that neither light-based nor efference-based theories alone can account for the diverse phenomena commonly encountered in the natural environment. A more comprehensive theory, synthesized from the narrower present positions, holds promise of broadened explanatory power through new insights regarding the interactions of optical and oculomotor information.

This chapter is also based on the premises that *both* light-based and efference-based information play vital roles in normal space perception, and that their roles are complementary. The processes underlying space perception have evolved to take advantage of the diverse and often redundant information provided by the environment and by the organism's interactions with it. Information about visual space varies greatly in the course of everyday experience. Both classes of information are richest, and perception is most accurate, in the daytime terrestrial environment, when the visual scene provides a wealth of information that serves both to specify spatial relations among external objects and to ensure precise oculomotor responses. But many organisms, especially humans, must also behave under conditions in which the information is not so rich. When the light-based information is diminished at sunset, in an empty sky, or in foul weather (and in many modern "artificial" environments), we must rely more heavily on efference-based information. At the same time, the fidelity of this information decreases because the central processes that control oculomotor adjustments depend on retinal stimulation for feedback. With reduced feedback comes a systematic loss of the precision and range of oculomotor control. One consequence of reduced feedback is the appearance of anomalous response biases and interactions among eye movement systems. Another consequence is the appearance of compelling misperceptions of the position, size, and motion of visible stimuli.

During the past decade, research from several laboratories has shown that a variety of perceptual problems encountered under degraded stimulus conditions are related to normal variations of oculomotor behavior. As light-based information is reduced, oculomotor adjustments are progressively biased toward the observer's characteristic resting or "tonus" state. This bias results, for example, in anomalous accommodation and vergence responses that can seriously impair one's ability to detect and identify weak stimuli. In addition, because contextual spatial information is not available, the efference-based information that accompanies such biased oculomotor responses can introduce systematic distortions of space perception (Owens, 1984). Other research shows that the resting state of the eyes can be modified by alteration of the usual relation between eye position and environmental space, and by unusual oculomotor effort, as with prolonged near work. These findings suggest that plasticity of the resting state may serve important functions for optimizing oculomotor performance and for coordinating perceptual and motor space (Owens & Leibowitz, 1983; Owens & Wolf, 1983).

The following sections summarize our research on the resting states of accommodation and binocular vergence and their influence on visual perception. Before presenting this work, however, it may be worthwhile to review basic aspects of accommodation, vergence, and their relation to perceived distance.

Oculomotor Adjustments and Distance

As recognized by Descartes, two oculomotor adjustments are required to see clearly at different distances. Binocular fusion depends on *vergence* eye movements that serve to eliminate foveal retinal disparity through action of the extraocular muscles. Contraction of the medial rectus muscles converges the eyes to fixate near stimuli, and contraction of the lateral rectus muscles diverges the eyes to fixate distant stimuli. At the same time, clear focus is maintained by visual *accommodation*, which is accomplished by variations of the curvature of the crystalline lens. To focus near stimuli, the ciliary muscle acts, in combination with elastic properties of the lens capsule and suspensory fibers, to increase the curvature of the lens, thus increasing its refractive power. To focus distant stimuli, the ciliary body decreases the curvature of the lens, thus decreasing its refractive power.

Contemporary models describe accommodation and vergence as parallel, interacting servo-control systems that require different types of retinal feedback (Hung & Semmlow, 1982; Toates, 1972, 1974). The central mechanisms controlling accommodation depend primarily on feedback about the blur or spatial contrast of the retinal images (Wolfe & Owens, 1981), whereas those controlling vergence require feedback about the disparity of the retinal images (Westheimer & Mitchell, 1969). The two systems are strongly interactive. A response by either accommodation or vergence is almost always accompanied by a synergistic change of the other response (Fincham & Walton, 1957). Thus, both systems continue to operate even when one lacks its normal light-based feedback, although such synergistic responses are generally less accurate than those obtained with sensory feedback. In the absence of adequate sensory feedback, both accommodation and vergence return to the individual's characteristic resting state.

As noted earlier, both vergence and accommodation have long been considered to be potential determinants of perceived distance. With the emergence of experimental psychology, this relationship was one of the first topics of investigation. One of the earliest studies was Wundt's (1862) attempt to quantify the effects of vergence and accommodation on the perception of distance and depth. He measured the ability to estimate the absolute distance and to discriminate shifts in depth of a vertical black thread seen through a tube against a uniform white background. The accuracy of these judgments was somewhat disappointing. Monocular impressions of distance were so uncertain that no meaningful measurements could be taken. Although binocular judgments were consistently more accurate and less variable, distance was consistently underestimated. The superiority of binocular judgments was later confirmed in studies by Baird (1903), Swenson (1932), Grant (1942), and many others, leading to the generalization that, although both accommodation and vergence provide distance information, binocular vergence is more effective. These studies did not always replicate Wundt's tendency to underestimate distance, however. Instead, some found a tendency to overestimate distance (e.g., Helmholtz, 1867) while others found a tendency to underestimate long distances and to overestimate short distances (Foley, 1980; Grant, 1942). This lack of precision and high intersubject variability contributed to the widely held view that oculomotor information is less effective than monocular cues for distance.

In the interests of experimental control, most investigations of the role of vergence and accommodation in space perception have used "reduced" stimulus conditions. Such conditions are not necessary, however. The potent influence of oculomotor adjustments in a bright "full-cue" environment can easily be observed through simple demonstrations that the reader may wish to try. The effect of vergence posture can be seen in the well-known "wallpaper illusion." While viewing a repetitive pattern, such as wallpaper or bathroom tile, one can voluntarily converge the eyes to fuse spatially separate sections of the pattern. At first this may induce blur because accommodation shifts synergistically with convergence toward a nearer focus, but if one holds steady fixation of the fused patterns, accommodation soon "unlocks" from convergence and focuses the actual stimulus surface. When this happens, the fused pattern clearly appears to be smaller and nearer than normal, an illusion that increases with greater convergence. Quantitative measures of the wallpaper illusion indicate that the apparent size and distance of the fused pattern are determined by vergence posture, even when accommodation corresponds to the stimulus surface (Lie, 1965).

A similar, though less dramatic, effect can be produced monocularly by holding a pencil about 50 cms away, so that its point is superimposed on a larger distant object, and varying accommodation to focus alternately the distant object and the pencil point. If accommodation is sufficiently flexible to accomplish this alternation, one will see obvious changes in the clarity of the superimposed images. At the same time, the distant object appears to shrink with near accommodation despite possible image spread due to blur. Both this effect and the vergence-induced wallpaper illusion, can be explained in terms of changes of perceived distance that result from variations of the observer's oculomotor adjustments. Consistent with the "size-distance invariance hypothesis" (Epstein, Park, & Casey, 1961), the perceived size of an object is directly proportional to the apparent distance of the object. Thus, fixated objects appear to shrink as vergence or accommodation adjust to a nearer distance and to grow as these systems adjust to a farther distance.

These illusions demonstrate that oculomotor processes can strongly influence space perception in the presence of light-based information that might specify constant position and dimensions of the stimulus array. Ordinarily, the observer's oculomotor adjustments and the light-based information are not contradictory. Rather, they provide redundant information for localizing objects and for scaling their dimensions and motions. Redundancy has obvious advantages. Many important biological functions are served by multiple mechanisms, and visual space perception appears to follow this rule (Leibowitz, 1971). Although in many situations both light-based and efference-based information contribute to normal space perception, this redundancy is lost when stimulation is degraded. Furthermore, as noted earlier, the remaining oculomotor information is less effective because central control mechanisms lack adequate sensory feedback. Many of the perceptual problems encountered under reduced stimulus conditions appear to be related to changes in the behavior of accommodation and vergence. The resting state of the eyes appears to be a key concept for understanding these changes.

THE RESTING STATE OF THE EYES

The Dark Focus

According to traditional theories (Helmholtz, 1867; Maddox, 1893), and modern textbooks, the eyes relax at the far point of their operating range. This view assumes that oculomotor effort is required only to see near stimuli, and that passive forces, such as the elasticity of supporting tissues, are responsible for shifting focus and fixation from near to distant stimuli. Several authors during the 1930s and 40s challenged this view (Cogan, 1937; Luckiesh & Moss, 1940; Morgan, 1946; Schober, 1954), proposing instead that accommodation relaxes at an intermediate distance. This view was appealing because it offered a simple explanation for anomalous refractive errors, which seemed paradoxical from the classical viewpoint (Leibowitz & Owens, 1978). The data base was slim, however, and this novel hypothesis had little impact on mainstream theory and practice.

The resting-state issue received little further attention until development of the laser optometer (Hennessey & Leibowitz, 1972), which had important advantages over earlier techniques for studying accommodation. One of the first phenomena studied with this device was the behavior of accommodation in total darkness. Measurement of the "dark focus" in college students confirmed the intermediate resting-state hypothesis and revealed unexpectedly wide differences among subjects who had normal vision. The average dark focus of the sample illustrated in Fig. 9.2 was 1.3 diopters (D) of "myopia," which corresponds to a focal distance of 76 cms. Individual dark focus values were widely dispersed, with a few subjects resting at optical infinity as predicted by traditional theory, while others focused as near as 25 cms in darkness (Leibowitz & Owens, 1978). Such wide individual differences of the resting focus had not been detected by previous investigators; it seemed likely that they would influence visual performance in low-visibility conditions.

Studies of the dark focus showed that biases of accommodation toward the resting state are responsible for anomalous refractive errors, which had long been

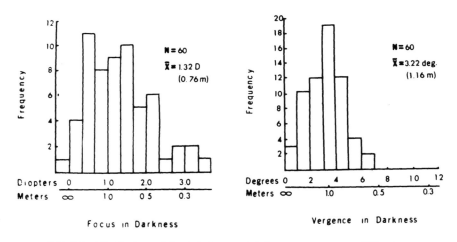

FIG. 9.2 Distributions of the dark focus and dark-vergence postures of 60 college students. Although both resting states usually correspond to an intermediate distance, they are not closely correlated. From D. A. Owens and H. W. Leibowitz, "Accommodation, convergence, and distance perception in low illumination." *American Journal of Optometry & Physiological Optics, 57,* 540–550. © The American Academy of Optometry, 1980. By permission. See also Fig. 9.8 (from Owens & Leibowitz, 1980).

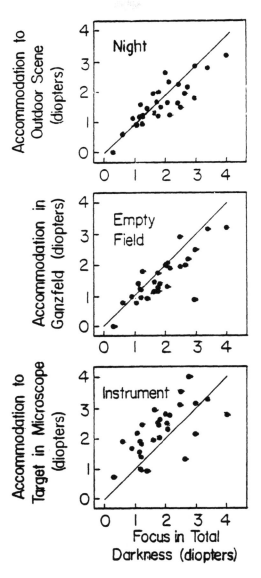

FIG. 9.3 Scatter diagrams illustrating correlations between the dark focus and anomalous refractive errors that occur in low illumination, a bright empty field, and when using optical instruments. From H. W. Leibowitz and D. A. Owens, "Anomalous myopias and the intermediate dark focus of accommodation" *Science, 189,* 646–648. Copyright 1975. Reprinted by permission of the American Association for the Advancement of Science.

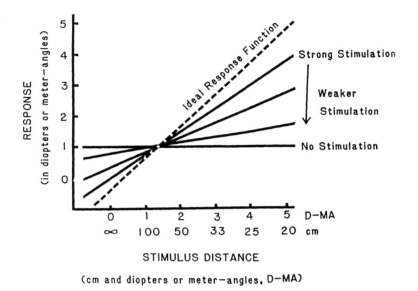

FIG. 9.4 Hypothetical functions illustrating the effect of reduced stimulation on the accuracy of accommodation and vergence. As stimulation is degraded, responses are progressively biased toward the observer's resting posture (100 cm, 1 diopter or meter-angle). This bias results in "myopic" or "esophoric" errors for distant stimuli and "hyperopic" or "exophoric" errors for near stimuli.

a problem for clinical vision and human factors specialists (Knoll, 1966; Maskelyne, 1789; Whiteside, 1952). In one study, we used the laser optometer to compare the dark focus with the magnitude of "anomalous myopias" occurring in three situations while viewing: (1) an outdoor scene through a filter that simulated nighttime illumination; (2) a bright, uniform *Ganzfeld* that simulated an empty sky; and (3) a grating pattern, seen through a microscope that had been focused by the subject. The results (Fig. 9.3) showed that all three "anomalous myopias" were highly correlated with the individuals' characteristic dark focus values (Leibowitz & Owens, 1975).

This and other experiments showed that the "anomalous myopias" are not refractive errors in the usual sense; that is, they are not due to structural characteristics of the eyes. Rather, they are focusing errors that result from *normal* variations in the behavior of accommodation. Accurate accommodation requires feedback regarding the effects of defocus on the contrast of the retinal image (Charman & Tucker, 1978; Owens, 1980; Wolfe & Owens, 1981). Whenever this feedback is diminished, focusing responses are increasingly biased toward the resting focus, resulting in "myopia" for distant stimuli and "hyperopia" for near stimuli. The same kind of response bias is also exhibited by the vergence system when retinal disparity information is degraded (Francis & Owens, 1983;

Ivanoff & Bourdy, 1954). Thus, a major insight from research on the resting state of the eyes is that the operating range of accommodation and vergence decreases progressively as stimulation is reduced.

One practical outcome of this research was the development of new techniques for predicting and correcting anomalous refractive errors (Hope & Rubin, 1984). Of closer relevance to the present discussion, these findings suggested that normal variations of oculomotor behavior may also be related to problems of space perception under reduced stimulus conditions.

The Specific Distance Tendency

We have known since the earliest experiments on space perception that individuals vary greatly in their judgments of size and distance (Epstein et al., 1961), especially under reduced stimulus conditions. One recurrent finding has been that errors often reflect a bias towards intermediate distances (e.g., Foley, 1980; Grant, 1942). This perceptual bias was studied most intensively by Gogel and his colleagues, who refer to the phenomenon as the "specific distance tendency" (*SDT*). They argue that many illusions of size, depth, and motion encountered under impoverished conditions occur because, in the absence of light-based information, perception is inherently biased toward the observer's "specific distance." The *SDT* is thought to be an intrinsic (or "autochthonic") determinant of perceived space, which has increasing influence as extrinsic information decreases. It is also interesting to note the the *SDT* varies widely across subjects, ranging from 30 cm to over 8 m, with an average value of about 2 m (Gogel, 1969, 1977, 1978).

The *SDT* is a heuristic concept because it explained a variety of illusions in terms of a common process, a systematic bias of perceived distance that occurs when light-based information is reduced. At the same time, this concept raised new questions. Although the *SDT* identified a common characteristic of many spatial illusions, it did not tell us *why* perception is biased toward an intermediate distance. Nor did it tell us why different people are biased toward different specific distances.

Because the experimental conditions used to measure the *SDT* eliminated all distance information except oculomotor adjustments, we hypothesized that such misperceptions might arise from errors of accommodation. To test this possibility, we measured accommodation and distance perception while subjects viewed a monocular point of light at distances ranging from 50 to 400 cms (Owens & Leibowitz, 1976). Focusing responses and the dark focus were measured with a laser optometer; perceived distance was measured by an indirect technique devised by Gogel to minimize verbal and other cognitive response biases. This method requires the subject to move her/his head back and forth laterally while fixating a stationary point of light in the dark. Gogel and Tietz (1973) discovered that the stimulus appears to move concomitant with head

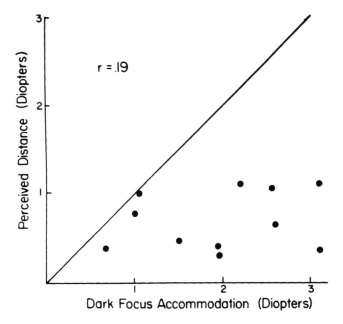

FIG. 9.5 Scatter diagram comparing measures of the dark focus and the specific distance tendency. From H. W. Leibowitz and D. A. Owens (1976). "Oculomotor adjustments in darkness and the specific distance tendency." *Perception & Psychophysics, 20*(1). 2–9. Reprinted by permission.

movements whenever its perceived distance differs from its actual distance. The direction of "illusory concomitant motion" is opposite the head movements if the target appears to be nearer, and it is the same as the head movement if the target appears to be farther than its actual distance. Since the light point appears to be stable when its position matches its perceived distance, the *SDT* can be measured by varying the distance of the stimulus until no apparent motion is seen during lateral translations of the head. In most cases, the illusory motion disappears with two or three head movements, so subjects were instructed to report their first impression of motion.

The results (Fig. 9.5) showed that, although the average dark focus and *SDT* values both corresponded to intermediate distances (41 and 145 cms, respectively), they were not significantly correlated (r = 0.19). This outcome disproved the hypothesis that the *SDT* is related to errors of accommodation, but it did not rule out the possible involvement of binocular vergence.

This hypothesis seemed unlikely at first because vergence and accommodation are normally tightly correlated, and we therefore assumed that they would correspond to the same distance in darkness. A previous study indicated that this assumption might be wrong, however. Fincham (1962) had reported evidence that accommodation and vergence dissociate "in the absence of retinal images."

This finding suggested that accommodation and vergence might rest at different distances. If so, then the *SDT* might be related to binocular vergence rather than accommodation.

Dark Vergence

We conducted a second experiment that compared the *SDT* and the resting position of binocular vergence. As in the previous experiment, perceived distance was measured indirectly by Gogel's head motion technique. The resting position of the vergence system, referred to as dark (or tonic) vergence, was measured by a technique similar to clinical tests of lateral heterophoria, except for the important difference that no accommodative stimulus was provided (Owens & Leibowitz, 1976, 1983). The subject was asked to report the relative positions of two dichoptic stimuli that were flashed briefly in the dark. Over a series of presentations, the lateral separation (retinal disparity) of the dichoptic stimuli was varied until the stimuli appeared to be aligned vertically. From this measure, it was easy to compute the distance and the convergence angle corresponding to the subjects' vergence posture in darkness.

This time the results (Fig. 9.6) showed a significant correlation ($r = 0.76$) between the resting position and the *SDT*. Subjects with a near dark-vergence posture tended to exhibit a nearer specific distance than those with a more distant dark-vergence posture (Owens & Leibowitz, 1976).[3]

These results were interesting for two reasons. First, they reinforced Fincham's (1962) finding that vergence and accommodation dissociate in the dark. This implies that although the *actions* of accommodation and vergence are mutually synergistic, their resting states are independent. Secondly, they indicated that the perceived distance of a weak stimulus viewed in the dark can be predicted from the observer's dark-vergence distance. Of course, this correlation does not necessarily mean that vergence determines the *SDT*. It is possible that the converse is true, or that both dark vergence and the *SDT* are determined by a third unknown factor. In any case, our findings indicate that errors of accommodation have little or no effect on space perception and that vergence biases may contribute to spatial illusions encountered under reduced stimulus conditions.

This conclusion is consistent with the claim that binocular vergence is more important than accommodation for space perception, but one must be cautious about generalizing to other conditions. The perception of size and distance can be varied by changing only the optical distance of a bright, monocular stimulus (McCready, 1965; von Holst, 1954). This phenomenon, sometimes referred to as

---

[3]To minimize variance unrelated to distance perception, we subtracted the lateral heterophoria of each subject from his/her dark vergence before computing the correlation illustrated in Fig. 9.6. Comparison of the data before normalizing the dark-vergence values for individual differences in heterophoria also yielded a significant, but lower, positive correlation ($r = 0.56$).

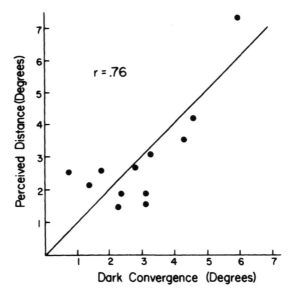

FIG. 9.6 Scatter diagram comparing measures of dark vergence and the specific distance tendency. From H. W. Leibowitz and D. A. Owens (1976). "Oculomotor adjustments in darkness and the specific distance tendency." *Perception & Psychophysics, 20*(1). 2–9. Reprinted by permission.

"micropsia," shows that accommodation can influence distance perception when adequate blur stimulation is available. Such findings are difficult to interpret, however, because they might result from variations of vergence, which invaribly accompany significant changes of accommodation (Fincham & Walton, 1957; Morgan, 1968). The question of *which* response contributes to space perception under bright, naturalistic conditions is an old one, but it may be ill conceived. The two systems interact, and their interactions apparently affect space perception.

Illusions of Size and Motion

Further research is necessary to determine the range of perceptual phenomena that are related to the dark-vergence bias. Our data suggest that it produces systematic errors of distance perception under conditions in which light-based information is minimal, and that it may help to account for the wide individual differences typically found in studies of distance perception. To the extent that perceived (or "registered") distance is fundamental to other aspects of space perception, biases toward the dark-vergence posture might also influence perception of size, depth, and motion.

The role of dark vergence in anomalies of size perception, such as the Moon Illusion, has not yet been investigated, although some evidence suggests that it may be a relevant factor. Size judgments of luminous, unfamiliar stimuli, viewed in the dark, are typically biased toward an intermediate value. This finding was one of the first phenomena presented as evidence for the existance of a *SDT* (Gogel, 1969). We know that vergence responses are biased toward the resting posture under reduced stimulus conditions (Francis & Owens, 1983). It is possible that such biases produce a corresponding "misregistration" of distance that influences perceived size. This hypothesis is consistent with evidence that size perception is quite accurate when the only information about distance is provided by oculomotor adjustments, provided that stimuli fall within the range of distances (25–200 cms) for which vergence and accommodation are most accurate (Leibowitz & Moore, 1966; Leibowitz, Shiina, & Hennessy, 1972). It would be interesting to know whether individual differences in anomalies of size perception, such as the loss of size constancy at long distances, are related to differences in dark vergence.

Although the role of the dark-vergence bias in size perception is still unclear, recent work by Post and Leibowitz indicates that this bias can affect motion perception. Recall that Gogel and Teitz (1973) discovered that a stationary target, seen in the dark, may appear to move during lateral translations of the head. The direction and magnitude of this "illusory concomitant motion" depend on the target's distance.

According to Post and Leibowitz (1982), this illusory motion arises from an anomalous interaction of smooth eye movement systems resulting from the dark-vergence bias. Their explanation rests on a fundamental distinction between two eye movement systems that evolved to serve different functional aspects of gaze stability. One system, which is phylogenetically older and has been referred to as *Stiernystagmus,* maintains stable gaze reflexively during movements of the head and body. This reflexive system is present in all mammals and in many lower orders. Its most familiar manifestations in humans are the smooth components of the optokinetic and vestibulo-ocular reflexes. The second system, referred to as *Schaunystagmus,* evolved later in conjunction with specialization of the central retina. This system permits voluntary foveal pursuit of moving stimuli and is fully developed only in higher species. Superficially, voluntary pursuit eye movements may appear indistinguishable from their smooth reflexive counterparts, but they are controlled by different central mechanisms (Dichgans, 1977), and they serve different perceptual functions.

Smooth eye movements have long been thought to provide oculomotor information for perception of object motion (e.g., Helmholtz, 1867), but this effect is mediated only by the voluntary pursuit system. A classical example can be seen if one pursues an afterimage (or a troublesome mosquito) viewed against a uniform background. Although the retinal image contains little or no motion, the fixated stimulus appears to move in the same pattern as the eyes. In contrast, the smooth eye movements that maintain stable fixation during self-motion do not contribute to perception of object motion. This is easy to see if one observes the position of a fixated object (or afterimage) while turning the head from side to

230 OWENS

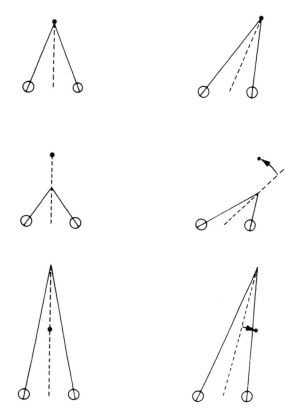

FIG. 9.7 Schematic illustration of the effect of vergence errors on the vestibulo-ocular reflex (VOR) during a head movement to the left. The solid lines represent vergence distance, which is appropriate in the top row, too near in the middle row, and too far in the bottom row. The dashed lines represent the direction of gaze that is maintained reflexively by the VOR. Arrows in the middle and bottom rows indicate the pursuit effort that is needed to maintain fixation in the presence of inappropriate vergence and VOR gain. This anomalous pursuit effort is thought to contribute to "illusory concomitant motion." From R. B. Post and H. W. Leibowitz (1982). "The effect of convergency on the vestibulo-ocular reflex and implications for perceived movement." *Vision Research, 22,* 461–465. Copyright (1982), Pergamon Press, Ltd. Reprinted by permission.

side. Although the eyes move smoothly in their orbits, the fixated stimulus appears stationary.

The latter type of smooth eye movement results from the vestibulo-ocular reflex (VOR). Whenever the head moves, the resulting vestibular stimulation rapidly initiates a smooth counterrotation of the eyes. This response is usually highly efficient, maintaining stable fixation during all sorts of complex head movements. For optimal gaze stability, the magnitude or "gain" of the VOR must vary inversely with fixation distance; the eyes must counterrotate more during near fixation than during far fixation. Although the mechanism that modulates VOR gain as a function of distance has not been established, binocular vergence is a likely candidate (Biguer & Prablanc, 1981; Hine, 1985).

Post and Leibowitz (1982) showed that, under conditions in which subjects see illusory concomitant motion, particularly during lateral translations of the head, VOR gain is inappropriate. They proposed that these "errors" of VOR gain result from the dark-vergence bias. When such errors occur, activation of the pursuit eye movement system is necessary to maintain stable fixation, and this anomalous pursuit effort gives rise to illusory object motion. Their account of the relation between vergence posture, VOR gain, and the smooth pursuit system is illustrated in Fig. 9.7. When vergence corresponds to the distance of the stimulus (top row), VOR gain is appropriate, holding fixation stable during head movements. If vergence corresponds to a distance nearer than the stimulus, however, VOR gain is too high, and would cause the eyes to counterrotate too far (middle row). Consequently, the subject must exert pursuit effort in the *same* direction as the head movement to maintain fixation. The opposite condition is obtained when vergence corresponds to a distance beyond the stimulus (bottom row). Now the VOR gain is too low, so the eyes do not counterrotate enough, and the subject must exert pursuit effort in the direction *opposite* the head movement to maintain fixation. In short, whenever vergence does not correspond to the distance of the fixated object, the VOR is not appropriate, and it must be supplemented or opposed by pursuit effort to maintain steady fixation. This anomalous pursuit effort, arising indirectly from the dark-vergence bias, produces illusory motion of the fixated object.

In addition to providing a parsimonious explanation of illusory concomitant motion, Post and Leibowitz's account highlights an important aspect of oculomotor innervation that has generally been neglected by efference-based theories of space perception. Their analysis of motion illusions emphasizes the fact that the extraocular muscles receive control input from multiple central processes. Although at a peripheral level, these inputs and the resulting eye movements can be very similar, their visual functions and perceptual consequences may be quite different. This may prove to be a key insight for understanding the contributions of oculomotor information to perception.

THE FUNCTIONAL VALUE OF OCULOMOTOR INFORMATION

At this point, one might question the general value of oculomotor information because, under optimal conditions, it seems to add relatively little to the information given by light-based stimulation and, under impoverished conditions, it exhibits systematic biases that often tend to distort perception (Turvey, 1979). A partial answer to this query is that, although oculomotor information tends to be imprecise under reduced stimulus conditions, it is often the best, and sometimes the only, information available. The greatest perceptual distortions are obtained only under the most degraded conditions. Even then, the oculomotor information may serve the important function of providing perceptual structure for stimulation that is otherwise quite ambiguous. Humans and other organisms must frequently act under nonoptimal conditions. Despite the occurance of perceptual distortions, oculomotor information may be essential for coordinating and guiding this behavior, especially under difficult visual conditions.

Contributions to Visually Guided Behavior

A particularly striking example of the utility of oculomotor information is provided by the research of Hansen and Skavenski (1977) on visually guided hammer blows. They asked their subjects to use a pointed hammer to hit targets that were presented at random locations over a horizontal range of 70 degrees. This task was carried out in both a fully illuminated room and total darkness, where all light-based information for target position had been eliminated. Their results showed that the hammer blows were quite accurate (within 5 arcmin) under *both* conditions, implying that oculomotor information was adequate to localize the targets. A second study showed that hammer blows were still surprisingly accurate (within 15 arcmin) when the target was flashed for only 25 msec in total darkness *while the subject was executing a saccadic eye movement.*

The second finding was particularly surprising because psychophysical judgments of visual direction indicate that localization is highly inaccurate during saccadic eye movements (Matin, 1972). It appears that "motor localization" (e.g., hammer blows) is more accurate than "cognitive localization" (e.g., verbal responses) when only oculomotor information is available to specify the position of a target (Bridgeman, Lewis, Heit, & Nagle, 1979; Bridgeman, Kirch, & Sperling, 1981; Skavenski & Hansen, 1978). This interpretation suggests that there is no single internal representation of space, but rather there are multiple representations that may be employed separately for different types of spatial tasks. Whatever the basis for differences between "cognitive" and "motor" localization, oculomotor information is clearly useful for interacting with objects seen under impoverished conditions, and for that matter, it may serve the same function in a bright complex environment.

A fuller account of the value of oculomotor information should include its role in calibrating the relationship between visual perception and behavior. Extensive literatures on ocular motility (Crone & Hardjowijoto, 1979) and on perceptual adaptation to optical displacements (Welch, 1978) indicate that we are remarkably good at adapting to systematic modifications of the relationship between eye position and light-based information about object position. Nearly everyone who has acquired new spectacles or bifocals has experienced this adaptation process. Such new lenses optically transform the relation between eye position and the optic array, and they initially cause some difficulties in judging the height of curbs, climbing stairs, and even in reaching for objects. With a little experience, however, these problems disappear, at least until it is time for a new prescription. Clinical and experimental studies suggest that this adaptation depends in large part on oculomotor processes.

Related research on animals indicates that oculomotor information is essential for the development of normal visuo-motor coordination. Studies of cats and monkeys show that normal visually guided locomotion and reaching do not develop if the animal is deprived of the opportunity to view its limbs and the environment during active behavior. A monkey reared without sight of its arms, for example, will readily fixate and can learn operant responses to obtain a piece of candy, but it cannot reach with its unseen hand in the direction of the candy (Bauer & Held, 1975). Similarly, a dark-reared cat can fixate, but initially cannot walk toward, a visual target (Hein & Diamond, 1983). These severe behavioral deficits rapidly disappear if the animal is allowed to behave freely in a fully illuminated environment.

The importance of eye position information for this calibration process was demonstrated by a fascinating series of experiments recently reported by Hein and Diamond (1983). In one of their experiments, they surgically interrupted innervation to the ocular muscles of one eye in kittens that had previously been confined to darkness; innervation to the muscles of the companion eye remained intact. Consequently, these animals received both optical and oculomotor information from one eye but only optical information from the other (immobilized) eye. The kittens were later introduced to the normally lighted laboratory environment and allowed to locomote freely for 3 hours each day, with either the intact or the immobilized eye occluded on alternate days. After 2 weeks, their visuo-motor coordination was tested with each eye separately in an obstacle course of wooden blocks and a "bridge-box," in which the subject must step over a small gap onto a bridge leading to food. These tests revealed dramatic differences between the behavior enabled by the two eyes. Although the kittens displayed normal visually guided locomotion and reaching with the intact eye, they were never able to acquire visually guided behavior with the immobilized eye alone. This implies that the dynamic optical (light-based) information provided by head and body movements is not adequate for developing or calibrating visual-motor space. It is as though without oculomotor information the animal does not know where it is looking. Evidence such as this weighs heavily against the presumption that light-based information alone is sufficient for normal perception and action.

Parallels in Oculomotor and Perceptual Plasticity

Returning now to human subjects, research on plasticity of distance perception has often used experimental glasses containing ophthalmic prisms with their bases oriented in the temporal (base-out) or nasal (base-in) directions. Consider,

234 OWENS

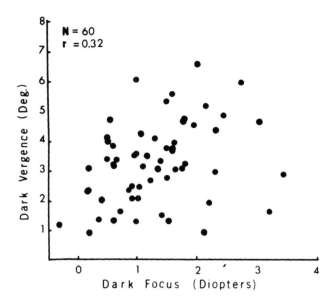

FIG. 9.8 Scatter diagram comparing the dark-focus and dark-vergence postures of 60 college students (distributions are given in Fig. 9.2). The low correlation suggests that the strong synergy exhibited by active accommodation and vergence is not present in the resting state. From D. A. Owens and H. W. Leibowitz, "Accommodation, convergence, and distance perception in low illumination." *American Journal of Optometry & Physiological Optics, 57,* 540–550. © The American Academy of Optometry, 1980. By permission.

for example, the effects of base-out prisms, which force the subject to converge more than usual to fixate binocular stimuli. This increased convergence initially causes objects to appear smaller and nearer, and subjects underreach for objects if they are prevented from watching their hand, a technique called "open-loop pointing." After a short period of active experience in a normal environment, the subject again perceives distance and reaches accurately despite the increased convergence. If the experimental glasses are then removed, she/he shows new errors of distance perception, now overreaching for objects. This aftereffect usually persists for several minutes until she/he "readapts" to normal (Ebenholtz, 1981; von Hofsten, 1979; Wallach, Frey, & Bode, 1972).

Because our previous experiments indicated that the *SDT* is related to the observer's dark vergence, we decided to test whether the dark-vergence bias might also be involved in prism adaptation. This question offered an opportunity to use a paradigm quite different from that of our first study. We used open-loop pointing, rather than the head-movement technique, to measure perceived distance, and we looked for within-subject as opposed to between-subject covariations of dark vergence and distance perception. This approach also presented an opportunity to look more closely at the dissociation of the resting states of vergence and accommodation, and it allowed us to examine a new question: What are the effects of the subjects' activities during exposure to the prism glasses on the adaptation process? Earlier research had shown that active experience in a bright environment greatly facilitates adaptation to laterally displacing prisms (Held, 1965; Welch, 1978), suggesting that adaptation involves processes that mediate sensorimotor coordination. Another hypothesis, which was appealing for its simplicity, proposed that prism adaptation results from changes in extraocular muscle, similar to posttetanic potentiation, which are induced by unusual or sustained effort (Ebenholtz, 1974; Paap & Ebenholtz, 1976).

Our subjects wore spectacles containing base-out prisms and negative lenses of equivalent power, so that their accommodation and convergence were forced to increase equally (Owens & Leibowitz, 1980). The subjects were divided into three groups, who performed different activities during the exposure period. One group, called the "Walkers," walked through the Psychology Building, participating in a variety of complex activities such as table tennis and pitch-and-catch. A second group, called the "Riders," followed the same path but rode in a wheelchair and did not participate in the perceptual-motor tasks. The third

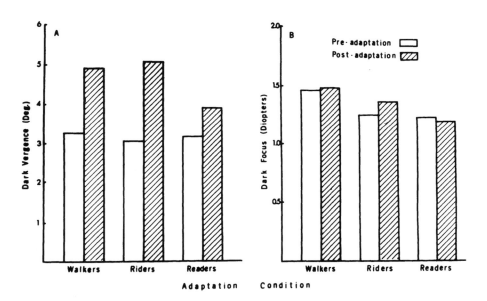

FIG. 9.9 Mean dark-vergence and dark-focus measures obtained before and after three groups of subjects were exposed to spectacles containing prisms and lenses that forced increased convergence and near-accommodation. Vergence exhibited significant adaptation, whereas accommodation showed no change. From D. A. Owens and H. W. Leibowitz, "Accommodation, convergence, and distance perception in low illumination." *American Journal of Optometry & Physiological Optics, 57*, 540–550. © The American Academy of Optometry, 1980. By permission.

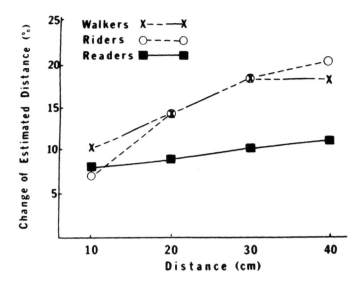

FIG. 9.10 Mean percentage change in open-loop pointing responses to a light point presented in darkness following exposure to spectacles containing base-out prisms and negative lenses. Differences among the three groups are similar to differences in adaptation of dark vergence shown in Fig. 9.9. From D. A. Owens and H. W. Leibowitz, "Accommodation, convergence, and distance perception in low illumination." *American Journal of Optometry & Physiological Optics*, 57, 540–550. © The American Academy of Optometry, 1980. By permission.

group, called the "Readers," remained seated in a dark room, reading an illuminated magazine at a fixed distance, while an experimenter turned pages. Before and after these activities, we measured each subject's dark focus, dark vergence, and perceived distance for a single point of light.

Preadaptation measures again indicated that accommodation and vergence rest at different distances in the dark. Their average values are significantly different (Fig. 9.2), and although weakly correlated ($r = 0.32$), the resting states do not exhibit the close correspondence found with responses to adequate stimulation (Fig. 9.8). Post-adaptation measures provided additional evidence for independence of the dark focus and dark-vergence postures. Fig. 9.9 summarizes the average values before and after adaptation for each of the three exposure conditions. These data show that dark vergence shifted toward a significantly closer distance (increased convergence) during adaptation, and that this effect was more pronounced for the Walkers and Riders than for the Readers. In contrast, there was essentially no change of the dark focus in any of the exposure conditions.

The data on distance perception (Fig. 9.10) revealed adaptive changes that paralleled those of dark vergence. Consistent with earlier studies, our subjects reached significantly farther after removing the experimental glasses than they did before adaptation, indicating that the perceived distance corresponding to a given vergence angle increased during adaptation. Of greater interest, our results show that, similar to changes in dark vergence, changes in distance perception were greater for the Walkers and Riders, who moved through the environment, than for the Readers, who remained seated in a dark room. This finding is consistent with Held's (1965) view that interactions with the environment facilitate adaptation. It is difficult to reconcile, however, with the hypothesis that adaptation is due entirely to a peripheral process such as eye-muscle potentiation (Ebenholtz & Wolfson, 1977). In view of their respective tasks, the Readers probably converged their eyes more than either the Riders or the Walkers. Therefore, the Reading condition should have induced greater eye-muscle potentiation and greater consequent changes in perceived distance. Instead, the differences among exposure conditions indicate that adaptive changes in vergence and perceived distance depend on interactions with the environment as well as on increased convergence activity. This suggests the involvement of processes that mediate sensorimotor coordination.

Vergence Tonus, Effort, and Distance Perception

At present, little is known about the processes by which oculomotor activity comes to affect distance perception. But whatever the process that transforms binocular vergence into perceived distance, its calibration is readily modifiable. When the usual relation between vergence posture and distance is altered, subjects initially misperceive size and location, and they misreach accordingly. After only a brief period of interaction with the environment, perception and visually guided behavior recover normal coordination. These observations, as well as the negative aftereffects obtained immediately after restoration of the original conditions, demonstrate that the relationship of vergence position and perceived distance is quite plastic, rapidly acquiring a new functional calibration under appropriate conditions. This phenomenon had been studied by a number of investigators, who have favored various theoretical interpretations (e.g., Ebenholtz & Wolfson, 1975; Held, 1965; Wallach, et al., 1972). The major contribution of our research was the discovery that adaptation of distance perception is accompanied by parallel variations of dark-vergence posture. This raised the possibility that oculomotor tonus is involved in calibrating the relationship between efference-based information and space perception.

The "Reafference Principle" of von Holst and Mittelstaedt (1950) has been one of the most influential theories of the role of efference in space perception. In addition to their well-known treatments of perceived direction and motion, von Holst (1954) proposed that size constancy depends on oculomotor efference. He observed that, even when the peripheral actions of accommodation are blocked by atropine, "an intention for near-accommodation will start a motor impulse, which cannot be nullified by any reafference, and, therefore . . . All objects in the visual field become small" (p. 93). In other words, the "registered" distance that determines perceived size is mediated by efferent commands to accommodation.

Although subsequent research supports von Holst's contention that oculomotor efference is an important source of distance information, two aspects of his formulation require revision. First, activity of the vergence system is at least as important as that of accommodation, and it should be included. It is not clear why von Holst chose to emphasize the role of accommodation, because an "intention for near-accommodation" would also produce efferent commands for convergence. Secondly, in accord with traditional theory, von Holst assumed that the eyes rest at infinity and, therefore, that efferent commands must always signal a nearer distance. Implicit in this view is the assumption that perceived distance should correspond to infinity in the absence of oculomotor activity. We know now that the eyes rest at an intermediate distance and require active effort to adjust to farther as well as to nearer distances. This implies that efferent commands to accommodation and vergence, which might serve as distance information, must act relative to the intermediate resting position rather than to optical infinity.

Von Hofsten (1976) presented a new theory of the role of vergence in space perception that incorporated the changes needed by von Holst's original proposal. According to von Hofsten, perceived distance is not related directly to the angle of convergence, but rather it depends on the extent to which a vergence response departs from the physiological resting state. This is consistent with von Holst's argument that oculomotor efference is a primary source of distance information, but unlike von Holst's view, it emphasizes the importance of vergence effort, and it invites definition of vergence effort with respect to the observer's resting posture. We have argued (1) that the dark-vergence posture represents the physiological resting state of the vergence system, and (2) that it may serve as an "anchor" or "set point," which corresponds to a fundamental reference value for distance perception (Owens & Leibowitz, 1976, 1983). These assumptions, in combination with von Hofsten's theory, provide a simple framework for interpreting the adaptive changes illustrated in Fig. 9.9 and 9.10. According to this view, fixating a target located at the dark-vergence distance would require no vergence effort, so it is perceived at the individual's characteristic "reference" distance. Fixation of targets beyond the dark-vergence distance would require divergence effort, which gives rise to increased perceived distance, and fixation of targets nearer than the dark-vergence distance would require convergence effort, which gives rise to decreased perceived distance.

It follows that modification of the usual relationship between vergence angle and fixation distance has three effects, which are closely related. Introduction of base-out prisms, for example, deviates both visual axes in the temporal direction so that the dark-vergence posture corresponds to a greater distance than usual, and the vergence effort necessary to fuse a binocular stimulus at any distance is altered. Thus, as illustrated in Fig. 9.11, base-out prisms initially displace the dark-vergence (resting tonus) position to a distance that is beyond the perceptual "reference" distance. This shift of resting tonus would reduce the amount of

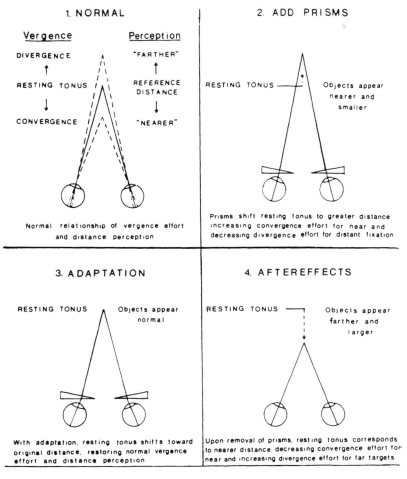

FIG. 9.11 Schematic illustration of the parallel changes in vergence tonus, vergence effort, and distance perception that occur during adaptation to base-out prisms. The resting posture is thought to correspond to a constant perceptual "reference" distance, whereas divergence and convergence effort are thought to signal increased and decreased perceived distance, respectively.

divergence effort required to fixate more distant stimuli, and it would increase the amount of convergence effort required to fixate nearer stimuli. All these changes have a common perceptual consequence: They cause the observer to underestimate the distance of fixated objects.

Exposure to base-out prisms induces a shift of the resting tonus toward a more convergent posture (Fig. 9.9). This shift is interpreted as an economical way to restore the original relationship between fixation distance, vergence effort, and perception. In effect, it moves the dark-vergence posture toward its original fixation distance despite the prisms. This change counteracts the effect of the prisms on vergence effort, restoring its usual correlation with fixation distance. When viewing through the prisms, the subject's dark-vergence distance again matches the perceptual "reference" distance, and the usual levels of convergence and divergence effort are required to fixate stimuli nearer and farther than the reference distance. So vergence effort is again a veridical source of distance information (Fig. 9.11, panel 3). When the prisms are removed, however, this new calibration is no longer veridical. The new resting posture now corresponds to a distance nearer than the reference distance and, consequently, less convergence effort is needed to fixate near stimuli and more divergence effort is needed to fixate distant stimuli (Fig. 9.11, panel 4). As a result, the subject overestimates distance until vergence tonus returns to its original level, again restoring the usual relation between the dark-vergence posture, vergence effort, and fixation distance.

According to this view, complete adaptation requires a change in dark-vergence posture that is opposite in direction and equal in magnitude to the optical deviation of the prisms. The results (Fig. 9.9) indicate that this adaptive process was not complete in our study. The prisms deviated vergence adjustments by 4.58 degrees ($8^\triangle$), and the shift in dark vergence (for Walkers and Riders) was about 1.7 degrees, or about 37% of the prism power. It is possible that greater adaptation would have been obtained with longer exposure to the experimental glasses or if postexposure measures had been taken immediately after removal of the glasses.[4]

Evidence from the literature on ocular motility indicates that changes in vergence tonus do compensate fully for prismatic corrections. Prisms would seem to offer a simple noninvasive technique for correcting heterophoria and even ocular tropias. Such corrections are generally not effective, however, because although they initially provide the desired ocular alignment, the original deviation often reappears with the prism in place (Campos & Catellani, 1978). Correction of concomitant esotropia (crossed-eye) with a base-out prism, for example, can result in a gradual increase of the esotropia until it restores the original misalignment despite the prism correction, a phenomenon referred to clinically as "eating the prism." Similarly, common lateral heterophoria can be eliminated by adding prism to one's spectacle correction, but later measurements usually show that the original phoria has reappeared with the correction in place. This is thought to be an important aspect of normal binocular vision, sometimes referred to as "orthophorization" (Carter, 1963; Crone, 1969). From a clinical standpoint, the changes in dark vergence shown in Fig. 9.9 might be seen as just another example of orthophorization. Although the basis for these clinical phe-

---

[4]The subjects in our study wore the experimental glasses for 20 minutes, and postexposure measures of the various dependent variables were taken in counterbalanced order so, on the average, postmeasures of dark vergence were made 7–10 minutes after the end of the exposure period.

nomena is not understood, theorists seem to agree that fusional processes and particularly vergence tonus are relevant mechanisms (Carter, 1965; Crone & Hardjowijoto, 1979). It may be that these processes serve the interests of normal space perception as well as ocular motility.

THEORETICAL IMPLICATIONS

The concept of resting tonus is not new, but its potential role in space perception has just been recognized during the past few years. Tonus in skeletal muscles was described at least as early as Galen (Scheerer, this volume), and it has been acknowledged as a property of extraocular muscle since the earliest investigations of eye movements and perception (e.g., Maddox, 1893). Although the physiological basis of oculomotor tonus is not understood, research on muscle physiology has revealed features of extraocular muscle and its innervation that may well be involved. In addition to two types of "twitch" fibers found in skeletal muscle, extraocular muscle contains another class of slow fibers which are referred to as "tonus bundles" and are not found elsewhere in mammals (Breinin, 1971; Burian & von Noorden, 1974; Granit, 1970). These fibers have very small diameter, they receive innervation through "en gappe" motor endings from multiple small (gamma range) motor neurons, and they maintain contracture for minutes with application of constant current or acetylcholine. Their function has not been determined, but some evidence suggests that they are the source of tonic activity in extraocular muscle.

Historically, there has been a long-standing controversy over the question of whether eye position information is provided primarily by efferent ("outflow") or proprioceptive afferent ("inflow") activity. Although a review of the inflow–outflow debate is beyond the scope of this chapter, oculomotor tonus may represent a conceptual "missing link." The phenomenon of oculomotor tonus seems directly relevant to this issue because tonus determines the length of the muscles and the position of the eye at rest. Therefore, a change in tonus would surely alter *both* the "outflow" and the "inflow" associated with a particular eye movement. Consider, for example, the vergence effort required to fixate an object at a distance of 50 cms (i.e., 2.0 meter-angles, MA). Assuming that vergence angle is a linear function of effort, one whose resting posture corresponds to 150 cms (0.67 MA) must exert about twice as much effort, or "disjunctive efference," as one whose resting posture corresponds to 75 cms (1.33 MA). This approach can also be extended to the problems of visual direction and motion. In this case, the "conjunctive efference" required for voluntary saccadic or pursuit eye movements is dependent on the *direction* of the eyes at rest. Consistent with this hypothesis, Shebilske (1981; 1985) has shown that illusions of visual direction following sustained eccentric gaze are accompanied by changes in the direction of gaze at rest, which he refers to as "Minor Motor

Anomalies." From the present point of view, these changes are not anomalous, but rather they reflect normal adaptation of oculomotor tonus.

Although "outflow" theories have generally been considered more persuasive than "inflow" theories (Howard & Templeton, 1966), they cannot handle all of the evidence (Hein & Diamond, 1983; Steinbach & Smith, 1981). For this reason and because extraocular muscle contains stretch receptors, which may be influenced by gamma-like input, contemporary theorists have argued that a more complex formulation than von Holst's "Reafference Principle" is required to account for the role of efference in space perception (Matin, 1972; Shebilske, 1977). Perhaps the concept of oculomotor tonus can help to simplify this reformulation. Muscle tonus obviously requires efference. As illustrated by Post and Leibowitz's analysis of the role of smooth eye movements in motion perception, however, it is a mistake to assume that all efference is functionally equivalent. Rather, efferent commands to the ocular muscles have multiple sources, which have evolved to serve different visual functions and are likely to produce different perceptual consequences. In this context, "tonic efference" should be classified with that of the reflexive eye movements subserving gaze stability. Its primary role is postural, and it has no *direct* effects on perception. Modification of tonus does influence perception *indirectly*, however, because such changes modify the effort (efference) required for voluntary eye movements. Thus, as illustrated in Fig. 9.11, changes in tonus can account for the fact that ostensibly equivalent eye movements (or steady-state fixation) may, on different occasions, produce different perceptual consequences.

Although the relation of afference and tonus is less clear, there is reason to suppose that proprioceptive feedback plays a role in modulating tonus. The evidence indicates that strong oculomotor effort, such as prolonged near fixation or eccentric gaze, induces a shift of tonus in the direction of the effort. Following the principles of control theory, Ebenholtz (1981, 1983) has described this effect as "hysteresis." Schor (1983) has characterized it as resulting from a "slow" control process, which may contribute to orthophorization and has important implications for clinical (orthoptic) visual training. From a functional perspective, we have proposed that this phenomenon serves to relieve the effort required by strenuous visual tasks (Owens & Leibowitz, 1983; Owens & Wolf, 1983).[5]

---

[5]Recent research has shown that reading can induce significant near shifts of *both* the dark focus and dark-vergence postures. These changes are greatest for subjects whose resting position initially corresponds to a far distance, and they are related to dissociable perceptual consequences. In general, myopic shifts of the dark focus induce transient myopic refractive error, but they are not related to subjective ratings of fatigue. In contrast, shifts of dark vergence are positively correlated with subjective ratings of visual fatigue. These findings suggest that changes in resting posture may serve to "reset" the system's operating range so that the visual task, in this case reading, is less stressful (Owens & Wolf, 1983). Parallel work by Shebilske, Karmiohl, and Proffitt (1983; Shebilske, Proffitt, & Fisher, 1984) indicates that adaptation of distance perception, as well as vergence tonus, can occur as a result of near work. This suggests that many commonplace activities involving near work may modify the relationship between vergence and space perception.

Although the source of these slow "hysteresis" effects is not known, it is possible that they depend in part on afferent feedback from muscle spindles, tendon organs, or "palisade" endings in the extraocular muscles (Granit, 1970; Richmond, Johnston, Baker, & Steinbach, 1984). If this were the case, then the effects of eye-muscle afference on visually guided behavior (e.g., Hein & Diamond, 1983; Steinback & Smith, 1981) could be explained as a consequence of changes in efferent signals that result from a shift in oculomotor tonus.

A final comment regarding mechanisms that determine tonus: Evidence discussed in a preceeding section indicates that adaptive modification of vergence tonus is facilitated by interactions with the environment (Owens & Leibowitz, 1980), suggesting that "higher order" processes are involved in variations of the resting posture. This interpretation might seem inconsistent with the possibility that eye-muscle afference affects tonus, for the latter possibility suggests the operation of a peripheral neural "loop." Theories of motor control indicate, however, that the existence of parallel mechanisms for postural control are not inconsistent but rather are commonplace, at least in skeletal muscles (Granit, 1970). The famous "stretch reflex," for example, illustrates the effectiveness of postural control by peripheral neural loops, as afferent signals from the muscle spindles trigger alpha innervation to extrafusal fibers controlling muscle length. Superimposed on this peripheral servo-control process is the gamma-spindle system, which modulates the postural "set point" maintained by the spindles. This is accomplished by means of gamma efference, originating at higher centers, to the intrafusal muscle fibers which contain the spindle receptors. This hierarchy of control greatly simplifies the difficult problem of coordinating multiple muscle groups; it permits higher order processes to adjust posture and to initiate complex actions without specifying absolute levels of innervation (Pew, 1984). Without straining the analogy too much, one might speculate that control of the extraocular muscles is also superimposed on a background of tonic postural activity, and further, that this tonic activity is determined by two sources: (1) peripheral feedback from the ocular muscles themselves, and (2) gamma-like input from "higher order" processes. In the case of the vergence system, the "higher order" processes might be concerned with integrating optical (light-based) and oculomotor (efference-based) information about the layout of the environment.

Although the mechanisms and functions of oculomotor tonus and effort remain to be clarified, this approach is appealing for several reasons. In the context of theories of perception, it helps us avoid the assumption of mentalistic computations to derive spatial information from eye movements, and it provides a simpler explanation than associative learning for maintaining appropriate calibration of eye position, perception, and visually guided behavior. From the practical standpoint, it has already been applied with some success to a variety of visual problems, including anomalous refractive errors and spatial illusions that occur under reduced stimulus conditions, adaptive modification of perceived distance, and symptoms of visual fatigue. Similar concepts may be equally applicable to clinical phenomena such as orthophorization and some aspects of concomitant strabismus.

This approach is also satisfying from the philosophical standpoint because it emphasizes the importance of sensorimotor *interactions*, and it seems to invite further investigation. While it stands on assumptions that go beyond our present data base, it also suggests a variety of straight-forward experiments that may enlarge our understanding of both the processes involved in oculomotor control and those mediating our perception and interaction with the environment.

ACKNOWLEDGMENTS

Preparation of this chapter was supported by the Zentrum für interdisziplinäre Forschung der Universität Bielefeld, Franklin & Marshall College, and Grant EY-03898 from the National Institutes of Health. I thank Richard Aslin, Deborah Harris, Herbert Heuer, Herschel Leibowitz, Eckert Scheerer, and Wayne Shebilske for comments on an earlier draft of this chapter. I also gratefully acknowledge the aid of Annie Vinter and Deborah Harris in translating Descartes.

REFERENCES

Baird, J. W. (1903). The influence of accommodation and convergence upon the perception of depth. *American Journal of Psychology, 14*, 150–200.

Bauer, J., & Held, R. (1975). Comparison of visually guided reaching in normal and deprived infant monkeys. *Journal of Experimental Psychology: Animal Behavior Processes, 4*, 298–308.

Berkeley, G. (1709). An essay towards a new theory of vision. In A. D. Lindsay (Ed.), *Berkeley: A new theory of vision and other writings*, London: J. M. Dent & Sons, 1972.

Biguer, B., & Prablanc, C. (1981). Modulation of the vestibulo-ocular reflex in eye-head orientation as a function of target distance in man. In A. F. Fuchs & W. Becker (Eds.), *Progress in oculomotor research*. New York: Elsevier North Holland.

Breinin, G. M. (1971). The structure and function of extraocular muscles—an appraisal of the duality concept. *American Journal of Ophthalmology, 72*, 1–9.

Bridgeman, B., Kirch, M., & Sperling, A. (1981). Segregation of cognitive and motor aspects of visual function using induced motion. *Perception and Psychophysics, 29*, 336–342.

Bridgeman, B., Lewis, S., Heit, G., & Nagle, M. (1979). Relation between cognitive and motor-oriented systems of visual position perception. *Journal of Experimental Psychology, 5(4)*, 692–700.

Boring, E. G. (1942). *Sensation and perception in the history of experimental psychology*. New York: Appleton–Century–Crofts.

Burian, H. M., & von Noorden, G. K. (1974). *Binocular vision and ocular motility*, St. Louis: C. V. Mosby.

Campos, E. C., & Catellani, C. O. (1978). Further evidence for the fusional nature of the compensating (or 'eating up') of prisms in concomitant strabismus. *International Ophthalmology, 1*, 57–62.

Carter, D. B. (1963). Effects of prolonged wearing of prism. *American Journal of Optometry, 40*, 265–273.

9. OCULOMOTOR INFORMATION ABOUT SPACE   245

Carter, D. B. (1965). Fixation disparity and heterophoria following prolonged wearing of prisms. *American Journal of Optometry, 42,* 141–152.
Charman, W. N., & Tucker, G. (1978). Accommodation as a function of object form. *American Journal of Optometry & Physiological Optics, 55,* 84–92.
Cogan, D. G. (1937). Accommodation and the autonomic nervous system. *Archives of Ophthalmology, 18,* 739–766.
Crone, R. A. (1969). Heterophoria: I. The role of microanomalous-correspondence, and II. Fusion and convergence. *Albrecht von Graefes Archiv für klinische und experimentale Ophthalmologie, 177,* 52–74.
Crone, R. A., & Hardjowijoto, S. (1979). What is normal binocular vision? *Documenta Ophthalmologica, 47,* 163–199.
Descartes, R. (1637). La Dioptrique, Discours VI. In C. Adam and P. Tannery (Eds.) *Ouvres de Descartes* (Vol. VI, pp. 130–147). Paris: Librarie Philosophie J. Vrin, 1973.
Descartes, R. (1664). Le Mond. Traite de L'Homme. In C. Adam & P. Tannery (Eds.), *Ouvres De Descartes* (Vol. XI, pp. 155–161, 183–185). Paris: Librarie Philosophie J. Vrin, 1967.
Dewey, J. (1896). The reflex arc concept in psychology. *Psychological Review, 3,* 357–370.
Dichgans, J. (1977). Optokinetic nystagmus as dependent on the retinal periphery via the vestibular nucleus. In R. Baker & A. Berthoz (Eds.), *Control of gaze by brain stem nerouns* (pp. 261–267). Amsterdam: Elsevier.
Ebenholtz, S. M. (1974). The possible role of eye-muscle potentiation in several forms of prism adaptation. *Perception, 3,* 477–485.
Ebenholtz, S. M. (1981). Hysteresis effects in the vergence control system: Perceptual implications. In D. F. Fisher, R. A. Monty, & J. W. Senders (Eds.), *Eye movements: Visual perception and cognition.* Hillsdale, NJ: Lawrence Erlbaum Associates.
Ebenholtz, S. M. (1983). Accommodative hysteresis: A precursor for induced myopia? *Investigative Ophthalmology & Visual Science, 24,* 513–515.
Ebenholtz, S. M., & Wolfson, D. M. (1975). Perceptual aftereffects of sustained convergence. *Perception and Psychophysics, 17,* 485–491.
Epstein, W., Park, J., & Casey, A. (1961). The current status of the size-distance hypothesis. *Psychological Bulletin, 58,* 491–514.
Fincham, E. F. (1962). Accommodation and convergence in the absence of retinal images. *Vision Research, 1,* 425–440.
Fincham, E. F. & Walton, J. (1957). The reciprocal actions of accommodation and convergence. *Journal of Physiology (London), 137,* 488–508.
Foley, J. M. (1980). Binocular distance perception. *Psychological Review, 87,* 411–434.
Francis, E. L., & Owens, D. A. (1983). The accuracy of binocular vergence for peripheral stimuli. *Vision Research, 23,* 13–19.
Gibson, J. J. (1979). *The ecological approach to visual perception.* Boston: Houghton Mifflin.
Gogel, W. C. (1969). The sensing of retinal size. *Vision Research, 9,* 1079–1094.
Gogel, W. C. (1977). The metric of visual space. In W. Epstein (Ed.), *Stability and constancy in visual perception: Mechanisms and processes,* New York: Wiley.
Gogel, W. C. (1978). Size, distance, and depth perception. In E. C. Carterette & M. P. Friedman (Eds.), *Perceptual processing, handbook of perception* (Vol. 9). New York: Academic Press.
Gogel, W. C., & Tietz, J. D. (1973). Absolute motion parallax and the specific distance tendency. *Perception and Psychophysics, 13,* 284–292.
Granit, R. (1970). *The basis of motor control.* New York: Academic Press.
Grant, F. W. (1942). Accommodation and convergence in visual space perception. *Journal of Experimental Psychology, 31,* 89–104.
Hansen, R. M., & Skavenski, A. A. (1977). Accuracy of eye position information for motor control. *Vision Research, 17,* 919–926.
Hein, A., & Diamond, R. (1983). Contributions of eye movement to the representation of space. In A. Hein & M. Jeannerod (Eds.), *Spatially oriented behavior.* New York: Springer–Verlag.

Held, R. (1965). Plasticity in sensory-motor systems. *Scientific American, 213*, 84–94.

Helmholtz, H. (1867). *Handbuch der physiologischen Optik,* Leipzig: Voss. (Or see English translation of 3rd ed., which is essentially as first with addition of commentaries by later workers, by J. P. C. Southall, New York: Dover Publications, 1962).

Hennessy, R. T., & Leibowitz, H. W. (1972). Laser optometer incorporating the Badal principle. *Behavior Research Methods and Instrumentation, 4,* 237–239.

Hine, T. (1985). The effects of accommodation and vergence on the VOR. Personal communication. *Investigative Ophthalmology and Visual Science,* Supplement, 26, 269.

Hope, G. M., & Rubin, M. L. (1984). Night myopia. *Survey of Ophthalmology, 29,* 129–136.

Howard, I. P., & Templeton, W. B. (1966). *Human spatial orientation.* New York: Wiley.

Hung, G. K., & Semmlow, J. L. (1982). A quantitative control theory of sharing between accommodative and vergence controllers. *IEEE Transactions on Biomedical Engineering,* BME-29, No. 5, May 1982.

Ivanoff, A., & Bourdy, C. (1954). Le comportement de la convergence en nocturne (The behavior of convergence in night vision). *Annales d'Optique Oculaire, 3,* 70–75. (Eng. trans available from DAO)

Knoll, H. A. (1966). Measuring ametropia with a gas laser. *American Journal of Optometry, 43,* 415–418.

Leibowitz, H. W. (1971). Sensory, learned, and cognitive mechanisms of size perception. *Annals of the New York Academy of Sciences, 188,* 47–62.

Leibowitz, H. W., & Moore, D. (1966). Role of changes in accommodation and convergence in the perception of size. *Journal of the Optical Society of America, 56,* 1120–1123.

Leibowitz, H. W., & Owens, D. A. (1975). Anomalous myopias and the intermediate dark focus of accommodation. *Science, 189,* 646–648.

Leibowitz, H. W., & Owens, D. A. (1978). New evidence for the intermediate position of relaxed accommodation. *Documenta Ophthalmologica, 46,* 133–147.

Leibowitz, H. W., Shiina, K., & Hennessy, R. T. (1972). Oculomotor adjustments and size constancy. *Perception and Psychophysics, 12,* 497–500.

Lie, I. (1965). Convergence as a cue to perceived size and distance. *Scandinavian Journal of Psychology, 6,* 109–116.

Luckiesh, M. & Moss, F. K. (1940). Functional adaptation to near vision. *Journal of Experimental Psychology, 26,* 352–356.

Maddox, E. E. (1893). *The clinical use of prisms: And the decentering of lenses* (2nd ed.). Bristol, U.K.: John Wright & Sons.

Maskelyne, N. (1789). An attempt to explain a difficulty in the theory of vision, depending on the different refrangibility of light. *Philosophical Transactions of the Royal Society of London, 79,* 256–266.

Matin, L. (1972). Eye movements and perceived visual direction. In D. Jameson & L. Hurvich (Eds.), *Handbook of sensory physiology: Vol. 7. Visual psychophysics.* New York: Springer-Verlag.

McCready, D. W. (1965). Size-distance perception and accommodation convergence micropsia—a critique. *Vision Research, 5,* 189–206.

Morgan, M. W. (1946). A new theory for the control of accommodation. *American Journal of Optometry, 23,* 99–110.

Morgan, M. W. (1968). Accommodation and vergence. *American Journal of Optometry, 45,* 415–454.

Owens, D. A. (1980). A comparison of accomodative responsiveness and contrast sensitivity for sinusoidal gratings. *Vision Research, 20,* 159–167.

Owens, D. A. (1984). The resting state of the eyes. *American Scientist, 72,* 378–387.

Owens, D. A., & Leibowitz, H. W. (1976). Oculomotor adjustments in darkness and the specific distance tendency. *Perception and Psychophysics, 20,* 159–167.

Owens, D. A., & Leibowitz, H. W. (1980). Accommodation, convergence, and distance perception in low illumination. *American Journal of Optometry and Physiological Optics, 57*, 540–550.

Owens, D. A., & Leibowitz, H. W. (1983). Perceptual and motor consequences of tonic vergence. In C. Schor & K. Ciuffreda (Eds.), *Vergence eye movements: Basic and clinical aspects*. Boston: Butterworths.

Owens, D. A., & Wolf, K. S. (1983). Accommodation, binocular vergence, and visual fatigue. *Investigative Ophthalmology & Visual Science (Suppl.), 24*, 23.

Paap, K. R., & Ebenholtz, S. M. (1976). Perceptual consequences of potentiation in the extraocular muscles: An alternative explanation for adaptation to wedge prisms. *Journal of Experimental Psychology: Human Perception and Performance, 2*, 457–468.

Pew, R. W. (1984). A distributed processing view of human motor control. In W. Prinz & A. F. Sanders (Eds.), *Cognition and motor processes*. New York: Springer–Verlag.

Post, R. B. & Leibowitz, H. W. (1982). The effect of convergence on the vestibulo-ocular reflex and implications for perceived movement. *Vision Research, 22*, 461–465.

Richmond, F. J. R., Johnston, W. S. W., Baker, R. S., & Steinbach, M. J. (1984). Palisade endings in human extraocular muscles. *Investigative Ophthalmology & Visual Science, 25*, 471–476.

Ross, H. E., & Ross, G. M. (1976). Did Ptolemy understand the moon illusion? *Perception, 5*, 377–385.

Schober, H. (1954). Über die Akkommodationsruhelage. *Optik, 6*, 282–290. (Eng. trans. available from DAO)

Schor, C. M. (1983). Fixation disparity and vergence adaptation. In C. Schor & K. Ciuffreda (Eds.), *Vergence eye movements: Basic and clinical aspects*. Boston: Butterworths.

Shebilske, W. L. (1977). Visuomotor coordination in visual direction and position constancies. In Epstein, W. (Ed.), *Stability and constancy in visual perception: Mechanisms and processes*. New York: Wiley.

Shebilske, W. L. (1981). Visual direction illusions in everyday situations: Implications for sensorimotor and ecological theories. In D. F. Fisher, R. A. Monty, & J. W. Senders (Eds.), *Eye movements: Cognition and visual perception*. Hillsdale, NJ: Lawrence Erlbaum Associates.

Shebilske, W. L., Karmiohl, C. M. & Proffitt, D. R. (1983). Induced esophoric shifts in eye convergence and illusory distance in reduced and structured viewing conditions. *Journal of Experimental Psychology: Human Perception and Performance, 9*, 270–277.

Shebilske, W. L., Proffitt, D. R. & Fisher, S. K. (1984) Efferent factors in natural event perception can be rationalized and verified: A reply to Turvey and Solomon. *Journal of Experimental Psychology: Human Perception and Performance, 10*, 455–460.

Skavenski, A. A., & Hansen, R. (1978). Role of eye position information in visual space perception. In J. W. Senders, D. F. Fisher, & R. A. Monty (Eds.), *Eye movements and higher psychological functions*, Hillsdale, NJ: Lawrence Erlbaum Associates.

Steinbach, M. J., & Smith, D. R. (1981). Spatial localization after strabismus surgery: Evidence for inflow. *Science, 213*, 1407–1409.

Swenson, H. A. (1932). The relative influence of accommodation and convergence in the judgement of distance. *Journal of General Psychology, 7*, 360–379.

Toates, F. M. (1972). Accommodation function of the human eye. *Physiological Review, 52*, 828–863.

Toates, F. M. (1974). Vergence eye movements. *Documenta Ophthalmologica, 37*, 153–214.

Turvey, M. T. (1979). The thesis of efference-mediation of vision cannot be rationalized. *Behavior and Brain Sciences, 2*, 81–83.

von Hofsten, C. (1976). The role of convergence in visual space perception. *Vision Research, 16*, 193–198.

von Hofsten, C. (1979). Recalibration of the convergence system. *Perception, 8,* 37–42.
von Holst, E. (1954). Relations between the central nervous system and the peripheral organs. *British Journal of Animal Behaviour, 2,* 89–94.
von Holtz, E., & Mittelstaedt, H. (1950). Das Reafferenzprinzip: Wechselwirkungen zwischen Zentralnervensystem und Peripherie. *Naturwissenschaften, 37,* 464–476.
Wallach, H., Frey, K. J., & Bode, K. A. (1972). The nature of adaptation in distance perception based on oculmotor cues. *Perception and Psychophysics, 11,* 110–116.
Welch, R. B. (1978). *Perceptual Modification: Adapting to altered sensory environments.* New York: Academic Press.
Westheimer, G., & Mitchell, D. E. (1969). The sensory stimulus for disjunctive eye movements. *Vision Research, 9,* 749–755.
Whiteside, T. C. D. (1952). Accommodation of the human eye in a bright and empty field. *Journal of Physiology (London), 118,* 65.
Wolfe, J., & Owens, D. A. (1981). Is accommodation colorblind? Focusing chromatic contours. *Perception, 10,* 53–62.
Wundt, W. (1862). *Beitrage zur Theorie der Sinneswahrnehmung,* Heidelberg: C. F. Winter'sche Verlagshandlung.

10 Perceptual Learning by Saccades: A Cognitive Approach

Peter Wolff
Universität Bielefeld

INTRODUCTION

The phenomenon that caused me to consider perceptual learning by saccades was reported by Festinger, Burnham, Ono, and Bamber (1967), by Slotnick (1969), and by Taylor (1962/1975). It can be described as follows: If a prismatic contact lens, causing straight lines to appear curved, is attached to the eye, the subject initially perceives the environment or the display to be distorted. The perceived distortion is reduced, however, as the display is explored by saccadic eye movements with the head in a fixed position. Such visual adaptation remains even during fixation (Slotnick, 1969). Removing the prism lens produces an aftereffect: The environment is perceived to be distorted in the opposite direction to the prismatic deformation until, after a short period, the perceptual world corresponds again to the actual environment.

Adaptation to the prism contact lens occurs even if the explored line is actually curved but appears initially straight because of the prismatic modification (Festinger et al., 1967; Slotnick, 1969). Hence, adaptation is not merely due to the "Gibson-effect" according to which inspecting a curved line with the naked eye reduces the perceived curvature of that line (Coren & Festinger, 1967; Gibson, 1933). With the straight line, however, the Gibson-effect may be involved, because adaptation and after effects are larger than with the curved line (Festinger et al., 1967; Slotnick, 1969). Nevertheless, it must be concluded that the perceptual world can be adapted to reality merely by explorative saccades.

In the present chapter a cognitive approach to perceptual learning by saccades is outlined. Proceeding from the fact that the modification of the saccadic reafference initiates perceptual learning in the contact-lens paradigm, the first sections consider the role of reafference for intended saccades. In the next sections I argue that perceptual learning fulfills the function to reestablish intentional control of saccades. Subsequently the cognitive model is presented, based on the assumption that perceptual learning is the process of detecting the invariance behind the efference–reafference relationship.

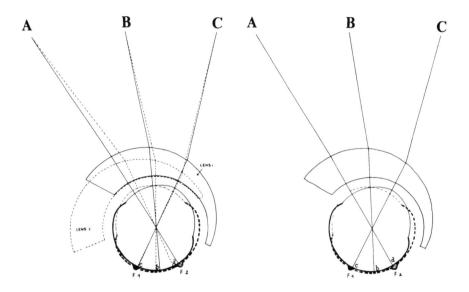

FIG. 10.1 Simplified illustration of the retinal effects produced by a prism lens. Capitals (A, B, and C) represent objects, lower case letters (a, b, and c) represent the retinal images of the objects. For simplification, first, the optical media of the eye are not taken into account. Second, projection center and rotation center are in line. Third, the inner face of the prism lens is illustrated as a sector of a circle around the projection center, i.e., rays through the projection center are not refracted by the inner face. Fourth, the retina is illustrated as a sector of a circle around the rotation center, i.e., the retina moves on that circle's periphery. Consequently, the *preexperimental* reafference has to be illustrated by the fact that, first, a, b, and c do *not* shift relative positions to one another, during saccade, and, second, the foveal distances of a, b, and c in angle of rotation is *identical* with the angle of rotation needed to fovealize a, b, or c.

FIG. 10.1a Illustration of the *contact-lens* paradigm: The lens moves with the eye. *Solid lines* apply to fixating C. The fovea takes position "F1", and the lens takes position "lens 1". *Dotted lines* apply to having moved the eye for fixating A. The fovea takes position "F2" and the lens takes position "lens 2". Figure 10.1a shows:

 1. a, b, and c move during the saccade relative to one another (modification of the saccadic reafference).
 2. A is missed because of the modification. (see later section)

SACCADIC REAFFERENCE AND PERCEPTION

To analyze the conditions for perceptual learning in the contact-lens paradigm, we have to look at the retinal consequences of the prismatic contact lens: The contact lens not only causes a distortion of the retinal image, i.e., of exafference but also modifies the way in which the retinal stimulation is changed by saccades, i.e., the saccadic reafference. The reason is that the contact lens moves with the eye (Fig. 10.1a; see also Howard & Templeton, 1966, p. 400; Taylor, 1962/1975, p. 223). Because the retinal conditions are the same as when the objects move during a saccade of the uncovered eye, saccades initially produce movement perception (Slotnick, 1969; so called "rubbery effects," Welch, 1978). If the prism is mounted in spectacles, the conditions are different: Although prism glasses modify the exafference basically in the same way as the contact lens does, they do not alter the saccadic reafference (Fig. 10.1b; see also Howard & Templeton, 1966, p. 402; Taylor, 1962/1975, p. 222). Therefore, with prism glasses, saccades are not accompanied by rubbery effects (Welch, 1978).

With prism glasses and the head fixed, saccadic exploration produces either no adaptation (Cohen, 1965, cited by Welch, 1978), or merely the Gibson-effect (Festinger et al., 1967). Thus, the modification of the reafference is a necessary condition for perceptual learning (cf. Hein & Held, 1962).

It seems that perception depends on the systematics of the saccadic reafference, a fact that becomes obvious when saccades and retinal change are decorrelated:

Using blue polarized light whose plane of polarization rotated, Coren (1971) produced a "Haidinger's brush" (HB), an entoptic phenomenon that constitutes a point-symmetric rotating retinal image whose center is situated exactly on the fovea (see also Ditchburn, 1973). HB is perceived as a rotating propeller-shaped shadow centered at the fixation point (Fig. 10.2). If the rotation of the polariza-

---

3. Although the saccades are missing, they reduce the foveal distances of a, b, or c. Thus, if the missed target is tracked by a sequence of corrective saccades, target discrepancies become increasingly smaller, until, ultimately, the target is met (see later section).

FIG. 10.1b Illustration of the *prism-glass* paradigm: The prism does not move with the eye. The *solid lined eye* applies to fixating C, whereas the *dotted lined eye* applies to having moved the eye for fixating A. All other solid lines apply to both cases. The saccade's retinal effects, shown in Figure 10.1b, are identical with those which have to be illustrated for the preexperimental case (see earlier):
1. a, b, and c do not shift relative position to one another during the saccade (no modification of the saccadic reafference)
2. A becomes fixated as a result of the saccade. The saccades remain successful, in spite of the lens.

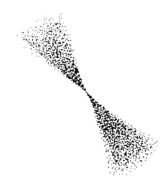

FIG. 10.2 Haidinger's brush (HB). HB's perceived size corresponds to a diameter of ca. 3.75 deg. (Coren, 1971). In contrast to the present Figure, HB is a homogenous shadow.

tion plane stops, HB becomes retinally stabilized and, therefore, disappears perceptually very rapidly. Because saccades do not influence HB's rotations, saccades and retinal changes are decorrelated as with retinal stabilization. As a result of decorrelation the perception of the rotating HB disappeared after some minutes. Decorrelation of saccades and retinal change can also be reached by moving the capillary shadow experimentally (Sharpe, 1972): Whereas the moving shadow is perceived initially, the perception disappears after a while.

The results suggest that the systematics of the saccadic reafference is essential for perception. Perceptual learning by saccades, therefore, must be related to the function of saccadic reafference.

FUNCTION OF SACCADIC REAFFERENCE

Intended Saccades

Saccades do not only fulfill the function of enlarging the foveal angle over time (cf. Wolff, 1984), rather, they are used to select information for realization, i.e., initiation and control of action (Neumann, 1980, 1983, 1985a, b, and this volume). This is illustrated, e.g., by the fact that subjects while exploring a visual scene under different task instructions, frequently look at those objects that are relevant for solving the task (e.g., Gould, 1976; Hochberg & Brooks, 1978; Kolers, 1976; Reinert, 1985; Yarbus, 1967). Further, during read out from iconic memory (Neisser, 1967), saccades are directed to the locations of the previously presented objects (Bryden, 1961; Hall, 1974; see also Teichner, LeMaster, & Kinney, 1978).

As an instrument for controlled selection, the saccade must be guided by the wanted information, which is the saccade's original goal. Thus, the motor movement is merely a mean to produce a specific retinal change (cf. MacKay, 1957, 1973, 1978, 1984; MacKay & Mittelstaedt, 1974; Mittelstaedt, 1971). In order to control saccades by their possible outcomes, the systematics of the saccadic reafference has to be taken into account. But, this is not why the reafference of a given saccade must be eliminated, as cancellation theory (e.g., Matin, 1972, 1982; Shebilske, 1977, 1984) assumes. Rather, the systematics of the saccadic reafference is needed in order to utilize the saccades for controlled selection.

According to the present view intended saccades are guided by anticipating their effects, according to the principle formulated by Bernstein (1967) that supposes that voluntary movements are controlled by anticipating their results (cf. Greenwald, 1970; Prinz, 1985, and this volume):

There is empirical evidence indicating that every intended saccade is preceded by an attentional shift to the perceived target position (Posner, 1980; Remington, 1980). Such an attentional shift seems to be obligatory for an intended saccade (Wolff, 1984; cf. Wurtz & Mohler, 1976), suggesting that the attentional shift specifies the retinal change the saccade is meant to produce. In a way, attention, like mental training, produces the result of the motor movement before the movement itself has been executed. Such an attentional shift could be called an "inner saccade" (Scheerer, 1978).

In the following sections, the term *intention* refers to saccades that are guided by anticipating their retinal result. Intended saccades are to be distinguished from other voluntary saccades that are not of a cognitive origin and from unvoluntary saccades that are elicited by peripheral stimulation.

Perceptual Learning and Intentional Control

Guiding intended saccades by shifting attention to the perceived target location suggests that the programming of the intended saccade depends on the perceived target location. Consequently, agreement between perceptual world and environment is needed for intentional control of saccades. If so, perceptual learning starts, when intentional control of eye movements is lost. In fact, if the subject has not yet adapted to the contact lens, saccades will miss their targets, because the modification of the saccadic reafference can initially not be taken into account (see, Fig. 10.1a). In order to reestablish intentional control, the new systematics of saccadic reafference must be learned.

Consider the assumption that the function of perceptual learning is to reestablish intentional control of eye movements. In the case of decorrelation and retinal stabilization, the aim cannot be achieved. Consequently, in the case of stabilization, eye movements disappear during periods of perceptual loss (Tepas, 1961; cited by Festinger et al., 1967), and in the case of decorrelation, eye movements become atypically small (Coren & Porac, 1974). But, in the contact-lens paradigm, perceptual learning is successful.

Accordingly, the reason why the perceptual world changes with the contact lens as well as with decorrelation is not the change of the saccadic reafference per se, but the loss of intentional control that results from the change of the saccadic reafference. The conclusion is corroborated by the following finding:

Coren and Porac (1974) showed that the perception of a rotating HB diminishes only if the subjects try to track the outer wing tip of one blade of the rotating HB, a task which is impossible because HB's center does not shift retinal position. If, however, the subjects look to and fro between points presented on a display simultaneously with the rotating HB, the perceived clarity of the HB does not decrease more than when the subjects fixate the center of a rotating control display that looks like a HB or when they fixate the center of the HB. The latter task is easy to do, because the HB is centered at the fovea.

The results suggest that decorrelation of saccades and retinal change, in general: Changing the saccadic reafference, does not alter the perceptual world, as long as the targets can be fixated, as the points and the centers of the rotating HB and the control display. Thus, changing the saccadic reafference is not a sufficient condition for perceptual learning. Rather, the change is effective only, if it prevents realization of saccades' intentions, i.e., control of saccades by anticipating their perceptual outcomes. Accordingly, perceptual learning means learning to use saccades as an instrument for controlling the retinal stimulation.

Control of Retinal Stimulation

If anticipating the retinal change is a sufficient condition to permit the oculomotor system to execute the saccade automatically (Wolff, 1984), an important conclusion can be drawn: If the subject is adapted to prismatic distortion, the very retinal effects that have been anticipated will result automatically. Instead of saying that eye movements are controlled intentionally, we should say that retinal stimulation is controlled intentionally inasmuch as exactly those retinal effects are produced which correspond to the perceiver's intentions. According to this view, perceptual learning provides access to the laws enabling intentional manipulation of retinal stimulation. These laws that determine how retinal stimulation can be changed by efferent commands are bound to be an invariance underlying reafferent variation.

A COGNITIVE APPROACH

Immediate Experience during Exploration

There is evidence that the visual system is neither necessarily informed about the actual oculomotor behavior nor is it necessarily informed about the actual behavior of the environment: When a perceiver initiates a saccade while the eye is prevented from moving, a motion is perceived in the direction of the intended saccade (Brindley & Merton, 1960), or when the experimenter moves the subject's eye, the subject perceives a motion in the opposite direction to the passive eye movement (Brindley & Merton, 1960; Helmholtz, 1866; Skavenski, Haddad, & Steinman, 1972). The results suggest that retinal information is processed as if the eye behaved according to the efferent command, independently of the eye's actual behavior. Thus, when asking what the organism can immediately experience at any moment during visual exploration, the only conceivable answer is that it can experience no more and no less than the coincidence of efference and retinal change. Perceptual learning must, therefore, result from this experience.

Further it must be evident that the retinal change results from the subject's own actions. The latter condition is true: The perceived shifting of the saccadic target that occurs if the target is displaced by the experimenter, while the subject moves the eye to the target (e.g., Bridgeman, 1981, 1983; Mack, 1970), is directly experienced as caused by the subject's own eye movements. The subjects realize immediately that they themselves move the stimulus by way of their gaze (Brune & Lücking, 1969).

The Perceptus Model

In order to illustrate the principle of perceptual learning by saccadic exploration I use a simplified example. The simplification consists in the fact that both eye movements and retinal variation are shown as *one*-dimensional movements. I further, begin with a situation in which no perceptual world exists. Congenitally blind people find themselves in a comparable situation when they begin to see after an operation, as reported by v. Senden (1931), or when exploring their surroundings with a TV camera as in sensory-substitution studies (Bach-Y-Rita, 1972, 1984). At least with sensory substitution, the people can learn to perceive the environmental properties which structure the light, if only after intensive training.

Perceptus and His Environment. Figure 10.3 shows a slotted shield that covers a line. Looking through the slot, we can see a point of the line. The shield can be moved across the line with a motor. When the shield is moved the point in the slot is shifted to and fro. On the shield lives a little ghost, called Perceptus, who turns the wheel that is connected to the motor via servo-control. As soon as Perceptus moves the wheel to the left or the right, the motor analogously guides the shield up or down across the line, with Perceptus participating in the trip. He is unaware of the shield's movement, however, because his world consists only of what happens in the slot (Fig. 10.4).

In this model, the shield represents the eye, and the motor represents the oculomotor system. The movement of the shield demonstrates a saccade, and the

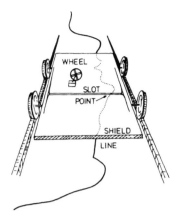

FIG. 10.3 Movable slotted shield covering a line. The slot reveals one point of the line. When the wheel is turned to the left or the right, the shield moves up (forward) or down (backward), and the point moves in the slot. The movement amplitude of the shield is analogous to the angle of the wheel rotation or to the number of wheel rotations.

line the environment, respectively. The one-dimensional slot corresponds to the two-dimensional retina, and the point position to the retinal image. Different point positions stand for different retinal conditions created when different objects are fixated. Perceptus represents the visual system whose efferences are symbolized by the wheel rotations. The point motions that Perceptus produces by rotating the wheel represents the reafferent variation of retinal stimulation.

Principle of Perceptual Learning in the Perceptus Model. How can the principle of perceptual learning be described by this model, especially if we assume that Perceptus has not yet learned anything?

As soon as Perceptus begins playing with the wheel, he becomes aware that

FIG. 10.4 Perceptus with wheel and Point. Perceptus should not conceived as a homunculus. His large eyes should merely symbolize that he is sensitive to changes of the slot state.

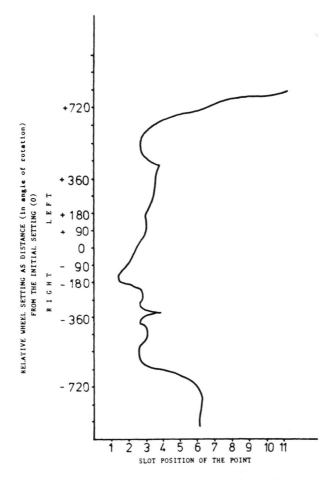

FIG. 10.5 Distribution of all possible wheel-point-coincidences. The determination of the initial wheel setting (0) is free. The units of the y-axis is determined by the invariant layout of point positions along the movement dimension.

with every wheel rotation he shifts the point. However, Perceptus cannot control *how* the point moves, only when it moves. How can he learn to use the wheel rotation as a means to control the point motion?

Because identical wheel rotations sometimes produce different point motions, and because identical point motions sometimes occur with different wheel rotations (depending on the momentary slot position relative to the line), there is no formal rule that can be used every time. The only real thing that exists in Perceptus's slotted universe are the coincidences of concrete wheel rotations and concrete point motions. The entirety of all possible wheel-point-coincidences is determined, however, because each coincidence can be reversed and, thus, repeated. Reversibility means that the wheel-point-relationship does not change with time. Instead, it changes with every wheel rotation. Thus the *relations* of all possible coincidences to one another are determined by an invariance that can be illustrated as a two-dimensional structure with the entries "slot position of the point" and "relative setting of the wheel" (Fig. 10.5).

The invariance determines all possible events in the slot, because it is the law that explains the wheel-point-relationship every time. However, the invariance contains neither point motions nor wheel rotations. Instead, the invariance is the qualitative layout or relative arrangement of all possible point positions whose relations define locations in a space through which Perceptus moves when he rotates the wheel. The point motion in the slot, coinciding with a given wheel rotation, is caused by the arrangement of those points in the invariance that are passed, i.e., by the passed locations. Thus, every effective wheel rotation is a voluntary movement in a space, and the coinciding point motion is the structure of the path. Every possible coincidence of wheel rotation and point motion constitutes a distance between two locations within the structure.

The line in Fig. 10.5 illustrates Perceptus's perceptual world. Although in the reference system of the slot the wheel-point-relations change continuously, it is clear that every single case, at every moment is determined by one and the same law, namely, a voluntary movement in a stable structure. To the extent that Perceptus learns the invariance, he learns, at the same time, his own actions, namely, that he moves himself within a structure when he turns the wheel.

Perceptual World and Reality in the Perceptus Model. To shift the point to a desired position in the slot, all Perceptus has to do is to move to the appropriate location in his perceptual world (attentional shift); moving within the perceptual world and turning the wheel is *one and the same* event. The same reality that, in the reference system of the slot, has to be described as a voluntarily caused point motion, is experienced in the perceptual world as an intended movement toward a location in a stable structure at a given moment. Both cases reflect the same event from different cognitive positions.

The control that Perceptus acquires is purely cognitive: He does not learn to influence events that were initially beyond his influence. Rather, he becomes able to choose wheel rotations according to their effects, a choice that in the beginning he was unable to make. That means at the same time, that Perceptus becomes able to *intend* saccades. Thus, intention emerges from perceptual learning.

To summarize: Perceptus can control his slotted universe by knowing the invariance underlying the wheel-point-relationship. The knowledge constitutes his perceptual world. It rests exclusively on information about sensory variation. Nevertheless, it is a stable structure that contains neither the point motions nor the wheel rotations but provides a space by the distribution of events that can be met by voluntary movements.

Application of the Model

Agreement Between Perceptual World and Environment. If the model is applied to perceptual learning by saccadic exploration, the underlying principle becomes less evident inasmuch as eye movement and reafference are two dimensional. But, the principle should remain the same: Voluntary control of retinal stimulation, (i.e., intentional control of eye movements) can be acquired only if the law that determines the reafferent variation of retinal stimulation is experienced as a voluntary movement in a stable structure. All possible retinal states are arranged relative to another along a continuum in such a way that all possible coincidences of efference and retinal change have to be described as distances within that continuum. The entirety of all possible coincidences is determined by an invariant topological structure, the perceptual world. The perceptual world offers the possible movements in terms of the retinal effects that the visual system can produce momentarily. If the offered retinal effects prove to be true, the perceptual world is veridical. It is not the validity, but the *reliability* that is important: The perceptual world tallies with the environment, if the perceiver is able to find his way. Thus, "agreement of perceptual world and environment" does not mean that two different structures—an objective external one (environment) and a subjective internal one (perceptual world)—exist that correspond with each other (cf. Bischof, 1966). The important point is that the relations between all possible coincidences of efference and reafference is invariantly determined. If so, the visual system will acknowledge the invariance. The knowledge constitutes the basis of the perceptual world and enables the visual system to control the retinal state. However, the invariance does not exist twice, i.e., both externally and internally; there is only invariance.

Saccade-Specific Perceptual World. In contrast to Perceptus limited actions, saccades are *two*-dimensional movements. Because I have illustrated Perceptus's perceptual world as a two-dimensional line, I ought to illustrate the perceptual world of the visual system as a three-dimensional structure, with the two dimensions of the voluntary movements on the one hand, and the third dimension of "retinal stimulation" on the other. This might be misunderstood, however, because the metrics of perceptual space are determined solely by the dimensions of the voluntary movement. Retinal stimulation merely provides the "substance" of which the spatial structure consists (see also the distinction between "space-filling" and "space-giving" sensations in Husserl's phenomenology, Scheerer, 1985a). Thus, the state of the slot lends to Perceptus's perceptual world the modality pertaining to the sensory quality of the slot. If the point motion causes visual sensations, Perceptus's perceptual world is a visual one.

Accordingly, saccades do not constitute a three-dimensional space, but only a two-dimensional plane, whereas the dimension of depth is provided by other movements (accommodation, convergence, head movements, and locomotion), perhaps along the same principle that underlies the Perceptus model. According to that principle, those environmental properties are perceived whose sensory projection is varied systematically by voluntary movements. In the case of the saccades, they are configurative properties, such as the curvature of a line. A hypothetical perceptual world produced by saccades alone would be as a two-dimensional configuration, if one neglects the perceived distance of the configuration from the perceiver. The term *perceptual world* is used, here, only in this sense.

Schematic Coincidences. The high-spatial resolution of the perceptual world is not only a consequence of the high precision of the oculomotor movement (e.g., Becker & Jürgens, 1979; Kornhuber, 1984), but also a result of the anatomical and neuroanatomical equipment of the eye. Both, the high sensitivity to sensory changes (e.g., Arendt, 1973) and the size of the visual angle guarantee that even minute movements as well as minute movement differences are registered sensorically. Therefore, the grain of the perceptual locations is fine, the spatial resolution is precise, and the structure of the perceptual world is detailed. The fine grain provides for the accuracy with which the eye can be controlled intentionally, as has been illustrated by Steinman (1976).

However, as is known, the spatial resolution of the perceptual world sharply decreases toward the periphery. According to the present model, the drop cannot be caused directly by the low-spatial resolution of the retinal periphery but, rather, should be a result of the inaccuracy with which oculomotor movements of wide amplitude are executed (cf. Carpenter, 1977). In the Perceptus model, this aspect can be described as follows: Suppose, the precision with which the motor guides the slotted shield across the line decreases when the amplitude of the movement increases. Although point motions that coincide with large wheel rotations are subject to an invariance, the latter describes only a stochastic relationship: Point motions coinciding with large wheel rotations cannot be reversed (and, hence, reproduced) exactly. The result is an imprecise, or as Neisser (1976) would say "schematic" coincidence between a group of large wheel rotations and a range of point motions within which a differentiation is not possible. Consequently, for large wheel rotations, Perceptus cannot learn to anticipate the final point position exactly. He can only anticipate an *area* of final point positions. The perceptual locations, which are far away from the one momentarily focused define an area that is not differentiated spatially. Therefore, Perceptus can shift only to this area in his perceptual world, not to a location within this area (cf. Wolff, 1984).

Differentiation and Anticipation. Although only one coincidence can be realized at one time, the present model does not imply that the visual system stores the single coincidences and integrates them to a coherent structure. The relations between all possible coincidences cannot be constructed by integration but, instead, must be experienced directly during explorative action.

The topological relation that determines the point motion coinciding with a momentary wheel rotation can only be detected on the basis of the coincidence's relation to all possible, i.e., previous as well as future, coincidences. Because the visual system is not capable of looking into the future, perceptual learning must be a process of progressive differentiation:

The first coincidence reveals the relation between two locations (A and B) whose places within the structure is yet unknown. The locations only exist through their mutual relationship. The subsequent coincidence reveals a further relation between location C and B. However, because B is solely determined by its relation to A, location C also depends on the first movement. Therefore, A, B, and their relations are not only included in C but are, at the same time, more precisely specified, namely, in respect to their new relation to C. C is location of the same spatial structure to which A and B also belong. But C is not simply added to A and B, rather, the whole structure becomes more differentiated by the second movement. Hence, the entire structure that contains only topological relations is included in every momentary coincidence.

Generally speaking: All previous coincidences determine the perceptual locations revealed by all subsequent coincidences in a common structure, and all subsequent coincidences specify more precisely the locations of all previous coincidences. Thus, the previously experienced coincidences are offered momentarily as movement possibilities even though they have been experienced in the past. Perceptual learning always depends on all previous experiences and leads to a differentiation of the entire structure. The basis is that only one movement can be performed at a time, and, therefore, every effective movement alters all subsequent movement possibilities. One has only to accept that it is not the single retinal image, but retinal stimulation *in variation* that contains the relevant information. The perception of the environment through the active variation of its sensory image is the basic idea underlying the present invariance principle (cf. Gibson, 1966, 1968, 1979).

Accordingly, an attentional shift within the perceptual world does not mean that some future event has been anticipated. The shift is nothing else than the intention to change the retinal state in a specific way, and the intended change is offered as a possible movement because the relation between the final retinal state to be produced by the movement and the momentary retinal state has already been experienced. What seems to an external observer to be an anticipation of a future event is, in fact, the selection of a movement possibility offered momentarily in terms of its retinal effect (see also the differentiation between "intention" and "expectation" in Husserl's phenomenology, Scheerer, 1985 b, and this volume). The basis for anticipation is the reversibility of the coincidences.

It is important to recognize that the perceiver does not explore his world like a picture but he lives in it. Stable structure and voluntary movements are two sides of one unified experience. Although the perceptual world is a stable structure, it is not a static framework, but a law in a dynamic activity. This law enables

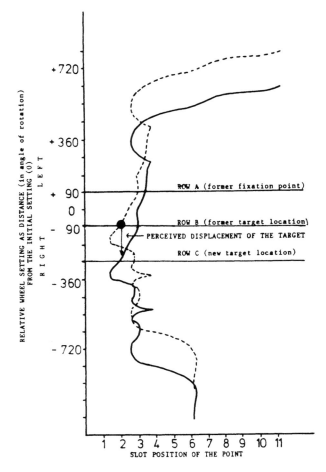

FIG. 10.6 Displacement perception: The figure illustrates the case in which the sensory state, in spite of a movement-intention, does not change. Row A represents the former gaze position; row B the new gaze position (which is the same as the former perceptual location of the target). The target is perceived to be shifted to row C.

programming the saccade according to an anticipated retinal change, rather than anticipating the retinal change according to a programmed saccade.

Displacement. When the actual retinal change does not agree with the anticipated one, the missed target cannot be perceived at its old location to which attention is directed now. According to the Perceptus model, the perceived location of an object is defined by the intended movement enabling the fixation of the object and producing the corresponding retinal state, according to the learned invariance. This is a corrective movement. Consequently, if the intention to fixate a target or to change the gaze to another target is not realized, the target should be displaced perceptually in the direction of the necessary corrective movement, independent of why intention was not realized. Thus, regardless of whether the subject's eye, during fixation, is moved experimentally (see previous section), or whether the eye is prevented from moving, while a saccade is intended (see previous section), or whether the target is displaced during the saccade (see previous section), the result is the same: The target is perceived to shift in the direction of the saccade that is necessary to fixate the missed target.

In the Perceptus model, perceptual displacement can be illustrated as follows (Fig. 10.6): Suppose that the point is at slot position 3, that the relative wheel setting is $+90°$, and that the gaze is directed to row A. If Perceptus decides to move to row B, he intends slot position 2, and he turns the wheel $180°$ to the right, namely, to the relative setting of $-90°$. In short, he shifts his attention to row B, which is the location of the target. If the slot position of the point does not change, for whatever reason, the same wheel rotation that Perceptus has already performed has to be repeated to shift the point from its unexpected slot position 3, his old one, to the intended slot position 2. Therefore, the target now has the same distance and direction in relation to the new gaze position as to the old one. The new target location differs from the former by the extent of the intended movement. The perceived target shifts with the gaze to row C.

Adaptation

Visual Adaptation. According to the Perceptus model, perceptual adaptation will occur, if the relations between all possible coincidences to one another change. Changing the relations is the case, when the qualitative arrangement of the point locations is altered (e.g., if the line under the shield is changed). The intended point motions cannot be realized until the new invariance has been detected.

Such conditions apply to the contact-lens paradigm: By modifying the systematics of the saccadic reafference, the contact lens changes the relations between all possible coincidences of efference and reafference. The relativistic layout of all possible retinal states, a layout that defines the efferences by which all possible retinal states can be transformed into each other, is qualitatively different from the preexperimental one. If the new invariance is detected, intentional control is reestablished. The new invariance offers the movements enabling a successful scanning of the display, i.e., the exposed line. Because this new invariance is as reliable as the preexperimental one, the line will be perceived with the same curvature as before the experiment with the naked eye.

How can the new invariance be experienced, although the targets are initially missed systematically?

As mentioned in an earlier section, control motivation initiates perceptual learning. If we assume that the intention will continue until there is no further movement offered for its realization, the corrective saccade will follow the unsuccessful main saccade automatically (Wolff, 1984). But the corrective movement will also miss the target. Presumably, the target is tracked within the perceptual world, automatically, that is, the movements of the gaze, and consequently the saccades, are in a sense unvoluntary as they are now controlled by the perceived target location. With the prism lens, however, the target discrepancies become increasingly smaller (see Fig. 10.1a) so that the original intention is finally realized.

The precondition for perceptual relearning, namely, that the target is attained ultimately is neither met in decorrelation and retinal stabilization where invariance is extinguished, nor in a situation where the relations between saccades and reafferences are inverted (Smith, 1962; cited by Schmidt, Gottlieb, Coleman, & Smith, 1974), because the target discrepancies are enlarged by the corrective movements.

Motor Adaptation. According to the Perceptus model, perceptual adaptation is not the only possibility to cope with a loss of intentional control: As a topological structure, the line in Fig. 10.5 does not depend on the Y-axis's scale (which is only for illustration). With different ratios of gearing between wheel and motor, which drives the shield, the same invariance would result, provided that the gearing ratio remains constant during exploration. The reason is that the invariance determines the scale of the y-axis and not vice versa, because the possible coincidences do not determine the invariance, but, in contrast, the invariance determines the possible coincidences. Thus, although a change of the gearing ratio alters the wheel-point-coincidences, it does not change the relations of the coincidences to one another. The topological structure remains the same, merely the y-axis's scale has to be changed. Thus, adaptation to altered gearing ratio does not require perceptual learning but merely motor learning. In order to reestablish intentional control Perceptus has only to alter the wheel rotations, but the perceptual locations to which Perceptus moves when he rotates the wheel remain the same as before.

Such conditions apply to learning situations where the loss of intentional control does not result from a qualitative change of the saccadic reafference, but from a change of the efferent commands needed to produce the intended result. According to the Perceptus model, motor learning will occur without any perceptual change.

In fact, the expectation is true: Miller and Festinger (1977) succeeded in producing oculomotor learning while their subjects scanned a U-shaped curve by saccades. The curve contained 3 equidistant geometric figures (Fig. 10.7). The subjects looked at these geometric figures, moving their eyes in alternating order from left-to-right and right-to-left. During each saccade the curve was moved in such a way that the eye, to be accurate, had to move on a horizontal path. In one

rigid shift condition   deformation condition

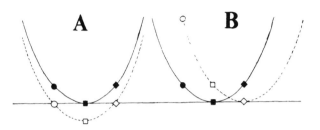

FIG. 10.7 Illustration of the Miller and Festinger (1977) paradigm: The subjects looked in alternating order from figure to figure (circle, square, rhombus, square, circle, . . . , etc.). The figure illustrates the situation where the subjects looked from square to rhombus. (Solid lines: pre-saccadic display, dotted lines: post-saccadic display.) In the "rigid shift" condition, the curve moved vertically during the saccade, leaving the relative curve positions of the figures to one another unchanged. In the "deformation condition", the curve moved horizontally, changing the relative curve position of the figures to one another. In both conditions the saccade's goals took the same horizontal position postsaccadically (horizontal line). (after Miller & Festinger, 1977).

condition (Fig. 10.7a), the curve shifted rigidly up and down. Thus, the systematics by which the retinal structure could be changed by saccades were not qualitatively altered. As a result of training, the subjects learned to compensate for the regular shifts of the curve: They moved their eyes mainly horizontally, as if the figures were arranged on a horizontal line. In spite of the oculomotor adjustment, the curve was not perceived as a horizontal. Rather, the perceptual change did not exceed the Gibson-effect.

The results are in line with many related experiments (Hajos & Frey, 1982; Henson, 1978; McLaughlin, 1967; McLaughlin, Kelly, Anderson, & Wenz, 1968; Miller, Anstis, & Templeton, 1981; Pola, 1976), in which the subjects had to look from a given fixation point to a target that was shifted during the saccade to a new position. In each trial, the subjects repeated the saccade from the same fixation point to the same target that was shifted in each trial in the same way. Thus, as in the Miller and Festinger study, the retinal change to be produced by the intended saccade was not changed, merely the motor movement needed to realize the intention was altered. As a result of training, the subjects looked directly to the postsaccadic target position, thus, compensating for the target's regular shift. Such motor adaptation, however, did not influence the perceived target location. Rather, the subjects did not notice that they adapted to the altered conditions, suggesting that the perceived gaze movement remained the same.

The conclusion also follows from a study by Mack, Fendrich, and Pleune

(1978): While their subjects moved their eyes horizontally, looking to and fro between the sides of a square, the square moved up and down, synchroneously with, and analogously to the horizontal eye movement component. As a result of training, the saccades adapted to the square's movements: The eyes no longer moved along a horizontal, but slanting path, i.e., partially compensating for the vertical movement of the square. At the same time, the detection threshold for the vertical movements during the saccades rose.[1] Rising threshold was not due to the fact that the vertical retinal slip, produced by the square's movement, was reduced by the obliquity of the saccades: When non-adapted subjects moved their eyes as oblique as the adapted subjects, they detected vertical stimulus movements during the oblique saccades as well as during horizontal saccades.

The results suggest that the *perceived* eye movement was not changed with the motor movement: The adapted subjects still intended horizontal saccades and "supposed" to look horizontally. In fact, when the adapted subjects moved their eyes to the *remembered* horizontal aim (without a cueing stimulus), they executed oblique saccades, i.e., in the direction in which the square had moved during adaptation. The Perceptus model explains the results by the assumption that the invariance behind the systematics of the saccadic reafference was not changed, but merely the "efference scale."

According to the Perceptus model perceptual learning will occur when the saccadic reafference is changed *qualitatively*. as it was the case in Miller & Festinger's second condition (Fig. 10.7b): When the figure's spatial relationship was *deformed* during the scanning saccades, the reduction of the perceived curvature, in fact, exceeded the Gibson-effect. Thus, perceptual learning resulted.[2]

The findings reported in the present section clearly disprove motor theory of perception (for a more detailed discussion of this point, see Wolff, 1985), according to which perception is based on the motor properties of the saccades needed to fixate and to explore the objects (Burnham, 1968; Festinger et al., 1967; Festinger & Cannon, 1965; Festinger & Easton, 1974; see also Coren, 1981; survey of motor theories in Weimer, 1977; historical survey in Scheerer, 1984).

In line with motor theory as well as with the scan path model of Norton & Stark (1971 a, b, c) according to which perception is based on ensembles of

---

[1]The result applies to stimulus movements in the same direction in which the square moved during adaptation. The threshold for movements in the opposite direction decreased. For simplification, only the former case is considered here.

[2]In Miller and Festinger's deformation condition (Fig. 7b), motor learning was also involved: The perceptual change was much too small to have caused the motor adjustment that was even stronger than in the rigid shift condition (Fig. 7A). Possible reasons are, first, that reafference of only the main saccades was changed, but not of the corrective saccades. Second, if the subjects, temporarily ignoring the instruction, executed saccades to other than the figures' locations, the reafference of those saccades was not *systematically* changed. Third, although the figures' positions relative to one another changed during saccades, the shape of the curve did not.

sensory-motor units, the Perceptus model assumes that the perceptual locations of objects are established by the eye movements required for fixating the objects successfully, and, that the objects's forms are established by the scanning movements necessary to explore the objects. However, motor information, although it is needed for saccadic exploration, does not *directly* bring about perception. Instead, perception is based on the reafferences, i.e., on the relations of all possible retinal states that can be produced voluntarily. Knowledge of these relations allow for cognitive control of scan pattern (Parker, 1978; Stark & Ellis, 1981, compare, however, Fisher, Karsh, Breitenbach, & Barnette, 1983).

CONCLUSION

According to the Perceptus model, the perceptual world is the topological structure of the qualitative layout of all possible reafferences, that is, the relations of all possible coincidences of eye movement-efferences and retinal changes to one another. The perceptual world informs the perceiver about the possible eye movements in the language of retinal effects that the perceiver can actually produce in his momentary environment. That information provides the perceiver with a basis for orientation that enables initiation and control of action by way of saccadic selection (previous section).

The perceptual world is not the result of a constructive process that interprets and completes sensory data and derives information from them about the environment indicated by the sensory data. In fact, in the Perceptus model, retinal stimulation does not function at all as a cue for another fact. The reafferent variation specifies nothing else than its own nature. Therefore, perception is direct: A mediating instance would be needed only if the perceptual world contained something other than the reafferent change of retinal stimulation. The perceptual world embodies the laws according to which retinal stimulation can be varied intentionally. And, it is this very law which is experienced in the process of perceptual learning, and constitutes the perceptual world.

ACKNOWLEDGMENTS

Thanks to Bruce Bridgeman, Don Graham, Herbert Heuer, Doug Mewhort, Odmar Neumann, Fred Owens, and Wayne Shebilske for helpful remarks on earlier versions and to Adelheid Baker for Translation and/or preparation of translation.

REFERENCES

Arendt, L. E. (1973). Spatial differential and integral operations in human vision: Implications of stabilized retinal image fading. *Psychological Review, 80,* 374–395.
Bach-Y-Rita, P. (1972). *Brain mechanisms in sensory substitution.* New York: Academic Press.

Bach-Y-Rita, P. (1984). The relationship between motor processes and cognition in tactile vision substitution. In W. Prinz & A. F. Sanders (Eds.), *Cognition and motor processes*. Berlin: Springer.

Becker, W., & Jürgens, R. (1979). An analysis of the saccadic system by means of double step stimuli. *Vision Research, 19*, 967-983.

Bernstein, N. A. (1967). *The co-ordination and regulation of movement*. London: Pergamon Press.

Bischof, N. (1966). Erkenntnistheoretische Grundlagenprobleme der Wahrnehmungspsychologie. In W. Metzger (Ed.), *Handbuch der Psychologie* (Vol. I, No. 1). Göttingen: Hogrefe.

Bridgeman, B. (1981). Cognitive factors in subjective stabilization of the visual world. *Acta Psychologica, 48*, 111-121.

Bridgeman, B. (1983). Mechanisms of space constancy. In A. Hein & M. Jeannerod (Eds.), *Spatially oriented behavior*. New York: Springer.

Brindley, G. S., & Merton, P. A. (1960). The absence of position in the human eye. *Journal of Physiology, 153*, 127-130.

Brune, F., & Lücking, C. H. (1969). Okulomotorik, Bewegungswahrnehmung und Raumkonstanz der Sehdinge. *Der Nervenarzt, 40*, 413-421.

Bryden, M. P. (1961). The role of post-exposural eye movements in tachistoscopic perception. *Canadian Journal of Psychology, 15*, 220-225.

Burnham, C. A. (1968). Adaptation to prismatically induced curvature with nonvisible arm movements. *Psychonomic Science, 10*, 273-274.

Buswell, G. T. (1935). *How people look at pictures*. Chicago: University of Chicago Press.

Carpenter, R. H. S. (1977). *Movements of the eye*. London: Pion.

Coren, S. (1971). The use of Haidinger's brushes in the study of stabilized retinal images. *Behavior Research Methods and Instrumentation, 3*, 295-297.

Coren, S. (1981). The interaction between the eye movements and visual illusion. In D. F. Fisher, R. A. Monty, & J. W. Senders (Eds.), *Eye movements: Cognition and visual perception*. Hillsdale, NJ: Lawrence Erlbaum Associates.

Coren, S., & Festinger, L. (1967). An alternative view of the "Gibson normalization effect." *Perception & Psychophysics, 2*, 621-626.

Coren, S., & Porac, C. (1974). The fading of stabilized images: Eye movements and information processing. *Perception & Psychophysics, 16*, 529-534.

Ditchburn, R. W. (1973). *Eye-movements and visual perception*. Oxford: Clarendon Press.

Festinger, L., Burnham, C. A., Ono, H., & Bamber, D. (1967). Efference and the conscious experience of perception. *Journal of Experimental Psychology Monograph, 74*, (4).

Festinger, L., & Cannon, L. K. (1965). Information about spatial location based on knowledge about efference. *Psychological Review, 72*, 373-384.

Festinger, L., & Easton, A. M. (1974). Inferences about the efferent system based on a perceptual illusion produced by eye movements. *Psychological Review, 81*, 44-58.

Fisher, D. F., Karsh, R., Breitenbach, F., & Barnette, B. D. (1983). Eye movements and picture recognition: Contribution or embellishment. In R. Groner, C. Menz, D. F. Fisher, & R. A. Monty (Eds.), *Eye movements and psychological functions: International views*. Hillsdale, NJ: Lawrence Erlbaum Associates.

Gibson, J. J. (1933). Adaptation, aftereffect, and contrast in the perception of curved lines. *Journal of Experimental Psychology, 16*, 1-31.

Gibson, J. J. (1966). *The senses considered as perceptual systems*. Boston: Houghton Mifflin.

Gibson, J. J. (1968). What gives rise to the perception of motion? *Psychological Review, 75*, 335-346.

Gibson, J. J. (1979). *The ecological approach to visual perception*. Boston: Houghton Mifflin.

Gould, J. D. (1976). Looking at pictures. In R. A. Monty & J. W. Senders (Eds.), *Eye movements and psychological processes*. Hillsdale, NJ: Lawrence Erlbaum Associates.

Greenwald, A. G. (1970). Sensory feedback mechanisms in performance control: with special reference to the ideomotor mechanism. *Psychological Review, 77,* 73-99.
Hajos, A., & Frey, D. A. (1982). Lernprozesse des okulomotorischen Sytems. *Psychologische Beiträge, 24,* 135-158.
Hall, D. C. (1974). Eye movements in scanning iconic imagery. *Journal of Experimental Psychology, 103,* 825-830.
Hein, A., & Held, R. (1962). A neural model for labile sensorimotor coordination: In E. E. Bernard & M. R. Kare (Eds.), *Biological prototypes and sythetic systems* (Vol. 1). New York: Plenum.
Helmholtz, H. v. (1866). *Handbuch der physiologischen Optik.* Leipzig: Voss.
Henson, D. B. (1978). Corrective saccades: Effects of altering visual feedback. *Vision Research, 18,* 63-67.
Hochberg, J., & Brooks, V. (1978). Film cutting and visual momentum. In J. W. Senders, D. F. Fisher, & R. A. Monty (Eds.), *Eye movements and the higher psychological functions.* Hillsdale, NJ: Lawrence Erlbaum Associates.
Howard, I. P., & Templeton, W. B. (1966). *Human spatial orientation.* London: Wiley.
Kolers, P. A. (1976). Buswell's discoveries. In R. A. Monty & J. W. Senders (Eds.), *Eye movements and psychological processes.* Hillsdale, NJ: Lawrence Erlbaum Associates.
Kornhuber, H. H. (1984). Mechanisms of voluntary movement. In W. Prinz & A. F. Sanders (Eds.), *Cognition and motor processes.* Berlin: Springer.
Mack, A. (1970). An investigation of the relationship between eye and retinal image movement in the perception of movement. *Perception & Psychophysics, 8,* 291-298.
Mack, A., Fendrich, R., & Pleune, J. (1978). Adaptation to an altered relation between retinal image displacements and saccadic eye movements. *Vision Research, 18,* 1321-1327.
MacKay, D. M. (1957). The stabilization of perception during voluntary activity. *Proceedings of the 15th International Congress of Psychology.* Amsterdam: North-Holland.
MacKay, D. M. (1973). Visual stability and voluntary eye movements. In R. Jung (Ed.), *Handbook of sensory physiology* (Vol. 7, No. 3), Berlin: Springer.
MacKay, D. M. (1978). The dynamics of perception. In P. A. Buser & A. Rouguel-Buser (Eds.), *Cerebral correlates of conscious experience.* Amsterdam: Elsevier.
MacKay, D. M. (1984). Evaluation: The missing link between cognition and action. In W. Prinz & A. F. Sanders, *Cognition and motor processes.* Berlin: Springer.
MacKay, D. M., & Mittelstaedt, H. (1974). Visual stability and motor control (reafference revisited). In W. Keidel, W. Handler, & M. Spreng (Eds.), *Cybernetics and bionics.* München: Oldenbourg.
Matin, L. (1972). Eye movements and perceived visual direction. In D. Jamesson & L. Hurvich (Eds.), *Handbook of sensory physiology* (Vol 7/4). Berlin: Springer.
Matin, L. (1982). Visual localization and eye movements. In A. H. Wertheim, W. A. Wagenaar, & H. W. Leibowitz (Eds.), *Tutorials on motion perception.* New York: Plenum.
McLaughlin, S. C. (1967). Parametric adjustment in saccadic eye movement. *Perception & Psychophysics, 2,* 359-362.
McLaughlin, S. C., Kelly, M. J., Anderson, R. E., & Wenz, T. G. (1968). Localization of a peripheral target during parametric adjustment of a saccadic eye movement. *Perception & Psychophysics, 4,* 45-48.
Miller, J., & Festinger, L. (1977). Impact of oculomotor retraining on the visual perception of curvature. *Journal of Experimental Psychology: Human Perception and Performance, 3,* 187-200.
Miller, M., Anstis, T., & Templeton, W. B. (1981). Saccadic plasticity: Parametric adaptive control by retinal feedback. *Journal of Experimental Psychology: Human Perception and Performance, 7,* 356-366.
Mittelstaedt, H. (1971). Reafferenzprinzip Apologie und Kritik. In W. D. Keidel & K.-H. Plattig (Eds.), *Vorträge der Erlanger Physiologentagung 1970.* Berlin: Springer.

Neisser, U. (1967). *Cognitive psychology.* New York: Appleton–Century–Crofts.
Neisser, U. (1976). *Cognition and reality.* San Francisco: Freeman.
Neumann, O. (1980). *Informationsselektion und Handlungssteuerung. Untersuchungen zur Funktionsgrundlage des Stroop-Interferenz-Phänomens.* Dissertation, Bochum, FRG.
Neumann, O. (1983). Über den Zusammenhang zwischen Enge und Selektivität der Aufmerksamkeit. *Bericht Nr. 19/1983, Arbeitseinheit Kognitionspsychologie,* Psychologisches Institut der Ruhr-Universität Bochum, FRG.
Neumann, O. (1985a). The limited capacity hypotheses and the functions of attention. *Report no. 23/1985, Research Group Perception and Action at the Center for Interdisciplinary Research (ZiF),* Bielefeld FRG.
Neumann, O. (1985b). Die Hypothese begrenzter Kapazität und die Funktionen der Aufmerksamkeit. In O. Neumann (Ed.), *Persektiven der Kognitionspsychologie.* Berlin: Springer.
Norton, D., & Stark, L. (1971a). Eye movements and visual perception. *Scientific American, 224,* 34–43.
Norton, D., & Stark, L. (1971b). Scanpaths in eye movements during pattern perception. *Science, 171,* 308–311.
Norton, D., & Stark, L. (1971c). Scanpaths in saccadic eye movements while viewing and recognizing patterns. *Vision Research, 11,* 929–941.
Parker, R. F. (1978). Picture processing during recognition. *Journal of Experimental Psychology: Human Perception and Performance, 4,* 284–293.
Pola, J. (1976). Voluntary saccades, eye position, and perceived visual direction. In R. A. Monty & J. W. Senders (Eds.), *Eye movements and psychological processes.* Hillsdale, NJ: Lawrence Erlbaum Associates.
Posner, M. I. (1980). Orienting of attention. *Quarterly Journal of Experimental Psychology, 32,* 3–25.
Prinz, W. (1985). Ideomotorik und Isomorphie. In O. Neumann (Ed.), *Perspektiven der Kognitionspsychologie.* Berlin: Springer.
Reinert, G. (1985). Schemata als Grundlage der Steuerung von Blickbewegungen bei der Bildverarbeitung. In O. Neumann (Ed.), *Perspektiven der Kognitionspsychologie.* Berlin: Springer.
Remington, R. W. (1980). Attention and saccadic eye movements. *Journal of Experimental Psychology: Human Perception and Performance, 6,* 726–744.
Scheerer, E. (1978). Probleme der Modellierung kognitiver Prozesse: Von der Funktionsanalyse zur genetischen Analyse. *Bericht No. 4/1978 Psychologisches Institut der Ruhr-Universität Bochum, Arbeitseinheit Kognitionspsychologie.*
Scheerer, E. (1984). Motor theories of cognitive structure: A historical review. In W. Prinz & A. F. Sanders, (Eds.), *Cognition and motor processes.* Berlin: Springer.
Scheerer, E. (1985a). The constitution of space perception: A phenomenological perspective. Paper to the Symposium on *"Sensorimotor interactions in Space Perception and Action,"* February 18–22. Bielefeld.
Scheerer, E. (1985b). Edmund Husserls Phänomenologie und ihre Perspektiven für die Kognitionspsychologie. In O. Neumann (Ed.), *Perspektiven der Kognitionspsychologie.* Berlin: Springer.
Schmidt, J. C., Gottlieb, M., Coleman, P. & Smith, K. U. (1974). Reversal of retinal feedback of binocular eye motions in depth vision. *American Journal of Optometrics and Physiological Optics, 51,* 382–399.
Senden, M. v. (1931). *Die Raumauffassung bei Blindgeborenen vor und nach ihrer Operation.* Dissertation, Kiel.
Sharpe, C. R. (1972). The visibility and fading of thin lines visualized by their controlled movement across the retina. *Journal of Physiology, 222,* 113–114.
Shebilske, W. L. (1977). Visuomotor coordination in visual direction and position constancies. In W. Epstein (Ed.), *Stability and constancy in visual perception: Mechanisms and processes.* New York: Wiley.

10. PERCEPTUAL LEARNING BY SACCADES 271

Shebilske, W. L. (1984). Context effects and efferent factors in perception and cognition. In W. Prinz & A. F. Sanders (Eds.), *Cognition and motor processes*. Berlin, etc.: Springer.

Skavenski, A. A., Haddad, G., & Steinman, R. M. (1972). The extraretinal signal for the visual perception of direction. *Perception & Psychophysics, 11,* 287–290.

Slotnick, R. S. (1969). Adaptation to curvature distortion. *Journal of Experimental Psychology, 81,* 441–448.

Stark, L., & Ellis, S. P. (1981). Scan path revisited: Cognitive models direct active looking. In D. F. Fisher, R. A. Monty, & J. W. Senders (Eds.), *Eye movements: Cognition and visual perception*. Hillsdale, NJ: Lawrence Erlbaum Associates.

Steinman, R. M. (1976). Role of eye movements in maintaining a phenomenally clear and stable world. In R. A. Monty & J. W. Senders (Eds.), *Eye movements and psychological processes*. Hillsdale, NJ: Lawrence Erlbaum Associates.

Taylor, J. G. (1975). *The behavioral basis of perception*. New Haven: Yale University Press. Reprint: Westport, CT: Greenwood Press.

Teichner, W. H., LeMaster, D., & Kinney, P. A. (1978). Eye movements during inspection and recall. In J. W. Senders, D. F. Fisher, & R. A. Monty (Eds.), *Eye movements and the higher psychological functions*. Hillsdale, NJ: Lawrence Erlbaum Associates.

Weimer, W. B. (1977). A conceptual framework for cognitive psychology: Motor theories of the mind. In R. Shaw & J. Bransford (Eds.), *Perceiving, acting, and knowing. Towards an ecological psychology*. Hillsdale, NJ: Lawrence Erlbaum Associates.

Welch, R. B. (1978). *Perceptual modification. Adapting to altered sensory environments*. New York: Academic Press.

Wolff, P. (1984). Saccadic eye movements and visual stability: Preliminary considerations towards a cognitive approach. In W. Prinz & A. F. Sanders (Eds.), *Cognition and motor processes*. Berlin: Springer.

Wolff, P. (1985). Wahrnehmungslernen durch Blickbewegungen. In O. Neumann (Ed.), *Perspektiven der Kognitionspsychologie*. Berlin: Springer.

Wurtz, R. H., & Mohler, C. W. (1976). Organization of monkey superior colliculus: Enhanced visual response of superficial layer cells. *Journal of Neurophysiology, 39,* 745–765.

Yarbus, A. L. (1967). *Eye movements in vision*. New York: Plenum.

11 Information-Processing Theory and Strong Inference: A Paradigm for Psychological Inquiry

Dominic W. Massaro
University of California, Santa Cruz

INTRODUCTION

Metatheory and research strategy are inseparable components of a paradigm of psychological science. The defensive half of the present essay begins with a defense of information-processing theory and a strong inference research strategy in psychological inquiry. The basic assumptions of this paradigm are described and briefly illustrated. Previous criticisms and alternatives are evaluated and found either lacking or restatements of the same paradigm. The offensive half of the essay illustrates the usefulness of the paradigm in the study of speech perception.

A series of tests addresses important issues in the evaluation and integration of auditory and visual sources of information in speech perception by eye and ear. Sources of information refer to the features or attributes of the environment that are utilized in perception and action. Questions include (1) whether there are both auditory and visual sources of information or just a single source, (2) whether or not the two sources are integrated, (3) the continuous versus categorical nature of the information from each source, (4) whether or not the sources are independent, and (5) the nature of the rule used to integrate the sources. Definite answers to these questions illustrate the value of the paradigm in psychological inquiry.

INFORMATION-PROCESSING THEORY

In information-processing theory, the individual is viewed as a processor of information (Broadbent, 1958, 1971; Massaro, 1975a; Neisser, 1967). It should be noted that the information-processing theory is a metatheoretical framework and is much more general than any particular methodology such as the additive-factor method (Sternberg, 1969). The researcher attempts to understand what happens to the information as it is perceived, interpreted, and acted upon by the individual. The processing of environmental information depends on the nature of the relevant sensory systems, some memory of past experiences, the relevant motor systems, and goals of the participant.

One central assumption of research within the information-processing paradigm is that observed performance in some domain involves a sequence of processing stages. The onsets of these processing stages are successive and each stage operates on the information available to it. The operations of a particular stage take time and transform the information available to it. The transformed information is made available to the next stage of processing. Two theoretical constructs are important in this approach. First, the memory construct describes or defines the nature of the information at a particular stage of processing. Second, the processing construct describes the operations performed by a stage of information processing. The information-processing paradigm provides a framework that can be implemented using a variety of experimental methods, manipulations, and dependent variables. Examples include the additive-factor method and backward recognition masking.

The information-processing approach has major implications for research. It is necessary to account for each of the processing stages in a task performed by individuals. This requires that the investigator make explicit the implicit assumptions inherent in the experimental situation. Failure to do so severely limits what can be learned from the results. The precise analysis given by the information-processing methodology can be thought of as a microscope. It allows the experimenter to see what is not directly observable. As an example, the additive-factor methodology has been reasonably successful in providing glimpses at recognition, memory search, and response selection processes (Massaro, 1984c; Sanders, 1980; Sternberg, 1975; Theios, 1975).

Limitations of Current Information-Processing Models

A prototypical information-processing model aims to specify (1) the time course of mental operations, (2) the nature of mental operations, and (3) the nature of memory structures that hold information. In contrast to what might be expected from their name, information-processing models have not really been all that concerned with information. Information is taken to mean the actual aspects of the environment that are informative. Noting the failure of an earlier enterprise, mathematical information measurement in explaining psychological phenomena, Neisser (1967) helped shape the view of information in the information-processing model: "Information is what is transformed and the structured pattern of its transformations is what we want to understand" (pg. 8). This statement seemed to give license to relegating information to a minor role in information processing.

Within the information-processing framework, many researchers sought to define the time course and nature of mental operations without really specifying the nature of the information used in particular domains. These researchers used rather arbitrary stimuli (tones, lights, letters, words) without really being concerned with their function in the real world. The implicit assumption was that the time course and nature of mental operations could be defined independently of the nature of the stimuli being processed. Although this research was a profitable enterprise, one obvious legacy was a model in search of a natural domain to describe.

The limitations of pure information processing became apparent to this writer when I and a group of students applied the model to language processing (Massaro, 1975b). Consistent with the information-processing approach, many facets of understanding language were illuminated by accounting for the stages of processing involved. For example, isolating the perceptual unit functional in speech perception required analyzing the memory structures and psychological processes involved in the task of perception. What became obvious, however, was that the language information was as important or more important than the processing of that information. A complete theory had to describe not only what is done with information but also what is used as information.

Consider the role of time. The time available for processing information is important in speech perception as it is in domains with simple artificial signals (Massaro, 1975b). However, time also is information in speech in that some speech distinctions such as vowel identity and consonant voicing are cued by the duration of the speech segments (Massaro, 1984b). Thus, the potential information in the language signal and its utilization by the language user had to be described as well as the time course of perception, decision, and memory. The information-processing paradigm was still the best game in town because it provided a coherent framework for the finding of analogous processes in speech perception and reading (Massaro, 1975b, 1978, 1979).

Alternatives to Information-Processing

Some of the opposition to the information-processing paradigm proposed that there should be a concern for natural environments. Theorists within the Gibsonian framework ask that investigators focus on the higher order structure of the environment and relate it to behavior (Gibson, 1979; Haber, 1983; Turvey, 1977; Turvey & Shaw, 1979). The implicit assumption in this proposal is that there are complex environmental invariants responsible for much of behavior and the goal is to discover these properties to explicate behavioral observations. Studying behavior in a natural situation follows naturally given this assumption. If these higher order invariants are eliminated as supposedly occurs in simple laboratory tasks, then they can not be discovered. Thus, we see that the neo-Gibsonians are concerned with one traditional problem in scientific inquiry called external validity or the degree to which one can generalize from the experimental to the natural situation.

The Gibsonian framework is similar in many important respects to the classical psychophysical approach inaugurated, by Fechner (1966), in which variation in the stimulus world is related to variation in performance. Both Fechnerian and Gibsonian paradigms dictate the discovery of relationships between objective and subjective worlds without fundamental concern for the intervening mental processes and representations. In contrast to the Titchenerian assumption of the whole being composed of component parts, however, the neo-Gibsonians, like the Gestaltists, believe that higher order invariants are directly perceived and will stand on the left side of the S–R chain. Both the component-cues and higher order invariants proposals bring the investigator into the domain of psychophysics.

These two approaches to the study of the world of information have produced somewhat disappointing results. Gibson and the neo-Gibsonians have not yet delivered with respect to discovering higher order invariants (see Shebilske and von Hofsten chapters, this volume). Looking out my window at grass, weeds, and trees, there is no apparent single higher order invariant that can capture my experience of depth and object constancy. The knowledge acquired in the psychophysical study of component cues has also been relatively limited (Rock, 1975). Although many cues have been proposed, very little insight has been gained into how the perceiver evaluates and utilizes the cues in perception. We have not learned the relative importance of the cues nor how the multiple cues work together. (A recent study by Cutting and Millard (1984) has, at least, begun to address the relative importance issue.) As we will see, one limitation in the traditional psychophysical approach has been the experimental design of asking how one cue works when other cues are neutralized or held constant. The single-cue paradigm not only fails to define how the particular cue would operate in a more natural situation, it also does not address the issue of how the perceiver evaluates and integrates multiple cues in perceptual processing.

INTEGRATING INFORMATION AND INFORMATION PROCESSING

My goal in this essay is to integrate the information-processing approach with the study of the world of information. The paradigm that makes this resolution possible can be attributed, in part, to Egon Brunswik (1952, 1955, 1956), who anticipated some of the trends currently in vogue in psychology. In contrast to Helmholtz's (1962) idea of perception guided by unconscious logic, he viewed perception as a primitive and autonomous process. This view subsumes Fodor's

11. INFORMATION-PROCESSING THEORY AND STRONG INFERENCE 277

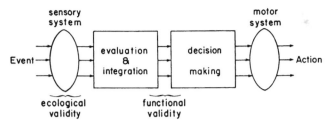

FIG. 11.1 Schematic diagram of the Lens model of Brunswik, illustrated in a more contemporary format. Ecological validity refers to the aspects of the physical and sensory world that are informative about some object or event. Functional validity refers to those aspects that are actually utilized by the observer in perception and action.

(1983) thesis of separate and autonomous modules for different psychological functions such as visual perception and language. Brunswik also called for the study of natural situation rather than artificial experimental tasks. Thus, calls to natural ecology in the study of perception such as those by Neisser (1976) and Haber (1983) were already existent in the psychological literature decades earlier. Brunswik also acknowledged multiple but ambiguous sources of influence on behavior. Brunswik proposed the concept of probabilistic functionalism based on the idea that there are many cues determining behavior. However, the cues were seen as equivocal and only probabilistically related to behavior. Brunswik (1955) stressed "the limited ecological validity or trustworthiness of cues. . . . To improve its (the organism's) bet, it must accumulate and combine cues" (p. 207).

Integrating multiple sources of information appears to be a natural human function. It appears to persist regardless of the intentions (goals and motivations) of the perceiver. Consider an early experiment carried out by Brunswik (described by Tolman, 1956). Subjects were asked to equate groups of coins that varied in number, area, and monetary value. Even though subjects were instructed to use just one of these three dimensions, their judgments were significantly influenced by the irrelevant dimensions.

One consistent generality in perception and cognition is the person's inability to selectively process only some aspect of the given environment. This principle is best illustrated in the Stroop color-word task. Subjects cannot ignore the name of a word when they intend to name the color of the word's type. Consider a similar effect in person impression. Subjects given a list of adjectives are asked to rate the person described by those adjectives and then to rate only one of the adjectives. The rating of the single adjective is influenced by the other adjectives in the list. This is called a positive context effect, because the likeableness value given the single adjective will be biased towards the values of the other adjectives in the list.

Brunswik is best known for his lens model, illustrated in Fig. 11.1 within a more contemporary format. With respect to the world of information, Brunswik distinguished between two kinds of validity. Ecological validity defines what cues are informative about the structure of the world. As an example, height in the vertical plane can be shown to be correlated with distance of the object from the observer. Functional validity defines what cues people actually use in perceptual processing. Given this distinction, it can be seen that a concern for ecological validity is not sufficient, because some ecologically valid property of the physical world may not be used and hence not be functionally valid. One might expect that functionally valid cues might always be ecologically valid, but many counterexamples exist. The gambler's fallacy of using the outcome of a preceding roll of the dice to guide prediction of the current roll is one of many ecologically invalid decision heuristics. A complete description of the environmental-behavior relationship requires an analysis of both ecological and functional validity.

Representative Designs

Complementing the theoretical notions of probabilistic functionalism, Brunswik (1955) proposed a unique methodological framework for psychological study. The framework called for representative designs or designs that are random samples of natural ecology. Thus, only correlational rather than experimental methods could be used because behavior must be studied within the context of the multiple cues as they co-occur in the natural world of the observer. In this regard, Brunswik anticipated Neisser's (1976) call to natural ecology by a few decades. Brunswik argued that single-factor and factorial designs are artificial because they decorrelate naturally occurring cues. For this reason, Brunswik contended that experimental results cannot be generalized to the real world. He made a distinction between internal and external validity. The results derived from a factorial design may be internally valid but yet may not be externally valid because they have no generality outside the experiment itself.

Brunswik's concept of representative design is nicely illustrated in a study of size constancy (Brunswik, 1944). The subject was asked to estimate the size of various objects in a natural setting across a wide range of sizes and distances. The subject judged the size of trees, telephone poles, bookcases, inkwells, and so on. The primary measure of performance was a correlation between the subjective estimates and objective physical size. In other studies, Brunswik and Kamiya (1953) found some ecological validity for the proximity of two lines as a cue to those lines defining the boundaries of a single object. Similarly, Seidner (Brunswik, 1956) found that vertical position of points was positively correlated with distance from the observer. It should be noted, however, that these latter two observations were only demonstrations of ecological validity because they did not evaluate functional validity in terms of the extent to which these cues are utilized in perception and recognition.

The finding of only moderate ecological validity for various cues probably contributed to Brunswik's development of probabilistic functionalism, meaning that objects and goals in the environment are only probabilistically related to the available cues. A cue such as height in the vertical plane is an equivocal, and thus a probabilistic cue, to depth in that it only predicts depth with some probability. Having been informed by the development of fuzzy sets (Zadeh, 1965) and continuous information (Massaro & Cohen, 1983a), however, we see that an equivocal cue might be better thought of as providing fuzzy rather than probabilistic information; that is, a depth cue provides continuous information about the degree to which a given depth is present.

Limitations of Representative Designs

Representative designs impose a major constraint on the type of psychological investigation that can be done. If two cues do not occur independently in the natural world, then they cannot be manipulated independently in the psychological investigations using representative designs. For this reason, representative designs are inadequate for psychological inquiry. The creation of artificial situations by utilizing factorial designs, on the other hand, can be very illuminating as I hope to demonstrate in our study of bimodal speech perception. With respect to external validity, one needs only a good theory that will allow generalization from a particular experiment to the real world even if the experiment is not representative of the real world.

Information-Integration Framework

Anderson (1981, 1982) can be viewed as an intellectual descendant of Brunswik's probabilistic functionalism, but not of representative designs. Within the framework of information integration, it is accepted that there are multiple sources of information; the goal is to define the sources of information and to assess how they are integrated in perception and decision. In contrast to Brunswik's representative design, however, information integration is studied by utilizing factorial designs that manipulate independently multiple aspects of the environment. In our study of bimodal speech perception, we combine the information-integration paradigm with the research strategy of strong inference.

RESEARCH STRATEGY

Falsification

The foundation for strong inference has been expressed most succinctly by Popper's (1959) falsification strategy in research endeavor. The central assumption is that hypothesis testing must follow deductive rather than inductive methods. Following Hume, Popper claims that we are not justified in inferring universal statements from singular ones. Any conclusion drawn inductively might always turn out to be false. Although we can generate many instances of positive results, the theory might still be exposed as false. As scientists, we should guard against simply trying to verify a particular hypothesis by demonstrating that it works in specific instances. Because new instances can always falsify a given statement, no experimental observation can verify a hypothesis. A critical feature of Popper's scientific framework is that verifiability and falsifiability do not have a symmetrical relationship. Although theories can be falsified, they cannot be truly verified.

Strong Inference

Platt's (1964) extension of Popper's framework encourages scientists to employ a strong inference strategy of testing hypotheses. In contrast to generating a single hypothesis, Platt would have the scientist generate multiple hypotheses relevant to a particular phenomenon of interest. The experimental test would be designed to eliminate (or in Popper's words, falsify) as many of these hypotheses as possible. The results of the experimentation would allow the generation of new hypotheses that could be subjected to further tests. Both Platt and Popper adhere to David Hume's axiom prohibiting inductive arguments. Given that the scientist should not attempt to confirm a single pet hypothesis, Platt's solution is more productive in that at least one of the multiple hypotheses under test should fail and can, therefore be rejected.

Criticisms of Falsification and Strong Inference

Falsification and strong inference have been criticized as scientific frameworks for psychological inquiry. In an influential paper called "You Can't Play Twenty Questions With Nature and Win: Projective Comments on the Papers on this Symposium," Newell (1973) makes two relevant points. The first point is that psychology, in its current style of operation, deals with phenomena. Clever experiments bring these phenomena into existence. As an example, by manipulating the relationship between successive lists of items to be remembered, one can demonstrate release from proactive interference or the progressive decrease in memorability with repeated learning of new lists of items. Newell's second point is that the guide to investigating these phenomena is one of construction of oppositions, usually binary ones. Thus, we test between nature versus nurture, central versus peripheral processing, or serial versus parallel processing, and so on. Newell listed both a large number of phenomena of psychology and many binary oppositions current in research, generated within the research framework of falsification and strong inference. Newell's argument is that our accumulation of phenomena and tests of binary contrasts are not really adding up to scientific progress in psychological inquiry.

Newell (1973) proposed the following solutions. First, know the method that your subject is using to perform the task. Second, never average over methods. Third, it is necessary to integrate research from a wide variety of domains. To achieve these solutions, Newell suggested that we need to develop complete processing models; analyze complete tasks; and construct a theory to perform many different tasks.

Newell's critique of strong inference is not convincing and, in fact, his dicta seem highly compatible with this research paradigm. Newell advocates exploring a complex task exhaustively, not simply in terms of the binary oppositions that can be defined for it. I am skeptical of this proposal if it represents theory-independent research, because data without theory are meaningless. The question we face is simply whether testing binary contrasts is a valuable approach to scientific investigation. The use of binary contrasts, such as in the question of the integration or nonintegration of information from different sources, appears to be fundamental to psychological inquiry. The interpretation of any experiment done with bimodal speech, for example, is critically dependent on whether or not subjects do in fact integrate the information from the multiple sources. Any theory that does not address this binary question could be wrong at a fundamental level because various results could be interpreted in terms of an integration process even though integration did not occur (Anderson & Cuneo, 1978).

Jenkins (1980) has also been critical of research carried our at an elementaristic or atomistic level based on the assumption of "bottom-up" inquiry. The goal within this paradigm is to find the basic laws of elementary processes with the belief that combinations of these basic laws will be sufficient to account for complex situations. Jenkins (1980) believes that this research enterprise is doomed to failure because it is "*relations* among elements that count rather than just the elements alone" (p. 223). As Jenkins (1979) has nicely illustrated, any generalizations about memory will have to include interactions with the nature of the subjects, the orienting tasks, the criterial tasks, and the materials. There are not simple one-dimensional rules of memory. As a solution, Jenkins (1980) proposes a research enterprise involving the close interaction between experiment and model building or analysis and synthesis, a solution highly compatible with the paradigm defended in this chapter.

In a review of progress in memory research, Tulving (1979) acknowledged the explosion of research and theory but remarked that "it is not clear that we know what all these facts and findings mean or what they add up to" (p. 27). Tulving believes that the science of memory has not yet obtained its first genuine Kuhnian (1970) paradigm. Until it does, Tulving offers the following advice. Don't spend too much time affirming what we already know, explaining the commonsensical, accounting for results of single experiments, and developing quantitative theories when the basic concepts are still lacking. These caveats by Tulving seem to have little substance. I agree that we should not simply affirm what we already know but we should test among alternative explanations of the facts. With respect to Tulving's advice against explaining the commonsensical, it may be the case that what on the surface seems commonsensical is actually the consequence of a set of interacting unintuitive processes. Accounting for the results of a single experiment is usually necessary to develop hypotheses to be tested in subsequent experiments. Finally, developing quantitative theories often leads to the discovery of basic questions and concepts.

Although Newell, Jenkins, Tulving, and others (e.g., Allport, 1980; Gopher & Sanders, 1984; Sanders, 1984; Stelmach & Hughes, 1984) have provided valuable reflections on aspects of research strategy, their advice does not seem to warrant rejection of the "information-processing" and "strong inference" paradigm. I believe that the best way to achieve Newell's goal of exhaustive analysis of a complex task is via information-processing theory and strong inference research strategy. If it is the relations among the elements that count, as Jenkins argues, one has to first understand what the elements are and only then how they relate. Building models requires the utilization of elementary processes and hypotheses about how these processes are organized to account for complex behavior. We are in complete agreement with Tulving's last piece of advice to be skeptical of intuitive and transparent theories and follow the precepts of "strong inference" (Platt, 1964).

One of the persisting criticisms of the information-processing approach is the failure to give satisfying accounts of how stages of processing work (e.g., Banks, 1983). We postulate recognition, memory search, and response selection stages but are chided for not delineating the exact nature of processing within any of these stages. As a reply to this criticism and as an illustration of the value of information-processing theory and strong inference in psychological inquiry, I review the research we have carried out on speech perception by ear and eye. The enterprise demonstrates how pure laboratory research can be designed to test between fundamentally different explanations and can facilitate the development of formal models of individual processing stages.

The processing of auditory and visual information in speech perception provides a relevant example of the apparent confounding of cues in the natural situation. One might expect that the validity and reliability of these two cues would be perfectly correlated. However, variation and noise in the environment and in the sensory systems could differentially modify the two sources of information and how they are processed. For example, the perceiver might have a varying view of the speaker's face and extraneous background noise might fluctuate randomly over time. Thus, for any particular speech event, the informativeness of the auditory aspect of the speech event is not necessarily correlated with that of the visual aspect of the event.

SPEECH PERCEPTION BY EYE AND EAR

The phenomenon stimulating this research has come to be known as the McGurk effect. McGurk and MacDonald (1976) reported a perceptual illusion when a

11. INFORMATION-PROCESSING THEORY AND STRONG INFERENCE 283

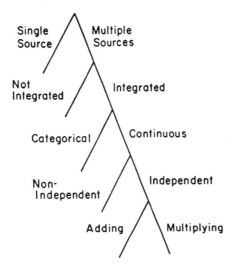

FIG. 11.2 Tree of wisdom illustrating binary oppositions central to the domain of speech perception by eye and ear.

given speech sound is dubbed onto a videotape of a different articulation. As an example, subjects reported *hearing* /da/ when the sound /ba/ was paired with a /ga/ articulation. Hearing was influenced by the corresponding visual information. As an aside, it should be noted that this discovery was only possible because of devising a situation that would *not* occur naturally. Thus, we have a violation of Brunswik's (1952) and Neisser's (1976) dicta for psychological research. What I aim to demonstrate is that the dissection of this phenomenon within the framework of binary oppositions, combined with the tools of information integration (Anderson, 1981, 1982) and model testing, illuminates not only the phenomenon itself but also more general problems of perception and pattern recognition.

The binary oppositions to be considered are arranged hierarchically in Fig. 11.2. In some cases, the question at one level is dependent on the answers to the questions at higher levels. As an example, the issue of whether or not multiple sources of information are integrated (combined) in perception requires that multiple sources rather than just a single source be available to the perceiver.

Single Versus Multiple Sources

The argument in favor of multiple sources of information in speech perception comes from the discovery of many different cues or features that contribute to the discriminable contrasts found in speech. The perceived distinction between voiced and voiceless English stop consonants in medial position such as /aga/ and /aka/ can be influenced by the preceding vowel duration, the silent closure interval, the voice-onset time, and the onset frequency of the fundamental. In addition to these bottom-up sources, phonological and semantic constraints function as top-down sources in recognition (Massaro & Cohen, 1983c; Tyler & Wessels, 1983).

The question addressed here is whether visual information also contributes to understanding speech. Anecdotal evidence comes from our dislike of dubbed movies and the seemingly extra effort to converse by telephone and to listen to narrative over the radio. The habit of watching a person speaking and the greater reliance on the speaker's visible articulations within noisy and distracting environments and with hearing loss also contribute to the impression of the visible domain of speech. A recent report provides some evidence that infants have some knowledge about the correspondence between the auditory and visual dimensions of the vowels /i/ and /a/ (Kuhl & Meltzoff, 1982). Although visual speech does not distinguish among all speech contrasts, it is ecologically valid to some degree. Of course, our question is whether visual speech is also functionally valid; that is, is it utilized by the perceiver. The McGurk effect seems to provide the most direct affirmative answer. What we see clearly influences but does not completely determine what we perceive in speech perception.

Integration Versus Nonintegration

The outcome of our first contrast indicates that both auditory and visual sources of information are utilized in speech perception. The answer to the next question might seem obvious to some because it is only natural for some to believe that the two sources are integrated. Integration of two sources of information refers to some process of combining or utilizing both sources to make a perceptual judgment. However, demonstrating that two sources are integrated in perceptual recognition is no easy matter. Consider a hypothetical experiment manipulating two independent cues to some distinction such as the height and width of rectangles as cues to their area (Anderson & Cuneo, 1978). Overall judgments of the area of the rectangles might reveal significant effects of both height and width even though these two cues were not integrated in the judgment of area. Some of the subjects may have used one cue, and other subjects may have used the other. Alternatively, a given subject may have used one cue on some trials and the other cue on other trials. Thus, a mixture of trials resulting from judgments on just a single cue can give results identical to that expected from a true integration of the two cues on each trial.

The two possible strategies of utilizing just one dimension versus integrating two dimensions are even more difficult to distinguish when the responses are discrete identification judgments rather than ratings. With discrete judgments, it might be impossible to eliminate the hypothesis of the single-cue strategy if subjects are tested only with a factorial combination of the cues. If it is possible to include discrete judgments of the single-cue conditions, however, the alter-

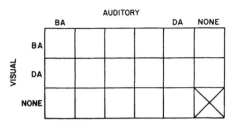

FIG. 11.3 Expansion of a typical factorial design to include single-auditory and single-visual cue conditions. The five levels along the auditory continuum represent speech sounds varying in equal steps between BA and DA. The BA and DA levels along the visual continuum represent BA and DA articulations. The level NONE for both the auditory and visual continua represents no information from that continuum.

native explanations might be tested. Consider the perception of bimodal speech events created by the combination of synthetic speech sounds along an auditory /ba/ to /da/ continuum paired with /ba/ or /da/ visual articulations. By adding the single auditory and single visual cue conditions to the factorial design as illustrated in Fig. 11.3, it is at least logically possible to reject the mixed-single-cue strategy. What is necessary is to find judgments of certain bimodal speech events that are not equivalent to judgments of either the visual or auditory dimensions presented alone.

Subjects were asked to identify bimodal speech events, auditory alone, and visual alone trials as illustrated in Fig. 11.3. The subjects were permitted an open-ended set of response alternatives. The results in Fig. 11.4 provide strong evidence against the mixed-single-cue strategy and for a true integration of the auditory and visual sources. The critical finding is the large proportion of /bda/ judgments given a visual /ba/ and an auditory /da/ when this same judgment is seldom given to either the visual or auditory information presented alone. We find over five times as many /bda/ judgments given to the bimodal events than to the visual-only condition, and the auditory-only condition almost never produces /bda/ judgments. It follows that the /bda/ judgments observed on bimodal trials could not have resulted from just one of the two sources and accordingly represent the outcome of the integration of both auditory and visual sources of information.

Evidence for the integration of auditory and visual information in bimodal speech perception also comes from the relative inability of subjects to selectively process either the auditory or visual dimensions of the speech event. Subjects were tested in three different conditions in the bimodal speech perception task. In one condition, subjects were instructed to identify the speech event as /ba/ or /da/ in terms of the information provided by *both* the visual and auditory sources of information. In the auditory selective attention condition, subjects were in-

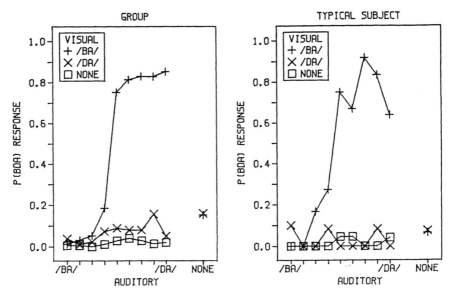

FIG. 11.4 Probability of /bda/ judgments to bimodal, auditory, and visual speech events. The left panel gives the group results, and the right panel gives the results for a typical subject. The nine levels between BA and DA along the auditory continuum represent speech sounds varying in equal steps between BA and DA and the Level None corresponds to no auditory speech (the visual condition).

structed to base their decision on only the auditory information, even though they were required to watch the speaker on the videotape. In the visual selective attention condition, subjects were instructed to base their identification decision on only the visual source of information, even though they would also hear auditory information for each speech event. In all conditions, subjects were limited to the response alternatives /ba/ and /da/.

Fig. 11.5 presents the results under two different attention conditions. The "Both" panel represents performance in terms of the probability of a /da/ identification as a function of the visual and auditory sources of information when subjects were instructed to make their decision of what was said on the basis of both sources. As can be seen, there is a strong effect of both variables. The right "Auditory" panel corresponds to the results when subjects were instructed to make their decision of what they heard on the basis of only the auditory information. There is only a small difference between these two conditions. Subjects are influenced by the visual information almost as much when they are told to selectively process just the auditory source as opposed to being told to process both sources of information. The right "Visual" panel in Fig. 11.6 presents the analogous results when subjects were instructed to make their decision of what they saw on the basis of only the visual information. Although

11. INFORMATION-PROCESSING THEORY AND STRONG INFERENCE 287

the influence of the auditory source seems to be somewhat attenuated in the visual selective attention conditions relative to the "Both" condition, there is still a substantial influence of the auditory information on the visual judgments. Thus, some integration occurs even though subjects attempt to process selectively only one of the two dimensions of input. These results indicate that subjects were not able to process selectively one dimension independently of influence of the other dimension. At least some integration appears to occur even against intentional selective attention.

One might argue that these results do not represent a definitive demonstration of integration. Even when subjects are instructed to report only what they heard, they might make their judgment on the basis of only the visual source on some subset of trials. This explanation seems unlikely, however, given that nonintegrated sources should be much easier to select than integrated ones. Furthermore, we might expect much larger differences in the selective and nonselective conditions if the sources have not been integrated. Our conclusion in favor of integration is furthered strengthened by the similar conclusion reached in the task with open-ended response alternatives.

The influence of both sources of information regardless of the set of the subject is another instance in which perceivers are not able to selectively process a single aspect of their perceptual world. This result is reminiscent of the Stroop effect (Stroop, 1935) in which the meaning of a word influences the pronuncia-

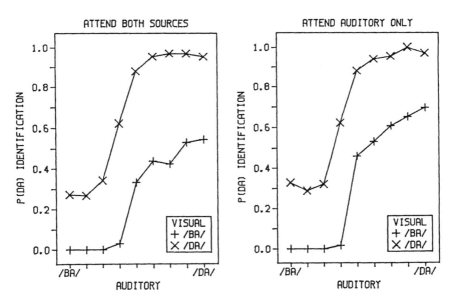

FIG. 11.5 Probability of a /da/ identification as a function of the auditory and visual sources of information under two attention conditions.

288 MASSARO

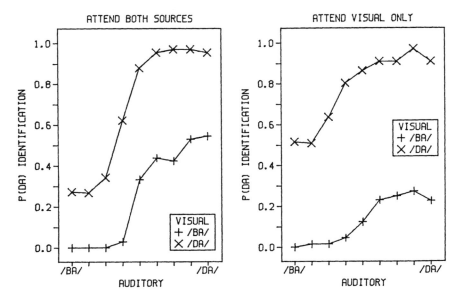

FIG. 11.6 Probability of a /da/ identification as a function of the auditory and visual sources of information under two attention conditions.

tion of the color of the type that the word is printed in. With respect to perception and action in the real world, this result at first glance might seem to be an inefficient way to design a perceptual mechanism. One would think that selectivity would be more optimal in the analysis of our perceptual world; however, if the perceptual world usually contains multiple sources of information, then selectivity can only be damaging to perceptual interpretation.

Given multiple sources of information, the more optimal strategy would be to evaluate and integrate all of the sources of information even though many of the sources at any one time may be ambiguous. The cost to a system designed as such would be the relative inability to process selectively single aspects or single dimensions of the perceptual world. In natural situations, the difficulty of selectivity is not usually a problem because we have available gross motor movements such as head and eye movements that allow us to selectively expose various sources of information. What these results demonstrate is that within a given view of the perceptual world, we find it difficult to selectively process one dimension independent of the influence of others.

Categorical Versus Continuous Information

The next branch on our tree of wisdom concerns the nature of the information available from each source. Categorical information implies that a discrete (phonetic) decision is obtained from each source before the sources of information are integrated. Continuous information implies that continuous information is available from each source for the integration process. Although these two hypotheses might seem to be easily distinguished, in reality, they are not. If only visual or auditory information is varied, the discrete as well as the continuous hypothesis can predict a continuous change in identification responses or rating responses with continuous changes along the stimulus dimension (Massaro & Cohen, 1983a).

A discriminating test between the hypotheses requires an analysis of the distribution of rating responses to repeated presentations of a stimulus event. Consider the bimodal speech events illustrated in Fig. 11.3 and the task of the subject is to rate each event along a nine point /ba/ to /da/ continuum. Categorical information predicts that the ratings to repeated presentations of a single event will come from two kinds of trials: those trials on which the event was identified as one alternative /ba/ and those on which the event was identified as the other alternative /da/. Thus, categorical perception predicts that the distribution of ratings to a given stimulus is a result of two different phonetic categorizations or a mixture of /ba/ identification and /da/ identification trials. On the other hand, continuous perception predicts that the rating is based on the outcome of the integration of the continuous auditory and visual sources of information. Hence, the distribution of ratings to a given speech event will result from a single kind of trial on which the perceiver has continuous information about the speech events.

Distributions of Rating Responses

As noted by Massaro and Cohen (1983a), analyzing the distribution of ratings can test between categorical and continuous models of speech perception. Fig. 11.7 gives the distribution of ratings for a typical subject in an experiment in which subjects were required to rate the /ba/-ness to /da/-ness along a 9-point scale. As can be seen in the figure, it is very difficult to see how these ratings could have resulted from a mixture of two different distributions. The categorical and continuous models were quantified to predict the distribution of ratings under the various experimental conditions. For all subjects, the continuous model gave a much better description of the results than did the categorical model. Thus we have evidence based on the distribution of ratings that the information along each dimension is perceived continuously rather than categorically.

Testings Models

Taking a second tack, Massaro and Cohen (1983b) and Massaro (1984a) formulated mathematical models of categorical and continuous perception of bimodal speech. The design involved a visual /ba/, visual /da/, or no visual articulation crossed with nine synthesized speech sounds equally spaced along a /ba/-/da/ continuum. Subjects watched and listened to presentations of the 27 aural-visual

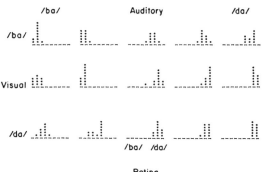

FIG. 11.7 Frequency distributions of ratings to bimodal speech events for a typical subject. The results are given for five levels along the synthetic speech auditory continnum between /ba/ and /da/ crossed with three levels along the visual continuum corresponding to a /ba/ articulation, no articulation, and a /da/ articulation. The ratings were on a 9-point scale between /ba/ and /da/. The categorical model predicts that repeated ratings to a given speech event result from two distributions, whereas the continuous model predicts that the ratings result from a single distribution.

events and identified the events as /ba/ or /da/ on each trial. We now derive the predictions of the two models for this experimental task.

Categorical Model. Following the logic of previous views of categorical perception, it is reasonable to assume that each dimension of the speech event is categorically perceived. There have been many conclusions that the auditory place continuum between /b/ and /d/ is perceived categorically (Eimas, 1963; Liberman, Harris, Hoffman, & Griffith, 1957; Repp, 1984). A similar logic might apply to the visual information (MacDonald & McGurk, 1978). According to a categorical model based on this logic, the listener has only categorical information representing the auditory and visual dimensions of the speech event. This model implies that separate categorical (phonetic) decisions are made to the auditory and visual sources and that these decisions are subsequently integrated (MacDonald & McGurk, 1978).

In the identification task, separate /da/ or /ba/ decisions would be made to both the auditory and visual sources and the identification response would be based on these separate decisions. Given categorical information from each dimension, there are only four possible outcomes for a particular combination of auditory and visual information: /da/-/da/, /da/-/ba/, /ba/-/da/, or /ba/-/ba/. If the two decisions to a given speech event agree, the identification response can follow either source. If the two decisions disagree, it is reasonable to assume that the subject will respond with the decision of the auditory source on some proportion p of the trials, and respond with the decision of the visual source on the

11. INFORMATION-PROCESSING THEORY AND STRONG INFERENCE   291

remainder $(1 - p)$ of the trials. In this conceptualization, the magnitude of p relative to $(1 - p)$ reflects the relative dominance of the auditory source.

The probability of a /da/ identification response, P(D), given a particular auditory/visual speech event, A_iV_j, would be:

$$P(D:A_iV_j) = \{1 a_i v_j\} + \{p a_i (1 - v_j)\}$$
$$+ \{(1 - p)(1 - a_i)v_j\} + \{0(1 - a_i)(1 - v_j)\}$$
$$= pa_i + (1 - p)v_j$$

where i and j index the levels of the auditory and visual stimuli, respectively. The a_i value represents the probability of a /da/ decision given the auditory level i and v_j is the probability of a /da/ decision given the visual level j. Each of the four terms in the equation represents the likelihood of one of the four possible outcomes of the separate decisions multiplied by the probability of a /da/ identification response given that outcome. In the experiment, nine auditory levels are factorially combined with three visual levels. In this model, each unique level of the auditory stimulus would require a unique parameter a_i, and analogously for v_j. Because p reflects a decision variable, its value also requires a unique parameter that would be constant across all stimulus conditions. Thus, a total of 9 + 3 + 1 = 13 parameters must be estimated for the 27 independent conditions.

Continuous Model. The continuous model will be formulated in terms of a fuzzy logical model of perception (Massaro & Cohen, 1983b; Oden & Massaro, 1978). Applying the model to the present task using auditory and visual speech, both sources are assumed to provide independent evidence for the alternatives /ba/ and /da/. Defining the onsets of the second (F2) and third (F3) formants as the important auditory cues and the degree of initial opening of the lips as the important visual cue, the prototypes are

/da/ : Slightly falling F2-F3 & Open lips

/ba/ : Rising F2-F3 & Closed lips

Given a prototype's *independent* specifications for the auditory and visual sources, the value of one source can not change the value of the other source at the prototype matching stage. In addition, the negation of a feature is defined as the additive complement; that is, we can represent Rising F2–F3 as 1-Slightly falling F2–F3) and Closed Lips as (1-Open lips),

/da/ : Slightly falling F2-F3 & Open lips

/ba/ : (1-Slightly falling F2-F3) & (1-Open lips).

The integration of the features defining each prototype is evaluated according to the product of the feature values. If a_i represents the degree to which the auditory

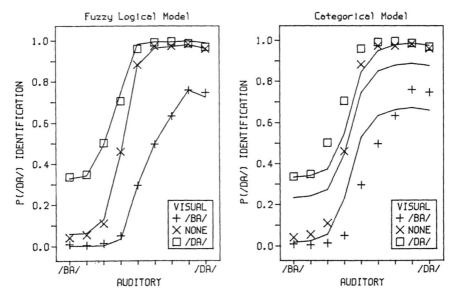

FIG. 11.8 Proportion (points) of /da/ identifications as a function of the auditory and visual levels of bimodal speech. The lines in the left panel give the predictions based on continuous perception of each source, whereas the predictions for categorical perception are given in the right panel.

stimulus A_i has Slightly falling F2-F3 and v_j represents the degree to which the visual stimulus V_j has Open lips, the outcome of prototype matching would be:

/da/ : $a_i v_j$

/ba/ : $(1 - a_i)(1 - v_j)$.

If these two prototypes are the only valid response alternatives, the pattern classification operation would determine their relative merit leading to the prediction that

$$P(D:A_i V_j) = \frac{a_i v_j}{a_i v_j + [(1-a_i)(1-v_j)]}$$

Given nine levels of A_i and three levels of V_j in the present task, the predictions of the model require $9 + 3 = 12$ parameters, one less than the categorical model.

Experimental Test. The points in Fig. 11.8 give the proportion of /da/ identifications as a function of the auditory level; the curve parameter is the visual condition. Both the auditory and visual sources influenced identification, with the contribution of visual source larger at the middle range of the auditory continuum. The lines in the left panel of Fig. 11.8 give the average predictions of the continuous model applied to the individual results of each of seven subjects. The right panel gives the predictions for the categorical model. As can be seen in the figure, the continuous model gave a significantly better account of the identification judgments than did the categorical model (Massaro & Cohen, 1983b). The advantage of the continuous model over the categorical model is preserved when the number of both stimulus and response alternatives is increased.

Independent Versus Nonindependent Evaluation of Sources

The next branch of the binary-opposition tree involves the issue of whether the two sources of information are nonindependent or independent. Independent sources of information imply that the information value determined in the evaluation of one source remains independent of the information value of the other. Nonindependent sources implies a violation of this principle. There are two approaches we have taken to answer this question. One of them is model free and the other is model dependent. In the model-free test, we have used reaction times to the single-dimension and bimodal events to determine whether the two dimensions show some form of intersensory interaction. If they do, then it should not be possible to account for the reaction times to a bimodal /ba/ in terms of simply the reaction times to a visual /ba/ and to an auditory /ba/. If the two dimensions are independent, we might expect reaction times to the bimodal event to be somewhat faster than those to the single-dimension events, but the advantage should be completely accounted for by statistical facilitation (Gielen, Schmidt, & Van Den Heuvel, 1983; Raab, 1962).

The reader might have realized that the predictions of independence appear to contradict those of integration; that is, the independence prediction implies that subjects respond to the auditory or visual source that is processed first, without waiting to integrate the two sources. Although this implication is correct, it does not necessarily mean that the two sources are not integrated, only that a response can be initiated before integration occurs. In the present task, the auditory and visual sources are completely unambiguous and they always agree with one another in the bimodal condition. Subjects are also instructed to respond as quickly as possible. Thus, although integration may still have occurred, it might not be observed in the reaction times because subjects could initiate a response based on just a single dimension whether or not integration of the two dimensions was complete.

Fig. 11.9 shows the distributions of reaction times of two subjects to the six stimuli. As can be seen in the figure, the subject is somewhat faster to the bimodal speech event but no faster than expected if the subject simply begins to initiate a response when either the auditory or visual dimension is identified. The advantage of bimodal trials can be accounted for simply in terms of the variability of the processing times along each dimension allowing the average reac-

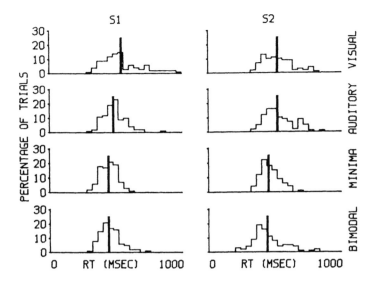

FIG. 11.9 Distribution of reaction times (RTs) for two subjects S1 and S2 to visual alone, auditory alone, and bimodal speech events. The minima distribution is that predicted for bimodal trials based on the auditory alone and visual alone trials. The solid bar gives the mean reaction time.

tion time to bimodal events to be shorter than to either dimension presented alone. These results also do not contradict the earlier conclusion that the two sources of information are integrated for perceptual recognition.

For the model-dependent test of the independence issue, we can ask whether a model assuming independence of auditory and visual information provides an adequate account of bimodal speech perception. The hypothesis of nonindependence must predict a failure of any model assuming independence (unless for some strange reason the independence model is mathematically equivalent to the nonindependence that exists). Independence models must assume that the information obtained along one source is independent of the information obtained along the other source. The models described in the test between categorical and continuous sources of information are independence models. Both models must fail if the auditory and visual sources are nonindependent. However, the adequate description of the continuous model provides evidence for independence and against nonindependence of auditory and visual information in speech perception.

Additive Versus Multiplicative Integration

The final branch to be discussed in this chapter involves the combination rule used to integrate the two sources. An additive or averaging rule is usually the

11. INFORMATION-PROCESSING THEORY AND STRONG INFERENCE 295

first to come to mind given the seminal work of Anderson and his colleagues (Anderson, 1981, 1982). This integration rule makes a strong prediction concerning the average rating response in an information-integration task; if the scale is an interval one, then the plot of the two factors should produce parallel curves. The theoretical reason to question the applicability of adding or averaging the evaluations of the separate sources of information is that this combination rule is nonoptimal. Averaging an ambiguous source of information with an informative source will tend to neutralize the judgment relative to the informative dimension being presented alone. In contrast, multiplying the sources of information within the context of the continuous model (Massaro, 1984a, 1984b, 1984c; Oden & Massaro, 1978) is functionally identical to Bayes rule and the Likelihood Ratio.

A test of the additive rule can be made in an experiment in which subjects rated on a 9-point scale bimodal speech events. The auditory source was varied along a continuum of nine steps between /ba/ and /da; and the visual source could be /ba/, neutral, or /da/ articulations. Fig. 11.10 gives the results of a typical subject in the experiment along with the predictions of additive and multiplicative integration rules. As can be seen in the figure, the results contradict the parallelism prediction of the additive rule. The results reflect instead that

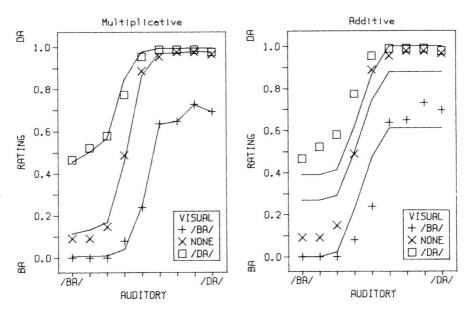

FIG. 11.10 Observed (points) rating judgments for a typical subject as a function of the auditory and visual levels of bimodal speech. The lines in the left panel give the predictions for a multiplicative integration rule, whereas the predictions for an additive integration rule are given in the right panel.

the contribution of one source has more of an impact to the extent the other source is ambiguous.

CONCLUSION

This short review of research carried out within the framework of information processing and strong inference should inform the introductory discussion concerning research paradigms for psychological inquiry. I discussed how the information-processing framework could be expanded to study the information that is used in information processing. The questions proposed in Fig. 11.2 could not have been answered in representative designs. As an example, only by manipulating the auditory and visual sources independently was it possible to assess whether the two sources are integrated in perceptual recognition. A factorial combination of the sources also allowed us to determine the categorical versus continuous nature of each source, whether the sources are evaluated independently, and how the sources are integrated in perception. Additonal studies that cannot be discussed here have addressed the questions of the relative influence of each source and developmental and individual differences in perception. With respect to Neisser's (1976) concern for natural problems, artificial experiments can be highly informative. Because one does not find independent variation of auditory and visual sources of information in natural speech, both Neisser and Brunswik would have to frown on the method of our research enterprise.

I believe that the enterprise was fruitful in providing insights into fundamental issues in perception and action. Although this enterprise might seem far removed from the book's theme of the relationship between perception and action, it makes apparent that perception involves the evaluation and integration of multiple sources of information. Theories of perception in the service of action must confront the important issues centered around how action is guided by the evaluation and integration of multiple sources of information. Although the laboratory is a far cry from nature, a good theory can bridge the gap between the two so that the distance seems shorter and shorter with every step.

ACKNOWLEDGMENTS

The writing of this chapter and the research reported in the chapter were supported, in part, by NINCDS Grant 20314 from the Public Health Service and Grant BNS-83-15192 from the National Science Foundation. The finishing touches on this chapter were completed while the author was a member of the project "Perception and Action," at the Zentrum fur Interdisziplinare Forshung der Universitat Bielefeld, Bielefeld, West Germany. The author would like to thank the other members of the group and the institute for providing an ideal environment for scholarship. Michaael Cohen made important contributions to the experimental work and Ray Gibbs, Herbert Heuer, and Andries Sanders provided helpful comments on a earlier draft of the chapter.

REFERENCES

Allport, D. A. (1980). Patterns and actions: Cognitive mechanisms are content specific. In G. Claxton (Ed.), *Cognitive psychology: New directions.* London: Routledge & Kegan Paul.

Anderson, N. H. (1981). *Foundations of information integration theory.* New York: Academic Press.

Anderson, N. H. (1982). *Methods of information integration theory.* New York: Academic Press.

Anderson, N. H., & Cuneo, D. O. (1978). The height + width rule in children's judgments of quantity. *Journal of Experimental Psychology: General, 107,* 335–378.

Banks, W. P. (1983). On the decay of the icon. *The Behavioral and Brain Sciences, 6,* 14–15.

Broadbent, D. E. (1958). *Perception and communication.* New York: Pergamon Press.

Broadbent, D. E. (1971). *Decision and Stress,* New York: Academic Press.

Brunswik, E. (1944). Distal focussing of perception: Size -constancy in a representative sample of situations. *Psychological Monographs, 56* (Whole No. 254), 1–49.

Brunswik, E. (1952). *The conceptual framework of psychology.* Chicago: University of Chicago press.

Brunswik, E. (1955). Representative design and probabilistic theory in a functional psychology. *Psychological Review, 62,* 193–217.

Brunswik, E. (1956). *Perception and the representative design of psychological experiments.* Berkeley: University of California press.

Brunswik, E., & Kamiya, J. (1953). Ecological cue validity of "proximity" and of other Gestalt factors. *American Journal of Psychology, 66,* 20–32.

Cutting, J. E., & Millard, R. T. (1984). Three gradients and the perception of flat and curved surfaces. *Journal of Experimental Psychology: General, 113,* 198–216.

Eimas, P. D. (1963). The relation between identification and discrimination along speech and nonspeech continua. *Language and Speech, 6,* 206–217.

Fechner, G. T. (1966). *Elements of Psychophysics* (Vol. 1). H. E. Adler, D. H. Howes, & E. G. Boring. (Eds. and Trans.).New York: Holt, Rinehart, & Winston. (original work published 1860)

Fodor, J. A. (1983). *The modularity of mind: An essay on faculty psychology.* Cambridge: Bradford books.

Gibson, J. J. (1979). *The ecological approach to visual perception.* Boston: Houghton Mifflin.

Gielen, S. C., Schmidt, R. A., & Van Den Heuvel, P. J. M. (1983). On the nature of intersensory facilitation of reaction time. *Perception and Psychophysics, 34,* 161–168.

Gopher, D., & Sanders, A. F. (1984). S-Oh-R: Oh stages! Oh resources. In W. Prinz & A. F. Sanders (Eds.), *Cognition and motor processes.* Berlin: Springer–Verlag.

Haber, R. N. (1983). The impending demise of the icon: A critique of the concept of iconic storage in visual information processing. *The Behavioral and Brain Sciences, 6,* 1–11.

Helmholtz, H. von (1962). *Treatise on physiological optics* (3rd ed.). J. P. C. Southall (Ed. and Trans.). New York: Dover. (original work published 1856–1866).

Jenkins, J. J. (1979). Four points to remember: A tetrahedral model of memory experiments. In L. S. Cermak & F. I. M. Craik (Eds.) *Levels of processing in human memory.* Hillsdale, NJ: Lawrence Erlbaum Associates.

Jenkins, J. J. (1980). Can we have a fruitful cognitive psychology? In Nebraska symposium on motivation. University of Nebraska Press.

Kuhl, P. K., & Meltzoff, A. N. (1982). The bimodal perception of speech in infancy. *Science, 218,* 1138–1141.

Kuhn, T. S. (1970). *The structure of scientific revolutions.* Chicago: University of Chicago press.

Liberman, A. M., Harris, K. S., Hoffman, H. S., & Griffith, B. C. (1957). The discrimination of speech sounds within and across phoneme boundaries. *Journal of Experimental Psychology, 54,* 358–368.

MacDonald, J., & McGurk, H. (1978). Visual influences on speech perception processes. *Perception & Psychophysics, 24,* 253–257.

Massaro, D. W. (1975a). *Experimental psychology and information processing.* Chicago: Rand–McNally.
Massaro, D. W. (Ed.). (1975b). *Understanding language: an information processing analysis of speech perception, reading and psycholinguistics.* New York: Academic Press.
Massaro, D. W. (1978). A stage model of reading and listening. *Visible Language, 12,* 3–26.
Massaro, D. W. (1979). Reading and listening (Tutorial paper). In P. A. Kolers, M. Wrolstad, & H. Bouma (Eds.), *Processing of visible language* (Vol. 1, pp. 331–354). New York: Plenum.
Massaro, D. W. (1984a). Children's perception of visual and auditory speech. *Child Development, 55,* 1777–1788.
Massaro, D. W. (1984b). Time's role for information, processing, and normalization. In J. Gibbon & L. Allan (Eds.), *Timing and time perception* (Vol. 423, pp. 372–384). New York: Annals of the New York Academy of Sciences.
Massaro, D. W. (1984c). Building and testing models of reading processes: Examples from word recognition. In P. D. Pearson (Ed.), *Handbook of reading research.* New York: Longman.
Massaro, D. W., & Cohen, M. M. (1983a). Categorical or continuous speech perception: A new test. *Speech Communication, 2,* 15–35.
Massaro, D. W., & Cohen, M. M. (1983b). Evaluation and integration of visual and auditory information in speech perception. *Journal of Experimental Psychology: Human Perception and Performance, 9,* 753–771.
Massaro, D. W., & Cohen, M. M. (1983c). Phonological context in speech perception. *Perception and Psychophysics, 34,* 338–348.
McGurk, H., & MacDonald (1976). Hearing lips and seeing voices. *Nature, 264,* 746–748.
Neisser, U. (1967). *Cognitive psychology.* New York: Appleton–Century–Crofts.
Neisser, U. (1976). *Cognition and reality.* San Francisco: W. H. Freeman.
Newell, A. (1973). You can't play 20 questions with nature and win: Projective comments on the papers of this symposium. In W. G. Chase (Ed.). *Visual information processing,* New York: Academic Press.
Oden, G. C., & Massaro, D. W. (1978). Integration of featural formation in speech perception, *Psychological Review, 85,* 172–191.
Platt, J. R. (1964). Strong inference. *Science, 146,* 347–353.
Popper, K. (1959). *The logic of scientific discovery.* New York: Basic books.
Raab, D. H. (1962). Statistical facilitation of simple reaction times. *Transactions of the New York Academy of Sciences, 24,* 574–590.
Repp, B. H. (1984). Categorical perception: Issues, methods, findings. In N. J. Lass (Ed.), *Speech and language: Advances in basic research and practice* (Vol. 10). New York: Academic Press.
Rock, I. (1975). *An Introduction to Perception.* New York: Macmillan.
Sanders, A. F. (1980). Stage analysis of reaction processes. In G. E. Stelmach & J. Requin (Eds.), *Tutorials in motor behavior* (pp. 331–354). The Netherlands: North–Holland Publishing.
Sanders, A. F. (1984). Ten Symposia on Attention and performance: Some issues and trends. In H. Bouma & D. G. Bouwhuis (Eds.), *Attention and performance X: Control of language processes.* Hillsdale, NJ: Lawrence Erlbaum Associates.
Stelmach, G. E., & Hughes, B. G. (1984). Cognitivism and future theories of action: Some basic issues. In W. Prinz & A. F. Sanders (Eds.), *Cognition and motor processes.* Berlin, Heidelberg: Springer–Verlag.
Sternberg, S. (1969). The discovery of processing stages: Extensions of Donder's method. *Acta Psychologica, 30,* 276–315.
Sternberg, S. (1975). Memory scanning: New findings and current controversies. *Quarterly Journal of Experimental Psychology, 27,* 1–32.
Stroop, J. R. (1935). Studies of interference in serial verbal reactions. *Journal of Experimental Psychology, 18,* 643–662.
Theios, J. (1975). The components of response latency in simple human information tasks. In P. M. A. Rabbitt & S. Dornic (Eds.), *Attention and performance.* London: Academic press.

Tolman, E. C. (1956). Egon Brunswik: 1903–1955. *American Journal of Psychology, 69*, 315–324.

Tulving, E. (1979). Memory research: What kind of progress? In L. B. Nilsson (Ed.). *Perspectives on memory research: Essays in honor of Uppsala University's 500th Anniversary*, Hillsdale, NJ: Lawrence Erlbaum Associates.

Turvey, M. T. (1977). Contrasting orientations to the theory of visual information processing. *Psychological Review, 84*, 67–88.

Turvey, M. T., & Shaw, R. (1979). The primacy of perceiving: An ecological formulation of perception as a point of departure for understanding memory. In L.-G. Nilsson (Ed.), *Perspectives on memory research: Essays in honor of Uppsala University's 500th anniversary*. Hillsdale, NJ: Lawrence Erlbaum Associates.

Tyler, L. K., & Wessels, J. (1983). Quantifying contextual contributions to word-recognition processes. *Perception & Psychophysics, 34*, 409–420.

Zadeh, L. A. (1965). Fuzzy sets, *Information and Control, 8*, 338–353.

12 Asymmetries in the Relationship Between Speech Perception and Production

Donald G. MacKay
*University of California,
Los Angeles*

What is the relation between perception and action? The present chapter describes a new theory of this relationship for the most proficient of human skills: the perception and production of speech. I develop the theory in two stages that reflect the classical dintinction between structure (hardware) and function (the real time processes that the hardware undergoes during production or perception). The structural issue concerns the relationship between the mechanisms for perceiving versus producing speech and represents a source of considerable controversy over the past several decades. Some, such as Lashley (1951), argue that perception and production share some of the same mechanisms because "the processes of comprehension and production of speech have too much in common to depend on wholly different mechanisms" (p. 186). Others have assumed separate rather than shared mechanisms for perception and production. For example, Wernicke used cases of aphasia to argue that production is localized in one area of the brain and perception in another, interconnected but separate area (see Straight, 1980). The motor theory (Liberman, Cooper, Harris, & MacNeilage, 1962; Studdert-Kennedy, Liberman, Harris, and Cooper, 1970) implicitly makes the same assumption because speech sounds such as stops are perceived with the help of the components that produce them in the motor theory, and this could only occur if the components representing stops differ for perception versus production.

MacKay (in preparation) examines in detail the available data bearing on this structural issue and argues that these and other theories that assume separate perception and production components are limited in detail and scope (e.g., none deal with the structural issue at the sentential level of the system) and are in a state of crisis (all have encountered fundamental phenomena that contradict their basic assumptions). The present chapter therefore attempts to develop a new theory wherein some of the components for perception and production are shared, and reviews various sources of evidence for these shared components (mental nodes representing higher level phonological units such as segments and syllables, and sentential units such as words and phrases).

The second, functional issue is in many ways more complex than the structural issue, even though structure places constraints on function. The issue is this: If there are shared perception-production components, how do they function in a theory of speech production? What processes involving these common components give rise to perception rather than production? And how do these processes involving shared components account for the basic facts of perception such as the regularities in perceptual errors?

The theory developed here addresses all these questions as well as some issues raised by a set of recently discovered asymmetries in the relationship between the perception and production of speech. For example, speech perception can proceed much more quickly than speech production: Computer-compressed speech remains perceptually intelligible at 5 to 7 times the rate that people can produce speech of equivalent intelligibility (Foulke & Sticht, 1969). I show here that this difference cannot be explained in terms of muscular or biomechanical factors but reflects a higher level processing difference between perception versus production. This raises the question of what these processing differences are that enable perception to proceed so much faster than production, especially if perception and production share identical higher level components. In reviewing this and many other processing asymmetries I discuss numerous empirical findings from various domains of inquiry (neuropsychology, psycholinguistics, cybernetics, motor control), but my main goal throughout is to develop the new theory of shared components in as detailed and general a manner as possible.

THE STRUCTURAL ISSUE: COMMON COMPONENTS

What are the common components underlying speech perception and production? I refer to these common components as nodes, i.e., processing units that share the same relatively simple structural characteristics and processing capabilities and respond to basic variables such as practice (repeated activation) in the same way (discussed later) during production and perception.

I begin by observing that not all of the nodes for perceiving and producing speech can be shared. The ear and associated auditory pathways register speech inputs but play no direct role in producing speech. Nor do the muscles for the respiratory, laryngeal, and articulatory organs contribute to speech perception. Here, then, are two separate systems that *do not* share both perceptual and production functions. One system contains sensory analysis nodes that represent the patterns of auditory input. The other system contains nodes that represent the patterns of muscle movement for producing speech sounds.

The hypothesis at issue is whether there exists another system of nodes that

12. SPEECH PERCEPTION AND PRODUCTION

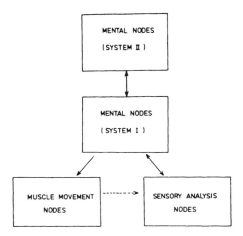

FIG. 12.1 An overview of the mental node hypothesis. The solid arrows represent internal connections between mental nodes, muscle movement nodes, and sensory analysis nodes whereas the broken arrow represents self-generated feedback.

represents neither sensory experience nor patterns of muscle movement *per se*, but higher level cognitive components common to both perception and production. Under this "mental node hypothesis," a common set of nodes is involved when we perceive or imagine perceiving a segment, word, or sentence, and when we produce these components, either aloud or within the imagination (internal speech). Although my examples here come from speech, this mental node hypothesis is not limited to speech but applies more broadly to all systems for everyday action and perception. Under the mental node hypothesis, a single set of mental nodes becomes involved when a chess player perceives and comprehends a sequence of grandmaster chess moves or generates the same sequence of moves either on the board or within the imagination. Such mental nodes are of course distinct from the sensory nodes that analyze the visual pattern of the chessboard and from the motor nodes that generate the sequence of muscle contractions for moving the pieces.

Fig. 12.1 provides a general overview of the mental node hypothesis. The mental nodes send "top-down" outputs to the muscle movement nodes for speech production and receive "bottom-up" inputs from the sensory analysis nodes for speech perception. These sensory analysis nodes analyze the input pattern for the speech of others as well as self-generated feedback, represented by the broken line in Fig. 12.1. Sensory analysis nodes are located in the sensory cortex and associated sensory pathways whereas muscle movement nodes are located in the motor cortex and associated motor pathways. Muscle movement and sensory analysis nodes have built-in connections at the lowest levels to different types of highly specialized end organs and achieve much greater practice (use) than mental nodes, so that their processing can proceed at a much faster

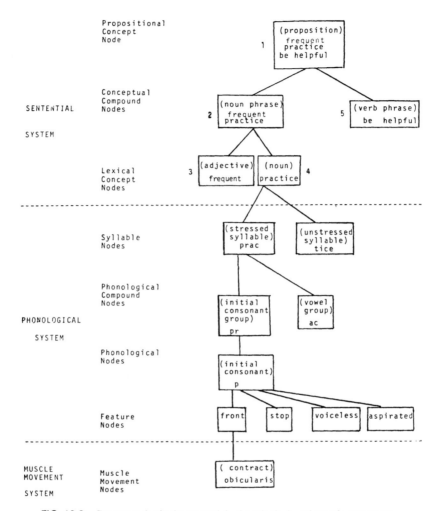

FIG. 12.2 Content nodes in the sentential, phonological, and muscle movement systems for components of the sentence "Frequent practice is helpful." The numbers adjacent the sentential components indicate order of activation during production (modified from MacKay, 1982). Lines between the phonological and sentential nodes represent both bottom-up and top-down connections. The connection to the muscle movement node (contract obicularis) is top-down only.

rate (see MacKay, 1982). However, mental, muscle movement, and sensory analysis nodes all speak the same "processing language" and communicate with one another in the same way (see following).

Mental nodes fall into three functional classes by virtue of how they connect with other nodes: *content nodes* for representing the form or content components of an action or perception; *sequence nodes* for activating and determining the order of the components; and *timing nodes* for determining when to activate the components. All three types of nodes play a role in both perception and production. However, I concentrate here on the connections between content nodes, setting aside sequence and timing nodes and how they interconnect until the subsequent section on processing.

Content nodes must become activated in producing a sentence and are connected to one another in hierarchical fashion. I illustrate these hierarchical connections in Fig. 12.2 by means of an arbitrarily chosen sentence, "Frequent practice is helpful." Following a notational convention developed in MacKay (1982), I refer to particular nodes by means of a two-component label: The content that the node represents appears in italics followed by its sequential domain (explained later) in brackets. Thus, the highest level node representing the entire thought underlying this sentence has the content *frequent practice be helpful,* occurs in the sequential domain (active declarative) and is labeled *frequent practice be helpful*(active declarative). This node is connected to two other nodes labeled *frequent practice*(noun phrase) and *be helpful*(verb phrase) (see Fig. 12.2). *Frequent practice*(noun phrase) is connected with the lexical nodes *frequent*(adjective) and *practice*(noun). These lexical nodes are connected with specific phonological nodes, representing syllables (e.g., *prac*), phonological compounds (e.g., *pr*), segments (e.g., *p*), and features (e.g., the one representing the frontal place of articulation of *p*.)[1]

A more complex but otherwise similar hierarchy of nodes underlies the control of muscle movements, but so little is known about the detailed nature and structure of connections within the muscle movement system for speech, that such a hierarchy cannot be represented here. Bottom-up hierarchies of sensory analysis nodes are likewise extremely complex and diverse, and beyond current analysis. For example, although Lisker (1978) was able to catalogue 16 acoustic differences that could serve to distinguish a single phonological feature (the voicing of /p/ vs. /b/) in a single phonological context, both the nodes that represent such acoustic differences and the structure of their interconnections are currently unknown.

Evidence for Mental Nodes

The mental node hypothesis predicts and explains many classes of phenomena, both detailed and general. Here I briefly mention four general classes, leaving more detailed phenomena and predictions for later in the chapter.

---

[1]Nodes are dynamic and sequential rather than purely descriptive units (see MacKay, 1982). Thus, the word *practice* in this example requires syllable nodes in order to sequence its components, but not all words require syllable nodes. For example, a monosyllabic word such as *desk* is a sequential unit only at the lexical level, which means that its lexical node *desk*(noun) may connect directly with the sequential units *d*(initial consonant) and *esk*(vowel group) rather than a syllable node such as *desk*(stressed syllable). The reader is referred to MacKay (1972, 1973b, 1978) and Treiman (1983) for detailed evidence supporting the syllable structure implied by the connections discussed and illustrated here.

Parallel Empirical Effects. As expected under the mental node hypothesis, many variables have parallel effects on perception and production. Practice is one of these variables: it facilitates both production (see MacKay, 1982) and perception (including recognition and discrimination thresholds; see Woodworth, 1938). Complexity is another. For example, Sphoer and Smith (1973) showed that the time to recognize tachistoscopically presented two-syllable words(e.g., *paper*) is longer than one-syllable words (e.g., *point*) equated for length in letters and frequency of occurrence, and, as predicted under the mental node hypothesis, Klapp, Anderson, and Berrian (1973) and others have demonstrated a parallel effect of syllabic complexity on the output side.

Interactions Between Perception and Production. The mental node hypothesis readily explains interactions between perception and production and vice versa, e.g., those demonstrated by Cooper and Nager (1975) and Cooper, Blumstein, and Nigro (1975) using adaptation techniques: As expected under the mental node hypothesis, repeated production of speech sounds (motoric adaptation) influences perception, and repeated perception (perceptual adaptation) influences production.

Shadowing Latencies. In shadowing experiments, a subject hears a word or sentence and simultaneously produces it aloud with as little lag as possible. The surprising result in these studies is that some subjects can shadow with lag times as short as 100 msec between acoustic onset of input and output, even with nonsense syllable stimuli; see Kozhevnikov and Chistovich (1965) and Porter and Lubker (1980). These shadowing latencies are faster than auditory reaction times for a single-alternative key press or for syllabic responses to a pure tone stimulus. These short shadowing times are all the more remarkable because shadowing involves a very large set of response alternatives, a factor normally associated with increased reaction time. There apparently exists a highly compatible relationship or direct connection between the mechanisms for perceiving and producing speech and this compatibility is directly explained under the hypothesis that the phonological nodes for perceiving and producing speech are identical.

The Units for Perception and Production. A hundred years of research into speech perception have confirmed the need to postulate a hierarchy of abstract units, including distinctive features (e.g., unvoiced), segments e.g., $\boxed{\text{p}}$, syllables e.g., *prac,* words e.g., *practice,* and larger sentential constituents such as *frequent practice*(noun phrase) or *is helpful*(verb phrase) (See Clark & Clark (1977) for a review of relevent data). Recent studies of speech errors indicate that these same units play a role in speech production (see Fromkin, 1973), a finding consistent with the mental node hypothesis. However, the speech error data in fact go beyond the perception data, indicating additional units as yet unexamined in studies of auditory speech perception. Within the structure of words the additional production units include word stems, stem compounds, prefixes and suffixes, all specific as to type, e.g., adverbial suffixes constitute a basically different type of unit from past tense suffixes (see MacKay, 1979), and within the structure of syllables the additional production units include the initial consonant group (or onset, i.e., the consonant or consonant cluster preceding the vowel), the vowel group (or rhyme, i.e., the vowel and subsequent consonants within the syllable), the final consonant group (or coda, i.e., the consonants following the vowel), the vowel nucleus (a simple vowel plus a glide and/or liquid), and the dipthong (simple vowel plus glide) (See MacKay, 1972, 1978, 1979; and Treiman, 1983 for supporting data).

The mental node hypothesis predicts that all of these recently discovered production units will play a role in perception, and more generally that each new abstract unit discovered in studies of production will exhibit a counterpart in perception, and vice versa. Needless to say, a great deal of additional research is needed to test this hypothesis and its implications. One of these implications concerns phonological complexity as revealed by production onset time. As noted earlier, several investigators have reported that production onset times are usually longer for two- than one-syllable words, and the reason is that most two syllable words require the activation of more mental nodes before their first segment node can become activated. However, as MacKay (in preparation) points out, number of activations prior to production onset is not correferential with length in either syllables or segments, so that the mental node hypothesis generates some new and more refined predictions concerning the relation between production onset time and the structure of words and syllables. For example, the theory predicts production onset time differences for some word pairs with equivalent length (e.g., *crome* vs. *court*) and predicts *equivalent* production onset times for other word pairs with different lengths in either syllables (e.g., *crome* vs. *color*) or segments (e.g., *cram* vs. *cramp*). The reader is referred to MacKay (in preparation) for details underlying these predictions.

FUNCTIONAL ISSUE I: A THEORY OF OUTPUT PROCESSES INVOLVING MENTAL NODES

How do mental nodes function in the perception and production of speech? My first step in addressing this issue is to outline a theory of *production* incorporating mental nodes. The theory is an extended version of the node structure theory proposed by MacKay (1982) for explaining how practice makes behavior more fluent (faster, less prone to error) and more flexible (adapting readily to changed circumstances and transferring readily from one response mechanism to another). Minor modifications have been introduced to accommodate present purposes (to develop a unified theory of perception and production incorporating shared mental nodes), but readers familiar with the earlier theory may be inclined to skip this section.

Dynamic Properties of Mental Nodes

Mental nodes have four dynamic properties that are relevent to both perception and production: activation, priming, self-inhibition, and linkage strength.

Activation. Behavior occurs if and only if the bottom-most muscle movement nodes in a hierarchy such as the one illustrated in Fig. 12.2 become activated. Activation is always sequential and requires a special triggering mechanism to determine when and in what order the content nodes controlling the action become activated. By way of illustration, numbers adjacent to the sentential nodes in Fig. 12.2 represent order of activation.

Activation is all or none and is self-sustained, continuing for a specifiable period of time, independently of input from the sources that led originally to activation. During this period of self-sustained activation, a node simultaneously primes all nodes connected to it. A period of self-inhibition (discussed later) follows activation. Unlike other uses of the same term, activation in the node structure theory never spreads and never changes with "distance" or fatigue or the number of other nodes a node connects to.

Priming. Priming is required for activation and refers to a transmission across a connection that produces increased subthreshold activity in a connected node. The degree of priming varies with "distance" from the source: An activated node primes its connected nodes most strongly (first-order priming) whereas a node receiving first-order priming primes its connected nodes less strongly (second-order priming). Third-order priming from a single node is negligible and can be ignored in theories of production. Thus, priming spreads but only to a limited degree, and unlike other propositional network theories, activation always requires deliberate application of a special activating mechanism.

Priming summates across all simultaneously active connections and increases during the time that any given connection remains active. Consider for example how top-down priming summates during production for the numbered nodes in Fig. 12.2. Top-down connections are one-to-many, which introduces anticipatory effects into the theory (see MacKay, 1982). For example, node 1 becomes activated first, which simultaneously primes nodes 2 and 5 (see Fig. 12.2). However, node 5 cannot be activated until 2, 3, and 4 have been activated, so that priming of 5 represents "anticipatory priming", which continues to summate during the time that nodes 2, 3, and 4 are being activated. This anticipatory priming accumulates over time and facilitates the eventual activation of 5 and all other "right-branching" nodes in an output hierarchy. However, anticipatory priming also increases the probability of anticipatory errors, the most common

12. SPEECH PERCEPTION AND PRODUCTION   309

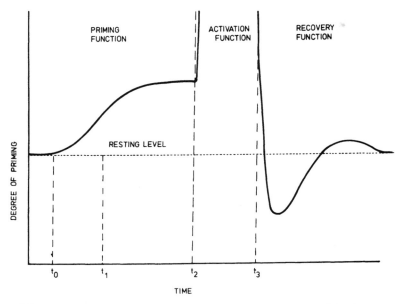

FIG. 12.3 The priming function (relating degree of priming and time following onset of priming, t_0), activation function (following application of the triggering mechanism at t_2) and recovery function (following onset of self-inhibition, t_3). See text for explanation (from MacKay and MacDonald, 1984).

class of error in speech production at either the phonological or sentential levels (see MacKay, 1982).

Unlike activation, priming is neither self-sustaining nor results in behavior when the bottom-most muscle movement nodes in an action hierarchy become primed: Priming between content nodes only summates to some subthreshold asymptotic level (see Fig. 12.3) and cannot directly cause a node to become activated. Also unlike activation, priming is order free or parallel in nature, requires no special triggering mechanism to determine when and in what order it occurs, and is not followed by a period of self-inhibition.

Self-Inhibition. After the nodes for producing components of skilled behavior become activated, they undergo a brief period of self-inhibition, during which their level of priming falls below resting level (see Fig. 12.3). Self-inhibited nodes then undergo a normal recovery cycle, which includes a period of hyperexcitability or postinhibitory rebound during which priming first rises above and then returns to resting level (see Fig. 12.3). Various sources of evidence for self-inhibition and the recovery cycle are discussed in MacKay (1986). With repeated activation of a node for prolonged periods of time (e.g., 5 minutes), fatigue sets in. During fatigue, the period of self-inhibition becomes extended, rebound from inhibition falls below normal resting level, and the node becomes generally less responsive to priming.

Linkage Strength. Linkage strength influences both the asymptotic level of priming and its rate of summation per unit time (represented by the initial slope of the priming function in Fig. 12.3). Linkage strength also determines how much and how rapidly priming becomes transmitted across a connection, and is itself determined by practice: the frequency with which a node has been activated via a particular connection in the past. As MacKay (1982) points out, linkage strength represents a long-term characteristic of a connection and explains a wide range of practice effects in the psychological literature.

The Sequential Activating Mechanism: Sequence Nodes

Mental nodes must be activated in proper sequence if an output is to be error free. Consider for example the mental nodes illustrated in Fig. 12.2. The highest level node *frequent practice be helpful*(active declarative) must be activated first. This simultaneously primes both *frequent practice*(noun phrase) and *be helpful*(verb phrase). However, only *frequent practice*(noun phrase) must become activated at this point, thereby simultaneously priming its connected nodes, *frequent*(adjective) and *practice*(noun), and so on down to the muscle movement nodes. The issue, then, is what mechanism causes ordered activation of simultaneously primed content nodes.

Sequence nodes represent that mechanism: They determine whether, when and in what order content nodes become activated. However, because each sequence node connects with and can activate any of the content nodes in its "domain," they are nonspecific in their effect (see MacKay (1982) for evidence in support of this nonspecificity). For example, the sequence node COLOR ADJECTIVE connects with and is responsible for activating all content nodes representing color adjectives (*red, green, blue, brown,* etc.), the set of nodes making up its domain. More generally, a sequential domain can be defined as set of response alternatives all of which share the same sequential privileges of occurence.

An activated sequence node multiplies the priming of every node connected with it by some large factor (e.g., 100) within a brief period of time. This multiplicative effect has no consequences for unprimed nodes but soon serves to activate (i.e., bring to threshold) the content node with the greatest degree of priming in its domain, normally the one that has just been primed from above via a connection from a superordinate content node. In producing the adjective *green,* for example, *green*(color adjective) must first become primed, either from above via a superordinate node such as *green apples*(noun phrase) or from below via say visual perception of either the color green or the printed word *green.*

Then COLOR ADJECTIVE must activate *green* (color adjective) as the most primed node in its domain. This "most-primed-wins" principle is extremely general and governs the activation of not just content nodes but sequence nodes as well (see MacKay, 1982).

A content node must of course attain some minimal degree of priming that can then be multiplied by the sequence node so as to achieve the threshold level required for activation. Below this minimal level, the degree of priming resulting from multiplication remains subthreshold, so that activation cannot occur.

Connections between sequence nodes represent serial order rules that determine order of activation for simultaneously primed sequence nodes. For the sentential system these serial order rules fall under the heading syntactic rules and for the phonological system, phonological rules. Thus, the sequence nodes ADJECTIVE and NOUN are connected in such a way as to represent the syntactic rule that adjectives precede nouns in English noun phrases.

An inhibitory connection is a simple means of achieving this order relation among sequence nodes. Under this proposal, ADJECTIVE inhibits NOUN and dominates in degree of priming when ADJECTIVE and NOUN receive simultaneous priming. However, once ADJECTIVE has been activated and returns to resting level, NOUN is released from inhibition and dominates in degree of priming, thereby determining the sequence (adjective + noun) for this and other noun phrases.

The Temporal Activating Mechanism: Timing Nodes

Timing nodes are the mechanism for the programming of timing in the node structure theory and are connected with sequence nodes in the same way that sequence nodes are connected with content nodes. Timing nodes also serve to organize the sequence and content nodes into systems. Thus, the sequence and content nodes in the aforementioned examples are part of the sentential system (see Fig. 12.2), and the sequence nodes for this system are connected with a sentential timing node. Sequence nodes within the phonological system are connected with a phonological timing node, and sequence nodes within the muscle movement system are connected with a muscle timing node.

Timing nodes become activated at specifiable points in time, priming the sequence nodes connected to them and activating the most primed one, following the most-primed-wins principle. By determining when the sequence nodes become activated, timing nodes therefore determine the temporal organization of the output. Different timing nodes have different periodicities or average rates of activation. For example, the sentential timing node exhibits a slower periodicity than the muscle timing node, because muscle flexions and extensions are produced faster than words and other sentential components.

Timing nodes also control speech rate. To determine the desired rate of speech, a speaker voluntarily adjusts the overall periodicity or pulse rate of the timing nodes (e.g., fast, normal, or slow). Control of the timing nodes also enables a speaker to selectively engage or disengage whole systems of nodes. During internal speech, the timing nodes for the sentential and phonological systems become active but not those for the muscle movement system. As a consequence, the phonological components for a sentence become activated in proper serial order and prime their corresponding muscle movement nodes (see MacKay, 1981) but no actual movement of the speech musculature ensues: Because none of the muscle sequence nodes have become activated, none of the content nodes within the muscle movement system can become activated.

A Simple Example

To illustrate how the timing and sequence nodes interact to determine whether, when and in what order the content nodes become activated in everyday speech production, consider the sequencing of the words *frequent* and *practice* in the sentence "Frequent practice is helpful." Fig. 12.4 illustrates the relevent content nodes (in rectangles), sequence nodes (in circles), and timing node (in triangle). Unbroken connections in the figure are excitatory, broken connections are inhibitory, and the dotted connection represents the inhibitory relationship between sequence nodes. Similar connections and processes are assumed for all sequentially organized mental nodes.

The node representing the sentential concept *frequent practice* (noun phrase) is activated first, simultaneously priming *frequent*(adjective)[2] and *practice*(noun), which immediately pass on second-order priming to their sequence nodes ADJECTIVE and NOUN. The inhibitory link between ADJECTIVE and NOUN temporarily reduces the priming level for NOUN so that ADJECTIVE becomes activated under the most-primed-wins principle following the first pulse from the timing node. ADJECTIVE therefore multiplies the priming of every content node in its (adjective) domain, and the one with the most priming in its domain, i.e., *frequent*(adjective), having recently been primed by *frequent practice*(noun phrase), reaches threshold soonest and becomes activated under the most-primed-wins principle.

Once a content node becomes activated, its sequence node must return quickly to resting level, because content nodes have a return connection to their sequence node that could cause reverberatory reactivation. Thus, once a content node becomes activated, it must quench or inhibit rather than further prime its

---

[2]Just as the domain of the words *green* and *red* is (color adjective), so the domain of *frequent* is (temporal adjective) rather than (adjective) as indicated here in order to simplify the illustration. Although all adjectives bear the same sequential relation to nouns in English, more specific domains such as (color adjective) and (temporal adjective) are needed in order to establish the appropriate sequencing among adjectives themselves. Thus, we say "frequent red lights" rather than "red frequent lights" following a sequential rule such as (temporal adjective + color adjective).

12. SPEECH PERCEPTION AND PRODUCTION

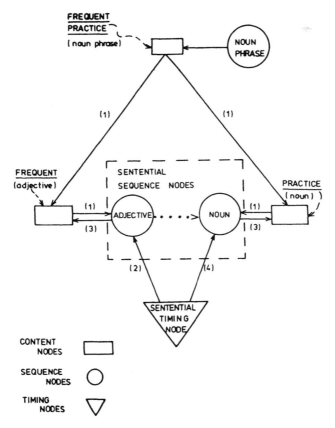

FIG. 12.4 The order of top-down processes (in brackets) underlying activation of content nodes (in rectangles), sequence nodes (in circles), and the concept timing node (in triangle) for producing the noun phrase *frequent practice* (from MacKay, 1982). The self-inhibitory and quenching mechanisms have been omitted for purposes of simplification.

corresponding sequence node so that only one content node becomes activated at any one time. This requires a special mechanism with a threshold, which if exceeded causes content nodes to inhibit rather than prime their sequence nodes.

Returning to the example in Fig. 12.4, quenching ADJECTIVE releases the inhibition on NOUN which now dominates in degree of priming and becomes activated under the most-primed-wins principle with the next pulse from the sentence timing node. NOUN therefore primes the entire domain of (noun) nodes, but having just been primed, *practice*(noun) has more priming than any other node in the domain, and becomes activated under the most-primed-wins principle.

STRUCTURAL ISSUE II: BOTTOM-UP CONNECTIONS FOR PERCEPTION

So far I have discussed some general phenomena which are consistent with the mental node hypothesis, and I have outlined a detailed theory of production involving activation of content nodes. Activation of a content node is also necessary for perception and proceeds via exactly the same structures (sequence and timing nodes) and dynamic properties (e.g., priming, and activation under the most-primed-wins principle) as production, a fact that must be kept in mind as we discuss Structural Issue II, the "bottom-up" corollary of the mental node hypothesis. Under this corollary, mental nodes are connected to one another via bottom-up connections that are necessary for perception. By way of illustration, bottom-up connections parallel the top-down connections in Fig. 12.2, so that each of the mental nodes illustrated there receive at least two bottom-up connections in addition to their single top-down connection.

To see why evidence for this corollary is needed, it is first necessary to note that top-down and bottom-up connections don't *always* run in parallel. Some nodes contribute bottom-up connections but receive no corresponding top-down connections in return. For example, there are neither logical nor empirical grounds for postulating top-down connections between phonological nodes and the visual nodes that represent facial movements such as lip closure. By way of illustration, hearing a speech sound over the telephone doesn't normally cause or enable one to visualize how its production might *look*.

However, there are good grounds for postulating bottom-up connections in the opposite direction. Consider the McGurk effect for example. McGurk and MacDonald (1976) had subjects observe a film of a person saying a simple syllable in synchrony with an auditory recording of a *different* syllable and found that visual features such as lip closure strongly influenced what phoneme the subjects reported *hearing*. Thus, with a conflict between visual [pa] and auditory [ta], subjects more often reported hearing [pa] rather than [ta]. This finding indicates that nodes representing visual events such as lip closure connect bottom-up with phonological nodes, thereby influencing which segment node receives most priming and becomes activated. And this means that top-down connections don't always parallel bottom-up ones.

Evidence for Bottom-up Connections

Parallel bottom-up and top-down connections help explain some otherwise puzzling speech production phenomena as well as some additional parallels between perception and production, discussed later.

Perceptually Based Production Errors. Irrelevant but simultaneously ongoing perceptual processes sometimes cause production errors, and this input-output interaction is difficult to explain in theories postulating separate components for production versus perception. Meringer and Mayer (1895) and Norman (1981) compiled several naturally occurring speech errors of this type, but the Stroop effect represents a well-known experimental demonstration of the same phenomenon (see Norman, 1981). Subjects in Stroop studies are presented with color names printed in several different colors of ink and the task is to ignore the word and name the color of the ink as quickly as possible. Errors are especially frequent when the color name differs from the name for the ink (e.g., the word *green* printed in red ink): subjects erroneously substitute the printed name (*green*) for the required name representing the color of the ink *(red)*.

This Stroop effect is readily explained under the node structure theory, where the same mental nodes are involved in perception and production and the most primed node in a domain automatically becomes activated regardless of its source of priming. A high-frequency word such as *green* will prime its lexical content node faster and more strongly than will a visually presented color, because the naming of a color is a relatively rare activity. This does not mean that Stroop interference is completely describable in "race model" terms because priming doesn't automatically cause activation in the theory. However, it *does* mean that color naming will either take more time or exhibit more errors with than without the competing color name, because in order to become activated and give rise to perception, the lexical node representing the color must achieve more priming than the lexical node representing the color name.

Top-Down Effects in Perception. The mental node hypothesis also explains top-down effects in both speech and visual perception. To illustrate one such effect, consider Leeper's (1936) experiment where an ambiguous figure such as Jastrow's rabbit-duck is presented along with instructions such as "Can you see the duck?" The subject will perceive the duck but not the rabbit because the instructions prime the nodes representing the conceptual components of ducks. With the added bottom-up priming from the figure itself, these "duck nodes" receive the most priming and become activated under the most-primed-wins principle, thereby causing perception of the duck. The "rabbit nodes" on the other hand only receive bottom-up priming and, being less primed, do not become activated, so that the rabbit goes unperceived.

Speed-Accuracy Trade-Off in Perception. The node structure theory was originally designed to explain the trade-off relationship between time and accuracy (errors) in motor and mental skills (see MacKay, 1982), and bottom-up connections readily capture speed-accuracy trade-offs in perceptual recognition. To recognize an object (or word), the highest level node representing the object (or word) must receive greater priming than any other (extraneous) node in its domain when the triggering mechanism is applied. Although extraneous nodes receive unpredictable amounts of priming, with a distribution over time approximating a Gausian curve with resting level as mean, priming for the appropriate or primed-from-below node summates systematically over time and must eventually exceed the priming of every other node in its domain if the stimulus is presented for long enough. But the shorter the stimulus duration, the greater the likelihood of error, i.e., the greater the probability that some other node receives more priming than the appropriate node at the time when the activating mechanism is applied.

FUNCTIONAL ISSUE II: THE PROCESSES UNDERLYING PERCEPTION

Having examined some implications of and evidence for bottom-up connections in a theory of production incorporating mental nodes, I turn now to processes that give rise to perception in the theory. Not only do mental nodes have the same dynamic properties in perception as in production, but the processes and mechanisms underlying the activation of a node are exactly the same in both. The only difference is that processes normally become initiated bottom-up rather than top-down in perception. Consider for example activation of the node *frequent*(adjective) following presentation of the word "frequent" in perception. Sensory analysis and phonological nodes provide strong and convergent (many-to-one) bottom-up priming that summates on *frequent*(adjective) and introduces second order priming to ADJECTIVE, just as in production. ADJECTIVE then becomes activated as the most primed sequence node following the next pulse from the timing node. Once activated, ADJECTIVE then multiplies the priming of all nodes in its (adjective) domain, but only the most primed one, normally *frequent*(adjective) reaches threshold and becomes activated.

As in production, the rate setting of the timing nodes in perception is partly individual specific and partly situation specific, determined by the perceived rate of input for example. In the node structure theory the input and perception of the input can proceed at different rates within wide limits: The rate setting for the timing nodes of speaker and listener need not match. The only requirements are that the perceiver's rate setting not be so slow that priming has largely decayed by the time the next pulse from the timer arrives, and not so fast that so little priming has built up that the probability of activating the wrong node exceeds the error criterion (see MacKay, 1982).

THE PRINCIPLE OF HIGHER LEVEL ACTIVATION

As already noted, activation is necessary for perceptual awareness. However, not all nodes in a hierarchy such as the one in Fig. 12.2 become activated during perception the way they do in production. Only higher level (e.g., sentential) nodes normally become activated and give rise to everyday perception. This principle of higher level activation is extremely general, applying to all types of perception. To illustrate the logical basis of this principle, I first show why activating lower level nodes is unnecessary in perception. I then show why activating lower level nodes is undesireable in perception and discuss the optimal level for activation to begin during everyday speech perception. Finally, I discuss various sources of evidence that support this principle of higher level activation.

Why Lower Level Activation is Unnecessary

Lower level nodes need not become activated during perception because of the efficiency with which they pass on priming to higher level nodes. This efficiency is attributable to two fundamental structural characteristics of bottom-up connections. One is the fact that bottom-up connections are many-to-one (see Fig. 12.2), which enables simultaneously occuring priming to converge and summate. Lower level nodes have an additional advantage in this summation process because convergent priming arrives either simultaneously or very closely in time at lower level nodes. For example, the priming from feature nodes converges simultaneously or nearly simultaneously on a segment node, whereas the priming from lexical nodes converges on a phrase node sequentially and over a period of a many hundreds of milliseconds. Without themselves becoming activated, lower level nodes can pass on enough temporally summated priming to enable higher level nodes to reach the minimum criterion required for multiplication to threshold (activation). Higher level nodes on the other hand must become activated during perception in order to transmit sufficient priming to enable the highest level nodes to become activated via priming multiplication.

The second structural basis for the principle of higher level activation is the fact that in general, lower level connections have greater linkage strength than higher level connections (see MacKay, 1982). Greater linkage strength means that low-level bottom-up connections pass on priming extremely efficiently. Thus, even when unactivated, lower level nodes transmit enough (second-order) priming to enable their connected (higher level) nodes to become activated via multiplication of priming.

By way of illustration, consider the hierarchy of bottom-up connections for the word *practice* in Fig. 12.2. To facilitate exposition, assume that the sensory analysis nodes representing the acoustic input provide the equivalent of first-order priming to the phonological feature nodes. Without becoming activated, each feature node therefore passes on somewhat weaker (second order) priming to their connected segment nodes. However, because each segment node receives simultaneous bottom-up priming from at least four feature nodes, this second order priming from all four feature nodes may summate to at least the level of first-order priming from a single node. The segment nodes pass on this summated priming to their connected phonological compound and syllable nodes, and again because of convergent summation, favorable timing, and high-linkage strength, the combined degree of second-order priming may remain comparable to that of first-order priming from a single *activated* node.

Why Lower Level Activation is Undesirable

A comparison of the costs of activation versus priming illustrates why unnecessary (i.e., lower level) activation is undesirable in everyday perception. Unlike priming, which is automatic and parallel or simultaneous, activation is nonautomatic, sequential, and time consuming: The activation mechanism (sequence node) must first receive a build-up of priming and then become activated via a pulse from the timing node. The sequence node must then activate its most primed content node via multiplication of priming. Activating more than one node at a time in a domain is virtually impossible and the rate of activation must not be so fast as to induce errors (see MacKay, 1982). This adds further to the temporal inefficiency of activation relative to priming and suggests that if activation is unnecessary, it should not occur. And because activating lower level (e.g., phonological) nodes is unnecessary (see foregoing), the principle of higher level activation postulates that only higher level nodes normally become activated during everyday perception.

The Optimal Level for Activation

Although activation incurs costs (not just time costs as discussed earlier but probably effort costs as well), activation is necessary for perceptual awareness, which becomes especially desirable at the highest possible levels to ensure appropriate or adaptive action (benefits). Consequently, there must be some optimal level where activation becomes cost effective: Below the optimal level, costs of activation (time and effort) outweight benefits, and above the optimal level, benefits of activation (perceptual awareness and adaptive action) outweigh costs. Two factors determine this optimum level; prior practice (linkage strength) and the time characteristics of convergent priming, and together these factors suggest that lexical content nodes represent the typical level where activation must first occur in the case of adults perceiving common words. On the one hand, unaided bottom-up priming *to* lexical content nodes probably surpasses the minimum level required for activation via multiplication (discussed earlier). On the other hand, the priming passed bottom-up *from* lexical content to phrase nodes may typically fall below this minimum criterion because of the poor temporal summation and weak linkage strength of the connections to phrase nodes. As a result, unless lexical nodes become activated, no higher level nodes whatsoever can be activated, making perceptual awareness impossible. In short, the principle of higher level activation must begin with lexical content nodes during everyday speech perception.

This is not to say that lower level nodes *cannot* become activated. As MacKay (in preparation) points out, the cost-effective level for activation varies with attention and the context or perceptual situation. For example, if an input is especially degraded or unfamiliar, activating phonological or even sensory analysis nodes may become necessary in order to provide sufficient bottom-up priming to enable higher level nodes to become activated via multiplication of priming.

Evidence for the Principle of Higher Level Activation

During *production,* phonological nodes must invariably become activated if the phonemes of a word are to be produced in proper serial order. However, during *perception,* phonological nodes become primed but not activated under the principle of higher level activation.[3] In addition to the logical arguments discussed previously, at least four lines of empirical evidence support this principle of higher level activation, as discussed below.

Perception of the Distal Stimulus. As expected under the principle of higher level activation, we normally perceive not the proximal stimulus or pattern of sensory stimulation but the distal stimulus or higher level conceptual aspects of an input. This phenomenon is of course not limited to speech but applies more generally to all perceptual systems, including vision and audition. For example, we perceive an object such as a lamp at some distance from ourselves but fail to perceive the disparate retinal images that provide the sensory basis for that perception. Similarly, we hear the sound of a car's horn as coherent and localized in space but fail to perceive the complex sensory events underlying this perception, e.g., differences in time of arrival of the sound to the two ears (see Warren, 1982). The reason is that priming from the sensory analysis nodes which represent these sensory events is passed on so automatically and so effectively that full-fledged activation and perception normally never occur at that level.

Phonemic Restorations. The phonemic restoration phenomenon provides further support for the principle of higher level activation. When an extraneous noise such as a cough or pure tone acoustically obliterates a speech sound in a word, the word sounds completely normal and subjects are unable to tell which speech sound has been obliterated (Warren, 1970). For example, when subjects

---

[3]One should not infer here that we are more aware of phonological segments in production than perception (because phonological nodes normally become activated during production but not during perception). Activation is only one of several conditions necessary for awareness.

listen to a sentence containing the word *legi*lature,* where the *s* has been masked by a cough*, the word sounds intact, and the missing *s* sounds as real and as clear as the remaining acoustically present phonemes (Warren, 1970). The subjects somehow synthesized the missing *s* and when informed that the cough replaced a single speech sound were unable to identify what sound is missing.[4]

The question of how this perceptual synthesis occurs is readily answered under the principle of higher level activation. For example, consider the sentence "The state governors met with their respective legi*latures convening in the capital city" (from Warren, 1970). Lexical content nodes become activated first under the principle of higher level activation, and for the word *legi*lature, legislature*(noun) will acquire greatest priming: even though the *s* has been obliterated in the acoustic waveform, no other node in the (noun) domain is likely to acquire as much top-down (contextual) and bottom-up priming. *Legislature*(noun) therefore becomes activated under the most-primed-wins principle and contributes top-down priming to its connected nodes, including *is*(vowel group) and *s* (final consonant group). By applying the most-primed-wins principle to the (final consonant group) domain, the *s* node can therefore become activated, causing clear perception of the obliterated *s.*

Consider now the cough and why it isn't perceived in its true (isomorphic) position in the sequence of speech sounds. The cough* is represented by nodes that are unconnected to the speech perception nodes—there are no nodes and serial order rules for representing the vowel group *i*,* syllable *gi*,* word *legi*lature* or lexical concept "legi*lature." This explains why the cough is poorly localized with respect to the speech sounds and why (in part) the cough seems to coexist in a separate perceptual space from the sentence (see Warren & Warren, 1970). Nonspeech noises are perceived via separate content and sequence nodes in a different perceptual system, analogous in some ways to a separate sensory system, even though speech and nonspeech noises share the same basilar membrane.

The Recognition of Segments Versus Syllables. The time it takes subjects to identify a segment versus a syllable within a sequence of nonsense syllables provides further support for the principle of higher level activation. The original experiment by Savin and Bever (1970) can be used for purposes of illustration because subsequent studies have replicated their basic findings and come to the same basic conclusion (see Massaro, 1979). Savin and Bever (1970) had subjects listen to a sequence of nonsense syllables with the aim of detecting a target unit

---

[4]Warren introduced an ingeneous control procedure to ensure that the missing sound was truly missing. In the control procedure, a word such as *legislature* was "mispronounced" as e.g., *legiklature,* and the mispronounced segment was replaced by the cough*. The results showed that again the subjects synthesized the missing *s.* Clearly then, this synthesis does not derive from coarticulatory cues present within the acoustic waveform because these cues differ for *s* versus *k.*

as quickly as possible. There were three types of targets; an entire syllable e.g., *splay*, the vowel within the syllable, i.e., *ay*, or the initial consonant of the syllable, i.e., *s*. The subjects pressed a key as soon as they detected their target and the surprising result was that reaction times were faster for syllable targets than for segment targets, either the initial consonant or the vowel in the syllable. Syllables apparently become perceived first, with perception of phonemes coming later.

These findings cannot be explained if all nodes in an input hierarchy must become activated, or if lower level activation is always necessary for higher level activation. However, the principle of higher level activation readily explains these findings: The subjects activated only the higher level (syllable) nodes on first encounter with the nonsense syllables, enabling immediate perceptual recognition of the syllable targets. Perception of the segment targets required an extra step: activation of segment nodes via multiplication of priming from the appropriate sequence node.

Aphasic Deficits. The principle of higher level activation predicts an asymmetry in the effects of brain damage on perception versus production (see MacKay, 1985) that receives support from recent studies of expressive and receptive deficits in aphasic, that is, the principle of higher level activation predicts that some lesions will impair only production whereas other lesions will impair both perception and production. Specifically, if a lesion selectively damages content nodes, then both production and perception will suffer under the theory. Selective damage to *sentential* sequence and/or timing nodes will likewise impair both production and comprehension, although the patient may still be able to produce and recognize *phonological* components. However, selective damage to *phonological* sequence and/or timing nodes will severely impair production, but will leave perception intact. The reason is that *phonological* sequence and timing nodes are unnecessary for the perception of common words, because phonological content nodes don't normally become activated (the principle of higher level activation). Moreover, for patients with intact comprehension, the theory predicts a specific type of production deficit involving the sequencing and timing of phonological components (see MacKay, 1985).

PERCEPTUAL ERRORS

As Freud (1901) and Meringer and Mayer (1895) pointed out, perceptual errors provide a means of (1) infering the otherwise hidden mechanisms of everyday speech perception, and (2) "testing" existing theories of perception, because theories that are incapable of explaining the errors that occur are incomplete or inadequate as accounts of the mechanisms underlying "veridical" perception. In this section I show how the node structure theory explains the regularities in perceptual errors that have been observed so far. I then outline some predicted regularities for future test.

Regularities in Perceptual Errors

In misperceptions collected from everyday speech, the misperceived units range in scope from distortions of entire words and phrases (e.g., *popping really slow* misperceived as *prodigal son*) to single features (e.g., *pit* misperceived as *bit*), and middle components of a word are more likely to be misheard than those at the ends (Browman, 1980). However, about 85% of all misperceptions are simple word substitutions: The listener mishears one word as another. This preponderance of word substitutions suggests that the word constitutes a particularly important unit in speech perception. Indeed, misperceptions almost never give rise to nonwords, as might be expected if words and phonemes had identical status as units in everyday speech perception. The principle of higher level activation readily explains why words predominate over nonwords in perceptual substitutions.

Slips of the ear sometimes resemble slips of the tongue (see Browman, 1980). By way of illustration, consider the misperception of *carcinoma* for *Barcelona* in the case of an individual who is for the moment concerned or preoccupied with this particular disease. Such substitutions represent a perceptual analogue of the Freudian slip and receive a parallel explanation under the node structure theory (See MacKay's (1982) explanation of Freudian slips). In this particular example, the perceptual substitution occurs because priming for *carcinoma*(noun), arising from the preoccupation (top-down) and from aspects of the acoustic stimulus (bottom-up) exceeds the priming for *Barcelona*(noun) arising from the input itself. As a consequence, the extraneous node *carcinoma*(noun) becomes activated under the most-primed-wins principle.

However, the similarities between errors in production versus perception are less striking than the asymmetries. One of these asymmetries bears on the distinction between mental, muscle movement, and sensory analysis nodes (see Fig. 12.1). For example, by masking incoming speech sounds, environmental noises can cause misperceptions but not misproductions, an asymmetry that follows directly from the independence of sensory analysis and muscle movement nodes. Less obviously but for the same reason, whole classes of production errors are absent from perception. An example is stuttering, a class of production errors that simply never occurs in perception. No one misperceives someone to say *pppplease* when they in fact said *please*. This asymmetry suggests that stuttering may usually originate within the system of muscle movement nodes (see MacKay & MacDonald, 1984) that are independent of both mental and sensory analysis nodes for perceiving speech.

The structure of bottom-up versus top-down connections contributes another set of asymmetries to errors in production versus perception. Thus, ambiguity causes problems for perception (see MacKay, 1970a) but not for production, because the top-down connections to lexical nodes are unique: The top-down connections from a node such as *the tall crane*(noun phrase) go to the node representing either one or the other of the meanings of *crane* (i.e., *crane 1*, the mechanical hoist, or *crane 2*, the bird) but not to both. By way of contrast, bottom-up connections are nonunique, so that an ambiguous word such as *crane* primes both *crane* 1(noun) and *crane* 2(noun).

On the other hand, psychological synonymy (see MacKay, 1973b) causes errors in production but not perception. Blends are the production errors. An example is *sotally*, a combination of the words *solely* and *totally* that occured in the context "He was sotally (solely/totally) responsible for that." Under the theory, blends occur whenever two nodes in the same domain, e.g., *solely*(adverb) and *totally*(adverb) receive exactly equal priming and via multiplication of priming become simultaneously activated. Lower level components of either one word or the other then become activated automatically depending on which one receives the most priming (see MacKay, 1973b), giving rise to errors such as *sotally*. Errors resembling blends never occur in perception because bottom-up priming from an acoustic input uniquely primes one or the other of the nodes representing synonyms.

Predicted Asymmetries between Perceptual Versus Production Errors

The node structure theory predicts three systematic differences that remain to be tested between slips of the tongue versus slips of the ear.

The Phonological Similarity Prediction. The node structure theory predicts that phonological similarity will play much more of a role in misperceptions than misproductions. As discussed earlier, production errors *sometimes* involve similar sounding words, but under the node structure theory, misperceptions should *virtually always* involve similar sounding words such as *carcinoma* and *Barcelona*. The reason is that bottom-up priming converges and summates to such an extent on the input side, that misperceptions must incorporate most of the phonological components of the actual input. However, during *production,* bottom-up priming only converges on nodes which are undergoing self-inhibition as a result of recent activation. As a consequence, only divergent bottom-up priming can cause phonologically similar word substitutions during production, and because divergent priming is second-order and relatively weak, the theory predicts that production errors will less frequently involve similar sounding words.

The Sequential Domain Prediction. The theory predicts that sequential class will play more of a role in misproductions than misperceptions. In production errors, words almost invariably substitute words from within the same sequential domain or syntactic class e.g., nouns interchange with other nouns and never with verbs or adjectives (see Fromkin, 1973; MacKay, 1979), but the theory predicts that misperceptions will frequently violate this syntactic class constraint. An example violation is the misperception of "descriptive" (an adjective) as "the script of" (a determiner, a noun, and a preposition, respectively) (from Browman, 1980).

In production, output alternatives are limited to a single sequential domain: Errors can only occur when an extraneous node in the same sequential domain as the intended word achieves greatest priming when the sequence node becomes activated. However, in perception, listeners cannot know with certainty what chunk of the acoustic waveform constitutes a word let alone what sequential class the word belongs to. Perceptual alternatives are not confined to a single sequential domain: Many sequence nodes become primed to some extent and an extraneous sequence node can sometimes receive greatest priming and become activated in violation of the syntactic class constraint. Thus, in the earlier example, *descriptive*(adjective) may receive and pass on less priming to its sequence node than *the*(determiner), *script*(noun) and *of*(preposition), in part because of the lexical frequency of *the* and *of* but perhaps also because of top-down (expectation) priming of *script*(noun). As a consequence, the extraneous sequence nodes DETERMINER, NOUN, and PREPOSITION become activated rather than ADJECTIVE and cause the observed violations of the syntactic class constraint.

The Sequential Error Prediction. Sequential errors involve the misordering of words or speech sounds just uttered or about to be uttered and are quite common in production. An example at the phonological level is the misproduction *coat thrutting* for *throat cutting* (from Fromkin, 1973). An analogous example at the sentential level is *We have a laboratory in our computer* for *We have a computer in our laboratory* (from Fromkin, 1973).

The node structure theory predicts many more sequential errors for production than for perception. One reason is that temporal sequences must be "constructed" during production but come built in during perception. Another reason is that the convergent bottom-up summation of priming that occurs in perception but not in production strongly constrains perceptual errors to resemble the actual input, and prevent sequential errors in perception which involve phonologically dissimilar words such as *laboratory* and *computer* in the earlier example.

ASYMMETRIES BETWEEN PRODUCTION AND PERCEPTION

I now examine how the node structure theory explains some additional, already observed asymmetries between perception versus production.

The Maximal Rate Asymmetry. The most striking difference between speech perception and production is that we can perceive speech at a faster rate than we can produce it. Foulke and Sticht (1969) summarized the evidence on the perception of speech sounds accelerated by means of computers that sample and compress acoustic signals without introducing pitch changes. The data indicate that compressed speech becomes difficult to comprehend and remember but remains highly intelligible up to 400 words per minute or about 30 ms per phoneme. In contrast, *producing* speech of equivalent intelligibility at remotely comparable rates is well beyond human capacity.

What accounts for this maximal rate asymmetry? An explanation in terms of the time and effort required to physically move articulators such as the jaw has several problems. One is the data on the rate of internal speech, which of course involves no movement of the articulators whatsoever. For example, MacKay (1981) had subjects produce sentences internally as rapidly as possible, pressing a key as they began and finished each sentence. Then after a 20-sec. pause the subjects repeated the same sentence internally, and so on, for a total of 12 practice trials at maximal rate. As expected, the maximal rate of internal speech increased systematically with practice but approached asymptote at about 100 ms per phoneme after seven practice trials. Although this asymptote is considerably faster than the maximal rate for producing these same sentences aloud and with equivalent amounts of practice, it nevertheless remains much slower than the 30 ms per phoneme rate for the perception of compressed speech. Because no movement of the articulators takes place during internal speech, this remaining difference indicates that muscle movement factors cannot completely explain the maximal rate asymmetry. However, the differences between perceptual vs. production processes discussed here provide a straightforward explanation. For example, activation takes time, and because not all nodes become activated during perception (the principle of higher level activation) perception can proceed at a faster rate than production. Similarly, the convergent summation of priming that occurs in perception but not production means that when it occurs, activation can proceed more quickly during perception than during production (see MacKay, 1982).

The Listening Practice Asymmetry. MacKay and Bowman (1969) reported a "conceptual practice effect" with an interesting but asymmetric counterpart on the perceptual side. The 1969 subjects were German-English bilinguals, who were presented with sentences one at a time and simply produced each sentence as rapidly as possible. An example is "In one corner of the room stood three young men." Following a 20-sec. pause, the sentence was presented again, for a total of 12 repetitions of the same sentence. Half the sentences were in English and the other half in German. The independent variable was practice and the dependent variable was the time to produce the sentence.

Practice had a significant effect: The rate of speech was 15% faster for the last 4 than the first 4 practice trials even though the subjects were attempting always to speak at their maximum rate. After practicing the sentence 12 times, the subjects received a "transfer" sentence in their other language, which they also produced at maximal rate. This transfer sentence was either a nontranslation (unrelated to the original sentence in meaning, syntax, and phonology) or a translation (with identical meaning but different phonology and word order from the original). The surprising finding was that subjects produced the translations significantly faster than the nontranslations (2.44 sec. per sentence vs. 2.24 sec. per sentence), indicating an effect of practice at the lexical concept level and above (see MacKay, 1982, for details and explanation).

Consider now the *perceptual* analogue of this conceptual practice effect. A *listening practice* condition was presented to determine whether repeated *listening* to a sentence leads to a conceptual facilitation effect similar to the physical practice condition discussed earlier. Twelve German-English bilinguals listened to a tape recording of the sentences repeated 12 times at maximal rate by the previous subjects. To ensure that subjects in this listening practice condition were paying attention to the input, they were instructed to indicate whether changes or errors occurred from one repetition to the next.

A transfer phase, identical to that in the physical practice condition, followed the 12 listening practice trials. During this transfer phase, subjects in the listening practice condition produced out loud and at maximal rate a sentence that was either a translation or a nontranslation of the sentence they had heard repeated 12 times, and as before, production times were faster for translations (2.31 sec.) than nontranslations (2.57 sec.), a 10% facilitation comparable to the 8% for physical practice. This facilitation effect is readily explained under the mental node hypothesis and suggests that repeated listening may suffice to develop the mental skill underlying the conceptual practice effect.

However, there was an asymmetry: Production times in the listening practice condition were longer than those in the physical practice condition, both for nontranslations (6% longer) and for translations (3% longer). One explanation of this statistically reliable difference is that subjects were less highly motivated during listening practice than during physical practice. However, we cannot yet rule out the more interesting possibility that physical practice is genuinely superior to listening practice. Listening practice may strengthen bottom-up connections while leaving top-down connections relatively weak, thereby facilitating performance less than physical practice, even for the highest conceptual levels of the skill.

The Word Production Asymmetry. Differences between perception versus production in the node structure theory help explain the word production asymmetry: the fact that we can usually recognize and understand a word long before we can use it in everyday speech production (Clark & Hecht, 1983). The main requirement for *recognizing* a word in the theory is the existence of previously formed bottom-up connections from phonological and sensory analysis nodes. However, *producing* the word requires the formation of several additional types of connections, which together may delay development of the production vocabulary. One is top-down connections from the lexical content node to the appropriate phonological and muscle movement nodes. Another is inhibitory connections between sequence nodes, which enable sequential production.

The Detection-Correction Asymmetry. Differences between detecting self-produced versus other-produced errors illustrate an additional asymmetry between perception versus production: Whereas speakers correct their own errors with about equal frequency across units of different size (Nooteboom, 1980), listeners detect errors involving larger units such as words with much higher frequency than errors involving smaller units such as phonemes and phoneme clusters (Tent & Clark, 1980). Thus listeners most easily detect errors which cause an obviously deviant meaning, whereas speakers detect all types of errors with equal sensitivity (see Cutler, 1982). This equi-sensitivity for the speaker is readily explained in the node structure theory: Output errors occur when an inappropriate node at any level in a hierarchy becomes activated, no matter what the size of the surface units involved (segment, segment clusters, syllables, or phrases), which predicts that speakers will perceive and correct errors about equally often for small versus large units (all other factors being equal).

The Missing Feedback Effect. Verbal transformation experiments illustrate another interesting asymmetry between perception versus production: the missing feedback effect. In the typical verbal transformation study, subjects listen to an acoustically presented word repeated via tape loop for a prolonged period and report hearing changes in the stimulus (Warren, 1968). For example, after many repetitions, subjects might misperceive the word *police* as *fleas, please* or *fleece*. These illusory changes are explained as follows under the node structure theory. When the word *police* is presented for the first time, it strongly primes the lexical concept node *police*(noun), and primes other nodes such as *fleas*(noun) and *fleece*(noun) to a lesser extent (depending on their phonological similarity to *police*), so that only *police*(noun) becomes activated under the most-primed-wins principle. However, after *repeated* presentation, the nodes for *police* become fatigued and respond less strongly, so that eventually *police*(noun) acquires less priming than say, *fleece*(noun), which therefore becomes activated under the most-primed-wins principle. The result is illusory perception of *fleece,* along with increasingly rapid perceptual shifts between the various other alternatives (*fleas, please, police, fleece*).

Consider now the missing feedback effect. Lackner (1974) had subjects repeat a word every 500 msec for several minutes and then listen to a recording of their own output. The subjects experienced the usual verbal transformations when they subsequently *listened* to the tape recording of their own output but reported no perceptual transformations whatsoever when *producing* the word. This asymmetry is curious because the acoustic events at the ear are identical in the two conditions. Why don't self-produced auditory inputs cause verbal transformations? Lackner (1974) and Warren (1968) attribute the missing feedback effect to a corollary discharge that accompanies the motor command to produce a word. This corollary discharge cancels or inhibits the external (proprioceptive and auditory) feedback resulting from producing the word, so that self-produced auditory inputs fail to induce the perceptual changes that occur in the typical verbal transformation experiment. However, the corollary discharge hypothesis has difficulty explaining both the many interactions between speech perception and production (discussed earlier) and aspects of Lackner's own data, namely that no *production errors* resembling the perception errors occurred when the subjects were repeating the words.

The node structure theory explains all of these phenomena by means of a common mechanism: the self-inhibition that follows activation of mental nodes. Under the theory, the mental nodes for producing and perceiving a word such as *police* are identical. As a consequence, when someone *produces* the word *police*, auditory feedback returns as priming to some of the just-activated nodes that produced it but arrives during their self-inhibitory phase and therefore has no effect. This explains why self-produced repeated inputs fail to cause verbal transformations, the missing feedback effect.

Consider now the absence of output errors during repeated *production* of a word. Repeating the word *police* causes fatigue of the corresponding mental nodes, but because top-down priming is unique (as aforementioned), only *police*(noun) and no other lexical node receives systematically increasing priming and becomes activated under the most-primed-wins principle. This reduces the likelihood of *production* errors resembling the ones that occur in perception and explains this additional asymmetry between the perception versus production of speech.

CONCLUSIONS

The asymmetries discussed earlier present problems for theories that assume a symmetric relation between processes for perception and production (see Gordon & Meyer, 1984). Identical components can represent both perception and production (the mental node hypothesis) in these theories, but perceptual processes are simply the reverse of the corresponding production processes, like the bidirectional reactions in chemical formulas (see Fodor, Bever, & Garrett, 1974).

This symmetry assumption is both simple and attractive: It enables researchers to devote all their efforts to studying perception, because solving the problem of perception also solves the problem of production under the symmetry assumption. Indeed, the appeal of the symmetry assumption may explain why psycholinguistics has until recently focused almost exclusively on perception rather than production or the relation between the two (see Fodor, Bever, & Garrett, 1974). However, the asymmetries discussed earlier indicate that studies of perception are by themselves insufficient and that comparisons of perception and production are both necessary and theoretically important. To further stimulate such comparisons, I conclude with a summary of the processes in the node structure theory that are asymmetric between production versus perception. Although some of these asymmetries have already received mention under other headings, summarizing them here provides a sharp contrast with "symmetrical" theories of the relation between production and perception.

The Sequential Activation Asymmetry. The logical order for activating mental nodes in production and perception is asymmetric under the node structure theory. By way of example, the numbers in Fig. 12.2 indicate the order in which the sentential nodes illustrated there must be activated during production (1, 2, 3, 4, 5), and the symmetry assumption requires the reverse order of activation during perception (5, 4, 3, 2, 1). However, this reverse order is logically impossible. If perception is to be error free and activation takes place during perception, the sequence must be something like 3, 4, 2, 5, 1 (where the numbers represent the corresponding nodes in Fig. 12.2 and left to right represents order of activation).

Convergent Versus Divergent Connections. Another important asymmetry between top-down versus bottom-up processes in the node structure theory stems from the fact that top-down connections are divergent or one-to-many in nature whereas bottom-up connections are convergent or many-to-one. The many implications of this asymmetry have already been discussed.

The Principle of Higher Level Activation. Under the principle of higher level activation, only higher level nodes become activated during everyday perception. Because of their linkage strength, timing characteristics, and convergent summation, lower level nodes pass on priming so efficiently that activation is unnecessary. This stands in contrast with production, where every node in the hierarchy must become activated if the output is to occur in proper serial order.

The Uniqueness Asymmetry. Top-down priming is generally unique: Only a single node in a given domain normally receives first-order top-down priming at any given time. Bottom-up priming, on the other hand is generally nonunique: more than one node in a domain normally receives first-order priming at any one time.

In conclusion, a great deal remains to be done to test and further develop the node structure theory. I am also aware of the sketchy and incomplete treatment here of various complex and sometimes controversial issues. Moreover, the sketchiness sometimes reflects multiple causes; both lack of space and lack of available data. For example, consider the perception and production of different types of phonological features. Like Cooper, Billings, and Cole (1976), Meyer and Gordon (1983) observed interactions between perceiving and producing the voicing feature but Gordon and Meyer (1984) found no such interactions for place of articulation. Cooper, Billings, and Cole (1976) likewise experienced difficulty using the selective adaptation technique to demonstrate interactions between perceiving versus producing place of articulation. Perhaps the sensory analysis and muscle movement nodes that represent what we now call place of articulation are connected directly with segment nodes, with no intervening mental nodes for representing place of articulation per se. Although this would explain the missing interaction, it seems too early, given our current state of knowledge, to commit a general theory on this issue: Omitting the issue was multiply determined.

Consider now the relation between the node structure theory and other theories of speech and cognitive skill. Like the motor theory of speech perception, the node structure theory gives speech a special place among systems for perception and action. Speech stimuli can be self-produced whereas one rarely produces stimuli such as the visual world (except marginally in drawing or writing). The node structure theory also makes speech special by incorporating a speech mode of perception, which is distinct from other perceptual modes: One and the same stimulus can be processed in the speech mode by activating the sequence nodes for the phonological system or in an auditory concept mode by activating the sequence nodes for the auditory concept system. The staggering degree of practice that speech normally receives (see MacKay, 1981, 1982) also makes speech special in the theory, as does the self-inhibitory mechanism that content nodes for speech require to deal with self-produced feedback. However, speech is not *fundamentally special* in the theory because similar node structures and degrees of practice can in principle be achieved for other perceptual and motor systems (see MacKay, 1985). Moreover, although different perceptual modes (systems) differ in nodes and perhaps also node structures (pattern of connections), they do not differ in fundamental principles of activation.

The node structure theory also bears a general resemblance to recent theories of word recognition (McClelland & Rumelhart, 1981) and of typing (Norman & Rumelhart, 1983) and participates in the current trend toward a focus on dynamic or process issues, in addition to static or structural ones. Like other recent theories, the node structure theory is concerned with underlying mechanisms and has the potential for mapping psychological constructs onto neuroanatomical ones (see MacKay, 1985), an exciting prospect because, as Ojemann (1983) points out, some such mapping seems essential for cracking the code of the brain.

However, the node structure theory provides some genuinely new mechanisms, units, and predictions. For example, the most-primed-wins principle bears a general resemblance to a principle built into McClelland and Rumelhart's (1981) theory of word recognition, but in order to produce speech as well as to recognize words, the node structure theory incorporates a fundamentally different (and much simpler) mechanism for achieving this principle.

The node structure theory also summarizes a wealth of results that in large measure are not accounted for in other theories and that have previously been considered to fall within four separate areas of inquiry: neuropsychology, psycholinguistics, cybernetics, and motor control. To complete the unification of these areas requires a great deal more theoretical and empirical work, and to achieve our ultimate goal, a unified theory of skill (speech being only one, albeit highly proficient example), will engage the field for many decades to come.

ACKNOWLEDGMENTS

The author thanks Robert Bowman for assistance in running the experiment and Drs. Dom Massaro, Herbert Heuer, Douglas Mewhort, Richard Warren, and Bill Cooper for comments on an earlier draft. This chapter was completed while the author was a member of the Perception and Action Research Group at the Center for Interdisciplinary Research (Z.i.F.) at the University of Bielefeld. The author acknowledges the support of Z.i.F. with appreciation.

REFERENCES

Browman, C. P. (1980). Perceptual processing: Evidence from slips of the ear. In V. A. Fromkin (Ed.), *Errors in linguistic performance: Slips of the tongue, ear, pen and hand* (p. 213–230). New York: Academic Press.

Clark, E. V., & Hecht, B. F. (1983). Comprehension, production and language acquisition. *Annual Review of Psychology, 34,* 325–49.

Clark, H. H., & Clark, E. V. (1977). *Psychology and language.* New York: Harcourt, Brace, Jovanovich.

Cooper, W. E., Billings, D., & Cole, R. A. (1976). Articulatory effects on speech perception: A second report. *Journal of Phonetics, 4,* 219–32.

Cooper, W. E., Blumstein, S. E., & Nigro, G. (1975). Articulatory effect on speech perception: A preliminary report. *Journal of Phonetics, 3,* 87–98.

Cooper, W. E., & Nager, R. M. (1975). Perceptuo-motor adaptation to speech: An analysis of bisyllabic utterances and a neural model. *Journal of the Acoustic Society of America, 58,* (1), 256–265.

Cutler, A. (1982). The reliability of speech error data. In A. Cutler (Ed.), *Slips of the tongue and language production* (pp. 7–28). Amsterdam: Mouton.

Fodor, J. A., Bever, T. G., & Garrett, M. F. (1974). *The psychology of language.* New York: McGraw–Hill.

Foulke, E., & Sticht, T. (1969). Review of research on the intelligibility and comprehension of accelerated speech. *Psychological Bulletin, 72,* 50–62.

Freud, S. (1901). *Psychopathology of everyday life* (A. A. Brill, trans. 1914). New York: Penguin.
Fromkin, V. A. (1973). Appendix. In F. A. Fromkin (Ed.), *Speech errors as linguistic evidence*. Paris: Mouton.
Gordon, P. C., & Meyer, D. E. (1984). Perceptual-motor processing of phonetic features in speech. *Journal of Experimental Psychology: Human Perception and Performance, 10*, (1), 153-178.
Klapp, S. T., Anderson, W. G., & Berrian, R. W. (1973). Implicit speech in reading reconsidered. *Journal of Experimental Psychology, 100*, 368-74.
Kozhevnikov, V. A., & Chistovich, L. A. (1965). *Speech articulation and perception*. Washington: *Joint Publications Research Service*.
Lackner, J. (1974). Speech production: Evidence for corollary discharge stabilization of perceptual mechanisms. *Perceptual and Motor skills, 39*, 899-902.
Lashley, K. S. (1951). The problem of serial order in behavior. In L. A. Jeffress (Ed.), *Cerebral mechanisms in behavior* (p. 112-136). New York: Wiley.
Leeper, R. A. (1936). A study of a neglected portion of the field of learning: The development of sensory organization. *Journal of Genetic Psychology, 46*, 42-75.
Liberman, A. M., Cooper, F. S., Harris, K. S., & MacNeilage, P. F. (1962). A motor theory of speech perception. In *Proceedings of the speech communication seminar*. Stockholm: Royal Institute of Technology.
Lisker, L. (1978). *Rapid* vs. *rabid:* A catalogue of acoustic features that may cue the distinction. *Haskins Laboratories Status Report on Speech Research, 54*, 127-132.
McClelland, J. C., & Rumelhart, D. E. (1981). An interactive-activation model of context effects in letter perception: Part 1. An account of basic findings. *Psychological Review, 88*, 375-407.
McGurk, H., & MacDonald, J. (1976). Hearing lips and seeing voices. *Nature, 264*, 746-748.
MacKay, D. G. (1970a). Mental diplopia: Towards a model of speech perception at the semantic level. In I. D'Arcais & W. J. M. Levelt (Eds.), *Recent advances in psycholinguistics* (p. 76-100). Amsterdam: North-Holland.
MacKay, D. G. (1970b). How does language familiarity influence stuttering under delayed auditory feedback? *Perceptual and Motor Skills, 30*, 655-669.
MacKay, D. G. (1972). The structure of words and syllables: Evidence from errors in speech. *Cognitive Psychology, 3*, 210-227.
MacKay, D. G. (1973a). Aspects of the theory of comprehension, memory and attention. *Quarterly Journal of Experimental Psychology, 25*, 22-40.
MacKay, D. G. (1973b). Complexity in output systems: Evidence from behavioral hybrids. *American Journal of Psychology, 86*(4), 785-806.
MacKay, D. G. (1978). Speech errors inside the syllable. In A. Bell & J. B. Hooper (Eds.), *Syllables and segments*. Amsterdam: North-Holland.
MacKay, D. G. (1979). Lexical insertion, inflection and derivation: Creative processes in word production. *Journal of Psycholinguistic Research, 8*,(5), 477-498.
MacKay, D. G. (1981). The problem of rehearsal or mental practice. *Journal of Motor Behavior, 13*(4), 274-285.
MacKay, D. G. (1982). The problems of flexibility, fluency and speed-accuracy trade-off in skilled behavior. *Psychological Review, 89*(5), 483-506.
MacKay, D. G. (1985). A theory of the representation, organization and timing of action with implications for sequencing disorders. In E. A. Roy (Ed.), *Neurological studies of apraxia and related disorders*. Amsterdam: North-Holland.
MacKay, D. G. (1986). Self-inhibition and the disruptive effects of internal and external feedback in skilled behavior. In H. Heuer, C. A. M. Brunia, J. A. S. Kelso, & R. A. Schmidt (Eds.), *The generation and modulation of action patterns*. Journal of Experimental Brain Research Supplement. Berlin: Springer.
MacKay, D. G. (in preparation). *The organization of perception and action: Fundamentals of theoretical psychology*.

MacKay, D. G., & Bowman, R. W. (1969). On producing the meaning in sentences. *American Journal of Psychology, 82*(1), 23–39.
MacKay, D. G., & MacDonald, M. (1984). Stuttering as a sequencing and timing disorder. In W. H. Perkins & R. Curlee (Eds.), *Nature and treatment of stuttering: New directions.* San Diego: College–Hill.
Massaro, D. W. (1979). Reading and listening. In P. A. Kolers, M. E. Wrolstad, & H. Bouma (Eds.), *Processing of visible language* (pp. 331–354). New York: Plenum.
Meringer, R., & Mayer, K. (1895). *Versprechen and Verlesen.* Stuttgart: Goschensche Verlagsbuchhandlung.
Meyer, D. E., & Gordon, P. C. (1983). Dependencies between rapid speech perception and production: Evidence for a shared sensory-motor voicing mechanism. In H. Bouma & D. Bouwhuis (Eds.), *Attention and Performance X*. Hillsdale, NJ: Lawrence Erlbaum Associates.
Nooteboom, S. G. (1980). Speaking and unspeaking: Detection and correction of phonological and lexical errors in spontaneous speech. In V. A. Fromkin (Ed.), *Errors in linguistic performance. Slips of the tongue, ear, pen and hand.* New York: Academic Press.
Norman, D. (1981). Categorization of action slips. *Psychological Review, 88*(1), 1–15.
Norman, D. A., & Rumelhart, D. E. (1983). Studies of typing from the LNR research group. In W. E. Cooper (Ed.), *Cognitive aspects of skilled typewriting* (pp. 45–66). New York: Springer–Verlag.
Ojemann, G. A. (1983). Brain organization for language from the perspective of electrical stimulation mapping. *The Behavioral and Brain Sciences, 2,* 189–230.
Porter, R. J., & Lubker, J. F. (1980). Rapid reproduction of vowel-vowel sequences: Evidence for a fast and direct acoustic-motor linkage in speech. *Journal of Speech and Hearing Research, 23,* 593–602.
Savin, H. B., & Bever, T. E. (1970). The nonperceptual reality of the phoneme. *Journal of Verbal Learning and Verbal Behavior, 9,* 295–302.
Spoer, K. T., & Smith, E. E. (1973). The role of syllables in perceptual processing. *Cognitive Psychology, 5,* 71–89.
Straight, S. (1980). Auditory vs. articulatory phonological processes and their development in children. In G. H. Yeni-Komshian, J. F. Kavanagh, & C. A. Ferguson (Eds.), *Child phonology: Vol. 1. Production.* New York: Academic Press.
Studdert-Kennedy, M., Liberman, A. M., Harris, K. S., & Cooper, F. S. (1970). The motor theory of speech perception: A reply to Lane's critical review. *Psychological Review, 77,* 234–249.
Tent, J., & Clark, J. E. (1980). An experimental investigation into the perception of slips of the tongue. *Journal of phonetics, 8,* 317–25.
Treiman, R. (1983). The structure of spoken syllables: Evidence from novel word games. *Cognition, 15,* 49–74.
Warren, R. M. (1968). Verbal transformation effect and auditory perceptual mechanisms. *Psychological Bulletin, 70,* 261–270.
Warren, R. M. (1970). Perceptual restoration of missing speech sounds. *Science, 167,* 392–3.
Warren, R. M. (1982). *Auditory perception: A new synthesis.* New York: Pergamon Press.
Warren, R. M., & Warren, R. P. (1970). Auditory illusions and confusions. *Scientific American, 223,* 30–36.
Woodworth, R. S. (1938). *Experimental Psychology.* New York: Holt.

13 Information Stores and Mechanisms: Early Stages of Visual Processing

D. J. K. Mewhort
Queen's University at Kingston,
and
University of Bielefeld

Suppose that a subject is shown a row of letters and is asked to name as many letters from the display as possible. If the letters spell a word, the subject may name the word rather than list the letter names. This chapter describes the mental activity involved in preparing the internal representation needed for such naming tasks. I start by outlining a model for tachistoscopic naming tasks that has been presented elsewhere (Mewhort & Campbell, 1981). After outlining the model, I show how it deals with sequential responses in whole-report letter naming and then show how it applies to word identification. In addition, I summarize how the model deals with two partial-report tasks, and I use the partial-report examples to discuss how the model fits with recent analyses of attention in vision. I conclude by reviewing some new evidence concerning the separation of stages described by the model.

THE NATURE OF THE MODEL

The model has been formulated in terms of an information-processing system and consists of a series of data buffers and data processors. The buffers are structured data stores that hold information temporarily, and the processors are mechanisms that carry out operations on the stored information, including operations that compress or abstract information taken from the display, operations that transform the data from one structured representation to another, and operations that add orthographic information to the data taken from the display. In addition to the main buffers, the processors may require local memory to store definitions and rules. Orthographic information, for example, is stored in local memory attached to the processors that apply it.

Within the constraints specified by interfacing rules, the data buffers and processing mechanisms described in the model can be used in several different combinations. Tasks that involve a multiletter sequential report, for example, will require both a temporally extended buffer to hold material during report and a processor to transform data from the initial parallel structure to the sequential one. Tasks that require report of only a single letter, in contrast, will not invoke such a processor, unless some other aspect of the task requires a temporally organized store. Because different tasks impose different processing requirements, they require a different subset of buffers and processing mechanisms. In general, we can think of each task's combination of buffers and processors as a processing system built in response to particular requirements; building a processing system amounts to ordering, assembling, and co-ordinating an appropriate set of processors and buffers for that specific task.

In developing the model, Mewhort and Campbell (1981) assigned responsibility for building an appropriate processing system for each experimental task to a problem-solving procedure, called the executive (see Logan, 1984, for a similar conception). The executive knows what buffers and processors are available to it, what function each can perform, and, hence, how each can contribute to the behaviour required.

To build a system for a particular experimental task, the executive starts by forming an internal representation of the task's requirements or goals. The representation is an internal description of the task from the subject's point of view. In virtually all cases, the experimenter provides the information needed to form the internal representation of the task's goals by virtue of his instructions to the subject. The executive takes information from the experimenter's description and combines it with its knowledge of the available mechanisms to form its internal representation.

After forming a representation of the experimental task's goals and requirements, the executive uses its representation to derive a processing system appropriate to the task; it compares the internal representation of the task against its inventory of processors and data buffers. The task may require the executive to formulate sub-goals repeatedly until it finds a match, that is, until it finds sub-goals that can be met with an appropriate sequence of existing mechanisms. Once the executive has derived a system by finding a match, it assembles the system by arranging the mechanisms in the correct order. The main constraints on the arrangements that can be built reflect, first, the limited number of mechanisms available and, second, the interfacing rules for successive mechanisms. Once the system has been assembled, the executive invokes the assembled system to perform the experimental task. Thus, from the perspective of the model, the processing systems that we study using "simple" experimental tachistoscopic tasks are constructed systems; they represent the executive's understanding of the experimental task in relation to the resources available to it.

BUFFERS AND PROCESSORS IN TACHISTOSCOPIC TASKS

The mechanisms available to the executive for use in tachistoscopic tasks include three structured data buffers and five processing mechanisms. By a structured buffer, I mean that the buffer is constructed from elements that preserve relations among the data contained in the buffer. In a spatial buffer, for example, in addition to the material contained in the buffer (the contents of the buffer), the structural elements of the buffer preserve spatial relations among the elements, namely distances among elements scaled in appropriate units.

The first two data buffers, named the feature buffer and the character buffer, are short-term spatial stores; they provide parallel access to their data. Both the contents and the structural elements of the first two buffers are subject to decay over an interval of about a second. The third buffer is a temporally structured buffer. It is a more permanent store, and it provides serial access to its data. Sequential maintenance operations (rehearsal) are required to sustain data in the temporal buffer after about one second of "free" storage.

Both *spatial buffers* preserve data in two-dimensional structures: The feature buffer holds precategorical feature elements; space is represented in the structure of the buffer and can be described in terms of a two-dimensional coordinate system. The *character buffer* holds postcategorical characters; space is represented in the structure of the buffer and can be described in terms of a two-dimensional coordinate system with integer coordinates. Attributes derived from the initial feature representation, such as color, are also represented. The *third buffer* holds postcategorical letters; time is represented in the structure of the buffer and can be described in terms of a vector with integer coordinates. In all three cases, of course, the contents of the buffer are abstract elements.

The third buffer shares some characteristics of traditional conceptions of short-term or working memory. The emphasis in traditional conceptions concerns coding systems, including systems based on phonemic, articulatory, and acoustic codes. The term code has come to mean a dimension derived from empirical relations concerning interference among presentation and storage conditions (see Richardson, 1984; Sanders, 1975). It is not clear what is meant by a code, in computational terms. Is a code a data structure or a kind of processing? In the present conception, the contents of the third buffer are elements stored in a temporal structure. In the traditional terms of an articulatory code, for example, the contents of the third buffer are better conceived as data for processors dealing with articulation rather than as part of an articulatory data structure. The important point is that the data, structured initially as a simultaneous parallel representation, have been restructured in a temporal representation.

The *first processing mechanism* is a letter-identification mechanism; it uses data in the feature buffer to identify characters and to determine their spatial position. The results of its decisions are data stored in the character buffer.

The *second processing mechanism,* the parser, is a data transformation mechanism; it accepts a string of characters from the character buffer in parallel and repackages the string as a set of syllable-like units. The repackaging rules are based on rules of orthography, and, therefore, the construction of the new units adds information to the data. After constructing the units, the parser passes them sequentially to the temporal buffer. By passing the units sequentially, the parser transforms the data from a parallel structure to a temporal one.

The *third processing mechanism* is an attentional mechanism; like the parser, it also accepts data from the character buffer and passes them to the temporal buffer. Although both mechanisms take data from the character buffer and pass them to the temporal buffer, they are based on quite different principles. The parsing mechanism is based on reading experience and uses orthographic information to assemble new units. The attentional mechanism, in contrast, is a selection device. Unlike the parsing mechanism, the attentional mechanism does not accept all data in parallel, and it does not integrate items to form new groups. Instead, it uses attribute tags or pointers associated with each item to search the character buffer for particular items.

The *fourth processing mechanism* is a rehearsal mechanism which recycles material through the temporal buffer; its purpose is to maintain the material until report. The *fifth processing mechanism* is a comparison mechanism that, like the rehearsal mechanism, uses data from the temporal buffer. Unlike the rehearsal mechanism, however, it does not recycle the data; rather, it uses the data to gain access to the lexicon.

EXAMPLES OF WORKING SYSTEMS

To describe the buffers and processing mechanisms in more detail, I outline how they might be used in three tasks, (1) the whole-report task with both words and pseudo-word stimuli, (2) the bar-probe task with pseudo-word stimuli, and (3) the digit-probe task with pseudo-word stimuli. In each case, I describe the assignment of mechanisms, explain the rationale underlying the assignment, and then review how the assembled systems account for performance. I start with the whole-report task because it illustrates how all three buffers might be used.

THE WHOLE-REPORT TASK

Assignment of Mechanisms in the Whole-Report Task

The whole-report task is, on the surface, quite simple: Characters are presented simultaneously, and subjects are required to report as many as possible. The task requires a processing system that can identify the items, organize a sequential report, and maintain the material until it has been reported.

The executive derives a processing system by considering the report requirements first and then building backward to the stimulus: The report is sequential and is extended in time. Thus, the task requires temporally structured data and a buffer that can store as many items as possible for the period of the report. Both requirements match the characteristics of the temporal buffer. Accordingly, the executive will invoke the temporal buffer. It will also invoke the rehearsal mechanism to sustain the material until report. Because the as-many-as-possible requirement matches the parser's ability to compress information by forming new units, the executive will use it to load the temporal buffer. The remaining parts following from interfacing requirements: Use of the parser implies use of the character buffer to store the data needed by the parser, namely postcategorical characters structured spatially. Use of the character buffer, in turn, requires use of the character identification mechanism and the feature buffer. To provide temporally structured material and to sustain it until report, the assembled system will involve all three buffers and three associated processors, the identification mechanism, the parser, and the rehearsal mechanism.

The Assembled System

The Feature Buffer. Visual feature detectors are memory elements that record the presence or absence of particular visual patterns, such as a line segment, a curve, or an intersection, at a particular location in the visual field. Each detector abstracts an aspect of the visual information. The model postulates that visual feature detectors are positioned to detect features from the whole visual field and that the display sets the current value for each detector. The set of values, that is, the information abstracted from the display, is stored in the first buffer, the feature buffer. The feature buffer preserves the physical characteristics of the display by representing a two-dimensional retinotopic image decomposed into primitive forms. Extent, for example, is represented in the buffer in real-number coordinates: the distance between features can be measured in terms of visual angle.

The quality of the featural representation is determined by structural factors in interaction with experimental manipulations. The amount of light and the contrast ratio of letters against their background, for example, have direct consequences for the quality of the representation. Likewise, acuity in the periphery is lower than in the centre of the visual field. Further, contours from adjacent characters can interact, and their interaction alters the simple acuity function (see Bouma, 1970, 1978). Finally, masking can destroy information in the buffer by writing over it; that is, the mask sets features previously absent and inhibits features currently set. The mask can alter information about both the location and the identity of particular features, and both kinds of information are subject to distortion over time.

Letter Identification. The model postulates an identification mechanism that knows the sub-set of features that comprise each character. After a display has set the values for each feature in the buffer, the identification mechanism notes the values at each position in the buffer and uses its tally to evaluate the weight of evidence for each character at each position. The blank character is a special case: It is defined in terms of the height-width relation of the adjacent nonblank characters. To decide among the candidates at each position, the identification mechanism combines the feature evidence with letter-frequency information (conditional on word length and letter position). Specifically, it uses frequency norms as the prior distribution in a Bayesian decision. The use of frequency information introduces a familiarity effect: The identification mechanism is biased for high-frequency letters (Campbell & Mewhort, 1980).

Information from all positions in the feature buffer is used in parallel; accuracy of identification is limited primarily by the quality of the feature data.

The Character Buffer. The character buffer holds the results derived by the identification mechanism. Whereas the feature buffer held image-like data represented as featural data abstracted from the display, the character buffer contains characters with associated properties or attributes. In contrast to the retinotopic representation at the feature buffer, for example, extent is measured in character units. One can think of spatial representation in the character buffer in terms of a list of items with pointers from an underlying ordinal structure to indicate absolute position information and pointers from letter to letter to indicate relative position. Other facts derived from the featural information—that it appeared in lower case, for example—are also represented as associated properties.

Both pointers and items can be lost over time, and masking can destroy either a letter or a pointer. If a position pointer is lost, the character's position is less clear; if precise position is needed for retrieval, the character may be inaccessible. Although information in the buffer is subject to distortion across time, the rate of loss is modest relative to that for loss of feature information from the feature buffer.

Loading Temporal Memory. The data in the character buffer are processed by the parser. It splits the character string into new units using orthographic rules to decide the boundaries. After the new units have been determined, they are passed to the temporal buffer in left-to-right order. By passing the units in order, the parser alters their form from a spatial to a temporal representation and, thereby, provides a sequential organization for rehearsal and report.

The use of left-to-right ordering reflects reading experience. English speakers spell words from left to right, and for English speaking subjects, left-to-right organization for alphabetic material is strongly biased by that experience (Bryden, 1967). The bias is clearly language based, however: Hebrew speakers develop an equivalent bias from right to left (Tramer, Butler, & Mewhort, 1985).

The parser developed from reading experience, that is, from the experience with a language-specific orthography. The orthographic rules are based on the vowel-consonant distinction and acknowledge certain morphological conventions such as the plural and adverbial suffix, and rules for clustering letters such as diphthongs. Parsing cannot occur without both abstract character information and accurate ordinal information, that is, parsing could not be achieved using the data in the feature buffer without an intervening step that acknowledges letter units.

For words or for pseudo words that conform to the language-specific orthography, the derived units are like syllables. If a pseudo word contains only consonants, however, it would not match any of the rules in the parser's grammar, that is, the parser's orthographic rules would not apply to the string. In such cases, single letters would be taken as units. Finally, when applying its orthographic rules, the parser may alter some characters, that is, it can correct errors produced by the identification mechanism.

Rehearsal and Report. The data in the temporal buffer are maintained by the rehearsal operator until report. The organization for rehearsal is normally based on the order of entry to the temporal buffer. If the circumstances demand it, however, the organization can be changed. If subjects are instructed to report in different orders, for example, rehearsal can be reorganized to suit. The organization of rehearsal must be set within about 750 ms, however, or some of the material will be lost (cf. Scheerer, 1972). In a word-identification trial, the match operator uses the data in the buffer to organize its access to the lexicon.

Applying the Model to Whole-Report Experiments

Because the assembled system is complex, it may be difficult to see how the mechanisms work together. Before I proceed, therefore, I describe how the model explains certain aspects of performance in whole-report tasks. The review is very selective for two reasons: First, the mechanisms that dominate performance in whole report, the scanning mechanism and the rehearsal mechanism, are peripheral to the main topic of the chapter, namely early-processing stores and mechanisms. Second, I have recently provided a review of the scanning and rehearsal mechanisms elsewhere (see Mewhort, 1984).

Order of Report. In whole report, subjects tend to report from left to right (Bryden, 1966; Mewhort, 1966), but the polarization is reduced with masking (Campbell & Mewhort, 1980). The model explains the left-to-right organization in terms of the parsing mechanism, but the relation is indirect: Subjects report from left to right because they rehearse in that order, and they rehearse in that order because the material is loaded into the temporal buffer in that order. Disorder in report introduced by masking reflects the mask's effect on location pointers at the character buffer. By destroying a pointer, the mask reduces the quality of spatial information within the character buffer and, thereby, disrupts the transfer of material to the temporal buffer.

The Familiarity Effects. Subjects can report more letters from a letter string that matches the statistical structure of their language than from a string of unrelated letters (e.g., Miller, Bruner, & Postman, 1954). In terms of the model, the familiarity effect reflects several processing mechanisms: It is not a single effect but a set of separate familiarity effects. The letter-identification mechanism is the first mechanism to contribute to the effect. Its contribution is small and reflects the use of frequency norms during the identification process. The parsing mechanism provides the next contribution. Its contribution is larger and reflects the use of orthographic rules (Mewhort, 1974; Mewhort & Beal, 1977). Rehearsal of material in temporal memory also contributes to the familiarity effect (e.g., Baddeley, 1964; Merikle, 1969); its contribution reflects the relative pronounceability of the units derived by the parsing mechanism. Finally, a modest contribution results from simple response bias during report: Subjects' guesses tend to match the statistical structure of English (see Mewhort, 1967, 1970, for a discussion of response bias).

Assessment of the familiarity effect is a complex problem. One experimental approach is based on the manipulation of stimulus properties. The idea is to see what kind of information the system is sensitive to (Henderson, 1982). A second approach is based on a manipulation of tasks while holding the stimuli constant. The idea, here, is to find tasks that invoke particular processing mechanisms and then to examine the contribution of those mechanisms to the overall familiarity effect.

Both approaches have strengths and weaknesses. The first assumes that orthogonal predictors can be isolated, an assumption that, quite frankly, I doubt can be met. The problem is that stimulus-selection techniques are inherently correlational. Thus, if one varies letter frequency, for example, one may covary featural complexity without intending to do so. Although one can select stimuli according to particular rules, any attempt to force orthogonal predictors leads to an infinite regression: the list of potential covariables is too long. Correlational techniques just do not yield the kind of experimental control one associates with laboratory manipulation. In addition, a pure manipulation of stimulus properties, that is, one made without a corresponding manipulation of tasks, leaves open the possibility that some mechanisms are sensitive to information that other mechanisms ignore.

The second strategy also faces difficulty. In particular, a manipulation of tasks using the same stimuli leaves open the possibility that the system is sensitive to properties not included in the test stimuli. Clearly, some combination of approaches is needed. The assessment of the familiarity effect offered by the model discriminates a number of separate contributors, but because most of the evidence is based on a manipulation of the task while holding the stimuli constant, the model does not provide a complete assessment of the information to which each mechanism is sensitive. I discuss this point in more detail after presenting evidence from partial-report tasks.

Nonexperimental strategies have been used to supplement the direct approaches. Mewhort and Campbell (1977), for example, implemented a computer model of the parser. They started with the grammar described by Smith and Spoehr (1974). It treats a word as a consonant (C) and vowel (V) string and provides simple rules for dividing the string into units depending on the pattern of vowels and consonants. Their grammar does not provide rules for diphthongs or for consonant clusters such as *ph* and *th*. Also, it does not distinguish silent from voiced vowels. Mewhort and Campbell extended the grammar to accommodate such problems, and the extended grammar deals with diphthongs, consonant clusters, and silent letters.

To test the simulation's success in predicting performance, Mewhort and Campbell (1977) examined individual differences in whole-report performance among a set of 160 eight-letter pseudowords (representing 40 examples from each of four orders of approximation to English). For each pseudoword, they derived a measure of relative difficulty by averaging performance across subjects. The scores were correlated with the number of units derived by the parser for the same pseudowords. They found a negative correlation that explained about 80% of the variance. In short, the familiarity effect can be described on a word-by-word basis in terms of parsing rules: Sequences that fit the rules can be split into a small number of compact units and yield high whole-report accuracy; sequences that violate the rules divide into a relatively large number of separate units (often single letters) and yield low whole-report accuracy. Such a result is encouraging, but as Mewhort and Campbell (1981, pp. 65–66) have noted, one can do almost as well with a parsing algorithm that merely counts vowels.

Configuration Manipulations. Blank characters normally define word boundaries, and the parsing mechanism treats a blank character between letters as a word boundary. Accordingly, imposing blank spaces between the letters of a pseudoword should trick the parser into placing characters that would normally fit together in the same unit into separate words. As a result, the number of units produced is increased and the familiarity effect is reduced (Campbell & Mewhort, 1980; Mewhort, 1966; Mewhort, Marchetti, & Campbell, 1982). Similarly, because parsing involves a left-right sequential sub-process, display configurations that do not permit such processing (such as a vertical or columnar display) should reduce the familiarity effect, a prediction confirmed by Bryden (1970), by Mewhort and Beal (1977, Expt. 3), and by Mewhort and Campbell (1980).

The parser creates units by applying orthographic rules to partition the character string into sub-sections. One can provide sub-sections of words directly, however, by presenting words in groups of two or three letters at a time. Some sub-sections are consistent with the parser's rules, that is, the parser can pass them on without modification (e.g., HOS-PI-TAL or AD-DI-TION). Other subsections form incompatible units, that is, units that do not fit the parser's rules (e.g., HO-SP-ITAL or ADD-IT-ION). Further, incompatible units cannot be modified because the fragmented display denies the parser access to the whole word in parallel.

Mewhort and Beal (1977, Expts. 2 & 3) and Mewhort and Campbell (1980) presented words displayed in either compatible or incompatible units. The fragments were created by spatial and temporal isolation techniques that either prohibited parsing altogether (e.g., a syllable in a vertical configuration) or that enabled parsing of the isolated sub-units (e.g., the same syllable in a horizontal display). When the isolation technique permitted parsing, word identification was good on average but depended on the kind of unit, that is, it was very good with consistent fragments but poor with incompatible units. When the fragmentation technique prohibited parsing, word identification was poor on average, and the kind of unit did not matter. Clearly, word identification depends on the system's ability to create appropriate units for itself.

Use of Position Information. Because the order of successive letters is critical to the use of orthographic rules, the parsing mechanism is sensitive to any disruption to the pointers that represent the position of letters in the character buffer: If position of letters is confused, the parser cannot yield the correct units, and accuracy of word identification should be reduced. To check the prediction, we need an experimental manipulation that affects the quality of spatial information but that does not affect information about the identity of the letters.

One such manipulation involves successive displays: If a row of letters is presented one letter at a time, subjects cannot retain information about their position unless the interval between successive letters is short (short means less than about 25 ms; Hearty & Mewhort, 1975). In terms of the model, the slow letter-by-letter presentation does not provide enough spatial context to generate the pointers that comprise the spatial representation at the character buffer. The interletter interval manipulation does not reduce the identification of unrelated letter strings, however (Mewhort, 1974). Thus, the manipulation provides a straightforward method with which to vary the integrity of position information independently of letter identification.

When words are presented in a letter-by-letter fashion, increasing the interval between successive letters reduces word identification. Further, if pseudowords are used instead of words, changes in the size of the familiarity effect parallel the reduction in word identification almost exactly (Mewhort & Beal, 1977, Expt. 1).

AN ANALYSIS OF TWO PARTIAL-REPORT TASKS

In a partial-report task, subjects are given a set of letters and a probe designating some of the items for report. The procedure was devised originally to permit the study of visual processing whilst excluding the complication of a large memory load (Sperling, 1960). A classic example is the bar-probe procedure reported by Averbach and Coriell (1961). They presented two rows of letters followed by an arrow (i.e., by a direct spatial indicator) that designated one of the letters for report. In addition to the bar-probe task, I consider a second procedure that has been derived from the bar-probe task, the digit-probe task. In the digit version, subjects are shown a row of letters and are required to report a single letter. Instead of a direct spatial indicator, however, the probe is a digit that indexes the item to be reported in terms of its ordinal position in the character string. From the perspective of the model, although the stimulus and the response required are identical, the two procedures involve different processing requirements. Comparison of the tasks offers, therefore, an ideal paradigm with which to study assignment of processing mechanisms.

THE BAR-PROBE TASK

Using a bar-probe task, Averbach and Coriell (1961) found that accuracy of report depends on the timing of the probe: Delaying the probe reduced accuracy systematically. The decrease in accuracy is widely taken to reflect decay of a precategorical buffer named iconic memory by Neisser (1967). Before describing how the model treats the task, I review the traditional position (see also Coltheart, 1984; v. d. Heijden, this volume).

Iconic Memory and Precategorical Selection

Iconic memory is thought to be a precategorical store subject to rapid decay. Furthermore, accuracy of report in the bar-probe task is thought to reflect the status of the feature data fairly directly. If the cue is early enough, for example, subjects should be able to use it to isolate the relevant features. If the features have not yet suffered decay, the subjects will be able to identify the material, and accuracy will be high. If the cue is delayed, however, iconic memory will decay over the delay interval and some features will be lost. Because of the loss, the cue will point to an incomplete or fragmented feature representation; the subjects will be less able to identify the material, and accuracy will fall.

A second aspect of the theory concerns masking. Following Sperling (1963), it has been generally held that a mask reduces performance by affecting the effective quality of precategorical data. Several variations have been proposed (e.g., Scheerer, 1973), but all agree that the mask either affects the feature data directly or affects the use of those data by disrupting the identification process. The point can be expressed in terms of a simple slogan: Precategorical data are subject to masking, but postcategorical data are stored in a form no longer subject to masking.

The traditional analysis explained the decrease in accuracy produced by delaying the probe in terms of the loss of feature data. That explanation implies a particular pattern for errors: If accuracy falls because too many features have been lost, the subjects' errors should reflect the same loss. In particular, their errors should represent guesses based on whatever features remain at the position probed. Although the data offer a straightforward test, the traditional analysis has largely ignored error data.

To report an item correctly, however, the subjects must not only identify the item correctly but also locate it correctly. The traditional iconic-memory analysis focused on the identification of material and largely ignored the localization component of the task. The assumption was, presumably, that localization errors are rare and that, in any case, accuracy reflects the integrity of the underlying featural representation. Granting the possibility of localization error, however, the iconic-memory position includes clear predictions for the resulting errors.

If subjects use the probe to decide what material should be identified, a localization error means that subjects have used the probe to isolate the wrong features for identification. What are the consequences for report? The answer depends on the timing of the probe. If the probe is immediate, the featural representation will be sound: The subject will identify an item from the wrong position in the array, and, having identified the wrong item, he will report it as if it were the correct item, that is, he will report an item from the display but not the item indicated by the probe. Such reports have been termed *location errors* in previous work (e.g., Mewhort, Campbell, Marchetti, & Campbell, 1981). If the probe is delayed, however, the featural representation will have decayed: The subject will be unable to identify the item, and, being unable to identify material from the display, he will generate a response by guessing on the basis of whatever features remain. Assuming both that the display is small relative to the experimental alphabet (e.g., 8 items out of 26 possible letters) and that it comprises a random sample from the alphabet, a guess has an 18-in-26 chance of yielding an item not present in the display. Such errors have been termed *item errors* in previous work. Other possibilities can occur, however: A guess has a 1-in-26 chance of being correct and a 7-in-26 chance of being scored as a location error. Thus, both correct reports and location errors are possible. Within the iconic-memory position, the consequences of a localization error are clear, however: With an early cue, if any errors appear, they ought to be location errors. With a late cue, however, item errors should outnumber location errors. Indeed, as the probe is delayed and accuracy decreases, the decrease ought to be complemented by an increase in item errors reflecting the loss of basic features through decay in the precategorical store.

Assignment of Mechanisms in the Bar-Probe Task

In contrast to the iconic-memory account, the present model explains performance in the bar-probe task in terms of retrieval errors at the character level

(Mewhort & Campbell, 1978). To understand how it deals with the task, however, one must adopt the perspective of the executive and see how an appropriate processing system can be built from the mechanisms available.

The bar-probe task is relatively straightforward: Only a single letter is required in the report. Hence, there is no need to develop a sequential report or to store several items during report: The task minimizes the rehearsal and response-organization problems that lie at the heart of the whole-report task. There is a trick to the task, however, a trick that concerns the way an item is designated for report. The bar is a direct spatial indicator. Thus, to permit the system to find the correct item, the executive must build a system (1) that uses a spatial buffer to permit a direct spatial instruction, (2) that uses a retrieval mechanism that handles individual items without merging them into new units, and (3) that holds the data in a form suitable for producing a verbal response.

The character buffer serves the first purpose; the attentional mechanism serves the second, and the temporal buffer serves the third. Hence, the executive will invoke the attentional mechanism to transfer an element from the character buffer to the temporal buffer in preparation for report. Thus, the main components of the processing system assembled by the executive are the feature and character buffers, the identification mechanism, and the attentional mechanism.

The assembled system allows two sources of error: The identification mechanism may err when loading the character buffer, and the attentional mechanism may err by selecting the wrong item from the character buffer. Faulty selection at the character level can result from three kinds of difficulty: probe alignment errors reflecting spatial drift during the target-probe interval, data inversion within the buffer itself, and mislocalization by the attentional mechanism. Inasmuch as the probe is not used to decide which features will be analysed, errors reflecting the identification process should be largely independent of the timing of the probe. Position information within the buffer, however, can change with time, that is, position information can be lost as the probe is delayed.

The traditional iconic-memory analysis supposes that one uses the probe at the feature level to decide what features to analyse. In van der Heijden's terms (e.g., v. d. Heijden, this volume), the iconic-memory account is an early-selection model. In the present account, however, the identification mechanism works in parallel to build the character buffer. Given a parallel identification process, it makes little sense to select particular features for identification analysis. Instead, the present model postulates that selection occurs at the postcategorical level, that is, it adopts the late-selection position.

Applying the Model in the Bar-Probe Task

In contrast to the predictions derived from early-selection theory (either the original version or the version extended to consider localization errors), Mewhort et al. (1981) have shown that the decrease in accuracy associated with a delayed probe is complemented, almost completely, by an increase in location errors. Assuming that responses classified as location errors—reports of items from the wrong position in the display—reflect mis-localization, that pattern of errors is exactly the result anticipated by the dual-buffer model. Because the probe is not used to select features for identification, the only sources of error are mis-localization at the character level and forgetting at the character level. Hence, as accuracy decreases, the dual-buffer model predicts the near complementary increase in localization errors. Thus, although the bar-probe task is usually thought to provide seminal evidence with which to define the concept, a detailed look at the errors indicates that the experiment does not, in fact, support the idea of an iconic memory. Instead, the pattern of results indicates that we must abandon the simple concept of iconic memory in favor of the late-selection view.

In addition to a manipulation of probe delay, Mewhort et al. (1981) reported five experiments that combined the bar probe with a manipulation of masking. There are several arrangements that combine the probe-delay factor with mask delay. Generalizing over the five cases, several features of the masking data confirm the dual-buffer idea at the expense of the traditional position. In general terms, accuracy increased as the mask was delayed. The increase was accompanied by a decrease in both item and location errors; the time course of their decrease was different for the two kinds of error, however. Although item errors started to decrease at short target-mask intervals, location errors remained high until the target-mask interval was relatively long. Indeed, increasing the target-mask interval did not start to affect location errors until its effect on item errors had reached asymptote (see Mewhort et al, 1981., Fig. 2).

Both the traditional iconic-memory conception and the dual-buffer model agree that masking disrupts basic feature data at a precategorical level. The dual-buffer account postulates, however, that a mask can also affect both location and identity information at the character buffer. The consequences of its double action are complicated, but the critical point is that subjects identify the material and then locate it.

Consider the case in which a mask has caused a localization error (that is, either the attentional mechanism is pointing at the wrong position within the character buffer, or the mask has inverted the data so that the attentional mechanism points at the wrong character even though it is pointing at the correct position). The subject will report the item addressed by the attentional mechanism. What kind of error will result? If target-mask interval is short, overall identification accuracy will be low, and all items in the character buffer are likely to be wrong. Thus, assuming that the subject reports the item addressed by the attentional mechanism, the response is likely to be an error that will be scored as an item error. If the target-mask interval is long, however, overall identification accuracy will be high, and most items in the character buffer will be correct. When the subject reports the item addressed by the attentional mechanism, the response is likely to be an error that will be scored as a location error. Thus, even though the mask caused errors of localization at short target-mask intervals, the scoring technique could not reveal that fact until the overall level of accuracy was relatively high. The same principle predicts the pattern obtained: assuming identification and localization reflect separate mechanisms but that a mask can affect both, delaying the mask must reduce item errors faster than it reduces location errors.

A Monte-Carlo Simulation of the Bar-Probe Task

The pattern of results for the bar-probe task is complicated. In the no-mask situation, delaying the probe reduces accuracy and yields an almost perfect trade off with location errors. In the mask situation, delaying the mask increases accuracy and yields an almost perfect trade off with item errors (until the decrease in item errors reaches asymptote). Once item errors reach asymptote, location errors start to fall. A sceptic might well wonder whether or not the dual-buffer model can deliver on its promise to predict such a complicated pattern of results. To expand the verbal description of the model, I present results from a preliminary simulation.

The simulation assumes that each trial involved an eight-item display composed of random letters. Following each display, one letter is designated for report. The simulation considers each trial separately and starts by building a character buffer. Each position is filled with one character: The proportion of characters correct is a parameter to the simulation; incorrect characters are supplied by guessing at random. Presentation of the probe is simulated by selecting a position randomly from the buffer. The trial may involve a localization error, and the probability of correct localization is a parameter to the simulation. The simulated trials are scored in the usual way.

Table 13.1 shows both accuracy and errors for two situations—the simple no-mask case and a mask case (e.g., cells 1 & 2 from Mewhort et al., 1981). For both, I have made an assumption that speeds the simulation. Specifically, I have assumed successive times (representing successive delays for the probe and/or the mask) introduce linear changes.[1]

For the no-mask simulation, I have assumed that the initial probability that each item will be identified correctly (i.e., placed in the character buffer) is 0.80; the initial probability of correct localization is also set at 0.80. Delaying the probe reduces the localization probability by 0.04 at each interval and introduces a 0.005 probability of forgetting from the character buffer.

---

[1] An exponential function would provide a better fit to the data presented by Mewhort et al., but it would be relatively slow to compute. The simulations were carried out on a Zenith Z-151 computer running under MS-DOS (2.11) and equipped with an 8087 coprocessor. The programme was written in Turbo pascal and used standard monte-carlo techniques. The results shown in the table reflect about 3 hours of processing time. Each data point is based on 20 simulated subjects who each received 1000 trials.

TABLE 13.1
A Monte-Carlo Simulation of the Bar-Probe Task Based on the Dual-Buffer Model

Percentage of Trials

A. No-Mask Case

Probe Delay	0	1	2	3	4	5	6
Correct Reports	65	62	57	54	51	47	44
Location Errors	22	25	29	31	34	38	41
	13	13	14	14	14	14	15

B. Mask Condition

Probe/Mask Delay	0	1	2	3	4	5	6	7	8	9
Correct Reports	24	27	29	31	34	35	38	40	44	46
Location Errors	39	39	40	40	39	40	40	40	39	38
Item Errors	35	33	31	29	26	24	21	19	17	16

For the mask case, the same initial assumptions hold. In addition, I have assumed that masking reduces the probability of correct identification (placement in the character buffer) by 0.35 and that it reduces the probability of correct localization at the character level by 0.30. As the mask and probe are delayed, I assume a gain at each interval for identification and localization of 0.05 and 0.04, respectively.

As is shown in the table, in the no-mask case, accuracy decreases with increased probe delay, and the delay is complemented almost perfectly by an increase in location errors; that is, the simulated results conform nicely to the pattern found by Mewhort et al. (1981) in the corresponding condition. Likewise, delaying the mask increases accuracy by reducing item errors, just as in the corresponding experiment. Note, in particular, that the simulation captures the counter intuitive aspects of the data—the flat curve for location errors as the mask is delayed and the almost flat curve for item errors associated with delayed probe in the no-mask cell.

THE DIGIT-PROBE TASK

The digit-probe task was derived directly from the corresponding bar-probe task, and from the perspective of the traditional concept of iconic memory, one would expect very similar results in both cases: There is nothing in the traditional idea to signal a contrary expectation. Indeed, some early experiments used the digit technique primarily to avoid visual interference (e.g., Merikle, 1974; Merikle & Coltheart, 1972). To derive predictions from the dual-buffer model, one must adopt the perspective of the executive (as before) and consider how an appropriate processing system can be assembled from the resources available.

Assignment of Mechanisms in the Digit-Probe Task

Like the bar-probe task, the digit-probe task requires report of a single letter. Hence, like the bar-probe task, report requirements do not force the executive to invoke mechanisms needed to support sequential report; the task minimizes report organization problems. Nevertheless, the assignment is not the same as in the bar task. The point follows because the probe is an indirect spatial indicator: To find the correct item, the system must be able to count across the array.

Counting implies categorization—items cannot be counted until they are discrete things. Further, counting is an operation extended in time. The temporal buffer is the only store available that supports temporally based operations; I assume that the rehearsal mechanism can count items as it recycles them. Hence, although it is not needed to support response organization, the executive will need the temporal buffer to permit counting to occur. To ensure that all items are counted, the system should load as many items into the temporal buffer as possible. Because the as-many-as-possible requirement matches the parser's capabilities, the executive will use it to load the temporal buffer. Hence, even though the task involves partial report, the assembled system will be the same as for a whole-report task, that is, it will include all three buffers, the identification mechanism, the scan-parse mechanism, and the rehearsal mechanism.

Applying the Model to the Digit-Probe Task

What predictions follow from the assignment of mechanisms in the digit-probe task? In general terms, performance should follow the pattern one sees in a whole-report task.

A first prediction concerns the familiarity effect that should obtain if one uses pseudo words of various orders of approximation to English. In whole report, imposing blank spaces between letters of a pseudo word reduces the familiarity effect. The same manipulation has almost no effect in a bar-probe task (Campbell & Mewhort, 1980; Mewhort, Marchetti, & Campbell, 1982). In the digit-probe task, the manipulation should produce the same interaction found in the whole-report case. Campbell (1979; see also Campbell & Mewhort, 1980) tested the prediction and found exactly the predicted result: The interaction of approximation to English with letter spacing is the same in both whole report and digit probe. The pattern of results across tasks is, of course, exactly what the model predicts from the assignment of mechanisms postulated for the two tasks.

G. T. Campbell (1981) has carried the comparison among the whole-report and the bar- and digit-probe tasks one step farther. She noted that the parsing mechanism is thought to be the main contributor to the familiarity effect in both the whole-report and digit-probe tasks. Because it applies orthographic rules that depend on the order of the letters, printing the pseudo words in reverse order (e.g., CRYSTEMP versus PMETSYRC) should reduce the familiarity effect, a prediction that she confirmed in both whole-report and digit-probe tasks. In the bar-probe task, however, the letter identification mechanism is supposed to be the main contributor to the familiarity effect. It does not use rules that depend on the order of the letters. Two predictions follow. First, the familiarity effect in the bar-probe task ought to be smaller than in the digit-probe task, a result clear in the data reported by Campbell and Mewhort (1980) and replicated by G. T. Campbell (1981). Secondly, printing the pseudo words in reverse order should have little effect in the bar-probe task on the size of the familiarity effect. G. T. Campbell (1981) also confirmed the second prediction; that is, although reversed spelling has a major effect in both the whole-report and digit-probe tasks, it has a null effect in the bar-probe task.

EVIDENCE CONCERNING THE SEPARATION OF STAGES

Separating Feature and Character Buffers

The idea that one must consider both pre and postcategorical buffers provides a convenient account for errors in the bar-probe task. We need, nevertheless, corroborating evidence. In this section, I describe some evidence that I interpret as corroboration for the dual-buffer idea.

The main points distinguishing the two buffers concern the level of abstraction associated with each; the feature buffer holds precategorical data whereas the character buffer holds identified letters. One way to confirm the need to suppose both buffers is to find operations that can impair the two levels of abstraction separately. Mewhort, Marchetti, Gurnsey, and Campbell (1984) used a bar-probe task to compare masking against a direct technique for degrading the stimulus. The new technique involved removing some of the dots used normally to define characters on the visual display. When dots are removed, accuracy of report decreases, presumably because basic feature data are not available to the identification mechanism. A similar reduction in accuracy can be produced by following the target with a mask. As noted earlier, however, the mask is thought to affect both buffers—it disrupts feature information at the feature buffer and both character and spatial data at the character level. Thus, although the reduction in accuracy produced by dot removal has a single cause, a similar reduction resulting from masking should reflect its role at both buffers.

Mewhort et al. (1984) confirmed the different effects of masking and dot removal by examining the errors associated with both kinds of manipulation. They first equated accuracy across the two techniques and then examined the errors associated with the different techniques. With the direct-degrading (dot removal) technique, there was a high percentage of identification errors, but with a mask, the bulk of the errors were localization errors. The pattern parallels predictions from the two-buffer idea. In terms of the model, the direct-degradation technique degrades basic feature data, and hence, it should produce errors reflecting the poverty of the feature store; that is, it should produce identification errors. A mask, however, is thought to degrade the feature representation, the identity of letters in the character buffer, and the quality of spatial data at the character level. Hence, by holding accuracy at the same level in the two conditions, the percentage of errors representing mis-localization should be much higher with a mask than with the direct technique. In short, there are two buffers, and we can manipulate their quality separately.

Do Location Errors Reflect Loss of Spatial Information?

The problem is straightforward: Location errors are defined as errors created by reporting letters incorrectly from the array. I have interpreted such errors as errors of localization. But, if a subject failed to identify anything and generated a response by guessing, he could very well guess a letter from the display, a response that would be scored as a location error. Therefore, some ambiguity exists concerning the cause of location errors. To corroborate the dual-buffer interpretation, we need independent evidence for the idea that spatial information is lost at the character level.

Mewhort and Leppmann (1985) provided a direct test suggesting that location errors do reflect loss of precise spatial information at a postcategorical level. In their first experiment, subjects were shown a row of eight letters for 50 ms and were asked whether or not a named letter had been present in the display. The name was spoken by a voice synthesizer at an SOA of -150, 0, 50, 100, or 200 ms. In their second experiment, the named letter was always present in the display, and the subjects were asked to identify its position. Accuracy of identification in the first task was independent of SOA but accuracy of localization in the second task dropped exponentially as SOA increased. Thus, subjects have little trouble retaining identity information but cannot retain the information needed to locate items in space, at least over the range of delays associated with studies of "iconic" memory. The results in the first experiment are very similar to those reported by Townsend (1973, Expt. 2) and both the first and second experiments are supported by data reported by Graves (1976).

CONCLUDING REMARKS

The chapter promised to outline the nature of the mental activity required to name letters and words presented tachistoscopically. To fulfill that promise, I have described the dual-buffer model in some detail, with particular emphasis on the front end of the model, that is, on its recognition and selection assumptions. Throughout, I have tried to show that the separate mechanisms described in the model have clear consequences in behavior. No doubt other explanations are equally plausible for individual experiments. To pursue such explanations piecemeal, however, misses the point of the exercise: A model stands on its structure and on the number or range of phenomena it can explain.

As van der Heijden (this volume) notes, the model represents one of a class of late-selection accounts. Although I agree with his assessment of the early–late dimension, he also describes the model as an unlimited capacity account, and the limited–unlimited capacity dimension is less clear. The model claims parallel examination of features, but it also claims that the identification mechanism can make mistakes. The parallel use of features is often associated with an unlimited-capacity position, but it usually also claims error-free performance: The suggestion that identification is error prone is a hallmark of limited-capacity models, not of the unlimited-capacity position.

The model has been able to deal with a fairly wide range of experiments using a small collection of operators and buffers. No doubt the list of operators will have to be expanded to accommodate new situations. Nevertheless, expansion is problematic: The basic discipline imposed by the model derives from its use of a small number of components to assemble different working systems in response to task demands. The model would become a parody of the approach if one needed a new operator for each new task.

It would be misleading, however, to end without pointing to some difficulties the model faces. One difficulty concerns the familiarity effect. The model claims that the identification mechanism uses position-sensitive frequency information but that the parser uses orthographic rules that depend on sequential relations among characters in a string. In support of the claim, I considered the effect of increased letter spacing and reversed spelling on the familiarity effect in whole-report, bar- and digit-probe experiments. Briefly, the tasks divide into two main sets corresponding to the kind of orthographic information associated with the processors used in each task. Thus, the bar-probe task yields a modest overall decrease in accuracy with increased letter spacing but no interaction of that variable with order of approximation to English. The digit-probe and whole-report tasks, in contrast, yield a large interaction of familiarity with letter spacing: Increased spacing reduces the familiarity effect. Similarly, the familiarity effect in the bar-probe task is not affected by reversed spelling whereas that in the whole-report and digit-probe tasks shows a large interaction: Reversed spelling reduces the size of the familiarity effect in the whole-report and bar-probe tasks.

The difficulty to be faced concerns the nature of the orthographic information the model grants to the identification and parsing operators, respectively. During feature analysis, however, subjects can exploit rules of the sort the model associates with the parser not with the identification mechanism (see Massaro, 1984, for both a review of the data and a defense of mathematical models used for their analysis). Massaro's experiments manipulated featural information directly, so there is little doubt that they address the feature-analysis stage. How can one fit his demonstration into the context of the model?

One possibility is to accept the demonstration as evidence for a fundamental limitation of the model. Most of the evidence for the model has been derived using the same stimuli (pseudo words of various orders of approximation to English). Massaro's experiments involved pseudo-words constructed to illustrate the use of particular orthographic constraints. Perhaps, the model is limited by overuse of a too narrow range of stimuli; perhaps, it requires repair that will attribute knowledge to processors differently.

A second possibility is to add a mechanism to the model that can deal with Massaro's demonstration. Adding a mechanism is dangerous but not indefensible. Massaro's results were obtained in forced-choice tasks. Virtually all the evidence cited for the model, however, has been obtained in response-production tasks. The two kinds of task are quite different: forced-choice tasks ask subjects to notice a just-discriminable difference; production tasks ask the subject to transform data until they are suitable for response production. It is quite possible that subjects are able to use information in forced-choice tasks that they cannot use to drive verbal response mechanisms. At present, however, the model lacks a mechanism that can bypass a verbal response.

ACKNOWLEDGMENTS

I wish to acknowledge support from the Natural Sciences and Engineering Research Council of Canada (Grant No. A318). I also thank Drs. E. E. Johns, A. H. C. v. d. Heijden, D. W. Massaro, and A. F. Sanders for valuable criticism and comment. The manuscript was prepared while I was a guest at the Centre for Interdisciplinary Research, University of Bielefeld: I owe many thanks to the centre for its splendid hospitality. Reprints may be obtained from the author at the Department of Psychology, Queen's University, Kingston, Canada K7L 3N6.

REFERENCES

Averbach, E., & Coriell, A. S. (1961). Short-term memory in vision. *Bell System Technical Journal, 40,* 309–328.

Baddeley, A. D. (1964). Immediate memory and the "perception" of letter sequences. *Quarterly Journal of Experimental Psychology, 16,* 364–367.

Bouma, H. (1970). Interactive effects in parafoveal letter recognition. *Nature, 226,* 177–178.

Bouma, H. (1978). Visual search and reading: Eye movements and functional visual field: A tutorial review. In J. Requin (Ed.), *Attention and performance* (Vol. VII pp. 115–147). Hillsdale, NJ: Lawrence Erlbaum Associates.

Bryden, M. P. (1966). Accuracy and order of report in tachistoscopic recognition. *Canadian Journal of Psychology, 20,* 262–272.

Bryden, M. P. (1967). A model for the sequential organization of behaviour. *Canadian Journal of Psychology, 21,* 37–56.

Bryden, M. P. (1970). Left-right differences in tachistoscopic recognition as a function of familiarity and pattern orientation. *Journal of Experimental Psychology, 84,* 120–122.

Campbell, A. J. (1979). *Mechanisms of letter and word identification.* Unpublished doctoral dissertation, Queen's University at Kingston, Kingston, Ontario, Canada.

Campbell, A. J., & Mewhort, D. J. K. (1980). On familiarity effects in visual information processing. *Canadian Journal of Psychology, 34,* 134–154.

Campbell, G. T. (1981). *Early visual processing: Performance without iconic memory.* Unpublished doctoral dissertation, Queen's University at Kingston, Kingston, Ontario, Canada.

Coltheart, M. (1984). Sensory memory: A tutorial review. In H. Bouma & D. G. Bouwhuis (Eds.), *Attention and performance X Control of language processes* (pp. 259–285). London: Lawrence Erlbaum Associates.

Graves, R. E. (1976). Are more items identified than can be reported? *Journal of Experimental Psychology: Human Learning & Memory, 2,* 208–214.

Hearty, P. J., & Mewhort, D. J. K. (1975). Spatial localization in sequential letter displays. *Canadian Journal of Psychology, 29,* 348–359.

Henderson, L. (1982). *Orthography and word recognition in reading.* London: Academic Press.

Logan, G. D. (1984). *Attentional control of thought and action: The psychology of the mental executive.* Paper read at Action, attention and automaticity, Centre for interdisciplinary research, University of Bielefeld, November 26–30.

Massaro, D. W. (1984). Building and testing models of reading processes Examples from word recognition. In P. D. Pearson (Ed.), *Handbook of reading research* (pp. 111–146). New York: Longman.

Merikle, P. M. (1969). Presentation rate and order of approximation to English as determinants of short-term memory. *Canadian Journal of Psychology, 23,* 196–202.

Merikle, P. M. (1974). Selective backward masking with an unpredictable mask. *Journal of Experimental Psychology, 103,* 589–591.

Merikle, P. M., & Coltheart, M. (1972). Selective forward masking. *Canadian Journal of Psychology, 26,* 296–302.

Mewhort, D. J. K. (1966). Sequential redundancy and letter spacing as determinants of tachistoscopic recognition. *Canadian Journal of Psychology, 20,* 435–444.

Mewhort, D. J. K. (1967). Familiarity of letter sequences, response uncertainty, and the tachistoscopic recognition experiment. *Canadian Journal of Psychology, 21,* 309–321.

Mewhort, D. J. K. (1970). Guessing and the order-of-approximation effect. *American Journal of Psychology, 83,* 439–442.

Mewhort, D. J. K. (1974). Accuracy and order of report in tachistoscopic identification. *Canadian Journal of Psychology, 28,* 383–398.

Mewhort, D. J. K. (1984). Scanning and the distribution of attention: The current status of Heron's sensory-motor theory. In W. Prinz & A. F. Sanders (Eds.), *Cognition and motor process* (pp. 139–148). Berlin: Springer–Verlag.

Mewhort, D. J. K., & Beal, A. L. (1977). Mechanisms of word identification. *Journal of Experimental Psychology: Human Perception & Performance, 3,* 629–640.

Mewhort, D. J. K., & Campbell, A. J. (1977). *Parsing and the problem of "perceptual" units.* Paper read at the meeting of the Canadian Psychological Association, Vancouver B.C.

Mewhort, D. J. K., & Campbell, A. J. (1978). Processing spatial information and the selective-masking effect. *Perception & Psychophysics, 24,* 93-101.

Mewhort, D. J. K., & Campbell, A. J. (1980). The rate of word integration and the overprinting paradigm. *Memory & Cognition, 8,* 15-25.

Mewhort, D. J. K., & Campbell, A. J. (1981). Toward a model of skilled reading: An analysis of performance in tachistoscopic tasks. In G. E. MacKinnon & T. G. Waller (Eds.), *Reading research: Advances in theory and practice* (Vol. 3, pp. 39-118). New York: Academic Press.

Mewhort, D. J. K., Campbell, A. J., Marchetti, F. M., & Campbell, J. I. D. (1981). Identification, localization, and "iconic memory": An evaluation of the bar-probe task. *Memory & Cognition, 9,* 50-67.

Mewhort, D. J. K., Marchetti, F. M., & Campbell, A. J. (1982). Blank characters in tachistoscopic recognition: Space has both a symbolic and a sensory role. *Canadian Journal of Psychology, 36,* 559-575.

Mewhort, D. J. K., & Leppmann, K. P. (1985). Information persistence: Testing spatial and identity information with a voice probe. *Psychological Research, 47,* 51-58.

Mewhort, D. J. K., Marchetti, F. M., Gurnsey, R., & Campbell, A. J. (1984). Information persistence: A dual-buffer model for initial processing. In H. Bouma & D. G. Bouwhuis (Eds.), *Attention and performance X Control of language processes* (pp. 287-298). London: Lawrence Erlbaum Associates.

Miller, G. A., Bruner, J., & Postman, L. (1954). Familiarity of letter sequences and tachistoscopic identification. *Journal of General Psychology, 50,* 129-139.

Neisser, U. (1967). *Cognitive psychology.* New York: Appleton, Century, Crofts.

Richardson, J. T. E. (1984). Developing the theory of working memory. *Memory & Cognition, 12,* 71-83.

Sanders, A. F. (1975). Some remarks on short-term memory. In P. M. A. Rabbitt & S. Dornic (Eds.), *Attention and performance V* (pp. 241-268). New York: Academic Press.

Scheerer, E. (1972). Order of report and scanning in tachistoscopic recognition. *Canadian Journal of Psychology, 26,* 382-390.

Scheerer, E. (1973). Integration, interruption and processing rate in visual backward masking I. Review. *Psychologische Forschung, 36,* 71-93.

Smith, E. E., & Spoehr, K. T. (1974). The perception of printed English: A theoretical perspective. In B. H. Kantowitz (Ed.), *Human information processing: Tutorials in performance and cognition.* Hillsdale, NJ: Lawrence Erlbaum Associates.

Sperling, G. (1960). The information available in brief visual presentations. *Psychological Monographs, 11,* (Whole No. 498).

Sperling, G. (1963). A model for visual memory tasks. *Human Factors, 5,* 19-31.

Townsend, V. M. (1973). Loss of spatial and identity information following a tachistoscopic exposure. *Journal of Experimental Psychology, 98,* 113-118.

Tramer, O., Butler, B. E., & Mewhort, D. J. K. (1985). Evidence for scanning with unilateral visual presentation of letters. *Brain & Language, 25,* 1-18.

III ATTENTION AND THE CONTROL OF ACTION

14 Beyond Capacity: A Functional View of Attention

Odmar Neumann
Universität Bielefeld

INTRODUCTION

Limitation has been regarded as one of the central aspects of attention ever since the concept of attention first appeared in ancient Greek philosophy. There has been a long tradition of discussing *how* it is limited, starting off with Aristotle's sophisticated consideration of the arguments for and against the assumption that the mind can attend to only one thing at a time (see Neumann, 1971). The modern research into attention that developed after the Second World War has largely centered around the question *where* attention is limited; i.e., whether its limitation restricts stimulus identification, or whether it affects only subsequent processes such as memory storage and decision making (for recent reviews see Allport, 1980; Broadbent, 1982; Kahneman & Treisman, 1984; Marcel, 1983; van der Heijden, this volume). By contrast, the question *why* attention is limited has so far attracted comparatively little interest.

One cause of this is probably that the limits of attention have, during the last decades, come to be largely identified with limited capacity, and that it has been taken for granted that the brain's processing capacity is limited, just as that of any other physical system. In other words, it has been assumed that capacity is limited (that there are limits to performance in attention tasks) because Capacity is limited (because the transmission or storage capabilities, or the computational power, or the energetical supply, of the brain or of parts of the brain, are limited). Limited *capacity* in the first sense of the term denotes an empirical fact in need of explanation, while limited *Capacity* in the second sense (which I will spell with a capital C in the following for the sake of clarity) refers to a theoretical construct that has been intended to provide this explanation.

Yet there are reasons to doubt that this is a satisfactory answer to the question why capacity is limited. A simple fact—that, however, Neisser (1976) seems to have been the first to point out with respect to attentional theory—is the lack of any physiologically established limit on the information that can be picked up at once. Neither are there obvious neurophysiological grounds for the assumption that dual-task performance is limited by the hardware properties of the brain. There is an immense amount of parallel computation going on simultaneously in the awake brain (see Anderson & Hinton, 1981; Creutzfeldt, 1983); and there are many subsystems that integrate information from different sources without an indication of limited capacity. For example, in the control of upright stance, visual information about contour and motion, vestibular information from the orthostate and the canals, and proprioceptive information from the joints, the muscles, and the skin are all processed in parallel and integrated (for a survey see Granit & Pompeiano, 1979). Thus, the brain's capacity is very large compared to the limits of attentional capacity in such apparently simple tasks as dichotic listening (e.g., Cherry, 1953), or reacting to two consecutive stimuli in the refractory period paradigm (e.g., Welford, 1952), or pressing a button in response to a tone while engaged in a simple matching task (e.g., Posner & Boies, 1971).

This chapter is concerned with the question how these and similar attentional limits can be reconciled with a realistic view of the brain's processing capabilities. I first review, and comment upon, some answers that have been suggested both from within Capacity theory and by theorists who reject the Capacity view of attention. In the second part of the chapter, I present a framework for a functional view of limited capacity. The main suggestion is that the limits of attention are not due to processing limitations, but rather result from the way in which the brain solves selection problems in the control of action.

WHY IS CAPACITY LIMITED? A SURVEY OF SOME ANSWERS

The main purpose of this section is to lay the ground for the considerations that are presented in the second part of the chapter. The following review is therefore biased and selective. (For a more comprehensive criticism of the Capacity approach see Neumann, 1985 a, b). I first briefly discuss four variants of Capacity theory with respect to how they try to explain capacity limits. Next there is a somewhat more detailed discussion of two contributions (Neisser, 1976, and Allport, 1980) that have suggested alternatives to Capacity theory.

Processing Load

Among the proponents of Capacity theory who have been clearly aware of the need to explain why capacity is limited was Broadbent (1971). In discussing the "late selection" view of attention proposed by Deutsch and Deutsch (1963), he writes: In one sense of course all the information from the senses must be available within the nervous system(. . .), and it may seem quite plausible that the detailed nature of the signal which has been delivered should in fact control whether or not it is selected" (p. 146). Broadbent (1971) believes, however, that this is not the case and gives the following functional reason: "If the presence or absence of all possible patterns from all the sense–organs is being analysed simultaneously, the number of possible combinations is very large; it is easy to suppose that all features present and absent can simultaneously be registered, but very hard to imagine that all conceivable combinations present can be detected at one time and distinguished from those which are absent" (p. 147). "Large though the brain is, any conceivable mechanism which could cope simultaneously with all possible states of the eye, the ear, and our other receptors, would probably be even larger" (p. 9).

Thus, Broadbent explains limited capacity by what AI researchers call the problem of a combinatorial explosion. The main argument against this explanation is that it fails to account for a basic feature of attention: The difficulty is not to combine stimuli, but rather to deal with them independently at the same time (see Allport, 1980; Neumann, 1978b). There are at least two lines of evidence for this:

First, monitoring and search tasks often show essentially no interference between simultaneous stimuli, unless two or more targets that require independent responses have to be detected simultaneously (e.g., Duncan, 1980; Ostry, Moray, & Marks, 1976; Pohlmann & Sorkin, 1976; Schneider, Dumais, & Shiffrin, 1984). Further, targets that converge on the same response (i.e., which are redundant) can—at least under certain conditions—be processed in parallel, producing on the average a shorter RT than single targets (e.g., Miller, 1982; van der Heijden, LaHeij, & Boer, 1983; van der Heijden, Schreuder, Maris, & Neerincx, 1984). Thus, capacity limits occur where stimuli have to be kept apart, not where they have to be combined. Second, combining stimuli may actually help to overcome interference, rather than producing it. Among the best-known examples is Cattell's (1885) finding that the "span of apprehension" for a letter array becomes identical to that of a single letter if the array forms a short, familiar word. Modern research has not only confirmed this but has in addition shown that performance in reading a word can, under certain conditions, even be superior to reading a single letter (the so-called word superiority effect; e.g., Reicher, 1969; Wheeler, 1970; for reviews see Massaro, Taylor, Venezky, Jastrembski, & Lucas, 1980; Paap, Newsome, McDonald, & Schvaneveldt, 1982). Similarly, an object superiority effect has been reported for lines embedded in the drawing of an object (McClelland, 1978; Wandmacher, 1981; Weisstein & Harris, 1974; for a review see Lanze, Weisstein, & Harris, 1982). Recently, Duncan (1984) has demonstrated that judgments concerning the same visual object (e.g., a line's tilt and whether it is dotted or dashed) can be made simultaneously without much loss of accuracy, whereas judgments concerning different objects (e.g., about a line's tilt and the height of an overlapping rectangle) cannot. Another interesting example, which points to the importance of perceptual integration as a means to overcome interference, is the parallel uptake of information from different sensory modalities if that information specifies the same event, such as hearing a speaker's voice and at the same time watching the lips (Massaro, 1985).

From these findings it can be concluded that capacity limits are related to limitations in processing stimuli *without* combining them. This is the exact opposite of what should be the case according to Broadbent's (1971) argument.

Mental Energy

A different attempt to bring the notion of limited Capacity into agreement with the known properties of the brain has been Kahneman's (1973) suggestion to view Capacity not as the capability to transmit and process information, but rather as an unspecific energetic input required by all processing structures, with the exception of early sensory processing. Capacity, or effort, denotes in this theory a construct that is linked to, but not identical with, physiological arousal. There are two basic problems with this notion of Capacity, one conceptual and one empirical. At the conceptual level, the problem is that this Capacity concept can easily be used to produce pseudo-explanations that are in fact mere translations of findings on attention into the language of Capacity (see Allport, 1980; Neumann, 1978a, 1983). The following citation illustrates how easily the explanandum (the fact of limited capacity) and the explanans (limited Capacity as a theoretical construct) are interchangeable in Kahneman's (1973) theory: "To explain man's limited ability to carry out multiple activities at the same time, a capacity theory assumes that the total amount of attention which can be deployed at any time is limited" (p.9). Most of Kahneman's assertions about Capacity— e.g., that its allocation becomes more uneven and less precise when arousal is high (p. 40), or that allocation is governed both by voluntary intentions and enduring dispositions (p. 42)—are mere empirical generalizations about attention, couched in a seemingly theoretical language.

The danger of providing a translation instead of an explanation can only be avoided by including into Capacity theory assumptions that do not simply reflect the known facts of attention. In Kahneman's (1973) version the major nontrivial assumption was that Capacity is unspecific, which predicts that dual-task interference should depend on task difficulty, and be equal for all task combinations at a given level of difficulty. This assumption has, however, turned out to be empirically untenable. At the time when Kahneman's book appeared, it had already become fairly obvious that, contrary to this prediction, dual-task interference can strongly depend on what types of tasks are combined (e.g., Allport, Antonis, & Reynolds, 1972; Brooks, 1968; Treisman & Davies, 1973; see also Bornemann, 1942, for early similar evidence). Kahneman's attempt at a solution was to suggest a second kind of interference, termed structural interference, which he assumed to occur when both tasks occupy the same mechanism of perception or response.

This additional assumption can, of course, only be successful in saving the unspecific-Capacity notion of attention, if structural interference can be empirically separated from Capacity-based interference, and if it can be shown that, after such a separation, the latter is unspecific. No serious attempt to achieve this has been made; probably because in the years after the appearance of Kahneman's (1973) book evidence quickly accumulated that patterns of specific interference—a strong performance decrement when the tasks are structurally similar; much less, or even no, decrement when they are dissimilar—are the rule rather than the exception in dual-task situations (for reviews see Sanders, 1979; Wickens, 1980, 1984). This has since led most students of attention to abandon the idea that capacity limits are due to a scarcity of general, unspecific Capacity. Instead, it has been assumed that there are different specific resources, each with its own limited Capacity.

Limited Resources

Usually authors have not been very explicit about what they mean by "resource". Typical definitions include "processing effort, the various forms of memory capacity, and communication channels" (Norman & Bobrow, 1975, p.45), "units, channels and facilities" (Navon & Gopher, 1979, p.233), or "memories, mechanisms, switches, and channels" (Schweickert & Boggs, 1984, p.224). There have, however, also been attempts to specify particular resources. Wickens (1980, 1984) suggested a three-dimensional system of resources consisting of stages of processing, codes (verbal vs. spatial), and input plus output modalities. Others have identified resources with brain structures, e.g., the hemispheres (Friedman & Polson, 1981; Hellige, Cox, & Litrac, 1979; Herdman & Friedman, 1985; Kinsbourne & Hicks, 1978). Sanders (1981, 1983; see also Gopher & Sanders, 1984) proposed three energetical supply systems (arousal, activation, and effort), selectively related to the assumed processing stages of feature extraction, response choice, and motor adjustment. Although these latter, concrete versions have succeeded in structuring part of the findings on specific interference and are therefore far preferable to the former, uncommitted versions, there are at least two problems with all variants of multiple resource theory.

One is that none of the proposed resource systems can account for the detailed pattern of results from dual-tasks experiments. The relevant literature has been reviewed elsewhere (Neumann, 1985 a,b). Briefly, the problem is that on the one hand interference is usually much more specific than would be predicted on the basis of a limited number of resources, and on the other hand there are cases of quite unspecific interference, that seem not to depend on any specific resource(s) being overloaded.

An example of the first difficulty is motor performance in dual tasks. It has been suggested that there is a resource reservoir for motor control (e.g., Gopher, Brickner, & Navon, 1982; Gopher & Sanders, 1984; Wickens & Kessel, 1980), implying that, as long as there are no other resources involved, motor interference should depend only on resource requirements, i.e., on task difficulty. However, the literature abounds of examples of specific interference *within* the motor domain. Well-known examples are more manual/manual than manual/vocal interference (McLeod, 1977), more interference between hand/hand than between foot/hand (Kinsbourne & Hicks, 1978), more interference between tracking/tracking or keypressing/keypressing than between keypressing/tracking (North, 1977), and more interference if the effectors have to perform different temporal patterns than if the patterns are identical or harmonically related (Duncan, 1979; Klapp, 1979; Peters, 1977, 1985).

The situation is similar on the input side. There is a tendency for stimuli from the same sensory modality to interfere more strongly than do stimuli from different modalities (for an overview see Wickens, 1980). However, this is not always the case (e.g., Lindsay, Taylor, & Forbes, 1968; Millar, 1975), and there are further specific sources of interference *within* each modality. For example, listening to two words or to two tones interferes more strongly than listening to a word and a tone (Treisman & Davies, 1973; see also Lawson, 1966). Similarly, attentional interference between visual stimuli has been reported to depend on what dimensions are to be attended simultaneously (Allport, 1971; Wing & Allport, 1972), where the relevant information is located (e.g., Hoffman & Nelson, 1981; Podgorny & Shepard, 1983), and whether or not the to-be-attended attributes belong to the same visual object (e.g., Duncan, 1984; Lappin & Ellis, 1970, exp.3; Treisman, Kahneman, & Burkell, 1983).

These findings indicate that the proposed resource systems are not specific enough to predict interference. Again, there are cases where interference is *less* specific than one would expect on the basis of what are assumed to be independent resources, i.e., where interference is apparently independent of the "resource composition" of the tasks. One example is the probe stimulus paradigm (for reviews see Posner, 1980; Poulton, 1981), where reacting to an unpredictable stimulus interferes with ongoing activity both across sensory modalities (Proctor & Proctor, 1979) and response modalities (McLeod & Posner, 1981; cited in Posner, 1982). Another example is provided by dual-task RT experiments. Here response latency in one task has been shown to depend on the number and complexity of S-R-pairings in the other task even with widely different RT tasks (e.g., Keele, 1967; Schvaneveldt, 1969).

Sure enough, resource theory can in principle handle these kinds of results by inventing the appropriate resources. For example, Wickens (1984) suggested that there may be a pool of general, undifferentiated resources in addition to specific resources; which would of course do away with the problem of unspecific interference. Similarly, specific interference found within the domain of a proposed resource could be handled by simply assuming the appropriate resources-within-resources. However, if resources proliferate as new examples of specific interference are being discovered, then we will end up with a pattern of resources that is the exact replicate of the pattern of results. This would be a description, not a theory. (For the sake of fairness, it should be noted that some theorists who are favorable to the resource notion have been well aware of this pitfall; e.g., Navon & Gopher, 1979; Sanders, 1983; Wickens, 1984; and especially Navon, 1984).

This lack of theoretical depth is the second general weakness of resource theory. Suppose that we were able to attribute limited capacity to the existence of a certain number of resources—would this answer the question why capacity is limited? It clearly would not, because we would still have to explain *why* these resources are as scarce as they seem to be. The problem that Broadbent (1971) attempted to solve with the combinatorial explosion argument, and that Kahneman (1973) tried to handle by invoking the metaphor of mental energy, seems to have been ignored by most resource theorists. Perhaps this is because of the analogies—e.g., with computers, or even with the resources of a national economy (Navon & Gopher, 1979)—that the "resource" metaphor suggests. The metaphor is a weak one, because there is no a priori reason to assume that similar limitations in the computational power of the brain exist and form the basis of attentional limits.

Input and Output Control

In the first decades of modern research on attention, the Capacity view was so widely accepted that limited Capacity was usually not regarded as a theoretical construct, but as a plain fact. As stated by Egeth (1977), it appeared "obvious that man has a limited capacity for processing information" (p.308). This firm hold of the Capacity notion on attentional theory began to wane in the late 1970s. There were two developments away from Capacity, a radical one and a less radical one. A radical alternative to Capacity was first suggested by Neisser (1976). Although his views seem to have had little direct impact on attention research, similar ideas were put forward by other authors in the years thereafter (Allport, 1980; Neumann, 1978a,b). Neisser's and Allport's proposals for an alternative to Capacity theory are discussed in the following sections.

The second, less radical but much more influential diversion from Capacity theory grew out of one of its variants, usually called the "late selection" view. (For a critical discussion and more precise definition of this term see van der Heijden, this volume). So-called late selection theorists place the Capacity bottleneck at a location where all stimuli have already been completely identified (e.g., Deutsch & Deutsch, 1963; for the present status of this idea see Allport, this volume; Duncan, 1980, 1981; Marcel, 1983; Posner, 1978, 1982; van der Heijden, this volume). Although this view assumes that there are processes, occuring subsequent to stimulus identification, that demand Capacity, it is not easy to see how it can interpret Capacity limitations as simply due to the brain's functional capabilities. If the brain is capable of processing all stimuli completely, why should it not also have the capability to perform all further processing operations without Capacity limitations? Thus, it is within the logic of the "late selection" approach to look for functional reasons of limited capacity.

One example is the treatment of the capacity issue in Posner's (1978) book. At the beginning of the chapter on attention and consciousness Posner presents the traditional view, postulating as the basis of limited capacity "a system that is so richly interacting that its efficient utilization for the processing of a signal code will usually reduce the efficiency with which it can process any other signal code" (p. 153). However, at the end of the same chapter a different view of capacity emerges. Posner (1978) asks what could be the evolutionary significance of consciousness and suggests as an answer that "the fact of its limited capacity may itself serve an important controlling function" (p. 181) by giving priority to a particular pathway, preventing other pathways from gaining access to action. This idea had previously been put forward by Shallice (1972; see also Shallice, 1978), with whom Posner finds himself in agreement. The mechanism of this control function, Posner suggests, is inhibition of the output of lower level systems.

A more explicit and more elaborate formulation of this idea appeared at the same time in a paper by two other members of the Oregon group, Keele and Neill (1978). They asked why there is interference near output, if there are (according to their analysis of the literature) no capacity limits in stimulus identification and memory activation. Keele and Neill (1978) propose that this is because a selector mechanism near output is needed "for coordinating information available from the environment with information regarding goals. . . The mechanism that determines one action or another appears, therefore, to be a major source of limitation, corresponding to what we mean by attention" (p. 23). Later on in their chapter they suggest that attention further serves to attenuate one source of information prior to memory access, if it conflicts with another; and that it also has the function of coordinating information.

These are all interesting and productive ideas that transcend the sterility of explaining capacity by Capacity. On the other hand, they are also very general suggestions. I next turn to two authors (Allport, 1980; Neisser, 1976) who have presented more detailed explanations of the functional causes of limited capacity.

NonCapacity Limitations

Neisser's (1976) analysis of the performance limits that are usually attributed to limited Capacity can be paraphrased as follows: First, there may be peripheral problems both on the sensory and the motor side. In the motor periphery, it can happen that two actions are physically incompatible, such as writing and throwing a ball with the same hand. In the uptake of sensory information, stimuli may mask each other. Second, performance limits can be due to coordination problems. For example, two actions that have been learned separately may be difficult to combine because they are based on different timings and bodily positions. In order to become mutually compatible, they need to be reorganized, which demands additional learning. Another case for which Neisser offers a similar explanation is the breakdown of the simultaneous performance of two actions when an emergency occurs in one of them, e.g., a driver stops talking when the traffic situation becomes difficult. This, Neisser suggests, is because such emergency reactions are rare and people have therefore not learned to combine them with other actions.

The third kind of limitation is assumed to be related to information pickup and is explained within the framework of Neisser's schema theory: The same schema cannot be used for two incompatible purposes, and further according to Neisser (1976) there seems to be a "genuine informational impediment to the parallel development of independent but similar schemata" (p. 103), due to the problem how to apply new information to the correct schema. The first of these two principles is invoked to explain examples such as the interference between imagining a spatial arrangement and observing a different spatial arrangement (e.g., Brooks, 1968), whereas the second is, according to Neisser, the cause of attentional limits in tasks such as dichotic listening and observing two overlapping visual scenes (e.g., Neisser & Becklen, 1975).

This theory points to a number of important sources of performance limitations—overt, physical interference and problems in coordinating actions and integrating information—that have been largely ignored by Capacity theories. Still, it falls short of providing a satisfactory explanation of a number of aspects of these limitations.

As to physical interference between incompatible actions, it could play a part in real-life situations, but hardly in laboratory research on attention where experimenters of course see to it that the required tasks are physically compatible. In daily life, however, the interesting observation is not that actions may be physically incompatible, but rather that people—as well as animals—rarely attempt to perform such actions concurrently. Even split-brain patients only occasionally attempt incompatible actions (see, e.g., Sperry, 1966, p. 303f). One reason for this seems to be that the control of visual attention remains at least partially unified despite commissurotomy (Holtzman, Sidtis, Volpe, Wilson, & Gazzaniga, 1981). Thus, the possibility that actions may overtly interfere is a *problem* for attentional theory rather than providing an explanation: Physical interference is rarely if ever the cause of capacity limits that are attributed to attention; but the prevention of physical interference may well be one of the tasks of attention. This possibility is further explored later.

The coordination problems that Neisser mentions have certainly not received sufficient consideration by Capacity-oriented research, despite the ease with which they can be demonstrated experimentally (e.g., Duncan, 1979). Neisser's account contains, however, at least two shortcomings. First, in what sense are the timings and postures required by the to-be-combined actions incompatible? They can be so in a physical sense. Thus, in one of the examples given by Neisser, writing with one hand and throwing a ball with the other hand, the throwing movement can perhaps be only executed efficiently—at least as long as there has been no specific training of the combination—if the other arm is allowed to swing, making writing impossible. However, most coordination problems, especially in the timing area, are not in any obvious way dictated by such physical constraints. For example, tapping one rhythm with one hand does not demand a bodily posture that would be expected to interfere with tapping a different rhythm with the other hand; yet this is extremely difficult (e.g., Duncan, 1979; Klapp, 1979).

Second, Neisser is probably wrong in assuming that difficulties in combining different actions are just due to insufficient training. Although coordination problems can sometimes be overcome with sufficient practice (for example, well-trained pianists can apparently time the finger movements of their two hands independently; Shaffer, 1981), there are other task combinations where practice does not seem to abolish interference. Most notably, both lengthening of probe RT due to the concurrent performance of a second task (Salthouse & Somberg, 1982) and the "psychological refractory period" in responding to the second of two consecutive signals (Gottsdanker & Stelmach, 1971) seem to survive months of training.

Neisser's conviction that many instances of dual-task interference are due to insufficient practice in carrying out the two tasks concurrently motivated heroic experiments where subjects were trained for many months to pick up two verbal messages at the same time, one visual and one auditory (Hirst, Spelke, Reaves, Caharack, & Neisser, 1980; Spelke, Hirst, & Neisser, 1976). These studies showed impressive practice effects but also the limits of practice; a full conscious understanding of both messages was not achieved by the subjects (Hirst, Spelke, Reaves, Caharack, & Neisser, 1980, p. 114; see also Lucas & Bub, 1981, and Neisser, Hirst, & Spelke, 1981).

Of the two explanations that Neisser offers to account for limitations in information pickup, the first—that the same schemata cannot be used for two different purposes at the same time—seems to reintroduce limited Capacity through the backdoor. The question is, of course, *why* they cannot. The second explanatory principle is more explicit. It suggests that the simultaneous usage of independent but similar schemata may pose an insuperable problem, due to the danger of crosstalk. This is a starting point for a functional explanation and not simply the statement of a processing limit.

However, it is nothing more than a starting point, because it fails to specify how this difficulty can be overcome: If there are two sources of stimulation, A and B, that fit to a degree into both schema X and schema Y, then there is potential crosstalk, because B may be picked up by schema X, although it properly belongs to schema Y; and correspondingly for A. This problem cannot be solved by simply activating only one of the schemata, say X. This would still leave the system with a situation where both A and B fit into X. Thus, the problem of how to select the correct information would still prevail. It is basically not a problem of *cross*talk, but rather a problem of filtering out unwanted information in applying a schema.

In summary, Neisser (1976) suggested a bold new view of limited capacity, but in part he overshot the mark, and in part his explanations remained incomplete. In arguing against the theoretical notion of limited Capacity, he tended to assume that there are hardly any real limits to attentional capacity, which is against empirical evidence. He was aware of the importance of peripheral, physical interference between actions for understanding attention, but he regarded it only as a possible source of performance limitations and did not notice that preventing physical interference is a major control problem in the behavior of animals and men. Third, he introduced the important idea that attentional limits in the uptake of information are related to the problem of establishing the correct connections between input information and perceptual activity, but he did not work out this idea and failed to explain in which way this problem can be mastered by the system.

Data-Specific and Function-Specific Interference

Four years after Neisser's attack on the Capacity concept, Allport (1980) presented a detailed analysis of the major findings on attention and concluded that they point to the existence of different, specific sources of interference rather than limited unspecific Capacity. Although he did not exclude as a possibility the existence of limited-Capacity mechanisms that serve diverse functions, Allport suggested as a working assumption that all interference is specific; either function specific (caused by competition for the same category of action) or data specific (due to problems of crosstalk in attaching input information to the proper action). Further, he proposed limitations in keeping different goals active as an additional source of interference. Although Allport's (1980) account was much more sophisticated than Neisser's (1976)—both with respect to its degree of theoretical elaboration and to the scope of behavioral and physiological findings on which it was based—, its problems are rather similar.

Consider first function-specific interference. Like Neisser, Allport (1980) starts by pointing out that there are overt limitations on physical action. He notes that alternative actions are mutually incompatible within action categories such as producing speech or directing gaze. Hence there is a need to somehow establish momentary dominance which, Allport suggests, may be achieved by reciprocal inhibition. This is a clear and convincing example of function-specific interference. However, as was the case with Neisser's examples of physical interference, it is obvious that this does not explain the usual examples of attentional interference where physical factors are excluded. Hence this principle has to be extended to become useful as an explanation. After mentioning the speech and gaze examples, Allport (1980) suggests mutual inhibition not only in these cases, but also for similar categories of action by the right and left hand, and some lines further down he states: "In general, competition for the same, functionally specialized subsystem is a form of 'function specific' limitation. It seems plausible that function specific limitations are not confined to the control of overt action, but can arise from competition for many different kinds of specialized 'analyzers' " (p.145).

The problem with this suggestion is that it does not specify how these cases of competition for assumed subsystems relate to competition for the control of overt action. Is this a mere analogy, i.e., are these internal subsystems limited in capacity *just as* effector systems are? In this case we would not be far away from resource theory; and as noted earlier, we would be left with the question why these subsystems exhibit limited capacity (and why others do not, as Allport suggests to be the case, for example, for stimulus identification). Or, alternatively, are these subsystems limited in capacity *because* there are limits on overt action? This could possibly provide a functional explanation of capacity limits. For example, systems involved in the control of speech output might be restricted to sequential operation because speech itself is physically sequential. This type of interpretation was, however, not considered by Allport (1980).

The question why capacity is limited remains likewise open with respect to Allport's third proposed kind of difficulty, limitations in keeping different goals active. He mentions as an example concurrence costs, i.e., dual-task interference due to merely keeping ready for one task while performing the other (see e.g., Adler, 1977; Noble, Sanders, & Trumbo, 1981). Allport (1980) admits that this proposed type of effect "seems closest to the conjectures about limited control processes, that have sometimes been invoked as the basis of 'attention' limitations" (p.147). In fact, without a functional explanation why this kind of limitation exists, it bears a strong resemblance to Capacity theory, though restricted to a particular type of unspecific interference.

By contrast, the idea of data-specific limitations provides a functional explanation of attentional limits that does not fall back on Capacity. Similar to Neisser's suggestion that the simultaneous usage of similar, but independent schemata may entail the problem of how to apply incoming information to the correct schema, Allport points out the risk of crosstalk if the information to be connected to one task also provides an eliciting condition for the kind of action demanded by the second task. As a case in point he mentions Shaffer's (1975) finding that it is extremely difficult to read aloud one text while typing another, auditorily presented text, wheras the inverse task combination is much easier. The particular difficulty of the former condition would be due to the strong calling cues for speech output provided by the speech input that must, however, be kept disconnected from it according to task requirements.

As I mentioned earlier, Neisser failed to explain how this type of difficulty can be overcome. Allport (1980) was somewhat more explicit, suggesting that the "strategy most often adopted for coping with situations of this kind apparently has the effect of decoupling one set of inputs (or intermediate products) from potential command of all categories of action." (p. 145; see Neumann, 1980, p. 367, for an independent discussion of the same idea). Allport did not elaborate on this suggestion, which I take up in the next Section.

In conclusion, I believe that the shortcomings in both Neisser's (1976) and Allport's (1980) answers to the question: "Why is capacity limited?" are due to the fact that they did not go far enough in abandoning Capacity thinking. The basic idea common to all versions of Capacity theory is that limited attention is due to processing deficits. Not surprisingly, this deep-rooted belief was still very much with Neisser and Allport when they did their pioneer work. Neisser's attitude seems to have been that because the processing deficits proposed by Capacity theory do not exist, there should be few if any real limits of attention that do not yield to practice. He tended to deny (empirical) capacity limits because he did not believe in (the theoretical notion of) limited Capacity, implying the validity of the equation "Capacity = capacity". Allport was much more explicit about the existence of real capacity limitations, and he was aware of the relationship between attention and the control of overt action. However, he did not work out the possible positive functions of capacity limitations for action control, with the result that two of his three proposed mechanisms had to be based on unexplained resource limitations. The "decoupling" idea is an exception to this, because it implies that an apparent deficit (the inability to attend to both sources of stimulation) actually serves a functional purpose (preventing crosstalk). The framework that I sketch in the following Section makes extensive use of this type of explanation.

A FUNCTIONAL VIEW OF ATTENTION

Selection and Capacity

The selectivity of attention has traditionally been viewed as its second major attribute, besides limited capacity. Limited Capacity theories did not ignore the selection aspect, but they regarded it as a secondary consequence of limited Capacity. This view is well captured in the following citation in Johnston and Heinz (1978): "Since we cannot be fully conscious of all the inputs that continuously flood into our processing system, some selection of perceptual information is needed prior to consciousness. Since random selection would provide consciousness with an uninterpretable collage of perceptual data, systematic selection is prerequisite to a coherent and intelligible picture of the world" (p. 421). Or, as Broadbent (1971) put it: "The obvious utility of a selection system is to produce an economy in mechanisms. If a complete analysis were performed even of the neglected messages, there seems no reason for selection at all'' (p. 147). In Broadbent's (1958, 1971) model, selection was attributed to a special mechanism, the filter. In Kahneman's (1973) Capacity allocation theory as well as in present-day resource theories (e.g., Gopher & Sanders, 1984; Navon & Gopher, 1979; Wickens, 1980, 1984) no special selection mechanisms are proposed; selection is viewed simply as the process of allocating resources.

This view is at best incomplete. Independent of all Capacity considerations, selection is evidently needed for the control of action. Organisms must constantly select what to do and how to do it. In part, this is a problem of motivation. But motivation usually is not sufficient to determine action. For example, my motive to finish this manuscript on schedule neither specifies its notions, nor the formulations in which they are conveyed, nor the sequence of finger movements that I must perform to get the text into the word processor.

Some of these specifications can be provided by applying the appropriate skills from my repertoire. For example, once a formulation has been determined, I only need to use my typing skill to specify the appropriate sequence of finger movements. But most of the specifications involved in the writing task do not come out of the simple application of skills. There are many ways in which a theoretical thought can be phrased, but one must be selected. I could, at any moment in time, continue typing; or stop typing and reread the file to look for errors; or briefly lift my eyes from the monitor screen to observe a bird outside, and son on. These and many more actions and variants of actions would conform to my motive to finish the manuscript, but few if any could be performed concurrently.

The problem is how to avoid the behavioral chaos that would result from an attempt to simultaneously perform all possible actions for which sufficient causes exist, i.e., that are in agreement with current motives, for which the required skills are available and that conform to the actual stimulus situation. As mentioned earlier, organisms are extremely efficient in solving this kind of problem. The suggestion that I explore in the rest of this chapter is that this is due to mechanisms that also produce limited capacity. Whereas Capacity theories regard selection as a functional consequence of limited Capacity, this view conceives limited capacity as a necessary by-product of the solution of selection problems. Because there are several kinds of selection problems (see next Section), different selection mechanisms are needed. Hence "attention", in this view, does not denote a single type of phenomenon. Rather it should be viewed as the generic term for a number of phenomena each of which is related to a different selection mechanism.

This approach offers several advantages over the Capacity view: First, as the following Sections will hopefully show, it leads to a categorization of the different kinds of attentional phenomena that seems to fit the data better than either unspecific Capacity or specific resource models. Second, it produces new questions for research. Third, it promises to bring behavioral research into closer contact with the neurophysiology of attention (see Allport, this volume). I should caution the reader, however, that the approach as it is presented here is far from being a theory of attention. If it should turn out to be at least partially correct, then there is no point in seeking a unified theory of attention in the style of the Capacity theories. What we need to understand are the different mechanisms that subserve selection functions and thereby produce capacity limitations. This will require integrating data from psychology and the brain sciences, but not an integration in the sense of putting all data into the Procrustean bed of a single functional model of attention.

Selection Problems in Action Control

If it is true that attentional phenomena result from the solution of selection problems in action control, then an adequate treatment of attention has to start with some considerations of how actions are controlled. This can be done only very briefly here (see Neumann, 1983, for a more detailed discussion). The main purpose of this section is to analyze which selection problems must be solved if an organism's actions are to be controlled adequately.

The term *action* as it will be used here denotes a sequence of movements that is controlled by the same internal control structure and that is not a reflex. (I do not dwell on the distinction between reflexes and actions, because the transition is certainly gradual. Essentially, actions differ from reflexes in that they are much more flexible in adjusting to situational demands; compare, e.g., the patellar reflex to the kicking movement of a football player's leg that depends on the ball's position, size, and weight, the direction and distance of the goal, etc.). Internal control structures can either be innate or acquired. Acquired control structures that are stored in long-term memory will be termed *skills*.

Skills are assumed to have two main characteristics. First, they are abstract in the sense that a skill does not specify any particular movement sequence, but rather a class of movement sequences. For example, a football player's skill of kicking a ball is used to control the whole class of individually different kicking sequences that he executes during his career. Thus, skills are schemata as defined by Schmidt (1975, 1976, 1982). Second, skills are nested hierarchically. Kicking a ball is, for example, a subskill within the higher level skill of playing football. I assume that skills are used to attain action goals, and that goals are nested in a similar way. I do, however, not attempt to define or discuss the notion of action goal, which would lead to the intentionality issue. This is beyond the scope of the present chapter.

To attain action goals, either one particular skill or a combination of skills have to be selected and made available for the control of the motor apparatus. (The case where skills need to be combined requires action planning; this is taken up in a later section). In either case, there are two main selection problems, the problem of effector recruitment, and the problem of parameter specification.

The problem of *effector recruitment* refers to the fact that there is one very real Capacity limit for all animals, namely the scarcity of effectors. Skills have the function to control effectors, but evidently different skills do not have different, dedicated effectors at their disposal. All high-level skills that involve locomotion engage the whole body. In humans, effectors such as the mouth and the hands are used for a variety of different skills. Further, usage of many skills involves postural adjustments, even if only one effector actually moves (Neisser, 1976). In addition, functions controlled by the autonomic nervous system may have to be set at particular values for proper application of certain skills. For example, speaking demands a different respiratory pattern than running. All this dictates that the sufficient condition for a skill to control effectors cannot be that the appropriate motivational and environmental conditions are present. An additional selection process is required that regulates which skills are allowed to recruit which effectors at a given moment in time.

Parameter specification is a problem because skills are abstract and hence do not by themselves specify all the parameters that need to be specified if an action is to be carried out. To give two examples, the skill of speaking obviously does not specify what to say, and the skill of catching as an internal control structure does not specify when to move the arm and close the hand in order to catch a thrown object. The latter problem can partially be solved "locally" because apparently some high-level skills include subskills for picking up information that is suitable to specify parameters. This seems to be the case with catching (McLeod, McLaughlin, & Nimmo-Smith, 1985). If this mode of specification is sufficient to specify all required parameters, then the action is automatic, according to the definition suggested by Neumann (1984).

There are two types of situations where this automatic mode of parameter specification will not suffice. One is that the necessary environmental information is not present and/or a subskill for picking it up is not available. In this case the action can be said to be *underspecified* by the skill plus the environmental information. This is the case in speaking. By contrast, in oral reading most of the action's parameters can be determined by picking up information from the text (though a few, such as timing, cannot). Yet there is still a selection problem in this situation. It results from the fact that one can only utter one word at a time, whereas the text contains more than one word. Thus, there is what may be called *overspecification* of the action by environmental information. Selection mechanisms are needed to cope with these two, of course not mutually exclusive, variants of the problem of parameter specification.

In the next Sections I first discuss the problem of effector recruitment and suggest how its solution may be related to capacity limitations. These are cases where capacity is limited in an unspecific way. The final sections are concerned with the varieties of specific capacity limitations that, according to the present approach, result from the solution of the parameter specification problem.

Effector Recruitment

The problem of recruiting effectors in such a way that no mutually incompatible actions are attempted is similar to the problem of how to prevent train crashes in a railroad network where many trains use the same tracks. There are essentially two ways to solve this problem. One is to devise a schedule such that two trains will never be close to each other on the same track. This will be especially efficient if the schedule can be continuously updated, taking into account the current traffic situation. To achieve this, a central station is needed that monitors all trains and directs them. The other method is to divide the network up into sections and to let a train entering a section block this section for other trains, e.g., by automatic setting of signals. Modern railroad networks use both methods in combination. Each of them has its advantages and disadvantages. The first allows a better usage of the limited resource, railway tracks; but it needs a complex exchange of information, and errors in information transmission or in central scheduling can have disastrous consequences. The second method has the disadvantage of much more limited capacity, because each section can only be used by one train at a time. However, it needs less communication and coordination, and it is much less error prone.

Which of these two methods is used by animal brains to solve the effector recruitment problem? The solution suggested by the computer analogy would of course be the scheduling method. I will argue, however, that the brain basically uses the blocking method. Scheduling does possibly play an additional part, but it may be a special property of human action control and not available to animals (see the section on action planning).

Using the blocking method to regulate effector recruitment would mean to let only one high-level skill (or action plan) at a time have access to the effector system. This seems to be contradicted by the fact that people can do two things at a time, and especially by evidence of essentially interference-free dual-task performance under conditions where there is little functional overlap between the two required actions (e.g., Allport, Antonis, & Reynolds, 1972; Shaffer, 1975). I ask the reader to suspend this objection for the moment; I return to it later. The behavior of animals clearly indicates that they usually stick to one action at a time. As stated by Hinde (1970): "Undoubtedly the commonest consequence of the simultaneous action of factors for two or more types of behavior is the suppression of all but one of them" (p. 396). This behavioral inhibition can be experimentally induced by electrical brain stimulation (e.g., v. Holst & v. St. Paul, 1963). Inhibition of an action tendency does not necessarily result in its permanent disappearance. One common finding is that competing action tendencies alternate in the control of action (e.g., Halliday, 1980; v. Holst & v. St Paul, 1963; McFarland, 1974). Other outcomes, such as a compromise action or disinhibition of a third action tendency, can also be observed (see Fentress, 1973; Hinde, 1970, for reviews), indicating that inhibition is not always completely succeddful in producing dominance of one of the competing action tendencies.

Although the physiological basis of behavioral inhibition seems so far not to be well understood (see Shallice, 1978, for a discussion of some possibilities), there is certainly no a priori reason why it should be absent in the human brain. This would explain in a general way why capacity is limited: It is limited because one ongoing action inhibits all other possible actions. Yet one may wonder what is to be gained by this type of functional insight, if it does not explain more detailed aspects of attention. This criticism, which can also be raised against the similar approach of Shallice (1972, 1978), would be legitimate if theorizing would stop here. The following Sections are an attempt to develop this view of attention in more detail, in order to get it into contact with empirical data.

Interrupting and Initiating Actions

If the problem of effector recruitment is basically solved by blocking, then there is the obvious risk that the organism will become too inflexible in its reactions to environmental events. There is a need for an interrupt function that enables responding to unexpected, but potentially important stimuli. The orienting reaction (Sokolov, 1963; for a recent review see Rohrbaugh, 1984) seems to be well suited for this task. It includes a number of components, e.g., an increase in skin conductance and various other autonomic effects, and—more important in the present context—behavioral changes such as the inhibition of ongoing activity, realignment of head and receptor orientation, and postural adjustments. Among the stimulus attributes that elicit an orienting reaction are intensity, novelty, and also significance (e.g., Bernstein, 1979, 1981).

With respect to limited capacity, the orienting reaction is of interest for at least two reasons. First, it is relevant to the "early" versus "late" selection issue. Second, it can explain some of the findings that seem to point to unspecific capacity limitations. Without the need for an interrupt mechanism, there would be no functional requirement for processing more stimulus information than is used in the control of the action that has currently access to the effector apparatus. Indeed, any additional processing could only complicate the problem of parameter specification (see the "crosstalk" arguments discussed earlier). By contrast, in order for ongoing action to be interrupted by stimuli that possess certain attributes, these attributes have to be identified before becoming involved in the control of action. This is what is usually called preattentive processing.

If one views preattentive processing as providing the information needed to orient to unexpected, but possibly significant stimuli, this provides on the one hand a functional reason why stimuli should be processed preattentively up to the registration of their significance. On the other hand, it does not support the radical position that all stimuli are processed up to the "highest and most abstract levels" (Marcel, 1983, p. 244), or that all the processing that can be done is done (van der Heijden, this volume). If preattentive processing takes place only in the service of an interrupt mechanism, then it should differ from processing for action control in several important respects.

First, what should be registered are *signals* rather than objects and events; that is, there is no need for integrating attributes within and across sensory modalities. It seems to have been demonstrated that indeed this kind of integration is absent prior to attentional processing (e.g., Massaro, 1985; Treisman & Gelade, 1980; Treisman & Paterson, 1984; Treisman & Schmidt, 1982). However, contrary to Treisman's suggestions, preattentive processing should not be restricted to simple features but should include semantic attributes. There is some evidence that some of Treisman's results, concerning the appearance of so-called illusory conjunctions, can be replicated for semantic features (Virzi & Egeth, 1984; see also Prinzmetal & Millis-Wright, 1984).

Second, preattentive processing should not proceed beyond the matching of stimulus attributes to stored attributes. For verbal stimuli, this would exclude the extraction of meaning at the sentence level. This seems also to be borne out by data (Govier & Pitts, 1982; MacKay, 1973; Underwood, 1977). Third and perhaps most important, this view suggests a distinction between (1) "preattentive" processing in the sense of matching to a neuronal model (Sokolov, 1963) stimuli that do not elicit an orienting reaction, and (2) eliciting of the orienting reaction itself, which is also "preattentive" in the sense that it of course occurs before attention is directed towards the signal. Many of the results that are usually cited in favor of late selection models may be attributable to (2) rather than (1). For example, it has been reported that words in the unattended channel in dichotic listening influence the processing of stimuli in the to-be-attended channel (Lewis, 1970; Treisman, Squire, & Green, 1974) and elicit a galvanic skin response that has previously been conditioned to them, or to semantically related words (Corteen & Wood, 1972; Dawson & Schell, 1982; Forster & Govier, 1978; Govier & Pitts, 1982). What this may mean is that these words, because of their significance and/or their semantic relatedness to the to-be-attended words, elicited an orienting reaction that was, however, insufficient to lead to conscious awareness (see Neumann, 1984, Section 4.3 and Neumann, 1985b, Section 4.2, for a further discussion). Thus it may be erroneous to generalize from these results to the processing of all stimuli.

The second aspect of the orienting reaction that is of interest for the capacity problem is that it inhibits ongoing action. As Rohrbaugh (1984) notes, this aspect has received relatively little experimental investigation. However, it might be present in a standard experiment in attention research, the probe stimulus paradigm. It was mentioned earlier that the interference between a main task and the task of pressing a button to a probe signal seems to be fairly unspecific and resistent to practice effects. I have argued previously (Neumann, 1984) that this is because the probe stimulus paradigm demands initiating a new action while a different action is going on. This would be a typical case of the "interrupt" function of the orienting reaction, leading either to a decrement in the main task, or to a lengthening in probe RT (if the main task is protected against interruption), or to both.

Action Planning

So far the question has been left open how dual or multiple activity is possible at all, if it is assumed that behavioral inhibition ensures the dominance of one action over all competing actions. Shallice's (1978) answer was that competing action systems can use all effector units not required by the dominant system. This is, however, improbable for a number of reasons. First, as pointed out by Allport (1980), there are dual tasks where no activity can be said to be dominant. Second, it is hard to imagine how this policy of leaving for other activities what is not required by the dominant action system could lead to orderly behavior. In most cases, the nondominant actions would get something, but not as much as they need, resulting in incomplete or abortive actions. Moreover, it is unclear how the available effectors should be divided between the nondominant action systems, if there are more than one of them. Finally, this hypothesis fails to explain why humans are able to perform concurrent activities, whereas animals apparently are not.

An alternative explanation that I wish to suggest is that multiple activity is no exception to the principle of behavioral inhibition. Concurrent actions are not independent actions. What makes them special is that they are not integrated within a common supraordinate *skill*. But this does not imply that there is no integration at all. Rather, I suggest, actions that depend on separate skills can be performed concurrently because they can be integrated in a different way, by means of *action planning*.

The capability of constructing and implementing action plans is in all probability an evolutionary acquisition that distinguishes man from other animals. It is mainly localized in the prefrontal lobes, as indicated by the deficits that result from lesions in this area of the brain (Fuster, 1980; Luria, 1980; for a recent review see Bridgeman, in press). In the absence of systematic behavioral research on action planning (for some tentative attempts see Logan, 1985; Neumann & Koch, 1986; Rosenbaum, 1984) it would be premature to speculate on mechanism. Basic questions—e.g., regarding the role of language and of imagery in action planning—have barely been formulated, let alone attacked experimentally.

What seems clear from everyday experience is that action planning enables combining skills without any training. This is the basis of almost every psycho-

14. ATTENTION AND CAPACITY 381

logical experiment. For example, when we instruct subjects to press a button if two briefly presented letters are identical, and to press another button if they are different, we ask them to construct and execute an action plan that combines perceptual, cognitive, and motor skills that they have, if they are naive subjects, never before used in this combination. Still we expect them to act according to the instruction as soon as the experiment starts.

Dual tasks demand in principle the same kind of combining various skills. The only difference is that execution more or less overlaps in time. This introduces additional capacity limits, which will be treated later. Let us first consider those limitations that may result from action planning as such.

One major capacity limitation that appears in single as well as dual tasks is a rise in the time to start execution as the number of condition-action-rules that make up the action plan is increased. The best-known example is the dependence of choice reaction time (CRT) on the number of alternatives (e.g., Hick, 1952; Merkel, 1885). Adding a second task that demands action planning will usually increase the number of condition-action rules in the combined action plan. It should therefore have the same effect as an increase in the number of alternatives in a CRT task, even if the second task does not have to be performed in that experimental trial, or if it has to be performed only subsequent to the first task. As mentioned previously, this is indeed what happens.

Task combinations where two reactions have to be executed simultaneously may be viewed in a similar way. For example, Schvaneveldt (1969, exp.2) presented single numerals in different spatial positions. Subjects had to respond to a numeral's identity by uttering the corresponding letter of the alphabet, while at the same time pressing an appropriate button in response to its position. As is to be expected from Hick's law, RT in each of these tasks increased with the number of alternatives in this task. However, it also increased with the number of alternatives in the other task. Plotting RT against the combined information load in both tasks (which Schvaneveldt did not do) even reveals that this seems to be the major variable to predict RT.

Thus, part of the dual-task interference between tasks that are controlled by a combined action plan may result from a capacity limit that is equally present in single tasks. What could be its functional basis? One possibility is that it is just another manifestation of the general principle, assumed by the present approach, that capacity limitations result from the solution of selection problems. The problem to decide which condition-action rule to apply in a given situation could possibly become insuperable if many such rules were kept available simultaneously as components of the same action plan. On the other hand, there may be real hardware limitations involved. For example, one might speculate that holding a selected number of neuronal connections in a transient state of activation ("selective coupling" in the terms of Allport, this volume) is difficult in a system such as the brain, where there is an extremely high interconnectivity between neural units (see e.g., Braitenberg, 1977). Keeping them separate and preventing activity from spreading to other connections may be a difficult task, restricting the manageable number of such connections (see Schneider, 1983, for a similar consideration).

These must for the present remain speculations. With respect to empirical findings, the suggested approach offers an explanation for unspecific dual-task interference, and it predicts when it should occur: Increasing the difficulty of one task should affect the other task if—and only if—the difficulty manipulation has its effect on the number and/or complexity of condition-action rules, as for example in the study of Schvanveldt (1969), or the similar experiments by Keele (1967). By contrast, when difficulty is manipulated in a way that presumably does not affect the action plan (e.g., varying tracking difficulty does not change the instruction, which is to keep the pointer on the target) the phenomenon termed *difficulty insensitivity* by Wickens (1980) should be observed (provided that there are no other sources of interference; see next Section): Though performance is somewhat lower than in single-task control conditions, there is no increase in interference due to different levels of difficulty in the other task (e.g., Briggs, Peters, & Fisher, 1972; Israel, Chesney, Wickens, & Donchin, 1980; Roediger, Knight, & Kantowitz, 1977).

This analysis can also provide a clue to the observation that seemingly easier tracking tasks sometimes suffer more interference than more difficult tasks. This was found by Trumbo, Noble, & Quigley (1968) when tracking was made easier by making it more predictable. According to the present interpretation, predictability would increase the demands on action planning, though it improves performance and thus makes the task seemingly easier. Introduction of a secondary task that also involves action planning should reveal this.

This account of dual-task interference is, however, not complete. There are additional causes of interference not due to action planning as such. One has already been mentioned: Initiating a new action should interfere with an ongoing action. I now turn to a further source of interference, which is related to parameter specification.

Parameter Specification and Practice Effects

In an earlier section the process of parameter specification was analyzed with respect to two potential problems, underspecification and overspecification. Underspecification was said to exist when a skill, in conjunction with input information, is insufficient to specify all parameters of an action. The term overspecification was suggested for the case where pieces of environmental information are simultaneously available that specify the same parameter(s) in mutually exclusive ways. This Section is concerned with underspecification. Overspecification is discussed in the next Section. One possible solution to the underspecification problem is the default assignment of parameter values, for example in the case where an animal exhibits a certain behavior in the absence of stimulation (so-called "vacuum activities"). In humans, one major possibility is action planning. Before a task-specific skill, say for typewriting, has been acquired, people can nevertheless master the task, albeit slowly, by using some general skills from their repertoire, combining them appropriately, and determining the necessary parameters by way of action planning. As practice proceeds, a new specific skill apparently develops to enable specifying these parameters directly and/or by picking up environmental information. Anderson (1982) has described this process as the transition from a declarative to a procedural form of representing knowledge.

One effect of practice seems thus to be the relief of the action-planning mechanisms from the task of specifying some of the action's parameters. This should reduce the kind of unspecific interference that is due to action planning. Indeed, unspecific dual-task interference is progressively reduced as a skill is practiced (e.g., Bahrick & Shelly, 1958; Fisk & Schneider, 1983; Mohnkopf, 1933). Interestingly, unspecific interference is also small or absent, if an action's parameters can be specified in a direct, highly "compatible" way by input information (McLeod & Posner, 1984), as should be the case according to the present considerations.

Much of dual-task interference is, however, specific. I have argued that it is too specific to be explainable by a limited number of resources. I now briefly describe an alternative to the resource view. Parameter specification demands that each parameter is given exactly one value at a time. (A movement cannot go into different directions at the same time, the speech apparatus is not equipped to simultaneously pronounce two words, etc.) This can only be guaranteed if the process of parameter specification is organized in such a way that different values of the same parameter of the same skill cannot coexist. One possible way to ensure this—which need of course not be the one actually used by the CNS—could be coding the different parameter values by different activity patterns of the same population of neurons (see Anderson, Silverstein, Ritz, & Jones, 1977; Arbib, 1981; for examples of this type of idea in different theoretical contexts). Whatever the mechanism, it should work not only if a given skill is used to control a single action, but also if an action plan has been set up that demands using the same skill for two *different* actions. Concurrent actions should therefore be possible only to the degree that they can use separate skills.

This will of course depend on the similarity between the two tasks, but likewise on the person's repertoire of skills. The more general the available skills, the greater the chance that the to-be-combined actions will depend on the same skills and therefore cannot be performed concurrently. Acquiring more specific skills should therefore be a way to overcome dual-task interference. The literature seems to be in general agreement with this view. Thus, Heuer (1984) cites a number of studies that indicate a progressive reduction of functional overlap between tasks in the course of training. A further factor that may be involved in practice is the acquisition of a coordination between the skills, for example with respect to timing (e.g., Kalsbeek, 1964; Wehner & Stadler, 1982). One way of viewing this is that the initially separate skills become integrated into a higher order skill, so that the situation factually ceases to be dual task. At least in some cases this view seems to be commonly shared by researchers. For example, reading while concurrently articulating different words or sound patterns is an often-used dual-task paradigm (e.g., Baddeley, Eldridge, & Lewis, 1981; Kleiman, 1975; Levy, 1977). Basically the same situation exists when skilled readers read aloud, for there is an eye-voice span of several words, and hence a word is being read while a different word is being uttered. Yet this is usually not regarded to be dual-task performance.

Object Selection

The problem of overspecification exists because in most natural—and in some laboratory—settings information that is suitable to specify part of an action's parameters is present in several variants. Take, for example, the situation where one wants to pick an apple from a tree (Neumann, 1980, 1983): There are probably a number of apples that my arm could reach and that thus could be used to specify the grasping movement. Obviously I cannot grasp all of them at the same time; so it has to be decided which one will be used for this purpose.

At first sight, this problem may look deceivingly simple. One might think that it suffices to somehow select the most attractive apple and then to grasp it. There are two reasons why the problem is not that simple. First, different attributes of each apple provide the information to specify different parameters of the action. For example, an apple's vertical and horizontal distance from my shoulder joint specify the target of my arm movement, whereas an apple's size and possibly weight specify the clutching movement of my fingers when grasping it. One apple may be attractive in one respect, and the other in another respect. Yet I cannot reach towards one apple and then grasp another. This is the problem of the *consistency* of selection. Second, one apple may be the most attractive at one moment, whereas a moment later a different apple may be more attractive. This could easily lead to an inefficient oscillation between different apples. Hence there is the further problem to guarantee the *continuity* of action, once a decision has been made.

The basis of solving both problems is, I suggest, provided by structural aspects of the real environment (Wolff, 1977): The world's structure is such that each apple differs from all others with respect to its position in (three-dimensional) space, and further, that all the apple's attributes are located at that position. Thus, by directing myself towards a position in space, I can solve the consistency problem (all attributes that I select belong necessarily to the same apple) as well as the continuity problem (as long as I maintain this direction, I will not be lured by other apples into revising my decision).

Of course many selection problems of this kind are more complicated. For example, both the animal and the target object may be mobile. Nevertheless the basic principle is, in my view, the same: In order to solve the overspecification problem, an animal selects one of the competing objects by directing itself towards its position in space. There are three kinds of "directing": One that involves the whole body—e.g., a predator selects a prey animal out of a flock by running in its direction—; one that involves parts of the body or receptor organs (e.g., head or eye movements, or turning the ears); and finally there is covert orienting by merely directing attention towards the selected object. I propose that these three kinds of directing are related in two ways: They complement each other (for example, one or the other may be the most efficient, depending on the "grain size" of the selection problem); and there are control relations between them: Exploratory movements of the receptor organs can provide the information needed to direct the whole body, and attentional focusing can serve to control both the receptor organs and the whole body (one example is the presaccadic attention shift; see Wolff, 1984).

One may wonder why the selection—at least the attentional selection—of an object to specify parameters of one particular action results in the rejected objects being decoupled from all action. The answer could be that there is nothing to be lost and much to be gained by such a mechanism. There is nothing to be lost because, according to the present view, simultaneous independent actions are impossible anyway. The benefit is that by excluding competing objects from being connected to any action the ongoing action is protected against interruption, which should contribute to the necessary balance between stabilizing action and interrupting it if important changes occur in the environment.

This approach leads to a view of sensory attention that seems to be in line with much of the experimental literature (Neumann, 1980, 1983, 1985a, b; Wolff, 1977). Demonstrating this by analyzing experimental data is beyond the scope of this chapter. In conclusion, I just briefly mention some types of findings that seem to conform to it.

The approach suggests that attentional selection (focusing) is the selection of objects (or, possibly, higher order perceptual units such as groups of objects). To my knowledge, Wolff (1977) was the first to put this forward explicitly. More recently, similar views have been expressed by several authors (e.g., Allport, this volume; Duncan, 1984; Kahneman & Henik, 1981; Kahneman & Treisman, 1984; Neumann, 1980; van der Heijden, Hagenaar, & Bloem, 1984). This implies that whether or not visual information can be attended to simultaneously is not a matter of information load but of structural factors, especially of spatial arrangement.

This has been supported in many experiments. Thus, features that belong to different dimensions of the same object (e.g., form and color) can be simultaneously processed without interference (e.g., Allport, 1971; Biederman & Checkosky, 1970; Saraga & Shallice, 1973). If figural elements form part of a supraordinate perceptual unit, they can in some cases even be processed better than when presented in isolation (word superiority effect and object superiority effect; see above). Separate figural units can, to a certain extent and under appropriate display conditions, be processed simultaneously if they appear in close proximity (e.g., Hoffman & Nelson, 1981), belong to one perceptual group (Treisman, 1982), or form a spatially compact configuration (Podgorny & Shepard, 1983). When these conditions are absent, capacity limits appear, e.g., with superimposed pictures or scenes that are unrelated to one another (Duncan, 1984; Goldstein & Fink, 1981; Neisser & Becklen, 1975).

The same structural factors also determine whether unwanted information can be efficiently ignored. The clearest example is the Stroop effect (Stroop, 1935), which is greatly reduced if word and color cease to be attributes of the same visual object (Goolkasian, 1981; Kahneman & Henik, 1981; Neumann, 1977, 1980; v.d.Heijden, Hagenaar, & Bloem, 1984).

CONCLUSION

The aim of the present chapter has been to present a view of attention, and more specifically of limited capacity, that regards "attention" as based on an ensemble of mechanisms that the brain needs to cope with different selection problems in the control of action, rather than as the expression of processing limitations.

In the first part, I have reviewed different answers to the question why attentional capacity is limited. Those that explain (the empirical fact of) limited capacity by (some theoretical construct(s) of) limited Capacity have been found to be unsatisfactory. There have been, however, several developments away from Capacity thinking that I have discussed with critical sympathy.

The main assumption of the framework developed in the second part of the chapter has been that there are basically two types of selection problems to be solved by animals as well as humans: The problem of effector recruitment (Which skills, related to action goals, are given access to the effector system?), and the problem of parameter specification (Which of the possible specifications of an action's parameters is put into effect?). I have tried to convince the reader that these problems offer a clue to a functional understanding of the different categories of interference that appear in the attention literature. Of course this is not more than a first small step towards more adequate models of the mechanisms of attention.

ACKNOWLEDGMENTS

I thank Alan Allport, Bruce Bridgeman, Dom Massaro, Doug Mewhort, Lex van der Heijden, and Andries Sanders for helpful discussions and comments on an earlier draft.

REFERENCES

Adler, A. (1977). *Die Wirkung eines zusätzlichen Reizes im Gesichtsfeld auf den Verlauf der Metakontrastfunktion: III. Ein Kontrollexperiment mit objektiven Leistungsmaßen.* Unpublished thesis, Department of Psychology, Ruhr-University Bochum, Germany.

Allport, D. A. (1980). Attention and performance. In G. Claxton (Ed.), *Cognitive psychology—new directions.* London: Routledge & Kegan Paul.

Allport, D. A., Antonis, B., & Reynolds, P. (1972). On the division of attention: A disproof of the single channel hypothesis. *Quarterly Journal of Experimental Psychology, 24,* 225–235.

Anderson, J. A., & Hinton, G. E. (1981). Models of information processing in the brain. In G. E. Hinton & J. A. Anderson (Eds.), *Parallel models of associative memory.* Hillsdale, NJ: Lawrence Erlbaum Associates.

Anderson, J. A., Silverstein, J. W., Ritz, S. A., & Jones, R. S. (1977). Distinctive features, categorical perception, and probability learning: Some applications of a neural model. *Psychological Review, 84,* 413–451.

Anderson, J. R. (1982). Acquisition of cognitive skill. *Psychological Review, 89,* 369–406.

Arbib, M. A. (1981). Perceptual structures and distributed motor control. In V. B. Brooks (Ed.), *Handbook of physiology, Sect. 1: The nervous system. Vol. 2: Motor control,* Part 2. Bethesda, MD: American Physiological Society.

Baddeley, A., Eldridge, M., & Lewis, V. (1981). The role of subvocalisation in reading. *Quarterly Journal of Experimental Psychology, 33A,* 439–454.

Bahrick, H. P., & Shelly, C. (1958). Time-sharing as an index of automatization. *Journal of Experimental Psychology, 56,* 288–293.

Bernstein, A. S. (1979). The orienting response as novelty and significance detector: Reply to O'Gorman. *Psychophysiology, 16,* 263–273.

Bernstein, A. S. (1981). The orienting response and stimulus significance: Further comments. *Biological Psychology, 12,* 171–185.

Biederman, I., & Checkosky, S. F. (1970). Processing redundant information. *Journal of Experimental Psychology, 83,* 486–490.

Bornemann, E. (1942). Untersuchungen über den Grad der geistigen Beanspruchung. *Arbeitsphysiologie, 12,* 142–172.

Braitenberg, V. (1977). *On the texture of brains.* New York & Berlin: Springer.

Bridgeman, B. (in press). *The biology of behavior and mind.* New York: Wiley.

Briggs, G. E., Peters, G. L., & Fisher, R. P. (1972). On the locus of the divided-attention effects. *Perception & Psychophysics, 11,* 315–320.

Broadbent, D. E. (1958). *Perception and communication.* New York: Pergamon Press.

Broadbent, D. E. (1971). *Decision and stress.* New York: Academic Press.

Broadbent, D. E. (1982). Task combination and selective intake of information. *Acta Psychologica, 50,* 253–290.

Brooks, L. R. (1968). Spatial and verbal components of the act of recall. *Canadian Journal of Psychology, 22,* 349–368.

Cattell, J. McK. (1885). The inertia of the eye and brain. *Brain, 8,* 295–312.

Cherry, C. (1953). Some experiments on the recognition of speech, with one and with two ears. *Journal of the Acoustical Society of America, 25,* 975–979.

Corteen, R. S., & Wood, B. (1972). Autonomic responses to shock-associated words in an unattended channel. *Journal of Experimental Psychology, 94,* 308–313.

Creutzfeldt, O. D. (1983). *Cortex cerebri.* Berlin: Springer.

Dawson, M. E., & Schell, A. M. (1982). Electrodermal responses to attended and unattended significant stimuli during dichotic listening. *Journal of Experimental Psychology: Human Perception and Performance, 8,* 315–324.

Deutsch, J. A., & Deutsch, D. (1963). Attention: Some theoretical considerations. *Psychological Review, 70,* 80-90.

Duncan, J. (1979). Divided attention: The whole is more than the sum of its parts. *Journal of Experimental Psychology: Human Perception and Performance, 5,* 216-228.

Duncan, J. (1980). The locus of interference in the perception of simultaneous stimuli. *Psychological Review, 87,* 272-300.

Duncan, J. (1981). Directing attention in the visual field. *Perception & Psychophysics, 30,* 90-93.

Duncan, J. (1984). Selective attention and the organization of visual information. *Journal of Experimental Psychology: General, 113,* 501-517.

Egeth, H. A. (1977). Attention and preattention. In G. H. Bower (Ed.), *The psychology of learning and motivation* (Vol. 7). New York: Academic Press.

Fentress, J. C. (1973). Specific and nonspecific factors in the causation of behavior. In P. P. G. Bateson & P. H. Klopfer (Eds.), *Perspectives in ethology.* New York: Plenum.

Fisk, A. D., & Schneider, W. (1983). Category and word search: Generalizing search principles to complex processing. *Journal of Experimental Psychology: Learning, Memory, and Cognition, 9,* 177-195.

Forster, F. M., & Govier, E. (1978). Discrimination without awareness? *Quarterly Journal of Experimental Psychology, 30,* 282-295.

Friedman, A., & Polson, M. C. (1981). Hemispheres as independent resource systems: Limited-capacity processing and cerebral specialisation. *Journal of Experimental Psychology: Human Perception and Performance, 7,* 1031-1058.

Fuster, J. M. (1980). *The prefrontal cortex.* New York: Raven Press.

Goldstein, E. G., & Fink, S. I. (1981). Selective attention in vision: Recognition memory for superimposed line drawings. *Journal of Experimental Psychology: Human Perception and Performance, 7,* 954-967.

Goolkasian, P. (1981). Retinal location and its effect on the processing of target and distractor information. *Journal of Experimental Psychology: Human Perception and Performance, 7,* 1247-1257.

Gopher, D., Brickner, M., & Navon, D. (1982). Different difficulty manipulations interact differently with task emphasis: Evidence for multiple resources. *Journal of Experimental Psychology: Human Perception and Performance, 8,* 146-157.

Gopher, D., & Sanders, A. F. (1984). "S-Oh-R": Oh stages! Oh resources! In W. Prinz & A. F. Sanders (Eds.), *Cognition and motor processes.* Berlin: Springer.

Gottsdanker, R., & Stelmach, G. E. (1971). The persistence of psychological refractoriness. *Journal of Motor Behavior, 3,* 301-312.

Govier, E., & Pitts, M. (1982). The contextual disambiguation of a polysemous word in an unattended message. *British Journal of Psychology, 73,* 537-545.

Granit, R., & Pompeiano, O. (Eds.), (1979). Reflex control of posture and movement. *Progress in brain research* (Vol. 50). Amsterdam: Elsevier/North-Holland.

Halliday, T. R. (1980). Motivational systems and interactions between systems. In F. M. Toates & T. R. Halliday (Eds.), *Analysis of motivational processes.* New York: Academic Press.

van der Heijden, A. H. C., Hagenaar, R., & Bloem, W. (1984). Two stages in postcategorical filtering and selection. *Memory & Cognition, 12,* 458-469.

van der Heijden, A. H. C., La Heij, W., & Boer, J. P. A. (1983). Parallel processing of redundant targets in simple visual search tasks. *Psychological Research, 45,* 235-254.

van der Heijden, A. H. C., Schreuder, R., Maris, L., & Neerincx, M. (1984). Some evidence for correlated separate activation in a letter-detection task. *Perception & Psychophysics, 36,* 577-585.

v. Holst, E., & v. St. Paul, U. (1963). On the functional organization of drives. *Animal Behavior 11,* 1-20.

Hellige, J. B., Cox, P. J., & Litvac, L. (1979). Information processing in the cerebral hemispheres: Selective hemispheric activation and capacity limitations. *Journal of Experimental Psychology: General, 108,* 251–279.

Herdman, C. M., & Friedman, A. (1985). Multiple resources in divided attention: A cross-modal test of the independence of hemispheric resources. *Journal of Experimental Psychology: Human Perception and Performance, 11,* 40–49.

Heuer, H. (1984). Motor learning as a process of structural constriction and displacement. In W. Prinz & A. F. Sanders (Eds.), *Cognition and motor process.* Berlin: Springer.

Hick, W. E. (1952). On the rate of gain of information. *Quarterly Journal of Experimental Psychology, 4,* 11–26.

Hinde, R. A. (1970). *Animal behavior: A synthesis of ethology and comparative psychology.* New York: MacGraw–Hill.

Hirst, W., Spelke, E. S., Reaves, C. C., Caharack, G.,& Neisser, U. (1980). Dividing attention without alternation or automaticity. *Journal of Experimental Psychology: General 109,* 98–117.

Hoffman, J. E., & Nelson, B. (1981). Spatial selectivity in visual search. *Perception & Psychophysis, 30,* 282–290.

Holtzman, J. D., Sidtis, J. J., Volpe, B. T., Wilson, D. H., & Gazzaniga, M. S. (1981). Dissociation of spatial information for stimulus localization and the control of attention. *Brain, 104,* 861–872.

Israel, J. B., Chesney, G. L., Wickens, C. D., & Donchin, E. (1980). P300 and tracking difficulty: Evidence for multiple resources in dual-task performance. *Psychophysiology, 17,* 259–273.

Johnston, W. A., & Heinz, S. P. (1978). Flexibility and capacity demands of attention. *Journal of Experimental Psychology: General, 10,* 420–435.

Jonides, J. (1981). Voluntary versus automatic control over the mind's eye's movements. In J. Long & A. D. Baddeley (Eds.), *Attention and performance IX.* Hillsdale, NJ: Lawrence Erlbaum Associates.

Kahneman, D. (1973). *Attention and effort.* Englewood Cliffs, NJ: Prentice–Hall.

Kahneman, D., & Henik, A. (1981). Perceptual organization and attention. In M. Kubovy & J. R. Pomerantz (Eds.), *Perceptual organization,* Hillsdale, NJ: Lawrence Erlbaum Associates.

Kahneman, D., & Treisman, A. (1984). Changing views of attention and automaticity. In R. Parasuraman & D. R. Davies (Eds.). *Varieties of attention.* New York: Academic Press.

Kalsbeek, J. W. H. (1964). On the measurement of deterioriation in performance caused by distraction stress. *Ergonomics, 7,* 187–195.

Keele, S. W. (1967). Compatibility and time-sharing in serial reaction time. *Journal of Experimental Psychology, 75,* 529–539.

Keele, S. W., & Neill, W. T. (1978). Mechanisms of attention. In E. C. Carterette & M. P. Friedman (Eds.), *Handbook of perception, Vol IX: Perceptual processing.* New York: Academic Press.

Kinsbourne, M., & Hicks, R. E. (1978). Functional cerebral space: A model for overflow, transfer, and interference effects in human performance: A tutorial review. In J. Requin (Ed.), *Attention and performance VII,* Hillsdale, NJ: Lawrence Erlbaum Associates.

Klapp, S. T. (1979). Doing two things at once: The role of temporal compatibility. *Memory & Cognition, 7,* 375–381.

Kleiman, G. M. (1975). Speech recoding in reading. *Journal of Verbal Learning and Verbal Behavior, 14,* 323–339.

Lanze, M., Weisstein, N., & Harris, J. R. (1982). Perceived depth vs. structural relevance in the object-superiority effect. *Perception & Psychophysics, 31,* 376–382.

Lappin, S., & Ellis, St. H. (1970). The span of apprehension: Form identification as a function of amount of information displayed. *Perception & Psychophysics, 7,* 65–72.

Lawson, E. A. (1966). Decisions concerning the rejected channel. *Quarterly Journal of Experimental Psychology, 18,* 260-265.
Levy, B. A. (1977). Reading: Speech and meaning processes. *Journal of Verbal Learning and Verbal Behavior, 16,* 623-638.
Lewis, J. L. (1970). Semantic processing of unattended messages using dichotic listening. *Journal of Experimental Psychology, 85,* 225-228.
Lindsay, P. H., Taylor, M. M., & Forbes, S. M. (1968). Attention and multidimensional discrimination. *Perception & Psychophysics, 4,* 113-117.
Logan, G. (1985). Executive control of thought and action. *Acta Psychologica, 60,* 193-210.
Lucas, M., & Bub, D. (1981). Can practice result in the ability to divide attention between two complex language tasks? Comment on Hirst et al. *Journal of Experimental Psychology: General, 110,* 495-498.
Luria, A. R. (1980). *Higher cortical function in man.* New York: Basic Books.
MacKay, D. G. (1973). Aspects of the theory of comprehension, memory, and attention. *Quarterly Journal of Experimental Psychology, 25,* 22-40.
Marcel, A. J. (1983). Conscious and unconscious perception: An approach to the relations between phenomenal experience and perceptual processes. *Cognitive Psychology, 15,* 238-302.
Massaro, D. W. (1985). Attention and perception: An information-integration perspective. *Acta Psychologica, 60,* 211-243.
Massaro, D. W., Taylor, G. A., Venezky, R. L., Jastrembski, J. E., & Lucas, P. A. (1980). *Letter and word perception: Orthographic structure and visual processing in reading.* Amsterdam: North-Holland.
McClelland, J. L. (1978). Perception and masking of wholes and parts. *Journal of Experimental Psychology: Human Perception and Performance, 4,* 210-223.
McFarland, D. J. (1974). Time-sharing as a behavioral phenomenon. *Advances in the Study of Behavior, 5,* 201-225.
McLeod, P. D. (1977). A dual-task response modality effect: Support for multiprocessor models of attention. *Quarterly Journal of Experimental Psychology, 29,* 651-667.
McLeod, P., McLaughlin, C. & Nimmo-Smith, L. (1985). Information encapsulation and automaticity: Evidence from the visual control of finely timed actions. In M. I. Posner & O. S. M. Marin (Eds.), *Attention and performance XI: Mechanisms of attention.* Hillsdale, NJ: Lawrence Erlbaum Associates.
McLeod P. J., & Posner, M. I. (1982). *Probe RTs and central capacity limits with separate response systems.* Unpublished Manuscript, University of Oregon. 1981 (cited in Posner, 1982).
McLeod, P., & Posner, M. I. (1984). Priviledged loops from percept to act. In H. Bouma & D. G. Bouwhuis (Eds.), *Attention and performance X: Control of language processes.* Hillsdale, NJ: Lawrence Erlbaum Associates.
Merkel, J. (1885). Die zeitlichen Verhältnisse der Willensthätigkeit. *Philosophische Studien, 2,* 73-127.
Millar, K. (1975). Processing capacity requirements of stimulus encoding. *Acta Psychologica, 39,* 393-410.
Miller, J. (1982). Divided attention: Evidence for coactivation with redundant signals. *Cognitive Psychology, 14,* 247-279.
Mohnkopf, W. (1933). Zur Automatisierung willkürlicher Bewegungen. *Zeitschrift für Psychologie, 130,* 235-299.
Navon, D. (1984). Resources—a theoretical soup stone? *Psychological Review, 91,* 216-234.
Navon, D., & Gopher, D. (1979). On the economy of the human processing system. *Psychological Review, 86,* 214-225.
Neisser, U. (1976). *Cognition and reality.* San Francisco: Freeman.

Neisser, U., & Becklen, R. (1975). Selective looking: Attending to visually specified events. *Cognitive Psychology, 7,* 480–494.
Neisser, U., Hirst, W., & Spelke, E. S. (1981). Limited capacity theories and the notion of automaticity: Reply to Lucas and Bub. *Journal of Experimental Psychology: General, 110,* 499–500.
Neumann, O. (1971). Aufmerksamkeit. In J. Ritter (Ed.), *Historisches Wörterbuch der Philosophie* (Vol. 1). Basel & Stuttgart: Schwabe.
Neumann, O. (1977). *Steuerung der Informationsselektion durch visuelle und "semantische" Reizmerkmale.* Report no. 2, Cognitive Psychology Unit, Department of Psychology, Ruhr University, Bochum, Germany.
Neumann, O. (1978a). Aufmerksamkeit als 'Zentrale Verarbeitungskapazität'. Anmerkungen zu einer Metapher. In M. Tücke & W. Deffner (Eds.), *Proceedings of the 2nd Osnabrück Psychology Workshop.* Reports from Fachbereich 3, no. 10, Osnabrück University, Germany.
Neumann, O. (1978b). *Zum Mechanismus der Interferenz beim dichotischen Hören.* Report no. 5, Cognitive Psychology Unit, Department of Psychology, Ruhr University, Bochum, Germany.
Neumann, O. (1980). *Informationsselektion und Handlungssteuerung. Untersuchungen zur Funktionsgrundlage des Stroop-Interferenzphänomens.* Dissertation, Bochum, Germany.
Neumann, O. (1983). *Uber den Zusammenhang zwischen Enge und Selektivität der Aufmerksamkeit.* Report no. 19, Cognitive Psychology Unit, Department of Psychology, Ruhr University, Bochum, Germany.
Neumann, O. (1984). Automatic processing: A review of recent findings and a plea for an old theory. In W. Prinz & A. F. Sanders (Eds.), *Cognition and motor processes.* Berlin: Springer.
Neumann, O. (1985a). Die Hypothese begrenzter Kapazität und die Funktionen der Aufmerksamkeit. In O. Neumann (Ed.), *Perspektiven der Kognitionspsychologie.* Berlin: Springer.
Neumann, O. (1985b). *The limited capacity hypothesis and the functions of attention.* Report no. 23, Research Group on Perception and Action at the Center for Interdisciplinary Research, Bielefeld University, Germany.
Neumann, O., & Koch, R. (1986). *Action planning: An experimental paradigm and some preliminary results.* Report no. 108, Research Group on Perception and Action at the Center for Interdisciplinary Research, Bielefeld University, Germany.
Noble, M. E., Sanders, A. F., & Trumbo, D. A. (1981). Concurrence costs in double stimulation tasks. *Acta Psychologica, 49,* 141–158.
Norman, D. A., & Bobrow, D. S. (1975). On data-limited and resource-limited processes. *Cognitive Psychology, 7,* 44–64.
North, R. A. (1977). *Task components and demands as factors in dual-task performance.* (Technical Report ARL-77-2-AFOSR-77-2), Aviation Research Laboratory, Institute of Aviation, University of Illinois.
Ostry, D., Moray, N., & Marks, G. (1976). Attention, practice and semantic targets. *Journal of Experimental Psychology: Human Perception and Performance, 2,* 326–336.
Paap, K. R., Newsome, S. L., McDonald, J. E., & Schvaneveldt, R. W. (1982). An activation-verification model for letter and word recognition: The word-superiority effect. *Psychological Review, 89,* 573–594.
Peters, M. (1977). Simultaneous performance of two motor activities: The factor of timing. *Neuropsychologia, 15,* 461–465.
Peters, M. (1985). Constraints in the performance of bimanual tasks and their expression in unskilled and skilled subjects. *Quarterly Journal of Experimental Psychology, 37A,* 171–196.
Podgorny, P., & Shepard, R. N. (1983). Distribution of visual attention over space. *Journal of Experimental Psychology: Human Perception and Performance, 9,* 380–393.
Pohlmann, L. D., & Sorkin, R. D. (1976). Simultaneous three-channel signal detection: Performance and criterion as a function of order of report. *Perception & Psychophysics, 20,* 179–186.

Posner, M. I. (1978). *Chronometric explorations of mind.* Hillsdale, NJ: Lawrence Erlbaum Associates.
Posner, M. I. (1980). Orienting of attention. *Quarterly Journal of Experimental Psychology, 32,* 3–25.
Posner, M. I. (1982). Cumulative development of attentional theory. *American Psychologist, 37,* 168–179.
Posner, M. I., & Boies, S. J. (1978). Components of attention. *Psychological Review, 78,* 391–408.
Poulton, E. C. (1981). Human manual control. In V. B. Brooks (Ed.), *Handbook of physiology: The nervous system. Vol. 2: Motor control,* Part 2. Bethesda, MD: American Physiological Society.
Prinzmetal, W., & Millis-Wright, M. (1984). Cognitive and linguistic factors affect visual feature integration. *Cognitive Psychology, 16,* 305–340.
Proctor, R. W., & Proctor, J. D. (1979). Secondary task modality, expectancy, and the measurement of attention capacity. *Journal of Experimental Psychology: Human Perception and Performance, 5,* 610–624.
Reicher, G. M. (1969). Perceptual recognition as a function of meaningfulness of stimulus material. *Journal of Experimental Psychology, 81,* 275–280.
Roediger, H. L., Knight, J. L., & Kantowitz, B. H. (1977). Inferring decay in short-term memory: The issue of capacity. *Memory & Cognition, 7,* 167–176.
Rohrbaugh, J. W. (1984). The orienting reflex: Performance and central nervous system manifestations. In R. Parasuraman & D. R. Davies (Eds.), *Varieties of attention.* New York: Academic Press.
Rosenbaum, D. A. (1984). The planning and control of movements. In J. R. Anderson & S. M. Kosslyn (Eds.), *Tutorials in learning and memory.* San Francisco: Freemann.
Salthouse, T. A., & Somberg, B. L. (1982). Skilled performance: Effects of adult age and experience on elementary processes. *Journal of Experimental Psychology: General, 111,* 176–207.
Sanders, A. F. (1979). Some remarks on mental load. In N. Moray (Ed.), *Mental workload. Its theory and measurement.* New York: Plenum.
Sanders, A. F. (1981). Stress and human performance: A working model and some applications. In G. Salrendy & U. J. Smith (Eds.), *Machine pacing and occupational stress.* London: Taylor and Francis.
Sanders, A. F. (1983). Towards a model of stress and human performance. *Acta Psychologica, 53,* 61–97.
Saraga, E., & Shallice, T. (1973). Parallel processing of the attributes of single stimuli. *Perception & Psychophysics, 13,* 261–270.
Schmidt, R. A. (1975). A schema theory of discrete motor skill learning. *Psychological Review, 82,* 225–260.
Schmidt, R. A. (1976). The schema as a solution to some persistent problems in motor learning theory. In G. E. Stelmach (Ed.), *Motor control: Issues and trends,* New York: Academic Press.
Schmidt, R. A. (1982). *Motor control and learning: A behavioral emphasis.* Champaign, Ill.: Human Kinetics.
Schneider, W. (1983, November 18). *A simulation of automatic controlled processing predicting attentional and practice effects.* Paper presented at the Meetings of the Psychonomic Society, San Diego, CA.
Schneider, W., Dumais, S. T., Shiffrin R. M. (1984). Automatic and control processing and attention. In R. Parasurman & D. R. Davies (Eds.), *Varieties of attention,* New York: Academic Press.
Schvaneveldt, R. W. (1969). Effects of complexity in simultaneous reaction time tasks. *Journal of Experimental Psychology, 81,* 289–296.

Schweickert, W., & Boggs, G.J. (1984). Models of central capacity and concurrency. *Journal of Mathematical Psychology, 28,* 223-281.
Shaffer, L. H. (1975). Multiple attention in continuous verbal tasks. In P. M. A. Rabbitt & S. Dornic (Eds.), *Attention and performance V.* New York: Academic Press.
Shaffer, L. H. (1981). Performances of Chopin, Bach, and Bartok: Studies in motor programming. *Cognitive Psychology, 13,* 326-376.
Shallice, T. (1972). Dual functions of consciousness. *Psychological Review, 79,* 383-393.
Shallice, T. (1978). The dominant action system: An information-processing approach to consciousness. In K. S. Pape & J. L. Singer (Eds.), *The stream of consciousness.* New York: Plenum.
Sokolov, E. N. (1963). *Perception and the conditioned reflex.* Oxford: Pergamon Press.
Spelke, E., Hirst, W., & Neisser, U. (1976). Skills of divided attention. *Cognition, 4,* 215-230.
Sperry, R. W. (1966). Brain bisection and mechanisms of consciousness. In J. Eccles (Ed.), *Brain and conscious experience,* Berlin: Springer.
Stroop, J. R. (1935). Studies of interference in serial verbal reactions. *Journal of Experimental Psychology, 18,* 643-662.
Treisman, A. (1982). Perceptual grouping and attention in visual search for features and for objects. *Journal of Experimental Psychology: Human Perception and Performance, 8,* 194-214.
Treisman, A., & Davies, A. (1973). Divided attention to ear and eye. In S. Kornblum (Ed.), *Attention and performance IV.* New York: Academic Press.
Treisman, A., & Gelade, G. (1980) A feature-integration theory of attention. *Cognitive Psychology, 12,* 97-136.
Treisman, A., Kahneman, D., & Burkell, J. (1983). Perceptual objects and the cost of filtering. *Perception & Psychophysics, 33,* 527-532.
Treisman, A., & Paterson, R. (1984). Emergent features, attention, and object perception. *Journal of Experimental Psychology: Human Perception and Performance, 10,* 12-31.
Treisman, A., Schmidt, H. (1982). Illusory conjunctions in the perception of objects. *Cognitive Psychology, 14,* 107-141.
Treisman, A., Squire, R., & Green, J. (1974). Semantic processing in dichotic listening? A replication. *Memory & Cognition, 2,* 641-646.
Trumbo, D., Noble, M., & Quigley, J. (1968). Sequential probabilities and the performance of serial tasks. *Journal of Experimental Psychology, 76,* 364-372.
Underwood, S. (1977). Contextual facilitation from attended and unattended messages. *Journal of Verbal Learning and Verbal Behavior, 16,* 99-106.
Virzi, R. A., & Egeth, H. E. (1984). Is meaning implicated in illusory conjunctions? *Journal of Experimental Psychology: Human Perception and Performance, 10,* 573-580.
Wandmacher, J. (1981). Contour effects in figure perception. *Psychological Research, 43,* 347-360.
Wehner, T., & Stadler, M. (1982). Frequenzanalytische Untersuchungen zur kognitiven Steuerung von Mehrfachhandlungen durch Rhythmisierung. *Zeitschrift für Psychologie, 190,* 183-201.
Weisstein, N., & Harris, C. S., Visual detection of line segments: An object superiority effect. *Science, 186,* 752-755.
Welford, A. T. (1952). The "psychological refractory period" and the timing of high-speed performance—A review and a theory. *British Journal of Psychology, 43,* 2-19.
Wheeler, D. J. (1970). Processes in word recognition. *Cognitive Psychology, 1,* 59-85.
Wickens, C. D. (1980). The structure of attentional resources. In R. S. Nickerson (Ed.), *Attention and performance VIII.* Hillsdale, NJ: Lawrence Erlbaum Associates.
Wickens, C. D. (1984). Processing resources in attention. In R. Parasuraman & D. R. Davies (Eds.), *Varieties of attention.* New York: Academic Press.
Wickens, C. D., & Kessel, C. (1980). Processing resource demands of failure detection in dynamic

systems. *Journal of Experimental Psychology: Human Perception and Performance, 6,* 564–577.

Wing, A., & Allport, D. A. (1972). Multidimensional encoding of visual form. *Perception & Psychophysics, 12,* 474–476.

Wolff, P. (1977). *Entnahme der Identitäts—und Positionsinformation bei der Identifikation tachistoskopischer Buchstabenzeilen. Ein theoretischer und experimenteller Beitrag zur Grundlagenforschung des Lesens.* Dissertation, Bochum, Germany.

Wolff, P. (1984). Saccadic eye movements and visual stability: Preliminary considerations towards a cognitive approach. In W. Prinz & A. F. Sanders (Eds.), *Cognition and motor processes.* Berlin: Springer.

15 Selection for Action: Some Behaviorial and Neurophysiological Considerations of Attention and Action

Alan Allport
Oxford University

This chapter is about the processes that *selectively* couple perception to action (or sensory processing to motor control). It is to be emphasized that the ideas put forward are in a very preliminary stage of development. My intention in this chapter is to focus discussion on some of the issues involved, rather than to put forward a fully fledged theory of selection-for-action.

I. INTRODUCTION: BEHAVIORAL CONSIDERATIONS

I assume that perceptual systems have evolved in all species of animals solely as a means of guiding and controlling action, either present or future. Indeed, I find it difficult to get any clear conception of what "perception" might be, as a subject of scientific study, isolated from its role in the control of action. See MacKay (1966, 1981) for lucid discussion of this issue.

The systems that thus make use of sensory information—that couple "perception" to "action"—must deal moment by moment with two essential forms of *selection*. Put briefly, these are: Which action? and Which object to act upon?[1] (More precisely, which *category* and/or *mode* of action? and second, How and where is the action to be *directed*?) There is reason to believe that these two major forms of selection are organized somewhat independently. There is a large measure of anatomical dissociability between the various systems critically in-

---

[1]There is also, of course, the choice of *when* to act. In this chapter the important issues of the *timing* of action are, in large measure, simply ignored. With an equally bad conscience I have left out of consideration the reafferent effects of action on the time course of sensory events.

volved in these different aspects of selective, perceptual-motor control; different forms of cerebral injury can result in severe, selective deficits in *either* one, leaving the other relatively intact.[2] Some of the evidence relevant to this claim is referenced in Section II. Additional and perhaps even more direct evidence of the dissociability of these two major forms of selection can be seen in many everyday "slips of action" (Norman, 1981; Reason, 1979). The appropriate category of action is chosen, but it is directed to, or carried out on, the wrong object; conversely, the right object (or the right location) is selected, but the inappropriate class of action is performed. These errors of course represent breakdowns in the normal process by which the selection of a given *category* of action, and its selective *direction* in space and time, are integrated or coordinated together. Such a process of integration, or coordination, is manifestly essential for the coherence of action, hence for survival. How it may occur is the topic of this chapter.

Selection-for-action

To start off with, I attempt to characterize one aspect of the selective integration problem, which I call the problem of "selection-for-action." (Assume, for the moment, that the choice of a particular category of action is simply "given"). The action is, say, picking apples. Many fruit are within reach, and clearly visible, yet for each individual reach of the hand, for each act of plucking, information about just one of them must govern the particular pattern and direction of movements. The disposition of the *other* apples, already encoded by the brain, must be in some way temporarily decoupled from the direct control of reaching, though it may of course still influence the action, for example as representing an obstacle to be reached around, not to be dislodged, and so on. The same necessity of selecting, in respect of a given class of action performed by a given effector system, just *one* among a number of physically available objects to act upon appears to be essentially universal. A predator (a sparrowhawk, say) encounters a pack of similar prey animals, but she must direct her attack selectively towards just one of them; the fleeing prey must, with equal speed, select just one among the possible routes of escape. Very many examples of the same general pattern can be readily called to mind. Their common properties, it appears, have a common origin. Although the senses are capable of registering many different objects together, effector systems are typically limited

---

[2]Indeed, as we see later, responsibility for different components of the how and where of sensory-motor selection, in respect of particular classes of sensory input and particular classes of action (or particular effector systems), is evidently divided among many different, functionally separable subsystems.

to carrying out just one action of a given kind at a time. Hence the biological necessity, and the theoretical importance, of selection-for-action.[3]

In primates and in other species with foveal vision, visual selection-for-action is enormously facilitated by foveation and pursuit movements of the eyes. Clearly, however, the selection of an object as a target for an eye movement *precedes* foveation; moreover, as regards other classes of action, foveation, though facilitatory, is neither a necessary nor sufficient condition for selection. It thus appears that a mechanism of fundamental importance for the sensory control of action is one that can selectively designate a specified subset of the available, and potentially relevant, sensory information to have control of a given effector system, and can selectively decouple the remainder from such control. The need for such a mechanism (of selective coupling and decoupling of perceptual and motor processes) arises directly from the many-to-many possible mappings between domains of sensory input and of motor output within the very highly parallel, distributed organization of the nervous system.

Note that the *range* of possible sensory to motor mappings, although, for adult humans, combinatorially immense, is far from being unconstrained. The diversity of action is build on a vast array of privileged, or "compatible" sensory-pattern-to-action linkages (e.g., Brainard, Irby, Fitts, & Alluisi, 1962; Hofsten, this volume; Lee, 1980; McLeod & Posner, 1984; Umiltà & Nicoletti, 1985), just as action systems are coupled by powerful synergies among effectors (e.g., Biguer, Jeannerod, & Prablanc, 1985). The important point here is that not only can the preferred or compatible linkages be radically affected by long-term learning, but the couplings must be *also* subject to *very rapidly acting* (within fractions of a second) and *task-dependent* modulation (e.g., Posner, 1980; Reeves & Sperling, 1986).

Perceptual Integration

Further, when selecting for action one among an array of objects, information pertaining to different aspects of the *same object* must be selectively linked together, and kept separate from—decoupled from—equivalent information re-

---

[3]I also intend these ideas regarding selection-for-action to apply, *mutatis mutandis*, to purely imagined objects and imagined actions. It seems clear that we can select for the guidance and control of action not only objects in the current sensory environment but also internally generated (e.g., recalled or imagined) objects and events. It is also clear that conflicts occur in selection-for-action between internally generated and environmental information (e.g., Brooks, 1968). Further, the need for and the nature of selection-for-action appears essentially unchanged whether the action involved is itself purely implicit action, or is to be overtly executed. Internally generated representations are undoubtedly of critical importance in the planning and coherence of extended sequences of actions. Again, however, in this chapter I confine the discussion to selection among sensorily available information.

garding *other* objects. Thus, if my choice of apple to pick is to be guided by the combination of color and size, it is essential, first, that the particular values of these two attributes do indeed relate to the same object and, further, that this information is correctly linked to information specifying the distance and direction needed to reach that same object, and not to equivalent information regarding any of the other objects in my field of view. Again, the need for the selective linking or integration of information across different domains of attributes, and its decoupling from other, concurrently available information belonging to *other* objects, is entailed by the parallel, distributed nature of information representation in the brain, discussed in Section II below.

Behavioral evidence that further bespeaks the need for such a process of attribute-integration, as well as giving some indication of its effects, can be found in the *errors* generated by this process. These have been referred to variously as "segmentation errors" (Allport, 1977; Shallice & McGill, 1978) and "illusory conjunctions" (e.g., Treisman, 1977; Treismann & Schmidt, 1982); they can be observed in failures of temporal as well as of spatial integration (Lawrence, 1971; McLean, Broadbent, & Broadbent, 1983). The phenomenon of simultanagnosia, that is the acquired inability to respond selectively to one spatially designated object among an array of similar visual objects, while equivalent performance with a single, visually isolated object is preserved (Levine & Calvanio, 1978; Shallice & Warrington, 1977), presumably results from neural insult to one or more components of this integrative mechanism.

Multiple Actions and Crosstalk Interference

Although a given effector system is generally limited to executing only one action of a kind at any one time, certain different classes of actions, implemented by separate effector systems and in respect of different sense-objects, can evidently be performed concurrently. This appears to be true even for very complex actions (e.g., Allport, Antonis, and Reynolds, 1972; Shaffer, 1975). Thus, for example, oral repetition ("shadowing") of continuous speech can be controlled by an auditory input, while at the same time the subject copy-types an independent, visually presented text, with remarkably little mutual interference. In this and other examples it is clear that the brain is able to maintain and update independent representations of two or more complex messages in parallel and to preserve the integrity of these different information streams in the control of separate categories of action. In certain other cases, however, this separation breaks down. A dramatic example is provided by recombining exactly the same inputs and outputs as in the previous example, in the task of simultaneously reading aloud from one text while typing or writing another text to auditory dictation (tasks that, *individually,* are performed with great proficiency). In this case the two streams of information now produce massive crosstalk, and the integrity of performance of one or both constituent tasks collapses (Tierney,

1973; Shaffer, 1975). In this example the auditory text offers a particularly direct, or "compatible," specification for the control of speech, whereas the visual text provides the optimum orthographic specification for—or "ideomotor compatibility" with—the spelling sequences of written output (Greenwald, 1972; see also Allport & Funnell, 1981). In contrast, in reading aloud, and in audio-typing, these optimally compatible input–output mappings are precisely those that are *not* required. Individually, the "less compatible" tasks of reading aloud and of audio typing can be fluently performed, even in the presence of irrelevant input in the other (more compatible) modality. With practice, writing to dictation can also be effectively combined with silent reading (Spelke, Hirst, & Neisser, 1976). Evidently, therefore, spoken and written output can each be effectively isolated (decoupled) from their optimally compatible inputs and controlled instead by other, *less* compatible information sources. This is the case when either one or other output is required alone. When *both* spoken and written output are required controlled by their less compatible inputs, however, this separation apparently breaks down.

The principal limitation on the simultaneous control of independent actions by separate sensory inputs appears to be, precisely, the difficulty of keeping the multiple streams of information separate, i.e., of *preventing crosstalk* between them, particularly when, as in the example just given, they involve the *less* compatible mappings between input–output pairs. (The case for this general view of "attentional" limitations is summarized in Allport, 1980a,b.) In other words, within each task, each effector system must be selectively decoupled from all but a specified subset of the available, and *potentially* relevant sensory information. Performance in such dual-task combinations can thus be seen as an extended or special case of the general problem of selection-for-action.

A similarly clear-cut asymmetry of crosstalk interference is seen in variants of the Stroop task, where only *one* response is to be made. Thus, for example, with word-picture combinations, in a *naming* task words interfere with pictures but not vice versa; in a conceptual *categorizing* task, pictures interfere with words, but not vice versa (Glaser & Düngelhoff, 1984).

Summary

I have just touched on three issues here—the selection among a number of potentially appropriate objects for action, the perceptual integration of object-attributes, and the maintenance of integrity among multiple concurrent sensory-motor tasks. In each of these the need apparently arises for the temporary and contingent closure of communication channels, which in other circumstances can be open, and the selective opening of others, thus enabling particular information structures to be linked and to interact while other structures that *may* so interact are temporarily segregated. A rapidly acting, dynamic process (of selective coupling and decoupling) of this kind is, I believe, an essential and ubiquitous feature of neuronal computation. It seems by no means implausible that a similar process of dynamic linkage underlies such diverse phenomena as the separation of figure and ground, the effects of preparatory attentional set, and the selective and integrative processes involved in high-level imagination and planning.

In this chapter, however, I focus on the need for such a mechanism of selective dynamic linkage in the process that I have labeled *selection-for-action*. In Section II I briefly review some observable properties of sensory-motor coding in the brain in relation to possible mechanisms of selection-for-action. In particular I discuss the possible role, in this process, of selective enhancement of sensorily evoked activity, and I consider some speculative hypotheses regarding the selective coordination, and segregation, of neural activity. In Section III I then consider some implications of these ideas for current issues in the theory of selective attention.

II. CONSIDERATIONS OF REPRESENTATION AND SELECTION IN THE BRAIN

Coding of Sensory and Action-related Properties and Their Interaction.

I begin by outlining certain features of neural coding that, I believe, have implications for a theory of selection-for-action. First, an extremely general and striking characteristic of the behavior of individual cortical (and other) neurons is their strong selectivity of response. A given cell will respond vigorously to a certain range of stimulus properties, although remaining relatively unresponsive to others (e.g., Stone & Dreher, 1982; van Essen & Maunsell, 1983). This means, in general, that the property—or properties—that are being signaled depend on what units are firing. Different sets of units signal different properties. The strength of response signals the quality of the evidence for a given property. In this sense, the signaling (or "representation") of stimulus properties in the brain can be described as "activation-coded" and "content-specific." It thus contrasts with most man-made devices for representing or storing information (books, computers, magnetic tapes, etc.), in which the location of storage—the position on the page, say—in no way defines *what* is to be represented.

In vision (and analogously in other sensory systems), cells responsive to a particular range of attributes of the retinal image are found grouped together in distinct areas of the brain, frequently in the form of separate, spatiotopic "maps" of their respective attribute domains (Cowey, 1985; van Essen & Maunsell, 1983). Multiple representation is found also in "motor" systems; in primates, about a dozen or more, distinct cortical fields appear to be involved in coding different aspects of the control of movement (Wise & Evarts, 1981). Moreover, of particular relevance to the theme of this chapter, many different aspects of selective *sensory-motor linkage* are also distributed over many different, specialized local subsystem (see following paragraphs).

A small range of cell types has been found, principally in infero-temporal cortex, that show selective response to more complex visual features, such as "face" or "hand" patterns (e.g., Desimone, Albright, Gross, & Bruce, 1984; Perrett, Rolls, & Caan, 1982). However, very few such complex trigger features have as yet been securely identified. Beyond the infero-temporal cortex, for example in the lateral hypothalamus and substantia innominata, cells can be found whose response is clearly related to the learned significance of visual stimuli for particular categories of *action*—for example their learned acceptability as food (Rolls, 1981). However these units, like those in infero-temporal cortex, are largely or even completely insensitive to differences in (i.e., they "know nothing about") an object's *spatial location*. Conversely, the units in posterior parietal cortex that map the relative environmental location of visual (and other) objects appear similarly insensitive to the object's particular visual or categorical attributes; moreover, lesions in intraparietal and posterior parietal cortex that grossly impair performance based on spatial relations between objects (e.g., "landmark" tasks) do not affect the ability to discrimate the objects themselves (Gross & Mishkin, 1977; Lynch, 1980; Rolls, 1981; Ungerleider, 1985; Ungerleider & Mishkin, 1982).[4]

Channels linking perceptual and motor subsystems can be interrupted in an immense variety of space-, modality-, and material-specific ways. (See Heilman & Valenstein, 1979, for general overview.) To illustrate, unilateral lesions in the posterior parietal region can result in a condition known as optic ataxia (Damasio & Benton, 1979; Perenin & Vighetto, 1982). There is a selective inability to use visual information from the contralateral (noncentral) retina, specifically in the guidance of manual reaching and grasping. This inability is unrelated to any specific sensory or motor deficits. Thus it can be confined to the combination of one hand and one hemifield; the *same* hand may be guided normally when in the other visual hemifield, and the *same* hemifield can guide the other hand with normal accuracy. To give just one other example of modality- and material-specific sensori-motor disconnection: In "optic aphasia" (Beauvois, 1982), visually presented objects can be responded to appropriately in all sorts of (nonverbal) ways, but can not be named, whereas naming from nonvisual sources, from a verbal description, from touch, etc., is performed correctly.

As is well known, large-scale lesions in a number of sites, expecially in posterior parietal cortex (area 7) can result in the clinical syndrome of unilateral "neglect" in both monkey and man (DeRenzi, 1982; Heilman, 1979; Kinsbourne, 1977). The patient (or animal), fails to show appropriate "selection-for-

---

[4]These functional specializations among different cortical subsystems are to be distinguished from earlier suggestions (Schneider, 1969) about the different roles of cortical and subcortical visual systems.

action" of objects, or parts of objects, contralateral to the side of the lesion. The neglect can be confined to a particular sense-modality, and may differentially affect responsiveness in specific effector systems, or even specific classes of action.

Some recent experiments with monkeys, by Rizzolatti and his associates, illustrate some of these points (Rizzolatti, Gentilucci, & Matelli, 1985; Rizzolatti, Matelli, & Pavesi, 1983). Unilateral lesions in postarcuate frontal cortex (area 6) and in the inferior parietal lobule (area 7b) — both areas that are involved in sensory-motor organization of head and arm movements in space—resulted in deficits restricted to objects presented *visually within manual reach* of the animal. The deficit did not apply to objects presented further away from the animal, and there was no loss of ocular motility or visual exploration. Further, a lesion confined to the most rostral part of area 7b, where the mouth is represented, resulted in selective neglect of both visual and tactile stimuli, but only if they were presented *close around the mouth* and face (in "peribuccal space") on the side opposite to the lesion. There was no deficit in responding to stimuli presented further away, either within or beyond manual reach. In sharp contrast, lesions in the frontal eye fields (area 8) resulted in selective, unilateral neglect of visual objects *far* from the animal. Within a few days, at least, objects in near ("peripersonal") space were responded to equally on either side, whereas there was a marked and persistent unilateral neglect of more distant visual objects.

As discussed earlier, selection-for-action can evidently occur with some degree of independence in respect of actions performed by different effector systems and in respect of different sources of sensory input. The findings of Rizzolatti et al., just described, illustrate in a rather striking way that the mechanisms governing the selection-for-action of visual objects are distributed among a variety of specialized, effector-oriented, modular components.

Modulation of Sensory Neural Coding in Relation to Action

There is a variety of evidence showing that neural responses to sensory stimuli can be modulated in relation to the organism's *conditional readiness to respond behaviorally* to a certain object, or to a certain region, in the sensory environment. (See, for example, Hillyard & Münte, 1984; Hillyard, Münte, & Neville, in press.) Particularly striking evidence to this effect, in monkeys, showing *selective enhancement* of neuronal response, is provided in a series of studies reviewed by Wurtz, Goldberg, & Robinson (1980, 1982) and Wurtz (1985). The following is a brief synopsis of their findings.

First, in the superior colliculus and in the frontal eye fields (area 8), responses to the appearance of a visual stimulus are enhanced when that stimulus is the target for an eye movement. (The responses in superior colliculus have latencies of 35–60 msec; in the frontal eye fields they are around 80–120 msec; the reaction time for the monkey to make an overt eye movement is around 200 msec). The enhancement is spatially selective: When the eye movement is made towards a stimulus outside the cell's receptive field, the cell shows no such enhancement. It shows no suppression, either. The same cells do not discharge before spontaneous eye movements made in the absence of a visual stimulus, or in the dark. Further experiments indicate that the enhancement effect occurs in *anticipation* of an eye movement, regardless of whether the movement actually occurs or not. The enhancement apparently relates to a transient *readiness to respond* to a stimulus in a particular location. However, in both these areas (superior colliculus and frontal eye fields) the response in question appears to be specifically a saccadic eye movement. When the monkey is trained to respond to the occurrence of the target stimulus with a hand movement, while maintaining fixation on a different location, no such selective enhancement occurs.

In contrast, in a population of cells in the posterior parietal cortex (area 7) an equally large, selective enhancement effect is reported when the response to the target stimulus is to be a movement either of eyes or hand, or when the animal merely knows that he may have to respond to it. Again, the enhancement is spatially selective. It does not occur prior to movements made in the absence of a visual stimulus, showing that, as before, the enhancement is a selective modulation of the visual response rather than simply an anticipatory signal of movement per se. Further, the spatial selectivity of the enhanced parietal response apparently specifies the location of the *stimulus,* not that of the response to be made. Thus the enhanced response to a visually peripheral stimulus is seen when the monkey is about to reach out to touch that stimulus object itself, and when his response is to release a bar in a different, central location.

Area 7 evidently contains many, spatially interleaved subpopulations of cells, differing widely in their characteristic response (Hyvärinen, 1982; Lynch, 1980). Many units respond continuously so long as the animal maintains fixation on an "interesting" visual object, provided also that the object is *within manual reach.* Other units respond strongly in anticipation of a saccade towards such an object, or during smooth visual pursuit of such an object. Other units again, especially in the region of the intraparietal sulcus, appear to anticipate arm-reaching and hand manipulation (Lynch, Mountcastle, Talbot, & Yin, 1977; Mountcastle, 1978). However, in contrast to sites further downstream in the sensory-motor system, the timing of unit discharge recorded in area 7 is correlated with the time of *stimulus* onset and *not* with the timing of overt motor response (Lamarre, Spidalieri, & Chapman, 1985). It should be emphasized also that these patterns of neural response are elicited only by objects towards which the animal shows active "interest," that is towards which he shows a conditional *readiness to respond* behaviorally.

As already pointed out, area 7 cells are unselective—that is, they specify very little—about the figural characteristics of the selected object, its form, color, or texture. Area 7 neurones also appear indifferent as regards the "semantic" and motivational significance of the selected stimulus, and hence as regards the major categories of behavior appropriate to it—for example feeding or aversion (Rolls, Perrett, & Thorpe, 1979).

Selective response to sensory stimuli, modulated by conditional readiness for different categories (or different aspects) of *action,* can be observed in a number of different anatomical sites. For example, Rolls and his associates have recorded cells in the lateral hypothalamus, and elsewhere, that respond strongly to the sight of *food*-related objects, and that show a pattern of specialization essentially complementary to that seen in posterior parietal cortex (Rolls, 1981; cf. Rolls, Burton, & Mora, 1976). The sharply enhanced response of these cells, in the presence of objects associated in the animal's experience with food, is seen only when the animal is hungry and when he is in fact *about to accept the object as food.* Comparable responses were not found when the monkey looked at or reached for nonfood objects, nor when he grasped, smelled, or tasted the food in the dark, that is, these are evidently "visual" cells, whose discharge is nevertheless strongly modulated by readiness for a particular category of behavioral response, namely feeding. Further, in direct contrast to the unit response just described in posterior parietal cortex, the hypothalamic units are indifferent to the spatial *location* of the object concerned. However, in common with posterior parietal units and in contrast to the pattern of response in infero-temporal cortex, the same hypothalamic units respond equally to objects with very diverse *visual* characteristics (such as oranges, nuts, bananas, even the syringe from which the animal obtained glucose).

Selection by Enhancement

A striking feature of these results, obtained in a wide range of cortical and subcortical sites, is that the response of cells having an identifiable, *sensorily* defined pattern of input is modulated in terms of the animal's *behaviorally* identifiable, *conditional readiness to respond* to that input. Specifically, the neuronal activity is enhanced. It is not difficult to imagine that this kind of selective enhancement of sensory activity may play a significant role in the mechanism of selection-for-action.

How might this operate?

In a parallel, activation-coded system, *competition* between alternative messages, or data sources, occurs whenever two or more messages converge on a process having fewer degrees of freedom than in the combined incoming message. Such competition can only be won (assuming equal long-term *associative* strength) by the message having the greatest transmitted activation.

Simulation of this kind of convergent competition in simple, associative matrix systems (Anderson, Silverstein, Ritz, & Jones, 1977; Schneider, 1985) indicates that quite small differences between the transmitted vector strengths of converging messages can still produce a "winner-takes-all" final result. The time needed to reach this stable outcome—i.e., to overcome the interference caused by the competing messages—depends on the relative vector strengths. Exactly equal strengths can result in deadlock: Neither message can activate its associated vector in the shared channel. Relative priority may thus be assigned to different messages *before* their convergence point, in principle either by selective enhancement or by selective attenuation.

The neurophysiological data that I have reviewed points only to selective enhancement. (Wurtz et al., 1980, show that certain remote inhibitory effects in superior colliculus, which had been previously interpreted as possible evidence of active suppression, almost certainly result from passive sensory interactions between stimuli, unrelated to any hypothetical removal of "attention.") Anatomical considerations (e.g., Cowey, 1985) suggest that thalamically controlled selective inhibition, or attenuation, is also a possibility, but I have been unable, as yet, to find evidence suggesting that such a mechanism plays a behaviorally significant part in selection for action. There would, in any case, seem to be a clear biological advantage in a system that does not entail either the active suppression of information that has been already encoded to a high level, or the restriction of processing of all but a favored subset of sensory information at any early level of analysis. As a method of priority assignment, selective enhancement has the peculiar advantage that it need not entail the suppression, or exclusion of *other* information prior to the point of competitive convergence.

Convergence must undoubtedly occur somewhere in mapping the very large degrees of freedom of sensory information into overt movements. How "early" or "late" in the process of sensory-motor mapping this kind of competitive convergence occurs, however, is a question that may, in principle, have as many different answers as there are combinatorial pairings of possible sensory inputs in respect of possible motor outputs; the answers cannot readily be inferred from the available neurophysiology.

Notice, however, that the selective enhancement, i.e., the *cueing* or prioritization of favored information, may occur long before the point of convergence, provided that the enhancement is cascaded forwards through successive nonconvergent recodings. The temporal characteristics of the enhancement effects reported by Wurtz et al. from different recording sites certainly appears to favor such a possibility.

The Coordination of Neural Codes

A recurrent theme in the organization of sensory-motor coding, briefly reviewed above, is the parallel, domain-specific channelling of different aspects of sensory-motor control. In particular, I pointed to the marked segregation in the analysis of *categorical* information (what? what for?) and *positional* information (where?), in primate vision. Nevertheless, such apparently distinct domains of processing have to control the coherent action of a single organism. Positional and categorical aspects of the sensory environment and of the selected action have to be coordinated. If selective enhancement is to play a part in selection-for-action, the positional and categorical codes so enhanced should relate to the *same* visual object, when these coding domains must control aspects of one and the same action.

The problem of the coordination of selective enhancement in the visual modality might be overcome if the enhancement originated at a stage in the visual system at which it could propagate forwards through subsequent, anatomically divergent pathways. There is some indication, however, that this may not occur in striate cortex itself, since, in their studies, Wurtz et al. were unable to find evidence of *spatially selective* enhancement in primary visual cortex. So far, the earliest level at which spatially selective effects on unit activity have been consistently recorded in visual cortical pathways is in the prelunate visual "association" area (Boch & Fischer, 1983; Fischer & Boch, 1981). The origin of the selective enhancement, in any case, need not be cortical.

There is tremendously rich provision not only of cortico-cortical but of reciprocal cortico-thalamo-cortical pathways both within the visual system and linking (traditionally labeled) "sensory," "motor" and "association" cortex (e.g., Graybiel & Berson, 1981). Indeed, in almost every case the reverse projections from cortex to thalamus are at least as profuse, in terms of axon numbers, as the ascending thalamo-cortical projections.[5] In a number of thalamic nuclei, such as the pulvinar, the descending cortical projections (e.g., from prestriate cortex) numerically dominate all other, subthalamic ascending inputs (Ogren & Hendrickson, 1979). Moreover, all long connections from thalamus to cortex are excitatory. It is clearly a serious possibility that patterns of selective enhancement of cortical activity are directed and coordinated *via* thalamic nuclei. Bachmann (1984) has recently reviewed a variety of evidence concerning the possible role of temporally trailing, and spatially selective thalamocortical activation in visual masking. Bachmann argues, persuasively, that phasic, local enhancement of cortical activity, which he labels *perceptual retouch*, is necessary for phenomenal perceptual awareness. However, in his very interesting discussion he does not explicitly consider the problem of selective enhancement of cortical activity occurring in a variety of *different* cortical regions at the same time. Before proceeding with this question further, I need to introduce a powerful theoretical conception put forward by Von der Malsburg (Häussler & Von der Malsburg, 1983; Von der Malsburg, 1981).

Von der Malsburg is concerned with the general problem of dynamic integration of neural activity—and hence of the psychological processes that it embodies—that, in more limited scope, forms the topic of this essay. The essential postulate of Von der Malsburg's ambitious "Correlation theory of brain function" is that synaptic linkage can be *very rapidly modulated* by correlations in the temporal fine structure of activity in pre and postsynaptic signals. High

---

[5]The wealth of cortico-thalamo-cortical connections further cautions against the conception of a simple hierarchy of stages of sensory-motor analysis.

correlation (i.e., approximate synchrony) of firing in any pair of synaptically connected units allows their full "long-term" synaptic weight to become effective, as in conventional neural net theories; *uncorrelated* activity, however, temporarily reduces their effective synaptic weight to zero. Thus units that are active, but whose activity is temporally uncorrelated, become mutually, transiently decoupled; they no longer interact. In this way a number of *potentially* interacting subnetworks with uncorrelated activity patterns can coexist without interfering. Interaction between temporarily decoupled units may be restored by extrinsically imposed time structure, arising for example in sensory signals. More importantly, Von der Malsburg suggests, time-dependent correlations can be created by the tendency of cells to form rapid bursts of spike activity that are then transmitted to other cells. There is a great deal more to Von der Malsburg's theory. However, enough has been said, I hope, to indicate its most essential element.

It should be evident that this theory provides, in outline, a possible neuronal mechanism for the rapidly acting selective coupling and decoupling of ongoing sensory-motor processes that, I have argued, are entailed by the demands of selection-for-action. In principle even widely distributed neural networks may be enabled to interact quite selectively, once a burst or wave of approximately synchronous high-frequency activity has established the required level of temporal correlation across them, while at the same time having the effect of decorrelating, and hence isolating, activity in other adjacent networks.[6] Moreover, the same principle might be operative not only in the integration of *sensory* coding units, but also in re-setting *sensory-motor* linkage and in creating temporary "coordinative structures" of motor control.

Equally clearly, these theoretical proposals of Von der Malsburg must be recognized as highly conjectural. They have yet to face critical empirical test.[7]

III. SELECTION FOR ACTION AND THEORIES OF ATTENTION

Selection and "Attention"

There is an extensive literature on selective attention, much of which is concerned to establish at what level in a postulated hierarchy of processing of the

---

[6]It is not clear whether any of the selective enhancement effects, of which we have evidence, might be appropriate to create effective temporal correlations of the kind required in Von der Malsburg's theory.

[7]In a recent paper, Crick (1984) has put forward an elaborate set of proposals, whereby thalamic neurones may be triggered by cortical activity to return rapid burst discharge to the most active cortical regions, thus perhaps, following von der Malsburg's hypothesis, creating temporary "vertical assemblies" of concurrently active units. Crick proposes that such a process may implement an "attentional searchlight," following Treisman (Treisman & Gelade, 1980; Treisman & Schmidt, 1982). Several such attentional searchlights, Crick suggests, may operate concurrently.

sensory input "perceptual selection" can or must occur. Seen in terms of the traditional contrasting alternatives of "early" versus "late selection," it is fair to say that the issue is still essentially unresolved (e.g., Francolini & Egeth, 1980; Shaffer & LaBerge, 1979). One of the aims of this chapter is to take steps toward reconciling these conflicting views, by presenting a somewhat different conception of the alternatives at stake.

Unfortunately—and it is a major source of theoretical confusion—in this literature the notion of "attention" itself is generally left undefined, or defined by reference to subjective experience. ("Everyone knows what attention is"). In practice, the *observable* criterion for successful "attention" to (or awareness of) an environmental event invariably turns on the ability of the subject to *act* voluntarily, or arbitrarily, in response to that event either at once, or subsequently in "recall." According to the conception developed here, the process of selection-for-action among environmental events includes selection not only for immediate action but for potential future actions as well, including so-called "perceptual reports."

Before going further we need to consider what is entailed by the notion of "selection." In many discussions—particularly discussions of so-called "early" or "precategorical" selection, though certainly not confined to them—there is a strong implicit assumption that selection, defined as the *cueing* or *designating of task-relevant information,* must imply the rejection or exclusion of the noncued information from levels of analysis beyond that at which the selective cueing is held to occur. The conception that commonly underlies this assumption is that, beyond the level at which the "selection" (that is selective *cueing*) occurs, all further processing is intrinsically serial; or, if not strictly serial, it is liable to "overload" should the unwanted information not be successfully excluded. The classic example of such a conception, as well as its most subtle and influential exponent, is Broadbent (1958, 1971, 1982). It is therefore valuable to examine his view in a little detail here. Broadbent (1971) writes, "there must be a stage early in the mechanism at which simultaneous processing of information is possible. This stage is succeeded by a stage at which successive processing only is possible. . . . (The latter, i.e.,) the P system might, in some usages of the term "perception," be regarded as a perceptual mechanism. (As) the stages were defined by the simultaneous versus successive quality of the operations. . ." (p. 135). "The information-flow model of 1958 is to be modified largely by considering the working of the limited capacity system which formed part of it. That system is now thought of as producing *one* of a set of category states" (p. 17, my italics). "The occurrence of a category state. . . corresponds to the firing of *one* of Treisman's dictionary units" (p. 150, my italics). Clearly, for such a system, a mechanism is needed that selects the information to be passed on to the serial (or, *mutatis mutandis,* the "limited capacity") stage and which, *in so doing,* rejects or shuts out other information. This, of course, is Broadbent's filter theory. Thus, Broadbent (1971) states, "One can sum up these experiments as

15. ATTENTION AND SELECTION-FOR-ACTION   409

showing that the selection of one ear shuts out most of the information on the other'' (p. 140). Cf. "The involuntary reading of a distant color word can be prevented by focusing attention on the relevant visual object" (Kahneman & Chajczyk, 1983). "Activation of the meaning of an item may . . . be restricted to just those items that are deemed relevant" (Francolini & Egeth, 1980).

The assumption, that selective cueing of certain information necessarily entails rejection or *exclusion* of all other information beyond the level of processing *at which the selective cue itself is encoded,* is evidently unchanged when the assumption of strict seriality (firing of *one* dictionary unit at a time) is replaced by a unitary "limited capacity" system. Broadbent, 1982 states, "The notion that a single information channel must be a single processor, or deal with events serially, is a common confusion in this area. It is not so" (p. 285).

Much of the behavioral evidence advanced in support of the notion of "early selection" has been concerned with the relative efficiency of selection—in the sense of selective *cueing* of task-relevant information—under different "levels" (dimensions) of selection cue. Efficiency of selective cueing is typically assessed by the presence or absence of interference from the noncued information (e.g., Francolini & Egeth, 1980; Kahneman & Chajczyk, 1983). The really important point to recognize, however, is that selection, in the sense of selective *cueing,* in no sense logically entails rejection or exclusion of the noncued information from further *processing.* It has certainly not been empirically demonstrated that selective cueing *in fact* has this consequence. This being so, behavioral evidence about the relative efficiency of "selection"—i.e., the relative efficiency of *selective cueing*—is simply irrelevant to questions about the level of processing accorded to the "unselected information." To put it another way, the controversy regarding "early" versus "late" selection has systematically confused "selection" as selective *cueing* and "selection" as selective *processing.* Once the distinction is made clear, there may even be no controversy.[8]

To my knowledge, the first person clearly to recognize this basic point of logic was van der Heijden (1978, 1981). According to van der Heijden (1978, 1981, this volume) *selective cueing* operates predominantly in terms of physical, or "precategorical," sensory attributes, whereas *processing* of both cued and noncued information proceeds at least to categorical levels of analysis. Van der Heijden has called this "postcategorical filtering." In this case we would have "early selection," in the sense of selective *cueing* or specifying of the tasrelevant information, *and* "late selection" as regards the further *processing* of both relevant and irrelevant information.

Our earlier considerations (Sections I and II above) suggest in preliminary outline how this combination of "early" and "late" selection ("early" selective *cueing,* "late" selective *processing*) might be implemented in the brain. They

---

[8]For further discussion and behavioral evidence of the independence of these two issues, see Allport, Tipper, and Chmiel, 1985.

also suggest that the terminology of "early" and "late" with its underlying conception of a particular, linear sequence of sensory analysis, may be seriously misleading.

In a massively parallel, activation-coded system, selective enhancement provides a possible mechanism of selective cueing that need not entail the exclusion from further processing of the noncued information, beyond the level of encoding at which selective enhancement first occurs. Only when there is structural convergence of parallel channels (for example, onto a shared effector system) is selective *processing,* in the sense of *exclusive* competition between different streams of information, inevitable.

Sensory-motor communication proceeds in many parallel, specialized channels. The evidence reviewed in section II by no means favors the conception of a simple hierarchy of levels of analysis, certainly not one in which the encoding of environmental position is completed at an "early" stage, preceding in linear sequence the encoding of categorical object-identity. Further, those sensory dimensions that have been found to provide efficient selection cues for selective response (besides the explicit specification of spatial location) are also dimensions that appear to have intrinsic, *spatiotopic* representation in the brain. They are thus well suited to cueing spatiotopic selective enhancement. In contrast, for example, selection cued by a "physical" attribute such as angular versus curved letter-shape—an attribute that would *not* appear to be coded explicitly in its own spatiotopic feature-map—is actually less efficient that selection by letter versus digit category (Bundesen, Pedersen, & Larsen, 1984). I suggest that so-called "early" selective cueing (or "stimulus set") is in all cases, directly or indirectly, cueing by spatial location. However, spatial location is coded by different cortical (and subcortical) systems right through to premotor cortex. There is nothing uniquely "early" about it. Rather, the analysis of location and of object-identity appear to proceed in large measure in parallel.

As regards *spatial* selection, selective enhancement of activation may be sufficient to determine the direction of a move—for example, the conjugate movement of head, eyes, and hand towards the position of an object in space. How the selection of spatial location is coordinated with nonspatial, categorical information, however, is almost certainly more complicated. Little if anything is known at the neuronal level as regards this issue. It may require the active coupling and decoupling of different, concurrently active networks, perhaps along the lines of Von der Malsburg's correlation theory of neural integration. Thalamically controlled selective activation may play a critical role in such a process. These are speculative possibilities which surely merit further research.

Limited Capacity

The concept of a central limited-capacity system has exercised an hypnotic hold on theorists of "attention." Indeed, the loosely described "limited capacity" of perceptual awareness, as *phenomenon,* sometimes appears to be *simply identified* with a hypothetical "limited capacity attentional *system,*" as a postulated causal mechanism (e.g., "a limited capacity system that might be identified with conscious awareness," Posner, 1982, p. 171). Neumann (1985, this volume) gives a powerful critique of the successive twists and turns of the concept of central limited capacity, and of the failure of this concept to provide explanatory power. (See also Heuer, 1985.) The reluctance to abandon the idea of a central, "limited capacity system," in spite of its manifest weaknesses, as in some sense providing an *explanation* for the limited or selective nature of awareness (or "attention"), perhaps stems, in part at least, from the belief that no other explanation is in sight. Thus, discussing Deutsch and Deutsch's (1963) "late selection" proposals, Broadbent (1971) wrote, "If there were really sufficient machinery available in the brain to perform such an analysis for every stimulus . . . it is difficult to see why any selection at all should occur. The obvious utility of a selection system is to produce an economy in mechanism. If a complete analysis were performed even on neglected messages, there seems no reason for selection at all" (p. 147).

To the contrary, as I argue in this chapter, the biological necessity of a process of selection-for-action is paramount and indispensable. In a later section I set out to show how the selective nature of episodic memory and awareness may be causally linked to this same process. For the present, no obvious or compelling reason has been presented, a priori, why selection (in the sense of *exclusion* of information from processing) should occur at any earlier stage of sensory analysis prior to the stage of selection-for-action.

The behavioral phenomena attributed in the past to the limited capacity of a central processor are more appropriately conceptualized, I believe, as the expression of crosstalk interference between parallel processes. Crosstalk is a problem whenever the task-specified inputs are not the single most compatible among concurrently available inputs for the task-specified actions. "Wanted" and "unwanted" inputs must then be actively decoupled from the control of particular actions. Our understanding of this process is undoubtedly still very primitive. It is a radically different conception, however, from the earlier notion of a central, limited capacity, or even from that of multiple limited "resources." (For further discussion see, for example, Allport, 1980a, 1980b; Navon, 1985.)

The Units of Selection: Kahnemann and Treisman (1984)

My introductory discussion of selection-for-action was presented in terms of the selection of physical *objects* to be acted upon. But what, actually, is an "object"? (What counts as just one?) Our phenomenal experience may appear structured in terms of "objects," but we should be circumspect in proposing a concept, defined only in phenomenal terms, as a component in a would-be causal account of behavior. To do so would be to risk confusing the explicandum with the explanation.

The concept of physical object seems to elude definition, except in terms of possible *actions* of self or other agents that the object affords or prevents. Thus a physical object may be thought of as a region of the sensory environment that can be *separately* acted upon in some way, a region of the environment that is invariant with respect to a class of action that it can support. Depending on what action is selected, a forest, a tree, the vein of a leaf can each be viewed as a single object. Our perceptual experience, as well as our linguistic categories, I suggest, are predominantly structured in terms of *objects* and the actions and events in which they take part precisely because this is the level of description of the sensory environment that captures these action-related invariances, and that is needed for the coherent integration of action-choice and action-guidance. That is, the nature of phenomenal, episodic awareness is structured by—is functionally dependent on—the processes of selection for immediate and future action.

The suggestion that selection-for-action is related to an object-level representation is not new. In a recent and influential series of papers Kahneman (Kahneman & Chajczyk, 1983; Kahneman & Henik, 1981; Kahneman & Treisman, 1984) has proposed that "*attention* is assigned to *objects,* or the locations that objects occupy." "Attention to irrelevant parts of relevant objects is obligatory" (Kahneman & Treisman, 1984, p. 45).

The behavioral findings that Kahneman and Treisman put forward to illustrate their thesis are obtained, for the most part, in what they call the "filtering paradigm." An essential feature of filtering (or "cross-domain cueing") tasks is that selection between subsets of sensory information that should, or should not, control a subsequent response is cued by *one* property of the display, whereas the appropriate category of response is cued by a *different* property. For example, the stimulus-selection cue might be color, whereas the choice of response (e.g., in reading a word) could be based on shape. (The cued subset is called the "relevant stimulus," the remainder is "irrelevant.") Such tasks therefore involve communication ("cueing") between one attribute domain and another. Kahneman and Treisman provide a number of compelling demonstrations that the amount of interference (crosstalk) from the irrelevant information—observed either directly, or through the *cost* in speed and/or accuracy of performance in preventing this interference—varies with the degree to which relevant and irrelevant information is judged to be "perceptually" (i.e., *phenomenally*) grouped together. As already suggested, what is represented as *one* "object," *phenomenally*, must depend both on the action-related invariances present in the sensory environment, and on the categories of action for which the environment must provide control. Using other, cross-domain cueing tasks, Prinzmetal (Prinzmetal, 1981; Prinzmetal & Millis-Wright, 1984) has shown that crosstalk ("feature integration errors") in oral report is affected not only by Gestalt-like factors of "perceptual" (i.e., phenomenal) grouping but also by categorical and linguistic factors such as whether a row of letters forms a word, a familiar abbreviation or a pronounceable pseudoword (cf. also Virzi & Egeth, 1984).

The data cited by Kahneman and Treisman did not permit them to distinguish between "attention" assigned to integrated object-representations, and "attention" assigned to the spatial regions that objects occupy. Depending on the meaning of "attention," both alternatives may be correct. Our discussion, earlier, suggested that *selective cueing* (selective enhancement) can operate in terms of encoded *location*[9]; moreover, cross-domain cueing appears most efficient as between domains of sensory attributes having spatiotopic representation. On the other hand, *selective processing*—i.e., the final, exclusive competition for the control of action—may involve selection among competing, integrated object-representations.

At the conclusion of their important, recent review, Kahneman and Treisman (1984) proposed an analogy for the temporary representation of particular objects and events in terms of the concept of an "object file." In the object file, information is cumulatively entered regarding the initial location and time of occurrence, the sensory properties of the object and (later?) its categorical identity and previously learned facts relating to it. In terms of the object file analogy, Kahneman and Treisman (1984) then put forward the following hypothesis:

> A possible alternative to the early-selection hypothesis is that attention (1) has no effect on the buildup of information in the object file, (2) affects only the output of object files, and (3) can be directed to an object file only by physical characteristics. Such a mechanism would be an early selection device, in the sense that its selective functions are controlled by elementary features. However, the effect of attention, as in late-selection theories, would be to control access to executive devices that produce responses. (p.55)

This hypothesis appears identical in effect to the conception of "postcategorical filtering" proposed by van der Heijden (1981, this volume). The results reported by Allport, Tipper, & Chmiel (in press) offer further support for such a view.[10]

The object file analogy does not specify how information is assigned to one among "several concurrently active object files" rather than another. Clearly, the object file analogy should not be thought of as a solution to the problem of perceptual integration but rather as a restatement of the problem.

In an activation-coded, content-specific coding system, information cannot be

---

[9]There is an important distinction to be made between specification of spatial location in retinotopic terms and in terms of spatial relation to the head or body axis, or in relation to other environmental objects. Depending on the action or effector system, each of these specifications of "location" will be needed for different aspects of selection-for-action.

[10]Kahneman and Treisman's hypothesis is evidently in direct conflict with the earlier "feature integration" hypothesis of Treisman and Gelade (1980), which asserted that "attention must be focused on each object in turn" for this assignment to occur correctly.

freely transferred, or copied, from one register, file, etc. to another. Episodic relations ("conjunctions") among encoded attributes must therefore be represented in some other way. The ideas put forward by von der Malsburg provide a possible, basic mechanism.

Selection-for-action and Episodic Memory

I suggested earlier that the segmentation of the phenomenal world in terms of objects—as structured configurations (or "conjunctions") of spatial and categorical attributes—is conditioned by the demands of coherent action; and in particular I emphasized the demands imposed by the ever-present problem of "selection-for-action."

For the *immediate* guidance of action, structured relations among object-attributes need be represented only *temporarily,* for as long as the particular action continues to be directed towards the same objects. However, it is evident that some of these contingent or "episodic" properties and relations are encoded more durably and can be used to guide action again on *subsequent* occasions. They may also be explicitly recalled. Contingent, relational information, sufficient to discriminate later among thousands of different complex scenes can be encoded within a second or two, even within small fractions of a second (e.g., Potter, 1976; Standing, 1973). Equally, not all the information available to the senses—or even used in the momentary control of action—appears to be durably encoded "in memory." What *is* so encoded depends, so one popular formulation runs, on "attention." "*Unattended*" objects and relations, according to this formulation, are not "encoded into memory," neither do they or their categorical identities and configural relationships "enter awareness." Unhappily, the notion of "attention" that is here invoked appears to offer rather little explanatory power; its definition (like "depth of processing") risks mere circularity. Conscious awareness and encoding in long-term memory depend on attention. So what is attention? Why, attention is what is needed for conscious awareness and encoding in long-term memory.

In practice, as we have already noted, the observable criterion for successful "attention" to or awareness of an environmental event depends on the subject's ability to *act* voluntarily (i.e., arbitrarily, selectively) in response to that event. To be aware of some environmental event is, in principle, to be able to act on it—e.g., to "comment" on it. In effect, then, this criterion is the same as for selection-for-action.

It is noteworthy that the same processes that we have considered as a possible neurophysiological basis of selection-for-action would appear to provide the preconditions also for the consolidation of more durable, episodic records. Transient electrical stimulation of thalamic nuclei has been shown to result in long-term enhancement of retrieval, or reenactment, of the processes occurring during stimulation (e.g., Mateer & Ojemann, 1983). In terms of von der Malsburg's hypothesis, correlated or synchronous activity across different subnetworks should activate synaptic communication among them; continued activity, once established, should enable long-term potentiation of the active synapses. (There is clear evidence of long-lasting potentiation of synaptic pathways, resulting from brief (less than 1 sec) trains of high-frequency stimulation, both in in vivo and in vitro preparations (c.f. Lynch & Schubert, 1980); these effects have been found to endure for days and weeks, at least.) The same (thalamically driven?) selective cortical enhancement that, I have suggested, is involved in momentary selection-for-action may also constitute one of the necessary conditions for the creation of longer term episodic memory. At this level of analysis we may thus begin to account for the contingency between the construct of "Attention" and later recognition and recall.

ACKNOWLEDGMENTS

This chapter was prepared while I was a guest of the Centre for Interdisciplinary Research (ZiF) at the University of Bielefeld, as a member of the Project "Perception and Action." I am deeply grateful to the organizers and to members of the Project Group for their hospitality and for many valuable discussions. I particularly wish to thank Lex Van der Heijden, Steven Keele, Odmar Neumann, and the Editors of this volume for suggestions that have improved this chapter, and for their encouragement in its preparation.

REFERENCES

Allport, D. A. (1977). On knowing the meaning of words we are unable to report: The effects of visual masking. In S. Dornic (Ed.), *Attention and performance, 6.* Hillsdale, NJ: Lawrence Erlbaum Associates.

Allport, D. A. (1980a). Patterns and actions: Cognitive mechanisms are content-specific. In G. Claxton (Ed.), *Cognitive psychology: New directions.* London: Routledge & Kegan Paul.

Allport, D. A. (1980b). Attention and Performance. In G. Claxton (Ed.), *Cognitive psychology: New directions.* London: Routledge & Kegan Paul.

Allport, D. A., Antonis, B., & Reynolds, P. (1972). On the division of attention: A disproof of the single channel hypothesis. *Quarterly Journal of Experimental Psychology, 24,* 225–235.

Allport, D. A., & Funnell, E. (1981). Components of the mental lexicon. *Philosophical Transactions of the Royal Society of London, B295,* 397–410.

Allport, D. A., Tipper, S. P., & Chmiel, N. R. J. (1985). Perceptual integration and post-categorical filtering. In M. I. Posner & O. S. M. Marin (Eds.), *Attention and performance, 11.* Hillsdale, NJ: Lawrence Erlbaum Associates.

Anderson, J. A., Silverstein, J. W., Ritz, S. A., & Jones, R. S. (1977). Distinctive features, categorical perception and probability learning: Some applications of a neural model. *Psychological Review, 84,* 413–451.

Bachmann, T. (1984). The process of perceptual retouch: Nonspecific afferent activation dynamics in explaining visual making. *Perception and Psychophysics, 35,* 69–84.

Beauvois, M.-F. (1982). Optic aphasia: A process of interaction between vision and language. *Philosophical Transactions of the Royal Society* (London), B298, 35–47.
Biguer, B., Jeannerod, M., & Prablanc, C. (1985). The role of position of gaze in movement accuracy. In M. I. Posner & O. S. M. Marin (Eds.), *Attention and performance, 11*. Hillsdale, NJ: Lawrence Erlbaum Associates.
Boch, R., & Fischer, B. (1983). Saccadic reaction times and activation of the prelunate cortex: Parallel observations in trained Rhesus monkeys. *Experimental Brain Research, 50,* 201–210.
Brainard, R. W., Irby, T. S., Fitts, P. M., & Alluisi, E. A. (1962). Some variables influencing the rate of gain of information. *Journal of Experimental Psychology, 63,* 105–110.
Broadbent, D. E. (1958). *Perception and communication.* London: Pergamon.
Broadbent, D. E. (1971). *Decision and stress.* London: Academic Press.
Broadbent, D. E. (1982). Task combination and selective intake of information. *Acta Psychologica, 50,* 253–290.
Brooks, L. (1968). Spatial and verbal components of the act of recall. *Canadian Journal of Psychology, 22,* 349–368.
Bundesen, C., Pedersen, L. F., & Larsen, A. (1984). Measuring efficiency of selection from briefly exposed visual displays: A model for partial report. *Journal of Experimental Psychology: Human Perception and Performance, 10,* 329–339.
Cowey, A. (1985). Aspects of cortical organization related to selective attention and selective impairments of visual perception. In M. I. Posner & O. S. M. Marin (Eds.), *Attention and performance, 11*. Hillsdale, NJ: Lawrence Erlbaum Associates.
Crick, F. (1984). Function of the thalamic reticular complex: The searchlight hypothesis. *Proceedings of the National Academy of Sciences. 81,* 4586–4590.
Damasio, A. R., & Benton, A. L. (1979). Impairment of hand movements under visual guidance. *Neurology, 29,* 170–174.
De Renzi, E. (1982). *Disorders of space exploration and cognition.* Chichester: Wiley.
Desimone, R., Albright, T. D., Gross, C. G., & Bruce, C. (1984). Stimulus selective properties of inferior temporal neurons in the macaque. *Journal of Neuroscience, 4,* 2051–2062.
Deutsch, J. A., & Deutsch, D. (1963). Attention: Some theoretical considerations. *Psychological Review, 70,* 80–90.
Fischer, B., & Boch, R. (1981). Enhanced activation of neurons in prelunate cortex before visually guided saccades of trained Rhesus monkeys. *Experimental Brain Research, 44,* 129–137.
Francolini, C. N., & Egeth, H. (1980). On the nonautomaticity of automatic activation: Evidence of selective seeing. *Perception and Psychophysics, 27,* 331–342.
Glaser, W. R., & Düngelhoff, F.-J. (1984). The time course of picture–word interference. *Journal of Experimental Psychology: Human Perception and Performance, 10,* 640–654.
Graybiel, A. M., & Berson, D. M. (1981). On the relation between transcortical pathways in the visual system. In F. O. Schmitt, F. G. Worden, G. Edelman, & S. G. Dennis (Eds.), *The organization of the cerebral cortex.* Cambridge, MA: M.I.T. Press.
Greenwald, A. G. (1972). On doing two things at once: Time sharing as a function of ideomotor compatibility. *Journal of Experimental Psychology, 94,* 52–57.
Gross, C. G., & Mishkin, M. (1977). The neural basis of stimulus equivalence across retinal translation. In S. Harnod (Ed.), *Lateralization in the nervous system.* New York: Academic Press.
Häussler, A. F., & von der Malsburg, C. (1983). Development of retinotopic projections, an analytical treatment. *Journal of Theoretical Neurobiology, 2,* 47–73.
Heilman, K. M. (1979). Mechanisms underlying hemispatial neglect. *Annals of Neurology, 5,* 166–170.
Heilman, K. M., & Valenstein (Eds.), (1979). *Clinical neuropsychology.* Oxford: Oxford University Press.

Heuer, H. (1985). Some points of contact between models of central capacity and factor-analytic models. *Acta Psychologica, 60*, 135-155.
Hillyard, S. A., & Münte, T. F. (1984). Selective attention to color and location: An analysis with event-related brain potentials. *Perception and Psychophysics, 36*, 185-198.
Hillyard, S. A., Münte, T. F., & Neville, H. J. (1985). Visual-spatial attention, orienting, and brain physiology. In M. I. Posner & O. S. M. Marin (Eds.), *Attention and performance, 11*. Hillsdale, NJ: Lawrence Erlbaum Associates.
Hyvärinen, J. (1982). *The parietal cortex of monkey and man: Studies of brain function*. Berlin: Springer.
Kahneman, D., & Chajczyk, D. (1983). Tests of the automaticity of reading: Dilution of Stroop effects by color-irrelevant stimuli. *Journal of Experimental Psychology: Human Perception and Performance, 9*, 497-509.
Kahneman, D., & Henik, A. M. (1981). Perceptual organization and attention. In M. Kubovy & J. R. Pomerantz (Eds.), *Perceptual organization*. Hillsdale, NJ: Lawrence Erlbaum Associates.
Kahneman, D., & Treisman, A. M. (1984). Changing views of attention and automaticity. In R. Parasuraman, R. Davies, & J. Beatty (Eds.), *Varieties of attention*. New York: Academic Press.
Kinsbourne, M. (1977). Hemi-neglect and hemisphere rivalry. In E. A. Weinstein, & R. P. Friedland (Eds.), *Advances in neurology: Hemi-inattention and hemisphere specialization* (Vol. 18). New York: Raven Press.
Lamarre, Y., Spidalieri, G., & Chapman, C. E. (1985). Activity of areas 4 and 7 neurons during movements triggered by visual, auditory and somesthetic stimuli in the monkey: Movement-related *vs* stimulus-related responses. In A. W. Goodwin, & I. Davian-Smith (Eds.), *Hand function and the neocortex. Experimental Brain Research, Supplementum 10*.
Lawrence, D. H. (1971). Two studies of visual search for word targets with controlled rates of presentation. *Perception and Psychophysics, 10*, 85-89.
Lee, D. N. (1980). The optic flow field: The foundation of vision. *Philosophical Transactions of the Royal Society of London, B290*, 169-179.
Levine, D. N., & Calvanio, R. (1978). A study of the visual defect in verbal alexia-simultanagnosia. *Brain, 101*, 65-81.
Lynch, J. C. (1980). The functional organization of posterior parietal association cortex. *Behavioral and Brain Sciences, 3*, 485-534.
Lynch, J. C., Mountcastle, V. B., Talbot, W. H., & Yin, T. C. (1977). Parietal lobe mechanisms for directed visual attention. *Journal of Neurophysiology, 40*, 362-389.
Lynch, G., & Schubert, P. (1980). The use of *in vitro* brain slices for multidisciplinary studies of synaptic function. *Annual Review of Neuroscience, 3*, 1-22.
Mackay, D. M. (1966). Cerebral organization and the conscious control of action. In J. C. Eccles (Ed.), *Brain and conscious experience*. New York: Springer.
Mackay, D. M. (1981). Neural basis of cognitive experience. In G. Szekely, E. Labos, & S. Damjanovich (Eds.), *Advances in physiological sciences* (Vol. 30). Oxford: Pergamon.
Mateer, C. A. & Ojemann, G. A. (1983). Thalamic mechanisms in language and memory. In S. J. Segalowitz (Ed.), *Language functions and brain organization*. New York: Academic Press.
McLean, J. P., Broadbent, D. E., & Broadbent, M. H. P. (1983). Combining attributes in rapid serial visual presentation tasks. *Quarterly Journal of Experimental Psychology, 35A*, 171-186.
McLeod, P., & Posner, M. I. (1984). Privileged loops from percept to act. In H. Bouma & D. G. Bouwhuis (Eds.), *Attention and Performance, 10: Control of language processes*. Hillsdale, NJ: Lawrence Erlbaum Associates.
Mountcastle, V. B. (1978). Brain mechanisms for directed attention. *Journal of the Royal Society of Medicine, 71*, 14-28.
Navon, D. (1985). Attention division or attention sharing? In M. I. Posner & O. S. M. Marin (Eds.), *Attention and performance, 11*. Hillsdale, NJ: Lawrence Erlbaum Associates.

Neumann, O. (1985). Die Hypothese begrenzter Kapazität und die Funktionen der Aufmerksamkeit. In O. Neumann (Ed.), *Perspektiven der Kognitionspsychologie*. Berlin: Springer.

Norman, D. A. (1981). Categorization of action slips. *Psychological Review, 88*, 1–15.

Ogren, M. P., & Hendrickson, A. E. (1979). The morphology and distribution of striate cortex terminals in the inferior and lateral subdivisions of the *Macaca* monkey pulvinar. *Journal of Comparative Neurology, 188*, 179–200.

Perenin, M. T., & Vighetto, A. (1982). Optic ataxia: A specific disorder in visuomotor coordination. In A. Hein, & M. Jeannerod (Eds.), *Spatially oriented behavior*. New York: Springer.

Perrett, D. I., Rolls, E. T., & Caan, W. (1982). Visual neurones responsive to faces in the monkey temporal cortex. *Experimental Brain Research, 47*, 329–342.

Posner, M. I. (1980). Orienting of attention. *Quarterly Journal of Experimental Psychology, 32*, 3–25.

Posner, M. I. (1982). Cumulative development of attentional theory. *American Psychologist, 37*, 168–179.

Potter, M. C. (1976). Short-term conceptual memory for pictures. *Journal of Experimental Psychology: Human Learning and Memory, 2*, 509–522.

Prinzmetal, W. (1981). Principles of feature integration in visual perception. *Perception and Psychophysics, 30*, 330–340.

Prinzmetal, W., & Millis-Wright, M. (1984). Cognitive and linguistic factors affect visual feature integration. *Cognitive Psychology, 16*, 305–340.

Reason, J. (1979). Actions not as planned: The price of automatization. In G. Underwood & R. Stephens (Eds.), *Aspects of consciousness* (Vol. 1). London: Academic Press.

Reeves, A., & Sperling, G. (1986). Attentional gating in short-term visual memory. *Psychological Review, 93*, 180–206.

Rizzolatti, G., Gentilucci, M., & Matelli, M. (1985). Selective spatial attention: One center, one circuit or many circuits? In M. I. Posner, & O. S. M. Marin (Eds.), *Attention and performance, 11*. Hillsdale, NJ: Lawrence Erlbaum Associates.

Rizzolatti, G., Matelli, M., & Pavesi, G. (1983). Deficits in attention and movement following removal of postarcuate (area 6) and prearcuate (area 8) cortex in *Macaque* monkeys. *Brain, 106*, 655–673.

Rolls, E. T. (1981). Processing beyond the inferior temporal visual cortex related to feeding, memory, and striatal function. In Y. Katsuki, R. Norgren, & M. Sato (Eds.), *Brain-mechanisms of sensation*. New York: Wiley.

Rolls, E. T., Burton, M. J., & Mora, F. (1976). Hypothalamic neuronal responses associated with the sight of food. *Brain Research, 111*, 53–66.

Rolls, E. T., Perrett, D., & Thorpe, S. J. (1979). Responses of neurons in area 7 of the parietal cortex to objects of different significance. *Brain Research, 169*, 194–198.

Schneider, G. E. (1969). Two visual systems. *Science, 163*, 895–902.

Schneider, W. (1985). Toward a model of attention and the development of automatic processing. In M. I. Posner, & O. S. M. Marin (Eds.), *Attention and performance, 11*. Hillsdale. NJ: Lawrence Erlbaum Associates.

Shaffer, L. H. (1975). Multiple attention in continuous verbal tasks. In P. M. A. Rabbitt & S. Dornic (Eds.), *Attention and performance, 5*. New York: Academic Press.

Shaffer, W. O., & LaBerge, D. (1979). Automatic semantic processing of unattended words. *Journal of Verbal Learning and Verbal Behavior, 18*, 413–426.

Shallice, T., & McGill, J. (1978). The origins of mixed errors. In J. Requin (Ed.), *Attention and performance, 7*. Hillsdale, NJ: Lawrence Erlbaum & Associates.

Shallice, T., & Warrington, E. K. (1977). The possible role of selective attention in acquired dyslexia. *Neuropsychologia, 15*, 31–41.

Spelke, E. S., Hirst, W. C., & Neisser, U. (1976). Skills of divided attention. *Cognition, 4*, 215–230.

15. ATTENTION AND SELECTION-FOR-ACTION 419

Standing, L. (1973). Learning 10,000 pictures. *Quarterly Journal of Experimental Psychology, 25,* 207–222.

Stone, J., & Dreher, B. (1982). Parallel processing of information in the visual pathways: A general principle of sensory coding? *Trends in Neurosciences, 5,* 441–446.

Tierney, M. (1973). *Dual task performance: The effects of manipulating stimulus-response requirements.* BA Thesis, University of Reading, England.

Treisman, A. M. (1977). Focused attention in the perception and retrieval of multidimensional stimuli. *Perception and Psychophysics, 22,* 1–11.

Treisman, A. M., & Gelade, G. (1980). A feature-integration theory of attention. *Cognitive Psychology, 12,* 97–136.

Treisman, A., & Schmidt, H. (1982). Illusory conjunctions in the perception of objects. *Cognitive Psychology, 14,* 107–141.

Umiltà, C., & Nicoletti, R. (1985). Attention and coding effects in S–R compatibility due to irrelevant spatial cues. In M. I. Posner & O. S. M. Marin (Eds.), *Attention and performance, 11.* Hillsdale, NJ: Lawrence Erlbaum Associates.

Ungerleider, L. G. (1985). The corticocortical pathways for object recognition and spatial perception. In C. Chagass (Ed.), *Pattern recognition mechanisms.* Pontificae Academiae Scientiarum Scripta Varia.

Ungerleider, L. G., & Mishkin, M. (1982). Two cortical visual systems. In D. J. Ingle, M. A. Goodale, & R. J. W. Mansfield (Eds.), *Analysis of visual behavior.* Cambridge, MA: MIT Press.

van der Heijden, A. H. C. (1978). *Short-term visual information forgetting.* Ph.D. thesis, University of Leiden.

van der Heijden, A. H. C. (1981). *Short-Term Visual Information Forgetting.* London: Routledge and Kegan Paul.

van Essen, D. C., & Maunsell, J. H. R. (1983). Hierarchical organization and functional streams in the visual cortex. *Trends in Neurosciences, 6,* 370–375.

Virzi, R. A., & Egeth, H. E. (1984). Is meaning implicated in illusory conjunctions? *Journal of Experimental Psychology: Human Perception and Performance, 10,* 573–580.

von der Malsburg, C. (1981). *The correlation theory of brain function.* Max-Planck Institute for Biophysical Chemistry. Report 82–2.

Wise, S. P., & Evarts, E. V. (1981). The role of the cerebral cortex in movement. *Trends in Neurosciences, 4,* 297–300.

Wurtz, R. H. (1985). Stimulus selection and conditional response mechanisms in the basal ganglia of the monkey. In M. I. Posner & O. S. M. Marin (Eds.), *Attention and performance, 11.* Hillsdale, NJ: Lawrence Erlbaum Associates.

Wurtz, R. H., Goldberg, M. E., & Robinson, D. L. (1980). Behavioral modulation of visual responses in the monkey: Stimulus selection for attention and movement. *Progress in Psychobiology and Physiological Psychology, 9,* 43–83.

Wurtz, R. H., Goldberg, M. E., & Robinson, D. L. (1982). Brain mechanisms of visual attention. *Scientific American, 246*(6), 124–135.

16 Central Selection in Vision

A. H. C. van der Heijden
University of Leiden, The Netherlands

I. INTRODUCTION

Most current theories of human visual information processing and selective attention agree about a number of distinct processing stages in which sensory information is analyzed and/or transformed prior to the emission of responses. The theories disagree, however, with regard to two basic issues: (1) the limited capacity (LC) versus unlimited capacity (UC) processing issue, and (2) the early versus late selection issue.

With respect to the capacity issue two points of view are usually put forward. The first suggests that all information registered is processed automatically and in parallel up to a stage of memory activation. This is the UC-processing assumption (e.g., Deutsch & Deutsch, 1963; Morton, 1969; Shiffrin & Schneider, 1977). In contrast the LC view states that only a limited amount of information can be identified; either the assumption of a structural bottleneck early in the processing chain (cf., e.g., Broadbent, 1958, 1971) or the assumption that some of the early stages require the allocation of a limited resource system (cf., e.g., Kahneman, 1973) is used to characterize the processing aspect.

With regard to central selection, i.e., selection unaided by eye movements, there are also two dominating views. The first maintains that selection takes place at a stage prior to those concerned with categorization or identification. This is the early selection view (cf., e.g., Broadbent, 1958; Kahneman, 1973). In contrast the late selection view suggests that selection operates at a stage that contains identified information (cf., e.g., Deutsch & Deutsch, 1963; Norman, 1968).

It is of importance to note that the two points of view about the capacity issue

TABLE 16.1
Capacity and Selection Assumptions and Position of Prototypical Models and Derivatives with Regard to These Assumptions

		capacity assumptions	
		limited	unlimited
selection assumptions	early	Broadbent, 1958 etc.	
	late	1)	Deutsch & Deutsch, 1963 etc.

1) Broadbent's 1971, "response set" is a LC processing-late selection mechanism.

and those about the level of selection are independent. In principle therefore, four overall theoretical proposals are possible: (1) LC processing and early selection, (2) LC processing and late selection, (3) UC processing and early selection, (4) UC processing and late selection.

So far only two possibilities have been seriously considered. The first is the LC processing—early selection combination, with Broadbent's (1958, 1971) filter model as the prototype. Basically similar models have been proposed by Sperling (1963), Estes and Taylor (1964, 1966), Neisser (1967), Rumelhart (1970), Coltheart (1972, 1975), and Kahneman (1973). The second is the UC processing—late selection combination with Deutsch and Deutsch's (1963) model as the prototype. Again closely related models have been proposed by Norman (1968), Morton (1969), Keele (1973), Posner and Snyder (1975), and Posner (1978). Of course, there are a number of models that not easily fit in with this, dichotomy. Nevertheless, the hypotheses and models sketched previously and summarized in Table 16.1 capture most of the theorizing of the last 25 years.

Keele (1973) already concluded that these two sets of theories and the available data leave us with an unresolved dilemma. With regard to auditory information processing he remarks: "if selectivity occurs at the level of physical characteristics of the message, why does the meaning of the ignored message affect response to the selected message? If, on the other hand, selectivity occurs at the level of activated memory, why do physical characteristics of the sound, namely direction and frequency, affect selection?" (p. 151) In this chapter we illustrate this dilemma in the realm of visual attention for the partial-report and partial-report bar-probe task. Parts II and III present the relevant data and outline the problems with the two sets of theories. In part IIa we present the basic data and in IIb the conventional early selection-LC interpretation. In part IIc we briefly discuss the main problem with this interpretation. In part IIIa we present further data and in IIIb a more recent, late selection-UC, interpretation. In part IIIc we extensively discuss some problems with this interpretation. In the last part of this chapter, part IV, we briefly indicate an alternative direction for future theorizing.

IIa. PARTIAL REPORT I

In his Handbuch der physiologischen Optik (section 28), Von Helmholtz (1894) mentions a series of experiments that he regarded as a great importance.

> I refer now to the experiments . . . . with a momentary illumination of a previously completely darkened field on which was spread a page with large printed letters. Prior to the electric discharge the observer saw nothing but a slightly illuminated pinhole in the paper. He fixed his gaze rigidly upon it, and it served for an appropriate orientation of directions in the dark field. The electric discharge illuminated the printed page for an indivisible instant during which its image became visible and remained for a very short while as a positive after-image. Thus, the duration of the perceptibility of the picture was limited to the duration of the afterimage. Eye movements of a measurable magnitude could not be executed within the duration of the spark, and movements during the brief duration of the afterimage could no longer change its position on the retina. Regardless of this I found it possible to decide in advance which part of the dark field surrounding the continuously fixated pinhole of light I wanted to perceive, and then actually recognized upon the electric illumination single groups of letters in that region of the field, though usually with intervening gaps that remained empty. After strong flashes, as a rule, I read more letters than with weak ones. On the other hand, the letters of by far the largest part of the field were not perceived, not even in the vicinity of the fixation point. With a subsequent electric discharge I could direct my perception to another section of the field, while always fixating on the pinhole, and then read a group of letters there.
>
> These observations demonstrated, so it seems to me, that by a voluntary kind of intention, even without eye movements, and without changes of accommodation, one can concentrate attention on the sensation from a particular part of our peripheral nervous system and at the same time exclude attention from all other parts. (Von Helmholtz, 1894; Warren & Warren, 1968, translators).

Von Helmholtz (1871) referred to the same experiments and stated that he considered the observations of great importance because they showed that there "is a change in our nervous system, independent of the motions of the external movable parts of the body, whereby the excited state of certain fibers is preferentially transmitted to consciousness" (Warren & Warren, 1968, translators).

Von Helmholtz's task was rediscovered by Sperling (1960) and Averbach and Coriell (1961). Sperling (1960) presented displays with rows of letters or digits. The subjects were instructed to keep their eyes fixated on a central fixation point. Then the display was exposed for 50 msec, sufficiently brief to prevent eye movements. The subjects were asked to report only items from one row in the

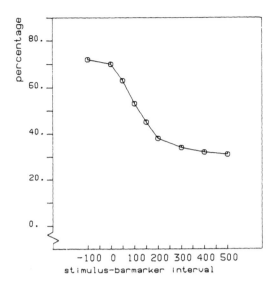

Fig. 16.1 Percentages correct reports in a partial-report bar-probe task as a function of stimulus-barmarker interval (after Averbach & Coriell, 1961).

display. The instruction as to which row to report was coded as a tone, occurring just before, during, or at various intervals after exposure of the display. A high, medium, or low tone specified report of the upper, middle, or lower row, respectively. It was impossible for the subjects to predict before the tone occurred, which of the rows would be specified. This is the partial-report task. Averbach and Coriell (1961) used a different form of stimulus sampling, called a (partial-report) bar-probe task. The stimulus displays contained linear letter arrays. A cue, an arrow or barmarker, was used to indicate the position of one of the letters. The exposure duration was 50 msec, and the barmarker appeared either before or at various moments after display presentation at a randomly chosen position. Subjects reported which letter (had) occupied the position indicated.

Figure 16.1 gives an impression of Averbach and Coriell's results. The proportion correct is rather high, when the barmarker or the tone is presented before the display. With increasing display-indicator intervals a fast decrease in proportion correct is observed, until, at an interval of about 250 msec, performance becomes asymptotic.

For present purposes two further topics in this field of research are relevant. The first concerns the question which types of stimulus attributes—besides location—are capable of producing this high initial level of performance and fast decrease of performance with increasing cue delays. It appeared that not only when the cue directly specified the position of the relevant items, but also when it indirectly specified the location via color of the items (see, e.g., Clark, 1969; Dick, 1969; Von Wright, 1968, 1972), via brightness (see, e.g., Von Wright, 1968), via shape (Turvey & Kravetz, 1970; Von Wright, 1968), or via size (Von Wright, 1970) the same pattern of results was found. Other studies showed that when the cue specified a subtle visual property such as upright letters versus letters rotated through 180 degrees (Von Wright, 1970) or a derived property such as letters versus digits ((Sperling, 1960; Von Wright, 1968, 1970; but see also Duncan, 1983 and Merikle, 1980), vowel versus consonant (Von Wright, 1970) or letters ending with the vowel /E/ versus letters ending with the vowel /i/ (Coltheart, Lea, & Thompson, 1974) this pattern of results failed to show up.

The second issue concerns the question which exposure or display parameters affect this pattern of results. From the vast literature we mention only a few findings. Exposure duration of the display has only a minor effect (Sperling, 1960). The decline of performance to the asymptotic level is much more gradual, i.e., extends over a much larger range of display-cue intervals, with a dark than with a light postexposure field (Averbach & Sperling, 1961). The higher the display luminance, the more elements reported with the shorter cue delays (see a.o. Eriksen & Rohrbauch, 1970a; Keele & Chase, 1967). A patterned visual stimulus, i.e., a mask, closely following the offset of the display seriously impairs report, the effect decreasing with increasing display-mask interval (see, for example, Lowe, 1975).

IIb. EARLY SELECTION AND LC PROCESSING

The results mentioned led to a coherent and nearly generally accepted view of an initial, large capacity, fast decaying, information store. Especially the availability of information *after* stimulus presentation was regarded the important and exciting finding.

The nature of the information retained in this store was mainly inferred from the results of investigations concerned with the problem which stimulus attributes were effective in selection. This led to the supposition that elementary physical attributes such as location, color, and brightness were represented and derived properties such as letter versus digit, or vowel versus consonant, not. Partial-report experiments addressed a stage of precategorical representation, containing solely raw or unprocessed information.

Sperling (1960, p. 26) identified "information storage" (i.e., what was experimentally observed) with a subjective "visual image." His reasons for this identification were phenomenological reports about legibility at the time a tone was heard when it followed the termination of the stimulus by 150 msec, the effects of different postexposure fields, and the known facts of visible persistence. So, in his opinion, the information in the initial high-capacity store was not only visual, but also visible. The information was stored as a rapidly fading image, or as a photograph loosing contrast over time.

Neisser (1967) summarized the early research and coined the term *iconic memory* for this persisting visual and visible analog of the stimulus.

Sperling (1960) and Averbach and Coriell (1961) also assumed that identity information did not become available automatically in their type of task. Identity information was neither in the initial visual store, nor somewhere else in the processing system. For identification items had to be "read," one after another. (See also Mackworth, 1962; 1963a, b, for this reading assumption.) Later this limited capacity reading process was variously named *synthesizing* (Neisser, 1967), *categorizing* (Broadbent, 1971) and *transfer to a more endurable memory* (Coltheart, 1975). This process, together with the short availability of the iconic material, was generally thought to be responsible for the fast decrease of performance with increasing cue delays. (See Coltheart, 1980a, pp. 186–187, for a detailed discussion of these assumptions.)

Although the main emphasis was on the visual image and its properties, central selection was not altogether forgotten. Sperling (Averbach & Sperling, 1961) stated "the finding that only 4 or 5 letters can be reported after a brief exposure dates back to the last century. My contribution has been, I think, to show that these few letters can be arbitrarily selected from a considerably larger number of letters which are available momentarily and shortly after the exposure" (p. 211). As we have seen, however, this finding also dates back to the last century. Nevertheless, the clear demonstration and objective measurement of central selective attention and its flexibility in a properly controlled situation was the major contribution of Sperling's (1960) and later iconic memory research.

It will be clear, that the information-processing model that emerged from this early research was clearly one of the early selection-LC type as described in the Introduction.

IIc. LC OR UC PROCESSING

The weak spot in the early selection-LC explanation of performance in partial-report and bar-probe tasks is the LC processing assumption. Several lines of research have suggested that this assumption is not generally valid and that automatic UC processing up to the highest levels of encoding cannot be excluded for this type of task.

First, it is of importance to note that the LC processing assumption is not really needed to explain performance in these tasks. Sperling (1963) thought that he had provided evidence in favor of the LC assumption in a task in which he varied exposure duration and presented a masking stimulus immediately after the display. Up to an exposure duration of 50 msec the number of items reported increased linearly. This result was taken as evidence for LC processing. But in

Marcel's (1983b) view, masking does not affect perceptual processing, so that, also under masking "All sensory data impinging however briefly upon receptors sensitive to them is analyzed, transformed, and redescribed, automatically and quite independently of consciousness, from its source form into every other representational form that the organism is capable of representing, whether by nature or by acquisiton. This process of redescription will proceed to the highest and most abstract levels within the organism" (p. 244). According to Marcel, masking interferes with the recovery or selection of identified information, not with the identification of the information (see Marcel, 1983a, for the experiments that led him to this position). A related point of view has been worked out by Van der Heijden (1981) and Mewhort and associates. The initial high level of performance and the decrease of performance with increasing probe delays need not be explained in terms of LC processing but can be explained as well in terms of selection of identified information. The possibility, that in lots of tasks not problems with the identification of information but with the selection of already identified information is what shows up in the data, cannot be ruled out.

Second, there is also positive evidence supporting the UC processing view. Although partial-report and bar-probe tasks are not especially suitable for demonstrating UC processing, some variations of the task nevertheless suggest this possibility and pose serious difficulties for LC processing. Mewhort (1967) presented two eight-letter pseudowords of either zero or fourth order of approximation. If one of the words was cued, the proportion of letters reported correctly was dependent not only on approximation order of the row indicated but also of the irrelevant word. Butler (1973, 1974) replicated this apparent effect of memory load. In a similar type of task Dick (1972) found that masking the irrelevant word enhanced performance for the relevant word. Di Lollo, Lowe, and Scott (1974) found the same effect when delaying the cued or the uncued words. Recently Merikle (1980, exp. 3) and Duncan (1983) demonstrated efficient selection based on alpha-numeric class when in a block of trials always letters (or digits) had to be named while the other category was consistently irrelevant. As stated, earlier research with mixed letter-digit reporting failed to show efficient selection. So, task relevance of the nontargets seems to be a factor of importance in partial-report tasks.

Yet a partial-report task is not the most appropriate paradigm for demonstrating UC processing. A better paradigm was used by Eriksen and associates (Collins & Eriksen, 1967; Eriksen, 1966; Eriksen & Lappin, 1965, 1967). They investigated performance in letter-identification tasks with accuracy as dependent variable. Their main interest was in establishing whether there are enough independent parallel visual processing channels. The general conclusion was that each occurrence of a target represented an independent opportunity for target detection when the letters were separated by more than 1 degree; with a separation of less than 1 degree the parallel channels appeared positively correlated. The same result has been found with latency instead of accuracy as dependent variable (Van der Heijden, Schreuder, Maris, & Neerincx, 1984; but see also Miller, 1982, exp. 4 & 5). If artifacts such as lateral interference, response competition and incompatible S–R mappings are ruled out, visual search tasks provide also evidence of UC processing (see, e.g., Fisk & Schneider, 1983; Schneider & Shiffrin, 1977; Shiffrin & Schneider, 1977; Van der Heijden, La Heij, & Boer, 1983).

There are also a large number of studies that clearly show that irrelevant elements are not excluded from processing, thereby strongly suggesting UC processing. Of special relevance are a number of variations of the Stroop task. Not only with integral combinations of words and colors a strong interfering effect of irrelevant information is found, but also with spatially separate color-word combinations (see, e.g., Dyer, 1973; Gatti & Egeth, 1978; Merikle & Gorewich, 1979; Van der Heijden, 1981), word–word combinations (Glaser & Glaser, 1982; Van der Heijden, 1981), color-color combinations (Van der Heijden, 1981) and letter–letter combinations (see, e.g., Eriksen & Eriksen, 1974; Eriksen & Schultz, 1979). These tasks are especially interesting because it has been shown that a series of selective operations in this type of task exactly describes whole-report performance as a function of exposure duration and can be used to adequately predict performance in partial-report tasks (cf. Van der Heijden, 1981).

In recent years so much evidence for the "breakthrough of the unattended" (Broadbent, 1982) had accumulated that Broadbent concluded that "advance uncertainty does affect the interaction between relevant and irrelevant stimuli. . . Two stimuli can well interfere, even though non-integral, particularly when the selective system is not operating" (p. 270). But advance uncertainty is one of the essential characteristics of partial-report and bar-probe tasks. And if it is valid as Broadbent (1982) states, that "Whatever the size of the beam [of the searchlight of selectivity] at any instant, everything within it obtains access to a further processing system" (p. 271), then there remains not much of the original LC assumption for partial-report and bar-probe tasks.

Given such a large amount of evidence consistent with UC processing, and so many examples showing that the meaning of the ignored messages affect response (Keele, 1973), it is worthwhile to briefly mention some of the reasons why LC processing was (and is) so widely held. At least three factors may be distinguished. First, the often used "reading" analogy with its serial, saccadic eye movements, connotation. Second, the initial failure to find efficient selection with the letter/digit criterion and the conclusion that this was proof that the materials had not been fully identified. A third, more general reason concerns the practice of mixing up data from visual and auditory information processing—for instance in theoretical papers (see, e.g., Allport, 1980a, b; Broadbent, 1982; Keele & Neill, 1978; Neumann, 1983)—and especially the tendency to use data obtained in dichotic listening tasks to also settle issues in visual information-processing research (see, e.g., Johnston & Dark, 1982). Fundamental properties of the visual system, for instance the retinal acuity gradient, are simply neglected (see, e.g., Broadbent's (1982) treatment of Eriksen and Schultz's (1979) data and Neumann's (1984a, b) interpretation of Gatti and Egeth's (1978) data).

IIIa. PARTIAL REPORT II

Besides the evidence in favor of UC processing also other evidence accumulated that forced theorists to a serious reconsideration of the basic assumptions of the "orthodox" iconic memory view. The first line of evidence is concerned with the relation between iconic memory and visible persistence; the second concerns data resulting from a detailed analysis of performance in bar-probe tasks.

Although Sperling (1960) was perfectly aware that his experiments only measured "information storage with the characteristics that were experimentally observed" (p. 22), he nevertheless identified this information storage with the persistence of vision ("visual image" or "persistence of sensation"), i.e., with what the observers saw. This identification opened the way to study iconic memory with "direct" methods. Instead of using the laborious indirect partial-report experiments, observers could also be asked to directly indicate in one way or another, how long they saw a shortly presented visual stimulus. Sperling (1967, p. 288-290) introduced these methods which were elaborated by Haber and associates (see, e.g., Haber & Standing, 1969, 1970). Since then, a large amount of direct methods have been developed and used to study iconic memory (see Coltheart, 1980a, b, and Long, 1980, for detailed reviews).

Recently, Coltheart (1980a, 1980b) has severely attacked the widely held assumption that the decaying visual memory as investigated in the partial-report experiments equals a visible memory that also can be studied "directly." Coltheart correctly argues that the identity of "informational persistence" and "visible persistence" should not be assumed, but demonstrated. Because both concepts are defined in terms of measurable aspects of observable behavior it is possible to investigate whether their identification is tenable. After careful study of the available evidence, Coltheart concludes that the identity assumption is wrong; informational persistence and visible persistence do not reflect a single underlying process, or, the processes investigated by direct methods do not correspond to the processes studied by the partial-report techniques.

Coltheart (1980a, 1980b) presents two major reasons for rejecting the identity assumption. The first is that stimulus duration and intensity have different effects on informational and visible persistence. The evidence Coltheart reviews strongly suggests two properties of visible persistence not shared by informational persistence: the inverse duration effect (the longer the stimulus duration the shorter its visible persistence after stimulus offset) and the inverse intensity effect (the intenser the stimulus the briefer the visible persistence after offset). The results of studies of stimulus duration and intensity on informational persistence have failed to show any evidence for an inverse relation.

The second reason is presented in Coltheart (1980b, but see also Coltheart, 1980a, p. 210). In Coltheart's view, visible persistence durations are much shorter than informational persistence durations. He argues that claims that the durations are roughly equal have overlooked an important factor. In partial-report experiments, the subject must decode the partial-report cue. Coltheart (1980b) states, "the time required to decode a partial-report cue was measured by Averbach and Coriell (1961), and in their experiment this time was about 270 ms. This means that a cue presented simultaneously with display offset is not applied to the contents of iconic memory until 270 ms later" (p. 64). In Coltheart's view estimates of informational persistence have to be corrected by adding this cue-decoding time. In that case the estimated durations of the two persistences are clearly different. To Coltheart's alternative approach to iconic memory, we return in section IIIb.

A second, important line of relevant evidence arose when it was appreciated that a detailed analysis of errors could add to the interpretation of the partial-report and especially the bar-probe tasks. With a few exceptions (see, e.g., Dick, 1974; Eriksen & Rohrbauch, 1970b; Townsend, 1973) only proportions correct were used as data in bar-probe tasks. These proportions correct were taken as unbiased measures of the identified items, i.e., errors were interpreted as failures of identification. But in a bar-probe task, there is more than item identification. Subjects must also locate the relevant item relative to the barmarker. Therefore, errors may reflect failures of identification, but also failures of localization. So, an analysis of errors is of crucial importance. Such an analysis of errors was presented by Eriksen and Rohrbauch (1970b), Townsend (1973), and Dick (1974), but especially Mewhort and associates have collected a complete set of relevant data.

Mewhort and associates used 8-letter linear arrays and a barmarker as a probe. Besides proportions correct, they distinguished two types of errors: intrusion errors and location errors. A response was scored as an intrusion error when a nonpresented letter was reported and as a location error when the subjects report another letter from the array than the one indicated. There were 8 letters in an array, 7 of which were nontargets, while 18 letters were not in the array. Hence in the case of random guessing, failures of identification should on the average result in numbers of intrusions and location errors in the proportion of 18 to 7. But that is not what was found. For our purposes, the most important results were: Appreciably more location errors than intrusion errors were made (see, Butler, 1980; Campbell & Mewhort, 1980; Mewhort & Campbell, 1978; Mewhort, Campbell, Marchetti, & Campbell, 1981; Mewhort, Marchetti, Gurnsey, & Campbell, 1984; Townsend, 1973; see also Fig. 16.2).

Most location errors consist of the correct response to an item adjacent to the item indicated by the probe (see, e.g., Campbell & Mewhort, 1980; Dick, 1974;

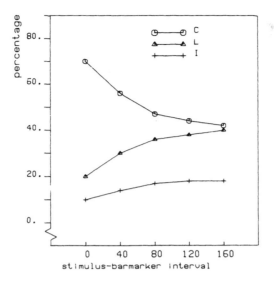

Fig. 16.2 Percentages correct reports (C), location errors (L) and intrusions (I) in a partial-report bar-probe task as a function of stimulus-barmarker interval (after Mewhort et al., 1981).

Eriksen & Rohrbauch, 1970b; Mewhort & Campbell, 1978; Mewhort et al., 1984; see for similar results in a different paradigm Estes, Allmeyer, & Reder, 1976; Estes, 1982).

The decrease in accuracy as the cue is delayed is largely matched by an increase in location errors and much less by an increase in intrusions (see, e.g., Eriksen & Rohrbauch, 1970b; Mewhort et al., 1981; Mewhort et al., 1984; Townsend, 1973; see also Fig. 16.2).

The decrease in accuracy as a result of a backward mask is largely reflected by an increase in location errors and only to a small extent by an increase in intrusions (see, e.g., Butler, 1980; Campbell & Mewhort, 1980; Mewhort & Campbell, 1978; Mewhort et al., 1981).

Location errors have an M-shaped serial position curve and mirror correct responses that have the complementary W-shaped serial position curve. So, the relative accuracy across the array is high when location errors are low and vice versa. For intrusions, this interrelated pattern of accuracy and errors is not observed (see, e.g., Campbell & Mewhort, 1980; Mewhort & Campbell, 1978; Mewhort et al., 1981).

This whole pattern of results, especially the large amount of location errors and the dissociation between the effect of probe delay on location errors (a large increase) and on intrusions (a minor increase) appears inconsistent with the orthodox iconic memory view in terms of a fading image. If errors resulted from identifying a degraded sensory image, a large initial amount and an equally large increase of intrusions is expected and a relatively small initial amount and increase of location errors. So the results are opposite to that predicted by the fading image analogy, and suggest that it are not problems of identification but problems of localization that impose the major limitations to performance in bar-probe tasks. Because the localization problems concern whole characters, the data also strongly suggest that the problems arise at a level where whole characters are available, i.e., after substantial initial processing or after identification of the items.

IIIb. LATE SELECTION – UC PROCESSING

Coltheart and Mewhort and associates have proposed rather similar alternatives to the orthodox iconic memory view. Coltheart (1980a) suggests "The alternative is that all items are identified, that is, reach their lexical entries. Iconic memory consists of the tagging of each of these entries with information about the physical manifestation of the word corresponding to that entry. This physical information decays away rapidly unless "lexically stabilized" by a "lexical monitor" of limited capacity" (p. 225). Of course, neither these tags, nor the tagged entries can be identified with visible persistence as measured in visible persistence studies; iconic memory and visible persistence are regarded as different processes (Coltheart, 1980a, p. 183). In this alternative the information about the physical manifestation is best regarded as some kind of abstract code at the lexical level (see also Coltheart, 1984).

To account for the results obtained in bar-probe tasks and a number of related tasks, Mewhort and associates have proposed a "dual-buffer" model. This model is the front end of a larger word-identification model (see Mewhort & Campbell, 1981, for a detailed description). Four components are involved in the bar-probe task: a feature buffer, an identifier, a character buffer, and an attentional mechanism. A representation of the stimulus first enters the feature buffer. The identifier, operating in parallel on all the information in this buffer, identifies the items and stores its results along with location information in the second store, the character buffer. The attentional mechanism operates on the identity and location information in this buffer and passes a code, suitable for output, to short-term memory.

This model, together with assumptions about differences in saliency of spatial information at different probe positions (to explain the W-shaped serial position curve), a faster loss of location information as compared to identity information in the character buffer (to explain the dissociation between the effect of probe delay on intrusions and location errors), and about an effect of a mask—besides its effect on the data in the feature buffer—on location information in the character buffer (to explain the differential effect of a mask on location errors and intrusions) is capable of explaining most of the results.

An essential assumption of the dual-buffer model is that selective attention operates in the character buffer and not in the feature buffer. It is of importance therefore to consider how the two buffers are defined.

Campbell and Mewhort (1980, p. 140) introduce the feature buffer as "a memory which stores the feature information. The visual persistence described by Eriksen and Collins (1968) and by Di Lollo (1977) likely reflects the operation of the feature buffer." Mewhort et al. (1981; see also Mewhort and Campbell, 1981, p. 61) add "The feature representation is precategorical, and the buffer's capacity is unlimited; that is, the buffer preserves spatial and other physical attributes of the display. Thus, the feature buffer holds raw data concerning the shape of each letter; for example, different features would be involved in upper and lowercase letters" (p. 51).

Campbell and Mewhort (1980; see also Mewhort et al., 1981, p. 51) describe the character buffer as "a visual-spatial buffer. The buffer preserves the spatial arrangement, but as the buffer is postidentification, it involves a more abstract representation than the idea of an image (or icon) would suggest" (p. 141). Mewhort et al. (1981, p. 51 and p. 62) identify the character buffer with the nonimage postidentification store studied by Rayner, McConkie & Zola (1980). The latter describe the information in this store as "independent of specific visual (case) characteristics." (Rayner et al., 1980, p. 224)

In summary, it seems that the feature buffer equals Coltheart's (1980a, b) visible persistence (see also Butler, 1981, p. 119). In the model, this is not the store addressed or used in the bar-probe task (see Mewhort & Butler, 1983, p. 33). For that task the character buffer is the relevant store. Although the character buffer is granted a role in visual perception, especially in the integration of information across eye movements and in the continuity of perception (see, e.g., Mewhort & Butler, 1983, p. 33; Mewhort & Campbell, 1981, p. 63; Mewhort et al., 1981, p. 62) it cannot be equated with visible persistence; details are lost (Mewhort & Campbell, 1981, p. 63; Mewhort et al, 1981, p. 51), the information is independent of specific visual characteristics (i.e., A = a at this level; Rayner et al., 1980, p. 224), or, is abstract. The character buffer exactly fits Coltheart's conception of informational persistence (see also Coltheart, 1984).

It will be clear that the views described in the preceding paragraphs are examples of late selection - UC processing models. The essential assumption is that all information is automatically processed up to the level at which identity information is available. It is assumed that the postcategorical level not only contains information about the identities of the visual stimuli, but also episodic information (cf. Coltheart, 1984, p. 260). Selective attention operates at this postcategorical level and uses the episodic information represented at this level (tags or relative spatial position) for distinguishing relevant and irrelevant information. While an initial, high-capacity, rapidly decaying visual feature buffer is still recognized, it plays no role in the selection of information in these models (see, e.g., Coltheart, 1984, p. 282).

IIIc. LATE OR EARLY SELECTION

The weak spot in late selection - UC processing explanations is the late selection assumption that information at the postcategorical level, such as tags, labels, or relative spatial position in a character buffer, is used for distinguishing between relevant and irrelevant information. Neither Coltheart's arguments, nor Mewhort et al.'s data are definitive proof that the representation, whose duration is measured in visible persistence studies, plays no role. First we discuss Coltheart's arguments, then we have a closer look at Mewhort et al.'s data.

With regard to Coltheart, the first issue is that visible persistence is not necessarily inversely related to target intensity and duration (Hawkins & Shulman, 1979; Long, 1980). The tasks used and especially the strategies adopted by the subjects seem to determine in large part the outcome of persistence studies. If subjects respond to the perceived offset of the stimulus, an inverse relation is found, but not, however, if the subjects really respond to target persistence, i.e., to the disappearance of the subjectively fading trace as distinct from target offset. Long (1980) concludes therefore that "the appealing parsimony of equating visible persistence and iconic memory, which has been the traditional view . . . , need not . . . be abandoned" (p. 814). Subsequent research seems to support Long's point of view (see Adelson & Jonides, 1980; Long & Beaton, 1982; Long & McCarthy, 1982), but a number of questions remains to be solved (see Coltheart, 1984 and Di Lollo, 1984).

Second, Coltheart's (1980b) conclusion that visible persistence durations are much shorter than information persistence durations is based on an erroneous interpretation of Averbach and Coriell's (1961) experiments. These authors were not interested in and did not really measure cue-coding time. They were only interested in estimating "effective storage time," i.e., the temporal extent of the newly discovered visual memory. For estimating this storage time they needed proportions correct for a range of "read-out-times" defined as the interval between onset of the display and subsequent appearance of a circle surrounding the indicated letter; in their view the circle instantaneously erased the marked letter. Observed performance was at a maximum of .75 with a read-out time of about 250 msec. The lowest valid read-out time used was 100 msec and yielded a proportion correct of about .20. For intermediate read-out times proportions correct increased linearly. It is far from clear how an average cue-decoding time can be derived from these data. Averbach and Coriell only conclude that *maximum* performance required 200 to 270 msec for detecting the presence of the marker and reading the marked letter. They ultimately arrived at "effective visual storage times" of 250, 250, and 300 msec for their three subjects. So average storage duration (and not average cue-decoding time) is about 270 msec. This value is well in line with estimated visible persistence durations.

We now turn to Mewhort et al.'s data. One of the most spectacular and consistent findings obtained with bar-probe tasks using linear arrays is the sharply W-shaped serial position curve for correct responses. (see e.g., Averbach & Coriell, 1961; Butler & Merikle, 1973; Campbell & Mewhort, 1980; Mewhort et al., 1981; Townsend, 1973). In the postcategorical dual-buffer model, this phenomenon is explained in terms of saliency of positional information in the character buffer.

It indeed appears that part of the W shape has to be attributed to the subject's limited ability to locate the probe relative to the display or to alignment difficulties. If subjects are asked to only indicate the position of the probe, the serial position curve of correct responses can also take on a W shape (see, e.g., Mewhort & Campbell, 1978; Tramer, 1981; but see Townsend, 1973, for a counter example). But this serial position curve is more flat, and therefore the subject's limited ability to locate the probe in space only accounts for part of the W function. There must be another factor involved. Is this factor saliency of positional information in the character buffer?

According to Estes (1978) there are two other factors the combination of which produces the W-shaped function. The first is the central-peripheral visual acuity gradient (see, for example, Haber & Hershenson, 1974, p. 51) and the second is lateral masking, i.e., the adverse effect on identification of a letter caused by a mask letter presented in close temporal and spatial proximity.

Recent research has provided substantial evidence for the importance of the latter factor. Lateral masking is not only observed with short but also with extended exposure durations (see, e.g., Estes et al., 1976; Taylor & Brown, 1972; Townsend, Taylor & Brown, 1971). It therefore appears to be a genuine visual factor and not a memory factor. Lateral masking is more detrimental in the periphery than in the fovea (Bouma, 1970; Mathews, 1973; Wolford & Hollingsworth, 1974) and with close target-mask spacing than with wide spacing (Bouma, 1970; Strangert & Brännström, 1975; Wolford & Chambers, 1983). The effect is asymmetric in the sense that masks placed on the peripheral side of the target are more effective than masks on the foveal side (Banks, Larson, & Prinzmetal, 1979; Bouma, 1970, 1973; Chambers & Wolford, 1983; Chastain, 1982a, b, 1983; Chastain & Lawson, 1979). Furthermore, lateral masking is probably to some extent feature specific, i.e., the accuracy reducing interaction effects are larger for identical or similar letters than for dissimilar letters (see, for example, Andriessen & Bouma, 1976; Bjork & Murray, 1977; Egeth & Santee, 1981; Krumhansl, 1977, and Krumhansl & Thomas, 1977; Santee, 1981; Santee & Egeth, 1980, 1982a, b, for the first suggestive evidence; see for example, La Heij & Van der Heijden, 1983; Shapiro & Krueger, 1983, for robust evidence obtained under a broad range of exposure conditions.) Estes (1972, 1974) proposed a model for generalised lateral interference and Bjork & Murray (1977) extended this model into what they called a "feature specific inhibition model."

In Estes' (1978, p. 188) view these two factors—retinal acuity and lateral masking—can account for the W function. Lateral masking would be greatest in the interior of the display where each letter has two neighbors, and least at the

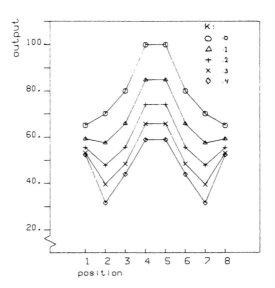

Fig. 16.3 Numerical example showing how lateral masking transforms an input function (.0) in W-shaped serial position curves (curves .1, .2, .3, and .4).

ends where the letters have only a single, foveal, neighbor, and a blank space at the peripheral side. In combination with the decreasing visual acuity from fovea to periphery, lateral masking explains the W-shaped serial position curve.

To illustrate the power of this type of explanation a numerical example is presented in Fig. 16.3. The upper curve in this figure (labeled .o) can be interpreted as an (8 letter) input function, I, to a system with lateral inhibition. The output functions, 0, were derived by using the sets of equations that characterize lateral inhibition between facets in the eye of the limulus (see Cornsweet, 1970). The relation between O and I is given by: $O_i = I_i - \Sigma K_{ji}O_j$. This equation can be read: The output value for the letter in positions, i, O_i, equals its input value, I_i, minus the sum of the inhibitory influences received from the other letters, $\Sigma K_{ji}O_j$. In our example all inhibitory coefficients, K_{ji}, were zero except those for adjacent letters. For the lines labeled .1, .2, .3, and .4 the coefficients used were .1, .2, .3, and .4, respectively. The figure shows that even with severe restrictions—an arbitrary input function, only inhibition between adjacent items, no asymmetry and all coefficients the same value—a broad range of W-shaped functions is obtained. So, Estes' (1978) explanation cannot easily be dismissed. (If lateral interference is in part feature specific, the lines in our figure have simply to be interpreted as resulting from averaging over a large number of trials with randomly varying adjacent letter similarities.)

Mewhort and Campbell (1981, p. 56) however reject Estes' explanation. If lateral masking has the effect of degrading representations in a feature buffer, misidentifications, and therefore mainly intrusions should be expected. Furthermore, these intrusions should mirror correct responses over serial positions. But that is not what is observed. Errors are mainly location errors and these location errors mirror correct responses over serial positions. Mewhort and Campbell therefore conclude that the shape of the accuracy curve reflects problems of localization and not identification.

There are two problems with this conclusion, however. First from the fact that mainly location errors are found it cannot be concluded that the basic cause is not lateral interference. If the barmarker points at letter X, and subjects name an adjacent letter Y than the conclusion is warranted that there were no problems with the identification of Y but not that there were no problems with the identification of X. A never explicitly reported but easily detectable feature of the data is pertinent here: The serial position curve for "supplied location errors" is also W shaped! It are the (adjacent) positions at which the *lowest* number of location errors are made, i.e., the positions with the *most salient* position information, that provide the names used to commit a location error if a position yielding a large number of location errors is probed; the names of items in the positions where a great number of location errors are made are only very sparsely used to commit a location error (see the tables in Mewhort et al., 1981). So it seems that the W-shaped function reflects overall item availability as suggested in the lateral masking view and has nothing to do with "saliency of position information in the character buffer."

Second, *feature-specific* lateral interference can explain in principle why location errors dominate, why these location errors are mainly close location errors and why the serial position curve for location errors mirrors the one for correct responses. The explanation consists of the orthodox iconic memory view with the feature-specific lateral interference assumption added. In fact, the explanation is rather simple. As a result of feature-specific lateral interference at some positions (see Fig. 16.3) there are identification problems. Identification may ultimately succeed but can also lead to a misidentification. Such an error will not be completely unrelated to the probed letter, but will often result in the name of a letter visually similar to the target (see Keele & Chase, 1967). These errors are mainly made just when visually similar letters flank the target because these cause the feature-specific interference. So, misidentifications are likely to consist of the name of an adjacent letter, that is visually similar to the probed letter. This explains the above chance occurrence of location errors (the 18:7 ratio is incorrect as a baseline because visual similarity plays a role), the finding that location errors are mainly near location errors (adjacent, visually similar, letters are the cause of the misidentifications), and the distribution of correct responses and location errors over probe position. It also follows that the strong positions provide the names for location errors; especially letters in these positions cause misidentifications if similar to the target and will tend to be named.

At the present it is not fully clear how the probe delay effect and the effect of backward masking have to be explained. It is however of importance to note that there are relations between these effects and the results obtained in feature-specific interference studies. Santee and Egeth suggest that uncertainty of target position and divided attention at the moment the display is presented (Santee & Egeth, 1982b, p. 499) and masking (Santee & Egeth, 1982a) seem to enhance the letter similarity effects (see also Santee & Egeth, 1980).

This section is concluded with two short remarks. First, a possible effect of letter similarity in bar-probe tasks has been recognized only very recently. There is no research directly concerned with this issue. Nevertheless, there is evidence that visual similarity and location errors are related. Mewhort and I reanalyzed the Mewhort et al. (1981) data and found positive correlations between a measure of similarity and number of location errors. Furthermore, in a series of experiments, some with colorpatches and some with letters as items, I used targets that were maximally dissimilar to the other elements in the display. There was no preponderance of location errors and, with increasing probe delays, intrusions increased at least as fast as location errors. (See Van der Heijden, 1984)

Second, there are other ways in which a relation between letter similarity and location errors can be explained. Estes (1982) suggests two possibilities based on generalized interference and target-neighbor similarity. In the first it is suggested that this similarity might hurt performance through increased positional uncertainty. In the second it is suggested that information concerning the similarity of two items will shift the observer's criterion for judging that the imperfectly perceived letter should be given the same name as the more clearly perceived one.

The main conclusion from this section is, that neither Coltheart's arguments nor Mewhort et al.'s data force us to assume that a precategorical feature buffer is not involved in partial-report and bar-probe tasks. It appears that the early selection assumption of the orthodox iconic memory view, together with the assumption of feature-specific interference, can adequately account for most of the results. Because the feature-specific interference component of this explanation is derived from a completely different field of research it deserves further attention. It is furthermore worthwhile to note that Estes' (1982) suggestions are phrased in terms of target-neighbor similarity. Similarity judgments require detailed feature information and are impossible with abstract letter information. So, also in Estes' view, the feature buffer has an essential role in these types of tasks.

IV. EARLY SELECTION AND UC PROCESSING

Sections II and III leave us with the same dilemma, Keele (1973) already pointed at. On the one hand, we have the early selection—LC account. It appears however, that the meaning of the irrelevant information affects responses to the relevant information. Therefore in models that try to account for performance in our type of task, UC processing is a more adequate assumption. On the other hand we have the late selection—UC account. But it appears that, given the available data, the use of an early representation of the physical features, cannot be ruled out for the tasks we are concerned with. Taken together, this suggests a combination of an early representation and UC processing.

In such a view, the early representation is not used for selective identification; the assumption is that all information is automatically identified. The only function the early representation can serve is in selection of relevant information from among identified irrelevant information. So, what we arrive at, is an early selection - UC processing model (see the scheme in the introduction).

Up till now, early selection -UC processing models have not received much attention and even appear unintelligible. It seems that mutually exclusive principles are combined. This apparent contradiction results from the prevailing views with regard to human information processing. In information transmission systems or serial digital computers what is selected is at the level at which the selector operates. Either a not yet transmitted (or not transformed) message is selected and then transmitted (or transformed), or, from among the transmitted (or transformed) messages one (or more) is selected for further transmission (or transformation). There is no sensible reason for selecting a message at stage A, when all messages have already arrived at a subsequent stage B.

Things change considerable, however, when we do not think in terms of computer models but of (pseudo) neural networks. (Allport, 1980a; Feldman & Ballard, 1982; Hinton & Anderson, 1981). A specimen of this kind of models— McClelland and Rumelhart's (1981) word recognition model—can serve to elucidate the early selection - UC notion.

In their "logogen model" McClelland and Rumelhart distinguish three levels: a level with feature detectors, letter detectors, and word detectors. For our present exposition only the feature level and the letter level are relevant (these two levels can be regarded as the set of input sides and the set of output sides of the logogens in Morton's, 1969, logogen model). In the model, feature detectors at the feature level are hardware connected by means of excitatory and inhibitory links with letter detectors at the letter level. A visual input, say an array of n letters, excites a number of spatially corresponding feature detectors (for our array, n spatially separated sets of feature detectors, one set of detectors for each letter presented). Activity at the feature level is automatically and nonselectively translated by means of the hardware connections into specific activity at the letter level(i.e., UC processing).

In this model, selective attention can in principle intervene at the feature level and at the letter level. Of course, for an early selection - UC combination we have to assume that selective attention intervenes at the feature level. The only means by which selective attention can intervene in the processing in this model is by changing the activity levels of a number of detectors. So, let us assume that selective attention increases the activity of one set of feature detectors (i.e., of the input side of one logogen). This operation at the feature level is immediately translated by means of the hardware links in an increased activity of one of the letter detectors at the letter level. This change in activity at the letter level can be identified with "being selected." This selection is early selection (the selective operation intervenes at the sensory level) but it is also postcategorical selection (identified letters are selected for further operations). And in this type of model, selection of an "untransformed" message results in the selection of a "transformed" message from among a number of transformed messages.

It is worthy of note that in this view the relevant features or relevant attributes are used for selection. In partial-report and bar-probe tasks these are the letter features, and in the Stroop-task, the color features; so both tasks are attribute selection tasks. The criterion attributes—in partial-report tasks the position, color, size, etc.—are not used for selection, but for what I termed *postcategorical filtering*, i.e., for locating the relevant information (see Van der Heijden, 1981, 1984; Van der Heijden, Hagenaar, & Bloem, 1984). So, at least two stages have to be distinguished in this view. The first stage concerns an operation in the feature buffer, or better, in the visual domain. Visual same–different tasks and search tasks can be used to further investigate the operations possible in this domain. The second stage is the selection stage as described earlier (see also Van der Heijden et al., 1984).

This early selection - UC processing model solves Keele's dilemma in a simple way. All information is processed, so the meaning of an ignored message can affect response to a selected message. Information in the visual domain is used for postcategorical filtering and selection, so, physical characteristics of the messages affect selection.

An early selection - UC model has further attractive features.

First it has to deal with the role of vision in central selective attention. The model leaves no opportunity to reduce vision either to some kind of preperceptual store as in early selection - LC theories or to some kind of postperceptual store as suggested in late selection - UC theories.

Second, the model is parsimonious because it does not require a duplication of information. So, neither tags in a lexicon—i.e., faint duplications of representations of physical features at the lexical level—, nor relative position information in the character buffer—i.e., a duplication of positional information in the feature buffer—are necessary in this model. The information needed is in the visual domain and can be used for selecting information in a lexicon or character buffer.

Third, the proposed operations are not altogether illogical. In fact, it is not too difficult to introduce this type of selection in McClelland and Rumelhart's (1981) model. A number of theorists have invoked operations like comparing, matching, cross-matching, checking and verifying to solve the problem how a precategorical and visual and a postcategorical, nonvisual representation are correctly related or integrated (see, e.g., Allport, 1977; Becker, 1980; Eriksen & Eriksen, 1974; Eriksen & Schultz, 1979; Keele & Neill, 1978; Morton, 1977). Such operations are evidently illogical because codes from different domains have nothing in common, and therefore their mutual comparison does not make sense. Comparisons are only valid within domains with compatible codes (Marcel, 1983b, p. 258; Prinz, 1984; Van der Heijden, 1981, p. 105–110).

Finally, the model is optimistic about the capabilities of the human information processor. It rejects the LC assumption and assumes that, given this world, this system and this point of view all identification is done that can be done. It also needs no assumption of failures of central selective attention to objects or to attributes (Broadbent, 1982; Neumann, 1984a, b). Given adequate information, subjects ultimately arrive at a correct response, even in the most difficult versions of the Stroop task. If selection fails, how does it ultimately succeed? In a number of laboratory tasks, however, the results of parallel monitoring of the environment for important information and the task requirements are not optimally combined. The resulting interference or delay is neither interpreted as a lack of capacity nor as a failure of selective attention. It is merely a sign that a system, optimally adapted to a normal environment, needs some time to adequately solve a problem in a highly artificial environment.

REFERENCES

Adelson, E. H., & Jonides, J. (1980). The psychophysics of iconic storage. *Journal of Experimental Psychology: Human Perception and Performance, 6,* 486–493.

Allport, D. A. (1977). On knowing the meaning of words we are unable to report: The effects of visual masking. In S. Dornic (Ed.), *Attention and performance VI.* Hillsdale, N.J.: Lawrence Erlbaum Associates.

Allport, D. A. (1980a). Patterns and actions: Cognitive mechanisms are content-specific. In G. Claxton (Ed.), *Cognitive psychology, new directions.* London: Routledge & Kegan Paul.

Allport, D. A. (1980b). Attention and performance. In G. Claxton (Ed.), *Cognitive psychology, new directions.* London: Routledge & Kegan Paul.

Andriessen, J. J., & Bouma, H. (1976). Eccentric vision: Adverse interactions between line segments. *Vision Research, 16,* 71–78.

Averbach, E., & Coriell, A. S. (1961). Short-term memory in vision. *Bell System Technical Journal, 40,* 309–328.

Averbach, E., & Sperling, G. (1961). Short term storage of information in vision. In C. Cherry (Ed.), *Information theory* (p. 196–211). London: Butterworth.

Banks, W. P., Larson, D. W., & Prinzmetal, W. (1979). Asymmetry of visual interference. *Perception & Psychophysics, 25,* 447–456.

Becker, C. A. (1980). Semantic context effects in visual word recognition: An analysis of semantic strategies. *Memory & cognition, 8,* 493–512.

Bjork, E. L., & Murray, J. T. (1977). On the nature of input channels in visual processing. *Psychological Review, 85,* 5, 472–484.

Bouma, H. (1970). Interaction effects in parafoveal letter recognition. *Nature, 226,* 177–178.

Bouma, H. (1973). Visual interference in the parafoveal recognition of initial and final letters of words. *Vision Research, 13,* 767–782.

Broadbent, D. E. (1958). *Perception and communication.* London: Pergamon Press.
Broadbent, D. E. (1971). *Decision and stress.* London: Academic Press.
Broadbent, D. E. (1982). Task combination and selective intake of information. *Acta Psychologica, 50,* 253-290.
Butler, B. E. (1973). Components of the familiarity effect in tachistoscopic recognition. *Journal of Experimental Psychology, 101,* 367-372.
Butler, B. E. (1974). The limits of selective attention in tachistoscopic recognition. *Canadian Journal of Psychology, 28,* 199-213.
Butler, B. E. (1980). Selective attention and stimulus localization in visual perception. *Canadian Journal of Psychology, 34,* 119-133.
Butler, B. E. (1982). Canadian studies of visual information processing: 1970-1980.*Canadian Psychology, 22,* 113-128.
Butler, B. E., & Merikle, P. M. (1973). Selective masking and processing strategy. *Quarterly Journal of Experimental Psychology, 25,* 542-548.
Campbell, A. J., & Mewhort, D. J. K. (1980). On familiarity effects in visual information processing. *Canadian Journal of Psychology, 34,* 134-154.
Chambers, L., & Wolford, G. (1983). Lateral masking vertically and horizontally. *Bulletin of the Psychonomic Society, 21,* 459-461.
Chastain, G. (1982a). Violation of the retinal acuity gradient in a detection task. *Acta Psychologica, 52,* 23-31.
Chastain, G. (1982b). Nontarget detectability and interference with parafoveal target identification. *Acta Psychologica, 50,* 117-126.
Chastain, G. (1983). Parafoveal identification asymmetry is a lateral masking effect. *The Journal of General Psychology, 109,* 77-81.
Chastain, G., & Lawson, L. (1979). Identification asymmetry of parafoveal stimulus pairs. *Perception & Psychophysics, 26,* 363-368.
Clark, S. E. (1969). Retrieval of color information from preperceptual memory. *Journal of Experimental Psychology, 82,* 263-266.
Collins, A. M., & Eriksen, C. W. (1967). The perception of multiple simultaneously presented forms as a function of foveal spacing. *Perception & Psychophysics, 2,* 369-373.
Coltheart, M. (1972). Visual information processing. In P. C. Dodwell (Ed.), *New Horizons in Psychology 2,* Harmondsworth: Penguin.
Coltheart, M. (1975). Iconic memory: A reply to professor Holding. *Memory & Cognition, 3*(1), 42-48.
Coltheart, M. (1980a). Iconic memory and visual persistence. *Perception & Psychophysics, 27*(3), 183-228.
Coltheart, M. (1980b). The persistences of vision. *Philosophical Transactions Royal Society of London.* B 290, 57-69.
Coltheart, M. (1984). Sensory Memory—A tutorial review. In H. Bouma & D. G. Bouwhuis (Eds.), *Attention and Performance X: Control of language processes.* London, Lawrence Erlbaum Associates.
Coltheart, M., Lea, C. D., & Thompson, K. (1974). In defense of iconic memory. *Quarterly Journal of Experimental Psychology, 26,* 633-641.
Cornsweet, T. N. (1970). *Visual perception.* New York: Academic Press.
Deutsch, J. A., & Deutsch, D. (1963). Attention: Some theoretical considerations. *Psychological Review, 70,* 80-90.
Dick, A. O. (1969). Relations between the sensory register and short-term storage in tachistoscopic recognition. *Journal of Experimental Psychology, 82,* 279-284.
Dick, A. O. (1972). Parallel and serial processing in tachistoscopic recognition: Two mechanisms, *Journal of Experimental Psychology, 96,* 60-66.
Dick, A. O. (1974). Iconic memory and its relation to perceptual processing and other memory mechanisms. *Perception & Psychophysics, 16*(3), 575-596.

Di Lollo, V. (1977). Temporal characteristics of iconic memory. *Nature, 267,* 241–243.
Di Lollo, V. (1984). On the relationship between stimulus intensity and duration of visible persistence. *Journal of Experimental Psychology: Human Perception and Performance, 10,* 144–151.
Di Lollo, V., Lowe, D. G., & Scott, J. P. (1974). Temporal integration in visual memory. *Journal of Experimental Psychology, 103,* 934–940.
Duncan, J. (1983). Perceptual selection based on alphanumeric class: Evidence from partial reports. *Perception & Psychophysics, 33,* 533–547.
Dyer, F. N. (1973). The Stroop phenomenon and its use in the study of perceptual, cognitive, and response processes. *Memory & Cognition, 1*(2), 106–120.
Egeth, H. E., & Santee, J. F. (1981). Conceptual and perceptual components of interletter inhibition. *Journal of Experimental Psychology: Human Perception and Performance, 7,* 506–517.
Eriksen, B. A., & Eriksen, C. W. (1974). Effects of noise letters upon the identification of a target letter in a nonsearch task. *Perception & Psychophysics, 16,* 143–149.
Eriksen, C. W. (1966). Independence of successive inputs and uncorrelated error in visual form perception. *Journal of Experimental Psychology, 72,* 26–35.
Eriksen, C. W., & Collins, J. F. (1968). Sensory traces versus the psychological moment in the temporal organization of form. *Journal of Experimental Psychology, 77,* 367–382.
Eriksen, C. W., & Lappin, J. S. (1965). Internal perceptual system noise and redundancy in simultaneous inputs in form identification. *Psychonomic Science, 2,* 351–352.
Eriksen, C. W., & Lappin, J. S. (1967). Independence in the perception of simultaneously presented forms at brief durations. *Journal of Experimental Psychology, 73,* 468–472.
Eriksen, C. W., & Rohrbauch, J. W. (1970a). Visual masking in multi-element displays. *Journal of Experimental Psychology, 83,* 147–154.
Eriksen, C. W., & Rohrbauch, J. W. (1970b). Some factors determining efficiency of selective attention. *American Journal of Psychology, 83,* 330–343.
Eriksen, C. W., & Schultz, D. W. (1979). Information processing in visual search: A continuous flow conception and experimental results. *Perception & Psychophysics, 25*(4), 249–263.
Estes, W. K. (1972). Interactions of signal and background variables in visual processing. *Perception & Psychophysics, 12*(3), 278–286.
Estes, W. K. (1974). Redundancy of noise elements and signals in visual detection of letters. *Perception & Psychophysics, 16*(1), 53–60.
Estes, W. K. (1978). Perceptual processing in letter recognition and reading. In E. C. Carterette & M. P. Friedman (Eds.), *Handbook of perception, Vol IX.* New York: Academic Press.
Estes, W. K. (1982). Similarity related channel interactions in visual processing. *Journal of Experimental Psychology: Human Perception and Performance, 8,* 353–382.
Estes, W. K., Allmeyer, D. H., & Reder, S. M. (1976). Serial position functions for letter indentification at brief and extended exposure durations. *Perception & Psychophysics, 19,* 1–15.
Estes, W. K., & Taylor, H. A. (1964). A detection method and probabilistic models for assessing information processing from brief visual displays. *Proc. Nat. Ac. Sc., 52,* 46–54.
Estes, W. K., & Taylor, H. A. (1966). Visual detection in relation to display size and redundancy of critical elements. *Perception & Psychophysics, 1,* 9–16.
Feldman, J. A., & Ballard, D. H. (1982). Connectionist models and their properties. *Cognitive Science, 6,* 205–254.
Fisk, A. D., & Schneider, W. (1983). Category and word search: Generalizing serach principles to complex processing. *Journal of Experimental Psychology: Learning, Memory, and Cognition, 9,* 177–195.
Gatti, S. V., & Egeth, H. E. (1978). Failure of spatial selectivity in vision. *Bulletin of the Psychonomic Society, 11*(3), 181–184.
Glaser, M. O., & Glaser, W. R. (1982). Time course analysis of the Stroop phenomenon. *Journal of Experimental Psychology: Human Perception and Performance, 8,* 875–894.

Haber, R. N., & Hershenson, M. (1974). *The psychology of visual perception.* London: Holt, Rinehart, & Winston.

Haber, R. N.. & Standing, L. G. (1969). Direct measures of short-term visual storage. *Quarterly Journal of Experimental Psychology, 21,* 43–54.

Haber, R. N., & Standing, L. G. (1970). Direct estimates of the apparent duration of a flash. *Canadian Journal of Psychology, 24,* 216–229.

Hawkins, H. L., & Shulman, G. L. (1979). Two definitions of persistence in visual perception. *Perception & Psychophysics, 25,* 348–350.

Hinton, G. E., & Anderson, J. A. (1981). *Parallel models of associative memory.* Hillsdale, NJ: Lawrence Erlbaum Associates.

Johnston, W. A., & Dark, V. J. (1982). In defense of intraperceptual theories of attention. *Journal of Experimental Psychology: Human Perception and Performance, 8,* 407–421.

Kahneman, D. (1973). *Attention and effort.* Englewood Cliffs, NJ: Prentice–Hall.

Keele, S. W. (1973). *Attention and human performance.* Pacific Palisades, CA: Goodyear.

Keele, S. W., & Chase, W. G. (1967). Short-term visual storage. *Perception & Psychophysics, 2,* 383–386.

Keele, S. W., & Neill, T. (1978). Mechanisms of attention. In E. C. Carterette & M. P. Friedman (Eds.), *Handbook of perception* (Vol. IX). New York: Academic Press.

Krumhansl, C. L. (1977). Naming and locating simultaneously and sequentially presented letters. *Perception & Psychophysics, 22,* 293–302.

Krumhansl, C. L., & Thomas, E. A. C. (1977). Effect of level of confusability on reporting letters from briefly presented visual displays. *Perception & Psychophysics, 21,* 269–279.

La Heij, W., & Van der Heijden, A. H. C. (1983). Feature specific interference in letter identification. *Acta Psychologica, 53,* 37–60.

Long, G. M. (1980). Iconic memory: A review and critique of the study of short-term visual storage. *Psychological Bulletin, 88,* 785–820.

Long, G. M., & Beaton, R. J. (1982). The case for peripheral persistence: Effects of target and background luminance on a partial report task. *Journal of Experimental Psychology: Human Perception and Performance, 8,* 383–391.

Long, G. M., & McCarthy, P. R. (1982). Target energy effects on type 1 and type 2 visual persistence. *Bulletin of the Psychonomic Society, 19,* 219–221.

Lowe, D. G. (1975). Temporal aspects of selective masking. *Quarterly Journal of Experimental Psychology, 27,* 375–385.

Mackworth, J. F. (1962). The visual image and the memory trace. *Canadian Journal of Psychology, 16,* 55–59.

Mackworth, J. F. (1963a). The relation between the visual image and post-perceptual immediate memory. *Journal of Verbal Learning and Verbal Behavior, 2,* 75–85.

Mackworth, J. F. (1963b). The duration of the visual image. *Canadian Journal of Psychology, 17,* 62–81.

Marcel, A. J. (1983a). Conscious and unconscious perception: Experiments on visual masking and word recognition. *Cognitive Psychology, 15,* 197–237.

Marcel, A. J. (1983b). Conscious and unconscious perception: An approach to the relations between phenomenal experience and perceptual processes. *Cognitive Psychology, 15,* 238–300.

Matthews, M. L. (1973). Locus of presentation and the selective masking effect. *Canadian Journal of Psychology, 27,* 343–349.

McClelland, J. L., & Rumelhart, D. E. (1981). An interactive activation model of context effects in letter perception: Part 1, An Account of basic findings. *Psychological Review, 88,* 375–407.

Merikle, P. M. (1980). Selection from visual persistence by perceptual groups and category membership. *Journal of Experimental Psychology: General, 109,* 279–295.

Merikle, P. M., & Gorewich, N. J. (1979). Spatial selectivity in vision: Field size depends on noise size. *Bulletin of the Psychonomic Society, 14*(5), 343–346.

Mewhort, D. J. K. (1967). Familiarity of letter sequences, response uncertainty, and the tachistoscopic recognition experiment. *Canadian Journal of Psychology, 21,* 309-321.
Mewhort, D. J. K., & Butler, B. E. (1983). On the nature of brief visual storage: There was never an icon. *The Behavioral and Brain Sciences, 6,* 31-33.
Mewhort, D. J. K., & Campbell, A. J. (1978). Processing spatial information and the selective-masking effect. *Perception & Psychophysics, 24,*(1), 93-101.
Mewhort, D. J. K., & Campbell, A. J. (1981). Toward a model of skilled reading: An analysis of performance in tachistoscopic tasks. *Reading research: Advances in theory and practice, 3,* 39-118.
Mewhort, D. J. K., Campbell, A. J., Marchetti, F. M., & Campbell, J. I. D. (1981). Identification, localisation, and "iconic memory": An evaluation of the bar-probe task. *Memory & Cognition, 9,* 50-67.
Mewhort, D. J. K., Marchetti, F. M., Gurnsey, R., & Campbell, A. J. (1984). Information persistence: A dual buffer model for initial visual processing. In H. Bouma & D. G. Bouwhuis (Eds.), *Attention and performance X, Control of language processes.* London: Lawrence Erlbaum Associates.
Miller, J. (1982). Divided attention: Evidence for coactivation with redundant signals. *Cognitive Psychology, 14,* 247-279.
Morton, J. (1969). Interaction of information in word recognition. *Psychological Review, 76,* 165-178.
Morton, J. (1977). Word Recognition. In J. Morton & J. C. Marshall (Eds.), *Psycholinguistics series II.* London: Elek.
Neisser, U. (1967). *Cognitive psychology.* New York: Appleton Century Crofts.
Neumann, O. (1980). *Informationsselektion und handlungssteurung.* Dissertation: Bochum.
Neumann, O. (1983). Uber den Zusammenhang zwischen Enge und Selektivität der Aufmerksamkeit. *Bericht Nr. 19/1983, Psychologisches Institut der Ruhr-Universität Bochum, Arbeitseinheit Kognitions-psychologie.*
Neumann, O. (1984a). Automatic processing: A review of recent findings, and a plea for an old theory. In W. Prinz and A. F. Sanders (Eds.), *Cognition and motor processes.* Heidelberg, Berlin: Springer.
Neumann, O. (1984b). Die Hypothese begrenzter Kapazität und die Funktionen der Aufmerksamkeit. In O. Neumann (Ed.), *Perspektiven der Kognitionspsychologie.* Berlin: Springer.
Norman, D. A. (1968). Towards a theory of memory and attention. *Psychological Review, 75,* 522-536.
Posner, M. I. (1978). *Chronometric exploration of the mind.* Hillsdale, NJ: Lawrence Erlbaum Associates.
Posner, M. I., & Snyder, C. R. R. (1985). Facilitation and inhibition in the processing of signals. In P. M. A. Rabbitt & S. Dornic (Eds.), *Attention and performance V.* London: Academic Press.
Prinz, W. (1984). Modes of linkage between perception and action. In W. Prinz & A. F. Sanders (Eds.), *Cognition and motor processes.* Heidelberg, Berlin: Springer.
Rayner, K., McConkie, G. W., & Zola, D. (1980). Integrating information across eye movements. *Cognitive Psychology, 12,* 206-226.
Rumelhart, D. E. (1970). A multicomponent theory of the perception of briefly exposed visual displays. *Journal of Mathematical Psychology, 7,* 191-218.
Santee, J. L., & Egeth, H. E. (1980). Interference in letter identification: A test of feature-specific inhibition. *Perception & Psychophysics, 27,* 321-330.
Santee, J. L., & Egeth, H. E. (1982a). Independence versus interference in the perceptual processing of letters. *Perception & Psychophysics, 31,* 101-116.
Santee, J. L., & Egeth, H. E. (1982b). Do reaction time and accuracy measure the same aspects of letter recognition? *Journal of Experimental Psychology: Human Perception and Performance, 8,* 489-501.

Schneider, W., & Shiffrin, R. M. (1977). Controlled and automatic human information processing: I. Detection, search, and attention. *Psychological Review, 84*(1), 1-66.
Shapiro, R. G., & Krueger, L. E. (1983). Effect of similarity of surround on target-letter processing. *Journal of Experimental Psychology: Human Perception and Performance, 9,* 547-559.
Shiffrin, R. M., & Schneider, W. (1977). Controlled and automatic human information processing: II. Perceptual Learning, automatic attending, and a general theory. *Psychological Review 84*(2), 127-190.
Sperling, G. (1960). The information available in brief visual presentations. *Psychological Monograph, 74*(11).
Sperling, G. (1963). A model for visual memory tasks. *Human Factors, 5,* 19-31.
Sperling, G. (1967). Successive approximations to a model for short-term memory. *Acta Psychologica, 27,* 285-292.
Strangert, B., & Brännström, L. (1975). Spatial interaction effects in letter processing. *Perception & Psychophysics, 17,* 268-272.
Taylor, S. G., & Brown, D. R. (1972). Lateral visual masking: Supraretinal effects when viewing linear arrays with unlimited viewing time. *Perception & Psychophysics, 12,* 97-99.
Townsend, J. T., Taylor, S. G., & Brown, D. R. (1971). Lateral masking for letters with unlimited viewing time. *Perception & Psychophysics, 10*(5), 375-378.
Townsend, V. M. (1973). Loss of spatial and identity information following a tachistoscopic exposure. *Journal of Experimental psychology, 98,* 113-118.
Tramer, S. (1981). *Data versus probe errors in the bar-probe task: A re-evaluation of the dual-buffer model.* Unpublished MA Thesis, Queen's University, Kingston.
Turvey, M. T., & Kravetz, S. (1970). Retrieval from iconic memory with shape as the selection criterion. *Perception & Psychophysics, 8,* 171-172.
Van der Heijden, A. H. C. (1981). *Short-term visual information forgetting.* London: Routledge & Kegan Paul.
Van der Heijden, A. H. C. (1984). Postcategorical filtering in a bar-probe task. *Memory & Cognition, 12,* 446-457.
Van der Heijden, A. H. C., Hagenaar, R., & Bloem, W. (1984). Two stages in postcategorical filtering and selection. *Memory & Cognition, 12,* 458-469.
Van der Heijden, A. H. C., La Heij, W., & Boer, J. P. A. (1983). Parallel processing of redundant targets in simple visual search tasks. *Psychological Research, 45,* 235-254.
Van der Heijden, A. H. C., Schreuder, R., Maris, L., & Neerincx, M. (1984). Some evidence for positively correlated separate activation in a simple letter-detection task. *Perception & Psychophysics, 36,* 577-585.
Von Helmholtz, H. (1871). Ueber die Zeit welche nötig ist, damit ein Gesichtseindruck zum Bewusstsein kommt. *Berliner Monatsberichte,* June 8, 333-337.
Von Helmholtz, H. (1894). *Handbuch der physiologischen Optik.* Hamburg, Leipzig: L. Vos.
Von Wright, J. M. (1968). Selection in visual immediate memory. *Quarterly Journal of Experimental Psychology, 20,* 62-68.
Von Wright, J. M. (1970). On selection in visual immediate memory. *Acta Psychologica, 33,* 280-292.
Von Wright, J. M. (1972). On the problem of selection in iconic memory. *Scandinavian Journal of Psychology, 13,* 159-171.
Warren, R. M., & Warren, R. P. (1968). *Helmholtz on Perception: Its physiology and development.* New York: Wiley.
Wolford, G., & Chambers, L. (1983). Lateral masking as a function of spacing. *Perception & Psychophysics, 33,* 129-138.
Wolford, G., & Hollingsworth, S. (1974). Lateral masking in visual information processing. *Perception & Psychophysics, 16,* 315-320.

Author Index

Italics denote pages with bibliographic information

A

Abbs, J. H., 95, 96, *100, 101*
Abraham, R. H., 8, 12, *27*
Abravanel, E., 60, *73*
Acuna, C., *166*
Adams, J. A., 78, 79, 81, 82, 83, *101*
Adelson, E. H., 434, *441*
Adkins, R. J., 151, *162*
Adler, A., 372, *387*
Adrian, E. D., 146, *162*
Akerboom, S., 93, *103*
Albright, T. D., 401, *416*
Alderson, G. J. K., 35, *45*
Allen, G. I., 134, *162*
Allers, R., 55, *73*
Allmeyer, D. H., 431, *443*
Allport, D. A., 90, 282, 361, 362, 363, 364, 366, 367, 368, 371, 372, 373, 377, 380, 385, 398, 399, 411, 413, 428, 439, 441, *101, 297, 387, 393, 415, 441*
Alluisi, E. A., 397, *416*
Anderson, J. A., 362, 383, 404, 439, *387, 415, 444*
Anderson, J. R., 383, *387*
Anderson, N. H., 279, 281, 283, 284, 295, *297*
Anderson, P. W., 6, *27*
Anderson, R. E., 265, *269*
Anderson, W. G., 306, *332*
Andriessen, J. J., 435, *441*
Andronov, A., 8, *27*
Anstis, T., 265, *269*
Antonis, B., 90, 364, 377, 398, *101, 387, 415*
Arbib, M. A., 34, 159, 383, *45, 162, 387*
Archer, T., 45, *46*
Arendt, L. E., 260, *267*
Arezzo, J., 112, 113, 114, 116, 117, 125, *128*
Arissian, K., 146, *162*
Aristotle, 173, 174, *192*
Armstrong, T. R., 97, *101*
Asanuma, C., 139, 140, 146, *162*
Asanuma, H., 146, 147, 151, *162, 165, 167*
Ashby, W. R., 7, *27*
Averbach, E. V., 345, 423, 424, 425, 426, 434, 435, *355, 441*

B

Baba, D. M., 19, *30*
Bachmann, T., 406, *415*
Bach-Y-Rita, P., 255, *267, 268*
Baddeley, A. D., 342, 384, *355, 387*
Baer, T., 27, *31*
Bahill, A. T., 20, *27*

447

AUTHOR INDEX

Bahrick, H. P., 79, 80, 86, 383, *101, 387*
Bain, A., 181, 186, 188, *192*
Baird, J. W., 220, *244*
Baker, R. S., 243, *247*
Baldissera, F., 18, *27*
Baldwin, J. M., 52, 67, *73*
Ballard, D. H., 209, 439, *211, 443*
Bamber, D., 249, *268*
Bandura, A., 52, 62, *73*
Banks, W. P. 282, 435, *297, 441*
Barnette, B. D., 267, *268*
Barret, G., 108, *130*
Bartlett, N. R., 70, *73*
Bartlett, S. C., 70, *73*
Bastian, Ch., 172, 191, *192*
Bates, J. A. V., 112, *128*
Bauer, J., 233, *244*
Beal, A. L., 342, 343, 344, *356*
Beaton, R. J., 434, *444*
Beauvois, M. F., 401, *416*
Becker, C. A., 441, *441*
Becker, W., 260, *268*
Becklen, R., 369, 386, *390*
Bell, Ch., 172, 181, 182, 183, 184, 185, 187, *192*
Bender, P. A., 88, *101*
Benignus, V. A. 121, *130*
Benton, A. L., 401, *416*
Berger, H., 105, *128*
Bergman, R., 33, *45*
Berkeley, G., 175, 178, 179, 217, *192, 244*
Bernhardt, M., 189, *193*
Bernstein, A. S., 378, *387*
Bernstein, N. A., 4, 23, 253, *27, 268*
Berrian, R. W., 306, *332*
Berson, D. M., 406, *416*
Bever, T. G., 320, 328, 329, *331, 333*
Beverley, K. I., 202, *212*
Bialystok, E., 66, *75*
Bichat, F. M. X., 181, *193*
Biederman, I., 385, *387*
Biguer, B., 196, 231, 397, *211, 244, 416*
Billings, D., 330, *331*
Bioulac, B., 139, *162, 165*
Bischof, N., 259, *268*
Bizzi, E., 10, 11, 149, *27, 162, 163*
Bjork, E. L., 435, *441*
Bloem, W., 385, 386, *388*
Bloom, W., 440, *446*
Blumstein, S. E., 306, *331*
Bobrow, D. S., 365, *391*

Boch, R., 406, *416*
Bode, K. A., 234, *248*
Boer, J. P. A., 363, 428, *388, 446*
Boggs, G. J., 365, *392*
Boies, S. J., 362, *392*
Boring, E. G., 171, 172, 173, 189, 190, 216, *193, 244*
Bornemann, E., 89, 364, *101, 387*
Bossom, J., 117, *130*
Bouma, H., 339, 435, *356, 441*
Bourdy, C., 225, *246*
Bower, T. G. R., 60, 62, 201, *73, 211*
Bowman, R. W., 325, *333*
Boylls, C. C., 23, *27*
Brainard, R. W., 397, *416*
Braitenberg, V. 381, *387*
Brännström, L., 435, *446*
Bray, N. W., 81, 82, *101*
Breinin, G. M., 241, *244*
Breitenbach, F., 267, *268*
Brickner, M., 366, *388*
Bridgeman, B., 197, 198, 232, 255, 380, *213, 244, 268, 387*
Briggs, G. E., 80, 382, *101, 387*
Brindley, G. S., 255, *268*
Brinkman, C., 141, *162*
Brinkman, J., 146, *162*
Broadbent, D. E., 273, 361, 362, 363, 364, 367, 373, 374, 398, 408, 409, 411, 421, 422, 426, 428, 429, 441, *297, 387, 416, 417, 442*
Broadbent, M. H. P., 398, *417*
Brodmann, K., 135, *162*
Brooks, L. R., 364, 369, 397, *387, 416*
Brooks, V. B., 140, 252, *162, 269*
Browman, C. P., 27, 322, 324, *27, 331*
Brown, C. M., 209, *211*
Brown, D. R., 435, *446*
Brown, Th., 172, 180, 181, 185, *193*
Brown, W., 70, *73*
Bruce, C., 401, *416*
Brune, F., 255, *268*
Bruner, J., 342, *357*
Brunia, C. H. M., 115, 126, *128*
Brunswik, E., 54, 276, 278, 283, *73, 297*
Bryden, M. P., 252, 340, 341, 343, *268, 356*
Bub, D., 370, *390*
Buffart, H., 66, *74*
Bundesen, C., 410, *416*
Bunz, H., 12, 16, 18, 20, *29*
Burchiel, K. J., 159, *168*

AUTHOR INDEX   449

Burian, H. M., 241, *244*
Burke, R. E., *163*
Burkell, J., 366, *393*
Burnham, C. A., 249, 266, *268*
Burnod, Y., 132, *164*
Burton, M. J., 404, *418*
Bush, B. M., 146, *162*
Bushnell, E. W., 63, *74*
Buswell, G. T., *268*
Butler, B. E., 340, 427, 430, 431, 433, 435, *357, 442, 445*

C

Caan, W., 401, *418*
Caharack, G., 370, *389*
Calvanio, R., 398, *417*
Calvert, T. W., 12, *31*
Calvet, J., 132, *164*
Campbell, A. J., 335, 336, 340, 341, 343, 344, 346, 347, 351, 352, 430, 431, 432, 433, 435, 436, *356, 357, 442, 445*
Campbell, G. T., 352, *356*
Campbell, J. I. D., 346, 430, *357, 445*
Campos, E. C., 240, *244*
Cannon, L. K., 266, *268*
Cardanus, H., 174, *193*
Carello, C., 4, 24, 26, 200, *32, 212*
Carlson, M., 137, *163*
Carmichael, L., 183, 184, *193*
Carpenter, R. H. S., 260, *268*
Carpenter, W. B., 48, 50, 54, *74*
Carter, D. B., 240, 241, *244, 245*
Casey, A., 221, *245*
Caspers, H., 106, *128*
Catellani, C. O., 240, *244*
Catsman-Berrevoets, C. E., 135, 151, *163*
Cattell, J. McK., 363, *387*
Cavallari, P., 18, *27*
Cecchini, A. B. P., 22, *28*
Chaikin, C. E., 8, *27*
Chajczyk, D., 409, 412, *417*
Chambers, L., 435, *442, 446*
Chapman, C. E., 138, 403, *163, 417*
Chapple, W., 10, *27*
Charman, W. N., 224, *245*
Chase, W. G., 425, 437, *444*
Chastain, G. 435, *442*
Cheal, M., 35, *46*
Checkosky, S. F., 385, *387*
Cheema, S. S., 151, *163*

Cheney, P. D., 134, 147, 150, 153, 156, *163, 164*
Cheng, D. W., 91, *101*
Cherry, C., 362, *387*
Chesney, G. L., 382, *389*
Chistovich, L. A., 306, *332*
Chmiel, N. R. J., 413, *415*
Ciuffreda, K. S., 208, *211, 212*
Civaschi, P., 18, *27*
Clark, E. V., 306, 326, *331*
Clark, H. H., 306, *331*
Clark, J. E., 327, *333*
Clark, M. R., 20, *27*
Clark, S. E., 425, *442*
Clayton, T. M. H., 41, 201, *46, 211*
Cogan, D. G., 222, *245*
Cohen, A. H., 12, *28*
Cohen, L., 18, *28*
Cohen, M. M., 279, 284, 289, 291, 293, *298*
Cole, K. J., 95, *101*
Cole, R. A., 330, *331*
Coleman, A., 22, *28*
Coleman, P., 264, *270*
Collins, A. M., 427, *442*
Collins, J. F., 433, *443*
Coltheart, M., 345, 351, 422, 425, 426, 429, 430, 432, 433, 434, *356, 442*
Condon, W. S., 70, *74*
Conrad, B. 140, 150, *163*
Cooke, J. D., 11, *28*
Cooper, F. S., 58, *74*
Cooper, W. E., 301, 306, 330, *331, 332, 333*
Corcos, D. M., 19, *28*
Cordo, P. J., 96, *102*
Coren, S., 249, 251, 253, 254, 266, *268*
Cornsweet, T. N., 436, *442*
Corrie, W. S., 133, *164*
Corriell, A. S., 345, 423, 424, 426, 434, 435, *355, 441*
Corteen, R. S., 379, *387*
Costa, L. D., 107, 112, *129, 130*
Coulter, J. D., 135, 137, 147, 151, *163, 165, 166*
Cowey, A., 400, 405, *416*
Cox, P. J., 364, *389*
Crago, P. E., 95, *101*
Creutzfeldt, O. D., 362, *387*
Crick, F., 407, *416*
Crone, R. A., 232, 240, 241, *245*
Crutcher, M. D., 140, *163*
Cuneo, D. O., 281, 284, *297*

AUTHOR INDEX

Cutler, A., 327, *331*
Cutting, J. E., 66, 200, 203, 276, *74, 211, 297*
Cvitanovic, P., 17, *28*

D

Damasio, A. R., 401, *416*
Damen, 126
Damos, D., 94, *101*
Dark, V. J., 428, *444*
Dawson, M. E., 379, *387*
Day, B. L., 146, 159, *165*
Darian-Smith, I., 138, *163*
Davies, A., 364, 366, *393*
de Condillac, E. B., 178, 179, 180, 185, *193*
Deecke, L., 107, 108, 110, 112, 116, 117, 122, 125, *128, 129*
DeLong, M. R., 140, *163*
DeMyer, W., 135, *166*
Denier van der Gon, J. J., 20, *32*
DeRenzi, E., 401, *416*
Descartes, R., 217, *245*
Desimone, R., 401, *416*
Desmedt, J. E., 149, 159, 195, *163, 211*
Deutsch, D., 363, 367, 411, 421, 422, *388, 416, 442*
Deutsch, J. A., 363, 367, 411, 421, 422, *388, 416, 442*
Dewey, J., 216, *245*
Diamond, R., 233, 242, 243, *245*
Dichgans, J., 229, *245*
Dick, A. O., 425, 427, 430, *442*
Diestal, J. D., 98, *103*
Di Lollo, V., 427, 433, 434, *443*
Ditchburn, R. W., 251, *268*
Dizio, P. 35, *45, 46*
Doane, B., 131, *165*
Dollard, J., 62, *75*
Donchin, E., 105, 382, *129, 389*
Dorfman, P. W., 39, 45, *45*
Dreher, B., 400, *419*
Dumais, S. T., 363, *392*
Duncan, J., 363, 366, 367, 370, 385, 386, 425, 427, *388, 443*
Düngelhoff, F.-J., 399, *416*
Dunlap, K., 70, *74*
Duthie, J. H., 100, *102*
Dyer, F. N., 428, *443*

E

Easton, A. M., 266, *268*
Ebenholtz, S. M., 196, 197, 198, 199, 200, 205, 208, 209, 234, 235, 237, 242, *211, 212, 245*
Eccles, J. C., 134, *163*
Eckmann, J.-P., 17, *28*
Edwards, M. W., 197, *212*
Egeth, H. A., 367, *388*
Egeth, H. E., 379, 408, 409, 413, 428, 429, 435, 438, *393, 416, 419, 443, 445*
Eimas, P. D., 290, *297*
Eisler, R., 177, *193*
Eldridge, M., 384, *387*
Ellis, S. P., 267, *270*
Ellis, St. H., 366, *389*
Elworth, C. L., 207, 209, *211*
Engel, J. J., 176, 177, 185, *193*
Epstein, W., 196, 206, 221, 225, *211, 245*
Eriksen, B. A., 428, *443*
Eriksen, C. W., 425, 427, 428, 429, 430, 431, 433, 441, *442, 443*
Estes, W. K., 422, 431, 435, 436, 438, *443*
Evarts, E. V., 116, 131, 132, 134, 138, 140, 143, 146, 147, 148, 149, 150, 154, 155, 156, 159, 161, 162, 400, *129, 163, 164, 167, 419*

F

Fechner, G. T., 276, *297*
Feldman, A. G., 9, 11, 22, *28*
Feldman, J. A., 439, *443*
Fendrich, R., 265, *269*
Fentress, J. L., 378, *388*
Festinger, L., 249, 251, 253, 265, 266, *268, 269*
Fetz, E. E., 132, 134, 147, 151, 156, 157, *163, 164*
Feynman, R., 27, *28*
Fick, E., 201, *211*
Fincham, E. F., 220, 226, 227, 228, *245*
Fink, S. I., 386, *388*
Finocchio, D. V., 132, 157, *164*
Fischer, B., 406, *416*
Fisher, D. F., 267, *268*
Fisher, R. P., 382, *387*
Fisher, S. K., 206, 208, 242, *212, 213, 247*
Fisk, A. D., 91, 92, 99, 383, 428, *103, 388, 443*
Fitch, H. L., 4, 12, 26, 71, *28, 74*
Fitts, P. M., 7, 80, 86, 92, 397, *28, 101, 416*
Flanders, J. P., 63, *74*
Flatt, A. E., 12, 22, *29*

AUTHOR INDEX 451

Fleishman, E. A., 78, *101*
Fodor, J. A., 276, 277, 328, 329, *297, 331*
Fogelgren, L. A., 210, *212*
Foley, J. M., 220, 225, *245*
Forbes, S. M., 366, *390*
Forssberg, H., 95, *101*
Forster, F. M., 379, *388*
Foulke, E. 302, 325, *331*
Fowler, C. A., 4, 12, 96, *28, 102*
Fraisse, P., 51, 70, *74*
Francis, E. L., 224, 229, *245*
Francolini, C. N., 408, 409, *416*
Freud, S., 321, *332*
Freund, H. J., 14, 140, *28, 164*
Frey, D. A., 265, *269*
Frey, K. J., 234, *248*
Friedman, A., 365, *388, 389*
Fromkin, V. A., 306, 324, *332*
Fromm, C., 132, 134, 140, 146, 147, 148, 149, 150, 151, 154, 155, 156, 159, 161, 162, *163, 164, 165*
Frykholm, G., 24, *31*
Fuchs, A. H., 80, 81, *101*
Funahashi, S. 143, *165*
Funnell, E., 399, *415*
Fuster, J. M., 116, 380, *129, 388*

G

Gaillard, A. W. K., 111, *130*
Galanter, E., 61, *75*
Galenos, 173, 174, *193*
Galilei, G., 175, *193*
Garrett, M. F., 328, 329, *331*
Gatti, S. V., 428, 429, *443*
Gazzaniga, M. S., 369, *389*
Gelade, G., 379, *393*
Gemba, H., 113, 114, 116, 139, *129, 130, 167*
Gentilucci, M., 402, *418*
Gentner, D. R., 98, *101*
George, L., 188, *193*
Georgopoulos, A. P., 140, *163*
Gerbrandt, L. K., 111, 112, *129*
German, D. C., 134, *164*
Geuze, R. H., 20, *32*
Gewirtz, J. L., 62, *74*
Ghosh, S., 147, *166*
Gibson, E. J., 33, *45*
Gibson, J. J., 4, 24, 174, 200, 201, 202, 216, 217, 218, 249, 261, 275, *28, 193, 211, 245, 268, 297*
Gielen, S. C., 293, *297*

Gilbert, P. F. C., 132, *164*
Gilden, L., 107, 108, 111, *129*
Gill, E. B., 43, *46*
Glaser, B. R., 399, *416*
Glaser, M. O., 428, *443*
Glaser, W. R., 428, *443*
Gleason, C. A., 107, *129*
Godaux, E., 149, 159, *163*
Godschalk, M., 143, *164*
Goetz, E. T., 78, *101*
Goff, W. R., 111, *129*
Gogel, W. C., 225, 229, *245*
Goldberg, M. E., 402, *419*
Goldscheider, A., 191, 192, *193*
Goldstein, E. G., 386, *388*
Goldstein, L., 27, *27*
Goodman, D., 12, 19, *30*
Goodwin, A., 138, *163*
Goodwin, G. M., 149, *164*
Goolkasian, P., 386, *388*
Gopher, D., 83, 282, 365, 366, 367, 374, *101, 297, 388, 390*
Gordon, G., 138, *164*
Gordon, P. C., 328, *332, 333*
Gorewich, N. J., 428, *444*
Gottlieb, M., 264, *270*
Gottsdanker, R., 93, 370, *101, 388*
Gould, J. D., 252, *268*
Govier, E., 379, *388*
Gracco, V. L., 95, *100, 101*
Granit, R., 241, 243, 362, *245, 388*
Grant, F. W., 220, 225, *245*
Graves, R. E., 353, *356*
Graybiel, A. M., 406, *416*
Green, J., 379, *393*
Greene, P. H., 7, 23, 27, *28*
Greenwald, A. G., 55, 60, 253, 399, *74, 269, 416*
Gregor, R. J., 98, *103*
Griffith, B. C., 290, *297*
Grillner, S., 95, *101*
Gross, C. G., 401, *416*
Gross, E. G., 117, *130*
Grözinger, B., 108, *128*
Gruithuisen, F. V. P., 181, 182, 185, *193*
Grünewald, G., 119, 120, 121, 124, 125, 126, *129*
Grünewald-Zuberbier, E., 119, 120, 121, 124, 125, 126, *129*
Grüsser, O. J., 187, *193*
Guckenheimer, J., 9, *28*
Guillaume, P., 52, 67, *74*
Gurnsey, R., 352, 430, *357, 445*

AUTHOR INDEX

H

Haber, R. N., 275, 277, 429, 435, *297, 444*
Haddad, G., 197, 255, *213, 271*
Hagenaar, R., 385, 386, 440, *388, 446*
Hajos, A. G., 265, *269*
Haken, H., 9, 12, 16, 17, 18, 20, *28, 29, 32*
Hall, D. C., 252, *269*
Haller, A., 181, *193*
Halliday, A. M., 108, *130*
Halliday, E., 108, *130*
Halliday, T. R., 378, *388*
Halwes, T., 58, *74*
Hamilton, W., 172, 174, *188, 193*
Hansen, R. M., 33, 232, *46, 245, 247*
Hardjowijoto, S., 232, 241, *245*
Harris, J. R., 363, *389*
Harris, K. S., 290, 301, *297, 332, 333*
Hasan, Z., 95, *101*
Hashimoto, S., 113, 114, *130*
Häussler, A. F., 406, *416*
Hawkins, H. L., 434, *444*
Hazemann, P., 109, *129*
Hearty, P. J., 344, *356*
Hecht, B. F., 326, *331*
Heilman, K. M., 401, *416*
Hein, A., 233, 242, 243, 251, *245, 269*
Heinz, S. P., 373, *389*
Heise, B., 122, *128*
Heit, G., 232, *244*
Held, R., 218, 233, 235, 237, 251, *244, 246, 269*
Hellige, J. B., 365, *389*
Helmholtz, H., 188, 189, 191, 218, 220, 221, 229, 255, 276, 423, *193, 246, 269, 297, 446*
Hempel, W. E., 78, *101*
Henderson, L., 342, *356*
Hendrickson, A. E., 406, *418*
Hendry, S. H. C., 137, 147, *165*
Henik, A. M., 385, 386, 412, *389, 417*
Hennessey, R. T., 222, 229, *246*
Henri, V., 181, 190, 191, *193*
Henson, D. B., 265, *269*
Herdman, C. M., 365, *389*
Hershenson, M., 435, *444*
Heuer, H., 87, 89, 90, 383, 411, *102, 389, 417*
Heywood, J., 138, *163*
Hick, W. E., 92, 381, *102, 389*
Hicks, R. E., 365, 366, *389*
Hikosaka, O., 138, *165*

Hillyard, S. A., 402, *417*
Hinde, R. A., 377, 378, *389*
Hine, T., 231, *246*
Hinton, G. E., 362, 439, *387, 444*
Hirst, W. C., 370, 399, *389, 390, 418*
Hochberg, J., 252, *269*
Hoffman, D., 149, *164*
Hoffman, H. S., 290, *297*
Hoffman, J. E., 366, 386, *389*
Hogan, N., 10, 22, *27, 29*
Hollerbach, J. M., 12, *29*
Hollingsworth, S., 435, *446*
Holmes, P. J., 9, 12, *28*
Holsapple, J., *163*
Holt, K. G., 7, 10, 11, 12, *22, 29*
Holtzman, J. D., 369, *389*
Hope, G. M., 225, *246*
Houk, J. C., 3, 95, 149, 150, *29, 101, 164*
Howard, I. P., 242, 251, *246, 269*
Hoyt, D. F., 17, *29*
Hubel, D. C., 131, *164*
Hubley, P., 60, *76*
Hughes, B. G., 282, *298*
Hughes, J. R., 199, *211*
Hulliger, M., 149, 150, *164, 166*
Hung, G. K., 208, 219, *211, 246*
Hume, D., 175, 176, 177, *193*
Humphrey, D. R., 133, *164*
Hyvärinen, J., 137, 403, *164, 417*

I

Iberall, A. S., 5, *32*
Ingle, D., 35, *46*
Ingvar, D. H., 140, *164*
Irby, T. S., 397, *416*
Israel, J. B., 382, *389*
Ivanoff, A., 225, *246*
Iwamura, 137, 138, *167*

J

Jacks, B., 139, *165*
Jacobson, L. E., 55, *74*
James, W., 49, 50, 54, 55, 59, 60, 78, 86, 189, 191, *74, 102, 193*
Jansson, G., 66, 200, *74, 211*
Jasper, H., 131, *165*
Jastrembski, J. E., 363, *390*
Jeannerod, M., 20, 197, 397, *28, 211, 416*
Jenkins, J. J., 281, *297*
Jenner, J. R., 148, *165*

Jennings, V. A., 156, 161, *163, 165*
Johansson, G., 66, 200, *74, 211*
Johnston, W. A., 373, 428, *389, 444*
Johnston, W. S. W., 243, *247*
Jones, E. G., 135, 136, 137, 138, 139, 146, 147, 151, *162, 163, 165*
Jones, R. S., 383, 404, *387, 415*
Jonides, J., 86, 87, 383, 434, *102, 389, 441*
Jordan, D. W., 12, 19, *29*
Jürgens, R., 206, *268*

K

Kaas, J. H., 137, *165*
Kahneman, D., 361, 364, 365, 366, 367, 374, 385, 386, 409, 412, 413, 421, 422, *389, 393, 417, 444*
Kalsbeek, J. W. H., 384, *389*
Kamiya, J., 278, *297*
Kantowitz, B. H., 382, *392*
Karmiohl, C. M., 42, 205, 209, 210, 242, *46, 213, 247*
Karsh, R., 267, *268*
Kasser, R. J., 147, *163*
Kato, H., 108, 110, *130*
Katz, D., 52, *74*
Kawarasaki, A., 117, *130*
Kay, B., 14, 18, 20, *29, 30*
Kay, H., 36, *46*
Keele, S. W., 3, 119, 366, 368, 382, 422, 425, 428, 437, 438, 441, *29, 129, 389, 444*
Keller, E., 110, *129*
Kelly, M. J., 265, *269*
Kelso, J. A. S., 3, 4, 5, 6, 7, 8, 9, 10, 11, 12, 13, 14, 16, 17, 18, 19, 20, 22, 23, 25, 26, 27, 96, 208, *27, 29, 30, 31, 32, 102, 211*
Kessel, C., 366, *393*
Kinney, P. A., 252, *271*
Kinsbourne, M., 365, 366, 401, *389, 417*
Kirch, M., 232, *244*
Klapp, S. T., 306, 366, 370, *332, 389*
Kleiman, G. M., 384, *389*
Knight, J. L., 382, *392*
Knoll, H. A., 224, *246*
Koch, R., 380, *391*
Koffka, K., 69, *74*
Köhler, W., 69, *74*
Kolers, P. A., 252, *269*
Kornhuber, H. H., 107, 108, 110, 112, 116, 117, 122, 260, *128, 129, 269*
Kosar, E., 151, *165*

Koss, B., 116, *128*
Kozhevnikov, V. A., 306, *332*
Kraft, C. L., 207, 209, *211*
Kravetz, S., 425, *446*
Kristeva, R., 110, *129*
Kröller, J., 156, *163*
Krueger, L. E., 435, *446*
Krumhansl, C. L., 435, *444*
Kubota, K., 143, *165*
Kubovy, M., 69, *75*
Kugler, P. N., 4, 5, 6, 7, 8, 11, 12, 22, 23, 24, *29, 30, 32*
Kuhl, P. K., 284, *297*
Kuhn, T. S., 281, *297*
Kurata, K., 141, 144, 145, 146, *165, 167*
Kuypers, H. G. J. M., 135, 151, *163*
Kwan, H. C., 147, *166*

L

LaBerge, D., 408, *418*
Lackner, J., 327, 328, *332*
La Heij, W., 363, 428, 435, *388, 444, 446*
Lamarre, Y., 138, 139, 403, *162, 163, 165, 417*
Lamour, Y., 161, *165*
Lancaster, B. S., 35, 36, 40, *46*
Lang, M., 122, *128*
Lang, W., 122, *128*
Lanze, M., 363, *389*
Lappin, J. S., 366, 427, *389, 443*
Laquanti, F., 20, *30*
Larsen, A., 410, *416*
Larsen, B., 142, *166*
Larsen, K., 146, *162*
Larson, D. W., 435, *441*
Lashley, K. S., 301, *332*
Lassek, A. M., 154, *165*
Lassen, N. A., 142, *166*
Lasslop, P., 171, 191, *193*
Latash, M. L., 11, 22, *28*
Lawrence, D. H., 398, *417*
Lawson, E. A., 366, *389*
Lawson, L., 435, *442*
Lea, C. D., 425, *442*
Lee, D. N., 24, 25, 26, 40, 44, 201, 397, *29, 30, 46, 211, 417*
Leeper, R. A., 315, *332*
Leeuwenberg, E. L. J., 66, *74*
Lehmenkühler, A., 106, *128*
Leibowitz, H. W., 208, 209, 219, 222, 224,

Leibowitz, H. W. (cont.)
225, 227, 229, 231, 235, 238, 242, 243, 212, 246, 247
Leifer, L. J., 121, 130
Leishman, J. R., 201, 211
LeMaster, D., 252, 271
Lemon, R. N., 132, 143, 147, 148, 149, 153, 156, 164, 165, 166
Leonard, J. A., 92, 102
Leppman, K. P., 353, 357
Levine, D. N., 398, 417
Levy, B. A., 384, 389
Lewis, J. L., 379, 390
Lewis, S., 232, 244
Lewis, V., 384, 387
Liberman, A. M., 58, 290, 301, 74, 297, 332, 333
Libet, B., 107, 108, 129, 130
Lie, I., 221, 246
Lille, F., 109, 129
Lindblad, I. M., 209, 212
Lindhagen, K., 36, 46
Lindsay, P. H., 366, 390
Lindsley, D. B., 115, 130
Lintern, G., 83, 101
Lipps, Th., 55, 74
Lishman, J. R., 26, 30, 46
Lisker, L., 305, 332
Litrac, L., 365, 389
Locke, J., 175, 176, 177, 193
Logan, G. D., 336, 380, 356, 390
Long, G. M., 429, 434, 444
Lotze, R. H., 49, 50, 55, 59, 60, 75
Lough, S., 41, 201, 46, 211
Lowe, D. G., 425, 427, 443, 444
Lubker, J. F., 306, 333
Lucas, M., 370, 390
Lucas, P. A., 363, 390
Luckiesh, M., 222, 246
Lücking, C. H., 255, 268
Luria, A. R., 380, 390
Luschei, E. S., 149, 164
Lynch, G., 415, 417
Lynch, J. C., 401, 403, 417

M

MacArthur, R., 197, 212
MacDonald, J., 282, 290, 314, 322, 363, 297, 332, 391
Mace, W. M., 24, 32
Mach, E., 188, 189, 190, 191, 201, 193, 211

Mack, A., 255, 265, 269
MacKay, D. G., 301, 304, 305, 306, 307, 308, 309, 310, 311, 312, 315, 316, 317, 318, 319, 321, 322, 323, 324, 325, 330, 379, 332, 333, 390
MacKay, D. M., 253, 395, 269, 417
MacKay, W. A., 147, 166
MacKenzie, C. L., 18, 19, 30
Mackworth, J. F., 426, 444
MacNeilage, P. F., 301, 332
McCabe, J. F., 97, 103
McCready, D. W., 227, 246
McCallum, W. C., 105, 129
McCarthy, P. R., 434, 444
McClelland, J. L., 330, 331, 363, 439, 332, 390, 444
McCollum, G., 17, 20, 31, 32
McConkie, G. W., 433, 445
McFarland, D. J., 378, 390
McGill, J., 398, 418
McGown, C., 11, 12, 31
McGurk, H., 282, 290, 314, 297, 298, 332
McLaughlin, S. C., 265, 376, 269, 390
McLean, J. P., 398, 417
McLeod, P., 86, 366, 376, 383, 397, 102, 390, 417
McLeod, R. B., 200, 211
Maddox, E. E., 221, 241, 246
Magendie, F., 131, 172, 183, 165, 194
Maine de Biran, F. P., 177, 185, 186, 188, 194
Mannell, R. C., 100, 102
Marcel, A. J., 361, 367, 379, 427, 441, 390, 444
Marchetti, F. M., 343, 346, 351, 352, 430, 357, 445
Maris, L., 363, 428, 388, 446
Mark, R. F., 35, 36, 40, 46
Marks, G., 363, 391
Marks, L. E., 63, 75
Marr, D., 209, 211
Marriott, A. M., 44, 46
Marsden, C. D., 94, 140, 143, 146, 149, 151, 159, 102, 165
Marsh, D. J., 5, 32
Marshall, P. H., 78, 101
Marteniuk, R. G., 19, 81, 30, 102
Maskelyne, N., 224, 246
Massaro, D. W., 45, 208, 273, 274, 275, 279, 284, 289, 291, 293, 295, 320, 355, 363, 364, 379, 298, 333, 356, 390
Mateer, C. A., 414, 417

AUTHOR INDEX 455

Matelli, M., 141, 402, *166, 418*
Matin, L., 196, 197, 232, 242, 253, *211, 212, 246, 269*
Maton, B., 132, *166*
Matthews, M. L., 435, *444*
Matthews, P. B. C., 149, 150, *166*
Maunsell, J. H. R., 400, *419*
Mauritz, K. H., 141, 143, *168*
May, M. T., 173, *194*
Mayer, K., 315, 321, *333*
Maxwell, J. C., 8, 9, *31*
Melbin, J., 22, *28*
Meltzoff, A. N., 68, 284, *75, 297*
Merikle, P. M., 342, 351, 425, 427, 428, 435, *356, 442, 444*
Meringer, R., 315, 321, *333*
Merkel, J., 381, *390*
Mermelstein, P., 27, *31*
Merton, P. A., 94, 255, *102, 268*
Merzenich, M. M., 137, *165*
Metral, S., 109, *129*
Mewhort, D. J. K., 335, 336, 340, 341, 342, 343, 344, 346, 347, 348, 349, 350, 352, 353, 427, 430, 431, 432, 433, 434, 435, 436, 437, 438, *356, 357, 442, 445*
Meyer, D. E., 328, *332, 333*
Meyer, E., *166*
Michaels, C. F., 200, *212*
Miles, T. S., 146, 147, 148, *168*
Mill, 181
Millar, K., 366, *390*
Millard, T. R., 276, *297*
Miller, G. A., 61, 342, *75, 357*
Miller, J., 264, 363, 428, *269, 390, 445*
Miller, M., 265, *269*
Miller, N. E., 62, *75*
Miller, S., 12, *31*
Millis-Wright, M., 379, 412, *392, 418*
Minorski, N., 8, 12, *31*
Mishkin, M., 137, 401, *166, 416, 419*
Mitchell, D. E., 219, *248*
Mittelstaedt, H., 138, 171, 184, 237, 253, *167, 193, 248, 269*
Mizuno, N., 114, *130*
Mohler, C. W., 253, *271*
Mohnkopf, W., 383, *390*
Mol, C. R., 20, *32*
Moore, D., 229, *246*
Moore, K., 68, *75*
Mora, F., 404, *418*
Morasso, P., 10, 11, 149, *27, 31, 162*
Moray, N., 363, *391*

Morgan, C. L., 61, 196, *75, 212*
Morgan, M. W., 222, 228, *246*
Morowitz, H., 5, *31*
Morse, R. W., 151, *162*
Morton, H. B., 94, *102*
Morton, J., 421, 422, 439, 441, *445*
Moruzzi, G., 146, *162*
Moss, F. K., 222, *246*
Monoud, P., 52, 60, *75*
Mountcastle, V. B., 138, 403, *166, 417*
Mowbray, G. H., 92, *102*
Mowrer, O. H., 62, *75*
Muakassa, K. F., 141, *166*
Muir, R. B., 132, 153, 156, *166*
Müller, G. E., 189, 190, *194*
Müller, J., 186, 187, 188, *194*
Munhall, K., 20, *31*
Münte, T. F., 402, *417*
Murphy, J. T., 147, 148, 149, *166*
Murray, E. A., 135, 137, 435, *166, 441*

N

Nagel, W., 182, *194*
Nager, R. M., 306, *331*
Nagle, M., 232, *244*
Nashner, L. M., 17, 96, *31, 102*
Naveh-Benjamin, M., 86, *102*
Navon, D., 365, 366, 367, 374, 411, *388, 390, 417*
Neerincx, M., 363, 428, *388, 446*
Neill, W. T., 368, 428, 441, *389, 444*
Neisser, U., 252, 260, 273, 274, 277, 278, 283, 296, 345, 362, 367, 368, 370, 371, 376, 386, 399, 422, 426, *270, 298, 357, 389, 390, 418, 445*
Nelson, B., 366, 386, *389*
Nelson, R. J., 137, 138, *165, 166*
Nelson, W. L., 20, *31*
Nessler, J., 43, *46*
Neumann, O., 86, 87, 89, 90, 252, 361, 362, 363, 364, 365, 367, 375, 376, 379, 380, 384, 385, 386, 411, 428, 429, 441, *102, 270, 390, 391, 418, 445*
Neville, H. J., 402, *417*
Newell, A., 280, 281, *298*
Newell, K. M., 82, 83, *102, 103*
Newsome, S. L., 363, *391*
Nice, R. S., 202, *213*
Nicoletti, R., 397, *419*
Nigro, G., 306, *331*
Nilsson, L. G., 45, *46*

Nimmo-Smith, L., 376, *390*
Noble, M. E., 80, 86, 372, 382, *101, 391, 393*
Noordergraaf, A., 22, *28*
Nooteboom, S. G., 327, *333*
Nordh, E., 149, *164*
Norman, D. A., 100, 315, 330, 365, 396, 421, 422, *102, 333, 391, 418, 445*
North, R. A., 366, *391*
Norton, D., 266, *270*

O

Oden, G. C., 291, 295, *298*
Ogren, M. P., 406, *418*
Ojemann, G. A., 330, 414, *333, 417*
Okano, K., 145, *167*
Olson, D. R., 66, *75*
Ono, H., 246, *268*
Ostry, D. J., 20, 363, *31, 391*
Otto, D. A., 121, *130*
Owens, D. A., 208, 209, 210, 219, 222, 224, 225, 227, 229, 235, 238, 242, 243, *212, 245, 246, 247, 248*
Owens, R. L., 209, *212*

P

Paap, K. R., 197, 198, 199, 235, 363, *212, 247, 391*
Palmer, J., 86, *102*
Palmer, St. E., 66, *75*
Pandya, D. N., 137, 138, *167*
Papakostopoulos, D., 112, 117, 118, 119, *130*
Park, J., 221, *245*
Parker, R. F., 267, *270*
Parton, D. A., 62, 67, *75*
Pastore, N., 178, *194*
Paterson, R., 379, *393*
Patla, A. E., 12, 18, *30, 31*
Pattee, H. H., 7, *31*
Pavesi, G., 141, 402, *166, 418*
Pawlby, S. J., 62, *75*
Pedersen, L. F., 410, *416*
Perel, M., 100, *102*
Perenin, M. T., 401, *418*
Perrett, D. I., 401, 404, *418*
Peters, G. L., 382, *387*
Peters, M., 366, *391*
Pew, R. W., 81, 97, 131, 243, *102, 166, 247*
Phillips, C. G., 133, 146, 147, 150, 151, *166*
Piaget, J., 52, 63, 64, 67, *75*

Pick, H. L., 42, 43, 44, 200, *211*
Picoult, E., 197, *212*
Pitts, M., 379, *388*
Platt, J. R., 280, 282, *298*
Pleune, J., 265, *269*
Podgorny, P., 366, 386, *391*
Pohlmann, L. D., 363, *391*
Pola, J., 265, *270*
Polit, A., 11, 149, *27, 162*
Polson, M. C., 365, *388*
Pomerantz, J. R., 69, *75*
Pompeiano, O., 362, *388*
Popper, K., 279, *298*
Porac, C., 253, 254, *268*
Porter, R., 133, 146, 147, 151, *166*
Porter R. J., 306, *333*
Posner, M. I., 253, 262, 266, 267, 268, 283, 397, 411, 422, *270, 390, 391, 392, 417, 418, 445*
Post, R. B. L., 209, 229, 231, *212, 247*
Postman, L., 342, *357*
Potter, M. C., 414, *418*
Poulton, E. C., 366, *392*
Powell, T. P. S., 136, 138, *165*
Prablanc, C., 196, 231, 397, *211, 244, 416*
Preston, J. B., 147, 148, 151, *167*
Preus, A., 173, *194*
Pribram, K., 61, *75*
Prinz, W., 57, 66, 69, 253, 441, *75, 270, 445*
Prinzmetal, W., 379, 412, 435, *392, 418, 441*
Prigogine, I., 9, *31*
Prochazka, A., 150, *166*
Proctor, R. W., 366, *392*
Proffitt, D. R., 42, 66, 205, 206, 209, 242, *46, 74, 213, 247*
Purdy, J., 33, *45*
Purkinje, J. E., 187, *194*
Putnam, C. A., 12, 19, *30*
Pylyshyn, Z. W., 66, *75*

Q

Quigley, J., 382, *393*

R

Raab, D. H., 293, *298*
Raaymakers, E., 93, *103*
Rand, R. H., 12, *28*
Randolph, M., 137, *166*
Rasband, P., 8, 9, *31*
Raymond, J. E., 209, *212*

Rayner, K., 433, *445*
Reason, J., 396, *418*
Reaves, C. C., 370, *389*
Reddish, P. E., 41, 201, *46, 211*
Reder, S. M., 431, *443*
Reed, E. S., 3, 7, 24, 208, *31, 32, 212*
Reeves, A., 397, *418*
Regan, D., 202, *212*
Reicher, G. M., 363, *392*
Reinert, G., 252, *270*
Remez, R. E., 12, *28*
Remington, R. W., 253, *270*
Repp, B. H., 290, *298*
Restle, F., 66, *75*
Reynolds, P., 90, 364, 377, 398, *101, 387, 415*
Rhoads, M. V., 92, *102*
Ricci, G. F., 131, *165*
Rich, S., 78, *101*
Richardson, J. T. E., 337, *357*
Richmond, F. J. R., 243, *247*
Richter, H., 50, 55, 56, *75*
Ritter, W., 105, 112, *129, 130*
Ritz, S. A., 383, 404, *387, 415*
Rizzolatti, G., 141, 402, *166, 418*
Robbins, C. A., 159, *168*
Robinson, D. L., 402, *419*
Rock, I., 276, *298*
Roediger, H. L., 382, *392*
Rohrbauch, J. W., 425, 430, 431, *443*
Rohrbaugh, J. W., 111, 115, 378, 379, *130, 392*
Roland, P. E., 137, 140, 142, 143, *166*
Rolls, E. T., 401, 404, *418*
Romanes, G. J., 61, *75*
Romanow, S., 81, *102*
Rosen, R., 5, 9, *31*
Rosenbaum, D. A., 380, *392*
Ross, G. M., 216, *247*
Ross, H. E., 216, *247*
Rossignol, S., 95, *101*
Rothwell, J. C., 146, 159, *165*
Rubin, M. L., 225, *246*
Rubin, P., 7, 12, 27, *27, 28, 29, 31*
Rumelhart, D. E., 330, 331, 422, 439, *332, 333, 444, 445*
Runeson, S., 24, *31*
Russel, J. R., 135, *166*
Russell, D. G., 84, *102*
Rustioni, A., 151, *163*
Ryan, L. J., 121, *130*
Rymer, W. Z., 3, 149, 150, *29, 164*

S

Sachs, C., 192, *194*
Saga, T., 143, *167*
Sakai, H., 135, *167*
Sakai, T., 151, *167*
Sakamoto, M., 138, *165*
Sakata, H., 117, 137, *130, 167*
Salthouse, T. A., 370, *392*
Saltzman, E. L., 4, 5, 10, 11, 12, 13, 14, 17, 18, 20, 23, 27, *27, 29, 30, 31*
Saraga, E., 385, *392*
Sander, L. W., 70, *74*
Sanders, A. F., 44, 274, 282, 337, 365, 366, 372, 374, *46, 297, 298, 357, 388, 391, 392*
Sanes, J. N., 149, 159, *167*
Santee, J. F., 435, 438, *443, 445*
Sasaki, K., 113, 114, 139, *129, 130, 167*
Savin, H. B., 320, *333*
Scaliger, J. C., 174, 177, *194*
Scheerer, E., 52, 58, 171, 241, 253, 259, 261, 266, 341, 345, *75, 194, 247, 270, 357*
Scheminzky, F., 55, *73*
Schell, A. M., 379, *387*
Schell, G. R., 139, 140, *167*
Schmidt, H., 379, 398, *393, 419*
Schmidt, J. C., 264, *270*
Schmidt, R. A., 3, 11, 70, 79, 82, 83, 84, 88, 91, 95, 97, 98, 99, 131, 293, 375, *31, 75, 102, 103, 167, 297, 392*
Schneider, G. E., 401, *418*
Schneider, W., 86, 91, 92, 96, 99, 363, 382, 383, 404, 421, 428, *103, 388, 392, 418, 443, 446*
Schober, H., 222, *247*
Schoen, J. H. R., 134, *167*
Scholz, J. P., 18, 26, *30*
Schöner, G., 12, 14, 18, 20, *29, 32*
Schor, C. M., 208, 242, *212, 247*
Schreuder, R., 363, 428, *388, 446*
Schubert, P., 415, *417*
Schuhmacher, H., 121, *129*
Schultz, D. W., 428, 429, 441, *443*
Schumann, F., 189, *194*
Schvaneveldt, R. W., 363, 366, 381, *391, 392*
Schweickert, W., 365, *392*
Scott, J. P., 427, *443*
Scott, P. D., 12, *31*
Semmes, J., 137, *166*
Semmlow, J. L., 208, 219, *211, 246*
Sessle, B. J., 147, *167*

AUTHOR INDEX

Shaffer, L. H., 90, 370, 372, 398, 399, *103*, *392*, *418*
Shaffer, W. O., 408, *418*
Shallice, T., 368, 378, 380, 385, 398, *392*, *393*, *418*
Shankweiler, D. P., 58, *74*
Shapiro, D. C., 83, 97, 98, *103*
Shapiro, R. G., 435, *446*
Sharp, R. H., 43, *46*
Sharpe, C. R., 252, *270*
Shaw, C. D., 8, 13, *27*
Shaw, R., 13, *32*
Shaw, R. E., 24, 25, 275, *32*, *299*
Shebilske, W. L., 42, 171, 196, 197, 199, 202, 203, 205, 206, 207, 208, 209, 210, 216, 218, 241, 242, 253, *46*, *194*, *212*, *213*, *247*, *270*, *271*
Sheeran, L., 60, *76*
Shelly, C., 86, 383, *101*, *387*
Shepard, R. N., 366, 386, *391*
Sherrington, C. S., 172, 192, *194*
Shibasaki, H., 108, 110, 112, *130*
Shibasaki, T., *166*
Shibutani, H., 117, *130*
Shiffrin, R. M., 91, 96, 363, 421, 428, *103*, *392*, *446*
Shiina, K., 229, *246*
Shinoda, Y., 151, *167*
Shulman, G. L., 434, *444*
Sidtis, J. J., 369, *389*
Siegel, R. E., 173, *194*
Silverstein, J. W., 383, 404, *387*, *415*
Skavenski, A. A., 33, 197, 232, 255, *46*, *213*, *245*, *247*, *271*
Skinhoj, E., 142, *166*
Slotnick, R. S., 249, 251, *271*
Smith, D. B., 111, *129*
Smith, D. R., 242, 243, *247*
Smith, E. E., 306, 343, *333*, *357*
Smith, K. U., 264, *270*
Smith, P., 12, 19, *29*
Smyth, M. M., 44, *46*
Snyder, C. R. R., 422, *445*
Sokolov, E. N., 378, 379, *393*
Solis, H., 161, *165*
Solomon, J., 4, 24, 26, 196, 206, 207, *32*, *213*
Somberg, B. L., 370, *392*
Sorkin, R. D., 363, *391*
Southard, D. L., 12, *30*
Speckmann, E. J., 106, *128*
Spelke, E. S., 370, 399, *389*, *390*, *418*

Spencer, H., 181
Sperling, A., 232, *244*
Sperling, G., 345, 397, 422, 423, 425, 426, 429, *357*, *418*, *441*, *446*
Sperry, R. W., 138, 171, 367, *167*, *194*, *393*
Spidalieri, G., 138, 403, *163*, *417*
Spoehr, K. T., 306, 343, *333*, *357*
Spring, J., 83, *103*
Squire, R., 379, *393*
Staats, A. W., 62, *75*
Stadler, M., 69, 384, *75*, *393*
Standing, L. G., 414, 429, *419*, *444*
Stark, L., 20, 197, 198, 266, 267, *27*, *213*, *270*
Stein, R. B., 3, 5, 12, *31*, *32*
Steinbach, M. J., 242, 243, *247*
Steinman, R. M., 197, 255, 260, *213*, *271*
Stelmach, G. E., 93, 131, 282, 370, *101*, *167*, *298*, *388*
Stengers, I., 9, *31*
Stephens, J. A., 148, *165*
Stephenson, J. M., 43, *46*
Sternberg, S., 44, 274, *46*, *298*
Stevens, J. K., 197, *212*
Sticht, T., 302, 325, *331*
Stingle, K. G., 62, *74*
Stone, J., 400, *419*
St. Paul, U., 377, 378, *388*
Straight, S., 301, *333*
Stränger, J., 52, *76*
Strangert, B., 435, *446*
Strick, P. L., 139, 140, 141, 147, 148, *166*, *167*, *168*
Stroop, J. R., 287, 386, *298*, *393*
Studdert-Kennedy, M., 58, 301, *74*, *333*
Sugitani, M., 138, *163*
Sully, D. J., 35, *45*
Sully, H. G., 35, *45*
Summers, J. J., 70, 119, *76*, *129*
Sur, M., 137, *165*
Suzuki, S., 84, *103*
Swenson, H. A., 220, *247*
Syndulko, K., 115, *130*

T

Takaoka, Y., 117, *130*
Talbot, W. H., 403, *417*
Tanaka, M., 138, *165*
Taniguchi, K., 143, *167*
Tanji, J., 132, 141, 143, 144, 145, 146, *163*, *164*, *165*, *167*

Taylor, C. R., 17, *29*
Taylor, G. A., 363, *390*
Taylor, H. A., 422, *443*
Taylor, J. G., 249, 251, *271*
Taylor, M. J., 118, 119, 120, 124, 125, *130*
Taylor, M. M., 366, *390*
Taylor, S. G., 435, *446*
Teichner, W. H., 252, *271*
Templeton, W. B., 242, 251, 265, *246, 269*
ten Hoopen, G., 92, 93, *103*
Tent, J., 327, *333*
Tepas, 253
Terzuolo, C. A., 20, 98, *30, 103*
Teuber, H. L., 131, *167*
Thach, W. T., 132, 139, 140, *162, 164*
Theios, J., 274, *298*
Thom, R., 22, *32*
Thomas, E. A. C., 435, *444*
Thompson, C. J., *166*
Thompson, K., 425, *442*
Thomson, J. A., 26, 201, *30, 46, 211*
Thorndike, E. L., 49, *76*
Thorpe, S. J., 404, *418*
Tiedemann, D., 178, 185, *194*
Tierney, M., 399, *419*
Tietz, J. D., 225, 229, *245*
Tinbergen, N., 61, *76*
Tipper, S. P., 413, *415*
Toates, F. M., 219, *247*
Todd, J., 41, *46*
Tolman E. C., 277, *299*
Tomovic, R., 5, *32*
Towe, A. L., 151, *162*
Townsend, J. T., 430, 431, 435, *446*
Townsend, V. M., 353, *357*
Toyoshima, K., 135, *167*
Tramer, O., 340, *357*
Tramer, S., 435, *446*
Treiman, R., 307, *333*
Treisman, A., 361, 364, 366, 379, 385, 386, 398, 412, 413, *389, 393, 417, 419*
Trendelenburg, A., 188, *194*
Trevarthen, C., 60, 62, *76*
Trumbo, D. A., 372, 382, *391, 393*
Tsukahara, W., 134, *162*
Tucker, G., 224, *245*
Tuller, B., 9, 13, 26, 27, 96, *30, 102*
Tulving, E., 281, *299*
Turvey, M. T., 4, 5, 6, 7, 8, 11, 12, 22, 24, 26, 66, 70, 196, 206, 207, 208, 218, 231, 275, 425, *29, 30, 32, 74, 76, 213, 247, 299, 446*

Tyldesley, D. A., 35, *46*
Tyler, L. K., 284, *299*

U

Ullman, S., 200, *213*
Umiltá, C., 397, *419*
Underwood, S., 379, *393*
Ungerleider, L. G., 401, *419*

V

Valenstein, E., 401, *416*
Vallbo, A. B., 149, 150, *164, 167*
Van den Heuvel, P. J. M., 293, *297*
van der Heijden, A. H. C., 345, 347, 354, 361, 363, 367, 385, 386, 409, 413, 427, 428, 435, 438, 440, 441, *388, 419, 444, 446*
van Essen, D. C., 400, *419*
Varela, F. J., 5, 6, 26, *32*
Vatikiotis-Bateson, E., 20, 96, *30, 102*
Vaughan, H. G., Jr., 107, 108, 112, 113, 114, 116, 117, 121, 125, *128, 129, 130*
Venezky, R. L., 363, *390*
Vighetto, A., 401, *418*
Vingerhoets, A. J. J. M., 115, *128*
Vinter, A., 52, 60, *75*
Virzi, R. A., 379, 413, *393, 419*
Viviani, P., 20, 98, *30, 32, 103*
Vogt, B. A., 137, 138, *167*
Volpe, B. T., 389, *389*
von der Malsburg, C., 406, *416, 419*
von Graefe, A., 188, *193*
von Hofsten, C., 24, 33, 36, 37, 38, 40, 42, 66, 200, 234, 238, 397, *29, 45, 46, 74, 211, 248*
von Holst, E., 138, 171, 184, 216, 218, 227, 234, 237, 238, 377, 378, *167, 193, 248, 388*
von Noorden, G. K., 241, *244*
von Senden, M., 255, *270*
von Wright, J. M., 425, *446*

W

Wade, M. G., 37, *46*
Wadman, W. J., 20, *32*
Wagner, H., 24, *32*
Wallach, H., 234, 237, *248*
Walters, R. H., 52, 62, *73*
Walton, J., 220, 228, *245*

AUTHOR INDEX

Wandmacher, J., 363, *393*
Wapner, S., 55, *76*
Warren, R. M., 319, 320, 327, 328, 423, *333, 446*
Warren, R. P., 320, 423, *333, 446*
Warren, W. H., 24, 25, *32*
Warrington, E. K., 398, *418*
Weber, E. W., 55, 177, 187, 188, *76, 194*
Wehler, A., 121, *129*
Wehner, T., 384, *393*
Weimer, W. B., 58, 266, *76, 271*
Weisstein, N., 363, *389*
Welch, R. B., 232, 235, 251, *248, 271*
Welford, A. T., 362, *393*
Wenz, T. G., 265, *269*
Werner, H., 55, *76*
Westheimer, G., 219, *248*
Wessels, J., 284, *299*
Wheeler, D. J., 363, *393*
White, J. L., 82, 84, *103*
Whiteside, T. C. D., 224, *248*
Whiting, H. T. A., 4, 35, 42, 43, *32, 46*
Whitsel, B. L., 151, *163*
Wickens, C. D., 90, 94, 365, 366, 367, 374, 382, *101, 103, 389, 393*
Wiesendanger, M., 116, 134, 141, 143, 145, 146, 147, 148, 151, 158, *130, 167, 168*
Willis, J. B., 12, *32*
Wilson, D. H., 369, *389*
Wing, A., 70, 367, *76, 393*
Wire, B., 58, *74*
Wise, S. P., 132, 135, 136, 141, 143, 148, 400, *164, 165, 168, 419*

Wolf, K. S., 210, 219, 242, *212, 247*
Wolfe, J., 219, 224, *248*
Wolff, P., 252, 253, 254, 260, 264, 266, 384, 385, *271, 393*
Wolford, G., 435, *446*
Wolfson, D. M., 237, *245*
Wong, Y. C., 147, *166*
Wood B., 379, *387*
Woodworth, R. S., 306, *333*
Woolsey, C. N., 137, 139, *168*
Wright, E. W., Jr., 107, *129*
Wrisberg, C. A., 83, *103*
Wundt, W., 175, 186, 189, 190, 191, 220, *194, 248*
Wurtz, R. H., 253, 402, 405, *271, 419*
Wyler, A. R., 159, *168*

Y

Yamamoto, L., *166*
Yarbus, A. L., 252, *271*
Yates, F. E., 5, 22, 24, *32*
Yin, T. C., 403, *417*
Young, D. S., 24, 40, 44, 197, 201, *30, 46, 211, 212*
Yumiya, H., 146, *162*

Z

Zadeh, L. A., 279, *299*
Zarzeki, P., 151, *167*
Zelaznik, H. N., 86, *103*
Zernicke, R. F., 98, *103*
Zola, D., 433, *445*

Subject Index

A

Accommodation, 65, 178, 199, 200, 208, 217, 219-222, 224-226, 228, 229, 235-237, 259, 423
Action plan, action planning, 375, 377, 380-383
Action system, *see* Perception-action system, 397
Activation, 308, 310, 311, 314-317, 319, 321, 323-325, 327, 329, 330, 381, 404, 410
  reverberatory, 312, 328
  sequential activation asymmetry, 329
Adaptation, *see* Perceptual adaptation, 7
  motor, 264-267
Adaptation technique, 306, 330
Additive-factor method, 274
After-image, 187, 229
Aiming, 37-38
Ambiguous figure, 315
Amputation, 188
Anesthesia, 188
Anticipation, 36, 40, 59, 260-261, 308, 403
Antidromic latency (ADL), 156
Aphasia, 301, 321
Area, *see* Cortex
Arousal, 364
Articulatory code, 337
Artificial Intelligence (AI), 363

Attention
  demands, 78, 120
  selective, 141, 285-287, 407, 421, 433, 439-441
  sensory, 385
Attentional
  focussing, 385
  mechanisms, 122, 338, 347, 348, 432
  processes, processing, 107, 124-125, 145, 379
  set, 400
  shift, 253, 258, 261, 385
Attenuation, *see* Selective attenuation
Attractor, 9, 23, 26
  point attractor, 10-12, 17
  periodic attractor, 12-17
Automaticity, 78, 85-92, 97, 98, 119, 376
Automatic processing, 91, 99
Awareness, 85, 86, 96, 178, 185, 216, 316, 318, 379, 406, 408, 411, 412, 414

B

Ballistic timing task, 82
Bar-probe task, 338, 345, 354, 422-440
Basal ganglia, 143
Bell-Magendie's law, 183, 185
Bifurcation, 17-19, 25-26
Bilinguals, 325

461

Bimodal speech, 285, 289, 294
Binary oppositions, 280, 281, 283
Blends, 323
Blocking, 377–378
Blur, 219
Brain stem, 133
Broken symmetry, 6
Buffer, 335–338
   character buffer, 337–352, 432–440
   feature buffer, 337–352, 432–440
   postcategorical buffer, 352
   precategorical buffer, 345, 352
   spatial buffer, 337, 347
   temporal buffer, 337–351

C

Capacity, *see* Processing, 86, 354, 361–362, 425, 433, 441
   limited capacity, 354, 361–386, 408–411, 432
   unspecific capacity, 364–365, 371
Cell columns, 106
Cerebellectomy, 139
Cerebellum, 108, 139, 183
Cerebral injury, lesion, 396, 401, 402
Cerebrum, 183
Channel, 365, 405, 409, 410, 427
Chess, 303
Circular activity, 67
Classification, 292
Closed-loop control, 22, 80–82, 90, 99, 134, 149, 150, 159
Coding, code, 66, 133, 337, 365, 400–407, 432
   activation-coded, 400, 410, 413
Combinatorial explosion, 363, 367
Commissurotomy, 369
Comparison mechanism, 338
Compatibility, *see* S-R compatibility, Ideomotor compatibility
Competition, 372, 380, 404–405, 413, 428
Concept learning, 66
Concurrence costs, 372
Condition-action rule, 381, 382
Conditioning, 62, 63, 132, 157, 159
Consciousness, 172, 178, 184, 186, 187, 188, 190, 368, 373, 423, 427
Consistency of selection, 384
Consolidation, 414
Contiguity, 49, 62
Continuity of action, 384

Contingent negative variation (CNV), 111, 115
Contrast ratio, 339
Controlled processing, 91
Controller, 4–5
Convergence, *see* Vergence
Corollary discharge, 138, 192, 197, 328
Correlation theory (of neural integration), 406–407, 410
Cortex
   association, 108, 406
   frontal, 140, 402
   motor, 108–116, 121, 133–146, 159, 303, 406
   parietal, 135, 138, 401–404
   perirolandic, 134
   precentral, 114, 145
   prefrontal, 143, 380
   premotor, 114–115, 135–141
   prestriate, 406
   sensory, 303, 406
   sensorimotory, 135–136
   somatosensory, 114–117, 134–138, 159
   striate, *see* visual
   supplementary motor, 135, 139, 141
   temporal, 401, 404
   visual, 35, 122, 406
(Cortical) cooling, 139, 145
Corticofugal systems, 136
Corticospinal cells, 133, 135
Craik's ration rule, *see* Ratio rule
Cross correlation, 134, 151
Cross-domain cueing, 412–413
Crossmodal correspondence, 63
Crosstalk, 370–373, 378, 398, 411–412

D

Dark focus, 208–209, 221–225, 236
Dark vergence, 208, 227–228, 234–240
   dark-vergence bias, 228–231
Dart throwing, 203–205
Deafferentation, 117, 139
Decay, 337, 345, 425, 429, 432, 433
Decision making, 361
Depth of processing, 414
Detection-correction asymmetry, 327
Detectors, *see* Feature detectors, 439
Dichotic listening, 362, 369, 379, 428
Difficulty insensitivity, 382
Digit-probe task, 338, 345, 350–354
Dipole, 106, 116
Direct perception, 196, 205, 206, 210

SUBJECT INDEX   463

Disparity (of retinal images), 219, 224, 227
Disturbance, *see* Perturbation
Divergence, *see* Vergence
Dual-buffer model, two-buffer idea, 348–354, 432–435
Dual-task performance, *see* Interference
Duplicity theory, 207
Dynamic control, 71
Dynamic control structure, 13–14, 18–21, 24, 27

E

Echokinesis, 50, 52–54, 68
Ecological validity, 278
Effector recruitment, 376–378, 386
Efference copy, 138, 184, 191, 192, 196
Effort
　effort of the will, 188
　feeling of effort, 172, 179
　mental effort, 85, 364
　oculomotor effort, *see* Vergence effort, 242–243
　sense of effort, 186
Electroencephalogram (EEG), 105, 108, 111
Electromyogram (EMG), 94, 108–121, 132–134, 143–146, 151–159
Emergency reaction, 369
End-point control, 23
Equifinality, 10–11
Equivalence,
　categorical, 64
　functional, 65
　conceptual, 65
　preconceptual, 65
Error,
　anticipatory, 308
　in information transmission, 377
　feature integration error, 412
　identification error, 353
　item error, 346–350
　intrusion error, 430–432, 437–438
　location error, 346–353, 430–432, 437–438
　perceptual error, 321–324
　production error, 322, 323–324
　segmentation error, 398
　sequential error, 324
　speech error, 306, 315
Error detection, 81–84, 327
Escapement, 12
Esophoric shift, *see* Phoria, 42, 205
Event perception, 195, 202–206

Event-related potential (ERP), 105
Evolution, 206–208
　of catching, 35–36
Executive, 336, 339, 347, 351
Expectation, 189, 261, 324
Exploration, 178, 182, 185, 259, 264, 267, 385, 402
External validity, 278–279
Eye movement, *see* Saccade, 20, 177, 178, 179, 186, 219, 229, 232, 241, 242, 255, 266, 267, 288, 385, 397, 403, 421, 423, 428, 433
Eye-muscle potentiation, 237
Eye-tracking, 36
Eye-voice span, 384

F

Facilitation, 153, 306, 326
Falsifiability, 280
Familiarity effect, 340–342, 351–354
Fatigue, 180, 192, 309, 327–328
Feature, 337, 354, 363, 365, 401, 435, 436, 440
Feature-detecting neurons, feature detectors, 138, 339, 439
Feedback, 67, 78–85, 112, 117, 119, 125–127, 134, 139, 140, 148–150, 158–159, 161–162, 218–224, 242, 243, 303, 330
　missing feedback effect, 327–328
Feedforward, 134
Filter, filtering, 371, 374, 408, 422
　postcategorical filtering, 409, 413, 440
Filtering paradigm, 412
Five-senses doctrine, 174
Force,
　concept of, 175–176, 185
　sense of, 187, 191
Forced-choice task, 355
Formant, 291
Foveal vision, 397
Freudian slip, 322
Frontal eye field, 402, 403
Functional overlap, 383
Functional validity, 278
Fuzzy sets, fuzzy logic, 279, 291

G

Galvanic skin response, 379
Ganzfeld, 224
Gating, 145

Gibson effect, 249, 251, 265, 266
Goal states, 52, 54
Guidance, 59, 117, 143, 395, 401, 414
   ideational, 54–55
   perceptual, 54–55
Gyrus,
   postcentral, 116, 135
   precentral, 116, 135

H

Haidinger's brush (HB), 251–252, 254
Hammering, 232
Hemispherectomy, 114
Hick's law, 92, 381
Hierarchy, 303, 306, 321, 375, 410
Higher order variable (structure, invariants), 202–206, 275–276
Human factors, 208
Human-machine interactions, 210
Hyperopia, 224
Hypothalamus, 401, 404

I

Idea, 178
Identification, 361–372, 426–439
   letter identification, 337, 340
   word identification, 335, 344, 432
Identification mechanism, identifier, 337–355, 432
Ideomotor compatibility, 399
Ideo-motor control, 48
Ideo-motor principle, 49
Illusory concomitant motion, 226, 229–231
Illusory conjunction, 379, 398
Image,
   kinesthetic, 58–59, 63–65, 69
   memory, 189–191
   retinal, 187, 190, 191, 216, 261, 319, 400
   retinotopic, 339
   sensory, 431
   visual, 179, 425, 426, 429, 433
Imagination, imagery, 303, 369, 380, 400
Indirect perception, 205, 206
Inflow, 171, 241, 242
Information,
   body-scaled, 42
   categorical, 288–293, 405, 410
   contextual, 215
   continuous, 279, 288–293
   dynamical, 8

efference-based, 195–221, 237, 243
   episodic, 433
   extraretinal eye position information (EEPI), 196–200, 218
   identity, 433
   indicational, 6–7
   light-based, 195–221, 225–233, 243
   multiple sources, 283, 284, 288, 293, 296
   orthographic, 336
   peripheral, 191
   positional, 405
   proprioceptive, 78, 84, 134, 184, 362
   propriospecific, 22, 23
   redundant, 218, 221
   retinal, 196–199, 255
   sensory, 77, 78, 195, 368
   somatosensory, 134
   specificational, 6–7
   symbolic, *see* indicational
   task-relevant, 409
   vestibular, 362
   visual, 283, 290, 339, 362
Information integration, 279–296, 433
Information-processing approach/theory, 44–45, 273–276, 282, 296
Inhibition, 153, 311–313, 368, 435
   behavioral, 377–378, 380
   lateral, 436
   reciprocal, 371–372
   selective, 405
   self-inhibition, 308, 309, 323, 328, 330
Innervation sensation, innervation feelings, 172, 186–190, 191
Input-output coupling, 147
Instinctive behavior, 61
Instruction, 85, 143–146, 336, 382
Integration rule, 295
Intention, 52, 54, 70, 71, 86, 96, 107, 237, 238, 250, 253, 254, 258, 261, 263, 264, 265, 277, 364, 375, 423
Interfacing rules, interfacing requirements, 336, 339
Interference,
   between stimuli, 363–366
   data-specific, 371–372
   dual-task, 86–89, 362–372, 377, 381–383, 398
   function specific, 371
   lateral, 437
   motor, 366
   physical, 369, 371
   proactive, 280

SUBJECT INDEX

structural, 365
unspecific, 383
Internal speech, 312, 325
Interneuron, 151, 156
Interrupt function, interrupting, 378–380, 385
Intersensory interaction, 293
Intersensory localization, 198
Intersensory mapping, 60, 63
Intrinsic metric, 25
Intuition, 179
Invariants,
    relational, 19
    movement, 97
Isomorphism, 69
Isopotential lines, 113

K

Kinematic control, 71
Kinesthesis, 191, 192
Kinesthetic sensitivity, 79
Knowledge of results (KR), 83, 126–127

L

Laser optometer, 222, 225
Lebenskraft, 181
Lens model, 278
Lesion, see Cerebral lesion
Lexical entry, 432
Limit cycle oscillator, 12–17, 21
Limulus, 436
Linkage strength, 310, 317, 318, 329
Listening practice asymmetry, 325–326
Lobe, see Cortex
Logogen model, 439

M

Magic pendulum, 48
Map, see Representation
Mapping, 61–64, 92
Masking, mask, 274, 339–341, 345, 350–353, 369, 406, 425, 427, 431–432, 438
    lateral masking, 435–436
Mass-spring system, 9, 10–12, 21
Matching, 64–72
    matching task, 362
Maximal rate asymmetry, 325
McGurk effect, 282, 284, 314
Mechanism, see Processor

Memory, see Image, Buffer,
    episodic, 411, 414–415
    iconic, 252, 345–353, 426–438
    long-term, 375, 414
    memory activation, 368, 421
    memory storage, 361
    short-term, 337
    structures, 274–275
    working, 337
Memory load, 427
Memory search, 274, 282
Mental energy, 364–365, 367
Mental faculty, 61
Mental node hypothesis, 306–307, 314–315, 326–328
Mental operations, 274–275
Micropsia, 228
Mind reading, 48
Minor motor anomaly (MMA), 208–210, 241–242
Mirror movement, 108, 110
Monte-Carlo simulation, 349–350
Moon illusion, 216, 228
"Most-primed-wins" principle, 311–331
Motion parallax, 218
Motoneuron, 148–156, 241
Motor adjustment, 365
"Motor field," 147, 153
Motor plan, 140, 141
Motor program, 97, 134, 139–141, 157, 159
Motor set, 138, 141, 143
Motor theory
    of mental imagery, 179
    of perception, 57–58, 266
    of speech perception, 301, 330
Movement,
    active and passive, 189
    articulatory, 20
    ballistic, 106, 119–127, 134, 139, 154–159
    bimanual, 17, 19
    corrective, 263–264
    cyclical, 14, 19
    distal, 133
    echokinetic, see Echokinesis
    event-synchronized, 51, 70
    exploratory, 138
    expressive, 56
    fine, 155–159
    goal-directed, 119, 125
    grasping, 138, 401
    orienting, 56
    pointing, 199, 203–205, 234

466   SUBJECT INDEX

Movement (*cont.*)
  positioning, 83, 120–121
  pronation, 154, 156
  ramp, 121, 150, 156, 161
  reaching, 20, 37, 44, 138, 233, 236, 401
  sequenced, 143
  self-paced, 107, 122, 143
  supination, 154, 156
  synkinetic, *see* Synkinesis
  voluntary, 55, 59, 117, 139, 147, 154, 159, 258, 259, 261
"Muscle field," *see* "Motor field"
Muscle sense, muscle sensation, 171–186, 191–192, 217
Muscle spindle, 149–150, 192, 243
Muscular feelings, 180
Myopia, 208, 222
  anomalous myopia, 224

N

Naming task, 335
Nativism, 179
Near work, 219
Network, 66, 407, 410, 414, 439
  network theory, 308
Neuronal model, 379
Neuron-motor response correlations, 132
Node,
  content, 304–321, 330
  "duck node," 315
  feature, 317
  lexical, 305, 315–323, 327
  mental, 302–330
  motor, 303–304, 308–310, 322, 327, 330
  muscle movement, *see* motor
  phonological, 305, 314–321, 327
  phonological compound, 318
  phrase, 317, 318
  "rabbitt node," 315
  segment, 307, 314, 317, 330
  sensory analysis, 302, 304, 316–322, 327, 330
  sequence, 304, 310–324, 327, 330
  speech perception, 320
  syllable, 318
  timing, 305, 311–321
  visual, 314
Node structure theory, 307, 311–316, 321–331
Nose visibility, 202

O

Object, 411–412
Object file analogy, 413
Object superiority effect, 363, 386
Oculomotor tonus, *see* Resting tonus
Ontogenesis
  of catching, 36–41
Open-loop control, 84, 97–99, 135, 140, 159
Open-loop pointing, *see* Movement
Operant conditioning, *see* Conditioning
Operator, *see* Processor
Optic array, 200, 201, 207, 216, 218, 233
Optic aphasia, 401
Optic ataxia, 401
Optic flow field, optic flow pattern, 24, 200, 202, 203, 207, 209, 218
Optical specification, 25
Orthophorization, 240, 242, 244
Oscillator, 12, 20, 21, 26
Orienting reflex, orienting reaction, *see* Reflex
Outflow, 171, 186, 241, 242

P

Pain, 181, 184, 192
Paralysis, 188, 197–198
Parameter specification, 376, 377–378, 382–384, 386
Paresis, 188
Parser, 337–344, 351–355
  parsing rules, 343
Partial report, 335, 343–345, 351, 422–440
Path planning, 22–23
Perception-action system, 26, 33–34, 39
Perceptual adaptation, perceptual plasticity, 232–237, 249, 263
Perceptual integration, 364, 397–398, 399
Perceptual retouch, 406
Perceptual world, 259–267, 330
Perceptus model, 255–258
Peribuccal space, 402
Perimeter, 198
Peripersonal space, 402
Peripheralistic determinism, 191
Persistence, 425, 429
  informational, 429–434
  visible, visual, 429–434
Perturbation of movement, 17, 94–96, 146–149, 159
Phase plane, 8, 12
Phonemic restoration, 319–320

Phoria, 199
  esophoria, 200
  exophoria, 200
  heterophoria, 199, 209, 227, 240
  orthophoria, 200
Pinocchio effect, 202
Place of articulation, 330
Plan, *see* Motor plan, Action plan
Polarized light, 251
Population stereotypes, 93
Positron emission tomography, 142
Postinhibitory rebound, 309
Postural aftereffect, 197–199, 203, 208
Potential (energy) function, 22–23
Potential field, 23
Potentials,
  Bereitschaftspotential (BP), *see* readiness potential (RP)
  motor potential (MP), 107
  negative shift (NS), 108, 118–125
  postsynaptic, 106
  premotion positivity (PMP), 107
  prefeedback potentials, 126
  readiness potential (RP), 107, 114–125
  relaxation potential, 125
  skilled performance positivity (SPP), 118
Potentiation, posttetanic potentiation, 199, 235, 415
Power grip, 156
Precision grip, 156
Preattentive processing, 378–379
Preparation
  for a movement, 107, 114, 126, 134, 141–143, 190
Priming, 310–329
Principle of higher level activation, 316–329
Prism
  contact lens, 249–251, 263–264
  spectacles, 42, 233–235, 238–240, 251
Priviledged sensory-pattern-to-action-linkage, 397
Probabilistic functionalism, 277–279
Probe stimulus paradigm, probe RT, 366, 370, 379–380
Processing,
  limited capacity (LC) 421–422, 425–429, 438, 440–441
  unlimited capacity (UC), 421–422, 426–429, 432–433, 438–441
Processing effort, 365
Processing load, 362–364

Processing mechanism, *see* Processor
Processing structure, 364
Processing system, 336, 339, 426
Processor, 335–345, 409, 411, *see* Identification mechanism, Attentional mechanism, Comparison mechanism, Rehearsal mechanism
Progression-regression hypothesis, 80–81
Proprioception, 192
Prototype matching, 291–292
Psychological refractory period (PRP), 92–93, 362, 370
Psychophysical mechanism, 60
Psychophysics, 276
Pyramidal tract, 133–135, 146, 154

R

Race model, 315
Ratio rule, 154
Readiness to respond, 402–404
Reafference, 172, 191, 253, 259, 263–267
Reafference principle, 171, 237, 242
Receptive field, 137, 147, 149, 403
Recognition, 274, 282, 315, 327, 330, 331, 439
Recovery cycle, 309
Reflex,
  autogenic, 96
  exteroceptive, 148
  long-loop, 94, 146, 148
  orienting, 178, 378–380
  phase-dependent, 95–96
  proprioceptive, 149, 159
  segmental, 149, 150
  short-latency, 145
  stretch, 94, 243
  transcortical, 135, 139, 146, 149
  vestibulo-ocular (VOR), 230–231
Refractive errors, 222, 224, 243
Refractoriness, *see* Psychological refractory period (PRP)
Regional cerebral blood flow (rCBF), 142
Regulator, 4–5
Rehearsal, 337, 341–347
  rehearsal mechanism, 338–341, 351
Reinforcement, 49, 62, 132
Representation,
  central, 59–66, 97
  conceptual, 68
  conscious, 192

468 SUBJECT INDEX

Representation (cont.)
 content-specific, 400
 declarative, 383
 higher-order, 72-73
 internal, 209, 335-336
 mental, 276
 multiple, 147-148, 232, 400
 precategorical, 425, 433
 procedural, 383
 retinotopic, 340
 sensorimotor, 137
 somatotopical, 141, 147
 spatiotopic, 400, 410, 413
 supramodal, 68
Representative designs, 278, 296
Resource, 87, 365-367, 377, 411, 421
 multiple resource theory, 365, 372, 374
Resting state, 219-231, 238
Resting tonus, 173, 239-243
Retinal acuity gradient, 429, 435
Retinal expansion, see Tau
Retinal flow, 42
RMS error, 80
Rubbery effects, 251

S

Saccade, 249-266, 403
 corrective, see Movement
 "inner" saccade, 253
Saint Vitus' dance, 48
Scan path model, 266
Schaunystagmus, 229
Schema, 369-375
Schematic coincidences, 260
Selection, 362, 373-386, 395-397, 440
 central, 421, 426
 early (precategorical), 347, 378, 408-426, 434-441
 late, 347-348, 354, 363, 367-368, 378, 408-413, 422, 432-438
Selection-for-action, 395-415
Selection mechanism, 374
Selective attenuation, 405
Selective coupling, selective decoupling, 381, 399
Selective cueing, 409-410
Selective enhancement, 402-405, 410, 413
Selective processing, 409-410
Self-organization, 5-6

Sensibility,
 epicritic, 177
 protopathic, 177
Sensorimotor coordination, see Visuomotor coordination
Sequential domain, 310
Servo-assistance, 150
Servo mechanism, 80, 150
Set, 287
Shadowing, 306, 398
Simultanagnosia, 398
Single-channel (model), 88, 93
Size-distance invariance hypothesis, 221
Skill, 374-384
 higher order, 384
Slips of the ear, 322, 323
Slips of the tongue, 322, 323
Somatotopical arrangement, see Representation
Span of apprehension, 363
Spatial structure, 51-52
Specific distance tendency (SDT), 225-227, 229, 234
Speed-accuracy trade-off, 315
Split brain, see Commissurotomy
S-R compatibility, 92-93, 306
S-R theory, 62
Stage, 87, 89, 274, 275, 282, 291, 365, 408, 421, 440
Stance, 95
Statistical facilitation, 293
Step cycle, 95
Stiernystagmus, 229
Stimulus onset asynchrony (SOA), 353
Strabismus, 244
Strong inference, 273, 279-282, 296
Stroop effect, Stroop task, 277, 287-288, 315, 386, 399, 428, 440, 441
Structural correspondence, 53
Structural displacement, 89
Structural limitations, 53
Structural similarity, 64, 365
Stuttering, 322
Sulcus,
 arcuate, 140
 central, 116
Superior colliculus, 402, 403, 405
Suppression, see Inhibition
Swing, 95
Sylvian fissure, 135
Synaptic linkage, 406
Synergistic muscles, 153
Synkinesis, 50-52, 68

SUBJECT INDEX

T

Table turning, 48
Tactile discrimination, 137
Task-related perception, 33
Task-relevance, see Information, 427
Tau (τ), 24–26, 41–42, 201
Temporal structure, time structure,
 temporal pattern, 51, 68, 72, 88, 366, 407
Thalamus, 108, 137, 139, 146, 405, 406, 410, 414
Time-sharing skill, 94
Time-to-contact, see Tau
Timing, 35, 38–39, 70, 79, 117, 126, 140, 305, 311, 329, 369, 370, 384
 relative timing, 97–98
Tonus state, see Resting state
Topological invariance, 13
Touch, 173–180, 401, 403
Trace, 67, 434
Tracking, 40, 79–81, 94, 123, 125, 154, 366, 382
Transcortical loop, see Reflex
Transcortical potential inversion, 113, 116
Transfer function, 197–204
Triggered reaction, 95, 134
Tropia, 240
 esotropia, 240
Two-hand coordination, 78–79
Typing, 336

U

Unilateral neglect, 401, 402
Uniqueness asymmetry, 329

V

Vacuum activities, 383
Verbal transformation, 327–328
Vergence, 42–43, 178, 199–200, 208, 217–238, 259
 vergence effort, 238–241
 vergence tonus, see Resting tonus
Verifyability, 280
Video display terminal (VDT), 210
Visual acuity gradient, see Retinal acuity gradient
Visual adaptation, see Perceptual adaptation
Visual angle, 339
Visual array, see Optic array
Visual fatigue, 243
Visual localization, 187
Visual search, 428
Visual speech, 284
Visual world, see Perceptual world
Visuomotor coordination, 195–205, 233, 235
Vitalism, 181, 183
Voice-onset time, 284
Voicing, 275, 330
Volition, 175, 176

W

Wallpaper illusion, 220
Weight lifting, 187, 189
Whole report, 338–344, 347, 351–354, 428
Will, 176, 186, 187, 190
"Winner-takes-all," 404
Wisdom of nature, 60
Word production asymmetry, 326
Word substitution, 322
Word superiority effect, 363, 386